NIRODBARAN'S
CORRESPONDENCE WITH
SRI AUROBINDO

The Complete Set

Nirodbaran's
Correspondence with
SRI AUROBINDO

THE COMPLETE SET
VOLUME TWO

SRI AUROBINDO ASHRAM, PONDICHERRY

First Complete Edition 1984
Second Complete Edition 1995

LOTUS LIGHT
PUBLICATIONS
Box 325
Twin Lakes, WI 53181 USA

Mother's Comments on the Correspondence

In the Introduction to the first volume I made a brief reference to the Mother's remarks on my correspondence with Sri Aurobindo. At the time I forgot to mention what she had said regarding the correspondence on a few other occasions, both to me and during conversations with another disciple. Since they are very interesting and significant, I am inserting them here. They should have appeared at the beginning of the first volume.

After I read out the portions on Karmayoga to the Mother, she asked me: "When are they appearing in the *Bulletin*?" "It will take time, Mother", I answered. "Oh, if I had them by my side, I could ask people to read them. Sri Aurobindo has answered all the problems in your letters. C'est merveilleux." I suggested, "We could give you typed copies, Mother."

"That is of no use, I can't read."

"There is the book where all the important letters have come out — the book of correspondence."

"Then it is all right."

January 2, 1972

"Mother, this morning I had a dream: You were telling me that Sri Aurobindo had given me everything; you had nothing else to give."

"It is true", she replied.

"But I want a lot of things from you", I rejoined. She smiled and, catching hold of my hands, said, "I mean that from the point of view of Yoga, he has said everything. It is marvellous! It is marvellous!"

She stroked my hands gently and looked into my eyes awhile, then closed her eyes and blessed me.

January 5, 1972

vi   MOTHER'S COMMENTS ON THE CORRESPONDENCE

Here is what she said to the disciple:

Nirod is reading out to me his correspondence with Sri Aurobindo, and it contains all the things (it's amusing), the things I said
long, long afterwards, and I didn't know that he had written them!
— exactly the same thing. I was very much interested.

In this correspondence, he told Nirod in a letter[1] (he said it
several times): "I may take a fancy to leave my body before the
supramental realisation . . ." He said that a few years before he
died. He had felt it.

(*Silence*)

But he spoke of a transformation that would come before the
advent of the first supramental being.[2] And that was what he told
me. He told me that his body was not capable of bearing this transformation, that mine was more capable — he repeated it.

But it is difficult. I told you so the other day.

Food, especially, is . . . it has become a labour.

January 19, 1972

Have you read the whole "Correspondence with Nirod"?

*I am translating it as I go along, so I haven't read the whole
thing.*

There are extraordinary things in there. He seems to be joking
all the time but . . . it's extraordinary.

You see, I lived — how many years? Thirty years, I think, with
Sri Aurobindo — thirty years from 1920 to 1950. I thought I knew
him well, and then when I hear this, I realise that . . . (*Mother
makes a gesture as if to indicate a breaking of bounds.*)

February 16, 1972

According to what Nirod is reading out to me now of his correspondence with Sri Aurobindo, it seems to have been the same thing
for Sri Aurobindo. Because, according to what he wrote (you will
see when you read it), I am always the doer. He says: "Mother says,

[1] March 30, 1935, p. 196.
[2] April 17, 1935, pp. 218–20; October 9, 1936, p. 704.

MOTHER'S COMMENTS ON THE CORRESPONDENCE vii

Mother does, Mother . . . " You see, as far as the organisation of the Ashram is concerned (relations with people and all that), it would seem that, quite naturally, all the time, it is all done through me.

And you know, from the point of view of humour, I have never read anything more wonderful, oh! . . . He had a way of looking at things . . . it's incredible. Incredible. But it seems that for him, the outside world was something . . . absurd, you know.

(. . .)

Oh! it's very strange. It's very strange. Since my childhood all my effort has been to (how can I put it?) achieve a total indifference — neither annoying nor pleasant. Since my childhood, I remember a consciousness which tried . . . That was what Sri Aurobindo meant — an indifference. Oh! it's strange. Now I realise why he said that I was the one who could attempt to effect the transition between the human and the supramental consciousness. He said so. He told me, and he says it, it is recorded in Nirod's thing. And I understand why . . .

Ah! I understand.

Yes, I understand.

April 26, 1972

I am hearing—through Nirod—things that Sri Aurobindo said, and he himself says that he contradicted himself a considerable number of times . . . (. . .) and that, of course, the two or three different ways are true.[1] So we can be as . . . as wide as he!

In fact his understanding was very flexible—very flexible. While listening to the things he said, I felt that I had understood very little of what he meant. And now that I am more and more in touch with the supramental Consciousness, I can see that it is extremely flexible—flexible and complex—and that it is our narrow human consciousness that sees things . . . (*Mother draws little squares in the air*) fixed and definite.

(. . .)

And I can see that when one goes above the mind, it becomes . . . it is like waves on the sea.

February 14, 1973

[1] December 22, 1934, p. 83.

NIRODBARAN'S

CORRESPONDENCE WITH
SRI AUROBINDO

The Complete Set

June 1936

I am feeling dry, dry, dry. But a mood of meditation creeps over the dryness.

Well, that's all right isn't it?

I find that my point of concentration usually goes between the eyebrows.

A quite useful place for concentration—O.K. so far.

Nothing happens though at times a feeling of স্তব্ধতা।[1]

Better and better!

I suppose that is enough for you, but unfortunately I want a little more.

Quite enough for a beginning—only at times, is insufficient; स्तब्धता[2] is quite the best ground for experiences and everything else.

Can you tell me why no experience is coming to me and why those that I had long, long ago, have stopped?

Too big a riot of mental activity and vital jumping.

If no joy is felt out of a creation after so much labour, what's the use, can you say?

The use of having no joy? It is no use.

I am thinking—after all what am I to do then? But thinking has no end either.

[1,2] *stabdhatā:* stillness.

Quite so. Stop thinking and become স্তব্ধ।[1]

> *Que faire? I suppose this dryness is due to your unexpected progress. That is the only consolation.*

Dryness, no! that is part of your own pilgrimage. The rest may be due to Add. Ab. Quite a number of people are trying to become স্তব্ধ, wide etc. without ever having intended it. I like to think my march may have something to do with it.

> *Addis Ababa — how far?*

Can't say. My rapidity slowed down much after D turned turtle and the correspondence avalanche restarted. However "nous progressâmes."[2]

> *Will you cast a glance at J's story — Russian Cat, which even Tagore liked?*

I shall try my Herculean best — I can't promise more.

> *Please give me some force for poetry now — without it I don't know how to come out of this condition.*

All right — shall try that also.

> *June 2, 1936*

> *You mean to say — "I am in Heaven. Everything is all right in the best of all possible worlds — in Sri Aurobindo Asram and with Nirod"!*

Quite so. All is well, if it ends well.

> *But how to make you realise that I welcome the stillness etc. . . . but it's not always there.*

I quite realise. Don't make such Herculean efforts to explain it.

---

[1] *stabdha:* still.
[2] We have advanced.

SRI AUROBINDO   605

> *No joy, no energy, no cheerfulness. Don't like to read or*
> *write — as if a dead man were walking about. Do you*
> *understand the position? Any personal experience?*

I quite understand; often had it myself devastatingly. That's why
I always advise people who have it to cheer up and buck up.

> *I asked Kanai for my diagnosis — he says some sort of*
> *trouble in the "prān"[1] positively; desire of ego. Just as a*
> *Kaviraj puts his finger on the pulse and diagnoses at once, so*
> *with this. What's required is purification.*

Diagnosis right—only should add an adjective disappointed pran
and ego. No active vital row; vital and ego lying back flat and
gloomy.

> *So, since I have to pass the time, how to do it? To bear the*
> *Cross gloomily, hoping for a resurrection?*

To cheer up, buck up and the rest if you can, saying "Rome was
not built in a day" — if you can't, gloom it through till the sun
rises and the little birds chirp and all is well.

Looks however as if you were going through a training in
vairagya. Don't much care for vairagya myself, always avoided
the beastly thing, but had to go through it partly, till I hit on *samata*
as a better trick. But samata is difficult, vairagya is easy, only
damnably gloomy and uncomfortable.

June 3, 1936

> *Vairagya! Good Lord! What next? A fellow who has always*
> *detested it, loved life and company, now undergoing a train-*
> *ing in vairagya!! Such is life, eh? Never dreamt of Yoga,*
> *and stumbled into it — vairagya now crowns it! Why D's*
> *phantom on me? His drive towards vairagya, I understand,*
> *was due to his past life's karma. But what past life's karma*
> *in my case, please?*

How do you know about your past life's karma? But perhaps it is

---

[1] *prān:* vital.

606 CORRESPONDENCE WITH

D's karma which is afflicting you, — your karma being that of getting caught up in the swirl of his tempestuous course.

> *And when I look at D's suffering due to this blessed vairagya, I shudder. I am only a small pot — then why this heavy burden on me?*

Well, why did you get into the track of the big pot?

> *And what kind of vairagya is this? It is encouraged by almost all yogis. Kanai understands by it a positive detachment from things of this life and a luminous aspiration within towards a higher spiritual achievement.*

Vairagya means a positive detachment from things of this life — but it does not *immediately* carry with it a luminous aspiration except for a few fortunate people. For the positive detachment is often a pulling away by the soul while the vital clings and is gloomy and reluctant.

> *I suppose you mean a different kind of vairagya in my case, suited to my nature?*

Yes, tamasic vairagya.

June 4, 1936

> *B.N. reported yesterday: "A snake has come out of my belly!" So he is germinating snakes now! Shall I give him santonin or rely on the Force?*

He is eating dirty food outside — so it is not surprising. But give him santonin.

June 6, 1936

> *A poem for you. I hope you will make out in it the fall of Adam (soul) from the garden of Eden. But what is it — symbolic, mystic or cystic?*

Symbolic mystic without being cryptic-cystic. Anyhow, pure in-

SRI AUROBINDO   607

spiration and very luminous. Something undeniably original, this
time, what?

> *A good piece of news: I find now three mules — mules,
> mind you, not horses — are trying to draw me on: (1)
> meditation, (2) silence (not of the mind but of the buccal
> cavity), (3) poetry.*

Well, mules are very useful animals. When Badoglio's motor-lorries
broke down, he bought 20,000 mules (I won't swear to the exact
number) and they did the trick. You have 3 mules and not 20,000
— but perhaps 3 will serve.

> *The buccal silence I can keep off from clashing with the
> other two. But the collision between meditation and poetry is
> inevitable unless I favour one of them.*

There are three ways of meeting that situation — (1) say "Yes,
yes" to both parties, — but that may create trouble afterwards,
(2) Be cryptic-cystic in your answers, so that neither will be sure
what you mean, (3) silence with an occasional profound "Ah, hum.
Yes, eh!" "Ah hum" always sounds unfathomable depths — and
if "Yes" is too positive, "eh" tones it down and corrects it. You
have not enough worldly wisdom.

> *I shall try with all my nerves to concentrate as far as prac-
> ticable — and I get also some not quite definitely pleasing
> sensation out of it.*

Well, that is good — I hope the indefinite will soon define itself.

> *As poetry also has come, I wouldn't like to give it up either.
> But how to harmonise?*

No need to harmonise by any set arrangement — only keep up
the concentration. One hour of packed concentration or even a few
minutes can do as much as three hours less packed. Do you say yours
is not packed? Well, striped, streaked, spotted, dotted or whatever it may be.

608   CORRESPONDENCE WITH

And do you "like to think" that it is all due to your march forward?

Of course I like and it may even be true.

By the way, my "tamasic vairagya" seems to be an epidemic. J also has the same symptoms.

That kind of vairagya is not new with J, so you need not take the credit of it.

She also added that Death would be a delivery from all these troubles and a renewal of this life.

What an idea! She would have the same things to face with less favourable conditions for overcoming them.

Please ask blessed Time to stand still behind you till your pen has run a 50 mile-gallop on this sheet.

Time can't stand still, but I have tried to make the fellow trot slower instead of cantering—with no great result.

[*Dilip sent my Bengali poem:* ālor pākhi (*The Bird of Light*)[1] *to Sri Aurobindo, saying: O Guru, Nirod has written a fine poem—albeit in a rather sad vein. The word-music is beautiful, what? No change I found necessary. Last night's result—the moonlight, voyez-vous?*]

Nirod's poem is exceedingly beautiful, full of the moonlight—he can't say any longer after that that he is not a poet.

June 7, 1936

Herewith a bhatiyāli[2]—*I hope you know this animal, don't you? I have used some native expressions. . . Of course, aristocratic expressions also abound, but that*

[1] *Swapnadīp*, p. 17.
[2] A boatman's song.

SRI AUROBINDO

> *doesn't matter, especially when this is a socialistic age.*
> *Nothing original, but hope not absolutely aboriginal?*
> *How do you find the animal?*

Admirable—No matter whether original, aboriginal or co-original—most good poetry is all three together. The animal is a fine animal and the plebeian spots on the aristocratic skin give it a very subtly attractive appearance.

June 10, 1936

> *T's pain in the finger is worse due to constant work.*

As she got nervous (pain and difficulty of doing her work) we sent her to R.

June, 11, 1936

> *Your answer[1] gave me a feeling different from other times.*
> *It didn't cheer me up; perhaps due to some atmosphere in the*
> *letter.*

I don't think there was any atmosphere in my answers.

June 12, 1936

> *... I have analysed and analysed myself, and have found*
> *that I have no real urge for the Divine. It seems more the*
> *unfavourable external circumstances that have brought me*
> *here. Had I been happy and in plenty there, would I have*
> *chosen this path?... Where is the sincerity in me?...*
> *So wouldn't it be better for you to let me go instead of*
> *wasting so much of your time and labour on me?*

Your analysis and reasonings are those of Grand'mère Depression which sees only what she allows to come to the surface for her purposes. There are other things that Madame suppresses because they don't suit her. It does not greatly matter what brought you here—the important thing is to go on till the psychic truth behind

---

[1] Unpublished.

610 CORRESPONDENCE WITH

all that becomes manifest. The inertia of your physical nature is only a thick crust on the surface which goes away slowly, but under the pressure it will give way. If you had some big object in the ordinary life and nothing to hope for here it might be different, but as things are it would be foolish to walk off under the instigation of this old Mother Gloom-Gloom. Stick on and you will get the soul's reward hereafter.

June 14, 1936

... You say I could help Y. How can I do so avoiding everything personal? If I can help at all, it is in her literary work — surely not in Sadhana! But there again you doubt. Tell me precisely what I should do — not "if you want to do this, you can do" sort of thing. How is the help to be there?

I put it as something that could be done on certain conditions. These conditions do not exist at present, for neither is free with regard to the other. But the conditions can come into existence.

It is not at all necessary to break off all contact with her, and drastic methods are only necessary in extreme cases. Too much contact has to be avoided at present and it should be kept limited to surface things. The main point is to get yourself inwardly and vitally free — neither vital pull nor impatient repulsion. Understand that they have to be got rid of and quell them down and reject them when they come.

June 15, 1936

Now I find that I am only a bundle of sex and nothing else! This is yogic transformation!

Nobody can be only a bundle of sex. Even a cat or a Casanova can't be that. It is the aboriginal coming up and figuring as if the whole man. But there are other bundles there even if this one is at the top for the moment.

The Mother kept quiet about B's case and asked not to apply atropine.

SRI AUROBINDO   611

Mother did not say not to treat her. She asked if it was not possible
to treat her without the atropine.

June 16, 1936

> *But how to treat B? Her headache is due to error of re-
> fraction. . .*

B told Mother she would never wear glasses. Has she said dif-
ferently to you?

> *Do you suggest to try purgatives, aspirin, stopping needle-
> work, etc. before going in for glasses?*

All that does not seem very promising.

June 18, 1936

> *My friend J's letter — he hears your voice, feels your Power
> acting, his mind and vital free from sex. Is it possible that
> one hasn't to struggle much for purification? Force does
> everything?*

It is quite possible if the psychic being takes the lead or is active —
not so easy otherwise.

> *How was this conquest done so easily considering that he
> is a married man, having a wife not very spiritually inclined?*

That is not the only "married man" instance.

> *While we who are here, in this atmosphere, find it so very
> difficult, though completely debarred from sex-life.*

In his case, as it seems from what he writes, the mind decisively
freed itself first. The difficulty with most is that the mind in parts
lends itself to the vital under one colour or another.

> *He actually says that a personal effort is only a small or
> ineffective help!*

612   CORRESPONDENCE WITH

Of course — personal effort without the supporting Force can do only a little, slowly, with much labour.

> *When I suffer, I don't see any Force coming and fighting my battle. I am paralysed for a time with pain etc., then the suffering disappears. I believe your Force works it out, but I want to feel, know and see.*

That is the difficulty. A full faith however can command the effects of the Force even without being conscious of the action of the Force.

> *Lastly, he has raised some points which invite your answers, if not tonight, some night.*

I don't know when, for his questions and subjects are of great amplitude.

> *P has two boils on a buttock which are stationary. She is constipated and feverish. I asked her to take enema or medicine, she will wait for permission, she says.*

Mother has not only given permission but order — but she is not going to latrine, not taking enema, because she fears the pain caused by the boil in evacuation!

R wants Amal, Ambu, Romen — all three his patients — to be weighed from time to time. Will you take Ambu to the hospital tomorrow and arrange to have it done and also arrange for general permission so that whenever three or any of them go for the purpose, they may be allowed?

                                                June 19, 1936

> *For S's constipation—I shall try tomorrow enema-turpentine.*

What's this turpentine enema? drastic effect? or what *gunas*?

> *A has pain in the left arm. On palpation a nut-sized hard swelling was found. She says it's increased latterly. It was caused by an injection in Africa. I don't think it will be dissolved by medicines. Excision is the only way.*

SRI AUROBINDO   613

Operation will not leave any undesirable after-effects?

June 20, 1936

> *Last night S had the same trouble, dyspepisa, with no relief. Gave one alkaline powder containing Bismuth — no effect!*

Bismuth is not constipative? I thought it was given for that effect. But if he is badly constipated already?

> *He can't tolerate any liquid nourishment. Some solid dry protein food would be good. I thought of egg.*

It can be tried — as it is not a liver case.

> *Pomegranate or orange juice would hardly be enough.*

Pomegranate juice not astringent and constipative?

> *S says as soon as the Mother was informed, he felt better. Why then all this medication? Make him altogether well!*

If he allows. L had acutely a similar illness and T in a milder form — they were cured without medicines. But S is such a pessimist and lamenter that I don't know if his body will respond in the same way.

> *I am rather worried about the fellow. I have asked his mother to come and help him whenever she is free.*

S has written (through Biren) asking for that on her behalf. But at the same time he writes that she doesn't sleep, doesn't eat, was weeping all night — If she does like that, how can she help him — she will only depress him farther. Otherwise it would be all right.

> *A's operation [of the arm] is not likely to leave any after-effects. It has to be done in the hospital. . .*

She jibs violently against operation.

614

Shall I remind you about the reply to Jatin's letter?

You did, but with no effect.

June 21, 1936

Bismuth and pomegranate are astringents, no doubt, but the former is also an antacid and as the latter is nourishing too, S seems to tolerate it. Found another possibility of the cause of his disease: worms. He has suffered from it for the last 15 years!

Then of course pomegranate is the thing. But what kind of worms do you suspect? I suppose the ordinary small intestinal worm betrays its presence without microscope. What kind does he have?

By the way, if you think R had better treat him, I have no objection. Whatever is in my power, I am doing. If any danger is ahead, you may transfer him.

I don't know whether it is possible. They are at daggers drawn for a long time past and S has written very bad things against him. Will he now accept him as doctor and obey all his directions? I suppose S will get all right; if once he can be made to take sufficient nourishment, the rest is at most a matter of time.

June 22, 1936

... One part in me has written about the difficulties and asks for help, another says and laments — You fool, you could have enjoyed yourself a little. Yoga, after all, is there before you — But meanwhile do you know what sandy deserts you have to cross?...

That is of course the whole difficulty — the division in the being. But even so the true being can and surely will prevail.

We're giving S calomel and mag. sulph to stimulate the flow of bile and a purge also.

Purge quite safe for his weakness?

SRI AUROBINDO   615

Please concentrate a little on his stomach.

Have been doing so — but the jaundice development (it must have been incubating from the first) is a nuisance.

Oh yes, giving also plenty of vichy water. Any comment?

Nothing much to say at present.

June 23, 1936

I would like to know if there are going to be any personal relations afterwards among sadhaks. To think that everybody will be equal to our eyes pains most of us.

Yes, it pains the outer vital, because that vital thinks it is a negative state of indifference and non-attachment, things that it hates because liking and disliking are its native atmosphere.

But with having psychic love for all, is there also going to be any pure divine love for a particular one?

But first you must realise what the "pure divine" love is!

Of course new friendships may come up and old ones break, but I am inclined to wonder whether such personal pure ties will be there or not.

But that is not the question your "inclination" asks — it is practically asking whether one can't keep up one's attachments and carry them into the higher atmosphere!

I gather from your reply to J that one will have the same deep psychic feelings for all.

Not the same psychic feelings for all, but different psychic feelings are possible.

We always think that all our relations will be impersonal. That is one of the reasons why we cling to our objects of love and desire.

616   CORRESPONDENCE WITH

That is not the reason—the reason lies in the clinging itself.

> *During meditation I had a vision of J lying dead in a room.
> Her death was accidental and not natural. Suddenly the door
> of the room opened and a hideous figure came in. It was so
> vivid that I still shudder to think of it. I was just sitting on a
> chair and looking at J's corpse. Is it J's mania of suicide
> from the subconscient?*

It looks on the surface like a nightmare vision of the vital. It might
refer to what you say—something shot up from a subconscient
impression into form. Or, who knows, it may mean simply the old
vital attachment by her lying dead and old vital Nature looking on
in a horrified disapproval!

I don't think it is much use writing about personal relations
in the true spiritual life (which does not yet exist here). None would
understand it except as a form of words. Only three points—

(1) Its very base would have to be spiritual and psychic and *not*
vital. The vital would be there but as an instrument only.

(2) It would be a relation flowing from the higher Truth, not
continued from the lower Ignorance.

(3) It would not be impersonal in the sense of being colourless,
but whatever colours were there would not be the egoistic and
muddy colours of the present relations.

> *It appears to me that women generally are not so disturbed
> because they deliberately eliminate from their mind any
> idea of physical sex contacts.*

They don't; but they don't want to face the dangers or the consequences of the vital physical impulse which *they* have to bear for
the most part.

> *Also their vitals are satisfied more easily by simple vital
> exchanges, e.g. walking, talking, at most holding hands.*

That is true of many women.

                                                June 24, 1936

> *I do believe that if one person loves another sincerely it will*

SRI AUROBINDO   617

> *have an influence on the person some day.*

It may have, very likely, but it isn't a necessary consequence.

> *A tells me that 3 or 4 days ago he saw in a vision that I was jumping into the Mother's lap. How miraculously you have saved me without any trying on my part.*

You called sincerely for the help, so the help came.

> *Jatin sends you another letter and wants a reply. Two letters. Can you reply either or both?*

This one is easier to answer. I keep it also.

> *May I have a cup of soup for S, for a few days, from Rajangam? D.R. soup is very watery.*

You mean some of our soup? I don't know how that can be arranged, but you can ask Champaklal if it is possible.

June 25, 1936

> *S—the pain and discomfort increased after 2 p.m. There is a tendency of salivation. Gave 2 doses of calomel.*

You are giving calomel—but is there no salt in his egg or any other food? Soup has salt in it. I think calomel should be stopped.

> *If you ask me to cut off all medicines or some of them, and rely on the Force, I am willing to do so.*

It seems a lot of medicine — but I doubt if in S's case we can rely on Force alone.

> *He can't digest milk, so I asked for the soup. It may be inconvenient to supply from your soup, so I can ask Dyuman to buy some soup vegetables and supply them. I think that would be best.*

618

No, it would not be best. We are asking Rajangam to manage somehow to prepare some more soup for the purpose.

June 26, 1936

> *S is not tolerating the milk well. Cream or creamed milk would have been better.*

Cream for jaundice? In France they actually took all cream out of the milk before allowing it!

> *Very little salt was given so far. I am adding a little now in the soup.*

The Mother's objection was to calomel+salt food. So long as calomel is not given, it is all right.

June 27, 1936

> *S tells others that he's better, though to me he hesitates to admit the fact. He asked B to write to you that he wasn't at all improving. When it was contradicted by facts he replied that his forbearance only has increased. I had a hearty laugh!*

He or rather B wrote to me a tragic tale. I told him this kind of illness took time to cure and meanwhile he had better practise quietness and cheerfulness — it would help the Force.

> *N.P. has pain near the spine, at the top of the right sacroiliac joint for the last 2 weeks.*

He has sent me a wail too about jerks and sleeplessness.

> *Please don't forget my book; if no time let it incubate another night, provided it hatches out fully.*

Had to. D took all my time with his woes and the opinions of Lawrence. It is the "Bases of Yoga" that has upset him!!! Moreover J's two letters, three urgently needed replies to sadhaks who have been waiting hungrily for weeks or days etc., etc. So —

June 28, 1936

SRI AUROBINDO   619

> *S—after taking eggs—had the sensation of vomiting and griping pain. Egg is responsible, I suppose.*

Yes, better suppress egg for the present.

> *He looks better but some discomfort will continue so long as the complete flow of bile is not established.*

Does it not always take long in these cases?

> *I propose to give some bitters with nux vomica etc.*

You can try.

June 29. 1936

July 1936

> *S is much better, feels happy. I forgot to write that jaundice usually takes 2-3 weeks.*

So I understood, even a month.

> *N.P. is dying more of fear, and thinking if he does this or that the pain may come back!*

That is why these things continue with him.

> *What about my private book or J's letters? Can't you send them?*

Not as yet. Could not make up arrears.

> *Today X seemed quite sane. So you see, Sir, after all it is your help that pulled her up.*

Of course as soon as you wrote I put the shower-bath on her.

> *[About J's novel:] If you say that she'd better follow what Y says, she is willing to do so. Her fury has toned down and*

she feels that after all there was nothing much to get upset about. The book belongs to the Mother.

Well, that is something.

I feel that Y would mind again if J did everything herself— and she won't be able to do it well. After all, Y has spent so much for the book, and he is determined to see that it brings a good sale. . .

You are quite right. Since Y has done everything about this book till now, it is better to let him finish. In future she can keep clear of any obligation to him, but here it will only create confusion and more trouble.

Another point — Y doesn't want J to send a copy of the book to Niren, for fear of criticism. . .

That is a point I cannot resolve.

July 1, 1936

For N — shall we try olive oil?

What for olive oil?

For his stomach-ache and constipation etc., yeast can be tried. It has been found very good in some cases.

Yeast ought to do him good, as he complains of weakness. You can have a try, before we plunge in R who is struggling with a difficult case just now. But I am afraid in N's body there is something that does not want to cure, for it finds itself more miserably interesting with constipation, ache and sciatica than without it.

I send you Nishikanta's version of my Bengali poem. He has tried to keep as far as possible my words, but even then it can hardly be called mine.

My God! he has pummelled you into pieces and thrown away all but a few shreds. No, you can't call it yours. Perhaps you can label

SRI AUROBINDO   621

it, "Nirod after being devoured, assimilated and eliminated by
Nishikanta."

> *Nishikanta has written so much that you can't do without
> tumbling into his influence.*

Your own version, if it takes things from NK is still not NK but
yourself.
                                                            July 3, 1936

> *Here is a poem — don't know if it is the outcome of your
> "shall try" or you didn't try at all?*

Just gave a pressure or two, that's all.

> *Opinion?*

Very beautiful.

> *I hope you won't disappoint me this week-end. I have waited
> long enough. One of J. B.'s letters must be answered. What?*

Can't say — so many people waiting for an answer.

> *A flower for Chand.*

Take from Nolini.
                                                            July 4, 1936

> *S's jaundice still seems to be the same. I propose to give
> him about half an ounce of mag. sulph. tomorrow.*

Mother suggests that a small lavement (cold) should be given him
daily until there is no bile. She doesn't think purgatives are much
use for jaundice.

> *Please try to give one or two more "pressures" for poetry.*

Shall try.

622

One answer to Jatin managed. Rest swimming on the wide wide sea.

July 5, 1936

> *I propose to give S, mag. sulph. not as purgation but to stimulate the bile flow from the liver. Any objection? However, I will do as Mother says.*

No, you can give the mag. sulph.

Mother was suggesting from her own experience, and the instructions of Doctors in France. But probably it differs with cases and people.

July 6, 1936

> [*Morning*]
> *I have no peace, no joy, no push for anything, and am physically an absolute rag. I wonder, after all, whether you have committed a mistake by telling me all that [an unpublished letter]; pardon my audacity. I doubt because I don't find any good result from it. Can you tell me why exactly you told me all that? Surely you must have had an end in view.*

You asked for it yourself, nor was there anything much more than I had told you on a former occasion — only one actual case of the general proposition. If the old thing rose up so violently, as a result, it shows that it was there all the time in the subconscient coming secretly in the way of the progress and the continuity or return of such experiences as you had. It seems to me that it was as well that it should come up and you should deal with it consciously and directly. If you want the Divine and the inner life, the old vital moorings must be cut.

> *In short, I am thinking of going out somewhere for a month. I can only think of A at Bombay who may be willing to keep me.*

That is D's proposition all over again! I have to spend a large part of the night writing letters to him so that he may not start for Cape Comorin and the Himalayas — now if you pile Bombay and A on

SRI AUROBINDO

623

these two ends of India, I for my part shall have to head for the Pacific Ocean.

> *I am feeling that the intimate personal contact you allowed me before — which is one of the big attractions — you are withdrawing. Perhaps I have committed some grave faults, or the necessity doesn't exist!*

I don't know where you got that rubbishy idea. I have told you that I am preoccupied with the old mass of correspondence — (now + D) + many important and pressing answers to people which in spite of their pressingness I can't get written. That is why I have not sent you back your personal book, as I need a less occupied mind to discuss such intricate and difficult questions as you have put this time. There is no question of withdrawing anything or grave faults or cessation of any necessity. For heaven's sake, don't begin striking this other Dilipian chord!

> [*Evening*]
> ... *You say I should deal with it consciously and directly. But how?*

I meant that you should fight it out.

> ... *You say it is all D. In everything I do, you find D.*

Because you say just the same things.

> *I didn't know at all that he has got it afresh — this idea of going away — perhaps over J's novel affair?*

No, the reason he gives is just the same as yours. . .

> *But if you head for the Pacific, well, I suppose I have to be swayed and billowed into the Atlantic, at whatever cost! You write, "If you want the Divine. . ." That is the whole question. Do I really want the Divine? Have I come for Him?*

I intended to write "If something in you wants the Divine," but dropped into the shorter form. Something must have wanted it,

624   CORRESPONDENCE WITH

otherwise the things you write or experienced formerly would be meaningless. Parts of the mind which are uppermost now may not want, but that is so with most people.

> *It is not so much the retention of my book that gave me that idea. From your short answers and from a wrong intuition perhaps.*

Short answers were due to the same cause.

> *But if you want to keep me here, do save me from this condition — no peace, no strength to fight, etc. Unless you save °me unconditionally, I am doomed.*

Quite ready.

> *Shivalingam has again had pain in the right ankle for the last 6 or 7 days. Thinking of trying Sod. Salicyl. injection; if that fails, then protein injection.*

[*No reply.*]

> *Mahatma Gandhi says in an article: "... I hold that complete realisation is impossible in this embodied life. Nor is it necessary. A living immovable faith is all that is required for reaching the full spiritual height attainable by human beings..." Your opinion on the matter?*

I do not know what Mahatma Gandhi means by complete realisation. If he means a realisation with nothing more to realise, no farther development possible, then I agree — I have myself spoken of farther divine progression, an infinite development. But the question is not that; the question is whether the Ignorance can be transcended, whether a complete essential realisation turning the consciousness from darkness to light, from an instrument of the Ignorance seeking for Knowledge into an instrument or rather a manifestation of Knowledge proceeding to greater Knowledge, Light enlarging, heightening into greater Light, is or is not possible. My view is that this conversion is not only possible, but inevitable in the spiritual evolution of the being here. The embodiment of life

SRI AUROBINDO   625

has nothing to do with it. This embodiment is not of life, but of
consciousness and its energy of which life is only one phase or force.
As life has developed mind, and the embodiment has modified
itself to suit this development (mind is precisely the main instrument of ignorance seeking for knowledge); so mind can develop
supermind which is in its nature knowledge not seeking for itself,
but manifesting itself by its own automatic power, and the embodiment can again modify itself or be modified from above so as to suit
this development. Faith is a necessary means for arriving at realisation because we are ignorant and do not yet know that which we are
seeking to realise; faith is indeed knowledge giving the ignorance
an intimation of itself previous to its own manifestation, it is the
gleam sent before by the yet unrisen Sun. When the Sun shall rise
there will be no longer any need of the gleam. The supramental
knowledge supports itself, it does not need to be supported by faith;
it lives by its own certitude. You may say that farther progression,
farther development will need faith. No, for the farther development will proceed on a basis of knowledge, not of Ignorance. We
shall walk in the light of knowledge towards its own wider vistas of
self-fulfilment.

July 7, 1936

No opinion about Shivalingam's injections?

You can try. But I thought you wanted to try salicylating first.

July 8, 1936

I am stuck up at the end of a poem. Your last "pressure"
[5.7.36] has failed. Give a little again please, so that I may
complete the poem tonight.

When do you work at night?

July 10, 1936

The trouble is that I have no definite time for working at
night, but usually it's at 9 p.m. Suppose when I intend
to write poetry, I inform you along with the report and wait
for the Force from 9 o'clock, wouldn't that be better?

626   CORRESPONDENCE WITH

I don't know that it would. It might work like that if I were always free to concentrate on particular things at a particular time; but that does not happen.

> *Doesn't your pressure work itself out or does it take a long time? Do you think if you put the Force at an exact time, say 9 p.m., it has a greater chance of immediate success?*

One can't make a rule like that. There is nothing more variable than the way the Force acts.

> *J was rather discouraged by a fall from her previous height and said there is no use then writing or labouring so much.*

She can't expect to succeed equally every time. No poet does. I have tried to explain that to her.

> *She says she also feels an urge for writing novels and does not know how to run two horses together. Is it possible to work part of the day on novel and part on poetry?*

It is quite possible to do it if one accustoms oneself to do it. But I suppose she gets absorbed in the novel or concentrated in the effort of poetry and the energy refuses to divert itself or gets disturbed if it is.

July 11, 1936

> *"They drink the Light from Heaven's golden cores. . ."*

How many "cores" do you think Heaven has? Singular, sir, singular!

> *If the Force is so variable, why then did you ask about my working time at night? Surely you had hit upon some idea!*

The exact knowledge of circumstances always helps the action, even if it does not follow a rule deduced from the circumstances.

> S says Asram bread does not agree with him, responsible for heaviness, want of appetite etc., asks for bazaar bread. What does the doctor say?

July 12, 1936

SRI AUROBINDO   627

I am obliged to keep N[1] for the usual reason. It is already beyond
time and my work unfinished.

> *I don't think Asram bread has anything to do with S's*
> *"non-agreement", for he takes only 1 or 2 slices in the*
> *morning. The real complaint is that he doesn't like curries.*

Is not I.K. cooking for him? He has sent me a letter asking for her
to cook this or that dish he wants. This is beyond me. I am not a
dietist — or whatever the proper word may be.

                                                           July 13, 1936

> *No, I.K. does not cook for S. He wants to stop soup, as it*
> *makes him heavy!*

What an idiot!

> *He wants to try semolina in milk. So shall I get some from*
> *M?*

You can ask M — I didn't know he had semolina.
  But don't yield too much to S's imaginations, he will become
impossible.

> *Any time for NK's poem?*

Forgot it on my table.

                                                           July 14, 1936

> *Jaswant writes: "Deepest Love to Sri Aurobindo. Do*
> *convey it if Papa writes blessings, if Jaswant comes up in*
> *memory. . ."*

Don't understand. What is to be conveyed? And how do the two ifs
relate together or with the "convey"?

> *I have begun two poems, one came on top of the other.*
> *A rush of ideas invading!*

---

[1] Nishikanta's poetry notebook.

628   CORRESPONDENCE WITH

Very good.

> *Please try if you can, to circulate some Force at night—*
> *9 p.m., and afternoon, just when you regain your curvilinear*
> *proportions—2.30 p.m.*

There is no such regularity about curvilineation. However I will circulate whenever possible.

S has sent me the accompanying letter. I absolutely refuse to ask the Mother or give orders upon his chits for food, so I refer it to you. I can't rely on him—here he asks for oil, but you had written that you had said no to oil. It seems to me if he takes oil and spices and greasy things before the bile is entirely out of his blood, it will be there for good. S has neither self-restraint nor common sense. His খেয়াল[1] is his guide. But are we to follow it?

> *. . . I am in sheer despair. I want to say—damn it all, damn*
> *it all. Let me—*

Don't damn, but lift up quietly.

July 15, 1936

> *Force, Force, please. I have begun four poems and none*
> *complete. Every day I get new lines at Pranam, but can't*
> *complete a single poem!*

Very well, let us try to bring them to completion.

> *Today S told me that he took a little rice, one potato, one*
> *brinjal-roast, one karela.*

Karela is good, potato passable—brinjal detestable, but I suppose less so roast than fried.

> *Today after a "storm" with X, everything is clear. And now*
> *I am completely out of the gloom, and am happy. How it*
> *came about—tomorrow perhaps.*

---

[1] *kheyāl:* whim.

SRI AUROBINDO   629

Very good. However it came about, the result is gratifying.

July 16, 1936

> *. . . But is it really "gratifying"? It may be so as far as my gloominess is concerned. But the ultimate result?*

The ultimate result is for the Ultimate to see—I was speaking in and of the immediate.

> *I am now determined to turn myself towards you as far as possible.*

Very good.

> *Have X and I formed our old attachments in this garb?. . .*

All that depends on the Ulterior (not the Ultimate). It is an advantage to have got to a friendly relation rather than a hard scraggy one which gave neither release nor quietude. The evolution from that basis depends on the future.

> *. . . A strong aspiration for more and more purity, sincerity, etc., is coming down. Contact with her gives me real joy. I see the vital receding. . . But are all these illusions? Will you explain?*

No use explaining. If you keep to the understanding and to your aspiration, psychology will take care of itself.

> *Give both of us your blessings and help to keep our relation pure, harmonious and happy. Will you?*

Yes.

> *Jatin says he can wait even for a year, for your reply. I hope it won't be as bad as that. I'll write that he need have no fear in these difficulties as your Force and protection are with him. Shall I?*

Yes.

S says he feels hungry now, will be absolutely all right in 4 or 5 days. Three cheers!!

What about bile?

July 17, 1936

Madan Gopal suddenly got high fever... Seems to be malaria which he had before... I might give him an injection tomorrow for quick action. Sanction?

If it is the antimalarial injection given to Jyotin, yes.

I asked N.P. to keep a watch over him; so N.P. should not go for work in the afternoon. He wants your permission.

Yes.

July 18, 1936

I hope I don't trouble you unnecessarily with detailed questions on poetry?

No.

D.L. has pain in the abdomen, fever, weakness, etc. She says whenever there is fever, there is this pain; I am inclined to think it is the other way round.

I should suppose so.

I'm afraid, her work, which is rather heavy, should be cut down.

The heavy part of the work is being done now by hired people. She is supposed only to supervise.

It seems to be ulcer. Some cases have been cured by just olive oil taken orally. I'll try it with simple diet...

All right. It can be tried.

July 19, 1936

SRI AUROBINDO   631

> *S is hardly better. We have to buy a few more pills. Sanction?*

Yes.

The fellow is thinking only of eating and renewing his ordinary life—he can't be allowed to chronicise his beastly jaundice.

July 20, 1936

> *V has had diarrhoea last 2 days. I wonder if it is due to cold in the stomach or the mangoes he had taken.*

Probably latter. It was at least Mother's first idea, though she knew nothing about the mangoes.

> *P's boil squeezed out. . .*

Mother gave a chit for one month yeast treatment; did you get it (from Tajdar)? With these boils always coming some blood purification is surely necessary.

July 23, 1936

> *D says: "If you want to publish your literary work, you must see that people understand it—not the public at large, but, as Virginia Woolf says, a select public. Otherwise don't publish at all. The very idea of publication means an appreciation, and how can one appreciate an unintelligible thing?"*

What is not understood or appreciated by one select circle may be understood or appreciated by another select circle or in the future like Blake's poetry. Nobody appreciated Blake in his own time—now he ranks as a great poet—more poetic than Shakespeare, says Housman. Tagore wrote he could not appreciate D's poetry because it is too "Yogic" for him. Is Tagore then unselect, one of the public at large?

> *D says that your case is different, because you don't care for publication!*

It is not for that reason.

Any light on the issue of the publication, and the public being the judge?

I don't agree at all with not publishing because you won't be understood. At that rate many great poets would have remained unpublished. What about the unintelligible Mallarmé who had such a great influence on later French poetry?

S still feels weak. His bile colour is improving. Shall I give him some iron and nux vomica?

Not iron as yet — let the bile go out first — Nux vomica yes.

July 24, 1936

One more poem completed.

Very beautiful.

I don't know its exact meaning and I am feeling rather shy to send it lest you also should find no meaning at all.

Plenty of meaning, but not "exact". Exact meaning is not the forte of this kind of poetry.

One suggestion please: can I use স্বপনিকা[1] for a she-dreamer? I find in the Bengali dictionary the word স্বপ্নক[2] meaning a sleepy person. If স্বপ্নক why not স্বপ্নিকা[3] or স্বপনিকা?

I have not met any স্বপ্নক in Sanskrit, but if there is one, his wife might very correctly be স্বপ্নিকা.

A question about Jatin's room business. I have found a single small room — rent Rs. 7 per month, no furniture, no light.

Does not sound promising.

---

[1] *swapanikā.*
[2] *swapnak.*
[3] *swapnikā.*

SRI AUROBINDO   633

> *Another house for Rs. 20, but people below go on playing*
> *music almost all the time.*

Don't know Jatin's financial capacities or his attitude towards
badly played music.

> *There is another house in front of your room. Rs. 15 per*
> *month. . .*

? Whose house?

> *You said nothing about J.*

What to say? Cure the fellow anyhow. The old Dr. used to regard
his sufferings as things of the nerves more than anything else.

> *D.L. still feels weak, shall I try arsenic and nux vomica?*

No objection to Nux Vomica. Arsenic? Well, if you think it might
be cautiously tried, but she is fatty already and may not be a fit
arsenical subject.

> *S has been having fever for the last 15 days, especially in*
> *the afternoons. I asked her to come in the afternoon to show*
> *the fever. She came in my absence and said to Mulshankar*
> *that as she was feeling all right no medicine was necessary!*

That was why we sent her to you that she might suddenly feel all
right. She used to go to Dr. Banerji with "high fever" which proved
to be not fever at all when he put the thermom.

                                                   July 25, 1936

> *I send you my poem with some changes made in the* chhanda
> *by Dilip and Nishikanta. I can't quite see their point; but*
> *as they are masters in metre I have to consider. What does*
> *your ear say?*

My opinion on metrical points is not of much value. I dare say
you are right, but the alterations made sound better.

634   CORRESPONDENCE WITH

> *Nishikanta says "red tears" is not very appropriate, for tears are associated with transparency. Can one use "red tears of pain" in English?*

Yes, in English one can, as poetical equivalent to the common phrase "tears of blood".

> *The third house I spoke to you about, for Jatin, belongs to the fisherman who, I understand, wanted to catch you in his net!*
> [*Sri Aurobindo underlined "catch you".*]

? Probably you are mistaking the identity. It was another member of the family.

> *Another poem by J! She seems to be flowering very rapidly.*

Yes.

> *But I can't pronounce upon the* chhanda *as I'm not a metrist. So I approach you.*

Neither am I.

> *J says that when she was writing it, she thought she knew what it meant, but after it was finished, it seemed strange to herself!*

It is strange, but admirable. More and more Blakish. One feels what it means, but mentally it is inexplicable. (I mean of course in the details; the general idea is clear.)

July 26, 1936

> *Today another poem by J. I'm staggered by her speed in writing. She says lines,* chhanda, *simply drop down, and she jots them down. She feels as if somebody is writing through her.*

But that is how inspiration always comes when the way is clear and the mind sufficiently passive. Something drops or pours down; somebody writes through you.

SRI AUROBINDO
635

> *I don't know that by one's mind one can write such things.*
> *What do you say?*

Not possible. There would be something artificial or made up in them if it were the mind that did it.

> *How has she opened to the mystic plane? Something akin*
> *to her nature or one just opens?*

It may be either.

> *Even when a thing drops down, isn't it rather risky to accept*
> *it as it comes, specially the* chhanda *part of it?*

If anything is defective, it can be only by a mistake in the transcription.

> *Does the* chhanda *also come down with inspiration or has*
> *one to change it afterwards?*

Yes, it comes and is usually faultless — if the mind is passive and the source a high, deep or true one. Of course metre as the Supraphysicals understand it!

> *I shall illustrate my point. J says she sometimes rejects*
> *lines because she doesn't understand their meaning. But*
> *since they repeatedly throw themselves on her, she accepts*
> *them. When the poem is completed the meaning becomes*
> *clear.*

The mind ought to be quiet till all is written. Afterwards one can look and see if there is anything to be altered.

> *All this is really funny. How has she got this Blakish opening*
> *without even reading him? Was she Blake or Mrs. Blake by*
> *any chance?*

Not necessarily. She was certainly not Blake. What I meant was not that they were just like Blake's or a reproduction of his, but simply that they have a kindred mystical stamp and come from a similar

A

636   CORRESPONDENCE WITH

source of inspiration. The figures, the form, the general vision are quite different from Blake's.

> *Lines come down in her meditation or she actually hears them!*

Why not? It is quite common with many here.

> *How do you find the metre of this poem? It seems a bit jerky to me. And how do you like the word* উল্লাসে ?[1]

I don't know really the law of Bengali metre in this respect. In an English stanza it would be quite natural to have these variations, especially if they go by pairs as here. But you should know better what is or is not admissible in Bengali. Of course Bengalically the last line may be dropped — but উল্লাসে spoils the symmetry of the sense a little, as it is intended to refrain the idea of the opening lines. However if necessary as metre, উল্লাসে will do very well.

> *You didn't write anything about Jatin's room business?*

Forgot, by Jove!

July 27, 1936

> *You say you don't know enough Bengali nor the metre, but all these discussions have revealed that your "don't know" is much more than "we know". Whether you know or don't know, we will write and please just opine on it.*

Very well, I will go on hazarding my perceptions of Form in the Formless. Metre and law can always take care of themselves.

> *My poetic fervour has volatilised away!*

Well, it was a good spirit anyway.

> *J says that even a few beautiful lines in a poem give her a thrill.*

[1] *ullāse:* in exultation.

SRI AUROBINDO   637

Well, that is the natural effect on a poet.

> *You know I have always complained of the lack of any such*
> *happiness. I write because I have nothing else to do. I say to*
> *myself, "It is not this, not this, neti neti, that I want. I want*
> *something deep, great and wide filling my whole being with*
> *ananda, peace."*

And yet you say there is no strand of Yogic seeking in you anywhere?
Neti neti with this longing for something deep and great in the
nature of Ananda filling the being and the vairagya for anything
less (নাল্পে সুখমস্তি ভূমা সুখমস্তি) [*nālpe sukhamasti, bhūmā sukha-*
masti] is the very nature of the Yogic push and impulse, at least
according to the Vedantic line.[1]

> *I seek for Ananda, it eludes me — Love, Peace are nowhere.*
> *If poetry doesn't give them, what's the use?*

Poetry does not give love and peace, it gives Ananda, intense but
not wide or lasting.

> *You will say that it is my mind that obstructs by its struggle.*

Your mind has obstructed the free flow of the poetry — but what it
has obstructed more is the real peace and Ananda that is "deep, great
and wide". A quiet mind turned towards the ভূমা[2] is what you
need.

> *I have written poems without much obstruction, but they*
> *didn't give me any joy except the last one: The Bird of Light,*[3]
> *which gave me just a thrill.*

Perhaps the beginning of Ananda of poetry, because it came from
a deeper than mental source.

> *Isn't it a fact that the best poetry, almost always, comes*
> *down without any resistance at all?*

[1] *nālpe sukhamasti, bhūmaiva sukham:* there is no delight in the small, the vast
itself is the happiness. (*Chhāndogya Upanishad* VII.23.1)

[2] *bhūmā:* vastness.

[3] A Bengali poem, "Alor Pākhi", in *Swapnadīp*, pp. 17–18.

638   CORRESPONDENCE WITH

Usually the best poetry a poet writes, the things that make him immortal, come like that.

July 28, 1936

> *Yes, there is a longing no doubt, for something deep, and নেতি নেতি* [1] *also is there; but I don't find vairagya for anything less as yet —*

নেতি নেতি is itself vairagya — the true vairagya.

> *For I am thinking of past vital pleasures, sweet memories of happy peaceful moments in a happy sunny or moony atmosphere, and am thinking — ah, if I could get back those rare moments!*

That is in another part of your vital — the lower.

> *So how shall I trust this নেতি as real or this "yogic strand"? All the time this blessed vital thought goes on! Yogic strand!*

Your argument is that because the Yogic strand is not the whole of the nature, it cannot be real. This is rather illogical. The Yogic strand is always in the beginning a strand, a movement or impulsion from one part of the nature, however veiled or small. It grows afterwards, slowly or quickly, according to people and circumstances, on the rest.

> *In spite of everything, a deep urge is there but a dissatisfaction too because I can't get it. Can this be a psychic sadness?*

It is the feeling of the higher vital which has been affected by the psychic.

> *I doubt.*

! That's the mind at it.

---

[1] *neti neti:* it is not this, it is not this.

SRI AUROBINDO   639

> *Anyway I have realised that without "something" deeply
> and lastingly settled in me, I can't do anything. I don't know
> what is that something or how to get it, so I lament.*

It is the wideness of the higher or spiritual consciousness with its
vast peace, light, knowledge, force, Ananda.

> *You say my mind obstructs, whereas I thought it is the vital
> hankering that hinders.*

Your mind obstructs with its perpetual "I doubt" (see above). The
vital of course by its hankerings.

> *Of course the mind is always thinking, worrying, but isn't
> it because the vital is restless?*

Partly or mostly, but also because it is the nature of the mind to
doubt, worry, eternally parliamentarise about things instead of
getting them done.

> *J sends a poem. She doesn't think much of it, as it was done
> so quickly. She says she heard the first few lines in sleep.
> After reading the whole poem, I have found it is impossible
> to write it simply from facility. It is an inspiration-poem.*

Of course it is impossible. There must be inspiration. The value of
the poem does not rise from the labour or difficulty felt in writing
it. Shakespeare, it is said, wrote at full speed and never erased
a line.

> *I don't know about the fineness of the poem, but the chhanda
> and her originality in thought and expressions move me so
> much.*

The poem is fine.

> *She says that while she was writing it, she felt some heavy
> pressure in the nape of the neck, then it came down and she
> was compelled to shut her eyes after which she felt all right
> and the poem came down quickly.*

640   CORRESPONDENCE WITH

The pressure is the sign of a Yoga-force at work.

> *You said that Blake put down with fidelity whatever came down.*

I didn't mean that he never altered — I don't know about that. I meant he did not let his mind disfigure what came by trying to make it intellectual. He transcribed what he saw and heard.

> *Will you circulate some Force towards me?*

Yes.

                                                            July 29, 1936

> *Yesterday I had a very strange dream — not exactly a dream. 3 or 4 of us were listening to D singing with his teacher Majumdar (now dead) who was playing the harmonium. Majumdar joined D in the song. Then the harmonium stopped; Majumdar, carried away by the* bhāva, *made very fine rhythmic movements, uttering some lines now and then. Oh, the whole thing was exquisite. Then the funniest thing happened; Majumdar was turned into D, and I found it was D who was uttering the lines and making the movements with a bare upper body. Then the bust became luminous and he went on singing, dancing and gradually his luminous bust rose in the air and vanished away! Someone cried out — he is an avatar, avatar. . . The whole thing so influenced me that even after my sleep broke, I remained quiet, thinking of that very pleasant vision. It was 3.15 a.m. What's this now?*

A very queer dream in the vital plane — rather mixed with contributions from the subconscient. Possibly it was the element of Majumdar that D had absorbed which you saw in that figure, then it disappeared into D himself, the inner progress he had made through his music being figured in the bust being luminous. But the vanishing away and the avatar beat me.

> *I enclose a poem of J with the corrected version which is*

SRI AUROBINDO   641

> *decidedly better than the original. She says formerly she*
> *used to aspire for things beautiful etc. instead of letting*
> *herself go. Now she remains passive — and this poem is the*
> *result. Any answer?*

There is no incompatibility between aspiring and letting the thing
come through. The aspiration gives the necessary intensity so that
what comes has a better chance of being a true transcription. In
this case probably the pain she felt in the neck etc. was a proof
of some fatigue in the physical parts which spoiled the transmission. . .

> *I am afraid there is plenty of work for you tonight. You can*
> *keep my poem.*

I am obliged to do so. I am issuing a notice for "Stop correspondence" but that need not deter you from sending your or J's poems
with comments.

July 30, 1936

> *Well, Sir, what about my epic?*

Splendid. This is a full-blown poem.

> *I notice some queer things happening in the realm of poetry*
> *between Nishikanta and myself. I wrote a line:* চলছে ভেসে
> চাঁদের তরী ওই সুনীলের সাগরে ,[1] *and did not follow it up.*
> *Two days later I find Nishikanta writing a poem wherein*
> *occurs the line* কে ভাসালে চাঁদের তরী ?[2] *Some time back*
> *a similar thing happened. These are about expressions;*
> *similar things are happening about* chhanda *also. Strange,*
> *isn't it?*

Nothing queer about that. You dropped the inspiration and did not
work it out; so it went off and prodded N who let it through. That
often happens.

[1] The moon-boat is sailing on the ocean of the blue sky.
[2] Who made it sail, the moon-boat?

642   CORRESPONDENCE WITH

NK's new poems strike me as if a new channel has opened up in him. The poems seem to become more simple and deep —psychic?

Yes—he has made a big jump forward. Formerly it was all vital; afterwards vital-mental (I am speaking of the transmitting agency, not the source of inspiration or its substance), now a new element has come in. Psychic? I don't know—perhaps psycho-mental-vital. At any rate something wanting has been filled up—a missing chord has come in.

He himself admitted that J's poems have helped him in this direction. I think this simple mystic-symbolic touch he got from J.

It is probable.

It seems I don't get joy in writing because I haven't yet got my own source and am writing only by the mind. If true, don't mental works give joy?

The mental by itself gives a kind of aesthetic রস,[1] but not ভোগ[2]— ভোগ comes from the excited participation of the vital, আনন্দ[3] from above.

But there is such a thing as an aesthetic thrill. Why don't I get it?

Probably the higher vital does not sufficiently participate.

D.L. has rashes. They are probably due to enema or salicylic acid.

It must be the salicylic.

July 31, 1936

---

[1] *rasa:* taste.
[2] *bhog:* enjoyment.
[3] *ānanda:* delight.

SRI AUROBINDO

August 1936

Please tell me if metre is, after all, not a question of the ear.

Mainly of the ear, but "number" also has something to do with it.

Wasn't the ear the first guide and then metre developed?

Yes, but in developing, metre modified the ear and created in it demands of a more complex kind.

What about Blake? Are his or other great poets' metres, absolutely orthodox?

English is different; it has a freer movement, I suppose, than Bengali. English metre is sometimes strict, sometimes breaks into irregularities.

J says she still feels that terrible pressure when she sits down to write. Is it due to resistance?

I suppose — if it is on the neck — that is the place of the expressing physical or externalising mind. As yet probably there is a strong resistance there — perhaps the result of something there that still expects or desires to write mentally, not mystically.

She was lying in bed trying to concentrate when she saw something like a thin wire coming towards her, with a rapid serpentine movement. The wire seemed to change into a snake. She had a joy out of it. She fears it may presage a bad event.

No need to fear. The wire implies a connection with some source — the snake the energy of that which was coming from the source. A snake is a bad symbol only when it comes from the vital or other lower plane.

D.L. complains of constant stinging pain in the abdomen. It is either ulcer or worms. I am thinking of treating her with

644   CORRESPONDENCE WITH

> *a milk diet in alkalies. If ulcer, then it is bound to produce results. On Monday I shall take her for X-ray.*

Is it not better to ascertain first by X-ray or otherwise before trying this treatment, as milk diet only may make her weak with a depressed resistance?

> *I asked S to take Asram food; he agreed but came back saying—"Let me go on one week more with the special diet." What's to be done?*

Go on for a week more, since the fellow insists. He may think himself into pains again otherwise.

August 1, 1936

> *I send you this magnificent poem of Dilip's along with his after-corrections. My impression is that most of the changes have spoiled the beauty of the poem. Do you agree with me?*

I have the same impression as you. It is always a little perilous to meddle afterwards with something that has come out in a full inspiration—"improvements" in such cases generally spoil the first spontaneous perfection.

> *I am again prosaic and gloomy. Everybody is changing here; no change for me.*

Everybody is who? Give me the good news.

> *Must I go on crying and crying?*

I hope not. Crying won't hasten the change.

> *Please put, at least, the shower of poetry on as you did a few days ago. Or is it gone?*

It can always come back.

> *What about my other book lying with you? Can you release it now?*

SRI AUROBINDO   645

I don't know. Not immediately at least.

> *You said that if the wrong medicine is given, the Force has to counteract that also. . .*

I only meant that it was so much obstacle to the Force which it has to overcome.

> *If the medical channel had opened in you like the painting vision, what a great help it would have been for you, and a boon for me!*

My dear sir, in that case I should have to do all the doctoring. So I take care not to let the Medico open. Simple measure of prudence.

> *J says no trouble at all now. . . . He is not willing to take any medicine. Cast him off?*

Bile gone? If so can finish.

August 2, 1936

> *J had never any bile! He complained of pain and weakness.*

Ah yes. I was under the impression it was S. I am always mixing them together.

> *You did not answer my question about the Force. What I asked you was that by the very fact of much obstacle, the Force or the giver of the Force knows that some mistake is being committed. Suppose you give a certain Force, but it fails to produce the desired result, then you say, "Oh that fellow has given wrong medicines — Swine!"*

Not at all. The Force (I am out of the picture here) feels a greater obstacle, but need not know that it is due to a wrong medicine. Force and Knowledge are two different things and in the consciousness below supermind may go together or may not.
  Swine is inappropriate — it should be some other animal.

August 4, 1936

X, in his latest poem, has used one of my expressions. Suppose his were to be published and then mine — I would be misjudged as borrowing from him. How far is it justifiable for a poet to take the bhāva and expression from others and use them?

Great poets have borrowed from small ones and small poets from great ones, and it is difficult to lay down any law in the matter. But to lift things bodily like that from unpublished poems shown in confidence, is not delicate — nor, I think permissible.

Shall we be petty and mean if we don't show our poems from such fear?

From the normal point of view it would be perfectly justified not to show your things — except of course for the fact that X and N have given you considerable help in forming yourselves as poets; but that is no reason why they should take things from your poems.

Please give the answer from the ordinary as well as the Yogic point of view.

From the Yogic point of view one ought to be indifferent and without sense of ownership or desire of fame or praise. But for that one must have arrived at the Yogic poise — such a detachment is not possible without it. I do not mind R's lifting whole sentences and paragraphs from my writings at the World Conference as his own and getting credit for a new and quite original point of view.

But if I were eager to figure before the world as a philosopher, I would resent it. But even if one does not mind, one can see the impropriety of the action or take measures against its repetition, if one thinks it worth while.

You will see that it is really a problem that concerns all writers, for I am also tempted to take and use others' expressions and bhāva but I don't know if I should.

You should not — if for nothing else for the sake of the poetry and right development of your own inspiration.

SRI AUROBINDO

> *A's umbilical pain is gone, slight liver pain. . . She says she wrote to Mother at 3.30 p.m. and since then her pain has stopped. She has these attacks, so I would like to know whether the medicine has done her any good or the Force alone.*

I suppose the medicine has done its part.

> *A worker in the hot water dept. had dysentery 3 weeks ago and was treated at home. Suddenly day before yesterday he had copious vomiting of dark blood. Came to us with chest pain. . .*

Dark blood can't be from the lungs? Not something wrong lower down?

August 5, 1936

> *What about my poem? I hope it is mentally quite clear!*

Very fine indeed, very. You have suddenly reached a remarkable maturity of the poetic power. Which seems to suggest that the periods of sterility were not so sterile after all or were rather an incubation period, a work of opening going on in the inner being behind the veil before it manifested in the outer. Let us hope the same is going on in the direct sadhana.

> *Today at Pranam I felt a somewhat "blocky" feeling, if you know what I mean?*

Yes, thought at first I was afraid you meant you felt blockheaded or felt foolish! but remembered in time the "block" of descent.

> *Is it the descent of Force?*

Usually the feeling comes from a mass of the higher consciousness coming down either as peace or as force.

> *Dr. Becharlal and I are again strongly suspecting D.L. of a double infection: hookworm with Trichomonas. . . We'll make another stool examination. . .*

648   CORRESPONDENCE WITH

By the way, I understand how hookworms get in, but how do these tropical Technomaniacs or whatever you call them, make their entry on the stage? Food? water? what?

> *S complains of hunger all the time. Five slices of bread are given in the morning, he wants one more! In spite of it, feels weak etc.*

He must have bad assimilation due to liver, so always hungry and no profit from food.

August 7, 1936

> *If you have thought it is the apparent period of sterility etc. that has produced this "maturity", I am afraid it is not quite so.*

I still think so and think that it is quite so.

> *For, this poem upon which you have based your opinion, was actually started, and one and a half stanzas were completed, on the 25th of July or so, i.e. before "the period of sterility". The rest only was done in these 2 or 3 days.*

It is not confined to you or this case but a general psychological principle — the action behind the veil, even the psychologists who do not believe in Yoga have begun to recognise the large part this plays in Nature.

> *So I'm a little puzzled about the "going in".*

I do not remember having said anything about "going in". I believe I spoke of something "going on" behind the veil during the time of apparent sterility in the outer being.

> *When you said "suddenly" did you mean that the maturity of power has come in fully in this poem?*

When I said suddenly I meant as I said, that it appears in these two bigger poems and was not there before. A progress was there, but not this.

I thought that development in poetry has a connection with the development in Yoga as well. But you mention the two separately.

If poetic progress meant a progress in the whole range of Yoga, NK would be a great Yogi by this time. The opening in poetry or any other part helps to prepare the general opening when it is done under the pressure of Yoga, but it is at first something special, like the opening of the subtle vision or subtle senses. It is the opening of a special capacity in the inner being.

Though maturity has come in, the substance and depth are remarkably lacking — I think they've come in J's poems.

There is a much greater ripeness in the thought-substance as well as the rest.

What is more visible and very vivid, it seems to me, is the word-beauty of the poem. It doesn't make one think or stir deeply with the discovery of some hidden treasure.

I don't know exactly what you mean by that — in yourself or in the reader? You say you have not the enthusiasm of creation, so your own feeling in the matter is not conclusive.

All this maturity etc. is all right, only it doesn't thrill me or give me satisfaction... No interest in life or its creative activities, especially when I see that I am the same Man of Sorrows... Please don't taunt me saying that it is all D!

No. D this time is making a valiant attempt to suppress the Man of Sorrows in him and seems so far to have succeeded. I hope you too will soon screw up your energy to the pitch of throwing off this encumbrance.

... I'm now trying to keep myself as busy as possible; it won't allow the mind to feed on those poisons.

Well, that is right — at least it helps.

*I don't know whether the Goddess of Poetry will withdraw
her boon because I don't care much for it.*

She doesn't seem to be doing so.

*Anyway, do you understand my psychology and, if you do,
will you give some answers, not mystic but mental?*

It is quite easy to understand if one realises that the natural being is
not of one piece, but made up of parts or quantums or whatever one
likes to call it. One part of your mind and vital has the need though
not yet the push for the Divine and that need is becoming very
prominent — . . . Another doesn't believe in, or hope for anything.
One part of the mind resorts to poetry but cannot wake the vital
enthusiasm, because the vital is besieged by the Man of Sorrows.
Then there is the man of sorrows himself mixing in everything.
Different parts of the mind take different sides and suggest opposite
things according as they are pushed by one force or another. As yet
no resolution of the central being to put all that into harmony,
expel what is to be expelled, change what is to change. I don't know
whether you call that mystic or mental answers, but I can't give
you any other that would be true.

*. . . Today D.L.'s stools were examined, again there were
swarms.*
[*Sri Aurobindo underlined the word "swarms".*]

What's this word? It looks like "swarms"! Swarms of what?

August 8, 1936

*I am satisfied with the answers exposing brilliantly the
symptoms and providing the diagnosis. Now the prognosis
and the treatment.*

That is more difficult. Panacea there is, but only one, which you have
indicated in your today's poem.[1]

How should I develop the push, the harmony and resolution

[1] A Bengali poem, "Nirbhar", published in *Swapnadīp*, p. 19.

SRI AUROBINDO   651

> *of the central being, and how should I wake up the vital enthusiasm for poetry? If there is one workable formula that will be a panacea, so much the better.*

For the rest there are several formulas which are not panaceas. The first is to get into touch with your central being and get it into action. That central may be the psychic, it may be the Self above with the mental Purusha as its delegate. Either of these once in action does the harmonising etc.

The second way is to act with your mental will on these things, not allowing yourself to drift and not getting upset by difficulties and checks, calling on the Mother's Force to assist and finally use your will. There are others, but I stop here.

> *I want urgently that part of the Divine which will help me keep my poise, calm, peace against any assault from the vital quarter...*

It is what is trying to come down in the block condition.

> *D.L. has less pain. Starts normal meals. She asked if she could take oranges and grapes. I said—yes.*

Grapes are safe? If she does not wash them in boiling water or a solution of permanganate?

> *By "swarms" I meant swarms of Trichomonas.*

The medicine had no effect? But if the Trichomonas are there in quantity, why is it necessary to search for Hookworms?

August 9, 1936

> *In your yesterday's answer you wrote that I have indicated the panacea in my poem. I thought I spoke of faith and surrender! Is that it?*

You described very admirably the attitude of perfect *nirbhar*[1] which is the great secret of the most perfect kind of sadhana.

---

[1] Reliance.

>*You have not said how to get into touch with the central being, and get it into action.*

There is no how. One decides to do it and one does it.

>*My mental will itself is weak.*

It can be made strong.

>*I can try to call down the Mother's force, but faith and surrender would require a wonderful Yogic poise and power possible only in born Yogis, I think.*

Not at all. A wonderful Yogic poise and power would usually bring self-reliance rather than faith and surrender. It is the simple people who do the latter most easily.

>*When you spoke of "poetic power" in my poetry, what did you mean? I asked D. He says "poetic power" means a dynamism, a vigorous living force which we find in Madhusudan. . . But we find in Shakespeare both power and beauty, while Swinburne has hardly power predominant.*

No power in Swinburne?

>*Did you mean by "poetic power" a power or capacity of expression?*

Of course that was what I meant. The other kind of power would not be prefaced by the epithet poetic. One would simply say "there is great power in his style" etc.

>*August 10, 1936*

>*Dr. Manilal examined D.L. . . She's extremely weak, he advises complete rest.*

I suppose there is no call for her to work.

>*. . . Is it possible for R to take her up?*

SRI AUROBINDO   653

I am asking R. You will have to tell him all about the case.

August 11, 1936

> *Chand has sent money to buy garlands for you. You can bless him without garlands, can't you?*

Yes, of course — quite able.

> *Jatin has brought me a pair of dhotis. I shall feel highly gratified if you will kindly use one.*

I have two drawers packed with dhotis already! Why not use both — your supplies being undoubtedly less?

> *Do you know what all these people say? That they feel peace, peace everywhere, which one never finds at any other place!*

Of course!

> *Jatin has been saying that Peace is coming as if in waves! Satuda the same, and Dr. Becharlal runs close, if not more! You must be very glad indeed to hear this news.*

It is not news! Numbers of people have said the same thing — even carry it to Europe and keep it there in the midst of the crush and confusion.

> *I wish I could get a little of this long-cherished and much-coveted basis of your Yoga.*

It is because you people here, having no infernal shindy outside themselves, create one inside it. The vital can't get on without a shindy — finds life dull otherwise.

August 13, 1936

> *NK sends you a poem on his Darshan impression.*

Kept him.

August 16, 1936

J wants to know why or how the mind-fag has come in and by what attitude or process it can quickly pass off . . .

There is nothing serious in it. Very often when the mind has been doing something for a long time (I mean of course the physical mind), something which demands intensity of work or action, not what can be done as a routine, it finds itself unable to do it well any longer. That means that it is strained, needs rest so that the force may gather again. Rest or a variation. A little rest given to it or a variation of work should set it right again.

I thought that one or two hours' work without undue effort might perhaps keep the channel open and at the same time produce no fatigue.

It is not a question of ordinary fatigue by overwork — but of a temporary inability to go on doing the same thing over and over any longer. That is what I mean by mind-fag. It is not the mere writing of poetry of any kind but the intensity necessary to bring down that kind of poetry that is in question. The channel in fact is not working because of the fag — it can work again only after rest. by not forcing oneself.

Dr. Manilal recommends arnica for Mulshankar's pain, and massage.

Massage best. No homeopathy without R's intervention is allowable.

S complains again of vague pains. Dr. Manilal says he must do only light work.

We gave him no work. It is his own spree.

A poem begun on the 6th and completed by Darshan. . . Well, any remark?

Sorry. Your poem got mixed up with Nolini's papers and I saw it

SRI AUROBINDO   655

only now. Glanced through but will have to study more carefully.
Will return with N's.

> Tomorrow, by the way, I am going to burst a little —
> Attention!

Eh what! Burst? Which way? If you explode, fizz only — don't
blow up the Asram.

August 17, 1936

> The Asram is quite safe! My explosion will burst me alone,
> but I will see if the Divine can as well be exploded. I ex-
> pected very much that your touch would relieve my burden,
> a little even, or would do something somewhere by which
> something at least would be tangible outwardly. Well,
> illusion it has been all. . .

Man alive (or of Sorrows or whatever may be the fact), how is it you
fell on such a fell day for your burst? There has been an explosion,
as D merrily calls it, beginning on the 14th but reaching now its
epistolary climax and I have been writing sober letters to excited
people for the last few hours. Solicit therefore your indulgence for a
guru besieged by other people's disturbances (and letters) until tonight. Send back the blessed burst and I will try to deal with it.

> My problem is: I have been trying to call down Peace
> but none comes. I admit that at times a stabdhatā comes
> down in meditation, but afterwards no peace, not to speak
> of Ananda etc.

The stabdhata is still the condition which announces the attempt of
peace to descend. It is a beginning.

> This miserable condition is continuing so long! It drives
> me to make big efforts in concentration, to push and push,
> but it seems the vital refuses to cooperate in the sadhana
> and hence there is no joy.

It is of course that; the mind is pressing the vital by concentration and otherwise, but the vital is not yet prepared to accept peace or renounce agitation and desire.

> *Is it because the food has been taken away from the vital that it non-cooperates?*

Partly that.

> *Or is it your Man of Sorrows who has besieged it?*

The Man of Sorrows only takes advantage of the vital resistance and restlessness to bring in despondency etc. and make things worse.

> *Who is this Man of Sorrows, really? Is it a force or a being that has possessed me? I feel as if something is keeping me down forcibly.*

Yes, it is so. But who it is, is a long story — He has not possessed, but is in control of part of your vital.

> *Whoever the devil he is, it seems to be impossible for me to dislodge him.*

Difficult at present but not impossible.

> *If it is because of D's company, I'll cut it off from tomorrow.*

No. D is less often upset and takes things in a more humorous way.

> *Or is it due to J's company? But that can't be cut off as the literary connection is there.*

Well, I can't say that has nothing to do with it — but cutting off may not make things better.

> *. . . I can't even walk, where I want to run. Really I am losing all hope again. . .*

That is the contribution of the Man of Sorrows.

SRI AUROBINDO   657

> *You said "nirbhar is the great secret",* [*10.8.36*] *but*
> *when one is besieged by so many things: mind restless,*
> *vital dead, what shall I do?*

"Nirbhar" means reliance on the Divine whatever the condition
or the difficulties. "Nirbhar" when all is going well, does not mean
much. It is a poise one has to take and you can grow into it as D is
growing into it.

> *Lastly, please ask Mother if I've been doing any wrong*
> *movement these 2 or 3 days. I feel some indication of that*
> *sort at the Pranam.*

Not to her knowledge.

> *Is the poem done?*

Yes. Very good, especially first half. But this flower and bee image
has been buzzing about since ages before Kalidas; needs a little
more polish to look entirely new.

August 18, 1936

> *I'm again passing through a period of* মন খারাপ[1] *due to*
> *the same old vital trouble.*

Ah that মন খারাপ! If you could only get rid of it — face the thing
calmly and steadily as something to be eliminated which necessarily
takes time but must and will be done!

> *. . . Now tell me how I should keep this* nirbhar *when the*
> *vital rises. Rejection? Detachment?*

D first — R with D.

> *How shall I detach myself when a subtle strain of dissatis-*
> *faction runs within?*

Detach from the dissatisfaction.

---

[1] *man khārāp:* bad mood.

> *Shall I cry out — "Damn it all ; don't worry even if the lower vital bursts up. Everything will be all right"?*

That is not nirbhar.

I fear all my answers[1] are scrappy as well as illegible, but this has been also a fell day (one letter 36 pages vernacular, 2 others each 8 pages of foolscap, others less in size (4, 2, 1 etc.) but ample in number — and this is no-correspondence period!) I have had to race against the old man Time.

August 19, 1936

> *You simply say "the difficulty is there"! I wonder if anyone else here had to work under such a condition. . . To "detach" — isn't it something Herculean for me?*

Well, but it is not individual to you. Everyone has to do that with his difficulties. Detach means that the Witness in oneself has to stand back and refuse to look on the movement as his own (the soul's own) and look on it as a habit of past nature or an invasion of general Nature. Then to deal with it as such. It may seem difficult, but it comes perfectly well by trying persistently.

> *If the mind goes on pressing and pressing, will the vital be prepared?*

It does in the end.

> *Otherwise to take up the vital violently like D, doesn't seem possible.*

Violently? I don't see how he did that.

> *To think that I will have to suffer like him for so many years before anything happens, freezes me!*

That is not necessary.

> *If time permits, a comprehensive answer, please.*

---

[1] Not published.

SRI AUROBINDO   659

When time permits.

Mother would like you to go to the Hospital and ask the Doctor
there what is really the matter with Swasti and how long they think
he will have to stay there. Between doctor and doctor.

August 20, 1936

> *All your answers for the cure of my troubles have been too
> strong for me, for you have thrown everything on my
> great self: "If you could do this, if you could do that, etc!"*

No, I have only made suggestions of what the great self could do to
help the Force and make an orientation for the Force to work upon
and carry out.

> *When I ask you how to do it, you reply—Oh one simply
> does it! If one could simply do it, why should I bother you?*

One simply does it, means that one tries a certain psychological
movement which is known by long experience to be effective and the
Force enters into it and one day one finds it done.

> *Tell me, if I pray for Peace, Calm, Force, Strength, etc.,
> will it be enough or not? After that, to be able to reject,
> detach, must be done by your Force. That's all I can do,
> please understand that.*

At any rate there must be the acceptance of the rejection or detachment for the Force to use—a kind of will to it. If you simply pray
and then say "All right, now, damn it, I have done all that is necessary; I can now lament or indulge"—that makes things a trifle
difficult.

> *On the whole, I feel better today. I could recall after some
> concentration the nebulous outlines of your face. Something
> is going to happen?*

Yes, of course.

> *Is it true that a greater and a vaster Force descended this Darshan?*

It is not a question of descent. We are nurturing the Force and it grows necessarily stronger and has more effect.

> *What about Jatin and his wife?*

Both of them very well and growing weller since they were here.

> *I want to ask you a host of questions on the psychology of the affair of D and Y...*

By the way, as you got better, D flopped down. Lost his incipient nirbhar and wants to walk off again.

> *Any time to circulate some Force for poetry?*

Yes.

N.B. I send you the lucubrations of the S fellow for your information. I absolutely object to his living in and on the Mother's force — he would be there like his own ball,[1] neither melted, nor plastic nor disappeared. Any remarks? Please return the gem as I may have to answer it.

August 21, 1936

> *I have been longing to ask you the mystery behind J's poetic flowering; but of late you have become awfully cryptic.*

That is perhaps because I am becoming more and more supramental.

> *You know her previous works were sporadic and simple with long gaps in between.*

That was because she was trying to write literature. That is often the first stage.

---

[1] The word "ball" was used by the patient to describe an accumulation of gas in the intestines.

> *When she was asked to compose songs the other day, we found a sudden transformation. Even the first few songs were not very striking, but they seemed to have opened a door and she has entered into your mystic kingdom. . .*

Opened the lyrical gift in her probably — began knocking for the spontaneous song in place of the mind-made article.

> *What she is writing seems to me exceedingly striking. We don't meet any such original ideas and expressions in Bengali literature.*

Of course not — she was not inspired this time by Bengali literature, but by the Faery International.

> *It is a great mystery to me. Comparing her original turn, expressions, speed, with her past work — what a miraculously rapid development!*

But, my dear sir, it often happens like that. I believe you were not here when D's poetry blossomed; but it was quite as sudden. Remember Tagore's description of him as the cripple who suddenly threw away his crutches and began to run and his astonishment at the miracle. Nishikanta came out in much the same way, a sudden Brahmaputra of inspiration. The only peculiarity in J's case is the source she struck — the pure mystic source.

> *I refuse to believe that it is she who has done it.*

Of course she didn't, nor D nor Nishikanta either. It is a way of speaking.

> *Has the inner mind opened up or what?*

A passage opened through it.

> *Please shed some light on it. If you want it to be kept a secret, I shall keep it — but a few lines on it.*

Well, if you think I knew how it's done! I hammer about till I hit the right spot. It hits quick sometimes, that's all.

Note however that there was always in J something that wanted or claimed to belong to another world. Perhaps by the pressure she got into contact with it.

> *How do you find the poem I am sending you? Does it deserve incineration?*

Well, as poetry it is some good — but I can't say it is distinguished or beautiful like the poems you have written since.

You needn't incinerate, but bury it in a drawer somewhere for the moment. Read it again after ten years (Horace's advice).

> *What about the refrain?*

Refrain? Man alive, if all were like the refrain, I should say "Bury, bury — burn, burn."

I have persistently forgotten to send you this letter. Can you give me any light on the subject? Do you know anything about these injections?

> [*Evening*]
> [*Regarding the letter.*] *My knowledge of leprosy is practically nil, so I approached Dr. Manilal. He says that since the servant has come in close contact with the family, all the members must take the injections as proposed. Though the treatment is palliative it may produce a greater prophylactic effect, at least the psychological effect.*

Good Lord — only that! Psychological effect needs injection?

> *Dr. Manilal says that servants working for 30 years in leper hospitals did not develop any leprosy. No intimacy in the contact?. . .*

Perhaps unconcern also!

SRI AUROBINDO   663

> *We have shed some light. Enough to illumine the supra-*
> *mental table?*

Umph!

August 23, 1936

> *Jatin's wife writes to her sister that she is extremely happy*
> *here. . . I can understand Jatin saying something like that,*
> *but she knowing nothing about spirituality likes the place*
> *so much — miraculous, what?*

Why? Plenty of people have felt that. E.g. the Yuvarani comes here
full of a secret sorrow for her lost son and goes back very happy.

> *Jatin had a dream of you as in the photograph, giving*
> *him instructions in his structural engineering work!!. . .*
> *It was Sri Aurobindo in his previous form, he says, why?*

I suppose, the present Sri Aurobindo having left all engineering
instructions to the Mother, the previous Sri Aurobindo had to come
and do it in this case.

> *We see then that Sri Aurobindo has come out, the least*
> *hope of which we don't entertain. For another thing, he has*
> *come out as an Engineer! Any possibility of the fruition*
> *of the dream?*

Anyhow what has it to do with coming out? Any number of people
meet me in dreams and get instructions or intimations about this
or that. It is an activity of the vital plane where I am not in strict
retirement — it has nothing to do with any future physical happening.

> *What's this threat, Sir? You are cryptic because you are*
> *becoming more and more supramental! [21.8.36]. For the*
> *Supramental's sake, don't be that yet. I have many things*
> *to know. . .*

Well, but haven't I told you that the supramental can't be understood by the intellect? So necessarily or at least logically, if I become

664   CORRESPONDENCE WITH

supramental and speak supramentally, I must sound unintelligible
to everybody. Q.E.D. It is not a threat, only the statement of a
natural evolution.

> *A carpenter beaten by a rat. . .*

Say, say! I never heard of a rat beating a man before! He ought to
go to the criminal court instead of the hospital.

August 25, 1936

> *At last you have given me an occasion for a question; let
> it be an occasion for a big reply, what?*

My dear sir, what is this extravagant ambition for bigness?
   With fifty letters a day raining on me in a "non-correspondence"
period, a supramental brevity is all of which I am capable.

> *You very often say "it is a meeting in the vital plane".
> Yesterday you said "an activity of the vital plane"—
> what does it mean? Are all happenings there as true as on the
> physical plane?*

Yes, except that sometimes the record is imperfect — but the happening is true.

> *Are they intimations of what would happen on the physical
> plane?*

No — the vital plane has an independent life of its own; the physical also.

> *My being meets you or the Mother in dreams, and receives
> your blessings. Has it any concrete value — as concrete
> as the Pranam touch?*

What do you mean by concrete? It is concrete there just as the Abyssinian or Spanish wars are concrete here.

> *Do you mean to say that people getting instructions from*

SRI AUROBINDO   665

> *you in dreams is as real, effective and correct as if you had*
> *written them on paper?*

Yes, if the record is correct.

> *If that be so, does Jatin's meeting mean that his future*
> *work* here *will be engineering?*

No, not necessarily.

> *Or does it mean that even there outside, he will be guided*
> *by the Mother?*

He may be, if he develops the supraphysical contact.

> *I am apt to think somewhat slightingly of these vital plane*
> *meetings. . .*

You are too physically matter of fact. Besides you are quite ignorant
of occult things. The vital is part of what European psychologists
sometimes call the subliminal, and the subliminal, as everybody
ought to know, can do things the physical cannot do — e.g. solve
a problem in a few minutes over which the physical has spent days
in vain etc., etc.

> *When I dream that you are writing big answers or the*
> *Mother blessing me profusely, I see exactly the contrary in*
> *my book and at the Pranam. Any explanation?*

What is the use of the same things happening on both planes? it
would be superfluous and otiose. The vital plane is a field where
things can be done which for some reason or other can't be done
now on the physical.

> *Please don't write supramentally. If being supramental,*
> *you can't write intelligibly, is there any earthly use of that?*

Certainly. Your inner self will understand and rejoice while the
outer stares and wobbles.
   N.B. There are of course hundreds of varieties of things in the

vital as it is a much richer and more plastic field of consciousness than the physical, and all are not of equal validity and value — I was speaking above of the things that are valid. By the way, without this vital plane there would be no art, poetry or literature — these things come through the vital before they can manifest here.

August 26, 1936

> *I had asked R long ago to get "Sudarshan" specially for A. He didn't listen; at the last moment he said he would write to Madras, but wrote to Gujerat, hence the delay.*

Very unbusinesslike and slipshod. Writing to Madras means that Mother will have to pay for inferior stuff while she can get free the best quality from Punamchand's father whose speciality it is.

> *X has inflammation inside the ear, I wanted to apply medicine, but he requires permission.*

You can. It was Mother who sent him to you for treatment.

> *S still complains of slight pain and discomfort. Thinking of trying enema on alternate days.*

Yes. Mother thinks it very necessary.

August 30, 1936

> *Yes, X told me that Mother had sent him, but when I went to apply medicine, he said — ask Mother!*

Nonsense! It is implied. Mother doesn't send him to the Dispensary for a promenade or to dance.

> *It seems J's irregularity of periods has been caused by excessive mental and physical strain due to poetry.*

Good Lord! If poetry is to be the parent of irregular menses!

August 31, 1936

SRI AUROBINDO

September 1936

I am sending you a few snaps — some samples of your supramental yogis. Isn't Dilipda splendid in a standing posture?

Superb!

What about his deep intellectual look in the sitting one?

Admirable!

And my noble self seems to be coming out of the grave or going there probably?

Asking where will be the end of this প্রনান্ত লীলা।[1]

My supramental forehead is merging with the Infinite, what?

Yes, dominating scornfully from there the pigmy universe.

Lastly, the Asram photos are very fine.

Very well done.

I give you a rare occasion for laughter. Please do laugh loud and share it with us!

No time to laugh! Can only smile.

As the cause of J's irregular menses it is not poetry I said, but the physical and mental strain. Coming here running with the poem, going back to meditation, then copying hurriedly the poem, then meal, etc. Going on thus day after day. Not enough to cause strain? No, not parent, it has become the issue!

[1] *pranānta līlā:* unending play.

668   CORRESPONDENCE WITH

You relieve me! I was thinking if poetry could be the parent of
i.m., what it would do to you and Dilip and Nishikanta.

September 1, 1936

*A is "slightly better". No fever, slight tenderness in the
liver region.*

Mother found him rather yellow at Pranam.? but if he has no fever,
I suppose it is all right.

September 2, 1936

*Again I have a blessed boil inside the left nostril — painful.
I feel feverish. A dose of Force, please!*

As the modernist poet says

O blessed blessed boil within the nostril,
How with pure pleasure dost thou make thy boss thrill!
He sings of thee with sobbing trill and cross trill,
O blessed, blessed boil within the nostril.

I hope this *stotra*[1] will propitiate the boil and make it disappear,
satisfied.
Is that why you tend towards home-eating?

*I asked R to return to us the duplicate key of the Dispensary.
He has now practically no connection with the Dispensary.
He has agreed, but puts a nonsensical suggestion that
whenever I go out I should leave the key with the gatekeeper.
He also says that if required, another key can be prepared
by Manibhai!!*

You ought to have shouted before. Now he has given order to Manibhai for another key.

September 5, 1936

---

[1] A hymn of praise.

SRI AUROBINDO

> *G has signs of inflammation in the left lung. Better to take an X-ray tomorrow; sputum examination if necessary after that.*

Better not X-ray etc. unless it is absolutely necessary. Feed him, tonic him, coddle with cod-liver oil and see how it works out before plunging into these soul-shaking measures.

> *Should be made a little civilised! He has hardly any bedding; no blanket, no mosquito net. He says there are not many mosquitoes.*

A blanket, banyan, mattress have been given. Mother did not know about mosquito net—but if he is not accustomed to it, he may find it rather suffocating. But you can ask Amrita for one if you think it indispensable. Civilisation is good, but not at all points for everyone.

> *I can't decide if he should be given any work, but if he sits all the time at home, that may act adversely.*

It will certainly act adversely.

> *At any rate, his wandering work has to be stopped.*

On the contrary, to move in the open is surely one of the best things for him — provided it is not under the rain. He has most probably not been eating enough and ought to be fed. Also cod-liver oil and tonic may be good for him. He must have got cold and neglected it.

> *What a powerfully effective "stotra"! the boil couldn't but burst. . . I couldn't make out one word. Is it "make thy bows thrill"?*

I thought you'd boggle over it. "Boss" man "boss" = yourself as owner, proprietor, patron, capitalist of the boil.

> [*Because of some inconvenience I wanted meals at home.*]
> *But if you want, the "home-eating" tendency can be stopped.*

670 CORRESPONDENCE WITH

D.R. says more and more people demanding home consumption—carrying capacity exhausted. Will have to double Dayabhai's work if this goes on—he will spend the whole day tiffin-carrying—and finally what will be the damned use of the Dining Hall? Your name among the home-consumers—so gave you a jog. If we omit the visitors, 50 per cent of the Asram are taking home-meals and most of these all meals at home. All do not take by cart, but even so the cart has to carry more than its proper capacity.

September 6, 1936

G did not have good sleep at night. . .

Said bad sleep was due to the beastly blanket and mattress. Prefers a bedsheet to wrap himself according to former custom.

> *He has to be given a tonic injection "une tous les deux jours"—on alternate days?*

Yes, if that is the direction.

> *His fever has to be brought down. Dr. Becharlal advises his native drug* galoye. . .

If it does not clash with the injections.

> *We must also give cod-liver oil, but I fear to begin at once as he has fever and may not be able to digest. Still I will try from tomorrow one teaspoon a day.*

You can wait till whenever it is suitable to give it. Perhaps the injections should be finished first.

> *"To move in the open" is surely the very thing, but don't you think with running fever of 101.4°, weakness, etc. it would be a little too much?*

That of course—The objection is to making him a permanently sedentary invalid—that is what so many are becoming.

SRI AUROBINDO   671

> *Till his fever comes down and weakness disappears, I think*
> *you will agree that his daily work has to be cut short.*

Mother has stopped his work.

> *Why not take A out of the doctors' hands now by pumping*
> *a big dose?*

Very refractory to big doses.

> *Dr. Becharlal prescribes butter for my amaigrissement and*
> *cod-liver oil by myself.*

?? [*Sri Aurobindo put 2 interrogation marks.*]

September 7, 1936

> *If any oranges can be spared for G, don't you think it will do*
> *him good?*

[*Mother:*] You can go to Champaklal, he will give two oranges
daily.

> *Why two interrogations, Sir, against my using butter?*

Butter and cod-liver oil — which is two.

> *Since the Force does not help, I have to seek fatness from*
> *butter and oil. Of course, Dr. Becharlal also added cheerful-*
> *ness to the prescription.*

Mother pours scorn on your idea that you are a jutting skeleton.
She says that you are less shockingly plump than when you came,
but that is all. But if you take butter and oil together, to say nothing
of cheerfulness, what will you become? Remember Falstaff.[1]

> *We understand that Mother asked Shanta not to take*
> *cod-liver oil with milk or water as it leaves a bad taste in the*
> *mouth.*

---

[1] A fat, witty, good-humoured old knight in Shakespeare's play, *Henry IV.*

Mother told her it might spoil her taste for milk—but did not forbid anything. Now Shanta says she can't take it even in milk, so renounces its use.

> *So we advised her to take it as it is though it is slightly bitter. But still she wants us to ask Mother how to take it!*

So what? Any substitute which she will not object to? She says she has pain in eyes and temples. Replaced fever?

September 8, 1936

> *This trouble of S's has become really a nuissance! Nothing seems to hit him at the right place.*

He has written me a furious letter denouncing you and all doctors and their wicked futile ways.

> *He is so much bent on having his diet increased in spite of our giving him quite a sufficient amount. His excessive hunger points towards some worm infection. Let us try Santonin, if you allow.*

But how try without being sure? Liver also gives alternations of not-eating and bouts of excessive hunger.

> *About me, did you say "less shockingly plump"! Good gracious, was I ever plump? Mother has only to see my bare upper body and exclaim—Oh, doctor like that!*

It's your clothes that made you plump?

> *Please circulate Force from 2 or 2.30 p.m., will you?*

Lord! my least forceful time or rather the fag-end of the same. Never mind.

September 9, 1936

> *What's the matter with my poetry? I tried yesterday's poem*

SRI AUROBINDO

> *again for a long time, nothing doing! The channel has*
> *choked up or what?... Remedy — try and try? or rest and*
> *rest?*

Both methods are possible and each has its advantages — or they
might be combined "Rest and rest and try and try."

> *I have been unusually happy after months!... Man of*
> *Sorrows was non-existent — kicked out? But unfortu-*
> *nately he is trying to poke his face again!*

Twist his nose.

> *We hear your Supermind is very near — not 50 years,*
> *I hope! Time to push us up a little, Sir, so that we may*
> *give you a proper reception, what?*

That's what the Force seems to be trying to do.

> *Don't forget to make us, at least, feel the Descent. 30*
> *years' sadhana, by Jove!...*

30 years too little or too many? What would have satisfied your
rational mind — 3 years? 3 months? 3 weeks? Considering that by
ordinary evolution it could not have been done even at Nature's
express speed in less than 3000 years, and would ordinarily have
taken anything from 30,000 to 300,000, the transit of 30 years is
perhaps not too slow.

> *In trying to solve the riddle of the Sphinx, Paul Brunton*
> *in his book,* A Search in Secret Egypt, *says, "That the*
> *Sphinx represents something divine or someone divine is*
> *suggested by the hieroglyph inscriptions on the walls of the*
> *Upper Egyptian temples, as at Edfu, where a god is pictured*
> *as changing himself into a lion with a human head in order*
> *to vanquish Set, the Egyptian Satan... If the force of a*
> *lion and the intelligence of man mingled their symbolisms*
> *in this crouching body, there was yet something neither*
> *bestial nor human in it, something beyond and above these,*

674   CORRESPONDENCE WITH

something divine!" [1] *He says there was some supernatural element in this stone being.*

Did the Egyptians or Atlanteans have the same conception or believe in the same evolutionary Avatarhood and hence the statue?

Maybe. But the Sphinx is rather the symbol of the whole evolution from subconscient to the superconscient Light.

He further asks whether the Pyramids are "vast and vain monuments" or are they reared merely to hold one Pharaoh's mummified flesh?

It is usually supposed by occultists to be a symbolic-scientific monument in which were performed some secret Egyptian Mysteries.

Two doses of Santonin will have no harmful effect on S. But, I suppose, the necessity no longer exists as he is furious with us and may even quit us.

If he doesn't quit and submits to Santonin we have no objection.

September 10, 1936

A says he feels heavy and sleepy and not refreshed. Is it the Force that does it?

Good Lord, no! It is forcelessness that does it.

September 11, 1936

D's letter gives me an occasion to ask you about the suicide of X's wife. You said something about Fate which is always a mysterious word.

Well, the determination of human life and events is a mysterious thing. Can't help that, you know Fate is composed of many things —

---

[1] Pp. 33-35.

SRI AUROBINDO   675

Cosmic Will + individual self-determination + play of forces +
Karma + x + y + z + a + b + c ad infinitum.

> *Suicides and accidents are supposed to be due to hostile*
> *Forces.*

Not Forces hostile to our work, but hostile to the suicide and to the
accidented fellow.

> *She died because "she was hostile to the Divine". So*
> *it can't be the action of hostile Forces, for it would be in*
> *their interest to keep her alive, so that X may be hampered*
> *in his aspiration.*

Was she hostile to the Divine? All I heard was that she was somewhat
in the way of X's sadhana—but so many wives and husbands are
like that and they don't get drowned.

> *And since X's turn to the Divine was much quicker than*
> *he thought, can one conclude from this accident that the*
> *Divine perhaps wanted to remove the obstacle? Of course*
> *it is a very drastic method.*

All that is simplificative reasoning—the truth is much more complex than that.

> *I was tempted to conclude so, because I heard you had said*
> *that X being a rare sattwic type, you wanted him sooner,*
> *or something like it.*

No. We were not particular about the time.

> *Some say the Divine's way would have been to try to turn*
> *the wife also this way or to help X to go through the ordeal—*
> *not this drastic step! A word or two please!*

God only knows what God does and why he is doing it. And God is
not in the habit of letting other people know—except when it
suits him.

A has malaise; not refreshed after sleep...

I have been without light, so blank, blank, blank. Keeping everything in hope of better luck today. (This has nothing to do with A's malaise, by the way. Only take advantage of bottom of page.)

September 12, 1936

Shall we put A on Sudarshan powder?

All right.

Try some Force please, A is getting disgusted, it seems!

Only getting? He is chronically disgusted, to my experience.

The hostile forces have made my life unbearable, sucking away every drop of blood gained after much pain and expense. Can't sit outside, even for a minute, under the breezy, starry sky. Their breeding place is in the thick canna bushes Manubhai has planted. Can't you direct him to strike them off and save my precious life? What will happen if the Asram doctor is to die of malaria?

My dear sir, Manubhai will have a fit and you will have to treat him and probably he will kill you into the bargain. You prefer a violent death to malaria? While there is life, there is hope, even if there are also mosquitos. Why not negotiate with Manubhai himself? If you plead with him in a sweet low pathetic voice, he may have mercy.

By the way, Shanta has consented to take the cod-liver oil after all, — so I have agreed to ask you for a whole bottle for her personal absorption. So send her a bottle of this divine but fishy nectar.

September 13, 1936

G says he feels "tous les bien"!

Good Lord! what's that? French?

SRI AUROBINDO   677

> *At times I think I am really useless as a doctor; I haven't
> the gift for it — wrong choice of profession altogether, like
> that of your Yoga, Sir! Both of them forced down my throat!
> I often feel like asking Mother to take off this responsibility
> from me and give it to some fitter person.*

To whom?

> *Those 5 years in Edinburgh weren't just play. I have done
> some studies surely, which are not worth a candle, for
> people with much less knowledge, quacks even, seem to be
> more successful.*

Book knowledge is necessary, but not much use by itself.

> *What are the elements then wanting in me? Lack of faith
> in the drugs given, lack of Faith in the Force?*

Lack of experience, lack of decision, vacillating intuition, want
of vision.

> *It is true that I haven't much faith in our drugs, but with
> these very drugs doctors are becoming enormously suc-
> cessful.*

They go ahead, don't mind how many people they kill, but they go —
human Motorcars.

> *It seems I don't know yet the right way to call down the
> Force, or is it because the "canalisation" hasn't been done
> yet?*

Right — that's it.

> *I am getting more and more disappointed in my doctorship,
> as in Yoga, since I hear that you are now trying more for
> transformation of nature than for experience.*

Because without transformation of nature, the blessed experience

678 CORRESPONDENCE WITH

is something like a gold crown on a pig's head — won't do. Picturesque perhaps, but —

> . . . *Please give me precise* practical *suggestions on the art of healing.*

My God, man! I am not a doctor.

> *What to do? How to bring down the Force?*

How? is there a how? You call, you open, it comes (after a time). Or, You don't call, you open, it comes. Or, You call, you don't open, it doesn't come. Three possibilities. But how — ? Well, God he knows, or perhaps he doesn't.

> *Seeing the miraculous effects of Homeopathy, Dr. Manilal asked me to study it with R. I don't know if it's any use — as study alone won't do. One must have the gift. Have I?*

Can't say! Had you the poetic gift some years ago?

September 16, 1936

> *As I thought — no help but to wait for canalisation and in the meantime carry on. I suppose all "lacks" will be removed by the descent of Force?*

Obviously, obviously!

> *You promised to write to me about Intuition, but like all your promises — !*

I promised to do so in some future age when I had time. That promise stands — if a promise stands. What more can you ask of it?

> *God knows what you are busy with now, with the correspondence also reduced?*

Who says it is reduced? For a few days, it was — now it has increased to half again its former size and every morning I have to race to get

SRI AUROBINDO

it done in time — and don't get it done in time. Thousand things are accumulating; inner work delayed.

> *I didn't mean by "practical suggestions", any medical ones, Sir! I meant about the Force. R, I saw once, put his hand on a patient's abdomen, and concentrated, God knows on what. . .*

On the Mother and her Force for which he was calling.

> *I hear he actually feels the Force descending and the patients also get relief for the time being.*

Yes, that has frequently happened.

> *Suppose I do the same, I know I won't feel any Force descending, but without feeling it, it may descend and act?*

Doubtful.

> *Regarding A, you said he was refractory to big doses. In that case, how will my calling help the canalisation of the hard granite?*

Even to small doses. Sometimes I get in a little surreptitiously and, as it were, against his will. He is much more granite than you.

> *You can be less mysterious in these explanations, si vous voulez.*

Not mysterious at all. Succinct and epigrammatic.

September 17, 1936

> *"Obviously, obviously"! What obviously, Sir? When will the blessed Force descend?*

That is irrelevant. The time of its descent has nothing to do with its obviousness.

680 CORRESPONDENCE WITH

> *Have been working these 2 or 3 days on this small poem, can't do it. Remarkable maturity of expression etc., etc. have all melted away!*

Not at all. They are there, only feeling shy and sitting modestly behind the pardah.

> *A, though "much more granite" than I, seems to receive very well in poetry.*

Ah, you think so! My dear sir, I have to do boring operations like digging an artesian well before I can get a few poems out of him — And afterwards it is one long wail "All gone! all gone! I am damned, doomed, dead, deteriorated, degenerated" for a whole day period. Sir, A is twice the Man of Sorrows you are.

> *If everything goes on so tremendously slow, isn't it enough to make one despair and sit and lament? Because one doesn't know how the devil one should proceed!*

If you appeal to the devil, you can't proceed.

> *Well, after the failure in poetry, I am thinking now of reading and writing any blessed thing that comes. But there's no joy in it. Everything seems a waste of time. Meditation is hard, doesn't bring any result, poetry won't come — this is the state of affairs.*

Present Discontents, what!

> *Fed up, fed up, damnably fed up! Work of the Spirit as complex as human nature!*

Of course it must be, because it is in human nature that it works.

> *You call, you open, you don't call, you open, you call, you don't open — no profounder mystery can there be than these phrases of yours!*

Not at all, plain as your nose. Excuses to the nose! I gave you three

SRI AUROBINDO   681

different cases, — don't mix them up together.

> *I have called for poetry, I have actually sat up for 2 hours, has it come?*

You called but did not open, so it did not come.

> *I am praying for A's cure, is there a response?*

You called, but A did not open, so it did not cure.
Both instances establish my case. Q.E.D.

> *You said once that it is the spiritual consciousness that my being wants and that this need was becoming very prominent, but not the push yet. It seems now the need also has pushed back?*

For the moment.

> *But if it is really the spiritual consciousness, how the dickens shall I get it by reading, say, Dickens, Lawrence or Nehru?*

Probably not! Especially Dickens.

> *Is that why I think it a waste of time?*

Possibly yes.

> *And yet I would like to read all the books. Have the attitude of* nirbhar *and do all these things?*

Why not?

> *Really, really, your Yoga is a puzzle and I haven't been able to catch the head or tail of it, shall never perhaps!*

You needn't catch either its head or its tail. It will be sufficient if you allow it to catch your head or your tail or both!
   Cheerio! Tails forward!

*G is now well. Shall we begin cod-liver oil now or after
the last 2 injections? Ah, if all patients were like him!*

Better finish injections first, then oil him.

September 18, 1936

Sri Aurobindo,
*There you are, Sir, with your paradoxical, mysterious
brevities! Dickens etc. won't give the spiritual consciousness
and it is a waste of time; again, they can be done with* nirbhar! *Then why should I do anything wasteful with* nirbhar?

If you want to understand my supramental brevities, you must read
carefully. You have absolutely ignored my pregnant "Possibly".
I never said that it must be a *waste* of time — but "possibly" yes or
"possibly" not. Reading Dickens merely cannot give you the spiritual consciousness — that is obvious. It would be a miracle if it did.
Reading the Oxford Dictionary might be more helpful in that direction. Unless of course a miracle took place; then even Dickens —
But otherwise it may evidently be a waste of time. D got helped by
Lawrence's letters — even J gave him dream-meetings with J and
his daughter. But most people would get little that is either occult or
spiritual from either. But things done with nirbhar can help — not
because of themselves, but because of the *nirbhar.*

*To try to be a literary man and yet not to know what big
literary people have contributed would be inexcusable. . .*

Why is it inexcusable? I don't know what the Japanese or the Soviet
Russian writers have contributed, but I feel quite happy and moral
in my ignorance. As for reading Dickens in order to be a literary
man, that's a strange idea. He was the most unliterary bloke that
ever succeeded in literature and his style is a howling desert.

*One may become, after hard studies of authors, a literary
man, but the supramental will keep its tail high up. What has
been the result? This is one great disharmonious problem
I haven't solved, neither have you helped me except by your
supramentally brief jokes.*

SRI AUROBINDO   683

To be a literary man is not a spiritual aim; but to use literature
as a means of spiritual expression is another matter. Even to make
expression a vehicle of a superior power helps to open the consciousness. The harmonising rests on that principle.

> *Considering the capacity, worth and qualities I have been*
> *born with, my aspirations or ambitions are too great. In*
> *J's words — "So much to be seen, so much to be done, so*
> *many fresh avenues to explore," in spiritual as well as non-*
> *spiritual domains. I haven't got a clear vision of what to do,*
> *how to proceed, how to establish a harmony between the*
> *Spirit and the mundane and then to be fired with dynamism.*

Ambitions of that kind are too vague to succeed. You have to limit
your fields and concentrate in order to succeed in them. I don't
make any attempt to be a scientist or painter or general. I have seen
certain things to do and have done them, so long as the Divine
wanted; others have opened in me from above or within by Yoga; I
have done as much of them as the Divine wanted. D has had dyna-
misms and followed them so long as they were there or as often as
they were there. You mentalise, mentalise, discuss, discuss, hesitate,
hesitate.

> *If by any chance I could throw away all troubles about*
> *progress in Yoga and push on with literature, that would be*
> *some solution.*

There is no incompatibility between spirituality and creative
activity — they can be united.

> *... At moments I have aspirations for being many-sided,*
> *then comes a voice — "Leave all those things, seek for*
> *something more precious, happy." The eternal contradic-*
> *tion!*

Fluctuating of course comes in the way of action and therefore of
success. One can do one or other or one can do both, but not fluc-
tuate eternally.

> *Can you now tell me something satisfactory, encouraging,*

hopeful, at the same time some practical suggestions — can't plead now that you aren't a doctor!

Give up the mentalising, hesitating, fluctuating habit. That is the one practical thing to do.

You say — I called, I didn't open. Isn't it mysterious when I called and sat up with paper and pencil for two hours and nothing came? Then all I can say is that opening is a mysterious business!

Who says it is not? Some people have the trick of always opening to a Force (e.g. Dilip, Nishikanta for creative literary activity), some have it sometimes, don't have it sometimes (you, Arjava, myself). Why make it a case of kicks and despair?

September 19, 1936

I had been to the pier with J. We were quietly resting on a bench with our feet up, when a Tamilian came with a stick in hand and ordered us to put our feet down. I was rather bewildered and put my feet down; so did J; but she asked "Why?" I said, maybe he is the guard of the pier, and it may be against rules. . . Behind us Purani and others were sitting with their feet up also, but he didn't tell them anything. This made J very excited and she said that he had insulted us. He was only a drunkard or a rogue. Then she accused me of cowardice for my abject submission; that it was not physical cowardice, but of the inner spirit. Because I didn't want to face him, I obeyed. The first thing a woman respects and admires in a man is courage! etc., etc. . .

Obviously what you ought to have done was to go baldheaded for the Tamilian, bang up his eyes, smash his nose, extract some of his teeth, break his jaw and fling him into the sea. Afterwards if the police came to arrest you, disable half the Force and slaughter the Inspector. Then J would have come to you in jail and wept admiringly over the mighty hero — That's what a "woman" expects of a "man" since the cave-days. It is also what a she-cat expects of a tomcat.

*Kindly tell me frankly and openly what was my movement —
was it cowardice? But this man was not at all strong, I
could have fought him, besides Purani and they were there.
Still why did I listen so meekly? Yet if he had come to
attack J, I don't think I would have drawn back. One of the
things I hate is cowardice.*

In this particular case if you thought it was against rules and the
man was a guard (as a matter of fact benches are usually supposed
to be sat upon with the feet down), there was no cowardice in
complying. Rules ought to be respected — the haughty self-assertive
disregard of civic rules is worthy only of savages.

Apart from that there is a passive quiet courage which becomes
aggressive only at need and is not partial to shindies, and there
is the aggressive courage. To show the latter on every occasion
is Irish, but not indispensable. Cowardice comes in only when you
do or abstain from doing out of a sense of fear. Were you afraid?
If not, it is not cowardice.

*I have seen many people physically weak, yet brave like
lions, while there are strong fellows who are cowards.*

Yes, of course.

*Is it something connected with the inner vital? Please
explain the situation and give a satisfactory reply on courage
vs. cowardice and the remedy.*

Fear is of course a vital and physical thing. Many people who have
shown great courage, were not physically or even vitally brave;
yet by force of need they pushed themselves into all sorts of battle
and danger. Henry IV of France, a great fighter and victor, was an
example. Just because his body consciousness was in a panic, he
forced it to go where the danger was thickest.

*On Saturday I had a dream that my complexion had become
absolutely golden. Y cried, "Oh, how beautiful you have
become!" Is it some inner beauty reflecting itself on the outer
being?*

686   CORRESPONDENCE WITH

If Y and her compliment had not been in the dream, we might say so. But—If we give it a symbolic sense, (leaving Y out of account as a contribution from the vital) then it is a beautiful vision not of the body but of the future change of the being. For gold is the colour of the Divine Truth. People who come down from the highest planes (when not white or blue) are usually golden in dreams and visions. Take your choice of explanations.

> *G's temperature normal today. 6 injections finished. Start the oil?* [*18.9.36*]

Yes.

> *Raghavan has eczema on right leg—not much benefit by mercury. Giving simple Zinc Oxide. Eczemas are beastly things. Wonder if we should give it up.*

Give up having eczemas? Certainly. Boils too.

> *I have one more blessed boil! Dr. Becharlal says it is a good sign, for it means purification!! If so I shall bear thousands!!!*

All that's a discovery. The boil is then truly a blessed one?

September 21, 1936

> *... If you approve of my all-round literary aim, then isn't it necessary that one should be acquainted with the best literatures of the world?*

Not indispensable,—even by being steeped in one literature, one can arrive. But useful of course.

> *What do you say about my plans to read Meredith, Hardy, Shelley, Keats and the French and Russian writers?*

Lord, Sir, I wish I had time to follow out a programme as massive as yours. I have none even to dilate upon yours.

> *You know I have hardly any experience of life and the world which helps in creation. That defect can, to a certain*

SRI AUROBINDO 687

> *extent, be removed by the study of these works.*

Is it so? There would be a danger of its being only derivative and bookish work. The great novelists like the great dramatists have been usually men who lived widely or intensely and brought a world out of the combination of their inner and their outer observation, vision, experience. Of course if you have a world in yourself, that is another matter.

> *. . . If I want to write poetry, I should read them side by side.*

? [*Sri Aurobindo underlined "them".*]

> *Now I am in a mood to read prose.*

No objection.

> *. . . I shall also read your books for 2 hours which will help my sadhana, opening of consciousness.*

Good.

> *My sex-trouble is also much less at present — my most heartfelt gratitude to Mother.*

Delighted to hear. Great pother and nuisance — the sex.

> *About that cowardice, I have thought and thought. . . Why should I have been afraid? I could have fought him any moment!*

Don't suppose it was cowardice.

> *I don't understand the first part of the explanation of my vision. Why Y and her compliment stand in the way of taking it as an inner purity? Because I want to look beautiful in her eyes?*

Yes — it creates a suspicion that it was golden vanity that created the golden vision — at least a desire to be gold in Y's eyes.

Rest of the explanation is also hazy but no matter.

Not hazy, only phosphorescent.

Who is this of France?

Henri Quatre, Henry IV of France — one of the most famous names in French history — what the deuce, Sir! never heard of him? Anyhow, he was a typical example of a great hero, victor in many battles who was yet physically a coward, but his mind and will prevailed over the fear in the body.

S has come back again! But I can't get the head or tail of his symptoms. Now he says one thing, now another.

Mother stopped his hot water and tiffin-carrier. He lamented about fever, liver pains and what not (that's his plea) for continuing them. I told him if he had such bad health, he must be under medical treatment, not rushing about everywhere and eating whatever he likes. He said doctor's treatment no good. But I suppose he has gone back either in the hope of your restoring his hot water and carrier or just to prove that cold water and Aroumé[1] don't agree with him.

Tomorrow, I think, we shall start Santonin, and watch.

Mother says why give santonine to a healthy fellow and spoil his health? She has a strong suspicion that S's illness may now have become diplomatic ache and strategic fever.

September 22, 1936

I have started writing, Sir. Not exactly a story, for I have just let myself go. . . . Should one have a rough outline of the plot or just begin somewhere and somehow?

It is done either way according to the author's *prakriti*.[2]

---

[1] The name of the Ashram Dining Room.
[2] Nature.

SRI AUROBINDO   689

> *And about style — should one try to improve it consciously or let oneself flow on?*

Same thing.

> *Good Lord, your writing is exceeding all limits, Sir!*

Transformation of handwriting. The self exceeds all limits, the handwriting should do so also.

> *"Lord, Sir, . . ."— I don't know what to make of it. [Letter of 22.9.36.]*

You seem to have made it out all right.

> *By having a world in oneself you mean what the Yogis say, having* brahmānda[1] *within by the power of Yoga?*

Or by the power of Nature.

> *Had a vision of a small pretty steam launch sailing at moderate speed in the sea. Meaning? Slow spiritual progress?*

Yes.

> *About D's gramophone record affair, rumours were that you refused him permission, but D insisted and brought the gramophone company people by special request. Well, D told us that they have come of their own accord with your permission.*

All that not true. They offered themselves to come and D took our permission. I have seen the correspondence. Who is spreading all these inventions?

> *S is running temperature 99°, morning and afternoon— "strategic"?*

Perhaps it is the grief of his lost tiffin carrier that gives him that.

---

[1] Creation—literally "egg of Brahman".

690   CORRESPONDENCE WITH

> *A says he can't work more than he would like to — i.e.*
> *till 12.*

What's that? Why should he want to work more than he would like
to? Do you mean "as much as" by any chance?

> *My boil has burst!!*

Hurrah!

> *G's afternoon temperature 99°.*

Tell him not to work too much. He is rushing about too much.
For some months he must do it only in small quantities. If the
temperature comes back, you will have to give the remaining four
injections — to be bought in town.

> *Shivalingam — Pain, swelling [leg] much less. Slight pain*
> *while walking. Shall I try protein injections? In such cases it*
> *gives good results at times, but might give febrile reaction.*

You can try. He is solid and stolid.

> *Or shall I let him go on with slight pain and swelling till*
> *the Supramental descends?*

No sir. Supramental does not want to have to deal with swelled
things, either heads, legs or stomachs.

September 23, 1936

> *A is better today. I suppose he got a dose of Force at night!*

Well, Thursday is the day he comes to Mother.

> *S was given Sudarshan yesterday—hasn't turned up at all*
> *today. Bitter has produced bitterness?*

By George! but that's a drastic remedy if he is malingering. He will
say again "Trust not in doctors."

September 24, 1936

SRI AUROBINDO   691

Nishikanta's leg is much better now.

What is actually the matter with N's leg? what's the cause of the
thing? He proposes to give it rest for one year! So as to cure it
entirely. But that seems to me the other extreme to straining it
unnecessarily by overstrenuous walking. After the year of rest, it
might want to rest all the life. What's your idea?

                                                September 25, 1936

*In my poem, Amal says "dim" and "dream" are too common.
He can't get any alternative. I am sure you have one up your
sleeve, what?*

My sleeve is empty.

*Please enjoy our poet H's sarcasm against "Aurobindo
and his best disciples" in* Agragati [*a Bengali journal*].

It is rather in H's silliest style.

*And what about our Indian Hitler's [S.T.] great mission to
save young brains of India by sending all Asrams to perdi-
tion?*

If he would save his own young brain first from the evident disposition towards softening his ambition betrays, it would be more
useful. It is S.T. himself or a fellow sheep of the modernist flock?

[*A note from the Mother:*]

Nirod,
    Devraj will wait for you to-morrow at 9 A.M. at the Canal side
entrance of the Hospital.
    It would be good if you could obtain that some care should be
given to the case —

                                                September 26, 1936

*Good Lord! R said Devraj has no organic trouble!! X-ray
shows definite and progressive T.B. — worse in the left lung.*

> *Tomorrow I shall see Valle or André (supposed to be a*
> *specialist in T.B.) But how R could have missed the diagnosis*
> *gets past me — with all his big cures!*

I think he did not take much interest in Devraj's case and was inattentive. But he has been at far from his best recently. He used in outside cases to send me detailed reports of some examinations that were very helpful for action — but in D.L.'s case I knew nothing except that it was only her and it was critical until I got your letter.

> *"The sparkling surges of the sea*
> *Roar and break. . ." — was the first version.*

Can't see how you got it in metrically. Besides the sea in poetry is always roaring and breaking. So why put it to that hard Sandow exercise once again?

> *"My consciousness flights fr̆ŏm. . ." — metre?*

It is not flighty metre, but a flighty use of language.

> *"Green trees" — no special significance?*

If they were yellow or red trees, then there would be a significance. "Green" is objectionable, because trees manage to be green always without any special significance.

> *Suppose it was ". . . like those green trees*
> *At evenfall"?*

That would successfully get rid of any significance.

> *There you are or there am I. . . Please divinise the animal*
> *by your Supramental Inspiration.*

Divinised! with quite fine results, though I say it.
Turns out to be a fine beast after all.

September 27, 1936

[*The first two medical reports were written by Dr. Becharlal.*]

SRI AUROBINDO   693

> *Yesterday noon S got temperature — 101.8°....*

What is the nature or cause of this fever?

> *... She wants to take curd thrice a day. I have asked*
> *her to take milk as long as the fever lasts — she says she*
> *doesn't like milk and it gives a pain in the stomach. Hence*
> *without Mother's approval, curd is not desirable in her*
> *present state.*

I believe milk does not agree with her, she finds it difficult to digest.
What then is she to eat? You must settle this and give word to D.R.

> *... By the way, please make a rule henceforth not to accept*
> *sadhaks before they pass a medical exam. Don't you realise,*
> *Sir, what potential troubles are ahead with so many invalids?*

You are quite right with a million times a million rightness.
   No time for comments on rest. Too many urgent calls from R.

September 30, 1936

October 1936

> *I don't know if you want a separate report from me of D.L.,*
> *apart from what I sent you through Pavitra. R surely writes*
> *everything and Pavitra tells you all. I have said that R*
> *doesn't agree with Valle's diagnosis and writes in today's*
> *report that it is "dyspeptic congestion of the colon"!! About*
> *Chlorodyne, Dr. Becharlal and I have given our opinion.*

The report you speak of has not reached me, so I don't know anything about the chlorodyne. There is a letter from R, but it gives only
the general condition during the day (hyper-pyrexin and a crisis due
to tympanitis), says that in spite of that there is some amelioration,
I understand from Pavitra that Valle found some amelioration in the
condition of the heart in the evening.
   As to the diagnosis. Valle, you say assigns a gynaecological cause
for the illness, so far that agrees with what was R's insistence all
along in his letters to me that there must be such a cause — he named

694   CORRESPONDENCE WITH

some such specific causes also — but he could not be sure because no
such cause was admitted at the time by the patient. That was when
there were the epigastric pains and before there was the generalisa-
tion. It is now over the present development that there is dispute.
But I gather from your report that, it being an advanced stage of
peritonitis, there is no hope. In a day or some days — or according
to R in some weeks, if it is peritonitis — she must go. But then it
does not seem to matter what treatment is given, — the best can
only give her some more days of suffering. Is this right? All are
agreed at least on that matter?

The only hope then is that it might not be peritonitis or that it
being peritonitis, R's optimism aided by any force I can give, which
cannot be much under the circumstances, will pull her through as
it did the others in R's cases whose lives were given up by the doctors.
But for this last miracle the conditions are not very favourable.
Perhaps if she lives through tonight and the next few days with an
amelioration there may be a chance. I put this all down in order to
have the situation clear in my mind. One thing only is a good sign
that the Mother's force + R's medicines blessed by her pulled
her out of the certain death which had come on her the other night;
but on the other hand it did not prove as it would have been in
another case, decisive.

October 1, 1936

[*The first report was written by Dr. Becharlal, regarding
S's illness, treatment, diet and work, and all the arrangements to meet her complaints.*]

Mother approves all your arrangements. If you think, she can do
light work for an hour. Is it advisable for her to leave her room or go
about? She has fancies about her room, disliking it, and thinks it
is her room that makes her ill.

*K vomited a small particle of bright red blood. . . Examined
the lungs and found that the lesion has extended more
than last time. Can you not consent again to an X-ray?
[26.12.35]*

Yes.

SRI AUROBINDO   695

> *If the diagnosis is correct, the treatment has to be pursued*
> *actively and regularly. The best thing would be to send her*
> *away. . .*

That's all very well — but she was ill before she came and the family,
X says, will do nothing for her treatment if she is sent back. What to
do then?

> *She has gone down in health, feels easily tired. Her food*
> *is very, very scanty. . .*

If so, how can she recover? In T.B. surely suralimentation is necessary.

> *It seems Mother strongly disapproved of D.L.'s taking up*
> *that rice-pounding work, but she insisted and Mother*
> *had to give way. The origin of her trouble or its recrudescence*
> *is traced to that heavy muscular work.*

All that is rubbish. The trouble was due to something else not
physical without which she could have gone on pounding another
fifty years without injury to her body.

> *. . . I must say that R's theories about diseases are absurd,*
> *however successful he may be as a homeopath-physician.*

You may say what you like about the homeopathic theories, but I
have seen R work them out detail by detail in cases where he had
free and unhampered action and the confidence of the patients and
their strict obedience and have seen the results correspond to his
statements and his predictions based on them fulfilled not only to
the very letter but according to the exact times fixed, not according
to R's reports but according to the daily long detailed and precise
reports of the allopathic doctor in attendance. After that I refuse
to believe, even if all the allopaths in the world shout it in unison,
that homeopathic theory or R's interpretation and application of it
are mere rubbish and nonsense. As to mistakes, all doctors make
mistakes and very bad ones and kill as well as cure — my grandfather and one of my cousins were patently killed by one of the

biggest doctors in Bengal. One theory is as good as another and as bad according to the application made of it in any particular case. But it is something else behind that decides the issue.

> *Just hear what grave errors he has committed. He said to me that he brought about the profuse menstruation in D.L.'s case by his drug, in order to get rid of some mischief there which the patient would not admit. He asked me if this excessive flow should be stopped. . . He had no justification at all to cause that profuse bleeding, when every drop of blood was precious.*

To bring out the latent illness and counteract it, is a recognised principle in homeopathy and is a principle in Nature itself. He misapplied it here because he was in ignorance of the full facts about the menstrual trouble.

> *As I understand from you, it was only from me that you came to know about her critical condition.*

No. I said he had told me her condition was very critical; but he had given no details. I learned the details from you.

> *Even after her fainting, he took her walking to the pier. Good Lord, an extremely debilitated, anaemic patient to be moved about like that!*

Never heard of the anaemia before or then. It was all a talk about stomach, worms or this or that stomachic ailment.

> *Chlorodyne contains morphia which, you know, is a sedative to the heart and respiration etc. Dr. Becharlal told R about its dangers, but R said, "I have given it already and the drugs to counteract its effects." Counteracting would be tantamount to making it useless and ineffective.*
> [*Sri Aurobindo underlined "tantamount to making it useless and ineffective".*]

Not according to homeopathic theory.

SRI AUROBINDO   697

> *Valle said, after D.L.'s death, that he was positive about*
> *the cause of death. All symptoms and signs were of peri-*
> *tonitis.*

May be or may not be. Neither Valle nor R are infallible. So often
I have seen a diagnosis made on all the symptoms which turned out
to be the wrong one. It is like a condemnation on circumstantial
evidence.

> *I believe Mother's Force had an effect on these medicines,*
> *but when R went out of those to this Chlorodyne, and didn't*
> *let you know, the danger was signalled. Of course, in any*
> *case, the condition was hopeless, but who knows?*

How can you believe that when everything is explained according to
medical science? There is no place left there for Mother's Force
or any force except Valle-Force.

> *Valle said D.L. would have passed away two or three days*
> *ago, but glucose, oxygen and injections kept her up. Beating*
> *our drum?*

Quite so.

> *Whatever was given to her: glucose etc., met with opposition*
> *from R.*

Quite natural for a homeopath, just as your sneering at homeopathic
theories and treatment is natural in an allopath.

> *It seems you were not very hopeful from the time I reported*
> *about her case.*

No. As I say, he told me it was critical.

> *If he had informed you before, wouldn't it have been better?*

No, it would not have been better.

> *Why do you say that the conditions were not favourable?*

698   CORRESPONDENCE WITH

They were unfavourable for working through R as we had worked in outside cases or as I have worked by myself in certain cases outside or inside.

> *Why didn't your Force prove decisive in this case? About the Supermind and its failure over hostile forces, I give you a chance to bombard me or else I shall!*

What has the Supermind to do here? Who told you that I was using the supramental Force? I have said all along that it was not the supramental Force that was acting. If you want the supramental Force, you had better go to Jogesh Mama of Chittagong. I hear from Chittagong that the supramental Force is descending in him.

I have put down a few comments to throw cold water on all this blazing hot allopathism. But all these furious disputes seem to me now of little use. I have seen the working of both systems and of others and I cannot believe in the sole truth of any. The ones damnable in the orthodox view, entirely contradicting it, have their own truth and succeed—also both the orthodox and heterodox fail. A theory is only a constructed idea-script which represents an imperfect human observation of a line of processes that Nature follows or can follow; another theory is a different idea-script of other processes that also she follows or can follow. Allopathy, homeopathy, naturopathy, osteopathy, kaviraji, hakimi have all caught hold of Nature and subjected her to certain processes; each has its successes and failures. Let each do its own work in its own way. I do not see any need for fights and recriminations. For me all are only outward means and what really works are unseen forces behind; as they act, the outer means succeed or fail—if one can make the process a right channel for the right force, then the process gets its full utility—that's all.

October 3, 1936

> *K's X-ray was taken. The previous lesion of the lung is healed. But a new one has appeared. For treatment, three things are necessary:*
> *1) She mustn't be always gloomy and depressed as she now seems to be.*

What remedy for that? It's her attachment to X that is the root—so

SRI AUROBINDO   699

long as she clings to that! But it's quite true. Nothing more favourable to T.B. than this kind of depression.

> *2) She must take plenty of food. 3) Plenty of fresh air also.*

Quite agree all points.

> *And cod-liver oil?*

If she can stand it, yes.

> *Don't know really what to do with S. Mother finds him quite healthy while he has 99° fever, pain in the abdomen, 4 or 5 motions a day!*

Not nowadays!

> *I see no go except Santonin.*

Heavens! Another?

> *Shivalingam has pain again! Given up the idea of injections hearing that "he is solid".*

Solidity was not stated as an objection.

> *M still passes 2 or 3 drops of blood in the urine. Feels a stone blocking the passage somewhere. I'm not quite sure whether it is a stone or a stricture from previous infections.*

Well! Preliminary medical examination very necessary for admission.[1]

October 5, 1936

> *M's urine was examined—contains pus; detailed report tomorrow. Now giving urotropine etc.*

Those are the hieroglyphics on the Valle paper? They are not Greek to me, but Amharic.

---

[1] See correspondence of September 30, 1936.

> *He had also syphilis! I consulted Valle, he advised serum injection. . .*

Christ! And yet you attribute the sufferings of these people to the Supramental Force!

> *By the way, what is happening, pray? Supramental descending? P is going fut. Some passing blood, some vomiting blood, another died devoid of blood!*

It appears that P has recognised that his Purushottamhood was indeed all fut! He says he felt some evil forces making him do and say these things, but he was so helpless that he was forced to obey them! That is a fall from Purushottama heights, but a return to sanity, if only temporary — (but let's hope it will increase). For that is evidently what happened.

> *All thought that he was doing serious sadhana.*

Serious? You mean not to sleep and all that sort of thing? Well, it is just that kind of seriousness which brings these attacks — Earnestness of this sort does call down that kind of Purushottama or rather call him in — for it is a horizontal not a vertical descent.

> *Purushottama descended in consequence of the earnest sadhana and hence he was calling Sri Aurobindo to come and bow to him! What next?*

Next? Perhaps he will want you also to come and bow to him and pummel you if you don't.

> *Makes me shake to the bones!*

Only the bones?

> *Already I am feeling awfully pulled down, on top of that M[1] sits; and the Purushottama crowns them all. I ask myself — whither, whither are you going, my friend, and what awaits you?*

---

[1] A difficult medical case.

SRI AUROBINDO   701

Perhaps the Paratpara Purusha beyond even the Purushottama.

But why this pulled downness? You are not pulling down Purushottama or any other gentleman from the upper storey, are you?
It is strain and want of rest, I suppose. Sleep, sleep! read Mark
Twain or write humorous stories. Then you will be quite chirpy
and even M won't feel heavy to you.

October 6, 1936

> *After M recovers, don't you think he had better go to Madras*
> *for a thorough check-up?*

Yes.

> *... We must know whether it is stone or tumour in the*
> *kidney or bladder — a thorough investigation is necessary.*
> *If you think that your Force will cure or R's treatment, then*
> *it is all right.*

Can't say without being sure what it is.

> *Regarding D.L. — R says he hadn't had her confidence*
> *from the beginning. Is that why you said that conditions*
> *were not favourable for working through R?*

He had the contrary — a strong anger, distrust and antipathy. But
that was only one part of it.

> *I am also rather eager to know what else was the trouble*
> *due to, if not physical, unless of course it is private.*

It is private, at present at least. Mother says it is an affair between
her and D.L.

> *You write — "... for me all are only outward means,*
> *and what really works are unseen forces..." [3.10.36].*
> *Could you amplify it a little further? And also explain*
> *how one can make oneself a right channel for the right Force,*
> *Faith, Intuition?*

Sir, do you think I have time for your interesting questions? I have had three nights' work to do in a single night — and in that my table lamp gone. In other perhaps fre-a-er off times.

J's poem held back.

October 7, 1936

Wretched, absolutely done for.
Feel like jumping into the sea,
Or hanging myself from a tree!

Why? Disburden yourself!

October 8, 1936

Disburden? You mean throw off the burden or place the burden at your door?

Both!

Please give me some Force for writing. But I wonder if you have time for circulating it.

Not as much as is necessary.

The atmosphere seems to be thick with doubt etc. A lull over the Asram.

Panic seems to be the order of the day as well as doubt.

Storm brewing?

The storm seems to have brewed. I am fighting it at present, having been obliged to give up my Abyssinian campaign and stop the march to Gore. However!

I have seen your letters to P.S. and Y. Comparing the latter's with mine — the one you wrote after S's death [25.3.35], I find that there is a lot of difference between them. Your views have changed immensely. In the letter to me, there was a very high optimistic, almost a certain tone about the conquest of death. Now it appears that you no longer hold

SRI AUROBINDO   703

> *that view, and say that death is possible because of the lack*
> *of solid mass of faith. It has to be conquered by Sadhana!*

In what does this change of views consist? Did I say that nobody
could die in the Asram? If so, I must have been intoxicated or
passing through a temporary aberration.

As for the conquest of death, it is only one of the sequelae of
supramentalisation — and I am not aware that I have forsworn my
views about the supramental descent. But I never said or thought
that the supramental descent would automatically make everybody
immortal. The supramental descent can only make the best conditions for anybody who can open to it then or thereafter attaining
to the supramental consciousness and its consequences. But it
would not dispense with the necessity of sadhana. If it did, the
logical consequence would be that the whole earth, men, dogs, and
worms, would suddenly wake up to find themselves supramental.
There would be no need of an Asram or of Yoga.

But my letters to Y and P had nothing to do with the conquest of
death — they had to do with the conditions of the sadhana in the
Asram. Surely I never wrote that death and illness could not happen
in the Asram which was the point Y was refuting and on which I
confirmed him.

> *A solid mass of faith? Surely that is a very heavy*
> *Himalayan condition you impose. For instance, do you*
> *expect old tottering N to have that solid mass in his liquid*
> *body?*

N was not old and tottering when he came and if he had kept the
living faith he would not have been tottering now.

> *Or do you either hope that by his sadhana he will have the*
> *conquest?*

That depends on whether he is still alive and not quite liquified and
able to open physically when the conditions change.

> *By that letter you have struck terror into many hearts, I am*
> *afraid, and henceforth we shall look upon death as quite a*
> *possibility, though not as common as it is outside.*

The terror was there before. It came with the death of D.L. and the madness of P and not as the result of my letter. It was rushing at the Mother from most of the sadhaks at Pranam every day.

> *The physical condition of many sadhaks and sadhikas, is not cheering in the least —*

Far from it.

> *You know best about the condition of their sadhana.*

Very shaky, many of them.

> *However, it is my impression that you have changed your front.*

It is not mine.

> *Formerly I thought you said—faith or no faith, sadhana or no sadhana, you were conquering death, disease, i.e. everything depended on your success; now it seems a lot depends on us poor folks, in this vital matter.*
> *[Sri Aurobindo underlined "this vital matter".]*

Why vital? What is vital is the supramental change of consciousness —conquest of death, is something minor and, as I have always said, the last physical result of it, not the first result of all or the most important—a thing to be added to complete the whole, not the one thing needed and essential. To put it first is to reverse all spiritual values—it would mean that the seeker was actuated, not by any high spiritual aim but by a vital clinging to life or a selfish and timid seeking for the security of the body—such a spirit could not bring the supramental change.

Certainly, everything depends on my success. The only thing that could prevent it, so far as I can see, would be my own death or the Mother's—But did you imagine that that success would mean the cessation of death on the planet, and that sadhana would cease to be necessary for anybody?

SRI AUROBINDO   705

> *If increase of numbers stands in the way, if doctors and*
> *medicines shake the faith, well, it is very easy to solve the*
> *problem, isn't it?*

Increase of numbers brought in all sorts of influences that were not
there in the smaller circle before. Doctors did not matter so long
as faith was the main thing and a little treatment the help — But
when faith went, illness increased and the doctor became not
merely useful but indispensable. There was also the third cause, the
descent of the sadhana into the physical consciousness with all its
doubt, obscurity and resistance. To eliminate all that is no longer
possible.

> *We have also an impression, considering the sudden wave*
> *of diseases, that it is due to some Force descending, so that*
> *wherever there is resistance there will be a rushing up.*

What Force?

> *Since the action is to go on in the subconscient physical*
> *at present with the Supramental descending (hail Supra-*
> *mental!!), all sorts of physical troubles will be rampant now.*

Rubbish! You repeat always this imbecile absurdity that the
Supramental is descending into the sadhaks — as P thought it had
descended into him! The sadhaks are miles away from the supramental. What I spoke of was not the descent of the Supramental
into the sadhaks but into the earth-consciousness. If the Supramental had descended into the sadhaks, there would not be all
sorts of troubles, but all sorts of helps and progress.

> *But you seem to sneer at the supposition and say things*
> *will happen that way if sadhaks believe like that.*

Yes, certainly.

> *I find that everything seems to happen here* ensemble : *a*
> *general wave of doubt, depression, going away, etc.*

706 CORRESPONDENCE WITH

Yes, general in the sense of many undergoing it — not all. There has been no time when everybody was depressed, everybody doubting, everybody taking the train homewards.

> *The rosy side also may be true—as you said a general stillness was felt.*

In the atmosphere, it may be so. But what has that to do with the Supramental descent?

> *I asked M to start tomorrow for Madras. He says he has to go to Calcutta—written there and is waiting for a reply...*

He is talking of starting on Sunday.

> *About S, the "coldish" feeling was absent. A lot of sweating at night, fever in the afternoon—99.8°.*

He has been sleeping with J who has developed occult terrors since P's outbreak and contracting the terror himself and had [. . .]¹ etc. of a bloodcurdling character. We must allow for S's vivid literary style. But I send you the document as you are in medical charge.

> [*A note from the Mother in the morning:*]

9-10-36

Nirod

   T is anxious about her health and wishes to be radiographed. Will you take her to the hospital for the purpose?

> [*Evening*]
> *Got your note* [*regarding T*]*, just a little too late! Now I am afraid we have to wait till Monday. But X-ray of what? Lungs? What symptoms? They will ask me. A recent victim of doubt?*

Not lungs — she has never had any difficulty there. Stomach, — she will indicate the place. She has had violent pains there off and on

¹ One word illegible.

SRI AUROBINDO   707

for periods ever since the Flood. She had them I believe in Hyderabad. There is a history of medical means to stimulate the action of
some gland to produce thinness and by God, it seems to have been
successful—for thin she has been ever since. I don't know if this
had anything to do with it. Confidential informations, sir.

Doubt can't be said to be recent—she has had it in big black
doses every time she had a vital fit which was almost always, but
there was always a sort of faith behind. Latterly the psychic part has
been growing and the fits less bad and rarer and shorter; but the
general disturbance in the Asram due to D.L.-P upset her and her
stomach and produced a passionate thirst for keen radiographic
knowledge. This is confidential also.

Mother tells me she is vacillating in her preference between ulcer,
worms and cancer! But hush! don't let her know I told you.

> [*The following 3 reports were written by Dr. Becharlal.*]
> *For getting sleep, X should be quite free from mental wor-*
> *ries—complete mental rest is necessary.*

That she simply can't do—unless when she is in a good inner
condition. Of course it is the right thing if she can do it.

> *A cup of hot milk at bed-time. Hot bath or hot foot-bath*
> *with mustard oil massage; evening walk etc...*

All these are very good; you must choose one that she will accept.

> *If my Mother approves to give her any other medical*
> *treatment, I propose to give her Hingwastak Churna,*
> *acid hydrochloride dil., etc...*

Mother quite approves of all that. I have said that you will give her
treatment and asked her to take it. So you can see to it.

October 9, 1936

> *L got hurt in the finger—a barrel fell on it day before*
> *yesterday!... Don't you encourage immediate treatment*
> *for these things?*

708   CORRESPONDENCE WITH

These things ought to be treated at once — but these women always hold back and don't want to go.

> *[The following 3 reports were written by Dr. Becharlal.]*
> *T passed blood in the urine. . . I pray my Mother, to grant Nirod and myself general sanction to treat T with every change of drug etc. and see the case.*

You can certainly have full sanction to treat according to discretion and do all that is needful.

> *T says he needs 2 attendants: one in the daytime, and one at night. He proposes A and M.*

I don't think either A or M can keep up at night. I suppose in daytime M can come. For the night you might enquire if anyone can come — it must be someone who will have time to rest in the day.

> *As for the medical treatment, T leaves it for Mother to decide whether he should take medicines from the dispensary.*

To what is the blood due? As for the treatment you will advise what is to be done.

                                              October 10, 1936

> *From your answer I couldn't very well make out whether I should go and see T, but I went once in the morning.*

Yes, that was included in "all that was needful".

> *What strikes me is that T is so terribly afraid, goodness knows why. I am dumbfounded to see him so! I had always a great admiration for the fellow's bravery. D.L. has unmanned his manliness?*

He was a very courageous man. Of course, even courageous men are not always courageous at every point and perhaps he was always robust and healthy so never tested at this point. But what I see is that it is part of the terror that has fallen on many others and

SRI AUROBINDO 709

has manifested in him in spite of his natural temperament because he absorbed something from D.L. during her illness — something that was the cause both of his malady and of his fear. Mysterious? Well, these occult things always are.

> *I feel somehow that you don't want me to attend to the case. Anyway Dr. Becharlal comes and tells me and we consult things.*

Whatever is "needful".

> *5 p.m. Dr. B reports that T is better. By the way, the fear in T has to be* executed mercilessly *by your letters and advice.*

Umph! He wanted his brother to come and receive his last will and testament. I told him I saw no pressing need for troubling the brother.

> *Since no poetry is on the horizon, what about my trying to write some prose, say, stories? Give me some Force please, in that direction, if you see any possibility.*

As an experiment? All right.

> *I hope my defective style won't come in as a hostile force, against future poetic development.*

I suppose it won't.

<u>Nirod</u>

I forward you two pages of a letter from M. Will you and Becharlal at once find somebody to replace M in the attendance on T? M is evidently not meant to be there. I don't want him to see the ghost and the condition of his head is a thing I don't like. Mother was thinking you might consult the Surgeon again to know if any precautionary measures were necessary. Anyhow please keep an eye on his head — for these accidents often produce their subtler results long after.

SRI AUROBINDO
October 11, 1936

> *You wrote to A.K. that "there is an increasing pressure now for sadhaks who really intend to do sadhana, to stop feeling, living, acting according to the ordinary nature." I don't know if your "pressure" includes in its action my precious self. If it does, I would be glad; if it doesn't, I would pray to be included. Even if I don't feel the pressure, it matters little; let it act surreptitiously and my nature break, what?*

The pressure is general, but necessarily it is felt or received without feeling it in accordance with the readiness of the sadhak. It includes everybody who can be included and aims at drawing in those who can't.

> *Is it possible to sanction some tea? I am rather ashamed as almost immediately after intending to do sadhana, I want to live according to "ordinary nature".*

You can ask Champaklal, Mother is giving a chit.

> *As you know the stomach remains at the level of the umbilicus, but, in T's case, it has descended into the pelvis and is sitting snugly there. It is called ptosis or atony of the stomach. As for the cause and treatment, we have to get the proper history. . .*

Can it have anything to do with the fact that she was fat in Hyderabad, took a medicine for becoming thin and did become suddenly from fat very thin?

> *S says — "I have no hunger", but when pressed he says, "Yes, I like food better now." There is S!*

He says the Mother has entered his stomach and is occupying it!! I say, confidential you know! Such secrets are precious.

> *M's vomiting etc. is not a new thing, it was his companion long before the accident. I shall study his case, then take him to the Surgeon. So why are you worried, Sir?*

SRI AUROBINDO   711

Because it is accompanied by the ghost.

One thing — P says A is getting back his old ill health and "fears"
a relapse — but A is not likely to acknowledge. Attributes it to
T-strain and T-strain to D.L. gap. Rather clever? If you get a chance
to send A without letting him know the indiscretion—P recommends rest—he is probably right.

> *Goodness knows what inspired you to pick up such a blessed
> place for your Asram! A most hopeless hospital with hardly
> any facilities! A heaven indeed for a Supramental colony!
> About M, we are wavering between cystitis and nephritis —
> which could have been settled in a second, in a well-equipped
> hospital.*

Had no medical standards in view when I came to Pondicherry —
nor any views about establishing an Asram. A supramental colony
obviously ought to have a first-class hospital, but no such colony
was then intended.

October 12, 1936

> *My eyes, was T ever fat? And from fatness she has come to
> this!*

It was one of those newfangled glandular explosives. Based on the
idea that some gland (Thyroid, no?) growing hyperactive makes
thin (and apparently keeps you so in spite of eating well — T's case).
There is another which keeps you fat even if you eat only once a
day (Suvrata's case).

> *I couldn't make out one word in your long letter [9.10.36]
> about T. Is it "Menses"?*

Nonsense, sir! The same thing — thinness.

Have you said anything to T? She was alarmed by the silence of
the doctors, so the Mother told her, indicating that it was not
dangerous, only certain precautions against trouble etc. If you
speak, don't be vivid and alarm her.

You have not said anything about remedies. French Medical
Dictionary says "lie down one hour after meals" (Mother had

recommended that long ago)—Some contrivance for support of the viscera (rather bandaging in this climate)—abdominal exercise for strengthening walls (parois) so as to support viscera. But if person thin, then "cure de lit" and fattening before any remedial course. T would kick at "cure de lit" I am afraid.

X says her right arm fails her often and becomes dead and useless for work. Would not massaging (perhaps with some effective ointment) be necessary?

October 13, 1936

I didn't imagine death would cease on the planet by your Supramental descent, or that sadhana would be unnecessary. When did I say that the Supermind is descending into the sadhaks? [9.10.36]

It is implied if they are to get the conquest of death by the mere descent.

What I said or meant was that you have conquered death or gained a great mastery over it...

In what sense?

You had said that it is the Overmental Force that has been acting and has been effective enough to ward off death, except in two cases—and they were not sadhaks. Well, it doesn't mean that it has the infallible victory, but it amounts to that, doesn't it?

How is that? Holding off an enemy and infallible victory are not the same thing.

Once the Supermind descends into you or into the earth-consciousness, the question of faith or sadhana becomes irrelevant as regards death, for death is a Force and, when you have a control or conquest over it, it means that its supremacy is lost in this part of the world, whether I have faith or not, do sadhana or not.

SRI AUROBINDO   713

Good Lord, man. What is this reasoning? Everything is a force —
why should the supramental descent into me or earth assure complete and universal immediate conquest of this Force only or
specially among so many?

> *... Even if one does sadhana, illness may come and snatch
> one away: then one's chance of doing sadhana for the
> change of consciousness, and, if possible, supramentalisa-
> tion is lost. I consider it a vital matter — not immortality —
> to be able to do that.*

Well but that is simply warding off death. Perhaps the supramental
will do that — (it can, if it wants) — but not for ever. I mean if a
man wants 200 years to supramentalise himself, it can't be promised that he will be kept alive till then.

> *If you say that so long as one is not supramentalised, death
> is a possibility, then I have no grounds left except to do
> sadhana in a spirit of surrender... I don't see then how
> faith can help one to avert death.*

Faith does help and has helped. It is a fact.

> *You have also said that to prevent death sadhana is neces-
> sary.*

To make the control of death absolute, not provisional and relative.

> *What I plainly ask is whether by your supramentalisation
> death would be impossible in the Asram, independent of our
> sadhana.*

Not in the sense that anybody can seek refuge in the supramentalised Asram against death and sit comfortably there without any
intention of doing sadhana.

> *... The Supramental Force can create the best conditions
> which the Divine Force can't?*

Yes.

714   CORRESPONDENCE WITH

> *. . . But surely the action of the Supramental Force would be different from that of the Divine Force.*

Yes.

> *. . . or would they be fundamentally the same, only different at points?*

No.

No time to expatiate or divagate.

What's this typescript? Extremely private matter, sir, for nobody's perusal except the body addressed. I keep it for want of time.

> *If two oranges per day are not possible, can pamplemousse juice be given to T, as long as he is on liquid diet?*

[*Mother:*] Champaklal will give you two oranges daily for T.

> *S's stomach is no more "gloomy" — bright and cheerful today. I am tempted to dance in glee. Is it the Force or Pancrinol, or both?*

You forget that the Mother occupied it. What's this Pancrinol? All-hair?[1] All-what? or has it to do with the Pancreas?

> *What the French Dictionary says is exactly the right treatment for T. Abdominal support would be very uncomfortable, as you say. If we can persuade her to "cure de lit" in the beginning, we can see later on.*

I doubt her attitude to the *cure de lit*, but it is not likely to be enthusiastic. For the support she is willing. Mother wants you to make a sketch showing the places, measurements to be entered and the whole sent to the Bombay firm (address will be given) asking them if they can provide. What do you say?

> *In your letter of yesterday, on the "glandular explosives", what's this, Sir — "Based on the idea that some gland (They — ?)"? What a pity really, if one has to sacrifice even a single word!*

---

[1] *pan* (Greek) = all; *crinis* (Latin) = hair.

SRI AUROBINDO   715

It is (Thyroid—no?) to be taken as a parenthetical question after
"gland".

> *A is bleeding from piles. It has to be stopped. V seems to be*
> *very enthusiastic over him!*

What's that? Enthusiastic over his bleeding? V's enthusings are
generally catastrophic to the enthused over.

                                                    October 14, 1936

> *You have kept that type-script? I am finished then! I know*
> *it will have the same fate as the previous one [on Avatar-*
> *hood, 6.3.35]! However, I send the book in the off-chance*
> *of an* expatiation *or a divagation.*
> *[Sri Aurobindo filled the gap I had left, with "expatiation".]*

None, none, none! I prefer to excavate instead.

> *By the way, after a long time I enjoyed two or three days'*
> *true Nirodian, i.e. unyogic, jollity; but the yogic Nirodian*
> *gloom has restarted! Goodness knows why these glooms and*
> *blooms come and go!*

Goodness doesn't know why, nor does anybody else.

> *You have finished the prospective action of the Supra-*
> *mental Force by two "yes"s and one "no" [14.10.36].*
> *Evidently you are shy about it, or time is shy?*

Time and I both are shy, good reason why.
   (Nishikanta says rhyme is quite common in Bengali prose, so
why not in English also?)

> *I am afraid I don't know about the practical aspect of the*
> *abdominal support for T. I have to consult books if they've*
> *given anything. Meanwhile she can surely lie on her right*
> *side for some time, if not "cure de lit".*

That of course. You told her about the "right side". Mother gave

716   CORRESPONDENCE WITH

only a general prescription for lying down for an hour or more if necessary after meals.

October 15, 1936

> *T is better ; not yet started milk. There is still considerable albumin in the urine (albuminorrhea).*

When there is albuminorrhea then is it considered safe to give salted food? On the other hand he seems to be asking for more food than the Doctors are prepared to give him.

October 16, 1936

> *T's case—Salt is usually withheld when there is oedema or puffiness anywhere. Since there is neither, and the kidney is functioning well, we thought we could give it in a small quantity. . . Any food given him should have carbohydrates —fluids—till the albumin is reduced to a minimum. . . We can safely allow him to consume his surplus fat a couple of days more. No other go—unless you find something.*

No. I find nothing—go ahead and minimise the albumin.

> *For U's lipoma, Vijayanand suggested to try a mild mercury ointment. He claims to have cured a goitre by it. Glandular swellings do, at times, respond to mercury, especially if syphilitic. On lipoma, I don't know. But it may irritate. Opinion?*

It is for doctors to decide. The only question is whether any harm is possible by its use. As it is, the lipoma is, I believe, harmless though not ornamental. Mercury being irritant is it likely to make it less benign if there is failure? If not—well.

> *7.30 p.m.*
> *M came in just now and said about her boil-medicine, "Mixture very bitter, may I take* pān *after it?" I said, "You may." Now I hear she is telling people that I've advised her to take* pān*. Ladies in the Asram are really wonderful!!*

SRI AUROBINDO   717

My dear sir, such ladies are quite wonderful outside the Asram also. M didn't need to come here to be marvellous in that way.

> *Reading about T, S, etc., confirms my disgust. You have made fine specimens of them.*

Were they all reasonable and consistent in their former life?

> *You have made them believe that medicines and doctors are no good, but at the same time could not infuse into them sufficient faith in you. Result — they have fallen between two stools!*

Well, T and S used both to get cured without need of medicines once on a time. The later development has evidently come for your advantage, so that you may have elementary exercises in samata.[1] I have had a lot of schooling in that way and graduated M.A. Your turn now.

> *They come to the doctors only to be disgusted with the treatment; obviously they come without any faith. . .*

If you had treated them in the pre-Asram period, do you think their comments if not at once cured would have been more filled with a holy awe and submission to the doctors?

> *Really, they are so touchy, so funny! The more one sees, the more one wants to see! Perhaps you will say — "Judge not lest ye be judged!"*

Exactly — for these are poor little uneducated people. But are the big brains at bottom less unreasonable and inconsistent? All alike, sir, in one way or another. Man who is a reasoning animal no doubt, but not a reasonable one.

October 17, 1936

> *I am sending you an excerpt from a medical book regarding the abdominal support for T. An abdominal support should*

---

[1] Equanimity.

fit closely to the symphisis pubis and Poupart's ligaments below; above, it should not extend higher than the umbilicus. . .

In the French dictionary they speak of a special thing for this ptosis of the stomach, in French of course. These things seem rather unconvincing. And if it is to fit closely to certain Latin things as well as to Poupart's affairs, how can it be done without measuring?

T's temperature shot up suddenly to 103.4°, and has remained so. Don't know why. Maybe constipation.

? Merely with constipation this persistence of high fever?

His urinary symptoms are better.

How far? and in what way? No pain? no albumen? or very little?

Y says he felt a descent of Power producing an indescribable sensation in the head, and followed by numbness of the extremities, feeling like nausea, throbbing in the head, giddiness, etc. All these symptoms point towards a high blood-pressure which, he says, is normal. . . Can descent produce such a havoc?

A descent cannot possibly produce nausea and vomiting etc. There can, if one pulls down too much force, be produced a headache or giddiness; both of these go if one keeps quiet a little, ceases pulling and assimilates. A descent cannot produce blood pressure, madness or apoplexy or heart failure or any other illness.

What I gather from Y's letter and D's is that he felt great intensity of descent (much greater than he had before) and got into a panic (because of the indescribable sensation) and thought he might be going mad like P (P's madness was *not* the result of a descent), so nervous that he upset his stomach and possibly his circulation also. That is the only possible explanation if it is not an attack of illness on which it is for the doctors to pronounce, not me.

October 18, 1936

SRI AUROBINDO   719

> *[The first report was written by Dr. Becharlal.] L came to the Dispensary and said she had fever, cough, cold for the last three days. She refused to take anything internally, without Mother's permission.*

She has full permission to take any medicine or treatment you think necessary.

> *About U's lipoma—we don't see the rationale of the treatment by mercury, so don't know its effectiveness. We can try it in small quantities.*

If it grows it will have to be cut. As to this treatment, well, I don't know—

> *For T's support—I don't know whether the equipment will fit her thin structure. Even then the adjustable ones may do.*

Can't she measure herself, if she is shown the designs?

> *S is better now. All Pancrinol exhausted. Shall we buy more or wait and see?*

"Wait and see" is always a very good formula.

> *Y's trouble is much less, still a sort of nondescript sensation is there.*

What the deuce is this nondescript? How is it he can't describe it? There are sensations that are due to descent and not troublesome or dangerous at all, there are others that are physical. But the description is necessary in order to distinguish.

> *He says he can't read or write. Lies down quietly for a time, but all on a sudden the thing descends and produces the sensation. Fears if something may happen at night.*

The difficulty is that he has got the fear and the association in his mind of the descent with the disturbance.

720   CORRESPONDENCE WITH

You wrote to him at the end: ". . . before there can be a resumption of the sadhana." Does it mean he should not go to pranam or meditation?

I meant by sadhana the positive side (descent etc.). What I indicated was that there was a part of the being which was afraid of the descent, didn't want it and by its fear got this trouble. This must be found out and put right before calling any descent again.

I wasn't thinking of pranam and meditation — he can go there; if he finds it all right to go, he can continue.

He had no vomiting, only nausea.
[Sri Aurobindo underlined "nausea".]

Well, that's a physical ailment, not a Yogic phenomenon. Can't it be got rid of? Whatever the cause, there is evidently disturbance of the stomach.

From your replies I presume that it may have been the descent, but since he got into a panic, he got these nervous troubles. Or was it the result of pulling?

That seems most probable unless there was an illness already breeding there (digestion, circulation?). But you say you found none.

Y showed me a letter of yours where you have said that it is not due to pulling; it is the right tapasya. And he has been following the same practice since then and has now a control. It can't be the effect of a dark Force.

Not through the descent, but through the fear a dark Force might strike in. That is what it is trying with many people.

If illness rises up by the descent of Force or a hereditary taint of madness manifested later on, it would be a very bad affair.

Illness does not rise up by the descent of the Force; nor hereditary taint nor madness. They come up of themselves, as in D.S.'s case

SRI AUROBINDO   721

who never had even the smallest grain of a descent or a Force
anywhere. It is only after he went off his centre that we are putting
Force (not as a descent, but as an agent) to keep him as straight
and as sound as possible.

> *In this case, though the descent wouldn't be the cause of*
> *these troubles, would it not indirectly flare up a latent focus?*

No. I never found it doing that.

> *And in such an experience as Y's, some amount of fear*
> *is inevitable, isn't it?*

What experience? Descent? Sensation in the head? Plenty of people
have had that here and elsewhere but no one got into a panic or
nervous upset.

> *N told me that Mother didn't approve of Y's staying at*
> *D's place...*

Up to that, it is correct.

> *...because adverse forces may act on D also and harm him.*

This must be N's own interpretation. The Mother said nothing to
that effect. D had already got into a depression by J's visit, next Y's
upset, finally something else and was preparing to head for Cape
Comorin — so naturally Mother didn't want visible food for that
to be supplied him. She said nothing of all that to N.

> *Do you go by the description of one's experience to decide*
> *whether it was an experience or the action of a dark force*
> *or the recrudescence of an illness?*

Yes, certainly — just as you go by the symptoms of a case as seen
by you and as related by the patient.

> *I thought that it is not possible for us to have spiritual*
> *experiences, especially major ones, without your previous-*
> *ly knowing that so and so will have such and such experiences.*

Previously? My God, we would have to spend all our time prevising the sadhaks' experiences. Do you think Mother has nothing else to do? As for myself, I never previse anything, I only vise and re-vise. All that Mother prevised was that there was something not right in Y, some part of him at odds with his aspiration. That might lead to trouble. That is why, entre nous, I want him to find out what part of him didn't want the descent.

October 19, 1936

> *S is much better in the morning nowadays, but troublesome in the afternoon. Getting cured by halves?*

Let us hope so. Half by half is better than nothing.

> *T has given measurements, but wouldn't it be better to enquire first from the Company if they have any supports for this trouble? If not, whether they can prepare according to measurements given. All this will take some time, but it is not very urgent, is it?*

No. You are right, of course.

> *Dr. Sircar has a touch of cold! Please save me; no more patients, especially big and bulky ones!*

Well, well, prevent the cold from becoming bulky.

> *7.30 p.m.*
> *Y is all right except for a tense feeling on the left side of the neck.*
> *[Sri Aurobindo underlined "tense feeling on the left side of the neck".]*

Not physical? Circulation?

> *M has been troubled by D.L.'s "ghost". He told me he had a dream and heard a voice calling him and clasping him— voice unerringly of D.L.*

Sorry, have to postpone M's ghostly troubles till tonight. Ter-

SRI AUROBINDO   723

rible night the last! (No, no — wasn't attacked by a pseudo-D.L.,
only by the demon of correspondence.) Have written, trying to
cheer him up in the meanwhile.

> *Today his trouble began again. Any link?*

Well, you said, did you not, that this headache was of long standing?
If so, the link with D.L. must be later — or only a mental association.

> *Why should he have these dreams connected with D.L.?*

Many people have been seeing or dreaming of the ghost of D.L.

> *I asked M to get rid of his fear. He has no hereditary taint of
> insanity. But seeing D.S.'s off-centre, is it possible?*

Don't know if there was any insanity in the family. D.S. is only
insane at one point which can be touched at any time. But apart
from that he is though narrow and extreme in all things, yet intellectually brilliant, an admirable linguist, reasoning and seeing
with extraordinary acuteness and clearness when he chooses. He
is more "intimate" with French than any Indian here — understands
the spirit of the language, reproduces it in his writing. A clear and
accurate observer too.

> *Why has D.L. such a special fascination for him, in coming
> to call him? Is it really possible that some part of D.L. is,
> after all, hovering over the Asram and trying to create some
> mental, vital or nervous havoc? Or some other force taking
> D.L.'s shape or voice trying to push in?*

D.L. does not call him; it is not she at all. When she got ill something
possessed her body and physical consciousness and turned everything against her recovery. When she died the Mother separated
this from her — but still there was a strong earthly attachment left in
her vital form — attachment to husband, food, comfort, relatives
etc., etc. This part threatened to become a "ghost", and Mother had
to work hard to get rid of it. But it went and there is no ghost, that is
no vital stuff walking about as a separate entity with the soul gone

out of it. But the suggestion was left in the Asram atmosphere and some Force has got hold of it making all sorts of dreams and fears in the minds of those who admit them. But I think that too is fading out gradually. Sorry to inflict all this occultism on you. . .

I somewhat understand M's involvement. You know he had an experience: hurried loud breathing, semi-conscious condition, etc., with one hand on D.L.'s abdomen, as if some Force had descended and possessed him. We looked admiringly at him and thought the Mother was working through him; unfortunately the fellow took it all wrong, as your letter showed.

M's disturbance was due to his wrong movement at the time of D's [D.L.'s] death. He had a propensity to become a big Yogi and a mighty instrument. At the time I was putting and so was the Mother a stupendous force to give D a last chance. M was trying to pull. Perhaps he felt and was shaken by the Force which was not intended for him at all — because he pulled it. He pretended to himself that he was doing it in an egoless fashion. Rubbish! Self-deception! He was delighted at being so great an instrument and at the admiration of others. I had to interfere because like that he might pull some wrong force on himself. It may be even that he did get something, not much I think, of the other dark Force that was there. This prepared the field for undesirable suggestions. My letter also bowled him over — but that was unavoidable. I suppose it will be all right, but for a moment he was shaky.

October 20, 1936

Jatin has sent snaps for your signature. Will you give it?

Yes.

Yesterday's feeling I can't locate — probably in the abdominal cavity. Today again something happened — but not any fear. It was an ingoing, perhaps, for I came out just as a fish comes out of water, with a sigh (?) or for taking air?

Don't quite understand. Yesterday you wrote that there was no fear, but a feeling that something unpleasant might happen and you must get over it again. But if it was like a fish in water, that

SRI AUROBINDO   725

could not be unpleasant.

Your present description would be a going inside of the vital (abdominal cavity) into its deeper self, perhaps in search of the psychic which lies behind. If so, very useful movement.

> *There was no drowsiness — understandable?*
> [*Sri Aurobindo underlined the word "drowsiness", which was written rather badly.*]

Your writing is sometimes no more understandable than mine. It took me some time to understand whether this word was Bengali, Sanskrit or English with a mixture. But I suppose it is drowsiness?

> *Y has gone, but I understand, he wants to come back — to be fitted into his old place?*

God knows. You must know that when he came back last time, he was only tolerated on trial owing to his own urgent insistence. Next time — well! He will have to be considerably changed before we say Yes.

> *He asked our opinion about his going to Calcutta for treatment. I said, "Why not ask Mother?" He replied, "I haven't that much confidence in Sri Aurobindo and Mother, to tell you frankly." That shows where the root of the trouble was. Was it deeper still?*

According to what Mother was seeing all along, it was deeper still. A certain falsehood in his being which he refused to recognise, but kept cherished under a veil of justifying reasons, not intending to change. He never really recognised that he had been wrong at any time. Yet it was treachery to the Mother — with what she calls a strain of hypocrisy in it.

> *But then he was crying also because he had to go. Queer, isn't it?*

No, not queer. Very usual. A divided being. One black, one wanting to be white.

I saw your letter to him... You were almost suspecting there was some twist in his nature.

More than suspicion — a knowledge.

What could have been the cause of such a havoc? Vital desires? Attachments?

He had these; but that was not the chief difficulty.

Or was it lack of confidence and faith in the Mother?

There was that, of course — but lack of faith was not enough to produce such an upsetting. It was something in opposition and hiding itself, that got terrified when it saw its companion pulling down the Force. For after all he did pull. Mother felt him doing it even last time he came to Pranam.

I am afraid all of us have these things, to some degree. I am a little shaken because of your hint at the resistance or the lower nature's unwillingness to change, for who hasn't that?

That was a euphemism, as I wanted him to look at and acknowledge to himself (acknowledging to us would not be enough, as he might do it "with the end of his lips" only) and get rid of it.

Mere unwillingness to change is not enough. Everybody has that in part of his being — if it were enough to produce disaster, nobody could do Yoga.

Some light on M's report of yesterday, please.

Obliged to postpone it again.

October 21, 1936

I had a dream last night: the Mother had become a little girl and was talking to a boy of her age, before a vast gathering. There was something very unusual about her. We were wondering whether it was really the Mother. How had she

SRI AUROBINDO   727

> *turned so young? and to this little girl we made pranam!
> What significance?*

It was in the vital world, I suppose; there anything may happen.
Can't say that I catch any symbolic significance in it. Perhaps
your vital was trying to find a ground for বাৎসল্য ভাব.[1]

> *Had a dream of a death also in the Asram. . .*

Well, if you go on dreaming like that!

> *What B.P. is doing is, you know, something criminal. . .
> Why not buy him a ticket?*

Evidently! We have already tried to chuck him once, but failed, —
because he had nowhere to go. I will have a try again, even if we
have to buy him a ticket for Nowhere.

> *I don't know why the boy D and his mother are here. Do
> you really think that they will be doing Yoga any day?
> If not, why this encumbrance?*

Quite right, sir, — perspicaciously right. The original idea was
that they would live separately — M.G. only being a sadhika, but
as usual once people are anywhere near they push in.

> *Your Force is acting, Sir, and many pots will break. Am I
> one, I wonder!*

Need not be. Hope you have no inclinations that way.

> *Can you not give one or two concrete instances of false-
> hood and treachery of Y, that called in this catastrophe,
> simultaneously with the descent?*

Concrete instances came before. It was he who indoctrinated M to
leave the Asram and go back to her husband and gave her the suggestions of how to justify herself etc. The story is too long. But it

---

[1] *vātsalya bhāva:* parental affection.

was what I referred to as the reason why Mother did not permit him to come, —finally he came without permission. I hear he once encouraged D in his depression to go away from here. All that had not changed—he pretended under the pressure of D, S to repent, but in reality he always considered that he had done no wrong. This part of him was so false that it erected its falsehood into right. The Mother spoke always of his hypocrisy. See, he told D "There is no love lost between myself and Sri Aurobindo and the Mother, but I am sincere in my Yoga." That means he was seeking after something not connected with us. Yet he wrote that when the Force came down which was at will, he felt the Mother's presence in him and was happy. All that is what the Mother speaks of as hypocrisy. Then when the Force threatened to come in earnest, this part of him got terrified and shaken—for it had rejected the Mother's protection and did not want her Force at all, but something that it could appropriate. It felt that it was "something not himself", and got into a panic. There does not seem to have been any illness, for you would have found some sign. Coming Madness? I doubt. He was in clear possession of his wits. Then fear only. As soon as he knew he was going away, the fear went, this part became exultant and all went away. It seems to me on the data that this interpretation is the only possible one.

Please see if you can be "obliged" to reflect on M's condition. Then I shall write my St. Augustine's confessions!

Have written.

October 22, 1936

What? You are "sorry to inflict all this occultism" on me? [20.10.36] Please, try to percolate a little more of it through the thick sieve of your correspondence. I lost all hope, you know, and was depressed, dejected and downcast. It is so very interesting — this occultism!

All right. I can flood you when I have time and occasion.

I am preparing my confession! Perhaps tomorrow!

Very good. Shall await the revelation.

SRI AUROBINDO   729

L seems to be damnably constipated.

Has been for years except for a brief period when R treated her,
but before he had finished his treatment she got proud and said
only the Force was good enough for her and stopped with a kick
for him. After some time of halcyon openness of the bowels the
whole thing came back. She complains of sleeplessness last three
nights.
October 23, 1936

S all right or jogging along?
I should like to know about K. I have been given secret information (how far reliable, I don't know) that she is vomiting blood
but concealing it from the Doctors to avoid being sent away, also
that she has *dhatukshay* which the Guj. dictionary translates as
continuous gleet. What according to your knowledge is the state
of things about her?
October 24, 1936

. . . S's pain must be stopped. Fever is there but not so bad.

What a painful fellow!

May we get Pancrinol for him?

Very well.

*K denies all symptoms: no cough, no bleeding, no fever.
P says she is better; there is no more bleeding, cough is
also intermittent. Has anybody seen the bleeding? But
gleet one can't see!*

Confidentially I may say it was P who wrote—she says K herself
told her and of the rest she has seen evidence and was troubled
about possible contamination. Of course P like others and like
K herself, is a liar, but—
October 25, 1936

*You wrote to me that we should drop the mixing together
and cooking. How to drop the mixing, Sir?*

I did not write "mixing"—I wrote "messing"—food, sir, food; eating in common, sort of psycho-gastric communion forming a spiritual culinary joy. If you want occultism, you shall have it with a vengeance.

> *If one has a double attachment, would it not be an insincerity?*

It depends on the ideal. If it were a matter of the union of two lives, it would be an insincerity, a faithlessness. But for the vital? Its character is to change, sometimes to multiply, to run here and there. Unless of course it is caught, glued to a single attraction or passion for a long period or for a lifetime. But in such gluings it is generally one of the two that is entangled, the other skirmishes around dragging his living appendage or else leaving it half-glued, half-dropped.

> *All my problems would have been solved if you hadn't been sitting so tight on my notebook, Sir. All this psychology would have helped me in my story writing.*

Sir, it is a melancholy subject I don't like to go into just now. I would rather tell you when you can look back with a retrospective interest, than inflict it on you now.

> *By the way, what do you say to my asking Dr. Sircar to teach me* The Life Divine?

Fire away.

> *A complains of slight bleeding per rectum. Beginning of piles?*

Irritation somewhere in the intestine? No signs of dysenteric tendency. Or a passing accident. He only mentioned having it twice.

> *We have advised some fresh air after work and is it possible to alternate his sedentary work with some activity?*

That is what we have advised him—although diminishing his sed-

SRI AUROBINDO 731

entary work may make other sedentary people more sedentary.
Don't know exactly how it is to be done, but it must be.

> *What about giving him some mixtures containing Soda
> sulph., Ammon. chlor., etc.?*

You can give if A is willing to take.

> *Here is M's autobiography of headache and vomiting...*

Queer history!

> *These days he is keeping well, it appears. Perhaps the
> "ghost" has been dissolved!*

I hope so. I have done my best to that end.

October 26, 1936

> *What, Sir? No comment, not a line or a word or even a
> scratch![1] Felt heavy the whole day thinking of this mystery!
> Will you cast a look back?*

No mystery. Simply a case of adhyaropa of Shankaric illusion.
Made mental answers and thought they were there physically in-
scribed on your blank page.

> *You surprise me by the revelations of D.S. What a pity
> that all his brilliances should have met with such a destiny!*

But look here, his brilliances came after his madness. Before that he
was earnest, industrious, eager for knowledge, ambitious, but
nothing more. I don't contend that his madness made him a genius,
though it would agree with the immortal theory of Lombroso that
genius is madness or at least always tied to abnormality and mental
and physical unsoundness. It may have been the result of our

---

[1] It refers to the correspondence of the 26th in my private notebook where Sri
Aurobindo didn't write anything at first. After this remark of mine he wrote the
first 4 responses.

A

constant pouring of force into him to keep his mind bright and coherent and clear.

> *His touchiness seems to have come from an inferiority complex, the cause of all his trouble.*

Don't believe much in complexes.

> *I am not very cheerful about his prognosis. The isolation, complete suspension of speech are abnormal states.*

Why complete? He was talking to Amal at least.

> *Some believe that he is not only all right but much better. Their judgment is based on the Mother's gracious smiles to him.*

What queer logicians!

> *I doubt if he will ever take charge of the Dispensary.*

Not likely.

> *Is his off-centre due to a possession?*

A very partial one perhaps.

> *You have written about D.L. that something possessed her body. How? And did that something take her away against Mother's and your Force? How could you allow it to possess her before your very eyes, especially in her weak moment?*

What's the row? If the mind and vital can be possessed, as happened to B and N and others, why can't the body? As for allowing it, sir, if people have an inner revolt, they take the risk and, if they refuse to give up the possession, or call it back when it goes, they have none but themselves to blame.

> *If you knew that there was very little chance of saving*

SRI AUROBINDO 733

> *her, what could be the meaning of sending a stupendous Force to her as a last resort?*

Why not?

> *Did you even then hope that perhaps the scales might turn?*

Of course, they might. It was a question of a battle of Forces.

> *Was that stupendous Force spoiled by the intervention of M?*

Can't say.

> *I understand that she was very sincere in her work, faithful to the Mother.*

At the end, she got disgusted with it, critical of the Mother, attached to husband, relatives, food, all earth-desires. It was that that made the difficulty of her soul's passage and the danger of the ghost. For it is these violent earth-attachments that keep the vital hovering about the place after death.

> *Another problem which puzzles me is that when you accepted her, did you think that she was likely to be cut off from the path?*

Destiny is not an absolute, it is a relative. One can alter it for the better or the worse.

> *You say, "the suggestion was left in the Asram atmosphere." [20.10.36] Suggestion by whom? Sadhaks or that vital form?*

The suggestion that came from what possessed her "I will remain as a ghost". The sadhaks simply received the ghost of the suggestion, and saw the ghost of a ghost.

> *Even a suggestion could be caught hold of by a Force? Where are we, eh?*

What's the idea? Forces are always making suggestions — why can't they catch hold of one that is in the air and ease their labour?

> *Do you mean to say that the Force that Y was drawing at first, was not the Mother's Force, but something different which he could control?*

Who said that? It was a higher Force at least, even if not taken from the Mother, but drawn down by himself. But it was coming in small doses and he played happily with it. When it threatened to come in earnest and a great mass, he got frightened.

> *And when the Mother's Force descended he got frightened feeling it "not itself" by these reactions?* [22.10.36.]

"not *him*self", separate from himself.

> *L has general weakness. . . How to treat her inordinate constipation?*

Don't know. R got it cured for a spell, — but she stopped his treatment. Surely there must be an allopathic way of curing her obstinacy?

> *I am sure if J's poems were published, it would be like Blake's state—a century later people would appreciate her. . .*

What you predict is extremely probable—unless she writes hereafter something they can understand. Then they will say these were her mystic amusements by the way. A great poetess, but with a queer side to her.

October 27, 1936

> *Here is the photo of the two sisters J speaks of. Aruna, one of them, seems to have written to you. Both of them are keen on Yoga.*

From Aruna's letter I couldn't say that they know very much about what Yoga is!

SRI AUROBINDO 735

> *They seem to be quite healthy soldieresses. . . We want*
> *healthy people, Sir, not marasmics or plethorics!*

Health is needed but health is "not enough". Besides, trust not
in appearances. Soldiers and soldieresses sometimes become
pathological — nerves, shell-shock etc.

> *I woke up at 3 a.m. and tried to meditate. No sooner had*
> *I sat down than I felt a* স্তব্ধতা[1], *and the atmosphere around*
> *was so quiet that I felt or imagined some presences there.*
> *I thought—if at this hour some of these presences catch*
> *me, what shall I do? I got very frightened. Were there any*
> *presences?*

What the deuce did you get afraid for? Supposing any were there,
you could have waited at least to see whether they were good
presences or bad. If good, no harm; if bad, you have only to tell
them to skedaddle. But I expect it was only a feeling of yours.
Generally the স্তব্ধতা is either empty of presences and formations
or only one Presence is there, that of one's self or that of the Divine.

> *Now I am wondering why really I was afraid—thereby*
> *losing a beautiful opportunity for gaining something.*

Quite so. If one gets afraid, the experience can't go on.

> [*After a long report of K's medical case:*]
> *Have women a substance equivalent to men's seminal*
> *fluid which is said to be the basis of physical energy? Our*
> *medical science is silent about it.*

You really don't want me to deliver to a doctor a lecture on physio-
logy or genetics? Nonsense!

October 28, 1936

> *Guru, now I remember it was not exactly* স্তব্ধতা. *It is so*
> *difficult to express it — as though something was going to*
> *happen to me with which I was totally unfamiliar. I was*

---

[1] *stabdhatā:* stillness.

736   CORRESPONDENCE WITH

>*going away somewhere, getting as quiet and still as the at-*
>*mosphere around. Going to lose the consciousness of the*
>*surrounding things?*

Well, that is the beginning of some kind of samadhi.

>*And if some forces were to invade at that moment—this*
>*was my fear.*

Why the hell should they? But if there is any chance of that, call
the Mother's protection around you.

>*But do you say that* স্বধতা *is empty of other presences?*

Certainly.

>*Isn't it a fact that some adverse force may come and try*
>*to attack us in meditation?*

In meditation it may, but not in স্বধতা. All meditation is not
স্বধতা.

>*S told me that once while he was meditating at the dead*
>*of night, a force came and gripped his neck (?).*

Well, that's quite possible. If it does, one has only to kick it away
and say, "Get off, you fool." Or if you are not vigorous enough to
do that, call the Mother's force.

>*Anyway this fear must go.*

Exactly.

>*People come in contact with so many planes, beings and*
>*forces in meditation, and if one gets afraid, there is a chance*
>*of madness.*
>[*Sri Aurobindo underlined "a chance of madness".*]

Not necessarily madness. Plenty of people get afraid without
getting mad. Madness is exceptional. What fear does is to stop

SRI AUROBINDO

the experience or else it exposes you to blows from the vital beings. If you don't fear, they can't hurt you.

> *J's uncle was one.*
> [*Sri Aurobindo drew a line indicating "one".*]

One what? Got mad with fear?

> *So fear must go.*

Fear must not enter in Yoga. As Vivekananda said, the Yogi must be অভী.[1]

> *The other day Dr. Sircar asked me what is the yogic process you adopt in curing people. I told him what you have said about the medical aspect — when the diagnosis is definitely clear you concentrate on that so that when the root is handled, symptoms disappear gradually. . .*

Not always. Most often I deal with the symptoms also.

> *"It is a Science which he alone knows, to others it is a sealed book or a forbidden tree. . ."*

Why he alone? What about the Mother? Plenty of people besides, have felt forces.

> *"We have tried to pluck the fruit, but he is very strict and does not allow."*

How's that??

> *Any comments or light on this occult business? How far am I right in enunciating or enumerating your method?*

All right, subject to the comments above.

> *By the way, if it is a question of forces, how or where the*

[1] *abhī:* fearless.

*deuce do these millions of blessed bacilli and viruses come in?
Has each Force a definite bacillus as its agent?*

What is the difficulty? You are like the scientists who say or used to say there is no such thing as mind or thought independent of the physical brain. Mind and thought are only names for brain quiverings. Or that there is no such thing as vital Force because all the movements of life depend upon chemicals, glands and what not. These things and the germs also are only a minor physical instrumentation for something supraphysical.

Or do the Forces diminish the general resistance of the body in an occult way and germs according to their individual characteristics try to capture the body?

They first weaken or break through the nervous envelope, the aura. If that is strong and whole, a thousand million germs will not be able to do anything to you. The envelope pierced, they attack the subconscient mind in the body; sometimes also the vital mind or mind proper — prepare the illness by fear or thought of illness. The doctors themselves said that in influenza or cholera in the Far East 90 percent got ill through fear. Nothing to take away the resistance like fear. But still the subconscient is the main thing.

But diseases like cholera, plague etc. are supposed to outbreak by contamination.

If the contrary Force is strong in the body, one can move in the midst of plague and cholera and never get contaminated. Plague too, rats dying all around, people passing into Hades. I have seen that myself in Baroda.

You will say then that flies, bugs etc. that contaminate food, are sent to people by these forces and they were meant to be infected?

They were open to the Forces in some way.

Buddha, they say, died of dysentery due to pork-eating.

SRI AUROBINDO   739

Modern scholars have cleared Buddha of that carnivorous calumny.
They say it was a vegetable root called *sukarakhanda* which ignorant commentators have mistranslated "piece of a pig".

> *Dysentery, as you know, is caused by a germ.*

It isn't. It is instrumentated by a germ.

> *And germs got into the pork by flies and flies were there
> at the instance of forces?*

What about the vegetable root? Flies also. But why should not
flies be instruments for illness just as you are an instrument for
curing?

> *What about Ramakrishna's cancer? You will perhaps chide
> me for bringing in these instances, but logically they have
> to be there. And if Buddha's illness may not be believed,
> can Ramakrishna's? "How does it invalidate the theory of
> forces, you fool?" you will thunder.*

What did he himself say about it — that it was the sins of his disciples which constituted the cancer. There is a physical aspect to things
and there is an occult supraphysical aspect — one need not get in
the way of the other. All physical things are the expression of the
supraphysical. The existence of a body with physical instruments
and processes does not, as the 19th century vainly imagined, disprove the existence of a soul which uses the body even if it is also
conditioned by it. Laws of Nature do not disprove the existence of
God. The fact of a material world to which our instruments are
accorded does not disprove the existence of less material worlds
which certain subtler instruments can show to us.

> *But Ramakrishna was an Avatar, Sir! An Avatar to be at-
> tacked and given insufferable pains!*

Why should he not? Why on earth limit the possibilities of an
Avatar?

> *Last night L called Dr. Becharlal for tympanites. He saw*

> *there was no tympanites at all. . . She had also a good motion today.*

That's it! Constipation she has got but she bloodcurdles herself into any number of other things.

> *S asked for meals at home. Because of the rainy weather he says he feels unwell. How can I refuse when a healthy fellow like myself— ?!*

What delicate people all are becoming! A feather will hunch them down. Can't bear this, can't stand that. Evidently they are approaching the heights of supramental Yoga!

> [*In the medical report, I wrote the name of the patient as* Ambala *instead of Ambalal.*]

I say! this is the name of a town, not of a person.

October 29, 1936

November 1936

> [*The following medical report was by Dr. Becharlal about Shanta who had pain in the back and chest. She had weak eyes and lungs, and did a lot of knitting, embroidery, etc.*] *She should not work for more than an hour in bent position. She should try to sit straight.*

That is all right. Mother had suggested that already in cases of fatigue of back from similar cause.

> *She should go for a walk in the open air every morning and evening.*

She starts, then loses interest or feels tired or something and drops it.

> *She should take cod-liver oil for a longer period.*

SRI AUROBINDO   741

You must persuade her to do that.

> *She may be given such work as may not fatigue the eyes,
> press upon the chest — picking dry leaves, flowers, watering
> plants, etc.*

She used to do some gardening before but dropped it.

> *J asks Mother whether bath salts get spoiled if a dozen
> bottles are bought at a time.*

No, they don't get spoiled.

> *Herewith Powell's letter regarding T's abdominal support
> It looks like an adjustable type.*
>
> *[20.10.36]*

It is a steel affair? I doubt whether T could stand that.

> *I hope she will be able to manage the measurements wanted.*

Lying down? it may be difficult for her.

> *Guru, this is the month when your thrice-blessed disciple
> came into the physical world. Please see that the supra-
> physical projects some more of its invisible rays. But
> thinking again — what will the poor Guru do if the big
> disciple doesn't fulfil the conditions? Is that so?*

The one hope is then that he may last on to fulfil the conditions
without his knowing that he is doing it! What do you think of that
device?

> *November 1, 1936*

> *What do I think of that "device"? What can I think, Sir?
> That is the only straw I am obliged to clutch at, but it
> may prove too weak for my burden. I am doubtful of the
> device because you must have tried it also in many other
> cases that have failed.*

742   CORRESPONDENCE WITH

The cases that have failed are those that have gone the wrong way — which is another kind of difficulty altogether.

> *Yes, T's support is a steel affair. Otherwise it won't be tight enough. But why can't she stand it?*

Because it is very painful when one is thin with no fat to protect one. So instead of relieving her pains, it would [cause] others.

> *Sir, how to solve her lying down problem, I don't know.*

Rack your brains and solve it.

> *Should I resume my hospital visits now? But cycles aren't allowed to be taken out in rainy weather, so?*

It is because the rider gets wet and the bicycle rusted. But if you can arrive at an understanding with Benjamin[1] —

There is an application for permanent residentship — X, son of B, husband of A. He had made himself something like a physical wreck in Africa, says he is all right now. Mother wants you to be very strict in your examination; also I have told him to give past history. First result of your suggestion for a preliminary examination of candidates!

> *November 2, 1936*

> *By the way, R was also suggesting about the medical board, after D.L.'s death. Can't he be included?*

There would be much confusion. He would say something quite different from the rest of you.

> *November 3, 1936*

> *We have brought one dozen packets of bath salts for Mother. Wouldn't it be better to send them now?*

Very well.

---

[1] A sadhak in charge of the cycles.

SRI AUROBINDO   743

> *I have found a line which seems quite good, but no more!*

Go ahead. Open the tap.

November 4, 1936

> *Guruji, I send you this incomplete masterpiece of mine. Such a one that I feel tempted to throw it head down, into—. Still, to be fair, the first 8 lines, I suppose, can stand on their feet. But the rest?*

Yes. These are all right. Afterwards you seem to have haled down by the hair of the head some lines which don't quite know where they are or what you are driving at. They have therefore not much life in them. Is there not a stop in the middle of the ninth line? If possible, after repairing the inspiration a little, you might start off from there again and produce a less abruptly evolved conclusion.

November 8, 1936

> *D.H. Lawrence says that one can only write creative stuff when it comes, otherwise it is not much good. In his own experience some sort of an urge—his daemon—has seized him, and he has created. Writing is a kind of passion to him—like kissing!*

All statements are subject to qualification. What Lawrence states is true in principle but in practice most poets have to sustain the inspiration by industry. Milton in his later days used to write every day fifty lines; Virgil nine which he corrected and recorrected till it was within halfway of what he wanted. In other words he used to write under any other conditions and pull at his inspiration till it came.

> *Perhaps the best creations are those which come by sudden inspiration, either in poetry or in prose.*

Yes. Usually the best lines, passages etc. come like that.

> *How to make writing a passion? Is one born with it?*

744   CORRESPONDENCE WITH

Usually. But sometimes it comes gradually.

> *With me it is neither a passion nor an urge! You've seen in my latest poems how my power of expression has deteriorated and resistance increased.*

I think you have been rather influenced by so much study of J's poems and are trying to follow a similar inspiration and it is not quite assimilated.

> *If I can make you believe that I am able to write stories after all, I shall ask you for some Force.*

I don't see why you should not be able to write.

> *I have been furiously thinking what is the use of blessed literature after all, if the nature remains just the same?*

Good heavens! where did you get this idea that literature can transform people? Literary people are often the most impossible on the face of the earth.

> *Is literature ever going to transform the nature?*

I don't suppose so. Never did it yet.

> *I have neither the strong will nor the sustained effort to transform my nature. The best way is to surrender — I am forced to do it — and keep quiet, quiet for years and years, which I am trying to do. But, Sir —!*

According to the affirmation of people acquainted with the subject, the preliminary purification before getting any Yogic experiences worth the name may extend to 12 years. After that one may legitimately expect something. You are far from the limit yet — so no reason to despair.

November 10, 1936

> *What do you think of the beginning of this poem, and the possibility, if any?*

SRI AUROBINDO   745

An energetic beginning — many possibilities.

> *Yes, I think I have been influenced by "so much study"*
> *of J's poems. But is it wrong to be thus influenced? Is it going*
> *to be an imitation?*

No, but it is a transition from one inspiration to another — and a
transition is often difficult.

> *A similar inspiration can have a different manifestation,*
> *can't it?*

Yes, of course.

> *Should I stick to my own domain? but what then is my*
> *own domain?*

Can't say very well; but it was distinctive enough.

> *I didn't mean that literature can transform people. We may*
> *have progressed in literature, but the outer human nature*
> *remains almost the same.*

Outer human nature can only change either by an intense psychic
development or a strong and all-pervading influence from above.
It is the inner being that has to change first — a change which is not
always visible outside. That has nothing to do with the development
of the faculties which is another side of the personality.

> *Wouldn't it be wiser to use my effort and labour in the*
> *direction of sadhana?*

That is another question altogether. But such sadhana means a
slow laborious work of self-change in most cases (twelve years
you know!), so why not sing on the way?

> *Literary people are hyper-sensitive, it seems. But why*
> *they alone? All artists, I am afraid, are like that.*

Of course.

746   CORRESPONDENCE WITH

> *The bigger one is, the greater the ego and the greater
> the sensibility or sensitiveness. I believe that if the artists
> were not so sensitive, they wouldn't be able to create!*

Not quite that. Sensibility, yes — one must be able to feel things.
Exaggerated sensitiveness not necessary. Men of genius have
generally a big ego — can't be helped, that.

> *Lawrence is terrible that way. He says he doesn't write
> for "apes, dogs and asses", and yet when these asses
> criticise him, he goes mad!*

Of course — T weeps oceans if criticised, Lawrence goes red etc.
It's the mark of the tribe.

> *What about yourself in your pre-yogic days? I hear that
> James Cousins said about your poem "The Rishi" that
> it was not poetry at all, only spiritual philosophy. I wonder
> what your poetic reaction was!*

James Cousins does not date from my preYogic days.
I never heard that. If I had, I would have noted that Cousins
had no capacity for appreciating intellectual poetry. But that I knew
already, just as he had no liking for epic poetry either, only for
poetic "jewellery". His criticism was of "In the Moonlight" which
he condemned as brain-stuff only except the early stanzas for which
he had high praise. That criticism was of great use to me — though I
did not agree with it. But the positive part of it helped me to develop
towards a supra-intellectual style. As "Love and Death" was
poetry of the vital, so "Ahana"[1] is mostly work of the poetic
intelligence. Cousins' criticism helped me to go a stage farther.

> *D said to us once that he spoke to Mother about his hyper-
> sensitiveness, and she replied that an artist has to be that —
> he must have finer, acuter feelings to be able to create his
> best.*

He has to be "*sensible*" in the French sense of the word.

---

[1] The reference is to the early version, not the one revised and considerably re-
written later.

SRI AUROBINDO   747

> *Only in Yoga one has to turn it towards the Divine. What do you say?*

I prefer he should drop the hyper-sensitiveness and be hyper-"sensible" (French sense, not English) only.

> *You have again hit me with the number of years in Yoga plus Virgil, Keats and Milton in poetry. I am preparing a hit-back!*

There was no hit in that — I was only answering your question about writing only when the inspiration comes. I pointed out that these poets (Virgil, Milton) did not do that. They obliged the inspiration to come. Many not so great do the same. How does Keats come in? I don't think I mentioned him.

> *J asks if A's letter can be sent now.*

Well, she can send. I will see at leisure.

November 11, 1936

> *Guru, what else could it be if not a "hit" or at least shutting my mouth? Every time I complain of a great difficulty, no inspiration, you quote the names of Virgil, Milton, etc. Same in Yoga — you say 10 years, 12 years, pooh!*

I thought you were honestly asking for the truth about inspiration according to Lawrence and effort; and I answered to that. I didn't know that it was connected purely with your personal reactions. You did not put it like that. You asked whether Lawrence's ideas were correct and I was obliged to point out that they were subject to qualification since both great and second class and all kinds of poets have not waited for a fitful inspiration but tried to regularise it.

> *When hour after hour passes in barren silence bringing unspeakable misery, these examples of great poets — Miltons, Virgils — who cannot be compared with small ones are no consolation at all. (Keats you mentioned on another occasion.)*

All that about great poets is absolute imbecile nonsense. There is no question of great or small. It is a question of fluency or absence of fluency. Great, small and mediocre are alike in that matter — some can write fast and easily, others can't.

> When you bring in the examples of Milton and Virgil in poetry and the number of years in Yoga, you forget that they had no Supramental Avatar as Guru to push them on, Sir!

Considering that the Supramental Avatar himself is quite incapable of doing what Nishikanta or Jyoti do, i.e. producing a poem or several poems a day, why do you bring him in? In England indeed I could write a lot every day but most of that has gone into the Waste Paper Basket.

> If you mean seriously that I have to wait 12 years, you will drive me to commit suicide, I tell you. Things are bad enough, Sir, and "sing on the way" indeed!

The rule of 12 years is one enounced not by me, but many Sanyasis and people who know about Yoga. Of course they are "professionals", so to speak, while this is an Asram of amateur Yogis who expect quick results and no labour — and if they don't get it, talk about despair and suicide.

> God knows when I shall be above all this vital desire, sex, etc. When I think of the first 2 years, I heave a sigh thinking of such a retrogression, a fall. You have said that falls and failures bring something better and richer; what have they brought for me?

There is nothing peculiar about retrogression. I was also noted in my earlier time before Yoga for the rareness of anger. At a certain period of the Yoga it rose in me like a volcano and I had to take a long time eliminating it. As for sex — well. You are always thinking that the things that are happening to you are unique and nobody else ever had such trials or downfalls or misery before.

> I have no other way but to surrender to the Divine, leaving

SRI AUROBINDO 749

> *Him to lead me through fires or flowers as He decides best.*
> *Can I "sing", honestly?*

I don't see why not? Dilip used to sing whenever he felt suicidal.

> *Amal says Cousins ignored your poem "The Rishi" while*
> *speaking of the others. Isn't that far worse?*

Neither worse nor better. What does Cousins' bad opinion about the "Rishi" matter to me? I know the limitations of my poetry and also its qualities. I know also the qualities of Cousins as a critic and also his limitations. If Milton had written during the life of Cousins instead of having an established reputation for centuries, Cousins would have said of Paradise Lost and still more of Paradise Regained "This is not poetry, this is theology". Note that I don't mean to say that "Rishi" is anywhere near "Paradise Lost", but it is poetry as well as spiritual philosophy.

November 13, 1936

> *You surprise me very much, Guru, by this "volcanic anger"*
> *of yours. People say that they never heard a single harsh,*
> *rude, angry word from your mouth here in Pondicherry.*
> *But how is it that this "volcano" flared up in Yoga when*
> *you were noted for its rareness in pre-Yoga? Subconscient*
> *surge?*

I was speaking of a past phase. I don't know about subconscient, must have come from universal Nature.

November 14, 1936

> *What do you mean by "feminine women"? as opposed to*
> *"masculine women"?*

Feminine is not used in opposition to masculine here, but means only a wholly unrelievedly feminine woman—a capricious, fantastic, unreasonable, affectionate-quarrelsome-sensual-emotional, idealistic-vitalistic, incalculable, attractive-intolerable, never-knows-what-she-is-or-what-she-isn't and everything else kind of creature. It is not really feminine, but is the woman as man has made her. By the way, if you like to add some hundred other epithets and double-epithets after searching the Oxford dictionary, you can freely do so. They can all be fitted in somehow.

I am tempted to ask you a delicate personal question about X. She seems to be in a good state of sadhana though I find that she spends much of her time in a very ordinary manner. . . Still she seems very happy and her sadhana must be very good, as she has no depression. . .

You forget that for a long time she was often keeping much more to herself, to Y's great anger. During that time she built up an inner life and made some attempt to change certain things in her outer — not in the outward appearance but in the movements governing it. There is still an enormous amount to be done before the outward change can be outwardly visible, but still she is not insincere in her resolution. As for her not having any depression [it is] because she has established a fundamental calm which is only upset by clashes with Y; all the rest passes on the surface ruffling it perhaps, but not breaking the calm. She has also a day or two ago had the experience of the ascent above and of the wideness of peace and joy of the Infinite (free from the bodily sense and limitation) as also the descent down to the Muladhar. She does not know the names or technicalities of these things, but her description which was minute and full of details was unmistakable. There are three or four others who have had this experience recently so that we may suppose the working of the Force is not altogether in vain, as this experience is a very big affair and is supposed to be, if stabilised, the summit of the old Yogas — For us it is only a beginning of spiritual transformation. I have said this though it is personal so that you may understand that outside defects and obstacles in the nature or the appearance of unYogicness does not necessarily mean that a person can do or is doing no sadhana.

I want to know the secret of it. Is she all the time thinking of the Mother within? I think she has a great love for the Mother. Is that the secret?

Partly. She got hold of the sadhana by the right end in her mind and applied it — just the thing Y failed to do because of his doubts,

SRI AUROBINDO   751

pride of intellect and denial etc. — so in spite of serious defects
of nature she has got on.

> *Is it enough for progress, if most of the time is passed in
> the way she does?*

She passes her time so because she can now do it and yet keep within
her inner condition and her sadhana. So she says at least. Possibly
if she did it less she would go on faster.

> *Guru, day after tomorrow is my blessed birthday. The
> year has gone round and the prophecy that at the age of
> 32, my troubles will be over, has well — ! [3.11.35]*

Thirty-second year over? Perhaps in the "will be over" over has
a different significance!

> *G says he doesn't want to take any more cod-liver oil,
> as he is quite all right and doesn't want to get fatter.*

Perhaps he could be given a rest from the oil for a time. But if he
thinks himself fat, that is an illusion.

November 15, 1936

> *M.G. says the doctor (M.B. only) at Calcutta didn't advise
> quinine without blood exam.*
> [*Sri Aurobindo put a question mark above "M.B. only".*]

What's this algebra?

> *His case looks like malaria. Is it necessary to examine
> blood?*

Examine blood for what? To see if it is malaria?

> *G has been taking half a cup of extra milk. He wants to
> give it up now. Should he cease?*

No. He must continue — unless he prefers cod-liver oil.

752   CORRESPONDENCE WITH

I send you one of Z's missives. The last para is private and non-medical but apart from that you may perhaps convey to Becharlal the substance of this despatch — the horrible tale of the alarming Lila that is going on in her stomach.

Please return the epistle.

November 16, 1936

Guru, any impression of Mother's on my birthday? I am afraid I wasn't calm but the whole day I felt peaceful.

Mother's verdict is "Not at all bad — I found him rather receptive." So, sir, cherish your receptivity and don't humbug about with doubt and despondency and then you will be peaceful for ever!

Quinine was given to M.G. But I suppose it is not any more necessary, as is evident. I know your views against quinine but what can we give instead?

Don't know. If it is a necessary evil, it must be administered, I suppose.

I return Z's "epistle", with thanks. Dr. Becharlal will look after the "Lila", but are these people living in an illusory world of their own or are we in a sceptical world of ours? She says every atom is merging peacefully and beautifully into the wideness of the Mother, and yet this alarming "Lila" of the stomach and the whole body! Is the Spirit separating itself from Matter and enjoying all this, while giving an impersonal account of material suffering?

Z is a humbug and I don't believe in her atoms. She has had experiences but on the mental and vital plane. It is only a real descent of the higher consciousness from above that can give a peaceful and beautiful merging of the atoms (?) into the wideness of the Divine — that is to say one feels the very cells sharing in that peace and wideness. This is possible even if the material body is ill. In most cases it is the subtle body that feels like that, but as the subtle penetrates everywhere the gross physical, the physical body also feels like that. But then it does not feel disturbed by the pains or motions

SRI AUROBINDO   753

of the illness — they do not affect its peace or Ananda.

November 17, 1936

> *May I ask Ardhendu to play a little sitar here in the dis-*
> *pensary, at night? I shall invite just a few friends.*

I suppose it can be done.

> *Chand has asked your advice and protection for going*
> *to Chittagong in January.*

Protection is possible, advice not.

November 18, 1936

> *Guru, Mother said I was receptive? But how? I don't*
> *know really.*

How the devil can you know, when you are not conscious?

> *That is the whole trouble in your Yoga, Sir, that everything*
> *goes on in an unconscious stream.*

It always does in the earlier stages.

> *All I know is that I tried to be calm and silent, forgetting*
> *by mind-effort that an outer world exists. That is recepti-*
> *vity?*

Nonsense! It is only the proper condition for receptivity. Naturally,
it is the proper thing to do if you want to be receptive or become
conscious of inner things. So long as the mind is jumping about or
rushing out to outside things, it is not possible to be inward, collected, conscious within.

> *The Mother said to me in the interview that my inner*
> *mind asked for vital stability and faith, which can be esta-*
> *blished by bringing the psychic to the front. How to do that?*

I consulted your books and found that by silence, self-offering and aspiration, it has to be done.

Yes, that is the proper way.

But aspiration for what?

Aspiration for the Divine or aspiration for faith and consciousness and the perfection of self-giving—aspiration for divine love, bhakti, anything that connects the soul with the Divine.

Does the psychic come to the front even if the vital is impure?

Well, it may; anything is possible; but if it does, it will certainly say "Fie, fie, what! all this dirt in the temple. Sweep me the temple clean."

Or the emergence of the psychic purges the vital of its impurities?

Yes, provided you give your assent.

I find that so long as sex is strong, no ascent or descent is possible.

That is not true. It is possible but damnably unsafe.

But in spite of these things which you say are not mine alone, if I could get rid of these two devils—doubt and despondency!

They are not uniquely yours either.

J does not claim to know any sadhana but still to have an inner peace and joy. It must be true, for I find J very happy and cheerful.

Well, yes, many people are like that. Calm or peace or happiness or cheerfulness, so long as there is no cause for disturbance; but immediately there is, then boil, seethe, simmer, growl, howl, yowl.

SRI AUROBINDO   755

The calm which causes of disturbance cannot disturb is the thing.

> *You say the working of the Force is not altogether in vain in spite of serious defects in people's nature. But surely they must have satisfied some essential conditions for gaining the experiences.*

Yes, of course. But it varies with different people. It may be faith, it may be earnestness and persistence. It may be love for the Divine. There are many other things it may be. Like the Mahomedan with his tuft, you must give a handle somewhere for the Angel of the Lord to catch hold of you and lift you up.

> *Otherwise I could have those experiences as well, but I can't, why?*

Mind bubbling, vital disturbed and despondent, physical inert.

> *Or would you say that it has taken those people 7 or 8 years?*

Yes, it has — what you would call damned slow progress — but, slow or not, they arrive.

> *It seems to me there must have been some difference between X and me, for instance, for which she had the experiences and I didn't. She took sadhana by the "right end" you said, which means surely that she had no doubt or despondency?*

No, sir, she had these in fits and very bad fits too like everybody else almost. But she preferred to believe, to be devoted, to fight against herself and conquer. She did not like Y take a pride in doubting and using the intellect for the purpose, was sensible enough to see that that wasn't what she came here for. She didn't want to question everything and be satisfied in her limited intellect before she took the way of spiritual self-giving and inner experience.

> *How did this "fundamental calm" get established in her?*

It came of itself through the sincerity of her will to open and to live for the Divine — there was insincerity and ego on the surface but the psychic could make itself heard owing to this — so the inner being slowly grew.

November 19, 1936

> *I have a bad frontal headache, feeling feverish, hope no complication of left frontal sinus suppuration! Help, Guru!*
> [*Sri Aurobindo drew an arrow from the word "suppuration".*]

What's all this? Is this a time to start suppurating sinuses? Drop it, please.

November 20, 1936

> *Guru, O Guru,*
>   *My head, my head*
>   *And the damned fever!*
>   *I am half-dead!*
>   *With pain and pressure*
>   *But blessed liver*
>   *Functions quite well,*
>   *Please send the others*
>   *To hell, oh to hell!*

Cheer up! Things might have been so much worse. Just think if you had been a Spaniard in Madrid or a German Communist in a concentration camp! Imagine that and then you will be quite cheerful with only a cold and headache. So

> Throw off the cold,
> Damn the fever.
> Be sprightly and bold
> And live for ever.

> *What's to be done? How to drop it? Is it the blessed cold only or any Force to boot that is causing havoc in the head?*

I don't know of any Force. Do you think it is some pressure making the difficulty in the head ooze out of it? If so —

SRI AUROBINDO   757

> *For it started, you know, on the very night I came from the Mother...*

Receptivity?

> *Very funny that every time I make a resolution regarding poetry or sadhana, something happens and ties me down. Why?*

Probably the adverse forces get frightened and put in an undercut or overcut to knock you out of tune.

> *I was proud that I was immune to illness! But a mere cold pulls me down, and that too at Darshan time! Again Fate, Sir! There is a proverb in Bengali which says that one who is unlucky, is unlucky everywhere; even in a* নেমন্তন্ন[1] *he doesn't get anything. I hope you remember the familiar word* নেমন্তন্ন*!*

I do, though it belongs to the far-off past for me.

> *November 21, 1936*

> *I am better today, Sir. But feverishness is there, which I hope will pass off tomorrow. But what about the lack of interest in everything?*

Don't understand. You want to get rid of the interest in everything or to get rid of the lack of interest?

> *Imagination of Madrid or the Concentration Camp will have a reverse effect!*

What reverse effect? Increase of cold and headache?

> *By the Guru! Please don't forget to give a supramental kick to my main impediments at Darshan; only no after-effects, please, what?*

---

[1] *nemantanna:* an invitation for a feast.

758   CORRESPONDENCE WITH

"By the Guru"! What kind of oath is this? But the object of the
imagination was not to liberate your nose or forehead, but to liberate your soul.

Kicking is easy. As to the effects or after-effects, that has to be
seen.
                                                November 22, 1936

> *Guru, I feel I must seriously write now — take the Muse
> by the forelock. Otherwise she is too high and proud; but
> your help is needed. You said afternoon is your fag-end, so
> every time I feel unsupported then. I will shift it to the
> lonely quiet night, to get your bright and energetic beginning.
> What? Approve?*

Not objected to at least provided you don't stay wrestling with the
Muse till the small hours of the morning.
                                                November 25, 1936

> *[The following report was written by Dr. Becharlal:]
> S said last evening that she was much better. But today
> she has not come for the medicines.*

She has written that she got worse with the medicine, so she stopped
it. I have told her that she ought to report to you instead of doing
that.

> *A perfect sonnet! (1) What do you think of the first line,
> Sir: "My clouded soul, do you know where you are?"
> Flat? and the* clouded *soul?*

(1) Flat? by God, sir, abysmal! The soul can get as clouded as it
likes but do you know where you are? In Pondicherry, sir, in Pondicherry — the most clouded soul can know that. You might just as
well write "My friend, do you know that you are an ass?" and call
it metre and poetry.

> *What about the thought, sequence, etc.? Please show the
> defects with your opinion and criticism. Is it a metaphysical
> or philosophic poem?*

SRI AUROBINDO   759

God knows! But the matter is that the metre of some of your lines
is enough to make the hair of a prosodist stand on end in horror!
I have marked all the quadrupeds you have created *in situ* — also
put in the margin my five-footed emendations of them. . .

November 27, 1936

> *After reading your remarks on yesterday's poem, oh
> what a joy I felt! In spite of your calling me an "ass", Sir!*

I only made you call somebody else one.

> *Let me whisper to you that after this Darshan something
> somehow has happened somewhere to make me cheerful
> and jolly, though you didn't seem to have given me a very
> warm reception — because of my damn cold?*

There was no absence of warmth — it may be your cold that made
it seem so to you.

> *And though Mother now and then rolls her eyes, which
> makes me roll in misery for one or two hours. . .*

Rubbish!

> *D also says he is very happy. So we both combine to give
> you this good news. You may congratulate yourself on some
> tremendous success you have achieved! What's the secret,
> Sir? Supramental in view?*

Supramental "in view" long ago. To reach is the thing.

> *Danger zone crossed?*

Can't say that, yet.

> *Ah, if this joy remains so! will it?*

Let us hope so.

I forgot to narrate to you a funny experience I had on Darshan day. Just after darshan, I sat in the Asram for a while, then went home and lay down. From 10 to midday I slept heavily. But throughout those 2 hours, I had the feeling that I'd lose all that I had received at darshan. Suddenly I felt myself sleeping in Ardhendu's room, listening to kirtan.[1] *But the funny part is that my body seemed to be lying on the bed and another part of me was up and listening to the* kirtan. *Was it the subtle body? What significance?*

Why funny? Quite natural.

Why the deuce do all you people ask always what significance? If you walked out of your house in boots, leaving your slippers or sandals behind, that would be a fact, but with no significance except that you had boots. You went out in your subtle body and listened to the kirtan of the vital plane in Ardhendu's room, leaving your body to snore (or not) in yours. Quite a common affair, only shows that you have become aware of the boots, i.e. of your subtle body and its exits.

November 28, 1936

Boil again inside the right nostril! But perhaps you will ask me to imagine being a Spaniard, German, Jew, the Japanese-German pact and the Russian inflammation against it etc., etc. All right, Sir, I will imagine all these if you will imagine giving me a dose of Force, what?

It is for you to do that. I can only send Force.

November 29, 1936

U has pain in the left elbow. Siju or Oriental Balm recommended by the Divine seems to have failed! We might try some other liniment.

Try.

[1] A particular style of devotional song.

SRI AUROBINDO   761

> *R has a glandular swelling on the right side of the neck now.*

What about other matters? Eruption on arm? Lice in hair?

> *Boil paining, what to do? Suffer with a smile?*

Smile awhile.

> *Some years ago G hurt his scrotum; there was a swelling as a result, since then any time he has fever or pain in his knee, the swelling of the testis appears. Right testis somewhat enlarged due to the fluid — sign of orchitis.*

? Not very coherent statement. Any connection between knee, fever any time and orchitis?

                                                          November 30, 1936

December 1936

> *Mulshankar still complains of pain in the hip joint. There is a loud cracking sound in some positions. Dr. Becharlal says the dislocation hasn't been set right, perhaps.*

It may be only rheumatism settled there. Sometimes a fracture even if set right perfectly leads to that. But you can see again if you think there is any chance of its not having been put right.

> *Sonnet emended by Amal. He has changed the metrical errors, as well as lines which seemed to him un-English.*

And what errors, my God! For heaven's sake don't try the irregular dodge yet. It doesn't succeed with you.

> *In J's poem, she says that by Nature's or the Bride's rhythm, roses live in hope? How? Why?*

What do you know about roses and their response to rhythm?

                                                           December 2, 1936

No, I don't know anything about the roses being opened by the rhythm of Nature or the Bride. Hence the question to know what you know.

What I know, is ineffable.

You seemed to have been in the worst of moods, due to heavy correspondence?

No, the best.

I hope you have had your fill of supramental glee by the merciless whipping on the inframental!

It was all done for your good with the most philanthropic motive.

But I don't understand your point in spite of such whipping. Is poetry to be felt only, only to have an inner thrill, tremor and quiver?

What's the use of saying poetry, with a universal sweep like that? It is a question of mystic poetry, not of all poetry.

Perhaps one must not use the intellect to understand what exactly or apparently is meant?

Mystic poetry does not mean anything exactly or apparently; it means things suggestively and reconditely, — things that are not known and classified by the intellect.

Or should one be satisfied only with the fineries, embroidery, ornamental decorations outside, and not see what it is that they are covering?

What you are asking is to reduce what is behind to intellectual terms, which is to make it something quite different from itself.

Must not one see if the body that these ornaments decorate is as beautiful and precious or more than these fineries?

SRI AUROBINDO

It is not a question of the (intellectual) body, but of the mystic soul
of the thing.

You want it intellectually beautiful and precious or mystically
beautiful and precious?

> *The symbolic and spiritual images in your* Bird of Fire,
> *for instance, are so rich, high, poignant and poetic, but
> if one could follow the* bhāva *behind or through them, I
> believe the appreciation would become complete.*

What do you mean by following the bhava behind? Putting a label
on the bird and keeping it dried up in your intellectual museum,
for Professors to describe to their pupils — "this is the species and
that's how it is constituted, these are the bones, feathers etc., etc.
and now you know all about the bird. Or would you like me to
dissect it farther?"

> *Suppose one said: "Why the devil do you want to know
> the meaning and not rest satisfied with the beauty of the
> expression?"*

Why the deuce are you dwelling on the poetry of the expression
as if that were all one feels in a mystic poem and unless one dis-
sects and analyses it one can't feel anything but words?

> *The little explanations you gave here and there of J's
> mystic poems enhanced the* rasa.

It didn't to me — it simply intellectualised all the rasa out of it.

> *If the explanations are not necessary then Blake's poems
> lose half the charm. People have perhaps appreciated
> the poetic qualities of his works, but now that they under-
> stand the significance also they consider him very great.
> Isn't that so?*

They understand the significance? in what way? By allegorising
them?

Read the remarks of Housman on the magnificent poem of

764   CORRESPONDENCE WITH

Blake he quotes in full and the attempts of people to explain it.[1]
I quite agree with him there though not in his too sweeping theory
of poetry. To explain that poem is to murder it and dissect the
corpse. One can't explain it, one can only feel and live the truth
behind it.

> *What I mean to say is that intellectual understanding is
> necessary to fully appreciate the beauty and worth of a
> poem, otherwise one feels only a subtle tremor or quiver
> of joy.*

Rubbish!
Who is this "one"?

> *In symbolic or mystic poems one wants to know also the
> truths behind the symbols for proper appreciation.*

Intellectual truths? Do you think that the intellectual truth of the
Divine is its real truth? In that case there is no need of Yoga. Philosophy is enough.

> *For instance J has written "Crimson Rose", and by crimson
> has suggested the painful feeling. Now if one could catch
> that instead of simply visualising a red rose, the rasa be-
> comes more thick.*

It would become much more thick if you felt the mystic red rose
and all that it is in the subtle planes instead of merely visualising a
red rose and thinking about pain.

I may farther say about J's poem that I don't care a damn who
the woman is that is sitting there and I would rather not have a label
put on her. It leaves me free to feel all the inner possible meaning of
her waiting and what she is waiting for.

It is the same with the symbols in Yoga. One puts an intellectual
label on the "White Light" and the mind is satisfied and says,
"Now I know all about it; it is the pure divine Consciousness
light," and really it knows nothing. But if one allows the Divine

---

[1] "My spectre around me night and day. . .", *The Name and Nature of Poetry* by
A.E. Housman. pp. 43-44.

SRI AUROBINDO   765

White Light to manifest and pour through the being, then one
comes to know it and get all its results. Even if there is no labelled
knowledge, there is the luminous experience of all its significance —

December 3, 1936

*All that whipping for my good? "With the most philan-
thropic motive"? Gracious! The only good was to stop
me from asking questions about J's poem. But really
what's the motive? You want the mind to be completely
silent?*

At least decently silent — not always asking for an intellectual
definition of everything mystic.

*I have brought Housman and shall read him. I would like
to get this point cleared if it can be cleared. Your Future
Poetry may also give some idea if I can pick out the right
chapter.*

Don't know that there is one (right chapter).

*I don't get sufficient time at night, so I have been writing
in the afternoon also.*

That's all right.

*If that is your "fag-end" really, then can't Mother give
me some Force?*

Very inappropriate time for her also. Besides, it is I who am directly
running the Poetry Department. However I am now more sprightly
from 2.30 to 4.30. After that, correspondence — no chance for
poetry.

*If you object to my intellectual dissection, please mark the
striking lines as you did yesterday in my Bengali poem,
because at times I can see their beauty only after you've
marked them — as it happened yesterday.*

Strange! for they are full of poetic power and feeling and what Matthew Arnold would call "in the grand style".

December 4, 1936

> *Nishikanta says that taking my poetry as a whole, some command over expression and harmony is there, but the বক্তব্য[1] is not clearly expressed, either because I don't know what I want to say or because the power of expression hasn't yet developed.*

I don't know about that. The বক্তব্য is there, it seems to me, and expressed, but it does not come to so much as one would expect from the richness of the expression. I suppose he means that you have caught only a little of something that might be expressed — only a hair of the tail instead of the complete animal.

> *Perhaps it is true about the বক্তব্য, but the difficulty is that very often I don't know what will follow. I get a line to begin with and let myself go.*

That is not the case.
Very fine things can come in that way.

> *Can you give me your opinion? Is there no way to hasten the process?*

No, it will come all right as you grow. You are only an infant, just now.

> *I wrote to you about my happiness, but the very next morning a nebulous cloak of depression fell on me and I am still under it! Well!*

Tut, tut, tut! You really must get rid of this kind of thing, hang it all. Out of this kind of nebula no constellation can be made.

---

[1] *vaktavya:* theme.

SRI AUROBINDO   767

The funny thing is that S complains so much and says
hunger also is less, but he looks none the worse.

Are you sure he is not a "malade imaginaire"?—at least to a large
extent?
                                                        December 5, 1936

Guru, yes, unfortunately I am "an infant". But is infancy
the reason, really? I thought it is a question of opening of
some inner channel that is the secret. If that opens or is
opened up, then the infant can grow old in a day.

Here you are illegitimately changing the metaphor. What has a
channel to do with infancy and old age? You are doing in prose
what you don't want J to do in poetry.

J, you know, was no better than an infant and she ran equal
with me in poetry, didn't she? All of a sudden see where
she is!

Because there are infants and infants. Some grow quick, others
slowly.

She has not only caught the animal whole and alive, but
most marvellously and rapidly, while I have not been able
to catch even a hair of the tail!

My dear sir, she let the inspiration through and didn't mind whether
she understood it or not—or at least if she did mind, it didn't
stop her from following it.

She has written 4 sonnets today, and each one better than
my single production of 2 or 3 days' labour! Why haven't
I been able to do it?

Because of your mind which is active.

Next, what about D who couldn't write a single line and
flourished in so short a time?

768 CORRESPONDENCE WITH

That was his vital vigour and confidence. As for you, you refuse to enthuse.

> *Sir, the mystery is a little deeper, methinks. If you so wanted this instant, you could have made me an "old man" or at least more than an infant!*

Have to work under the conditions you offer me.

> *I began this poem night before last, wrote 3 stanzas quickly, but had to stop, as it was rather late. Perhaps I should have finished it then somehow, as the flow was coming?*

Yes, not good to stop the flow, unless you have got to the stage when you are sure of picking it up again.

> *By the way, I am thinking of reading some more English poems to be able to write better.*

It should certainly be a helpful thing.

> *So shall I devote the afternoon to reading instead of writing?*

Unless you feel a sudden inspiration. Then throw the book aside and write.

December 7, 1936

> *It is really difficult for me to understand how the mind comes in the way, for I seem to think that whatever comes I jot down.*

Well, but why doesn't it come down like a cataract as in J's case or as a flood in D's?

> *Of course, I want to see also if any better things are possible.*

See how? If better things come, it is all right; but if you try to find out better things, then that is mental activity.

> *But if you say whatever comes should be transcribed, I don't*

SRI AUROBINDO   769

> *know, for I have to wait and wait for an expression.*

Waiting is all right.

> *Should one then keep absolutely silent and go on waiting*
> *and waiting for the things to drop?*

What else then is to be done? To hunt about for them? If so, you
are likely to put in any damned thing, imagining it is better.

> *If you say the mind is active, I should think D's mind is no*
> *less.*

He often says "This has flowed through me." How could it if the
mind were active? I suppose you mean by mind the transcribing
agency? I don't mean the receiving mind. The receiving mind must
be passive.

> *Can you not elaborate that sentence: "you refuse to en-*
> *thuse"?*

Yes, you say you take no pleasure or joy in your poetry.

> *Lack of enthusiasm? All right, I shall work and work in*
> *whichever way you advise, sitting on depressions and des-*
> *pondency.*

That is not what I mean by enthusing. I mean by it the joy of the
inspiration both as it is coming and afterwards.

> *If you think afternoon will be better for giving Force, I shall*
> *write then. . .*

No importance. Force can come at any time.

> *I shall put plenty of vigour; about confidence I can't promise*
> *yet for it is my conviction that I haven't as much stuff as they*
> *have.*

It is a psychological condition, attitude or whatever you like to call it that you must get into it, — still, compact, receptive, vibrant to the touch when it comes.

> *By the way, I had a talk with D regarding mystic poetry. He doesn't seem to feel much in Blake's poetry.*

It simply means that he has not the mystic mind. It does not make any difference to the value or beauty of Blake's poetry.

> *And mystic poetry as a whole appeals to him less than poems with concrete meaning.*

Mystic poetry has a perfectly concrete meaning, much more than intellectual poetry which is much more abstract. The nature of the intellect is abstraction; spirituality and mysticism deal with the concrete by their very nature.

> *He says Tagore's poem: "All the pooja [worship] accomplished in life. . ."[1] is vastly more appealing to him than "O Beauty, how far wilt Thou lead me?. . ."[2]*

How is this less concrete than the other?

> *Or "I have harvested lots of paddy And while I was harvesting came down the rains."[3]*

Again how is it less concrete?

> *Mystic poetry will ever remain for him misty and mysterious and occupy a second place.*

That is another matter. It is a question of personal idiosyncrasy. There are people who thrill to Pope and find Keats and Shelley empty and misty. The clear precise intellectual meanings of Pope are to them the height of poetry—the emotional and romantic suggestions of the Skylark or the Ode to a Nightingale unsatisfactory. How the devil, they ask, can a skylark be a spirit, not a bird? What the

---

[1,2] *Gitanjali* by Rabindranath Tagore.
[3] *Shonār Tari* by Rabindranath Tagore.

SRI AUROBINDO   771

hell has 'a glow-worm golden in a dell of dew' to do with the song
of the skylark? They are unable to feel these things and say Pope
would never have written in that incoherent inconsequential way.
Of course he wouldn't. But that simply means they like things that
are intellectually clear and can't appreciate the imaginative connections which reveal what is deeper than the surface. You can I
suppose catch something of these, but when you are asked to go
still deeper into the concrete of concretes, you lose your breath
and say "Lord! what an unintelligible mess. Give me an allegorical
clue for God's sake, something superficial which I can mentally
formulate." Same attitude as the Popists' — in essence.

> *I can't deny that I got more joy from your explanation
> of J's poem. Though I felt the rasa before, when it came to
> "illuminations of Truth", it gave me more rasa. The feeling
> became concretised, so to say.*

You mean, it became more intellectually abstract. A glorious
concrete, an illumination of Truth is an abstraction, unless it is
seen and felt.

> *There lies the whole difference. You read a poem — mystic
> or otherwise and feel all the beauty without understanding it,
> but when the significance also is flashed, the feeling is more.*

Not only all the beauty, but all the life and truth of it.
What significance? allegorical significance?

> *How far can you say that your appreciation is a thing
> divorced from the flash of understanding that is revealed
> to you or your living behind the words?*

The trouble with you is that you can understand nothing unless an
intellectual label is put on it . . . You are like a person who could
not love and enjoy the presence of a beautiful thing or person
until you know the scientific category, class or botanical or other
description in Latin.

A has written twice about some eruption she is having — she said you would write to us about it, but there is no eruption in this book. Please let me know what it is. An "eruption" may mean anything from prickly heat to —

December 8, 1936

S.B. had no sleep at all last night. No trouble and yet no sleep. Mystery! Any yogic reason?

It is the new fashion with the Asram Yogis — not to sleep.

I send you a letter from S which will speak eloquently for itself. Please return after communicating the contents to Dr. B. I see she has horse-disease অশ্বরোগ¹ — I presume she means piles (?). Is the blood in her stools due to piles or something else?

December 9, 1936

Here is Jatin's letter. Why is he seeing visions of engineering, with the Super-engineer at his side? What significance, if any, of the dream? To be fulfilled here or there? He wants to be a yogi; don't you see?

He was moving in the vital plane which is not bound by the mental will or by the physical realities. There a certain capacity in him was being turned to the Divine Work and the building was symbolic of that, also the power of undertaking my suggestions without speech.

Why then all these un-yogic engineering dreams and visions, when he is concentrating all his efforts with the view to become a super-yogi?

You must dismiss these mental limitations if you want to understand the occult worlds. The vital world has its own law of working, system of events and symbols — it is not bound by the waking mind.

Please give him a satisfactory reply, and what about his letter remaining with you for eternity!

¹ aṣwarog; arśarog: piles.

SRI AUROBINDO 773

Which letter? there is more than one, I believe.

Mark that he gets tremendous peace by thinking of you.

Naturally, as he meets in me the source of Peace.

December 10, 1936

Nishikanta [conjunctivitis of both the eyes] is better than he was yesterday.

Mother is not satisfied with the condition of his eyes. Why the increase? Too strong medicines?

December 11, 1936

Guru, I don't know why the Mother looked at me like that during Pranam. Was I anywhere in the wrong?

Mother knows nothing about it.

I went over the whole incident [personal] and didn't find anywhere that I have misrepresented facts.

No.

Or is it because I was bothering myself and you over a trifle?

No.

It was not an illusion. Some meaning was there.

Yes? But then it must have been a meaning in your mind, not the Mother's. So only you, its mother, can find it out.

Today Nishikanta is better.

Slightly.

And mercury? Its strength is only 1% and used like anything in the hospitals and recommended in books.

774

CORRESPONDENCE WITH

Maybe, but many people suffer much from it. Probably the method is to irritate Nature until she reacts? If so, — well!

> *The D.R. servant seems to have sciatica. Can he be treated with Salicylates?*

Try whatever you think best.

> *Or should he go to the hospital?*

I think not.

December 12, 1936

> *J's poems are getting beyond me. Give me either the feeling and consciousness or the mental notes.*

She seems to be passing from Blake towards Mallarmé, though she has not quite got there yet. Sorry for you. The poem is fine but enigmatic.

December 13, 1936

> *Do you mean to say that because I have no joy in writing poetry, it is taking so long for the channel to open? But I don't see why joy should be a necessary condition for writing poetry.*

Art is a thing of beauty and beauty and Ananda are closely connected — they go together. If the Ananda is there, then the beauty comes out more easily — if not, it has to struggle out painfully and slowly. That is quite natural.

> *I will put in any amount of labour and that should be enough for things to pour down.*

Labour is not enough for the things to pour down. What is done with labour only, is done with difficulty, not with a downpour. The joy in the labour must be there for a free outflow. You have very queer psychological ideas, I must say.

SRI AUROBINDO   775

> *How can I have any joy when what I write seems such poor
> stuff and delivered with much perspiration?*

That is your confounded nature. How can the man of sorrows feel
joy in anything or any self-confidence? His strain is "O how miserable am I! O how dark am I! Oh how worthless is all that I do,"
etc., etc.

But apart from the M of S, you seem to suffer from a mania
of self-depreciatory criticism. Many artists and poets have that;
as soon as they look at their work they find it awfully poor and
bad. (I had that myself often varied with the opposite feeling,
Arjava also has it); but to have it while writing is its most excrucia-
ting degree of intensity. Better get rid of it if you want to write
freely.

> *But I get a lot of joy reading J's poetry — I can't describe
> it...*

I suppose it is because it is what Housman calls pure poetry — stirs
with joy the solar plexus.

> *Where you marked so many fine lines in my last poem,
> I had hardly felt the thrill while writing them.*

That's the pity of it.

> *Please give some Force to complete the incomplete poem
> I have been at. I fear to touch it lest the coming lines should
> fail in their quality.*

Well, it's that kind of thing that stands in the way.

> *The first portion I wrote quickly and almost dosing. God
> knows why dosing?*
> [*Sri Aurobindo wrote z above the s of "dosing".*]

This is a medical spelling.
Probably in order that your waking mind might not interfere.
Dozing is often a form of semi-samadhi in which the waking mind
retires and the subliminal self comes bobbing up.

776

Have you finished with Jatin's long letter regarding dreams, sleep-walking etc.? The reply is overdue, Sir!

I have often tried to begin that, but it is a long affair and before putting pen to paper my courage wilted away.

Guru, sorry? Really? I am very glad, you can be sorry, for then you will do something for me. . . Why do you say "She seems to be passing etc., etc."? That simply infuriated J, ". . . I am writing all this hard stuff which nobody understands, not even Sri Aurobindo! . . . I shall stop writing then. And now I am passing from one funny poet to another (Mallarmé)."

Well, if she thinks it derogatory to be compared to such great poets as Blake and Mallarmé! Blake is Europe's greatest mystic poet and Mallarmé turned the whole current of French poetry (one might almost say, of all modernist poetry) into a channel of which his poems were the opening.

"Mallarmé's works are, in one word, 'unintelligible'. Why on earth should I write such things?"

Then why did they have so much influence on the finest French writers and why is modernist poetry trying to burrow into the subliminal in order to catch something even one quarter as fine as his language, images and mystic suggestions?

We told her that she is only an instrument of the Force, and she must surrender to it. "But how can I be sure that it is the Force and not my own making? If Sri Aurobindo assures me of it, I shall be satisfied."

If it were her own making, she would have written something different. Its very character shows that her mind has not made it.

Is it really true that Mallarmé used to write with a set determination to make his works unintelligible? Can one really do it in that way?

SRI AUROBINDO   777

Certainly not. The French language was too clear and limited
to express mystic truth, so he had to wrestle with it and turn it
this way and that to arrive at a mystic speech. Also he refused
to be satisfied with anything that was a merely intellectual or
even at all intellectual rendering of his vision. That is why the
surface understanding finds it difficult to follow him. But he is so
great that it has laboured to follow him all the same.

> . . . J doubts that her poems have enough poetry.

The doubt is absurd — they are poetry sheer and pure.

> Our saying and feeling don't matter much, you see. Sri
> Aurobindo, Tagore, etc., etc. must acclaim.

I can't answer for Tagore — . . .

> Please acclaim, acclaim!

Clamo, clamavi, clamabo.[1]

December 14, 1936

[*This medical report was written by Dr. Becharlal.*]
P complains of indigestion.

In her letter to me today she complains of headache, giddiness —
also of vomiting every third day. She says when she takes medicines
it stops, afterwards she is as before.

December 15, 1936

> Guru, please read pages 19-21 of this book.[2] There Kastner
> seems to say about Mallarmé just what I have said, though
> he speaks of him as being an acknowledged master, and
> of his great influence on contemporary poetry.

---

[1] In Latin; I acclaim, I have acclaimed, I shall acclaim.
[2] *A Book of French Verse — From Marot to Mallarmé*, selected by Prof. L. E.
Kastner.

778   CORRESPONDENCE WITH

He can't deny such an obvious fact, I suppose—but he would like to.

> He says, "*A purely intellectual artist, convinced that sentiment was an inferior element of art, Mallarmé never evokes emotion, but only thought about thought; and the thoughts called forth in his mind by the symbol are generally so subtle and elliptical that they find no echo in the mind of the ordinary mortal.*"[1] *Do you agree with all that he says about Mallarmé?*

Certainly not—this man is a mere pedant; his remarks are unintelligent, commonplace, often perfectly imbecile.

> He continues: "*Obscurity was part of his doctrine and he wrote for the select few only and exclusively. . .*"[2]

Rubbish! His doctrine is perfectly tenable and intelligible. It is true that the finest things in art and poetry are appreciated only by the few and he chose therefore not to sacrifice the truth of his mystic (impressionist, symbolist) expression in order to be easily understood by the multitude, including this professor.

> "*Another cause of his obscurity is that he chose his words and phrases for their evocative value alone, and here again the verbal sonorities suggested by the tortuous trend of his mind make no appeal except to the initiated.*"[3] (*I suppose here he means what you meant about the limitedness of the French language?*)

Not only that—his will to arrive at a true and deep, instead of a superficial and intellectual language. I gave two reasons for Mallarmé's unusual style and not this one of the limitedness of the French language only.

> "*His life-long endeavour to achieve an impossible ideal*

[1] *ibid.*, pp. 19–20.
[2] *ibid.*, p. 20.
[3] *ibid.*, p. 20.

SRI AUROBINDO   779

> *accounts for his sterility (he has left some sixty poems*
> *only, most of them quite short) and the darkness of his*
> *later work, though he did write, before he had fallen a victim*
> *to his own theories, a few poems of great beauty and per-*
> *fectly intelligible."*[1]

60 poems, if they have beauty, are as good as 600. It is not the mass
of the poet's work that determines his greatness. Gray and Catullus
wrote little; we have only 7 plays of Sophocles and seven of Aeschylus (though they wrote more), but these seven put them still in the
front rank of poets.

> *He says that "Mallarmé's verse is acquired and intricate"*
> *i.e. a thing not of spontaneity, but of intellectualisation.*
> *Saying that Verlaine is an inspired poet, he seems to mean*
> *the contrary about Mallarmé.*

If these two magnificent sonnets (the last two)[2] are not inspired,
then there is no such thing as inspiration. It is rubbish to say of a
man who refused to limit himself by intellectual expression, that
he was an intellectual artist. Symbolism, impressionism go beyond
intellect to pure sight—and Mallarmé was the creator of symbolism.

> *I don't say that this author is an authority, but I found*
> *this reference interesting and send it to you for your opin-*
> *ion. . .*

I don't find it interesting—it is abysmally stupid.

> *. . . X also seems to have the same view as the writer's.*

I hope not.

> *In fact it was X who said about Mallarmé's set determi-*
> *nation to make his works unintelligible* [14.12.36]. *He*
> *writes in an article: Hopkins, in seeking for the secret*

---

[1] *ibid.*, p. 20.
[2] "Le cygne" and "Les fleurs" (*ibid.*, pp. 314–16): Les fleurs is in fact **not** a
sonnet.

780   CORRESPONDENCE WITH

> *of sound which is the soul of poetry, has done such rigorous
> Hathayogic sadhana with rhythm that it strikes us as an
> astonishing feat. (For instance he has turned the expression
> "through the other" into "throughter" ["throughther"?].)*

That is a question of language—how far one can do violence to
the form of a language. It is a different question altogether.

> *He says that Mallarmé adopted the path of arduous* tapa-
> syā *with language because the French language is too
> simple, clear and transparent etc., etc. And then he remarks
> that just as in spirituality simple* (sahaj) *sadhana leads to
> truth, so also in poetry simplicity leads to beauty.*
>
> *Would it mean then, that due to Mallarmé's acrobatics
> with words, his poems are not beautiful and won't lead you
> to beauty—if written in that way?*

Only X can say what he meant, but to refuse beauty to Mallarmé's
poetry would be itself an acrobacy of the intellect. For what then
is beauty? Simplicity and beauty are not convertible terms. There
can be a difficult beauty. What about Aeschylus then? or Blake?

> *I tried to break that nut of his (no. 199)*[1]—*an exposi-
> tion of it is also attached. But,* pardi! *It was a hard nut,
> Guru. Really what a tortuous trend and how he has turned
> the images!*
> *["... Va-t-il nous déchirer avec un coup d'aile ivre*
> *Ce lac dur oublié que hante sous le givre*
> *Le transparent glacier des vols qui n'ont pas fui!"]*
> *"The transparent glacier of flights haunting the hard
> lake under the frost"! The frost or snow has become the
> glacier (icefield) and the icefield composes the lake—
> that's what I imaged.*

How does hoar-frost or rime become the glacier? "Givre" is not
the same as "glace"—it is not ice, but a covering of hoar-frost
such as you see on the trees etc., the congealed moisture of the
air—that is the "blanche agonie" which has come down from

---

[1] *ibid.*, pp. 315–316, "Le vierge, le vivace et le bel aujourd'hui." (Le Cygne)

SRI AUROBINDO   781

the insulted Space on the swan and on the lake. He can shake off
that but the glacier holds him; he can no more rise to the skies,
caught in the frozen cold mass of the failures of the soul that refused to fly upward and escape.

> *I tried hard to understand the construction, can't say I
> have it!*

You haven't.

> *What do you think of this sonnet [Le cygne]?*

One of the finest sonnets I have ever read.

Magnificent line, by the way, "le transparent glacier des vols
qui n'ont pas fui!" This idea of the denied flights (imprisoned
powers) of the soul that have frozen into a glacier seems to me as
powerful as it is violent. Of course in French such expressions
were quite new — in some other languages they were already possible. You will find lots of kindred things in the most modern
poetry which specialises in violent revelatory (or at least would-be
revelatory) images. You disapprove? Well, one may do so, — classical taste does; but I find myself obliged here to admire.

> *What's this "evocative value" of words and phrases? Sug-*
> *gestiveness? Taking away imagination beyond the expres-*
> *sions or words? "According to Mallarmé's own definition,*
> *the poet's mission is either 'to evoke gradually an object*
> *in order to suggest a mood, or, inversely, to choose an*
> *object as a symbol and disengage from it a mood by a*
> *series of decipherments'."*[1]

It is a very good description of the impressionist method in literature. Verlaine and others do the same, even if they do not hold the
theory.

> *I don't understand what he means, but it seems to be some-*
> *thing different from what Housemann means.*
> *[Sri Aurobindo put a question mark above "Housemann".]*

[1] *ibid.*, p. 19.

782   CORRESPONDENCE WITH

What's this spelling? He is not a German.
Housman is not a symbolist or impressionist in theory — V[1]

> *He [Housman] says a poet's mission is to "transfuse emotion" which Mallarmé had not!*

Indeed? because the professor says so? How easily you are impressed by anybody's opinion and take it as final!

> *Some reply please — I have left a whole page blank.*

I do not know what you mean by emotion. If you mean the surface vital joy and grief of outer life, these poems of Mallarmé do not contain it. But if emotion can include also the deeper spiritual or inner feeling which does not weep or shout, then they are here in these two sonnets.[2] The Swan is to my understanding not merely the poet who has not sung in the higher spaces of the consciousness, which is already a fine idea, but the soul that has not risen there and found its higher expression, the said poet being, if Mallarmé thought of that specially, only a signal instance of this spiritual frustration. There can be no more powerful, moving and formidable expression of this spiritual frustration, this chilled and sterile greatness than the image of the frozen lake and the imprisoned Swan as developed by Mallarmé.

I do not say that the spiritual or occult cannot be given an easier expression or that if one can arrive at that without minimising the inner significance, it is not perhaps the greatest achievement. (That is, I suppose, X's contention.) But there is room for more than one kind of spiritual or mystic poetry. One has to avoid mere mistiness or vagueness, one has to be true, vivid, profound in one's images; but, that given, I am free to write either as in Nirvana or Transformation, giving a clear mental indication along with the image or I can suppress the mental indication and give the image only with the content suggested in the language — but not expressed so that even those can superficially understand who are unable to read behind the mental idea — that is what I have done in the

[1] Incomplete in MS.
[2] See the last paragraph of 22.12.36, p. 786.

SRI AUROBINDO 783

"Bird of Fire". It seems to me that both methods are legitimate.

December 16, 1936

[*This medical report was written by Dr. Becharlal.*]
*S has been asking for white bread instead of our Asram
bread. We are not in favour of it.*

It would not be good for him.

*J asked me to concentrate on the Mother, before writing
poetry. Concentrate on the Mother: her eyes, feet, hands
etc., etc., then keep quiet for a moment, and jot down
whatever comes. As I tried the method, I went somewhere
very deep within and heard some lines (which however I
couldn't catch), on waking I wrote down those very lines!*

I suppose, having concentrated on the Mother, you were taken
by her to the world of art and poetry and heard something there.

December 17, 1936

Mother thinks that the health of S needs special care. She is not
eating well and is becoming thin and anaemic. At this period of her
growth that would be disastrous and might affect her whole physical future. Mother thinks she should have some dépuratif for the
blood and at the same time something strengthening and tonic —
it has to be seen what will suit her. Mother would like you to look
into the matter and speak also to P.S. about it.
   What about I.K.? She has written to me today that she is not
well, nausea, inability to eat etc.

[*In the reply of the 18th there was a word I had underlined
in red, for Sri Aurobindo to decipher.*][1]

Man, you can't expect me to read my own writing after so long
a time!
   It looks like sideless, but can't be.

December 18, 1936

----

[1] See the last paragraph of 23.12.36, p. 788.

784   CORRESPONDENCE WITH

Enquired about S. She does not seem to take enough food and says she doesn't feel hungry. I think she should take lots of vitamins — do you believe in them?

Certainly.

She should take oranges, apples, butter, raw tomato if available. . .

Tomato not available just now.

I consulted P.S. He says he is not in favour of medicines. In Calcutta too, doctors were rarely called. I told him that home-conditions were lacking here, regarding food. Then he said, "Whatever Mother says must be done."

It is not medicines that Mother wanted to give; but on the one side fortifying foodstuff (like cod-liver oil, but all cannot stand cod-liver oil) and on the other something for purifying the blood (e.g. in France they give chicory *tisane* for that). All that will not be necessary if she takes sufficient food. If you can see to that, these other things will not be necessary. What Mother wants is that she should not be allowed to be weak and underfed at this age which is important for the growth.

I have to admit now that poetry can be taken as sadhana — for whatever makes you think of the Mother, is sadhana, isn't it?

Yes.

And I have some hope in poetry, after all, what?

A great deal of hope.

December 19, 1936

P.S. consents to give her a new preparation with ergosterd, a vitamin. It is a concentrated product, only 4 to 6 drops to be taken a day.

Mother doubts. Better have vitamins in the ordinary way.

SRI AUROBINDO   785

> *I don't know if chicory is available here.*

No; besides, she would not take it. It is too bitter.

> *You kept silent about butter.*

Quite agree to butter.

> *What about prunes, dates, raisins?*
> *[Sri Aurobindo underlined "prunes, dates, raisins".]*

Also.

> *Nolini has given me an article (sent by the Mother) on*
> *The Effects of Pān-Supāri.[1] As far as I know, in India*
> *people believe that* pān *helps the digestion, and* choon
> *(calcium?) is good for health.*

Even if it stimulated momentarily, that would not prevent from
wearing it out in the end. But the idea is probably a superstition.

> *. . . Some believe that chewing* supāri *is a good exercise*
> *for the teeth, especially here where we don't take any*
> *meat!*

Lord! I have known people who lost all their teeth at an early age
by the habit.
   Meat is good for the teeth? Always heard the contrary — Besides
millions who don't take meat have as good teeth as anybody in the
world and don't need pan supari either.

> *A European eye specialist of Calcutta said that many eye*
> *diseases are due to* pān-supāri, *and he was a dead enemy*
> *of them.*

Very probably — Teeth and eyes are closely connected.

> *But what should I do with this typed copy given by Nolini?*
> *To enforce on patients? Or others also? A was repeatedly*
> *told but — !*

[1] Betel leaf–betel nut.

786   CORRESPONDENCE WITH

That's like one of my uncles who preferred taking his pan betel to keeping his teeth.

> *But, Guru, you must admit that* pān *has a sweet taste, or perhaps you are an utter stranger to it?*

Have taken it — can't say I found it very attractive or enticing. ভিন্ন রুচিরহি লোকঃ।[1]

December 20, 1936

> *J's finger was incised on suspicion of pus, but there was hardly any. He says now there's much burning and throbbing paih.*
> [*Sri Aurobindo underlined "incised"*]

Premature incision not safe, I believe, in this kind of thing.

December 21, 1936

> *Your belief is right, Guru! I didn't feel happy yesterday. However, nothing untoward has happened; almost no pain, but the swelling persists, asked to foment.*

Mother suggests hot water 1 part peroxide, 3 parts water and dipping the finger for 15 minutes. Some of these things are cured by that — it ought really to be done immediately, but even now it may be effective.

> *You wrote about "two sonnets" [16.12.36] of Mallarmé (last two). The other on Edgar Poe? I thought you meant "Les Fleurs", but it is not a sonnet.*

Sonnets was a mistake — I meant the last two poems including the Swan sonnet.

December 22, 1936

> *Why, that is almost exactly what we have advised J to do from the very start, only peroxide was not given.*

---

[1] *bhinna ruchirhi lokah:* people have different tastes.

You are taking daily almost exactly the same thing as Anglo-Indians take in their clubs i.e. a peg. Only brandy and soda are not there — but the water is.

> *Amidst the wonderful silence of the trees, the blue vast sea and sky, what a queer poem I wrote. Gracious Lord! I went there to enjoy myself and this discordant poem was the result; making me sad throughout the day. I was so sad, till suddenly I thought, the poem may be the cause.*

Maybe. You may have made an unconscious excursion to somewhere undesirable.

> *Have you ever heard such a story of any poet?*

Why not? Poets are always queer cattle.

> *Did I make an excursion to an occult plane, or did the occult precipitate itself into the poem?*

May be either.

> *Very funny, really, if this is the reason of the sadness; even if not, why such a bizarre poem should come out in a beautiful place?*

Quite usual. The better things are, the more melancholy one can become. Luxury of contradiction proper to the vital nature. Funny for the intelligence, quite natural according to vital logic.

> *... Guru, I am not at all satisfied with my poems. I'll have to stop writing.*

Are you ever satisfied? That's not a reason for stopping.

> *Shall I give up sonnet writing?*

No.

> *Good God, I didn't ask you about that word* [18.12.36]

> *at all, for I read it the very next day. But that is no reason why you shouldn't recognise your own writing, Sir!*

A marker was on that page, so I thought you were returning[1] my writing by imposing on me the impossible task of reading it after many days!

December 23, 1936

> *I am floored today by my own poem; mystic, I think. Written yesterday. Opinion?*

Why floored? It is as easy as a nursery rhyme.

December 25, 1936

> *Dr. Manilal says there is nothing wrong with S...*
> [*Sri Aurobindo underlined "nothing wrong".*]

It looks like it. Malade very imaginaire.

B says she feels giddy at times with so much quinine and in spite of it her 99° is still going on — so she wishes to drop quinine for a time and be given "some other medicine as may be proper." Well?

December 26, 1936

> *For A, Dr. Manilal advises only one emetine injection and try its effect since she had so many attacks of dysentery. Well?*

She writes that Manilal has told her to live on milk and take no other food (except lemon water when she is thirsty). I am searching in your reports but find nothing. What's the row? Is it a fact? Most of these women, I believe, are cooking and eating food of their own fancy and going wrong in the stomach.

> *I'm trying hard to get rid of J's influence in poetry, but I can't succeed. I don't know how to do it.*

Persevere and call for something new, then it will come.

---

[1] Doubtful reading.

SRI AUROBINDO   789

> *Can you not send me one or two of your mystic sonnets?*

Which sonnets? I have written the two sonnets of spiritual realisation[1] which were circulated. I don't remember any others; except
poems of a more philosophical cast — these I did not circulate.

December 27, 1936

> *I heard that X has a deep, very deep respect for you, if*
> *nothing else. He has followed closely your development,*
> *always. . . Hasn't he said after the interview with you—*
> *"You have the Word and we are waiting to accept it from*
> *you. . ."?*

That was a long time ago. He is disappointed that I have not
come out and started giving lectures in America and saving humanity. Sorry, but I have no intention of doing these things.

> *Though he seems to have criticised some principles enun-*
> *ciated by you, I think he has a genuine belief in your mission,*
> *and a faith that a new creation will start from you as the*
> *fountain-head. Am I wrong, Guru, though you make us*
> *wait and wait for years and years?*

You want me to start going about and giving lectures? Sorry again,
but quite out of the question.

> *His prose-poems are not good, if you have seen any. Is*
> *it because his grey matter has become greyer by age?*

It is quite natural — he is fagged out. It is true Sophocles wrote
one of his grandest dramas when he was — well, was it 70 or 80
years old?

> *Or is it because you don't support him any longer with*
> *your force?*

?[*Sri Aurobindo put a question mark.*]

---

[1] "Transformation" and "Nirvana", *SABCL*, vol. 5 (*Collected Poems*), p. 161.

7A

> *But look at his prose. It seems to be becoming more and more brilliant. Why this difference?*

Prose is a different matter. One can always write prose.

> *You kept silent about the sonnet. If your pen can't gallop, you can ask it to trot?*

Very little chance of it. The only time I tried, a surrealist poem came out[1] — so I have dropped the attempt.

> *My poetic judgment seems to be very poor, Guru, or is it because my own poem is now in question?*

Nobody can really form a proper judgment of his own poetry — or at least only one poet here and there can perform that miracle.

> *Really, I don't know what to do now — how to strike a new path? Already the difficulty in writing is great, and then to avoid J's influence! I don't know if I shall be able to write at all. My head is`threatening to break!*

As usual, anticipating trouble and misery! Your position is always "That's got to be done. Oh *what* a bother. I shall never do it" — while it should be "Ah, that's to be done? All right then, it's going to be done."

> *I have lost all my distinctiveness — can't find a new one. And yet you say "Are you ever satisfied?" Sadhana sluggish, poetry bosh, joy and peace vaporised!*

Poetry is not bosh — and joy, peace need not vaporise·unless you pump them out of yourself instead of into yourself.

> *Why, Sir, dissatisfaction itself is a sign of a greater seeking, isn't it?*

It is generally a twisting round and round in the same place round the centre of one's own dissatisfaction.

---

[1] "Surrealist", *SABCL*, vol. 5 (*Collected Poems*), p. 113.

I don't know that you are satisfied with my condition either.

I am not depressed by it at any rate.

You promised to send me a sonnet to show how a "direct prayer" can be made strong in the couplet — don't you remember?

That was not a sonnet.

But now I ask you for either that or to compose a mystic poem with the lines I have suggested. It won't take you more than 5 minutes.
[Sri Aurobindo underlined "5" and put a question mark against it.]

Nonsense, I am not such a galloper.

By the way, please have a glance at page 12 of The Hindu, *regarding K's opinion of Guruship. We thought him a sensible fellow, especially after his big sacrifice — giving up all the huge estates that were given to him.*

He seems to be a well-intentioned fellow but rather a bit of an empty sort of goose. The twaddle he talks is simply awful.

J is puzzled by her poems. . . If she is puzzled, hardly necessary to speak about myself.

Will see whether I can wrestle with it tomorrow.

December 28, 1936

I understand that the curry given on Thursday evening is the residue of the soup, with some potatoes added. It has not much nutritional value since boiling for a long time takes all the stuff out, except a dead residue of cellulose. I propose humbly to the Mother to change this meal.

792   CORRESPONDENCE WITH SRI AUROBINDO

We don't know anything of the kind. According to chemical analysis in France, *half* of the nutritive elements goes into the soup, half remains in the vegetables and these are eaten in France so as to have the full value of the food used.

I am afraid it is not good for the stomach either.

Why are you afraid? This soup affair on Thursday is done on the principle of the French national dish called *pot-au-feu* (as much the national dish as beefsteak is for England) in which the food is boiled in the soup and then the soup and the vegetables etc. cooked in it are taken. If it is so bad for the health, how is it that the French are not a nation of dyspeptics with bad stomachs and livers?
I have answered from the scientific and health point of view above. But since there is this prejudice and auto-suggestion as well probably as a strong dislike for it, Mother has stopped the whole soup affair. It is a very costly business and there is no use in spending so much if there is a dislike for the arrangement.

December 30, 1936

1937

Hirendranath Dutt, theosophist and philosopher, in one of his articles on Rāslīlā, asks why mystics and yogis use so much the imagery of passion, wine etc. in their description of experiences of Divine Love. Then he quotes Underhill to say "... it [human love] most certainly does offer upon lower levels a strangely exact parallel to the sequence of states in which man's spiritual consciousness unfolds itself and which form the consummation of mystic life."

I don't agree—unless it is a sadhana of the vital plane which then naturally expresses the vital being = love-excitement, love-quarrels, *viraha*,[1] revolt, despair, rupture etc., etc., frequent surrenders, unions, partings.

Dutt has said that according to the Ancients, pleasure of the sex-act is something akin to the Ananda of Brahman. Why? In answer to this, Ouspenski, a famous Russian philosopher, has said: "Of all we know in life, only in love is there a taste of the mystical, a taste of ecstasy..."

Leave out the "only"—and to a certain extent one can agree—but "love"—not "sex".

The interpreter continues: "Nothing else brings us so near to the limit of human possibilities beyond which begins the unknown. And in this lies, without doubt, the chief cause of the terrible power of sex over human life... Love, 'sex', these are but a foretaste of mystical sensations."

Love and sex are the same, then? There can be no love without sex? This is piffle.

---

[1] The separation of lovers.

794   CORRESPONDENCE WITH

> *He says further: "Mystical sensations are sensations of the same category as sensations of 'Love', only infinitely higher and more complex."*

There is much else besides in mystical experience — there are not only sensations.

> *He asks: "If that is so, why then is man averse to this intensely pleasurable mystical activity? Because principally he gets the taste of that mystical pleasure in the sex-act, and he is satisfied with it."*

What rubbish! Brahmananda is a substitute?

> *The sexual creative act is admittedly the supreme and most desired gratification of the senses.*

Not to everybody.

> *The sexual creative act is an exact counterpart of the mental and creative processes of which, the East maintains, it is merely the reflexion.*

Don't catch on. How is sex-gratification a reflex of mental processes — e.g. of the solution of a mathematical or scientific problem or even of the creation of a poem or picture? Because there is a kind of joy in all these things? but it is not the same kind of joy.

> *The transient character of sex-gratification is regarded in the East as an ordinance of Nature so that man may be led to seek the more sustained delight of mental and spiritual creative effort.*

In the East? by whom?
I don't believe it for a moment. To suppose that if sex-gratification were a more prolonged business, Shelley and Shakespeare would not have cared to write poetry — is blank brutal nonsense — They had something else in them besides the mere animal.

SRI AUROBINDO   795

> *Do you agree with all this, Guru, especially with Ous-*
> *penski's opinion?*

What a question to ask me! As if it were at all possible that I would
agree to bring down all values to the level of the animal pleasure.

> *Love may perhaps be a foretaste of mystical sensations,*
> *but sex-love also? But people say that sex-pleasure and*
> *Brahmananda [Bliss of Brahman] are brothers.*

The only truth in that is that all intense pleasure goes back at its
root to Ananda — the pleasure of poetry, music, production of
all kinds, battle, victory, adventure too — in that sense only all
are brothers of Brahmananda. But the phrase is absolutely in-
accurate. We can say that there is a physical Ananda born of
Brahmananda which is far higher, finer and more intense than the
sexual, but of which the sexual is a coarse and excited degradation —
that is all.

> *If the transient nature of the sex-act is an ordinance of Nature*
> *to lead man to a more sustained delight of higher things,*
> *I fail to see why there is so much pleasure attached to it*
> *that they compare it to a foretaste of Brahmananda. You*
> *say that it is meant for procreation, but the act of pro-*
> *creation could have been managed without this pleasure.*

Certainly, Nature gave it to encourage her aim of procreation.
The proof is that the animal does it only by season and as soon
as the procreation is over, drops it. Man having a mind has discovered that he can do it even when there is not the need of Nature
— but that is only a proof that Mind perverts the original intention
of Nature. It doesn't prove that Nature created it only to give man
a brief and destructive sensual pleasure.

> *I won't lengthen my perorations and human reasonings.*
> *Will you give a satisfactory reply to all these questions*
> *tonight or tomorrow?*

Well, it can't be tonight, as there are three tons of correspondence.

796   CORRESPONDENCE WITH

(It may be less of course in actual weight, I am giving the psychological estimate.)

[*In the medical notebook:*]

I have added against your notes of the 30th certain remarks which
I had no time to write then. You may perhaps pass a glance over
them.

January 2, 1937

> *N.P. complains of much pain in the eyes — frontal head-*
> *ache after half an hour's reading, eyes watering etc. Manilal*
> *advises him to use glasses. He says glasses will cure it.*

Glasses cure it, means what? The weakness will disappear and he
will be able to read without glasses after a while?

> *... About the pot-au-feu, apart from all these, may I*
> *point out a little flaw in your argument? French people*
> *are used to taking a mixed meal, so the quantity of the*
> *vegetable would be very small in proportion.*
> [*Sri Aurobindo underlined "very small".*]

Don't understand. It is a question of the healthiness for the stomach.
There is quite enough vegetable in a pot-au-feu to test the stomach
and it is not taken once a week only, but often.

> *Moreover, what French people can take and digest, I am*
> *sure Indians can't. Physically Indians are a far inferior*
> *race to the Europeans — an admitted and deplorable fact.*

It is the other way round. Indians can digest foods (chillied, curried,
strongly spiced) which would send a European to his grave in a
short time. Indians have a shorter life but dietetically a much more
spicy and hot life.

January 3, 1937

> *I was very surprised to read a statement of G — he says*
> *that a few months ago he felt in sleep as if he wanted to see*
> *a woman. He was shocked to find such an impulse in him*
> *after over 40 years of struggle to conquer the sex-instinct.*
> *He says also that it was one of the blackest moments in*

SRI AUROBINDO 797

> *his life and if he had succumbed to it he would have been ruined...*
>
> *Imagine a man over 60 and practising absolute sex-control for over 40 years, as well as control in speech, thought, food, so sincerely, having such a bout.*

There is nothing astonishing in that. First of all, even if it had been in waking, it is to be expected. G's method is ethical, a stern mental control, নিগ্রহ.[1] That keeps down the sex fellow, but does not eliminate him. He can start up at any moment. Secondly, it was in sleep when the mind is not in control, unless you have specially practised control of sleep. I don't quite understand the black moment and the potential succumbing. Succumb to what? Does he mean that the effect of the desire continued after waking from sleep or he was shocked in the sleep itself, resisted in the sleep?

> *L, I hear, had a fall from spiritual height, and he is enjoying the life of "Krishna". What then will be our lot? Alas, alas, where shall we be?*

But why did he fall? Because he justified the fall as a great spiritual progress? Of course if you and others do the same, you can't expect to fare better than he did. But then there is no ground for crying "Alas, alas, where shall we be?"

> *Isn't it the same sex-impulse as G's flaming up in another garb in L's case? And the sex-impulse who is said to have known heights in Yoga?*
>
> [*Sri Aurobindo underlined "the sex-impulse who is".*]

Meaning? It was precisely because L considered the sex-impulse to be a height in Yoga that he went for it.

> *I have been* infligé *with doubts, and these things are wearing and tearing the soul. Felt almost like rushing away somewhere.*

Don't you think it is rather silly to allow examples like G's who is

[1] nigraha.

not even a sadhak or L's who did the sadhana of sex-yielding to depress you, as if they had any relation or bearing on the Yoga here.

Any answer or "tons of correspondence" still?

Plenty of tons. But the answer will be given when I have the questions and some leisure together.

About N. P., Manilal says glasses can't cure the disease and once he takes to glasses, he may have to change them every two years or so.

That of course, but it can't be called cure.

But that can't be helped unless his eyes are suspended from reading etc., for if he goes on with his occupations with the defect, it may increase. Of course rest to the eyes wouldn't do it, nor would he feel any pain. So?

Well, is he prepared to wear specs and accept the sure deterioration of his eyes under their protection?

I am trying to have a dash at Herbert's French class which begins at 8.15 p.m. So have to change Dispensary time at night — after meditation to 8 p.m. Mother's approval and a notice can be put up?

Yes.

January 4, 1937

Jatin asks me to send you these questions saying· "The answer is immanent but it wants clarification and there is Sri Aurobindo who will do it in a minute." So will you do it in a minute?

No. You must not ask impossible miracles from me.

He says all sorts of questions arise and temporarily block the way, and he is rather "agitated".

SRI AUROBINDO   799

What is agitating him, the mental question or the problem in a
practical form? Anyhow I have tried to answer.

                                                                  7-1-37
Nirod
P has been recommended by Dr. Manilal to put two medicines
for her eyes. Mother told her to go to the Dispensary, but she wants
a letter of authority so that she may be attended to a little. So here's
the letter. You will arrange.

                                                         SRI AUROBINDO
                                                         January 7, 1937

> *One misgiving is pressing heavily on my soul. I sense
> and feel and see that the tone of your letters has suddenly
> become very grave, rough, stiff and gruff — the owl-like
> severity with which you had once threatened me. I don't
> know what I have done to deserve such a punishment.
> Or is it because you are getting supramentalised day by day
> that you are withdrawing yourself so? There must be a reason
> if my "sense feel" is correct. Well, if you want to press me
> between two planks and pulverise me. . . Well, I don't want
> it, you know!*

I think your sense feel has been indulging in vain imaginations,
perhaps with the idea of increasing your concrete imaginative
faculty and fitting you for understanding the unintelligible. As
you have now much to do with mystic poetry, it may be necessary.
But why object to being pulverised? Once reduced to powder,
think how useful you may be as a medicine, Pulv. Nirod. gr II.
Anyhow disburden your soul of the weight. I am not owled yet,
and my supramentalisation is going on too slowly to justify such
apprehensions. Neither am I withdrawing, rather fitting myself
for a new rush in the near or far future. So cheer up and send the
Man of Sorrows with his planks to the devil.

> *I don't understand why P wanted a letter of authority.
> Has she been made to wait or neglected?. . . I find that
> patients here, especially ladies, want to be served quickly —
> 5 minutes at the most! They can't wait, they must go, they
> have work, etc., etc.*

Important people, you see — necessary for the world action, লোকসংগ্রহায় চ,[1] can't be kept waiting.

> *A seems much reduced and has become a pucca hypochondriac. We have decided to keep him mainly on milk diet. Vegetables and dal don't agree with him.*

It seems to me that this ought to reduce him more and more. To my experience, not taking food simply eternises the dyspepsia. It is all right for a few days, but to make it a rule kills the stomach. Here I agree with R's principle of reeducating the stomach and intestines. But all that is only a standpoint. If the medical Science does not admit it, I don't insist.

> *And we shall give some assimilable form of cod-liver oil.*

No objection to that —

> *Lastly, he must be given some sedentary work.*

But he has his classes?

January 8, 1937

> *Oh, Guru, you missed my poem altogether? What a disappointment for me!*

Didn't see your book was there, I believe — otherwise would have commented.

> *By the way, is it again the correspondence that burdens your soul?*

Very badly.

> *My soul is disburdened though, and I am happy and bright.*

Good!

January 9, 1937

---

[1] *lokasangrahāya cha:* And for holding together the people.

SRI AUROBINDO   801

> *A has no classes. They have been stopped long ago.*

If he has nothing to do, it is natural he should be engrossed with
his stomach.

> *Guru, what do you say to this poem of J's? I am damned
> if I understand anything of it. Blakish, Mallarmic? Me-
> thinks it exceeds both.*

There is no necessity of going beyond Blake and Mallarmé. Their
things are often more difficult than this.

> *Have you any more of these mystic members to compare
> her with?*
> [*Sri Aurobindo put a question mark above "members"
> which was not very clearly written.*]

What's this mystic word?

> *At the rate she is going, I don't know, Guru, where she
> will end. Do you see the end?*

Why should there be an end?

> *I don't know if anyone will make out anything of her
> poetry, except your Supramental Self. The explanations
> of the last two poems, by Jove, are explanations indeed!*

You mean they are more unintelligible than the thing explained?
That about Dawn and Evening was difficult to swallow, but the
end of the 51* seems to me to offer no difficulty at all. It is a magnificent rendering of the large movement of the soul towards the
Silence — but of course it may be meaningless to a posterity that
will, we may assume, know nothing about either Soul or Silence.

> *I sometimes try to project my third eye into posterity
> and see the reactions in its mind regarding J's poetry.
> I at once cover up the sight.*

---

* The poem's number.

Is it your posterity that your third eye sees or posterity in general? Posterity has not had the reaction you speak of with **B & M**— their reputation grows with the lapse of time.

> *They will say—Sri Aurobindo gave expositions of this poetry—ha, ha! and he praised it and gave Force for it! The poetess was undoubtedly "queer", but the Guru?*

But do you then find that it is bad poetry? for at fine poetry posterity will not say ha! ha! but at most "Oof! how difficult!" It is only contemporary opinion that is foolishly contemptuous of grand poetry.

> *Now then, have you any time to help us?*

I am afraid I have not sufficient time. Won't you try again and wrestle with the গভীর[1] instead of having visions of posterity?. . .

January 10, 1937

> *I am slightly depressed about my poetry, Guru. It seems all mind-made.*

It is an extremely beautiful poem. What a grumbler you have got inside you! After writing a thing like that, you ought to be licking your lips in satisfaction.

> *Apart from this depression, these last two days I have been feeling unaccountably rotten, sad, irritated, why? Force, please, O please, please, for heaven's sake!*

No reason. If the Man of Sorrows gets grounds to wallow in agony, he wallows on the ground—if he doesn't he wallows in the waters—if waters are denied to him, he will wallow in the air. If no he will wallow in the void. But wallow he must. Even if you had written a poem as deep as the sea and as splendid as the sunrise, he would still wallow, if that was his fancy— "wallow and luxuriously wail to the world and its Witness."

January 14, 1937

---

[1] *gabhīr:* deep, profound.

SRI AUROBINDO   803

> *About "licking lips", I shall perorate tomorrow.*

It is the licked or the unlicked lips that are going to be vocal?

January 15, 1937

> *I have used the word প্রমীলা[1] in a new sense, meaning fatigue, drowse, slumber. D objected to কৃষিমা[2] saying it wouldn't do. . . Funny thing — this word coinage! Sometimes people accept it, sometimes they reject.*

After all when one coins a new word, one has to take the chance. If the word is properly formed and not ugly or unintelligible, it seems to me all right to venture.

> *If it is not accepted it will remain a blot in the poem. Tagore coined the word তৃণাঙ্কিত[3] but he laments that people have not accepted it.*

Why a blot? There are many words in Greek poetry which occur only once in the whole literature, but that is not considered a defect in the poem. It is called a "hapax legomenon", "a once-spoken word" and that's all. তৃণাঙ্কিত for instance is a fine word and can adorn, not blot Tagore's poetry even if no one else uses it. I think Shakespeare has many words coined by him or at least some that do not occur elsewhere.

> *Any opinion, Guru, and does your intuition say anything on প্রমীলা ?*

I really can't say what প্রমীলা it is. I think, a rare Sanskrit word. Most people wouldn't understand it, perhaps.

> *In your letter of day before yesterday I could not make out a word. Is it: "he wallows in the grave — "? Gracious!*

---

[1] *pramīlā.*

[2] *krishnimā.*

[3] *triṇānchita:* covered with grass.

804

Ground, sir, not *grave*. A ground need not be a grave.

J is still upset. Please, open your tap a little.

She is terribly unreasonable, and she feels herself too easily "tapped" on the head or otherwise.

If God wills, please will or shall something in this fully blank page.

Nothing to write. You have got the essentials, and I have a damned lot of letters to write.

January 16, 1937

Behold! From where comes this unknown Creeper
Along the woodland path anointed by the rising Moon?
All pain she has tinged with the blue of Heart-stream,
She has made Heaven unveil and break out into murmuring
billows.

The magic of her compassion flowers in her hand,
And the thunder-roar that booms the world's end is hushed
suddenly;
In the morn that is the death of the naked skeleton
She stalks over the world, a gathered Fire, voicing her
approach.

The Dark One has put on a golden garland,
And on her delicate forehead burns the flame of red sandal—
She, the Eternal Memory, from within the forgetfulness of
earth's depths
Kindles the first spark of the Word born of the churning.

The eye of the waxing Moon at night-end
Pours out of its blue the golden gleam of a dark collyrium.
[Translated by Nolini Kanta Gupta from the Bengali.][1]
I don't know what this is driving at.

I am afraid I don't know either. You have suddenly shot beyond

[1] The original Bengali version was sent to Sri Aurobindo. The translation was done on 19.1.37.

SRI AUROBINDO   805

Mallarmé, J and everybody else and landed yourself into the Surrealism of the most advanced kind. Such a line as বিবসনা কঙ্কালের মরণপ্রভাতে [1] would make any surrealist poet's heart wild with joy. I think however you should put up a petition to your Inspiration to rein in this gallop towards and beyond the latest Modernism and give us something less progressive and startling.

The only lines I can make something out of are the first two — the creeper (of the unknown new life) in the woodland path of the moonrise, (spiritual opening) — অভিষিক্ত [2] with the moonbeams, I suppose and the third quatrain which is rather remarkable. The Energy (secret in the physical centres) accepted (?) the golden Garland (the garland of the Truth) and She (this Kundalini Shakti) who carries in her the eternal Memory of all things secreted in the apparent Inconscience kindles from the oblivious depths of Earth (the material Nature) the first lightning of the Word of the churning of the Depths i.e. the first bringing up of all that is concealed and undelivered in the consciousness of Matter.

It is a very cryptic but also very significant poetic description of the working of the closed-up Energy in the physical centre when it wakes. The couplet *might* mean that the white-blue moonlight (spiritual light) pours the golden script of the Truth from its eyes (power of vision). The rest *may* mean a preliminary consequence of the opening in which the wave of Manifestation of Paradise comes and brightens up the anguish of the Man of Sorrows in you with a stream of soul-blue, with the result that the tempest is stopped, there is the day of death for the confounded Naked Skeleton (of the dead old Adam in you) and a concentrated Fire pervades everything. After which, as I have said, the Yoga Shakti uncoils in your physical centre and starts serious business. Great Scott! I think I have unexpectedly solved the riddle. But বজ্রের রাগিনী [3] still baffles me.

> It has some meaning, I suppose, but all mixed up. Do you
> find any meaning in it?

Well, if my prophetic soul has rightly interpreted it, it is not mixed

---

[1] In the morn that is the death of the naked skeleton.
[2] Anointed.
[3] *vajrer rāginī:* the thunder-roar.

806   CORRESPONDENCE WITH

up but it is recklessly audacious in its whirlingness of cryptic images. Spiritual surrealism with a vengeance.

Unfortunately I had no time—A mass of work standing over from the week and no time to finish even that. I will look more carefully into the poem tomorrow.

Chand's letter, if you can make out anything.

Have made something out of it by my immense power of divination.

January 17, 1937

So, you have found a splendid meaning in yesterday's poem, Sir!

Quite involuntarily—it dawned on me as I wrote.

You have asked me to send a petition to my Inspiration, but when the Inspiration is your Supramental Self?

Excuse me, no. This is not supramental poetry—so the inspirer can't be my supramental Self.

January 18, 1937

Excuse you? What do you mean, Sir? You give inspiration only for supramental poetry? Startling news, Sir!

Where have I said that I give inspiration for supramental poetry either only or at all? You said that your inspirer for this or for any other poem of yours was my supramental self. I simply said that it can't be, because a supramental self would produce or inspire supramental poetry—and yours is not that, nor, I may add, is J's or D's or my own or anybody's.

We fondly believe that you give inspiration, set apart a time for it, and now you say that you are not the Inspirer?

I say that my supramental Self is not the inspirer—which is a very different matter.

SRI AUROBINDO

807

> *Pray tell me the mystery. Why shirk the responsibility now, because a surrealist poem has come out? You are responsible for it, I think.*

Excuse me, no. As the Gita says, the Lord takes not on himself the good or the evil deeds (or writings) of any. I may send a force of inspiration, but I am not responsible for the results.

> *But did you seriously mean that I should send a "petition"?*

Not very seriously. I was only afraid that you might land us in the poetry of the 22nd century — and that might be a long time to wait for somebody to understand us.

> *All that I do is to remember you and call for your help, and whatever comes I jot down. If I hadn't done this I would have missed these poems. Tell me then what to do.*

No need to do anything, but continue.

> *If spiritual surrealism is what is in that poem [on Kundalini], then it's not at all bad. But Nolini thinks that there is not much of spiritual surrealism there.*

Well, if spiritual is objected to, let us say mystic surrealism. The European kind is vital swapnic.

> *Why not send me that surrealist sonnet of yours?*

No such thing exists, for it was not a sonnet.

> *By your statement we fear that a mixture is coming up in our poetry, and you will exclaim one day: "What? Am I the inspirer of these?!"*

Not at all. In fact I made no statement.

> *Was there anything objectionable in yesterday's poem? Really, Guru, this disclaimer of yours is terribly mysterious; the more I think of it the more I am puzzled.*

But there was no disclaimer. I simply got my supramental self out of the way and left the brunt to be borne by my non-supramental self.

All this time we have known, believed and prayed that you give us the inspiration, and suddenly this?

Suddenly what? My statement that your poetry is not supramental? Surely you did not think it was!

Please give a satisfactory reply; otherwise this dread will haunt me whenever I take up pen and paper.

Rubbish! There is nothing to dread.

Nolini has been suddenly inspired to translate that sur-realist poem [17.1.37]. Will you have a glance at it at your leisure?

Very good translation.

January 19, 1937

You have relieved us by your answer. But I thought you have only one Self—the Overmental or the Supramental.

Why do you suppose me to be so poor in selves? When everybody has several, I must content myself with one?

Who is this "I" who sends the Force—which aspect, I mean?

"I" is a pronoun only = the Multifarious One.

It would be a pity to stop writing poetry till the 22nd century and have to wait for people to understand it. That would be unyogic, and being untrue to the poet also.

From one standpoint; from the other the prudence of postponing for the fitting century might be classed under যোগঃ কর্ম্মসু কৌশলম্ ৷ [1]

---

[1] *yogaḥ karmasu kaushalam:* Yoga is skill in works. (*Gita*, II.50)

SRI AUROBINDO   809

It would certainly be unpoetic.

> *What's your opinion about that bizarre poem—"Good"
> or "Grand"? what is the word? I can't flatter myself by
> taking it to be "grand", nor can my poetic being take it
> for "good" without pain.*

It was good. I forgot that you did not like "good" poetry, only
"fine" and even "very fine". Let us then promote it to "fine", but
stop short of "grand".

> *I can just make out the curve of the r. Please solve the
> mystery and soothe me a little.*

You are wrong; the "r" curve was conspicuous by its absence.
Perhaps I was trying to write in a certain kind of modern English
style "grood" = "really good".

> *I wrote a beautiful poem in the early morning, but I can't
> show it to you for it was done in sleep and I have lost it.
> Pity, isn't it?*

Great pity.

January 20, 1937

> *How can one like "good"? To you good, fine, very fine,
> extremely fine, may be all equal! Of course, to the Divine,
> yes.*

Generally one likes good things and dislikes bad things. But you
seem to dislike both, which is more Yogic in samata (of a negative
kind) than my attitude.

> *If only I had been your critic in your pre-Divine days and
> pronounced "good" about your poetry, I would have liked
> to see your reaction!*

My reaction would depend on whether it agreed with my estimate
or not. If all my poetry were pronounced good by an undeniable

810   CORRESPONDENCE WITH

authority, I should be very pleased and perhaps even might lapse from Yogic heights into egoism.

> *Like "good", I like "fine" less than "very fine" and "exceedingly fine", obviously.*

In that case, you must dislike very fine poetry also — and plump for the exceedingly fine only. But can any poet always and in every line and poem be exceeding?

> *I don't see how you can place fine, very fine, exceedingly fine, on the same level, or how you expect us to like them equally.*

They may not be on the same level, but they are all admirable — and good in its own way is admirable too.

> *Of course, if while saying only fine, you keep within yourself "exceedingly", it will be all equal to you. I can't see your within, Sir! "It is good", "not bad, etc." shows on the very face of it what it is.*

Well, but I can't be always turning my inside outside with a mathematical precision — especially at a first reading in a gallop. I put an impression or rather dash it down as it comes — and it seems to drop a "very" in the process or a good drops in = fine. In any case "good" does not mean "bad" or "poor".

> *I want to know from what angle you see and judge — subject-matter, poetry, plane, consciousness or what?*

I don't see and judge like that — I feel. I have said it is an impression — not an analysis. For an analysis I would have to consider, look from all points of view, analyse, synthetise — no time for all that.

> *Can one write poems from the same source and yet express different ideas in different ways? Or should one strike a different source?*

If you want to go to the same field quite allowable — but a different

SRI AUROBINDO   811

source in the same field gives a greater 'originality' e.g. in the poem
of tonight you did that.

> *J asks: if you have not much time, should she stop sending
> poems every day?. . . But, Guru, I hear you can read with
> electric rapidity, only writing has to be done at a paralysed
> speed, though I doubt it from the nature of your Supra-
> mental script. And much writing is only occasional. . .*

? Many mickles make a muckle — which translated into English
means — a lot of small notes takes a big amount of time.

January 21, 1937

> *I don't dislike "very fine" poetry. Anything short of that is
> not pleasant. And certainly I plump for exceedingly fine,
> not at once, but gradually. You can't object to that surely?*

Rather exacting to demand that everything written shall be very
fine.

> *In A's case, I'm suspecting T.B. of the intestine. But you
> know very little can be done, if it is that. After D.L.'s
> death, he has become such a hypochondriac. I don't know
> if we should take an X-ray of his intestine for any T.B.
> focus.*

An examination and suggestion of T.B. would probably finish
what little morale he has. To discover it is also not very useful since
you say that little = nothing can be done.

January 23, 1937

> *Then we have to try what we can for A?*

Yes.

> *I am a little discouraged by your answer regarding him.*

Why? because I did not favour T.B. research?

812   CORRESPONDENCE WITH

*Can we not pull him up in spite of everything? What should
we do for that?*

If you can get the preoccupation of death and grave illness out
of his head, that might help. It is his sense of being desperately
ill that prevents the force working.

*J asks whether she should send her poems every day or
twice or thrice a week.*

She can send every day. It is only that I have not time always to
make any long comments.

January 24, 1937

*J can send her poems on alternate days. You have written
that long notes are not possible, then we'll ask only in case of
absolute difficulty, when we can't help asking you.*[1]

Naturally — but if it [involves] careful reading and [. . .] writing,
I can't undertake [to] do it that very day; [besides] that I have masses
of [work] to do now — not only letters, [but] I have to prepare
something [for] A.P.H.[2] otherwise the house will collapse, as they
have been [waiting] long without a fresh book. There [are] also
translations into French [for journals] which Pavitra is [wanting]
me to see, etc. etc. [There] are letters from outside some [of] them
very important which are waiting months without [an] answer.
If I have to [write] an explanation of 2 poems (her poems are sometimes long) every day it would take too much time. That amounts
[to] more than I can do.

*She says, "If Sri Aurobindo won't see my poems whom should
I write for? I don't show my poems to anyone else."*

Where did I say I wouldn't see them? Too much femininity here!

I was discouraged by your answer regarding A's case,

---

[1] The original manuscript of the following reply is mutilated. The words in square
brackets have been partly or wholly reconstructed.
[2] Arya Publishing House, Calcutta.

SRI AUROBINDO 813

> *because the tone of your letter did not give much hope for his recovery.*

How can one be hopeful when he is morally down like that?

> *X-ray would help in a negative way. Clinical diagnosis is not always correct. Very often all the available methods of investigation are insisted upon in these difficult cases. If there were no positive X-ray findings, one could change one's diagnosis and treat accordingly. . .*

All that is merely the standpoint of medical convenience. You ignore my standpoint. If T.B. is declared, rightly or wrongly his consciousness receives a fatal blow and the spiritual action is as good as *enrayé*. Yet if it is T.B. of intestines, what is there but spiritual action that can do anything? Medical [Science] can only act in such a case if it changes its philosophy. On that I shall send you an article from the Presse Médicale which may throw some light. In France fortunately medical Science is beginning to open its eyes.

January 25, 1937

> *Is today's poem surrealist? If I am going too fast I may put a check. But these blessed images come in so alluring a way that I dance with joy.*

Surrealism means a dream-sequence poetry — and modern dreams are extravagant. The images may be all right but they get entangled and intertwisted or else on the contrary one jumps from one to another that seems unconnected.

> *Please ask Pavitra to send me the French medical journal.*

It is with me.

January 26, 1937

> *May I ask what is the nature of Mother's ailment?*

Occult, with a physical effect in the eye.

814   CORRESPONDENCE WITH

[*About my poem:*]

... Sir, this sounds terribly surrealistic — If it means anything it is splendid — all of it — but what does it mean?

January 27, 1937

> *I am ashamed and at the same time devilishly glad that Guru has been floored! But isn't it really a huge joke? ... How is it you didn't catch any meaning in my poem of yesterday? Nolini sees no difficulty at all. It does mean something positively!*

If it means something palpable to you, why don't you let me into the secret?

> *You couldn't make out the meaning of the word বণিতা?*[1]

In Sanskrit বণিতা usually means a wife — I was wondering whose wife she was and suspecting adultery.

> *But why do you want the meaning of words? Poetry has to be felt, Sir!*

Provided there is something to feel. But if feeling is enough, why ask me or yourself for a meaning?

> *I have used the word ডালা*[2] *in today's poem. It means, as you must know, a sort of a dish in which* puja *offerings are carried to the temple, so this* ডালা, *can't it paint?*

Not known in the Royal Academy or any other — this painter.

> *What sort of poetry am I writing? Who is this Muse creating this havoc as to founder even the Guru?*

Surrealist — I suppose. My province doesn't go so far.

January 28, 1937

---

[1] *vanitā.*
[2] *ḍālā.*

SRI AUROBINDO

> *I knew that it meant something, but not palpably enough to let you in. It was palpable to Nolini who said moreover that it reminded him of Baudelaire.*

A very big compliment, but I don't know that the parallel can be enforced very far.

> *I have always said that feeling is not enough, but every time you stopped me, saying that mystic poems have to be felt, lived etc., and not understood. Well?*

As I say, feeling or living is quite enough, if there is something to feel or live. But in surrealism the thing to be felt is itself deliberately incoherent.

> *You have said that your province doesn't go so far. How then does the surrealist intervene between your Force and my transcription unless you want him to do so?*

The Surrealist can intervene anywhere, provided the logical mind consents to be a little drowsy.

> *This sort of thing has opened suddenly in me, as you know. I think after your surrealistic poem you have passed it on to me.*

It may be, but my surrealistic poem was clarity itself compared with this technique.

> *You must be having additional work now. So shall we stop sending poems?*

Well, I don't know. If they are not too many conundrums —

> *When there is an operation in the hospital, my services are required and it goes on sometimes till 11 a.m. In that case I may miss meditation. What should I do?*

I suppose it happens only once in a way? or is it frequent or the rule?

816   CORRESPONDENCE WITH

> *I hear Mother's ailment is "red eye". It may be then con-*
> *junctivitis or even iritis.*

It is neither.

> *Medical help no good for the Divine?*

Medicines no use for this even if Mother would take them — only
rest as complete as possible, especially from reading and writing
or any strain of the eye.

> January 29, 1937

> *The first line of my poem of today runs thus:*
> ওই তব পূর্ণ কুম্ভে কী রেখেছ সখি?[1]
> [*Another line:*]
> নিয়ে যাও, নিয়ে যাও সে বিষ-কলসী![2]
> *J says it is vulgar.*

I don't understand the use of the word vulgar here. I don't see anything vulgar in পূর্ণ কুম্ভ[3] or বিষ-কলসী.[4]

> পূর্ণ কুম্ভ *may mean breasts, but it takes another meaning*
> *in the poem: the inflamed desire of the flesh. Even so, is*
> *it vulgar?*

পূর্ণ কুম্ভ, if it means the breasts, would be described in English as
sensuous but not as vulgar. The word vulgar is only used for coarse
and crude expressions of the sensual, trivial or ugly. But it does not
seem to me that it should naturally be taken = breast, but indicate
the whole vital and physical being regarded as a vessel or jar which
can be filled with honey or water or poison. Nothing vulgar in that.

> *Why not send that surrealist poem? I would very much*
> *like to see what is spiritual surrealism.*

---

[1] With what have you filled your pitcher, my-beloved?
[2] Take away the pitcher filled with poison.
[3] *pūrṇa kumbha:* full pitcher.
[4] *vish kalasi:* pitcher filled with poison.

SRI AUROBINDO   817

It isn't spiritual, it is comic — and I am not going to send it. It is
Nonsense Surrealistic not Unfathomable-Sense S.[1]

> *Tomorrow, if you like, I won't send any poem, thus sparing*
> *you some time to send me your poem.*

No use not sending, as I am not going to send. My reference to
it was only a joke.

> *I hope Mother is better now.*

Somewhat.

                                                    January 30, 1937

> *Herbert said yesterday that though Baudelaire is a great*
> *poet, he is considered an immoral one.*

That is not anything against his greatness — only against his morality. Plenty of great people have been "immoral".

> *I had just a glance at Baudelaire's* Flowers of Evil *and I*
> *found this:*
> >   *"The Moon more indolently dreams tonight*
> >   *Than a fair woman on her couch at rest,*
> >   *Caressing, with a hand distraught and light,*
> >   *Before she sleeps, the contour of her breast."*
> *What a queer imagination, but vulgar or immoral?*

What is there vulgar in it or immoral? It is as an indolent distraught
gesture that he puts it. How does it offend against morality?

> *It is strange that I get a thrill from these bizarre images.*
> *Your inspiration will, I hope or fear, give me a Baudelairean*
> *fame — an immoral, vulgar poet!*

It is a terrible prospect.

                                                    January 31, 1937

---

[1] S stands for Surrealistic.

February 1937

A terrible prospect? Do you dread that I will find an "easy path into the world of macabre visions by hashish or opium"?

That's why I call it terrible! However let us hope that one day you will stop on the immoral path to Inferno.

Now a serious misgiving throttles me. It seems you don't like the poems I am writing at present. Why, Sir?

Why does it seem?

Are they worse than "slow scolopendras" which you like immensely?

Yes, but I don't like it seriously, only as fun. However, your poems are not scolopendras — so that is not relevant.

If you don't like, what's the use of writing such things which are neither fine as poetry nor perhaps helpful to sadhana!

But who says they are not fine as poetry?

In yesterday's sonnet the sestet seemed to have a Baudelairean turn. Was it due to faulty transcription?

No, it was a good transcription of Baudelaire.

Or perhaps a fine mystic thing was coming, but the surrealist intervened and spoiled it?

There is certainly a change in the inspiration at that point. Probably Nolini's suggestion has raised up or called down the spirit of Baudelaire and he is trying his best to write spiritual poems through you.

All these questions are in vain, I suppose, and over them you will give a cryptic smile!

SRI AUROBINDO 819

Exactly.

> *Really, Guru, you float easily through the complicated
> constructions of Dilip, NK and others, while I am your
> stumbling block. What?*

Well, sometimes your constructions are like a lot of finely dressed
people (words) crowded together in a dancing-hall, but I don't
know who is the wife of who, and who the bien-aimée, and who
the paternal uncle and who the maternal grand-niece. So I have to
ask and fix their genealogy and general relations.

> *There is a conspiracy among the gods to take away Mother
> into retirement: no Pranam henceforth. Sir, they have
> taken you away already and if Mother withdraws, well,
> we can do the same one by one.*

Well, if people withdraw into themselves, they might find the
Mother there!

> *We are already finding great difficulty in writing with-
> out the Touch. "Hé, writing!" you will shout. But writing
> is sadhana, Sir.*

Which sadhana? Ah yes, I see — অতিবাস্তব পন্থা.[1]

> *R came and said in a pitiable voice that Mother has ptosis
> of the eye-lids, which may persist, if neglected.*

What is ptosis?
Why do people make such prognostications? Suggestions of the
kind ought never to be made, mentally even — they might act
like suggestions and do more harm than any good medicines could
do.

> *He doesn't understand nor do I, why Mother doesn't take
> kindly to medicines and doctors when the trouble could*

---

[1] *ativāstava panthā:* surrealist path.

820   CORRESPONDENCE WITH

*be cured in a short time. Frankly, I don't know how much
our medicines, not homeopathy, can help.*

Then why don't you understand? If medicines can't help, what's
the use of putting foreign matter in the eye, merely because it is a
medicine? Medicines have a quite different action on the Mother's
body than they would have on yours or R's or anybody else's and
the reaction is not usually favourable. Her physical consciousness
is not the same as that of ordinary people — though even in ordinary
people it is not so identical in all cases as "science" would have us
believe —

February 1, 1937

*Did your remark "people withdraw into themselves" carry
a suggestion that "personal touch" is not necessary or essential?. . .*

It is not essential — the inner touch is the essential thing. But it
can be of immense help if properly received. For certain things it
is essential but these certain things nobody yet is ready for.

*Some people believe that whatever is necessary can be had
through meditation or otherwise.*

Whatever is necessary for the inner being, yes.

*As a matter of fact, plenty of people are glad as they can
now do whatever they please.*

But there was never any necessity for such people coming to the
Pranam! It is not obligatory.

*I know from my own experience that we have abused the
Pranam. . . Even then I believe very strongly that there is
something very great in the physical touch of the Mother,
and one can't afford to lose it under any circumstance;
of course one must have the right attitude.*

That is it. The Pranam (like the soup in the evening before) has
been very badly misused. What is the Pranam for? That people

SRI AUROBINDO   821

might receive in the most direct and integral way—a way that
includes the physical consciousness and makes it a channel—
what the Mother could give them and they were ready for. Instead
people sit as if at a court reception noting what the Mother does
(and generally misobserving), making inferences, gossiping afterwards as to her attitude to this or that person, who is the more
favoured, who is less favoured—as if the Mother were doling out
her favour or disfavour or appreciations or disapprovals there,
just as courtiers in a court might do. What an utterly unspiritual
attitude. How can the Mother's work be truly done in such an
atmosphere? How can there be the right reception? Naturally
it reacts on the sadhak, creates any amount of misconception,
wrong feelings etc.—creates an open door for the suggestions of
the Adversary who delights in falsehood and administers plenty of
it to the minds of the sadhaks. This apart from the fact that many
throw all sorts of undesirable things on the Mother through the
Pranam. The whole thing tends to become a routine, even where
there are not these reactions. Some of course profit, those who can
keep something of the right attitude. If there were the right attitude
in all, well by this time things would have gone very far towards
the spiritual goal.

> *Some people, especially ladies, missed the Mother when
> she withdrew from the Pranam. I didn't miss her much, why?
> Is it because my psychic is not very awake?*

Or perhaps because the physical consciousness is obscure and the
psychic not prominent enough.

> *There are others quite sincere who like the meditation
> instead of the Pranam.*

Yes, there are some who say they profit much by it.

> *Are they withdrawing into themselves and getting the
> Mother there?*

They are getting something at any rate.

> *What's the right attitude? To be psychically depressed,*

because Mother is not coming or to try to get her within?

Psychic depression (a queer phrase — you mean vital, I suppose) can help no one. To try to receive within is always the true thing, whether through meditation or pranam.

Can one pray for the Divine? Praying for the Divine to the Divine, not a contradiction?

The Divine Himself can pray to the Divine. There is no contradiction.

I am surprised to hear that even "prognostications" are very harmful. I thought these beliefs were just superstitions.

Prognostications of that kind should not be lightly thought or spoken — especially in the case of the Mother — in other cases, even if there is a possibility or probability, they should be kept confidential from the person affected, unless it is necessary to inform. This is because of the large part played by state of consciousness and suggestion in illness. I shall I suppose one day send you the Presse Médicale with my note (the journal is with me and I shall send it to you, it is no longer with Pavitra) and that will perhaps show the basis.

Ptosis means drooping of the upper eyelid by a paralysis temporary or otherwise.

But, confound it, there is nothing of the kind. The drooping of the eyelid was quite voluntary.

[In J's poem:] What is the blue bird? Aspiration for the Divine?

The Blue Bird is always a symbol of aspiration towards something Beyond.

February 2, 1937

I don't quite understand about "the physical consciousness" being obscure.

SRI AUROBINDO   823

The physical consciousness is that part which directly responds
to physical things and physical Nature, sees the outer only as
real, is occupied with it — not like the thinking mind with thought
and knowledge, or like the vital with emotion, passion, subtler
satisfaction of desire. If this part is obscure, then it is difficult to
bring into it the consciousness of deeper or spiritual things, feelings
etc. even when the mind or the vital are after these deeper things.

> *There is a flower called "Aspiration in the Physical", what*
> *does it mean?*

Aspiration means aspiration for the Divine, for higher consciousness etc.

February 3, 1937

> *About Mulshankar's vomiting, Manilal says that it is there*
> *from his birth, it has nothing to do with the accident. I*
> *wonder if it is the result of too much meditation and con-*
> *centration which he used to do.*

But surely he did not do a lot of concentration before birth?

February 4, 1937

> *I hear X has a deep affection, respect and admiration for Y*
> *and yet I know that she has suffered a lot at his hands.*
> *[Sri Aurobindo underlined "deep affection".]*

Of course. A womanly woman always appreciates a man who can
make her suffer, provided he has a dominating personality. Cave-
woman instinct.

> *X was given some home-truths today. She didn't like it*
> *very much. . .*

Of course not — nobody likes home-truths when they show one's
own inconsistent egoism. If they did not go home, they would be
more pleasant.

824   CORRESPONDENCE WITH

B has long-standing piles — painful and burning.

He wrote about something like a boil near about + protruding
piles and was afraid of being immobilised if it went on. Nothing
of the kind?

By the way, is there still trouble in Mother's eyes?

Somewhat.

I send for information another tragic letter from S — which
please return. It appears, it is only a resurrected S that is walking
about the Asram since yesterday afternoon!

I say — Dr. Hutchinson, President of the Royal Society of
Medicine, in London, says (vide Sunday Times, page 4) that if
all the doctors struck work for a year, it would make no difference
in the death-rate. The doctors' only use is to give comfort, confidence and consolation. Now what do you say to this opinion of
your President? Rather hot, isn't it?

February 6, 1937

*Friends have I none, Guru; to none can I open myself
except to you. Don't forsake me, please.*

Certainly not.

*I send you a book of poetry[1] to have your opinion on the
Bengali poems there. They strike me as very powerful and
original in the Tagorean age. I think they abound in surrealistic images and have some sort of similarity with my
recent poems.*

Have read two pages — very fine poetry. Shall read at leisure.
But up to now nothing surrealistic. So far don't find any identity
with yours except a certain fullness and boldness of language.

*Please don't keep the book for long. Otherwise Premanand[2]
will lose all his* prem *and* anand*![3]*

[1] Poetry by Mohitlal Majumdar.
[2] The Ashram librarian.
[3] Love and delight.

SRI AUROBINDO   825

He is always doing that and losing his hair too into the bargain.
If he objects to my keeping the book, I will give him a clout on
the head which will help to keep his hair on.

February 7, 1937

> *Did you write: "... I will give him a* club *on the head..."?*
> *He will die, Sir, but if he doesn't, a doctor will be needed!*

Clout, clout. A clout is a harmless thing — at most you will have
to put a bandage.

> *I read the script in Sunday Times, by Dr. Hutchinson. It is*
> *not only hot, but a little top-heavy it seems. If the doctors'*
> *function is only to give consolation, I fear many patients*
> *visiting us will leave, cursing us. Take B's case of piles. Will*
> *simple consolation suffice?*

It depends on the effectivity of your consoling words and confidence in giving drugs. Your words and cheery care may so raise
B's morale that it will affect his piles and, if it can't do altogether
that, your medicine may give so much confidence to the piles that
they will walk in and give up the ghost. But it's all a confidence trick
in reality. If the piles are crass and refuse confidence, well —

> *I asked V if he agreed to this "consolation" treatment.*
> *He said, "Certainly!" Then I asked him, "How is it then*
> *that your old malady has come back which was supposed to*
> *have been cured by R?"*

Well, that's the point. How did R or how does anybody cure? By
his medicines or by his "confidence" imparted to the subconscient
of the patient?

> *He answered, "But one doctor may fail and, besides, there*
> *is the Force!" Well?*

The Force is another matter. Your President Hutchinson or Hen-
derson (or what the deuce was his name?) wasn't thinking in terms
of Force.

But doesn't R cut short the course of a disease, doesn't his medicine help to alleviate the patients' sufferings?

Sometimes. But how?

Anyway, what is your opinion?

My opinion is that Allah is great and great is the mystery of the universe and things are not what they seem, etc.!

February 8, 1937

I have no energy to write or fight. Down in the pool!

Wade out and up.

I have glanced through your translation of J's poem. But can't you make some time and put it into metrical form, since you have done so much? The translation, though beautiful, loses much of the magnificence of the original.

This costs no trouble — done in ten minutes — to metrify is the very deuce.

I forgot to report about S. You know he has a cut just above the patella. Due to constant walking it's a gaping wound. Today while we were dressing it, he fainted! He said I frightened him by saying that it was serious. I said nothing of the kind — except that it may require stitches, which he took to be serious. Just a stitch will do. But he is so nervy! We may wait till tomorrow and see?

Mother has told him to take rest — perhaps with rest he may not need stitching. I don't think he is very courageous about these things.

February 9, 1937

About my new poetry which you call "surrealist", many expressions creep in, having hardly any meaning. Some-

> *times a poem becomes a "great success", at other times it is a misfire.*

When one develops a new kind of poetry or a new technique, one must not mind having to find one's way.

> *. . . At times I have to make a foolish face before people when I can't understand my own expression, and they'll think I'm writing rubbish. . .*

Why foolish? Make a mystic face and say "It means too much for owls." The difficulty is that you all want exact intellectual meanings for these things. A meaning there is, but it can't always be fitted with a tight and neat intellectual cap.

> *Your cryptic smiles and magnificent silence, don't lend themselves to any interpretation. You have a very easy way of escape, by saying "Surrealist".*

My "surrealist" is a joke but not a depreciatory one.

> *D also said "If this is surrealistic, I have nothing to say" — which, at times, is tantamount to saying that under that heading one can write anything blessed or non-blessed.*

If you are going to listen to D's criticisms or be influenced by them, you can't go on writing these things. His standpoint is an entirely different one. What his mind can't understand, is for him nonsense. He is for the orthodox style of poetry with as much colour as possible, but not transgressing by its images the boundary of the orthodox. This poetry is a modern "heresy" and heretics must have the courage of their non-conformity.

> *Now, what the deuce is this Surrealism? I gather that Baudelaire is its father, and Mallarmé its son.*

Surrealism is a new phrase invented only the other day and I am not really sure what it conveys. According to some it is a dream poetry reaching a deeper truth, a deeper reality than the surface reality. I don't know if this is the whole theory or only one side or phase of the practice. Baudelaire as a surrealist is a novel idea, nobody ever called him that before. Mallarmé, Verlaine and others used to be classed as impressionist poets, sometimes as symbolists. But now the surrealists seem to claim descent from these poets.

Does surrealism indicate that the meaning should be always unintelligible, if any? That there may be many expressions which have hardly any significance, coherence, etc.? If it has, so much the better; if none, well, it doesn't, in any way, affect the beauty of the poem?

This is the gibe of the orthodox school of critics or readers — certainly the surrealists would not agree with it — they would claim they have got at a deeper line of truth and meaning than the intellectual.

Yesterday, you used the term "surrealistic transitions". What did you mean?

Transitions that are not there of a mental logic.

Transitions that are hardly palpable on the surface?

Not palpable on the surface, but palpable to a deeper vision.

Or do they have no link or reason at all, and come in just as vital dreams come in?

How do you say that vital dreams have no link or reason? They have their own coherence, only the physical mind cannot always get at the clue by following which the coherence would unroll itself. For that matter the sequences of physical existence are coherent to us only because we are accustomed to it and our reason has made up a meaning out of it. But subject it to the view of a different consciousness and it becomes an incoherent phantasmagoria. That's how the Mayavadins or Schopenhauer would speak of it; the former say deliberately that dream-sequences and life-sequences stand on the same footing, only they have another structure. Each is real and consequent to itself — though neither, they would say, is real or consequent in very truth.

SRI AUROBINDO 829

> *I request you to give a brief discourse on Surrealism. D says, "I feel there is something in your poem, but I can't catch it."*

D has asked practically for the same, but I would have to study the subject before I could do so.

[*A letter written to Dilip Kumar Roy.*]

I really can't tell you what surrealism is, because it is something — at least the word is — quite new and I have neither read the reliable theorists of the school nor much of their poetry. What I picked up on the way was through reviews and quotations, the upshot being that it is a poetry based on the dream-consciousness, but I don't know if this is correct or merely an English critic's idea of it. The inclusion of Baudelaire and Valéry seems to indicate something wider than that. But the word is of quite recent origin and nobody spoke formerly of Baudelaire as a surrealist or even of Mallarmé. Mallarmé was supposed to be the founder of a new trend of poetry, impressionist and symbolist, followed in varying degrees and not by any means in the same way by Verlaine and Rimbaud, both of them poets of great fame. Verlaine is certainly a great poet and people now say Rimbaud also, but I have never come across his poetry except in extracts. This strain has developed in Valéry and other noted writers of today. It seems that all these are now claimed as part of or the origin of the surrealist movement. But I cannot say what are the exact boundaries or who comes in where. I suppose if Baron communicates to you books on the subject or more precise information, we shall know more clearly now. In any case, surrealism is part of an increasing attempt of the European mind to escape from the surface consciousness (in poetry as well as in painting and in thought) and grope after a deeper truth of things which is not on the surface. The Dream-Consciousness as it is called — meaning not merely what we see in dreams, but the inner consciousness in which we get into contact with deeper worlds which underlie, influence and to some extent explain much in our lives, what the psychologists call the subliminal or the subconscient (the latter a very ambiguous phrase) — offers the first road of escape and the surrealists seem to be trying to force it. My impression is that there is much fumbling and that more often it is certain obscure and not always very safe layers that are tapped. That accounts for the note of diabolism that comes in in Baudelaire, in Rimbaud also, I believe, and in certain ugly elements in English surrealist poetry and painting. But this is only an impression.

Nirod's poetry (what he writes now) is from the Dream-Consciousness, no doubt about that. It has suddenly opened in him and he finds now a great joy of creation and abundance of inspiration which were and are quite absent when he tries to write laboriously in the mental way. This seems to me to indicate either that the poet in him has his real power there or that he has opened to the same force that worked in poets like Mallarmé. My labelling him as a surrealist is partly — though not altogether — a joke. How far it applies depends on what the real aim and theory of the surrealist school may be. Obscurity and unintelligibility are not the essence of any poetry — and except for unconscious or semi-conscious humorists like the Dadaists — cannot be its aim or principle. True Dream-poetry (let us call it so for the nonce) has and must always have a meaning and a coherence. But it may very well be obscure or seem meaningless to those who take their stand on the surface or "waking" mind and accept only its links and its logic. Dream-poetry is usually full of images, visions, symbols, phrases that seek to strike at things too deep for the ordinary means of expression. Nirod does not deliberately make his poems obscure; he writes what comes through from the source he has tapped and does not interfere with its flow by his own mental volition. In many modernist poets there may be labour and a deliberate posturing, but it is not so in his case. I interpret his poems because he wants me to do it, but I have always told him that an intellectual rendering narrows the meaning — it has to be seen and felt, not thought out. Thinking it out may give a satisfaction and an appearance of mental logicality, but the deeper sense and sequence can only be apprehended by an inner sense. I myself do not try to find out the meaning of his poems, I try to feel what they mean in vision and experience and then render into mental terms. This is a special kind of poetry and has to be dealt with according to its kind and nature. There is a sequence, a logic, a design in them, but not one that can satisfy the more rigid law of the logical intelligence.

About Housman's theory: it is not merely an appeal to emotion that he posits as the test of pure poetry; he deliberately says that pure poetry does not bother about intellectual meaning at all,

SRI AUROBINDO   831

it is to the intellect nonsense. He says that the interpretations
of Blake's famous poems rather spoil them — they appeal better
without being dissected in that way. His theory is questionable, but
that is what it comes to; he is wrong in using the word "nonsense"
and perhaps in speaking of pure and impure poetry. All the same,
to Blake and to writers of the dream-consciousness, his rejection
of the intellectual standard is quite applicable.

SRI AUROBINDO[1]

February 12, 1937

[*A letter written to Dilip Kumar Roy.*]

About your points regarding surrealism:

1. I have answered this in my former letter. If the surrealist
dream-experiences are flat, pointless or ugly, it must be because
they penetrate only as far as the "subconscious" physical and
"subconscious" vital dream layers which are the strata nearest to
the surface. Dream-consciousness is a vast world in which there are
a multitude of provinces and kingdoms, but ordinary dreamers
for the most part penetrate consciously only to these first layers
which belong to what may properly be called the subconscious belt.
When they pass into deeper sleep regions, their recording surface
dream-mind becomes unconscious and no longer gives any transcript of what is seen and experienced there; or else in coming back
these experiences of the deeper strata fade away and are quite
forgotten before one reaches the waking state. But when there is
a stronger dream-capacity, or the dream-state becomes more conscious, then one is aware of these deeper experiences and can bring
back a transcript which is sometimes a clear record, sometimes a
hieroglyph, but in either case possessed of a considerable interest
and significance.

2. It is only the subconscious belt that is chaotic in its dream
sequences; for its transcriptions are fantastic and often mixed,
combining a jumble of different elements: some play with im-
pressions from the past, some translate outward touches pressing
on the sleep-mind; most are fragments from successive dream experiences that are not really part of one connected experience —

[1] *SABCL*, vol. 9, pp. 445-447. (Previously unpublished passages are included
here.)

as if a gramophone record were to be made up of snatches of different songs all jumbled together. The vital dreams even in the subconscious range are often coherent in themselves and only seem incoherent to the waking intelligence because the logic and law of their sequences is different from the logic and law which the physical reason imposes on the incoherences of physical life. But if one gets the guiding clue and if one has some dream-experience and dream-insight, then it is possible to seize the links of the sequences and make out the significance, often very profound or very striking, both of the detail and of the whole. Deeper in, we come to perfectly coherent dreams recording the experience of the inner vital and inner mental planes; there are also true psychic dreams — the latter usually are of a great beauty. Some of these mental or vital plane dream-experiences, however, are symbolic, very many in fact, and can only be understood if one is familiar with or gets the clue to the symbols.

3. It depends on the nature of the dream. If they are of the right kind, they need no aid of imagination to be converted into poetry. If they are significant, imagination in the sense of a free use of mental invention might injure their truth and meaning — unless of course the imagination is of the nature of an inspired vision coming from the same plane and filling out or reconstructing the recorded experience so as to bring out the Truth held in it more fully than the dream transcript could do; for a dream record is usually compressed and often hastily selective.

4. The word "psyche" is used by most people to mean anything belonging to the inner mind, vital or physical, though the true psyche is different from these things. Poetry does come from these sources or even from the superconscient sometimes; but it does not come usually through the form of dreams; it comes either through word-vision or through conscious vision and imagery whether in a fully waking or an inward-drawn state: the latter may go so far as to be a state of Samadhi — *svapna samādhi*. In all these cases it is vision rather than dream that is the imaging power. Dreams also can be made a material for poetry; but everyone who dreams or has visions or has a flow of images cannot by that fact be a poet. To say that a predisposition and discipline are needed to bring them to light in the form of written words is merely a way of saying that it is not enough to be a dreamer, one must have the poetic faculty and some training — unless the surrealists mean by this

SRI AUROBINDO   833

statement something else than what the words naturally signify.
What is possible, however, is that by going into the inner (what is
usually called the subliminal) consciousness — this is not really
subconscious but a veiled or occult consciousness — or getting
somehow into contact with it, one not originally a poet can awake
to poetic inspiration and power. No poetry can be written without
access to some source of inspiration. Mere recording of dreams
or images or even visions could never be sufficient, unless it is a
poetic inspiration that records them with the right use of words and
rhythm bringing out their poetic substance. On the other hand,
I am bound to admit that among the records of dream-experiences
even from people unpractised in writing, I have met with a good
many that read like a brilliant and colourful poetry which does hit —
satisfying Housman's test — the solar plexus. So much I can con-
cede to the surrealist theory; but if they say on that basis that all
can with a little training turn themselves into poets — well, one
needs a little more proof before one can accept so wide a statement.[1]

> [*I had asked Sri Aurobindo on 12.2.37, if I could put a
> stitch to S's small cut (9.2.37). There was no answer that
> day.*]

By the way did you do your tailoring work with S? I forgot to
write that you could stitch away at him as much as necessary.

                                                        February 13, 1937

> *Today I have written three sonnets, Sir, in one and a half
> hours! What do you say to that?*

Remarkable!

> *I have a fear that the fountain might dry up or that I might
> go on repeating the old thing.*

Why fear? If it happens, you will start something new. Perhaps
super-realism.

                                                        February 14, 1937

---

[1] *ibid.*, pp. 447-449. (A line previously unpublished is included here.)

834   CORRESPONDENCE WITH

> *What a disappointment! I thought yesterday's poem was
> very fine. It seems it is pretty hard to write exceedingly
> fine stuff in this kind of poetry.*

Well, well, I must reserve the adverbs, or I shall have nothing
to put in case you "exceed" yourself.

February 15, 1937

> *P said about my new poems that they seemed to be more in-
> tellectual, but there is not much power; for power comes
> only from the Psychic. I was rather surprised to hear that
> from him as I thought Power, Peace, vastness, etc., come
> from the spiritual consciousness from above. . .*

Power can be everywhere, on any plane. What descends from above
is power of the higher Consciousness — but there is a Power of
the vital, mental, physical planes also. Power is not a special
characteristic of the psychic or of the spiritual plane.

February 16, 1937

> *So you also fail to tell the precise meaning of the poem!*

Who the devil can give the precise meaning of inner things?

> *Then it will never be understood. People will sarcastically
> say, "Surrealist! W.P.B!"*[1]

"Write plenty of books"?

> *The other day Dilip said to M. Baron, "But one can't
> understand this surrealist poetry." He replied, "Why
> should you understand?"*

Exactly — why should you understand? When you can instand,
overstand, roundstand, interstand — what's the need of understanding?

---

[1] Waste-paper basket.

SRI AUROBINDO 835

> *If you don't understand, how do you pronounce fine, very fine, etc.? By simply feeling?*

Queer fellow! As if feeling could not go deeper than intellectual understanding!

> *Anyhow, it seems the poet has nothing to do but to submit himself to the Force. For, when he doesn't know what he is talking about, how is he going to improve?*

He need not understand, but he can know.

> *It is like casting a net and depending on luck to catch small or big fish as may be the case. Is there any other way?*

Of course there is. Find it out.

> *See for instance today's fish. Do you find any head or tail?. . .*

Very nicely coloured gleaming fish.

> *But seriously, how to write better this kind of stuff? What is the trick?*

The trick is to put your demand on the source for what you want. If you want to fathom (not understand) what you are writing ask for the vision of the thing to come along with the word, a vision bringing an inner comprehension. If you want something mystic but convincing to the non-mystic reader, ask for that till you get it.

> *What do you say to today's poem?*

Very fine, this time.

Well, let us put it in English — without trying to be too literal, turning the phrases to suit the Eng. language. If there are any mistakes of rendering they can be adjusted.

At the day-end behold the Golden Daughter of
                              Imaginations —
She sits alone under the Tree of Life —

A form of the Truth of Being has risen before her rocking
there like a lake
And on it is her unwinking gaze. But from the unfathomed
Abyss where it was buried, upsurges
A tale of lamentation, a torrent-lightning passion,
A melancholy held fixed in the flowing blood of the veins,—
A curse thrown from a throat of light.
The rivers of a wind that has lost its perfumes are bearing
away
On their waves the Mantra-rays that were her ornaments
Into the blue self-born sea of a silent Dawn;
The ceaseless vibration-scroll of a hidden Sun
Creates within her, where all is a magic incantation,
A picture of the transcendent Mystery—that luminous
laughter
(Or, A mystery-picture of the Transcendent?)
Is like the voice of a gold-fretted flute flowing from the
inmost heart of the Creator.

Now, I don't know whether that was what you meant, but it is
the meaning I find there. Very likely it has no head or tail, but it
has a body and a very beautiful body—and I ask with Baron, why
do you want to understand? why do you want to cut it up into the
dry mathematical figures of the Intellect? Hang it all, sir! In spite
of myself you are making me a convert to the Housman theory
and Surrealism. No, Sir—feel, instand, overstand, interstand, but
don't try to understand the creations of a supra-intellectual Beauty.

It is enough to feel and grasp without trying to "understand"
the creations of a supra-intellectual Beauty.

February 17, 1937

Will a simple "demand" give the thing?

A demand is an aspiration for something—it will bring its answer,
not always immediately, but in time.

But which source?

Whatever the source.

SRI AUROBINDO   837

Where is the time to ask for all that when one is busy writing?

Have it at any time as the thing you want — whenever you think
of your poetry.

*I thought of giving you a simple beauty today, but give
this instead for you to see if what I demanded from the
source has been granted.*

If it's something which means a big advance, you can't expect it all
at once.

Well, Sir, has the source responded?

Responded to what? What were you asking for?

*Where does the poem strike you — at the solar or lunar
plexus?*

It must be the Baron plexus. It is surely your contact with him
that has started you on this line.

February 18, 1937

*You are a most wonderful God, Sir! More queer than my
poems, if you don't mind my saying so. You have been
hammering this surrealism into my soul for such a long time
and now you say that I got it from Baron?*

You don't seem to have read carefully my letter to Dilip. I said
your poems belong to the Dream-Consciousness, but I had used the
word Surrealism lightly — i.e. your poems are not on a line with the
actual surrealism of the day, the thing to which the name is given.
   But this last poem is Baronic, (I don't know what Baron's poems
are like, but I mean they have the modern incoherence).

*If Baron has anything to do with it, it was only the other day
that I first met him.*

838 CORRESPONDENCE WITH

As this came soon after meeting Baron, I said as a joke that it must have been a real modern surrealistic influence from him.

Well, regarding yesterday's poem, you seem to have understood the surrealist lines, not the others.

Good Lord! the only lines I understood were those I marked as *not* entirely surrealistic.

I thought the reverse.

So did I.

Now I find that in spite of your long letters, I have not really grasped what this blessed surrealism is.

I wrote very clearly in my letter to Dilip that I did not know myself what Surrealism is since I have not studied either surrealistic theory or surrealistic literature. I gathered from what I have read — reviews, citations — that it was dream-consciousness of a lower type (therefore incoherent and often ugly). I also explained at great length in another letter that there was a Dream-Consciousness of a higher type. Are these distinctions really so difficult to understand?

February 19, 1937

What does this telegram from Chand mean? All I know is that this loan company is a company in Chittagong where he has kept deposits. Is it the position of his complex self or the self of the company that is risky? Which?

Both perhaps.

One thing is clear that he requires your protection. Well?

Difficult to protect such an erratic genius. However.

February 20, 1937

The difficulty I am faced with in my poetry is that some

SRI AUROBINDO   839

> *poems suddenly turn out to be very good, others fall below the mark.*

But that is quite usual in the work of all poets.

> *Everything depends on the Inspiration. But then I can't change any line or word since I don't understand what I am writing.*

From your explanations you seem to understand all right. The question is about the inspiration itself. It is sometimes more successful, sometimes less — for various reasons. What one has to see is whether what has come through is quite satisfactory in language, image, harmonious building, poetic force. If not, one can call a farther inspiration to emend what is deficient. At first one allows the inspiration to come through without interference, to establish the habit of free flow. But that does not mean one must not afterwards alter or improve — only it should be done not by the mind but by a fresh and better inspiration. If in the course of writing itself, a correcting inspiration comes, that can be accepted — otherwise one does the perfecting afterwards.

> *You advised me to demand from the source what I want. But I don't know what precisely I want. All I can say is that the writing should have greater beauty, depth, etc.*

That is rather too vague.

> *. . . I fondly cherish a hope that one day we shall be able to write like Harin.*

Better, I hope.

> *Perhaps we may not have his fluency.*

So much fluency is not necessary. He had perhaps too much.

> *Nowdays I am having more difficulty in writing. The "abundance" of inspiration seems to have vanished. In one hour I write just one sonnet. . . I find that plenty of old images and*

840   CORRESPONDENCE WITH

> *expressions try to come in, which I have to reject merci-*
> *lessly.*

It is probably because of your seeking for something better which
makes the mind hesitate — as also the bar put upon the constant
repetition of old images. But that is only a transitional difficulty.
Still perhaps you are thinking too much while writing?

> *I concentrate or meditate for a while before writing; at*
> *times I go within and then write. But the difficulty is no less.*
> *I have to pause after every expression.*

Pause to do what? Think? You have to cultivate the power of
feeling instinctively the value of what you write — either while writing or immediately you go over it when it is completed.

February 23, 1937

> *How is my aspiration for greater beauty, depth, etc.*
> *"vague"? How to be more precise when one doesn't know*
> *the meaning of what one is writing?*

Whatever the reason it is not precise, it is only a general formula
which in practice might mean a hundred different things.

> *The result of the Darshan was very queer: a heavy inert*
> *sleep during the day and night. The waking hours passed*
> *in vacancy. I felt like a corpse without a soul; even the*
> *thought of death passed across my mind.*

It looks like a plunge into physical or sub-physical inertia.

> *Perhaps it was due to fatigue: keeping awake on the Darshan*
> *night, for decoration?*

Might be. Fatigue sometimes brings that.

> *. . . Or have you done something in the sub-conscient phys-*
> *ical?*

SRI AUROBINDO   841

Done what? Raised up the subconscient in the form of a blank?
Had no such intention.

> *Some people had peace, joy, etc. I am not discouraged,*
> *but would like to know what happened, and pray to get me*
> *into a better state.*

Of course this kind of emptiness often happens when the physical
is being directly dealt with — the important thing is not to remain
in it, but to make it a passage to a new force and better consciousness.

> *By the way, do you think I should seriously take up French?*

I don't know that it is necessary just now.

> *Naik proposes that I join the French class they are or-*
> *ganising...*

Naik's class as proposed means an active part for everybody. It
depends on whether you feel like taking such a part.

> *February 24, 1937*

> *You spoke about a "formula" yesterday. If you could give*
> *it, we could aspire for it and get quick results.*

There is no formula — these things are not done by formulas. It
is the thing that you want for your poetry that you have to make
precise in your perception — and get it.

> *Or do you mean that one should first aspire for harmony,*
> *when that is established then depth, images, etc.?*

Harmony certainly, and as much depth as possible and the right
images and language giving the thing to be expressed as powerfully
built and living a form as possible. But I am not aware that there is
any fixed order like that in their coming.

842 CORRESPONDENCE WITH

You say sometimes images are forced — How to understand that? Inner feeling?

One can surely feel that if one tries.

My inner vision didn't tell me that "the book of the Ocean" was a forced image, nor did it tell me that the poem was not cogent enough. . .

Well then, the inner vision or the subtle sense of these things has to be developed till it is capable of feeling and seeing these differences.

I realise however that all this will take time to develop. Meanwhile one has to stumble, make mistakes and sometimes have good luck.

If one can't yet see one's way, one has to feel, if not by experiment.

February 25, 1937

So Dr. Becharlal has gone! Now perhaps the avalanche of the Dispensary work will roll down on me. Will you save and help me?

Help, I can. But save? Well, an avalanche is an avalanche.

February 28, 1937

March 1937

You find "funny" things in my poems? Then, Sir, you have only to ask me to stop writing.

But why do you object to fun? Modern opinion is that a poet ought to be funny (humorous) and that the objection to funniness in poetry is a romantic superstition.

How is it then that you give remarks "very fine" etc.?

SRI AUROBINDO   843

Well, it can be funnily fine or finely funny — can't it?

> *If they are really funny, why should I spoil my valuable
> time writing them when I could sleep comfortably for two
> hours?*

For the joy of the world, of course.

Funny however is used in the sense of "extraordinary". You
can't deny that these things are extraordinary?

> *Is that the reason why you don't give any explanations
> either? Very well, Sir!*

Why should I explain when you can understand and explain yourself? As Christ came to save sinners, not the righteous, so am I here
to explain the inexplicable to the non-understanding, not to the
understanding.

> [*There were a few friends who, inspired by my surrealistic
> poetry, were writing poems in the same vein, and I was
> sending them to Sri Aurobindo asking him to explain some
> of the difficult ones. After explaining once or twice he said
> that if it continued he would go on "strike".*]
> *But I don't see the logic of your threat of "strike". If people
> begin writing these surrealistic poems by your inspiration,
> am I to blame and suffer?*

The strike is supposed to be against the 4, 5, 6 ad infinitum, not
against the two.

My inspiration? When they catch it from you!

> *By the way, for whom have you to write explanations from
> set to dawn? One is my precious self?*

Yes.

> *And the other is J?*

Yes. I have to explain for her also.

> *But she is not a surrealist!*

844   CORRESPONDENCE WITH

Surrealist or symbolist, it comes to the same so far as need for explanation goes.

March 1, 1937

> *... In spite of your decrying my poems, Sir, there are plenty of beautiful conceptions, you must admit!*

Who decries it? Some are funny—I beg pardon, extraordinary—but the beauty is all there.

March 2, 1937

> *I suppose you have seen that letter of S's. I left it to the wisdom of the Mother to do what my wisdom failed to decide... What a letter, my God!*

Why get upset over such an entirely unimportant thing? S's letters are like that and nobody attaches the least value to them. I have thrown his letter into the W.P.B. which is the only place that suits it.

March 3, 1937

> *A has pain in the liver region and near the umbilicus. She was given acid Hydrachlor mix with Nux vomica for a long time. Now we have changed it to mix. Sod. and other salts.*

A writes that B told her to take curds when she had diarrhoea (?), and she has been doing so with the results that she is being washed out completely by thick leucorrhea, sometimes also intense shooting pains in stomach lower and upper—spine and loins paining day and night. Asks if she is to continue curds. Asks me to tell you.

By the way what was your objection to Kola for Arjava? I have forgotten. He complains of being very rundown in energy—Mother thought that ten days of Kola repeated whenever necessary (not continued for longer periods) might help to keep it up—and as we have fresh supply of Kola—well!

March 4, 1937

> *My objection was that Kola contains caffein which is a stimulant, so it can't be continued for a long period. But*

SRI AUROBINDO 845

> *surely it can be taken for 2 or 3 weeks — it will be a good*
> *tonic after this weakness.*

In that case you can give? If it is not with you, take from Pavitra.

March 5, 1937

> [*P suffering from a carbuncle.*] *He said that if it was going*
> *to be serious, he would as well start for home!*

If he wants to go, don't stop him — let him do so. He was allowed
to come here for a month's experiment to see whether the place
suited him and he suited the place. The carbuncle seems to be a
negative answer.

> *What's your opinion, Sir, on today's poem?*

Quite successful.

March 6, 1937

> *"Quite successful" only? When will this be followed by*
> *a little more warmth and exhilaration, can you predict?*

Well, I can write, if you want: "Superlative! Extraordinary! Un-
imaginable! Surprising! Inexpressible! Ineffable!" That ought to
be warm and exhilarating —

> *I told you that I have written two poems in an hour. Should*
> *I have written one instead and revised it to make it a better*
> *egg if possible?*

No such rule necessary.

> *But when this stuff itself is not very remarkable, can further*
> *labour improve it much?*

Only detail corrections needed.

> *Wouldn't it be a waste of time?*

Yes.

846

> *I could write instead another poem if it pours in?*

Yes.

> *Of course one can go on altering and altering till an altogether new poem is created. That is what you do, I understand.*

That is for "big" poetry. Short poems I usually revise only once and alterations are not many.

March 7, 1937

> *10. p.m.*
> *I heard just now that X is again troubled because of some "peacelessness", and intends to go to Calcutta. May I go to see him? I hope there is no harm in doing so? I know I won't be able to help him. . . He cheered me up in my last depression.*
>
> *I suppose it is useless to discuss, or to persuade either. What will be the best thing to do? I pray that he may give up this mad project. . . You must keep him, Sir!*

There is no harm in your going to see him, but it should be to cheer him and be helpful, not to dispute or lecture. To make him change his mind or cancel his going is difficult now because he has telegraphed to everybody—would be of little use. For something in him is strongly seized with this idea of Calcutta and Almora which has been long ripening and repeating itself, and it has been coming back and back every ten days or so. It would come back again and with greater vehemence. It is better to let him have his relief. He wrote a quite reasonable letter except for his usual silly nonsense about the "grimness" of the morning Meditation—and in answer I subscribed to his going for a few months, and staying at Calcutta and Almora. He was making his preparations quite cheerfully when suddenly he got the idea of taking Y with him (so it is reported) and went to her. She gave him a scolding and lecture. Result —he came gloomy to the Mother, found her "stern" (which she was not) and broke into a tragic despair, praying for death and saying that he would never come back or write again etc. If he is to go, it is surely better that he should go gladly and cheerfully and not in this spirit.

SRI AUROBINDO   847

As to the madness of the project it is certainly not the best thing
he could have done. But he has got into such a formation of ideas
and feelings against the Yoga as it is practised here (he had that
always almost) and is so unable to get rid of it that he is unable to
have any outward progress until it is broken and no progress (a
quiet inward psychic growth he does not want) throws him into fits
of despair after every calm period of a few days. He wants to escape
or get relief from it by going out. Well, let him try it, by a miracle it
might succeed. In any case to hold back always when he says he is in
turmoil here is not possible.

                                                      March 9, 1937

          L has a burning sensation in the mouth and throat.

What cause? She says from mouth to throat is carpeted with pepper
and covered with thin pomegranate grains and she suspects an
eruption there. Also you have medicated her throat but under the
tongue there is fire. Surrealist Poetry is not your monopoly — even
your patients write it.

S informed me the other day that her spine had already begun
breaking of itself into two.

                                                     March 10, 1937

          *Guru, I was badly hit by X's going away. . . The first ques-
          tion is: why has he gone?*

The marvel is that he did not go before.

          *You and Mother have poured and poured all heaven, as it
          were, on him—affection, sympathy, love, consideration,
          etc., and yet he complains of dryness of heart here!*

By dryness of heart, he means that the vital is not given free play.

          You have very admirably explained in NK's poem Jackal,
          *how the lower nature rushes towards the subconscient, and
          as soon as I read it I could not resist drawing the conclusion
          that this is X's present picture, word for word. Do you agree?*

Yes, it is that. A certain part of him which belongs to the lower

848   CORRESPONDENCE WITH

vital was always rushing and has dragged away the rest.

>*. . . Why has this lower nature become so vehement this time?*

But it has been rising again and again vehemently for a long time.

>*Many times he wanted to go but you stopped him; why have you failed this time?*

This time I didn't try. It was becoming like a dog pulling at his leash and moaning miserably. Can't go on with that sort of thing for ever. So I had promised his outing, Bangalore and Cape Comorin. He changed it to Baroda and Almora after Bangalore. I said, All right. He gave up Almora and perhaps Baroda. I said, All right. Finally no Bangalore, but Calcutta, Almora and anywhere else and several months at least. I said, All right—Then for some reason the old drama (for up till now all was fairly reasonable except the "grim Meditation" affair and the intolerableness of Mother's withdrawal and loss of the Pranam which had made his sufferings just tolerable), of Mother's sternness, desire of death, never never shall I come back here—finally joy of going accompanied with sentimental effusions. That's the whole story.

>*Will he come back with his lower fires run down and, thus a changed man, jump into the spiritual sea? For a time perhaps, but will not the hydra-headed monster rise up again?*

Yes, if there is no radical change. But only Mahakali can bring that about. Up to now we have given her no chance.

>*Isn't it true that in Yoga desires enjoyed are more harmful than rejected or repressed?*

At any rate in this Yoga.

>*Some say he hasn't gained anything substantial. Why, his psychic has surely developed in these 8 years. . .*

Rather say—it was beginning to develop by fits and starts interrupted by periods of vital violent reaction. Of course if he had

SRI AUROBINDO   849

stayed and gone through it, the psychic should have prevailed in the
end. But —

> Did he not realise that there is nothing, after all, in lower
> enjoyments?

He said so always.

> After this realisation can there be a fresh necessity for
> further enjoyment?

If there is no radical change, there can.

> Is it possible that he won't return at all, or will come back
> after many years?

With X everything is possible.

> "Won't return" seems impossible for have you not said that
> his success is sure and that you will carry him yourself to his
> goal?

I put a proviso, "If you are faithful to your seeking for the Divine".

> How is it that in spite of tremendous cost of Force and
> Energy, you could not change his views about your Yoga?

His mind changed somewhat, but his vital clung to the feeling
of frustration by the Yoga and therefore abused the Yoga. It wanted
either satisfaction of its play or brilliant experiences to replace
them or both together. Not getting its way, it damned the Yoga as
grim, horrible etc. All the time it refused to go on steadily with the
thing that would be effective.

> Quarrels with J, grimness of A, estrangement with N, etc.,
> etc., are they reasons for deserting this Yoga?

For a man with X's vital they seem governing reasons.

> He has read so many of your books, has had so many letters

*from you, yet he doesn't give any importance to inner things
— calm, silent, steady progress? What have you done then,
Sir?*

You are speaking as if it was his thinking mind that refused. His
thinking mind was changing its attitude. It was the vital mind that
refused inwardness, silence etc.

> *Unfortunately he seemed to think that Mother is harder
> than you: she is grim and doesn't love etc., etc.*

That is because Mother's pressure for a change is always strong —
even when she doesn't put it as force it is there by the very nature
of the Divine Energy in her. But it was just this change his vital did
not want — hence the feeling.

> *He will suffer terribly, I fear, outside. Is it then his soul's
> necessity for further experience? Has the soul any such
> need?*

If the soul had not, it would not be here in this world of Ignorance.
It is for the experience of Ignorance that it is here.

> *It baffles me to think that a man who had so much self-
> confidence regarding poetry, music, and achieved success
> with sheer industry, could do nothing in Yoga with so much
> of your Force. . .*

What a delusion! All the industry in the world could not have made
him a poet, a novelist, a prosodist, an effective writer on serious
questions. . . None of you realise that X had talent but no genius
before he came here — Tagore is right there, except in music — and
even there many criticised him as shallow, limited, superficial;
merely pretty, lacking in depth, power, greatness. I saw a letter of
an admirer the other day who told X that formerly his music had
been full of show and ostentation, but now there was an immense
change, it had become true and genuine. . . But he had a strong vital
and Mother and I saw that there was stuff here which could be made
into something. And we made it. . .

SRI AUROBINDO   851

>*He has supported himself in many things, saying that he*
>*had your sanction. You gave him absolute freedom. . .*

It was no use interfering—he would have done it all the same.
And these things—talks, food, sociality were not the crucial things
in his case. To press in his case on these points would only have
prevented all chance of his giving an opportunity to the sadhana.
It is not necessary in all cases to put this kind of pressure,—it depends on the case and the nature.

>*Another thing that hurt me was K's revolt. How could*
>*he say such things against you when he broke with X over*
>*you and Ramakrishna?*

My dear Sir, these fits are periodical with K—it is only the remarks
against myself that were new. Ever since he came here, he has been
announcing from time to time his departure.

>*He came here, I understand, on this earth, only for you!*

Eh, what?

>*What has been achieved if after 13 or 14 years of sadhana,*
>*there is a lack of faith in the Guru?*

Considering what K was, much has been achieved. But in a way
nothing is really achieved until all is.

>*Is that not enough to show that real faith is not yet there?*

Faith is there in parts of the being, absent in others.

>*Now, if K behaves in this way and X can leave the Asram*
>*after 8 years, two opposites—what about us?*

Opposites, but for the same reasons—a physical mind clinging
like a leech to its own wrong ideas of traditional sadhana and a
vital that does not want to surrender, to lose independence and its
own way of satisfaction.

What have you kept in store for us, Sir? Not sandesh and rasagolla! Will the sadhaks tumble one by one in this way as your Supramental comes nearer and nearer? Then with whom will you enjoy your Supramental? Night and day you are soaring and soaring.

Romantic one! I am not soaring and soaring—I am digging and digging, "Go to the ant, thou sluggard" sort of affair.

You don't even look to see what fires your wings are throwing on our mortal frames!

My wings are throwing no fire. If anything happens to your mortal frames, it is your own kerosene stoves that are responsible.

Why don't you give us any word of hope? When will your Gentleman come down, if he will?

Bother your words of hope. I am concerned with getting things done, (if people will kindly allow it and not be making a row all the time)—not with words.

I am shaken to the roots, for I fear I may share no better fate in your hands. Nevertheless all your promises will be fulfilled one day, for the Divine is eternal and so is the soul.

Well, that ought to be enough.

. . . How is it that a person professing a deep love for you is strongly attached to another one, and asks you to have trust in him or her? Isn't it a duplicity? I can't tolerate such conduct, and get rather disturbed. . .

You speak like a Daniel come to judgment. If you could only be calm like Daniel in the den of lions when these things happen, it would be all right.

. . . Seeing all this I have made up my mind to cut off all vital human relations. . .

SRI AUROBINDO   853

I say that all that is magnificent, if you can do it. But can't you see
that it is the inward change that is wanted — the inward plunge?
These dramatic outward breaks lead only to new joinings. Neither
you nor she can keep to it. If there comes a strong ingoing movement,
then it is another matter. That of itself would make it possible to
readjust the relations or to withdraw if necessary. But splashings
about on the surface — will it lead to anything? It does not look
like it.

> *If I have shown X's other side, it is needless to tell you that
> I have seen his finer side too, and have profited much by it.
> Affection can be there even when one criticises somebody,
> can't there?*

Yes, of course.

Outward breakings away and rejoinings, what's the use of that?
The remedy lies inside you. Try to go inward, find the Mother
there, find your true self, your psychic being. Afterwards J won't
matter — you may be her friend or her literary collaborator or
neither and it won't make a jot of difference — I have spoken.

> *You may congratulate yourself, Sir, on this invasion of
> surrealism [10.3.37]! But L is better. What have you done
> with S's spine? I saw her still going strong; result of your
> operation?*

The spine was surrealistic — her going it strong is realistic.

> *Krishnayya says that you have asked him to stop Hadensa
> as it is of no use now.*

Nonsense — it is he who wanted to stop, saying no improvement,
very costly — So I said, he could stop.

> *P's carbuncle is much better — says bandage is now bondage!*

Seems much struck by Mother's force as per cure carbuncle — no
gratitude to the doctor. Such is life!

March 11, 1937

854   CORRESPONDENCE WITH

*All interest in life has disappeared, Sir! Poems are a bore;
what prescription?*

Shift to a centre within.

Our chief centre has gone!

I suppose he will find plenty of radii in his new-old circumference.

*Poor fellow speaks about my affection in his letter. What
an illusion!*

Illusion? This is poetry, sir.

*Yes, Sir, such is life! But in P's case I must give more
credit to Mother, for his quick cure. Good he believes in
her Force, for you will have a disciple of the Warrior-land
[Punjab] of which you have none.*

Have several (not here, but there) but they are almost all neurasthenics!

Only, he is a little too old and too much chaperoned by V!

Great heavens! V has got hold of him — Poor fellow!

We have to get Hadensa tubes for B; shall we?

Yes.

Nishikanta has congestion of throat.

Result of Customs? or of custom?

March 12, 1937

*What about my book, Sir? Haven't decided where you will
begin and where you will end? or keeping it for Sunday?*

My dear Sir, if you write a Mahabharat, you can't expect the
answer however scrappy to be finished in one or two nights among

SRI AUROBINDO   855

a mass of other work? *Nous progressâmes*[1] — that's the state of things.

> *Still feeling bad — not for the loss of the centre, but don't know exactly.*

No? you don't feel অনাথ?[2]

> *Under P, you wrote: "They are almost all nervous thieves"? Gracious!*

I didn't. I wrote "neurasthenics" — neurasthenic Warriors, sir!

> *And about Nishikanta — "Result of — or of custom?"*

Customs (British). Reference to their outing with Dilip.

March 13, 1937

> *How did you hear of this remark* anāth?

Any number of vivid reports of the great event — this detail among others.

> *I find that as a result of your Force, A has had only one vomit today!*

Evidently my Force is growing just as my handwriting is improving!

> *Doraiswamy better; pain.*

Is it that he has a better pain? or that the fact that he has a pain shows that he is better; or that he is better but still has pain? An aphoristic style lends itself to many joyfully various interpretations.

March 14, 1937

---

[1] We have made some progress (i.e. "I have made a start on your letter").
[2] *anāth:* orphan.

Obviously, evidently, undoubtedly, Sir, your Force is growing! By the number of departees, one can see that!

They are not departees — yet. X gone on a spree — says he will one day come back. V sent as a missionary by the Mother — don't expect his mission will be very fruitful though. R went for her property — property and herself held up by family, as we told her it would be etc. So no sufficient proof of Force here. If they had all gone saying ফিরব না, কখন ফিরব না[1] as X threatened once, the proof would be conclusive.

March 15, 1937

About the "departees", they may come back all right, but why did they go? Because some pressure acted on the old knots and they had to give up the Yoga, at least temporarily. Once one takes up this Yoga, what is family, property or anything else?

But R didn't give up Yoga — she was going on very well. Only the idea of her property shut up in others' hands and ready to disappear, obsessed her. She wanted to bring it and give it to Mother. It was a mistake, for it was not worth the risk and trouble and interruption to Sadhana. But there was a vital push and attachment that made her recur always to the idea.

You have forgotten D.S. who went mad after 8 or 9 years of Yoga?

What Yoga? This idea of D.S. being a great Yogi is a queer thing.

Have you read the letter and poems by X? Anything to communicate regarding the letter?

Nothing special.

The poems seem extremely fine, don't they?

Yes, I said so.

[1] Never again shall I come back.

SRI AUROBINDO   857

*You can't call them sentimental this time, Sir, because
they are addressed to the Divine!*

Well, one can be sentimental with the Divine, if one particularly
wants to!

*X is having plenty of garlands, meetings, feastings etc.
Spree indeed! . . . Good enough for a change, what?*

Change, certainly.

*Are you writing a Mahabharat in reply to my "Maha-
bharat", I wonder!*

I was.

*Guru, I hope you won't "ash"[1] me for spoiling your after-
noon "spree", by this letter, will you?*

Where is the spree in the afternoon? Neither afternoon, evening,
night, nor morning. Spree, indeed!

*Laugh with the sonnets and cry with the letter [X's], if
you can. Very touching! If the "কোমল ব্যবহার"[2] of the
people there had not been so good, it would have been
splendid methinks.*

You recommend me a fit of hysteria? No, sir. The sonnets are as
usual, quite admirable. So, I dare say, was the কোমল ব্যবহার —
By the way, his uncle has developed a carbuncle! And X expects
me to cure it! A case for you, sir. After P!

*[Regarding a poem of J's:] The confusions of muddy eddies
of life are at an end?*

Wish they were! Jehovah!

How far down is your plume? Do you see the great Tail yet?

---

[1] Reduce to ashes.
[2] *komal vyavahār:* kind behaviour.

858   CORRESPONDENCE WITH

Tail is there — but no use without the head.

March 16, 1937

> *Why did you say "I was"? Have you stopped writing the*
> *Mahabharat, then?*

Because I can make no time — Night after night have to write
letters, letters, letters, not to speak of other things.

> *Everything seems to be queer in this world, Sir, especially*
> *in this yogic world! When a fellow [D.S.] works hard at*
> *French, medicine, trying to improve the Dispensary and*
> *himself, and thereby serve the Divine better, it is bad.*
> *Too much concentration and meditation is worse.*
> *[Sri Aurobindo underlined "and himself".]*

There is where you miss the truth and he missed it also — he did
not try to "improve himself", at any rate in any Yogic way — he
might try to aggrandise himself but that is another matter. Self-
aggrandisement does not save from collapse.

> *When one follows the rule "eat, drink and be merry"*
> *it is the worst.*

Well, I never heard that 'to eat, drink and be merry' was one of
the paths of Yoga — unless Charvak's way is one of Yoga.

> *I am coming to X's view that your Yoga will always remain*
> *yours. Nobody will ever catch its head or tail, except a*
> *few perhaps. Let us pin our faith on the "Head" now. The*
> *tail has noosed many!*

It is not my Yoga that is difficult to get the head or tail of — it is
your and X's and others' views about Yoga that are weird and
wonderful. If a fellow is brilliant in French and Sanskrit, you
think he is a wonderful Yogi, but then it is the people who are first
in the Calcutta B.A. who must be the greatest Yogis. If one objects
to spending all the energy in tea and talk, you say "What queer
gurus these are and what queer ideas", as if sociability were the
base of the Brahman — or on the contrary you think everybody

SRI AUROBINDO

must shut himself up in a dark room, see nobody, go mad with want of food and sleep—and when we object to that, you say "Who can understand this Yoga?" Have you never heard of Buddha's maxim "No excess in any direction"—or of Krishna's injunction "Don't eat too much or abstain from eating, don't drop sleep or sleep too much; don't torture the soul with violent tapasya—practise Yoga steadily, without despondency. Don't abstain from works and be inactive, but don't think either that mere work will save you. Dedicate your works to the Divine, do it as a sacrifice, reach the point at which you feel that the works are not yours but done for you etc., etc. Through meditation, through dedicated works, through bhakti—all these together, arrive at the divine consciousness and live in it." Buddha and Krishna are not considered to be unintelligible big Absurdities, yet when we lay [stress] on the same things, you all stare and say "What's this new unheard-of stuff?" It is the result I suppose of having modern-minded disciples who know all about everything and can judge better than any Guru, but to whom the very elements of Yoga are something queer and cold and strange. Kismet!

> *Have you heard that Y is also tottering, or has tottered already? Couldn't get over the shock of D.S.'s madness?*

Y has written to us already. He wants to make a marriage and farewell to the world trip, somewhat like X's. . . But he has been tottering, as you call it, ever since he was here, so that is nothing new. . .

> *Guru, Chand wants to know what will be the true spirit of surrender for him and how he ought to receive Mother's flower "Surrender" which he has been getting often.*

Why for him? Surrender is the same for everybody.

> *Any illumination?*

None.

> *There is some law point here and reference to A.P. House[1]*

---

[1] Arya Publishing House, Calcutta.

also. God knows who this B.K. is, who requires your permission to go into all this business. Well?

B.K. is a "disciple" and has been Manager of A.P.H. but is now to be relieved of his duties. He was at the head of some institution in Khulna — forgotten which. Don't know what status he has for the purpose. Probably he is or was a lawyer—but not sure. Permission be hanged!

March 17, 1937

> [*Morning*]
> *You perhaps had a hope that at least you would have some respite with no more of X's voluminous correspondence. Much mistaken, Sir! Much mistaken!*

So long as I have not to write voluminous answers.

> *I am sure next August will be a great victorious occasion with swarms of élites of Calcutta at your feet. Happy at the prospect?*

Horrifying idea! Luckily the élites are not in the habit of swarming.

> [*Afternoon*]
> *All these orations, successes, etc. of X, raise another question—whether the Divine also wanted that His name should be spread now.*

The Divine is quite indifferent about it. Or rather more privacy would be better for the work.

> [*Evening*]
> *What? X also has a "message"? But all I heard was that he had become restless.*

I said that his [Y's] outing was somewhat like X's — i.e. a social round.

> *What, Y has gone out to deliver a "message"? What message, Sir?*

SRI AUROBINDO   861

There is nothing about message. Marriage, marriage—two mar-
riages, in fact. Not that he is going to marry 2 wives, but he is
going to see the misfortune of two others consummated and
gloat over it.

> *But why exactly did D.S. tumble?—if not private. Self-
> aggrandisement only? Can't be!*

Why not? Never heard of megalomania?

> *I heard he was touchy regarding his wife and wife touchy
> about him—My God, grazes the skin, almost, Sir!*

Touchy means what? And how does touchiness graze the skin?

> *Now about X's tea and butter!...*

It isn't butter—it's "tea and talk".

> *All these were, it seems, generously granted by you to X.
> No bar, no restriction—full freedom, carte blanche...*

They were granted by me as a concession to his nature, because
by self-deprivation he would land himself in the seas of despair—
not as a method of reaching the Brahman. He was trying to do
what his nature would not allow. It was only if he got intense
spiritual experience that he could give up tea and talk without
wallowing in misery—Is it so difficult to understand a simple thing
like that? I should have thought it would be self-evident even to
the dullest intelligence.

> *You remember your reply to his "ascetic" letter about
> giving up cooking, shaving his head, etc., etc.? Well,
> what is this now? Sociability not the base of Brahman,
> surely? That's what we all thought, but your sanction and
> support that each has a different path etc., took our support
> away.*

Because I allowed him to talk, and objected to his making an
ostentatious ascetic ass of himself, does it follow that the talk and

tea were given as part of his Yoga? If the Mother allowed butter or eggs to Y for his physical growth, does it follow that butter and eggs are the bases of the Brahman? If somebody has a stomachache and I send him to the dispensary, does it follow that a stomachache, the dispensary, Nirod and allopathic drugs are the perfect way to spiritualisation? Don't be an a—, I mean a Gandhilike logician!

> *My poems are now getting less surrealistic and losing all charm of incomprehensibility . . .*

Necessary transition, I suppose.

> *Also the power of bold expressions, images, etc. are disappearing. . . Why?*

Get them in another way, bold and original but not surrealistic, so that people instead of crying "Very fine but what the devil does he mean?", will shout "Ah ha! Wah! wah!" in a chorus of approbation for your genius and personality much as X is getting in Calcutta. How do you like the prospect?

March 18, 1937

> *Nishikanta and Jyoti say, about my recent poems, that there is much improvement. They're more cogent, harmonious and still retain my originality and surrealism too.*

They are more cogent and harmonious; there is also plenty of individuality, fine images, lines and phrases. But the surrealistic *audacity* of phrase and image is in abeyance. My suggestion is that it has to come back without the surrealism and with this greater clarity and harmony and more perfect building. That's why I said "transition".

I say, there's a fellow in this world who says that besides occasional emissions of normal and orthodox kind with dreams, he gets almost daily slight discharges without dream in light sleep (day sleep or morning sleep renewed after waking) and there are *"internal" discharges* which don't come out until there is (after some days, I believe) a proper discharge. This he supposes due to a liquification of the semen due to former bad habits. When there

SRI AUROBINDO   863

are these internal discharges his head becomes empty and giddy,
and he expects if it goes on there will be no head left — or at least
nothing inside it. Now I have heard of internal haemorrhage but
not of internal discharges which seems self-contradictory in itself
as a phrase. I can understand habitual loss of semen or weakness
in retention due to past misuse, but what is this? Does your medical
science shed any light? have you had any experience in treatment
of such things so as to give me a direction for this distressed trav-
eller towards headlessness? What?

March 19, 1937

*I am afraid I can't throw much light on these "internal
discharges", unless it means that instead of coming out
they flow back to the bladder due to some obstacle in the
urethra. Hardly a possibility.*

They can be stopped halfway by will in an emission — but he does
not mean that.

*If there is constant excitement there might be a constant
dribbling also. . .*

But it is only in these two sleeps and without dream. He says
waking time is all right.

*Or there might be a gleety discharge which may be mis-
taken for semen.*

Hasn't spoken of that. But would it come only in special sleeps
like this?

What does R say on this matter?

Haven't asked him. Afraid of a resonant explanation which would
leave me gobbrified and flabbergasted but no wiser than before.

But is he really sure that they are seminal discharges?

Can't make out. He distinguishes them from emission, speaks of
slight discharges and internal discharges — same thing apparently.

Lastly, if his testes have undergone some degeneration, the internal secretion may be deficient.

How could that be described as internal discharges in two special kinds of sleep?

Is my surmise enough to understand the matter?

No.

J is very much fascinated by the variety in chhanda in Dilip's and NK's work, and doesn't want to rest content only with the old forms. You say both forms can be beautiful. Why not try then this modern form, since we are your "modern disciples"?

No objection to trying. But is the form of Dilip and Nishikanta general in modern Bengali poetry? I thought it was Dilip's departure and much criticised by many? I don't think a rule or school can be made of these things. Let each follow his own genius.

যুগধর্ম্ম[1] *must be satisfied. You can't pooh-pooh it, when you want things to be intelligible to people. Otherwise they will damn it.*

I don't follow the যুগধর্ম্ম myself in English poetry — There I have done the opposite; tried to develop old forms into new shapes instead of being gloriously irregular. In my blank verse, I have minimised or exiled pauses and overflows.

Lord, sir! If you want to be intelligible and read by people, why do you write symbolic and sometimes almost surrealist poetry?

In your comment on my poetry, why did you underline "audacity"? French sense?

If I had intended the French sense, I would have written *"audace"*.

The word means boldness, daring. Does it suggest anything more? I don't like these "suggestions". One has ego enough

---

[1] *yugadharma:* spirit of the age, Time-spirit.

SRI AUROBINDO   865

> *and to spare. So please don't write: you have done this,*
> *you have done that!*

Don't understand all this. I thought you would like to get the
"audacious" originality back again in full in better form, so I
suggested that the transition could very well be moving towards
that. What the hell has all that got to do with egoism or with personal effort either?

> *Why bloat the ego still further when you know that sug-*
> *gestions and that sort of thing are no use? In Yoga, you*
> *say surrender, and in poetry — this personal effort business?*
> *No, Sir, no!*

Wait a minute — Where have I said that there is to be no personal
effort in Yoga? Kindly read the passages in The Mother about
tamasic surrender and the place of personal effort in the sadhana.

March 20, 1937

> *I think my expressions were rather surrealistic, so you*
> *helled them.*

What expressions?

> *Well, what I meant by "suggestions" was that I shall be*
> *led to think it was I, my great personal effort, that brought*
> *in the boldness of images, audacity, etc. Won't that be*
> *egoism and personal effort business?*

Do you mean that you don't want your poetry to improve because
that would make you egoistic? Very queer, sir.

> *What about the book, Sir?*

What book?

> [*After I gave a brief interpretation of a poem of J's, Sri*
> *Aurobindo gave a further explanation.*]

... Very complicated operation. Kindly explain or translate or do something to remove my bewilderment. I am afraid your prose is becoming as surrealistic as your poetry — full of ellipses and suppressed concepts. Today it has bewildered me thrice (see your poetry book,) where I have had to ask "what expressions?" "what book?"

If these internal discharges can be stopped halfway by will, what happens to them? Do they go back to the vesicles or come out in the urine?

Don't know — they don't give any sign afterwards.

... But is it not usual to have losses without dreams in sleep?

Yes, but that is quite another matter.

I hear it is common in people who have misused their parts, and the fact of their getting them after sleep may be due to lack of voluntary nervous control.

In sleep.

Or if the prostates are enlarged, they may press on the vesicles more directly in the lying position, and thus cause the discharge.

Yes, constipation also produces discharge.

I can't think of any other possibility. Does he unconsciously do involuntary movements in sleep, I wonder!

Not likely.

March 21, 1937

Another letter from Chand — family matters and something about his Bank trouble! What a fine thing to be an Avatar, what?

SRI AUROBINDO   867

Why? You think an Avatar has to take in the Bank troubles of
his Chands? No fear!

> How the devil could I mean that I don't want my poetry
> to improve? I certainly want it to improve to its zenith,
> but it must not bring in the egoistic idea that I have done
> it by my own power, as your expressions "you have to do
> this", "you have to bring this etc., etc." is very likely to
> feed the egoism. That's all, Sir! Not clear?

Well, sir, if I can't say you, must I write "that body" or "the phenomenon of an apparent Doctor-poet"? Or there must be an impersonal commotion in the apparently personal part which might
be pragmatically called "doing this" or "bringing this". That would
discourage egoism; but it might discourage my writing also as
well as stifle your poetic inspiration while you stared at the round-
abouts.

> "What book?" you ask after 2 or 3 weeks? My "Maha-
> bharat", Sir, or Ramayana, if you like!

Good heavens! who would have thought of that?

> Yes, I tried reading The Mother, but the first chapters
> gave me a fright and made my blood freeze — "no use, no
> use" resounds everywhere, resulting in the idea of giving
> up even the ghost of Yoga!

I suggested to you to read the passages referring to the necessity
of effort so long as the Force does not take up the whole business.

> About "internal discharge", I had a talk with Rajangam.
> Could you please wait till tomorrow?

Yes, certainly.

                                                    March 22, 1937

> . . . I am now waiting only for the Mahabharat, and in
> the meantime sharpening my sword!

868   CORRESPONDENCE WITH

Well, don't brandish the sword in the void—that's all.

[*A long report on "internal discharge".*]

Any remedy?

March 23, 1937

Y asked me if I had written to you anything about X, she would like to see your answers. Will you take the trouble, Sir, to cross the portions of your letters that I can show her? [*Sri Aurobindo twice underlined "cross" and "can".*]

Good Lord, sir, I can't do that. You forget that I will have to try to read my own hieroglyphs. I have no time for such an exercise— I leave it to others.

Today I have written 3 poems, Sir, from 2.30–4.45 p.m. Remarkable, isn't it?

Colossal!

N had fever in the evening again. . . Couldn't find anything in the lungs. Still something incipient may be going on as he had already pleurisy. Anyway, we can give him some medicine—Ayurvedic or allopathic?

That's the doctors' business. Whatever has been good for him.

I took Sanganswami to the oculist. He will scratch the conjunctiva a little suspecting something there.
About the remedy I am afraid! [*I suddenly took up N's report.*]

Afraid of what? Will make things worse?

But, I suppose, some nerve tonics, sedatives and gland products will have an effect. . .

I read with amazement—thought it was all about Sanganswami's eye.

SRI AUROBINDO   869

> *J says she makes no mental effort; tries to keep quiet, yet
> nothing comes down.*

Difficulty of shunting the train.

March 24, 1937

> *Guru, here is a history, a prayer and a task! I hope you
> will note the dates of X's performances.* [1]

Noted, but he is sometimes late in his information. That doesn't
matter though.

> *He has given me some work—shall I ask Anilbaran and
> Nolini? But for Anilbaran your sanction is necessary.*

Sanction for what? The suggestion is rather vague.

> *Shall I send him Arjava's poems?*

If Arjava consents.

> *You will note, Sir, he writes that he does not doubt that
> his material success and fame and glory are by your Force,
> but all doubts are about his yogic success. Can't under-
> stand his contradiction. Does he mean he has capacities
> in some lines which the Divine can push, but yogic cap-
> acity nil, so the Divine can't pull?*

That's his latest idea—though not so late, for it was growing for
some time.

> *Anyhow... There is going to be plenty of money, Sir, of
> which Mother has great need!*

No objection if it comes.

> *Please explain your "shunting". How can the difficulty
> be solved?*

---

[1] X's musical recitals on the radio.

870   CORRESPONDENCE WITH

When one has run always on one line with great success, it is
difficult to shunt to another. Time, aspiration, inner working. Sorry
if I am indefinite, but—

> *... Despair doesn't seem to help.*

It doesn't.

> *On the other hand, it hinders, doesn't it?*

Yes.

> *A quiet aspiration with faith works best.*

Quite so.

> *Preaching?*

Very correct preach.

> *I told J confidently that poetry is bound to develop.*

Of course it will.

> *Today J named me an "angel of hope", Sir. From a "devil
> of despair" to an "angel of hope"? Your Yoga has worked,
> Sir! You can congratulate me a little.*

Mille félicitations!

March 25. 1937

> *"Mille félicitations"? Thank you, Sir! But just note that
> it was with regard to poetry only. Yoga has to come. With-
> out that no felicitations are any good, at least for me.*

Well, well—all in due time—*mille félicités* as well as *félicitations*.

> *A funny thing happened last night. It began this way:
> since 6.30 p.m. I had been feeling the Mother's Presence,
> and more vividly yours, until I went to bed.*

SRI AUROBINDO
871

> *In the evening when I went to the pier, for a while your
> entire face appeared vividly before my eyes. I was so happy
> that I forgot the moon above and was drinking in your
> Presence. Then gradually it dissolved, leaving only the
> outline. At times it seemed to be before me, at others as
> if the whole sky was pervaded by your Presence. I returned
> home, but went again to the pier at 9 p.m. with J. While
> she was talking, I was perceiving the outline of your Pre-
> sence, and no other thought came in or went out. J's talk
> had no effect on it. Within I was automatically uttering
> your name and the Mother's.*
>
> *At 10.30 p.m. I went to bed, after a short concentration.
> I was in a sort of semi-slumberous state wherein a great
> pressure was being exerted on the head. The whole body
> became hot and was perspiring. The pressure increased
> so much that I said I must come out of it or burst. It was
> such a possession. I relaxed myself and rolled into sleep.*
>
> *I hope you will pick the grain out of the chaff. What
> sort of an affair is this, Sir? Trying to cut my throat or
> burst my head?*

Very good indeed — that is something like a beginning.

Well, sir, the Presence not finding an entrance into your waking
mind easy, tried to take advantage of half sleep to do it. (Half
sleep is always a favourable condition for these things). But your
body consciousness, not being familiar with such spiritual pene-
trations, got into a stew — and as a stew is accompanied by heat
and steam, — so your body got hot and perspired.

Naturally, when it found so much resistance, it increased to
meet the resistance.

Obviously, to burst is undesirable.

Throat not in the picture — Tried to steal a march into your
head.

> *Did I do anything wrong by trying to relax?*

It is better to relax than to burst.

> *. . . Sometimes I have felt inclined to doubt the Presence,
> but I think I should not, what?*

872   CORRESPONDENCE WITH

Certainly not — doubt under such circumstances is perfectly imbecile.

> *Still a small snake of doubt says (not regarding yesterday's feeling, though), "It is all imagination—"*

Rubbish!

> *It goes on "If not. . . why have you to concentrate and call the Presence? By its very nature the Presence should at once make you see that it is there as if it were an object before you, without making you imagine things."*

Sir, is the Presence of a physical nature or a spiritual fact? And is the physical sense accustomed or able to see or feel spiritual things — a spiritual Presence, a non-material Form? To see the Brahman everywhere is not possible unless you develop the inner vision — to do that you have to concentrate. To see non-material forms is indeed possible for a few, because they have the gift by nature, but most can't do it without developing the subtle sight. It is absurd to expect the Divine to manifest his Presence without your taking any trouble to see it, — you have to concentrate.

> *Just now, as I am writing to you, I feel as if the Mother were looking at me and you too, but from your invulnerable fortress.*

It simply means you have a subjective sense of our Presence. But must a subjective sense of things be necessarily a vain imagination? If so, no Yoga is possible. One has to take it as an axiom that subjective things can be as real as objective things. No doubt there may be and are such things as mental formations — but, to begin with, mental formations are or can be very powerful things, producing concrete results; secondly whether what one sees or hears is a mental formation or a real subjective object can only be determined when one has sufficient experience in these inward things.

> *What should I do to develop this experience further? It is the very* Thing, *you see, isn't it?*

SRI AUROBINDO   873

Yes, of course. What you have to do is to grow and let the experience grow.

> *Is this what you call going inward?*
> *[Sri Aurobindo drew a line from the word "inward" leading to his reply.]*

No, not quite — but it is evidently the result of some opening from within — for without that opening one cannot become aware of Presences or Forms that are super-physical in their nature.

> *This experience, I feel, is the means of escape from worldly pleasures, isn't it?*

Yes.

> *I feel now some strength; nothing can disturb me in my relation with people. Good?*

Exceedingly good.

> *Please give me some necessary instructions, not depending on my notes, as to what should be done. If I have seen the tail it must lead me to the head!*

There is nothing to do but to go on concentrating and calling the Presence within and without you, the opening, the power to receive and let it come. The more the mind falls quiet during or as the result of concentration, the better (no other thought in or out). But no need to struggle for that, must come of itself by the concentration.

                                                              March 26, 1937

> *C is involved in a cheating case; by some compromises he can get out of it...*

What does he mean by compromises? Lies? If he goes on with this sort of thing, how the devil is he ever to come out of his messes?

> *...Z attributes her trouble to R's insufficient or even negligent treatment. Strange! I saw that R took much*

care and he cured her of that terrible attack of hiccough. Such is life, Sir! What?

Z is a liar and says anything she wants to — she is also semi-hysteric and believes anything she wants to. Such is life and such are humans.

Shall we try Fandorine? Her back-ache also is due to retroversion of the uterus, probably.

If it is retroverted uterus, Fandorine will have no effect. If it is bad circulation etc., then it is the best. Anyway you may try it.

S.B. has intense itching — the whole body is swollen and red.

But what nature of eruption? She has sent a howl — can't sleep, etc.

B complains of more pain!

Yes, he has also sent an epistolary howl.

Suggesting enema from tomorrow. Lead and opium lotion for injection. This lotion, as you see, is sedative and astringent.

I suppose it can do no harm?
Is not B too sedentary for a man with piles?

March 29, 1937

The trouble is that people expect their ailments to disappear by a miracle! Doctors are not Gods and Gods are not always miraculous, are they?

Miracles can be done, but there is no reason why they should be all instantaneous, whether from Gods or doctors.

Suddenly at 5 p.m. B's pain vanished. So I justify his epistle, Sir! His thundering scowl burst your ear!

SRI AUROBINDO   875

It wasn't a scowl, even a thundering surrealist one — it was a
tympanum-piercing howl — so one had to do something.

> *K gave her baby 2 spoons of milk of magnesia. Result —*
> *copious motions with blood and mucus discharge; no sleep,*
> *restlessness, crying, etc. . . Looks like irritation due to*
> *heavy dose of magnesia! Must K's babies have something*
> *every time she comes here?*

Well, if she gives them 2 spoons of milk of magnesia, they are
bound to. That was the way D's last baby got killed here, though
M began it before she came. But the result was a dysentery which
nothing can cure. But does your Science approve of purging babies
of that age? In France, Mother says, the doctors (those who speci-
alise for children at any rate) forbid purgatives being given *on
any excuse* to children under twelve months.

> *Some Force from you is wanted, for the baby can't aspire*
> *and surrender, Sir!*

Exactly! that's why milk of magnesia should not be given. Any
baby treated in that way will need much aspiration and surrender
to counteract the results.

> *[About the patient with the "internal discharge":] He says*
> *that only after slight sleep or rest he feels giddy, weak and*
> *the condition lasts for 2 or 3 days. From this he gathers*
> *that there has been the discharge.*

It is only gathered then! I was insisting that it was not possible,
but the fellow *ne voulait pas démordre*.[1]

> *But do you know that he is awfully, terribly and damnably*
> *constipated?*

I knew he was constipative, but not so adverbially.

> *By the way, I want to know, just as a piece of information,*

---

[1] The fellow stuck to what he said; the fellow wouldn't give up his point.

what Mother is going to do about the awful smell around Belle Vue.

Smell was that of Godard's prawns. The Municipality has just thundered at him and given notice to the prawns to quit. I am told that there is a sensible odorous amelioration since the last two days.

March 30, 1937

2 p.m.
I asked Mother through Nolini, whether I should give an emetine injection to K's baby, she said—No medicines to babies under 1 year.

Emetine injection to a child of that age is not approved.

What Mother says is that this is not an illness, but an accident caused by the purgative given. The tissues have been hurt and have to recover. What would be best is to give not a medicine properly speaking but something which would protect the injured tissues while they reformed. Mother does not know whether what is given to adults for that purpose can be administered to children.

They say that the pains seem to have decreased, as the child slept well.

As regards diet, he is given freely barley water, whey and glucose water. Shall we give milk?

Milk might be too heavy. The diet seems all right.

Now I am wondering if Nolini heard it right. Did Mother disapprove only of emetine or all medicines?

Mother had said to me about the purgatives, not about medicines. Emetine for a child like that she would of course never sanction.

[*Between 2 p.m. and 8.30 p.m.*]

31.3.37

Nirod
In view of the nature of the illness of K's child and its development, I think we cannot take any longer the responsibility—if

SRI AUROBINDO   877

you think best, we can call in Dr. Valle who, I hear, has a child
of his own and ought to have some experience with the maladies
of children. You might see him at once, if possible.

SRI AUROBINDO

[*Evening*]
*...Now emetine being out of the question, we can give
what we gave yesterday: 1) Bismuth 2) Soda Bicarb 3)
Kaolin...*

Kaolin was the kind of thing Mother was thinking of as utilisable.

*I asked Nolini, he said — no medicines, no medicines.
But your evening answer [to the note written at 2 p.m.]
doesn't say that. It says — no emetine, no purgative, but
"something which would protect the injured tissues..."
Again at the end you say "Mother had said to me about the
purgatives, not about medicines." It is all very puzzling
and I am in a fix...*

Well, since medicines have been used, and the atmosphere is not
the right one for No-medicine, you can go on, — but nothing
violent like emetine. The Mother offered to call Valle and in that
case of course the responsibility would be with him, but K has
refused.

*What do you say, Sir, about this poem? Somewhat forced
and artificial, no rhythm?*

I am afraid so. Rather drum-drum-drummy-brang-clangy.

I have marked in two places, please see if they jar your ears.

I am afraid they do.

March 31, 1937

878   CORRESPONDENCE WITH

April 1937

Have you ever had a headache by giving up tea?...

Yes, of course. Whenever you stop it suddenly, gives headache in revenge.

> *Today I stopped the habit of morning tea. The result:*
> *a headache since 11 a.m. Or is it the Force trying to break*
> *my precious head?*

No, it is the tea-habit, furious at being given up.

> *About K's baby — there seems hardly any improvement in*
> *the number of stools, except that blood has stopped. Don't*
> *you think the number should decrease now; if possible,*
> *stop altogether?*

Decrease certainly — slow down to nothing — but sudden stoppage might not be so good — although usually if it is the right medicine it does happen.

> *Does Mother favour Dover's powder? That will reduce*
> *the number which was 20 today.*

Can't suggest anything,—since medicine needed, must find your way.
    20 motions in a day too much for a child of that age.

                                                    April 1, 1937

> *4.30 p.m.*
> *Guru, finished! My concentration, peace, bliss, all gone!*
> *At this moment I am dull, dull like clay and hence am*
> *compelled to write and groan.*
>   *After I wrote about the experience, the thing gradually*
> *melted away. Why? The devil knows. All I have done, if*
> *they can come under any criminal section, is that I have*

SRI AUROBINDO   879

> *enjoyed some food with Anilkumar and Nishikanta, and narrated the experience to X.*

That would have been better left undone.

> *... Suddenly to drop into an underground cell is, I don't know what.*

Everybody drops. I have dropped myself thousands of times during the sadhana. What rose-leaf princess sadhaks you all are!

> *Sometimes I cannot but subscribe to S's opinion that this Yoga is not for us. . . Some say the preliminary stage is the same in all Yogas; only the later stage is difficult here. I don't think it is true, for here, from the very start, it works for the change of nature, working to the very details, which other Yogas know nothing about. They leave the nature out altogether.*

According to those who have practised them, in the old Yogas one has to be prepared to pass 12 years simply disciplining, disciplining without a single experience before one can expect as a right any single experience. If one gets experiences so much the better, but one can't expect or claim.

> *Therefore one has to build a strong foundation; consequently more time, more bricks, more work, more money, etc., are needed. Then how can the initial stage be the same as in other Yogas?*

Allow me to point out that here there are any number of people who have had experiences which would be highly prized outside. There are even one or two who have had the Brahman realisation in a single year. But it is the fashion here to shout and despair and say we have got nothing and nobody can get anything in this Yoga. I believe the pretensions of the Pondicherry sadhaks to have an easy and jolly canter to the goal or else think themselves baffled martyrs would be stared at with surprise in any other Asram.

880   CORRESPONDENCE WITH

> *Perhaps or certainly, you are giving Force to K's baby,*
> *but why no visible effect? He is an infant, no resistance on*
> *his side... You cured D's acute abscess in the abdomen,*
> *simply by your Force and no medicine. Where is the trouble*
> *here?*

Don't talk nonsense. It is because he is an infant that the Force cannot work easily on him. D is not an infant.

> *I am rather worried. No blessed opening in any direction.*
> *One has to grope and grope. You don't give any blessed*
> *intuition either!*

The Mother has no intuition for medicines for infants—You must find out yourself.

> *If you like, I will completely stop all medicines and leave*
> *him to you and Mother.*

That we cannot tell you to do. It could only have been guaranteed at the beginning and with a proper mental atmosphere in the people.

> *Shall I report twice a day about the baby?*

Yes, certainly.

April 2, 1937

> *(1.30. p.m.)*
> *I thought breast milk should be suspended for K's baby,*
> *when you said that milk is heavy [31.3.37].*

It was supposed that you meant cow's milk. Mother's milk, if the mother is healthy, is the best medicine for these things — Calomel is not to be given. Also it is better not to follow R's advice in these matters or to try too many medicines. The mother's milk and sleep are the most important things for cure — some medicine is a help at the most. More — too many medicines — make things worse rather than better. Anyhow what the Mother wants is for it to be possible for the mother and child to go to Madras tomorrow

SRI AUROBINDO   881

night with D. She has ordered K to that effect.

> [*Evening*]
>
> [*After the summary of A's prolonged treatment had been given:*]
> *So is it hopeful or hopeless?*

Hopeful on the whole.

> *I could not write poetry for 2 days. Along with the heavy work, a disgust for poetry has seized me, just when things were coming up. Misfortunes are usual with me, so no use complaining, what?*

Rubbish! Such "misfortunes" are usual with everybody—including myself.

                                                        April 3, 1937

> [*Afternoon*]
> . . . *It seems K and her child may go, though perhaps a little risky, as absolute rest is indicated.* . .

He will not be running about in the train. What is meant by absolute rest for a child of 4 months? To stay here is much more risky.

> *Mother's milk and sleep are now available, though the former not much. What about the number of stools? Can you help that?*

Medically, the effective treatment for the case and the person has not been found—Yogically, the mother has proved to be not a receptive instrument and the child also does not answer to the Force except for a short while and in a slight degree—the wisest thing for them is therefore to go.

> [*Evening*]
> *For heaven's sake don't include yourself in the misfortunes!*

But I never said that I was one of the misfortunes.

I am not Brahma to take them as part of the lila!

I thought everybody was Brahma, সর্ব্বমিদং ব্রহ্ম.[1] Anyway you are trying to do Yoga, so the sooner you adopt the lila attitude the better. Moreover, plenty of people undergo these "misfortunes" without lamentations—take them as the ordinary stuff of life.

No poetry today either! Hellish!

Well, you can try to straddle back into heaven tomorrow.

For K's baby, by "absolute rest" I meant that the jerkings in the train may not be very desirable.

I don't see why it should be worse than other rockings.

I have consulted all the writings on diarrhoea, all give only symptomatic treatment.

There you are in company for once with the homeopaths.

But whatever little the doctors have found by experience to be effective, is not acceptable to you. For instance they recommend Calomel, you say not to be given. . .

It is no use discussing these matters—the Mother's views are too far removed from the traditional nostrums to be understood by a medical mind, except those that have got out of the traditional groove or those who after long experience have seen things and can become devastatingly frank about the limitations of their own "science".

You remember Valle's treatment of Valentine? He gave all the blessed things one after another—2 or 3 emetine in spite of negative stools, opium, etc., till he cured her.

---

[1] *sarvamidam Brahma:* all this is Brahman.

SRI AUROBINDO   883

That is to say, he experimented at random—till Valentine cured
in spite of all this ill-treatment of her body. And yet you call medicine a "science".

> *If I had dealt with the case, I think you wouldn't have al-
> lowed me emetine at all? Why? Because of my inexper-
> ience or you don't want that anything drastic should happen
> by our treatment?*

Certainly not, under your responsibility. Doctors acting on their
own can try the kill or cure method—it's their own business.

> *I admit it is quite possible for Science to be wrong as it
> has been shown repeatedly.*

Very obviously.

> *I would have tried anti-serum and astringents, opium etc.
> and I think most of the doctors would have done that.*

Try everything one after the other and together and see if any
hits—that seems to be the method.

> *K doesn't believe that milk of magnesia is the predis-
> posing cause of the child's illness.*

Of course she won't, as that would make her responsible.

> *D says it is quite harmless. But it may be harmful also
> and it was so here.*

If it may be harmful, how can it be declared harmless?

> *Otherwise I don't see why after 6 or 8 motions, diarrhoea
> should have started.*

Ideas differ. Both the Mother and Pavitra were horrified at the
idea of a child of 4 months being given a purgative. The leading
Children's doctor in France told the Mother no child under 12

884   CORRESPONDENCE WITH

months should be given a purgative, as it is likely to do great harm and may be dangerous. But here, we understand, it is the practice to dose children freely with purgatives from their day of birth almost. Perhaps that and overadministration of medicines is one cause of excessive infant mortality.

You didn't say anything about the medicines for S.

What medicines? Sudarshan? you say she refuses.

April 4, 1937

Have you observed that the bodies of sadhaks and sadhikas have become abnormally sensitive? Even a small dose of medicine produces reactions. Good or bad?

It shows a more sensitive body consciousness—good, if it becomes more sensitive also to the Force.

Last evening's curry of potato and tomato didn't keep well, I am afraid. I took it at about 8.30 p.m. and found a bad smell.

Mother tasted it just after meditation—it was then very good still. But tomatoes can't be kept too long, especially in this hot weather—unless it is very carefully done. Up to 8.30 was probably too long and it must have turned.

April 5, 1937

I have scratched the whole poem out of existence! And yet when I completed it, I was so happy thinking it was something great! Fool!

Every poet is such a fool. His work is done in an exalting excitement of the vital mind—judgment and criticism can only come when he has cooled down.

Well, Sir, any good this poem, or goes to the same basket?

This one is very fine. No W.P.B., please.

SRI AUROBINDO   885

> *I can't get the current back. Even the taste has disappeared.*
> *On the contrary a fear has grown, lest my poems be good-*
> *for-nothing.*

Nonsense! No poet can always write well — If even Homer nods,
Nirod can often doze — that's no reason for getting morally bilious.

> *Once I asked you to give some advice as regards the treat-*
> *ment of a patient, you replied: ". . . I have no medico in*
> *me, not even a latent medico." [1.4.35]*

Of course not. If it were there, I would develop it and run the
Dispensary myself. What would be the need of a Nirod or Becharlal
or Ramchandra?

> *Then the other day regarding K's baby you wrote that the*
> *Mother has no intuition for infants.*

No intuition for stuffing infants with heterogeneous medicines.

> *Well then, if you have no latent medico and Mother has*
> *no intuition for infants, can you tell me how by the force*
> *of devotion, faith, surrender, etc., is one going to get*
> *guidance from you? If the Divine hasn't got it, where the*
> *deuce will it come from?*

What logic! Because Mother and myself are not Engineers, therefore Chandulal can't develop the right intuition in engineering?
or because neither I nor Mother are experts in Gujerati prosody,
therefore Punjalal can't develop the inspiration for his poems?

> *If the Divine can't guide me externally which is much*
> *easier, how can he guide internally, and if he has no medico,*
> *wherefrom will the medico come to him within?*

Oh Lord! what a question! To guide internally is a million times
easier than to guide externally. Let us suppose I want General
Miaja to beat Franco's fellows back at Guadalajara (please pronounce properly), I put the right force on him and he wakes up
and, with his military knowledge and capacity, does the right

886   CORRESPONDENCE WITH

thing and it's done. But if I, having no latent or patent military
genius or knowledge in me, write to him saying "Do this, do that",
he won't do it and I wouldn't be able to do it either. It is operations
of two quite different spheres of consciousness. You absolutely
refuse to make the necessary distinction between the two fields
and their processes and then you jumble the two together and call
it logic.

> *If the medico can be revealed from within, why could it
> not be revealed from without and tell me to give antidys.
> serum to K's baby, which I hear has been administered
> and found to be effective?*

Damn it, man! Intuition and revelation are inner things — they
don't belong to the outer mind.

> *If you or Mother can't guide me concretely, how will the
> guidance come later on, I wonder.*

Do you imagine that I tell you inwardly or outwardly what expressions to use in your Bengali poems when you are writing?
Still you write from an inspiration which I have set going.

> *Can you satisfy my logical brain box, Sir?*

Your logical brain box, sir, is such a rule-of-thumb, Dr. John-
sonian sort of affair that it is quite impossible to satisfy. If ever
you succeed in emptying the brain box of its miscellaneous contents and being mentally silent, then you will discover how these
things are done.

> *If I am to carry on the medical work well, I would like
> and expect to have an opening in that line. . . Please don't
> say that I cogitate and hesitate. It is precisely that that
> I want to avoid. Shall I adopt the surrealistic method, i.e.
> to keep quiet for a moment and whatever strikes first, go
> ahead with it; only be careful in case of poisons?*

There is a vegetable called "bubble and squeak". That describes
the two methods you propose. "Bubble" is to go on tossing symp-

SRI AUROBINDO   887

toms about in the head and trying to discover what they point to—
that's your method. "Squeak" is to dash at a conclusion (supported
by a quotation) and ram some inappropriate medicine down the
patient's throat,—that's X's method—But the proper method
is neither to bubble nor to squeak.

> *You remember once I told you of this surrealistic method
> and you cried Good Lord!?* [*28.10.35, p. 365*]

I did and I repeat it; I don't want this Asram transferred to the
next world by your powerful agency.

> *Once Mother asked me to try this method, i.e. instead of
> analysing the various possibilities and probabilities and
> then diagnosing by elimination etc., just keep quiet and
> go at it.*

Well, so that's how the Mother's statements are understood! A
free permit for anything and everything calling itself an intuition
to go crashing into the field of action! Go at it, indeed! Poor it!
   What the Mother says in the matter is what she said to Dr.
Manilal with his entire agreement—viz. Reading from symptoms
by the doctors is usually a mere balancing between possibilities
(of course except in clear and simple cases) and the conclusion is a
guess. It may be a right guess and then it will be all right, or it may
be a wrong guess and then all will be wrong unless Nature is too
strong for the doctor and overcomes the consequences of his
error—or at the least the treatment will be ineffective. On the contrary if one develops the diagnostic flair, one can see at once what
is the real thing among the possibilities and see what is to be done.
That is what the most successful doctors have; they have this
flashlight which shows them the true point. Manilal agreed and
said the cause of the guessing was that there were whole sets of
symptoms which could belong to any one of several diseases and
to decide is a most delicate and subtle business, no amount of
book knowledge or reasoning will ensure a right decision. A
special insight is needed that looks through the symptoms and not
merely at them—This last sentence, by the way, is my own, not
Manilal's. About development of intuition, afterwards—no time
tonight.

Regarding the vaccination you referred to, shall I ask the hospital doctor to come and do a few cases and then from the next day I can do; or shall I ask them to show me a few cases at the hospital? Either can be arranged for. Valle says all the members have to be vaccinated. André says all are not necessary. He has asked me to see him tomorrow morning.

The letter sent to us by Valle with Gaffiero's counter-signature expressly offered to us the management of the whole affair by our own doctors, so that there should be no intervention of the authorities with all its inconveniences — we have only to make a report of the persons vaccinated and their reactions. They, if we have to vaccinate at all, are just the conditions Mother wants. She does not want their doctors or infirmiers[1] to come in. So you will avoid that. Ask them to show you a few cases so that you can do the thing yourself-—that is the only course Mother sanctions.

Valle of course had to say that everybody was to be vaccinated, but really they are offering us by this arrangement some freedom in the matter which we shall not have if they come in. The Mother proposes to have the workmen and servants vaccinated and a small number of the sadhaks, especially those who go out and mix with the town people — enough to make a sufficient show on paper. She expects that Gaffiero will pass the thing and let the matter drop without insisting more — he is very favourable to the Asram. Only the thing had better be completed before he goes to Europe.

April 6, 1937

Valle seemed to say that one of their members has to be present, to write down the reports etc. which has to be done in a special way and on the spot. It can't be done by one person. I said we have assistants, we can very well manage it, once shown how. As I pressed my point, Valle seemed rather annoyed thinking, perhaps, "What's the harm if just a compounder or infirmier comes?"

In their letter they very distinctly stated that they did not want to

---

[1] Hospital-attendants.

SRI AUROBINDO   889

impose their doctors and infirmiers on us, we could do it well
enough on our own and they wanted only our report as to persons
vaccinated, reactions, etc. Now they are going back on what they
said. I suppose it is because you have shown too clearly that you
were somewhat new over the matter —

> *He also said, "It may not be effective, for the vaccine may
> solidify or get spoilt in some way."*

It is true of course about the vaccine.

> *André seemed more liberal yesterday. He said he would
> come and do the whole thing. He will perhaps bring an
> assistant.*

Do the whole? In a single day? with the same knife? with what kind
of sterilisation?

> *He didn't insist on all the members. So I suppose he can
> bring the compounder and finish the servants in one day.*

Certainly, all the members are not to be vaccinated. There are
people in ill health, some with weak hearts etc. You are going to
expose them also to the risk of 'the reactions'? Sometimes the
vaccination knocks people ill for a day or two. If many of the
workers are to be down together, who will do the work? People
in a state of debility, e.g., N, T, L, X, A, S, those who have already
fever, or skin disease, those who are otherwise contra-indicated
are all to be included in the hecatomb? The whole thing is pre-
posterous and you must not allow yourself to be hustled into
doing anything they tell you. We must first know what we are
prepared to do, who have not on any account to be exposed to
this poisoning, etc., etc. and do only what we consent to, not what
they insist on. I am farther informed that for two days after vaccination one is supposed not to do any physical work or exertion.
How then are you going to vaccinate all the servants or workmen
in one day? If there are 20 or 30 people down with fever together
are you going to trot about all day and night looking after all?
This won't do at all. Everything will have to be carefully considered and arranged beforehand and you must not allow yourself

890   CORRESPONDENCE WITH

to be hustled into any premature action and arrangements. There is no epidemic raging that all should be done in maddening haste — it must be done little by little in a manageable way. We have not to take them into confidence as to whom we vaccinate and whom we don't, either, or let them know that we are not doing it to all — unless they themselves say it need not be done to all.

The only way out for the vaccination seems to be that the compounder can come and do a few servants at a time (3 or 4) and you can be there and learn and afterwards you can take up the rest of the thing yourself.

> *Guru, C's letter! Do you notice what he says about outside disciples and D's going? Any truth?*

Can't make out anything from the fellow's Bengali flourishes. What does he say? I can only make out that B has told to him what Bishwanath told to B about what Mother told to Bishwanath; but what it was I can't make out — Only that for that reason D and others were allowed to flit. Kindly enlighten.

April 7, 1937

> *Today 4 persons were vaccinated. It is a very simple affair, but there is going to be trouble, it seems. The assistant says it is not possible for him to come every day only for 4 persons, neither can he leave the vaccines etc. without Valle's permission. He says there's hardly any reaction, except a slight fever in children. So what's the harm in vaccinating more people?... The thing is that they have stock vaccine tubes (sealed) for 50 people — not less than that. Once a tube is unsealed, it has to be used up in a day, or discarded. Today already we had to throw away some. If, by chance, there is none one day, we can simply drop that day. But for that, the assistant said, Valle's permission is required, otherwise we can buy from the pharmacy. If Valle doesn't allow the first, we'll be compelled to buy. But what a cost it'll be! I'm sceptical about Valle's permission, because he insists on the staff's presence and I don't know that he would like only 4 persons at a time. So what's to be done about it? Gaffiero will have no ob-*

SRI AUROBINDO   891

> *jection, I think. But Valle is in charge. And the difficulty*
> *is how to say all this in French.*

And yet it was Valle himself who wrote saying that they would
not impose their doctors or infirmiers upon us!

Valle and Gaffiero don't pull on well together.

Mother has asked Pavitra to see Gaffiero tomorrow. Pavitra
will be going at 9, so you must go to Pavitra's before 9.

April 8, 1937

> *"Creating language from the sleep of God", how can one*
> *do that?*

From where else are you going to do it? The Word comes out of
the Silence. I have myself written about Inspiration bringing
"thoughts Hewn from the silence of the Ineffable."[1] If anybody
can't understand, *tant pis pour lui.*[2]

> *I have fallen into the old pit of lack of enthusiasm. Source*
> *exhausted, it appears!*

Source of enthusiasm? The source of poetry seems to be there,
all right.

> *The vaccination business has been now fixed. If we do only*
> *4 persons, it will take too long. (Can't be finished be-*
> *fore Gaffiero goes in May.) Suppose, after seeing the*
> *reaction, if any, of the fellows done, we increase the number*
> *to 10—half from B.S. and half domestic, or half domestic*
> *and half sadhaks?*

Workmen not to be touched till the roof is finished—on Tuesday.
Then you can have 4 + 4 servants and workmen, +2 sadhaks.
But get a list of sadhaks done (in consultation with Amrita) and
we will mark off those who must *not* be poisoned. For the rest
you will have to do those whom you can induce to make them-

---

[1] *SABCL*, vol. 28, *Savitri*, Book I, Canto 3, p. 41.
[2] So much the worse for him.

selves victims on the sacred altar of Science, so that Valle can say with self-satisfaction "Ah ha! the Asram has been vaccinated."

> *How funny that Valle acceded to Pavitra and was an adamantine rock to me!*

Valle said it was only out of compassion for you because you said you knew nothing about it and were so much at sea! He did not put it in that figurative language but it was the purport of his plea.

> *I am afraid D [a child] has obstinate constipation. I am damned, for, except enema, castor-oil is the drug for children in our "Science".*

All "science" does not recommend castor-oil for children — I think it is a nineteenth century fad which has prolonged itself. The Mother's "children's doctor" told her it should not be done — also in her own case when a child the doctors peremptorily stopped it on the ground that it spoiled the stomach and liver. I suppose you will say doctors disagree? They do! When K's child reached Madras, the first doctor said "Stop mother's milk for three days", the second said "Mother's milk to be taken at once, at once!" So, sir. Anyhow for D Mother proposes diet first—small bananas Pavitra will give, very good for constipation—papaiya if available in the garden. Also as he is pimply, cocoanut water on an empty stomach. Afterwards we can see if medicine is necessary.

April 9, 1937

> *I wonder why you flared up at the idea of my using the surrealist method in treating patients.*

I didn't flare up. I was cold with horror.

> *By "go at it" I obviously didn't mean sending your Asram to the next world! No, not at all. I meant only this: say a case comes with pain in the stomach, loss of appetite, etc., I simply keep silent, suddenly comes to me the suggestion—gastritis, without any analysis of symptoms.*

SRI AUROBINDO   893

Doctors don't mean it, when they do that kind of thing. It is not deliberate murder with them, but involuntary or, shall we say, experimental homicide.

> *Mother told me to practise the intuitive method, I thought. "Go at it" was simply my military language! I thought this is one of the ways to develop intuition — if it can be developed. Otherwise how the deuce is it going to come? Going to open suddenly?*

She said that you have to stop jumping about from guess to guess and develop the diagnostic insight — seeing what comes from the intuition and then looking at the case to see if it is right. But to take the first thing that comes and *act on it*, is guessing pure and simple. If after a time you find that your perceptions turn out to have been automatically right each time, then you can be confident that you have got the thing.

> *How do the most successful doctors have intuition, by a flash or what you call an inner sight?*

Some have it by nature and develop it by experience.

> *Or do they get it by plenty of experience, treating, curing, killing, etc.?*

Well, there are some who after killing a few hundreds, learn to kill only a few. But that is not intuition; that is simply learning from experience.

> *Rajangam thinks that behind their success there is plenty of experience; their familiarity with various diseases, and manifestations, shows them immediately what's wrong with a case.*

Of course, experience is of great importance, but still it is not everything.

> *Book knowledge will not always succeed in practice, experience will do; but experience must stand on adequate*

book knowledge. Since you have neither book knowledge nor experience, you have no medico — so no intuition, I suppose.

Excuse me, you can have intuitions — without book-knowledge or even experience.

You will perhaps say that there are plenty of doctors with plenty of experience, but that they are not all successful. True, but the other thing is also true that successful doctors are supported by their varied experience.

Some succeed from the beginning.

How do you solve the tangle?

What is the difficulty? Experience is necessary, book-knowledge is useful for the man who wants to be a perfect doctor; observation and discrimination are also excellent provided they are correct observation and discrimination; but all these are only helps for the flair to move about supported by a perfect mental confidence in the flair.

Then about the inner and outer guidance: of course all this trouble comes from not knowing anything about the queer action of the complex Force formula.

There is also some inability to grasp the philosophy of things.

The internal guidance is possible only when the subject has sufficient receptivity, isn't it?

Certainly.

When one hasn't that receptivity, outer guidance will surely be the only course.

How is the outer guidance to give intuition? It only by itself supplies a ready-made course of action which the person blindly follows.

For instance, you give me Force for English poetry — some

SRI AUROBINDO   895

> *lines come all right, others are jumbled, wrong, etc., and*
> *these things you correct by outer guidance, i.e. by cor-*
> *recting, changing, etc. till I become sufficiently receptive*
> *and then only a few changes will be necessary.*

I do so in your English poetry because I am an expert in English
poetry. In Bengali poetry, I don't do it. I only select among alter-
natives offered by yourself. Mark that for Amal I nowadays avoid
correcting or changing as far as possible—that is in order to
encourage the inspiration to act in himself. Sometimes I see what
he should have written but do not tell it to him, leaving him to
get it or not from my silence.

> *You say the same thing about Gen. Miaja with his military*
> *knowledge and capacity. Exactly, if he has these things,*
> *he can receive your right Force.*

It does not follow. Another man may have the knowledge and
receive nothing—If he receives, his knowledge and capacity help
the Force to work out the details.

> *It seems that though you have no patent or latent military*
> *capacity, your Force has, and it wakes up in the man*
> *the right judgments etc.*

Not in this life.

> *This is all a mystery beyond my ken.*

May I ask why? Your idea is that either I must inspire him specif-
ically in every detail, making a mere automaton of him, or if I
don't do that, I can do nothing with him? What is this stupid
mechanical notion of things?

> *The Force having military knowledge, poetic power,*
> *healing virtues, etc., the embodiment of the Force also*
> *must have the latent general, poet, medico, etc.—sounds*
> *strange to me otherwise.*

Because you have the damnably false idea that nothing can be done in the world except by mental means — that Force must necessarily be a mental Force and can't be anything else.

> *The strangest thing of all is that if the Divine wills, why can't an effective drug in a case be revealed to him, medico or no medico?*

Why the devil should He will like that in all cases?

> *I am to induce the victims for the sacrifice? Good heavens! Do you want me to be sacrificed by your disciples? Please mark off those who are to be vaccinated, instead of the other way round.*

Can't do that.

Of course my suggestion of voluntary sacrifice was a joke. It is an official order from the Government department, and we can't contemptuously wave it aside — we can only minimise its incidence.

As to Force let me point out a few elementary notions which you ignore.

(1) The Force is a divine Force, so obviously it can apply itself in any direction; it can inspire the poet, set in motion the soldier, doctor, scientist, everybody.

(2) The Force is not a mental Force — it is not bound to go out from the Communicator with every detail mentally arranged, precise in its place, and communicate it mentally to the Recipient. It can go out as a global Force containing in itself the thing to be done, but working out the details in the recipient and the action as the action progresses. It is not necessary for the Communicant to accompany mentally the Force, plant himself mentally in the mind of the Recipient and work out mentally there the details. He can send the Force or put on the Force, leave it to do its work and attend himself to other matters. In the world most things are worked out by such a global Force containing the results in itself, but involved, concealed, and working them out in a subsequent operation. The seed contains the whole potentiality of the tree, the gene contains the potentiality of the living form that it initiates, etc., etc., but if you examine the seed and gene ad infinitum, still you will not find there either the tree or the living being. All the same the Force has put all these potentialities there in a certain

SRI AUROBINDO 897

evolution which works itself out automatically.

(3) In the case of a man acting as an instrument of the Force the action is more complicated, because consciously or unconsciously the man must receive, also he must be able to work out what the Force puts through him. He is a living complex instrument, not a simple machine. So if he has responsiveness, capacity, etc. he can work out the Force perfectly, if not he does it imperfectly or frustrates it. That is why we speak of and insist on the perfectioning of the instrument. Otherwise there would be no need of sadhana or anything else — any fellow would do for any blessed work and one would simply have to ram things into him and see them coming out in action.

(4) The Communicant need not be an all-round many-sided Encyclopaedia in order to communicate the Force for various purposes. If we want to help a lawyer to succeed in a case, we need not be perfect lawyers ourselves knowing all law, Roman, English or Indian and supply him all his arguments, questions, etc., doing consciously and mentally through him his whole examination, cross-examination and pleading. Such a process would be absurdly cumbrous, incompetent and wasteful. The prearrangement of the eventful result and the capacity for making him work his instruments in the right way and for arranging events also so as to aid towards the result are put into the Force when it goes to him, they are therefore inherent in its action and the rest is a question of his own receptivity, responsiveness etc. Naturally the best instrument even is imperfect (unless he is a perfected Adhar), and mistakes may be committed, other suggestions accepted etc., etc., but if the instrument is sufficiently open, the Force can set the thing to rights and the result still comes. In some or many cases the Force has to be renewed from time to time or supported by fresh Force. In some directions particular details have to be consciously attended to by the Communicant. All that depends on circumstances too multitudinous and variable to be reduced to rule. There are general lines, in these matters, but no rules; the working of a non-mental Force has necessarily to be plastic, not rigid and tied to formulas. If you want to reduce things to patterns and formulas, you will necessarily fail to understand the workings of a spiritual (non-mental) Force.

(5) All that I say here refers to spiritual Force. I am not speaking of the Supramental.

898   CORRESPONDENCE WITH

(6) Also please note that this is all about the working of Force on or through people: it has nothing to do with intuition which is quite another matter. Also it does not preclude always and altogether a plenary and detailed inspiration from a Communicant to a recipient — such things happen, but it is not necessary to proceed in that way, nor below the Supermind or supramentalised Overmind can it be the ordinary process.

> [*I sent a translation of C's Bengali letter where he wrote about his lapses.*]
> *. . . Well, well, I am not so bad after all, am I?*

No,—I should say that compared with most people you are quite decent!

> *But C seems to have made a lot of progress, hasn't he?*

Can't certify so long as the brothel walks about with him.

C writes about your letter "abortioning" him with regard to his falsehood. Can't you abortion him of his brothel? (I suppose it is some other word, but it reads like "abortioning".)

April 10, 1937

> *You may read, if you like, my letter of 2.4.37. The first part of the letter hardly requires the answer you gave, as fortunately I have got back the condition. But I would like to know if telling of experiences may have a bad effect.*

It may.

> *The difficulty of your Yoga, even in the first stage, seems to me to be greater compared with the other yogas.*

The difficulty is a myth. The difficulty is in the change of Nature or transformation which comes afterwards. Otherwise the difficulty in the beginning is the same for this or any other Yoga. Some go fast, some go slow here, also elsewhere.

> *Sir, here is the enlightenment on C's letter [7.4.37]: "I*

SRI AUROBINDO   899

> have heard from Benoy that Sri Aurobindo is now con-
> centrating on outside sadhaks. A day may come when
> his work may be done even by those staying outside. Benoy
> has heard it from Bishwanath who has been told by the
> Mother, that is why D and a few others have been allowed
> to come out. Any truth in it?"

No truth whatever! Mother said nothing to Radhakanta.[1] It is
probably one of Benoy's romances or it may have been built on
some casual remark of R—which was immediately turned into
"Mother's saying" with additional superstructures.

> This sort of notion is unfortunately current even in the
> Asram.

There are hundreds of false notions current in the Asram.

> The other day K was saying that you have written to him
> that, even living outside, sadhana can be done, for it is
> done by the psychic which can receive from anywhere.

Of course it can—there are plenty of people doing it outside in
Rangpur, Chittagong, Gujerat and elsewhere. How far they will
get is another matter.

> So staying here is not absolutely necessary; and simple
> staying won't give anything either.
> [Sri Aurobindo underlined "simple".]

Of course not. If simple staying did it, the servants and workmen
would be yogis by this time.

> ...I told him that there is surely a difference between
> doing sadhana here and doing it outside. There is a great
> thing in the Mother's touch etc... He said all that is
> ভাঁওতা![2]

[1] Manager of Arya Publishing House, Calcutta.
[2] bhā̃otā: bluff.

? Don't know the word.

Is it only for physical transformation that staying here is necessary? Otherwise sincere sadhana can be done elsewhere as well as here.

I don't suppose the later stages of the transformation including the physical would be possible elsewhere. In fact in those outside none of the three transformations seems to have begun. They are all preparing. Here there are at least a few who have started one or two of them. Only that does not show outside. The physical or external alone shows outside.

About the vaccination, Chandulal says some carpenters and painters will not be working on the roof building. So shall I start with them?

That is all right.

Then, as to the sadhaks, if you don't give a notice, I am afraid everyone will refuse or individually approach you for permission to be left out.

A notice would have to be given, of course. I am marking on the list with a red dot those whom we positively want omitted (but it does *not* mean all else have to be vaccinated) and with a blue dot those who ought to vaccinate without doubt because they go out and mix with town people or mix with them in some other way. A red line means visitors or short time residents who need not be bothered. Over the rest I am still cogitating.

Can your letter on Force be read out to a limited few?

Yes, but only a few. No copies.

April 11, 1937

Guru, another wire from Chand! "Nirod Asram Pondicherry Biswanath asks look arya Correspondence Tomorrow blessings." If you understand what he means, please give an answer, if any!

SRI AUROBINDO   901

You can wire to him that it is not sanctioned. Nolini will write
to Radhakanta.

> *Besides those whom you have vetoed for vaccination,
> I'm afraid many others have to be done so. I had to ex-
> clude M, J, B and S, for they had pox before.*
> [*Sri Aurobindo underlined "had pox before".*]

Those who have had pox once are not vaccinated? That's all
right. I forgot myself, I think, old Laxmi. Shailaja says he had
"got it" (I don't know whether vaccination or smallpox) a year
ago—I have told him to report the fact to you. Vithalbhai has,
I suppose, to be exempted, he has several ailments; he says he has
been twice vaccinated. Ambu and Nagin are under R's treatment,
the latter for debility—they also I suppose go out. There may be
others.

April 12, 1937

> *Why, Sir, you didn't know that smallpox fellows are not
> required to be vaccinated?. . . A book says one attack
> generally protects for life, but second attacks are not very
> uncommon and the protection tends to wear off in time.
> My theory smashed? Well, exception proves the rule, what?*

Well, there are people who say that smallpox attacks immunise
for only a few years. But if it is as you say, then there are others,
I suppose. There is Amani[1] among the servants for instance who
nearly died of smallpox. I myself had a slight attack in Baroda
soon after I came from England—so you needn't try to come up
and vaccinate me.

> *You have written to Shailaja that the effect of vaccina-
> tion lasts 5 years, and revaccination is not required within
> that period.*

That is what one book says.

> *But I gather that French regulation requires vaccination
> every year. . .*

[1] The Mother's servant.

902   CORRESPONDENCE WITH

Why not every week?

Whom are you vaccinating? Mother wants to have the report every day.

How do you like this poem,[1] Sir?

Well, the rhythm seems to me all right and the poem is exceedingly beautiful. A1.

Why the devil am I having a headache these last 2 days?

Supramental trying to find a place in your head?

[Regarding the interpretation of a poem of J's:] When there is no fire of Aspiration, the psychic opens the door?

It can, by a pressure from above. It may be that the preparation was over, so that the fire like everything else had sunk into silence, waiting for the descent under whose pressure the psychic door flew open.

That is hardly possible in your Yoga. No aspiration, no nothing — says your teaching.

Never taught anything of the kind. I got the blessed Nirvana without even wanting it. Aspiration is the first or usual means, that is all.

April 13, 1937

You seem to be, by the way, like Bernard Shaw in matters of vaccination. Do you deny the profits of one of the greatest discoveries of medicine? Not for yogis, but for the public?

Can't discuss that. Have not denied partial effectivity, though complete it is not, since it has to be renewed every year, as you say. The whole Pasteurian affair is to me antipathetic — it is dark and dangerous in principle, however effective.

[1] *"Alor gandha"*, Swapnadīp, p. 23.

SRI AUROBINDO   903

> *You struck me dumb with surprise, Sir! That poem was*
> *exceedingly fine? I thought absolutely otherwise. What*
> *does your "A" mean at the end?*

It is you who surprise me. I should have thought the poetical
quality of these stanzas would have been self-evident. On metre
etc. I cannot pronounce, for in Bengali metre I am not an expert —
so I only wrote that it seemed all right. What I wrote was of the
poetical quality and after reading it 2 or 3 times to make sure,
the estimate remains. It is A1 (not A) — A1 means of the first
quality.

April 14, 1937

> *We are short of three persons for vaccination; I propose*
> *to make them up tomorrow.*

Make up — how? I thought you had daily only enough for ten
vaccinations, and, if all were not used, those remaining over have
to be thrown away?

> *Well, don't discuss the effectivity of vaccination, if you*
> *don't like, but please enlighten us with your Supramental*
> *Light as we are rather hidebound in our glorious "science".*

No time for showing the glorious Science its errors. Too busy
trying to get the supramental Light down to waste time on that.
Afterwards, sir, afterwards.

> *Sada & Co. refuse the vaccination point blank! Till now*
> *none has succeeded in doing them, they say! Well?*

Nothing to be said, unless you tell them to go and be d—d in
their own way!

> *After reading so many Bengali poems and Dilipda's learned*
> *lessons on metre, you ought not to say that you are not an*
> *expert in Bengali metre, Sir!*

Read them? Flip-flopped through them, you mean — how could
all that strenuous technicality remain in the head?

Look at this Bengali sonnet. How is it?

Very fine indeed except for the concluding couplet which might be called a flat drop! What the deuce, sir!? What kind of coupletitis is this illness of yours? *anaemia finalis.*

> *Another letter from C, saying that your chiding had wonderful effect, Sir. Lots of worries gone! So it is not my "abortioning", Sir! [10.4.37] Yours entirely. I am not used to these things, not yet, at least! It was, by the way, "chastising". Gracious, chastising is miles away from "abortioning"!*

Can't be, can't be! You must have misread it. I stick to the abortion.

> *Can the observing of these moral obligations which C mentions be a help in Yoga?*

Yes, sir, if done in the right spirit, it will.

> *J says you called her also "sir"!*

So I did — but I was answering to you.

> *Guru, this poem seems a very fine poem, though I can't follow it.*

You are a very difficult follower. It is because you follow your own mind instead of identifying with the mind of the poem.

> [*Against a portion of the interpretation I had cancelled:*]

!!! What a confusion!

> . . . *Rather complicated, this.*

No, sir; it is your mind that has got complicated.

> . . . *After a talk with J, the poem seems clear and my criticism wrong* . . .

SRI AUROBINDO   905

Luckily I thought of reading the end first, otherwise I would have
had to swear at you at length all the way instead of growling slightly
here and there.

April 15, 1937

> *Identifying with the mind of the poem or the poet or with*
> *anything else — are all fine phrases to me, Sir.*

It is the only way in which poetry can be read — every lover of
poetry does it.

> *But how to do it? God alone knows. From your remark it*
> *seems to be very easy. Any process?*

No process needed; it is done automatically. Never heard of entering into the spirit of a poem? If you can enter into its spirit,
what is so difficult in entering into its mind?

> *You couldn't still resist swearing even when I cancelled a*
> *portion and corrected myself? Beast of Burden?*

Who? I? or you?
  Swore a little first, then went into the cancel. Had intended to
come back and swear more, but cancelled the farther intention
of swear.

> *What is it, Sir, Sada & Co. to be dead? dead!*

No, sir, not dead, but damned! damned! damned!

> *Very glad to hear, Sir, that you are "too busy". Only we*
> *have been hearing that so often and so long since, that by*
> *now the Supramental or any Light should have tumbled*
> *down!*

It isn't so easy to make it tumble.

> *But jokes apart, I hear, from reliable authority, that the*
> *Supramental Descent is very near. Is it true, Sir?*

I am very glad to hear it on reliable authority. It is a *great* relief.

> *What is this medical word, Sir? "What kind of* coupletitis*"?*

Yes, that's it—like neuritis, laryngitis etc. so coupletitis, illness of the couplet.
  It appears that D [a child] is getting 4 motions a day and today blood. Something will have to be done before it gets worse.

April 16, 1937

> *When we were discussing about the Force and the Spanish General Miaja [6.4.37], you said: "Let us suppose. . . I put the* right *force on him. . .", why did you say "right"? Is there also a wrong Force? Can't be, for it is the Divine Force.*

Don't remember what exactly I wrote—so can't say very well. But of course there can be a wrong Force. There are Asuric Forces, rajasic Forces, all sorts of Forces. Apart from that one can use a mental or vital Force which may not be the right thing. Or one may use the Force in such a way that it does not succeed or does not hit the General on the head or is not commensurate with the opposing Forces. (Opposing Forces need not be Asuric, they may be quite gentlemanly Forces thinking they are in the right. Or two Divine Forces might knock at each other for the fun of the thing. Infinite possibilities, sir, in the play of Forces.)

> *Even if it can't be wrong, its efficacy will vary with the power of the communicant. For instance there will be a difference between Ramakrishna's and Vivekananda's Force, and therefore in the resultant effectivity or ineffectivity.*

Naturally.

> *What I want to know is whether the Force, applied or directed, is always the right Force. Can there be any mistake in the Force, in its misapplication or in its failure to get the desired result?. . .*

SRI AUROBINDO   907

What is a mistake? Eventually the Force used is always the Force
that was destined to be used. If it succeeds, it does its work in the
whole and if it fails it has also done its work in the whole. ন তত্র
শোচতে বুধঃ ।[1]

> *My main point is the Intuition. The Force has evidently*
> *a close connection with the intuition or any other faculties*
> *which are awakened by the action of the Force.*

In what way? A Force may be applied without any intuition —
an intuition can come without any close connection with a Force,
except the force of intuition itself which is another matter. Moreover a Force may be applied from a higher plane than that of any
Intuition.

> *By the way, it seems your Supramental is a magnificent*
> *something wide apart by gulfs and seas from all other*
> *Powers and Forces.*

Certainly, otherwise I wouldn't be after it.

> *You won't say anything about the Supramental till it*
> *descends. It is this great mystery about it that makes us*
> *pin all our faith on it and the word Supermind goes from*
> *mouth to mouth. Ah, if we could have faint glimpses of it!*

Not much utility in this mouth to mouth business. If people set
themselves seriously to the task of psychic or spiritual opening or
development, it would be much more useful — even for the coming
of the Supramental. If I tried to explain about the Supramental,
it would be all UP with the Supramental. The rest of the lives of
the sadhaks would be spent in discussing the supramental and how
near Nirod or Nishikanta or Anilbaran was to the Supramental
and whether this was supramental or that was supramental or
whether it was supramental to drink tea or not etc., etc. and there
would be no more chance of any sadhana.

> *In my Bengali poem of yesterday, you asked me: "What's*

---

[1] *na tatra shochate budhah:* the wise man grieves not over that.

this word?" Well, I meant it to be ব্রস্ত,[1] but wrote instead স্রস্ত।[2] A স[3] sat on top, you could have cut it off.

Thought it ought to go off, but it snapped its fingers and said it was too big and clear and positive to be treated in that way.

Any necessity of making মূচ্ছিতা[4] *feminine?*

Hallo! I thought you were in favour of the feminine being used for everything, even words which were originally masculine and neuter?

স্মৃতি[5] *personified?*

স্মৃতি or memory is in all languages feminine and is personified as a goddess or a feminine form — yet you object! Queer! Anyway if she can have a বক্ষ[6] why can't she be figured as a person?

We examined D's stools — not dysenteric at all. . .
As regards treatment, how about trying one or two days greens? Boil them in water and give with rice?

Very good idea.

After that we may try a dose of castor-oil. I wonder if he has an anal fissure . . . The pain he complains of is at the anus and not around the umbilicus.

If so, can't it be discovered? If that's the thing Anthenor pommade is indicated after quarter litre wash — if he's too young for enema with the tube, a *poire* might be used.

S has a hard red swelling about the left elbow joint; no cause. . .

Sir, in this world there is nothing without a cause — unless you

---

[1] *trasta.*
[2] *strasta.*
[3] *sa.*
[4] *mūrchhitā:* one who swoons.
[5] *smriti:* memory.
[6] *vaksha:* bosom.

hold the ultra-modern view that causation does not exist.

> *We have been giving some perfumed toilet powder to C for sweating. K asked for it; now S also has asked for it. Don't know if it is for sweating or "contagion". Can't go on at this rate, can we?*

No. Can't give to everybody. They must get their anti-perspiration from the Prosperity normally.

April 17, 1937

> *D has no fissure. I have advised green vegetables for him.*

I forgot to say that the Mother puts her entire veto on castor oil for D.

> *No luck about Intuition?*

None! Too thorny a subject to tackle without leisure and space.

April 18, 1937

By the way S must be added to the list of vaccination impossibles. R asks me to warn you and Amal that if you vaccinate, you will get back your old friends the boils and Amal his old companion the stye. I pass on the warning to you without farther piling up the agony. A very nasty affair this vaccination, in any case.

> *Guru, this poem is in blank verse. The rhythm seems quite all right. Still the austerity and force have to come, I think, no?*

Yes, good rhythm, fine poetry.
Of course, it is not the epic style, but in its kind it is very good.

> *I don't like the sound of* phāṭi ṭuṭi, *do you?*

Sounds somewhat too much like somebody dropping and breaking cups and saucers — doesn't fit in with the rest of the style.

910   CORRESPONDENCE WITH

"I go mad when I see a deer in the spring woods . . ."

Not really?!!

April 19, 1937

Why ask and exclaim "Not really"? You told us that sincerity is not indispensable in poetry, neither true facts. You should have appreciated the beautiful figure of expression in that line.

Well, it was not a question of reality, but of verisimilitude. And then the vision of you gone mad over a deer was a little upsetting.

I have changed the line to: "In the spring woods I get excited like the bees . . ."

Umph! This is less upsetting.

I don't understand the poem. It says the swans, flowing in the shoreless vast, tumble into the sleep of creation. What is this sleep of creation? The swans don't seem to have come into creation at all, as they are still asleep. Or is it that after aeonic travels high up, the soul comes down into this Ignorance of creation?

Confound it sir, it was when it was above creation that it was awake—in creation it is asleep and dreaming—as you are when you are vaccinating people, though you mayn't think it—the vaccination is only an ugly dream. You were high up for ages in the Above and then you came down into the cosmic Dream to vaccinate people and write poetry. You are a Swan (or is it a Goose? হংস¹ you know) who fell asleep in the moonlight and tumbled into a dream of medicine.

What is the epic style? What elements are required for successful blank verse?

I spoke of epic style because you talked of austerity and force.

¹ *hansa:* swan; *has:* goose or duck in Bengali.

SRI AUROBINDO   911

Special austerity and ojas needed for epic style, not necessary in
other blank verse.

> *Speak of English blank verse, if you plead ignorance of
> Bengali.*

Good Lord! you don't want me to expatiate on all that now? I
believe I wrote about it to Amal[1] — I mean for English blank verse.
For Bengali I decline all authority.

> *Greens seem to have no effect on D. He still has 4 or 5
> motions, but no blood. We have to go into the details re-
> garding his diet, the number of motions and their relation.*

Yes. What about pastilles charbon both to help against diarrhoea
and also to fix time taken for digestion?

> *I quite agree with you, Sir, about the beastly nastiness of
> vaccination, though in which way, we may disagree.*

It is beastly and nastly in all ways, so there is no room for dis-
agreement.

> *S has been put out of the ring and so also Amal.*

Then add Ishwarbhai and Madanlal to the Vaccinatory Un-
touchables.

April 20, 1937

> *What is this I hear — U decamped last night! D's departure
> seems to have come as a tempest and blown away many.
> Victory of the hostile force you can't yet handle?*

I am not handling any hostile force.

> *U and A were apparently doing very sincere sadhana, no
> question about that.*

[1] *SABCL,* vol. 9, pp. 456–457.

A

912 CORRESPONDENCE WITH

What is meant by sincere sadhana? In the Mother's definition of sincere, it means "opening only to the Divine Forces" i.e. rejecting the others even if they come. If A and U were like that, how did they go? It would indeed be a miracle.

> *A seems to have gone for health...*

A went, not only for health, but to see his dear Guru who is preparing to shuffle off the mortal coil and for other motives of that kind. Quite natural, isn't it?

As for U, he has been going some dozen or dozen and a half times, only pulled back with great difficulty. Wants immediate siddhi in perfect surrender, absolute faith, unshakable peace. If all that is going to take time, can't do the Yoga. Feels himself unfit. Not being allowed to reach the Paratpara Brahman at once, had better rush out into the world and dissipate himself into the Nihil. Besides got upset by every trifle and, as soon as upset, lost faith in the Mother — and without faith no Yoga possible. Reasoning, sir, reasoning — the mighty intellect in its full stupidity. Understand now?

> *Each time somebody leaves the Asram, I feel a kick, a shock, a heartquake...*

May I ask why? People have been leaving the Asram since it began, not only now. Say 30 or 40 people have gone, 130 or 140 others have come. The big Maharattas, B, Y, H departed from this too damnable Asram where great men are not allowed to do as they like. The damnable Asram survives and grows. A and B and C[1] fail in their Yoga — but the Yoga proceeds on its way, advances, develops. Why then kick, shock and heartquake?

> *You said long ago that the Supramental won't tolerate any nonsense of freedom of movement or wrong movement. Is this the kick he is imparting from high up?... In these two months he has struck a tall tower like K and a fat buoy like D; how many of these!*

[1] Here A, B, C are not editorial substitutions.

SRI AUROBINDO   913

And what then?

> *In NK's letter you wrote that it is the hostile Force that*
> *is snatching away people, not the Divine Force that is*
> *driving them away. I hold the view that the Supramental*
> *is descending concentratedly and that those who resist,*
> *who are between two fires, have either to quit or to submit.*

Not so strongly or concentratedly as it ought, but better than
before.

Even if it were so, that is their own business. The Divine is driving
nobody out except in rare cases where their staying would be a
calamity to the Asram (for instance it could decide one day to
drive H out); if they cannot bear the pressure and rush away,
listening to the "Go away, go away" push and suggestion of the
Hostiles can it be said then that it was the Divine who drove them
away and the push and suggestion of the Hostile is that of the
Divine? A singular logic! The "Go, go" push and suggestion have
been successfully there ever since the Asram started and even before when there was no Asram. How does that square with your
theory that it is due to the concentrated descent of the Force?

> *The Supramental not tolerating any nonsense comes to*
> *that, doesn't it?. . . But really, if the more you are busy*
> *with getting down the Supramental Light, the more such*
> *things are happening, I am afraid you will have to stop the*
> *business or let whosoever drops be hanged.*

Why should I stop the business — that is to say postpone the
possibility for another millennium because A. or U gets shaky or
many others look homeward? Will that postponement change the
lower nature or get rid of the Asuras?

> *What's the idea? What's the occult secret? You promised*
> *to give me some lessons in Occultism — here is an occasion.*
> *Please expatiate, and pacify my nervous shocks. Otherwise*
> *I have to close down my poetry, vaccination, patients and*
> *every blessed thing, and gaze at the sky and exclaim —*
> *what? what? what chance?*

What occult secret? It is a fact always known to all Yogis and occultists since the beginning of time, in Europe and Africa as in India, that wherever Yoga or Yajna is done, there the hostile forces gather together to stop it by any means. It is known that there is a lower nature and a higher spiritual nature — it is known that they pull different ways and the lower is strongest at first and the higher afterwards. It is known that the hostile Forces take advantage of the movements of the lower nature and try to spoil through them, smash or retard the siddhi. It has been said as long ago as the Upanishads "Hard is this path to tread, sharp like a razor's edge"; it was said later by Christ "Hard is the way and narrow the gate" by which one enters into the kingdom of heaven and also "Many are called, few chosen" — because of these difficulties. But it has also always been known that those who are sincere and faithful in heart and remain so and those who rely on the Divine will arrive in spite of all difficulties, stumbles or falls. That is the occult knowledge pertinent here.

I have expatiated — but in the line of common sense, not occultism.

> *I have written 5 sonnets, Sir. Record! Gave a big dose?*
> *But are they only great in number, as in your young days?. . .*

Eh?

> *We are staggered at Romen's success in poetry. Metre*
> *free, blank verse, whatever he touches, comes out remark-*
> *able!*

Regular metre he has not yet done, but he succeeded remarkably in the free metre of his lyric.

> *While, in my case, after so many lessons in metre, you*
> *damned each one of them!*

Surely that's a misstatement. I believe I gave several of them nice compliments.

> *Don't you think D eats too much for his age?*
> *Morning   — some raisins, cocoa, 4 slices of bread +*
> *   banana*

SRI AUROBINDO   915

> *Noon*   — *3/4 bowl rice, curds, greens*
> *Afternoon* — *fruits*
> *Evening*   — *4 slices of bread, greens, milk*
> *Night*   — *oranges*

Greens and raisins can be stopped. But the diet does not seem otherwise excessive. Raisins may easily irritate.

April 21, 1937

> *By the way, you didn't understand me. I didn't mean that you damned my poems, but my metres or rather my innovations in metres.*

Oh that! Of course. Your irregulars were very rough with the poor English language. As for Romen, I understand he simply hooks on to the source and lets it tumble through him. That explains his success: যোগঃ কর্ম্মসু কৌশলং[1] — যোগ = joining on, hooking on.

> *Charcoal given to D. He has had 3 motions—all healthy, but rather bulky for his age. What does Mother say to a small dose of Mag. Sulph. or Soda Sulph.?*

No.

> *Sometimes deficient fat digestion, due to liver derangement, may produce bulky stools; but then it would be clay colour. Enema won't have action on liver.*

What is the need of purge or enema, when there is free motion, healthy, though in excess?

Do you know beforehand whom you will vaccinate? If so Mother also would like to know beforehand. (Question of experiments with Force.)

I am afraid I have to multiply exemptions — Khirod, (too busy to have leisure for fever,) Dikshit (do, also very bad health); Atal (do, too busy, also frequent previous vaccination).

By the way, I suppose you enquire before vaccinating, whether they ever had smallpox. Dasaratha Reddy, I believe had some kind

---

[1] *yogaḥ karmasu kaushalam:* Yoga is skill in works.

of pox here just before going but don't know if it was small or chicken.

> *Isn't it high time that you opened up the medical channel in me, Sir? I feel ashamed that being a doctor I can't cure cases!*

Medical channel? Rather rocky perhaps and sanded — but if poetry could open, why not medicine?

April 22, 1937

> *How is this sestet, Guru?*

Very pleasing. (Going to use new adjectives occasionally).

> *And this poem, how is it?*

Very pleasing also.

> *I dreamt last night that you said it was an exceedingly beautiful poem. Will it be fulfilled?*

I have already said it — so it would be nothing new.

> *Medical channel rather "vichy"? "Vichy"? and — what? It means anyhow the thing is not easy, but why not?*

Rocky, sir, rocky. Sanded — silted up with sand from both sides.
   No place for the current. Have to blast rocks, dig out channel, embank.

   What about D? He says you gave him a medicine — what medicine? And the result of the charbon? He says it came out after 5 hours. Is that correct? If so, the conclusion?

April 23, 1937

> *Some other new adjectives? Oh Lord, no! Have enough, your "pleasing" pleases me not!*

Dear me, dear me! I was tired of writing fine and beautiful (you

SRI AUROBINDO   917

forbid "good") and thought I was very clever in getting a variation. You are hard to please! What do you say to "nice"? "exhilarating"? "*épatant*", "*joli, très joli*", "*surprenant, mon cher*"?[1]
Let's have some variety, Sir.

> *Romen hooks on and Nirod cooks on? No, Sir, I too let*
> *it tumble now!*

Well, this has tumbled very well.

> *I am damned, Sir! The only medicine I gave D was one pill*
> *of charbon. . .*
> > *As regards diet, I would favour stopping banana and*
> *papaya, for they are laxatives, as you know.*

Yes, unless it is likely to lead to constipation. Anyhow you can try
and see the result.

> *If Mother sanctions, we can give small doses of Bromide*
> *and Tinc. Belladonna to inhibit the excessive nervous*
> *stimulation.*

No medicine.
   By the way, M has sprained his foot. You might enquire whether
he needs or wants any medical assistance.

                                                   April 24, 1937

> *D doesn't seem to be digesting curry . . . Why not try some*
> *olive oil?*

Yes. If olive oil difficult to digest, could mix a little lemon juice.

> *In place of banana and papaya, oranges can be increased.*

Yes.

> *[P had the point of a needle stuck in her palm.] Can't take*
> *it out. Tomorrow is X-ray. What does Mother say?*

---

[1] "splendid", "lovely, very lovely", "amazing, my dear sir".

918

You can take the X-ray.

M is all right. No medical service required.

Yes. He says it became suddenly and miraculously all right in the last hours of the night's sleep.

April 25, 1937

[A poem.] What adjectives, Sir? New or old?

Very pleasing again.

P's X-ray taken. Philaire will see the X-ray plate. If he decides to operate, can it be done? Or should the plate be shown to Mother first?

Mother would certainly like to know before any operation is made, where the thing is, how deep and what the operation would involve.

Some improvement in D's condition. He wants to eat something in the afternoon. Mangoes are laxative, so I disagree.

Mangoes — no! But care must be taken that it does not swing round to constipation again.

What can we give? Biscuits? He wants sweet biscuits.

Glaxo biscuits perhaps.

One thing, people from the Washing Dt. should not be vaccinated together or immediately one upon the other; but at intervals of a few days, so as to prevent any difficulty in the work in case of hives. The Aroumé depts. are those in which one has most trouble because of dropping off of workers for illness or any other cause.

April 26, 1937

What about this poem, Sir? Pleasing or pleasant?

Both at once and very!

SRI AUROBINDO   919

> *Sadhaks are getting rare for vaccination. Whomever we*
> *approach, says "no", alors?*

What's to be done? Must make the best of it.

> *Philaire says that P's needle can be extracted by operation*
> *under local anaesthesia.*

I suppose it has to be done and we can only hope that Philaire will
really prove skilful and manage with least trouble and least unfavourable incidence.

P is of the nervous type and with them there is usually the max-
imum of trouble.

> *D had 4 motions . . . given half an oz. of olive oil.*

Thought he was better!

                                                    April 27, 1937

> *By the way, am I also going into the Amalian relapse? These*
> *blessed poems don't seem to catch. I have now a positive*
> *distaste for writing.*

I don't see any relapse. Your Matra-brittas[1] are always excellent,
sonnets up to the mark — Perhaps you miss the glories of surrealism — the magnificent images and smiting lines? Anyhow you
have gained in harmony and finish. Perhaps when you magnify
and smite again, it will be in a more perfect way.

> *A spree will improve matters?*

Spree, sir, spree! what do you mean?

> *P's operation tomorrow at 9.30 a.m. Please circulate some*
> *Force!*

P in order to facilitate matters for tomorrow, has started menses
today. What cheer, brothers? In view of the fact that anaesthetic

---

[1] A type of metre and rhythm.

may be necessary it might be safer to postpone for two or three days — what?

> Tomorrow's list of people for vaccination: Krishnayya, Premanand, Nishikanta . . .

Krishnayya? not an unhealthy subject? won't bite? Besides D.R. badly off for workers. Leave it to you, sir.

> K has swelling of left ankle (old injury).

Why revived? She is talking of bone injury etc.

Amrita was to have offered himself as a victim on the altar of vaccination, but he has been kindly bitten by the dog of the Privy Councillor, so although there is no hydrophobic danger, it is better for him to cure before being bitten by the vaccinator.

April 28, 1937

> "What cheer brothers or bothers!" Never heard of such a phrase, Sir! Most 21st century, I am sure. Even Wodehouse hasn't that!

It is both. You don't know the story of Pavitra and Khitish and the bother? Pavitra who had just come here with a rather French pronunciation of English, said to K "I am a brother to you all" and Khitish cried out "Oh, no, no!" Pavitra insisted, but Khitish still cried out with pain and politeness in his voice "Oh, no! no! no!" It turned out K had heard all through "I am a bother to you all"! so brothers are bothers and bothers are constant brothers to us, insisting on inhabiting the Asram — or at least visiting it, like the vaccination, P's needle etc.

> "Why revived?" [K's swelling in the ankle.] God knows! If I know, it is her dancing gait that has brought it by some twist there. Bone injury indeed!

She has been weeping and saying nobody cares for her because you said it was nothing and I didn't jump to her bone suggestion. So Mother gave her Siju to embalm her wounded feelings.

SRI AUROBINDO

>*A few D.R. workers remain to be vaccinated: N, S, I.K., etc.*

Not very eager to have them bitten — what will become of D.R. kitchen if they go over? You don't want to eat?

>*. . .Vaccination today—if you allow Krishnayya.*

Allowed.

>*Here is an English poem[1] written between dozes!*

Compliments! you have reached the summit with one bound! Magnificent.

>*Don't quite follow what you meant by "magnify" and "smite again".*

Refer back to "magnificent" images and "smiting" lines.[2]

>*This poem [J's] is sent as an illustration of what follows.*

Tonight there is a mass of correspondence and I have not been able to deal with even half of it. So tomorrow.

>*J asks why it should be called blank verse. Is it simply because rhymes are absent?*

Yes.
   Blank verse means verse without rhyme; it is applied usually in English to the unrhymed pentameter.

>*Is this absence of rhyme made up for by other things?*

That is a question of the success of the blank verse as poetry — not of the metrical category into which a poem falls.

>*Is there a variation of pauses?*

---

[1] "First Word", *Sun-Blossoms*, p. 8.   [2] p. 919.

In English variation of pauses is not indispensable to blank verse. There is much blank verse of the first quality in which it is eschewed or minimised, much also of the first quality in which it is freely used. Shakespeare has both kinds.

> *Where is this poem different from a sonnet, except in rhymes lacking?*

That is because the sonnet turn or flow has been used without the rhyme which is an essential part of the sonnet structure.

> *J says she doesn't think she is really a poet. By Mother's pressure she has been led to write things.*

Mother's pressure means what? She wanted to write poetry and attempted, at first without much success. Afterwards the channel opened as it did with others.

> *If she were a poet, she wouldn't write with so much difficulty. She would spontaneously go on writing like a well gushing out.*

Every poet does not write like that. Some of the greatest have written with labour and constant self-correction.

> *She adds that she would not always fear Mother's displeasure if she didn't write etc., etc.*

Why should Mother be displeased if she didn't write? Is it a task that Mother or I have set her against her will?

> *She says that with the difficulty of blank verse, the dissatisfaction has grown to such a height that she feels like giving up poetry.*

Whether to write blank verse or not or to write poetry or not, is purely a matter for her choice. She asked for poetic inspiration and it was given her. Now she seems to complain because it has been given her — it is not her own, therefore not valuable.

SRI AUROBINDO   923

> *Well, Sir, she was saying that before writing today, she
> had some fear, a lack of confidence lest the blank verse
> become again unsuccessful.*

Why? The one hope of doing well is to write in a cheerful attitude,
without too much mental insistence and open herself to the Inspiration quietly and confidently till it comes. Fretting and fuming
can only block the passage.

> *Please give the factors that make blank verse successful.
> We have read your letter to Amal. Is that all?*

I don't know any factors by which blank verse can be built up.
When good blank verse comes one can analyse it and assign certain
elements of technique, but these come in the course of the formation
of the verse. Each poet finds his own technique — that of Shakespeare differs from Marlowe's, both from Milton's and all from
Keats'. In English I can say that variations of rhythm, of lengths
of syllable, of caesura, of the structure of lines help and neglect
of them hinders — so too with pause variations if used; but to
explain all that would mean a treatise. Nor could anyone make
himself a great blank verse writer by following the instructions
deliberately and constructing his verse. Only if he knows, the
inspiration answers better and if there is failure in the inspiration
he can see and call again and the thing will come. But I am no
expert in Bengali blank verse.

*April 29, 1937 **

> *I told you that D.R. and B.S. workers have almost all been
> vaccinated. Sadhaks, 30 done, and no more forthcoming.
> So shall we close the show here?*

I suppose it can be closed.

> *Thank you sir, for the compliments! I have reached the
> summit, but next time you will find me in the abyss!*

The abyss can also produce poetry.

* Except for the first reply, all the others must have been given on April 30, 1937.

If one could remain there!

In the abyss? why?

> *April 30, 1937*

May 1937

> *Shall go tomorrow to enquire about P's operation . . .*
> *I think it would be better to see it again on the screen to-*
> *morrow evening, for the needle may have shifted.*

Yes.

> *Why do these things — tooth trouble etc., come to the*
> *Mother? I hear that you throw them off very quickly when*
> *they try to come to you. The Mother could do the same.*

I have not to deal with the sadhaks — except through correspondence.

> *I am feeling feverish, cold in the head, bad headache. Due*
> *to sea bath and diving? What a pity!*

Pains of pleasure, I suppose.

> *Which is better:*
> *"To a motionless abode — intense hushed seas"? or "of*
> *deep hushed seas"?*

My God, sir, the line with its tangle of sh and s sounds would be unpronounceable like Toru Dutt's "Sea-shells she sells".

> *May 2, 1937*

> *Guru, from this quatrain you will see that I have tried a*
> *hell of a lot to improve or rewrite it and yet not successful!*
> *"Plunge there like pearls in timeless trance-repose;*
> *Culled from spring-garden of fire-coated seeds.*
> *The nectar-rays of heaven's golden Rose*
> *Shower on the calm expanse — like pollen beads."*

SRI AUROBINDO   925

So I see, but your plunging quatrain plunges and splashes a lot
without arriving anywhere near coherence. There is still no possible
connection between the ideas and images here and there that go
before and after.

> [*The following questions were put by J:*]
> *How may I learn the epic style of blank verse?*

I suppose it is best done. by reading the epic writers until you get
the epic rush or sweep.

> *Is it too early for me to learn it? Kindly say a few words,
> and if there is no harm in my trying it at present, please
> give some force and inner guidance for it.*

Epic writing needs a sustained energy of rhythm and word which
is not easy to get or maintain. I am not sure whether you can get
it now. I think you would first have to practise maintaining the
level of the more energetic among the lines you have been writing . . .

May 3, 1937

> [*The first 3 questions were put by J:*]
> *Kindly say who are the epic writers. I want to read them
> all. Is your "Love and Death" an epic, and "Urvasie", and
> "Baji Prabhou"?*

Love and Death is epic in long passages. Urvasie is written on the
epic model. Baji Prabhou is not epic in style or rhythm.

> *Are your 12 recent poems[1] too in epic style?*

No, they are lyrical, though sometimes there may come in an epic
elevation.

> *Will "Paradise Lost" and "Paradise Regained" help? And*

---

[1] Transformation, Nirvana, The Other Earths, The Bird of Fire, Trance, Shiva,
the Inconscient Creator, The Life Heavens, Jivanmukta, In Horis Aeternum,
Thought the Paraclete, Moon of Two Hemispheres, Rose of God. *SABCL*, vol. 5
(*Collected Poems*).

who are the other epic writers in English? Kindly mention all the epic writers in all the languages — it is good to know them, at least.

"Paradise Lost", yes. In the other Milton's fire had dimmed. In English Paradise Lost and Keats' Hyperion (unfinished) are the two chief epics. In Sanskrit Mahabharat, Ramayan, Kalidasa's Kumar Sambhav, Bharavi's Kiratarjuniya. In Bengali Meghnadbodh. In Italian Dante's Divine Comedy and Tasso's (I have forgotten the name for the moment[1]) are in the epic cast. In Greek of course Homer, in Latin Virgil. There are other poems which attempt the epic style, but are not among the masterpieces. There are also primitive epics in German and Finnish (Nibelungenlied, Kalevala) —

Our vaccination list is ready. Will send a duplicate to Mother tomorrow, before submitting it to the hospital.

You will send a copy to Pavitra, for he will have to write to Valle as it was to him that their original letter came.

S has been complaining of her extreme weakness, pains etc. which are so great that she is on her way to death—her ribs can be counted, her stomach etc. have become microscopic; her pains terrible; often she can hardly get up from her bed in the morning; often her breath comes gaspingly through weakness. She says she took medicines from you for eight long days without any change; when she told you, you said "It's the only medicine I have", so she dropped treatment. On my telling her that she may have to go to Bombay side for treatment, she says she will prefer to die near to the Mother — not a comfortable prospect for the Mother, but she may live if we give her one cup more milk a day and butter — which have been accorded. Ah yes, before the demand for butter, she wrote that she can't eat — she feels too ill.

It is true that Mother finds her looking very down and seedy. Any enlightenment from Science?

I send you the poem again. How do you find the effect, on the whole? I have very little credit though, this time.

---

[1] *Jerusalem Liberated.*

SRI AUROBINDO   927

. . . I think between us — putting aside all false modesty — we have
made a rather splendaceous superrealist poem out of your surrealist
affair.

>   *Still, something, what?*

Certainly. Mine are only the finishing touches.

>   *May 4, 1937*

>   *I hear D is having the same number of motions. Is there*
>   *any harm in giving an enema?*

It could be given with guimauve in it, provided the stock of guimauve is unspoilt with no insects in it. But it is a French medicine
with special proportions etc. — you have prepared before? for
they won't know how to do it.

>   *May 5, 1937*

>   *Yes, we have prepared it before. . . Shall give it tomorrow*
>   *afternoon or day after morning?*

Very well.

>   *I have been thinking of studying medical books daily one*
>   *hour, but can hardly manage it, though at the same time*
>   *inflicted with doubts as to the utility of studies and lacking*
>   *in practical experience, I do not know what to do. Please*
>   *give some Force. Must run two horses, what?*

Why not?

>   *The difficulty is still lack of living interest in it — what you*
>   *call* enthousiasmos!

Enthousiasmos does not mean living interest or enthusiasm — it
means the inrush of the creative force or godhead, আবেশ[1] — You
don't need that for chewing medical books.

>   *May 6, 1937*

---

[1] *āvesh.*

I consulted doctors in the hospital about D's case. They say it is a mild form of colitis, and recommend Stovarsol—which is a very strong drug; or Biolactyl—a product of intestinal flora, which is very mild. Perhaps Mother won't favour any medicine.

No. Neither stova nor flora.

A is complaining very much of his ill health, physical depression, lack of energy, which are constantly increasing, so much so that it is impossible for him to do any mental work. Something has to be done. But first we must know the cause. Anémie cérébrale? slow poisoning by liver or kidney? something else? Mother wants you to arrange for the usual examinations (urine, blood) so that it may be found out.

May 7, 1937

[*A's case.*] Anémie cérébrale! *Good God, no! It is anaemia hepaticus.*

Who is this hermaphrodite? [*Sri Aurobindo changed "hepaticus" to "hepatica".*]

... Is blood-examination necessary? for what? Malaria or simple blood-count?

I don't know—it is to satisfy A. He thinks he has a colonisation of colon bacilli — spreading where they ought not to be (like certain nations) or else liver poisoning or kidney poisoning—he feels in the morning as if he had been poisoned in his sleep. It is to decide between these scientific theories that so many examinations were suggested.

About the treatment, I don't give anything today depending on your remarks + results of urine exam etc.

Must know first what he has.

Please give some Force tonight to rewrite two poems. A great bother this chiselling business — and uninteresting

SRI AUROBINDO 929

> *too. But perhaps it's pleasant for you as you cast and re-*
> *cast ad infinitum, we hear, your poetry or prose.*

Poetry only, not prose. And in poetry only one poem, "Savitri".
My smaller poems are written off at once and if any changes are
to be made, it is done the same day or the next day, and very rapidly
done.

> *By the way, you said that these two lines of Amal's poem:*
> *"Flickering no longer with the cry of clay*
> *The distance-haunted fire of mystic mind",*
> *have an Overmind touch. Frankly speaking, I thought the*
> *first line I too could have written myself. Can you show me*
> *where its super-excellence lies?*

What super-excellence? as poetry? When I say that a line comes
from a higher or overhead plane or has the overmind touch I do
not mean that it is superior in pure poetic excellence to others
from lower planes — that Amal's lines outshine Shakespeare or
Homer, for instance. I simply mean that it has some vision, light
etc. from up there and the character of its expression and rhythm
are from there.

> *I appreciate the previous lines much more. Amal too is*
> *puzzled. Is it definable? Is it in assonances, dissonances,*
> *rhythm or what?*

No. You do not appreciate probably because you catch only the
surface mental meaning. The line ["Flickering no longer with the
cry of clay"] is very very fine from the technical point of view, the
distribution of consonantal and vowel sounds being perfect. That,
however, is possible on any level of inspiration.

These are technical elements, the overmind touch does not consist in that but in the undertones or overtones of the rhythmic
cry and a language which carries in it a great depth or height or
width of spiritual truth or spiritual vision, feeling or experience.
But all that has to be felt, it is not analysable. If I say that the second
line ["The distance-haunted fire of mystic mind"] is a magnificent
expression of an inner reality most intimate and powerful and the

first line with its conception of the fire once "*flickering*" with the "*cry*" of clay, but now no longer is admirably revelatory — you would probably reply that it does not convey anything of the kind to you. That is why I do not usually speak of these things in themselves or in their relation to poetry — only with Amal who is trying to get his inspiration into touch with these planes. Either one must have the experience — e.g. here one must have lived in or glimpsed the mystic mind, felt its fire, been aware of the distances that haunt it, heard the cry of clay mixing with it and the consequent unsteady flickering of its flames and the release into the straight upward burning and so known that this is not mere romantic rhetoric, not mere images or metaphors expressing something imaginative but unreal (that is how many would take it perhaps) but facts and realities of the self, actual and concrete, or else there must be a conspiracy between the "solar plexus" and the thousand-petalled lotus which makes one feel if not know the suggestion of these things through the words and rhythm. As for technique, there is a technique of this higher poetry but it is not analysable and teachable. If for instance Amal had written "No longer flickering with the cry of clay", it would no longer have been the same thing though the words and mental meaning would be just as before — for the overtone in the rhythm would have been lost in the ordinary staccato clipped movement and with the overtone the rhythmic significance. It would not have given the suggestion of space and wideness full with the cry and the flicker, the intense impact of that cry and the agitation of the fire which is heard through the line as it is. But to realise that, one must have the inner sight and inner ear for these things; one must be able to hear the sound-meaning, feel the sound-spaces with their vibrations. Again if he had written "Quivering no longer with the touch on clay" it would have been a good line, but meant much less and something quite different to the inner experience, though to the mind it would have been only the same thing expressed in a different image — not so to the solar plexus and the thousand-petalled lotus. In this technique it must be the right word and no other, in the right place, and in no other, the right sounds and no others, in a design of sound that cannot be changed even a little. You may say that it must be so in all poetry; but in ordinary poetry the mind can play about, chop and change, use one image or another, put this word here or that word there —

SRI AUROBINDO   931

if the sense is much the same and has a poetical value, the mind
does not feel that all is lost unless it is very sensitive and much
influenced by the solar plexus. In the overhead poetry these things
are quite imperative, it is all or nothing — or at least all or a fall.

May 8, 1937

> *Guru, my Bengali poem was not even pleasing this time?*
> *Alas! Or did you forget it in the sweep of the cataract that*
> *came down into your pen?*

Quite forgot all about him! Anyhow not very successful — pretty
but wobbly — like someone unsure of his legs but just drunk enough
to be sentimental.

> *... It is quite possible, I am sure, to write such lines like*
> *Amal's, without knowing the technique etc.*

Of course.

> *Amal says the lines didn't come originally ready-made*
> *like that. He had to change and alter, being guided solely*
> *by the ear or some vague feeling, and stuck on to the right*
> *thing.*

Necessarily — until the ear and feeling are satisfied, one has to do
that. For overhead poetry to come with a faultless rush one must
be very very.[1]

> *You talk about inner vision, inner feeling, etc., but the*
> *blessed writer himself doesn't know very often he has visioned*
> *something; all the same he writes.*

That you must have in order to understand and judge about the
source, touch etc. But one can write without knowing anything.

> *Last night, by Jove, was a trial indeed! After constructing*

[1] See correspondence of May 17, 1937, p. 939.

> *the first 6 lines, I was dozing and dozing, and in full doze, wrote the whole poem. So much was the "trance" that after finishing the poem I couldn't even revise it properly and went to bed. Sleep came immediately! ... Really, Sir, your Inspiration or Force has a very queer way of working: by dulling, benumbing and paralysing the senses.*

Of course. If you could write in a doze, perhaps you could even achieve something supramental.

> *You found the original line nice, but no meaning. That is the trouble, Sir! Sometimes you say, "Why the deuce do you want the meaning?" Another time, "Nice line, but meaning?" A contradiction, Sir.*

Well, but the other lines have a meaning or try to have. If you wrote all nonsense, then it is different.

No contradiction! Nonsense hangs together and meaning hangs together — but nonsense intervening in sense hangs apart.

> *Amal says that "concentrated blood" is very fine but how can it be lost in the night?*

Concentrated blood sounds like condensed milk. It's the blood that's lost or the night?

Sorry, but I had to rewrite the last lines. As they stand they are simply magnificent nonsense.

> *D, they say, is getting better... One or two more washes, if necessary, will perhaps set him right.*

Yes. We can see for 2 or 3 days and give another if necessary.

May 9, 1937

> *You seem to have "transformed" the sun into a majesty of night!*

No, it's condensed milk — oh, I mean, blood.

SRI AUROBINDO   933

> *To tell you frankly, today's poem[1] seems to me very fine,*
> *Sir. But you will find many flaws, probably.*

It is an English poem and shows that, in spite of lapses in detail,
you are getting hold of the language and its poetic turn. It is not so
original as the first one, but excellent poetry.

May 10, 1937

> *I am sending you today's poem so that you may show me*
> *the un-English overtones and undertones and other defects.*

What the deuce! Overtones and undertones are not English or
unEnglish; but I have pointed out the unEnglish ambiguities.
Perhaps you will say that it is a surrealistic poem? But it has too
much an air of logical building for that.

> *If you have time, I would like to know what exactly are*
> *these overtones and undertones [8.5.37].*

I was speaking of rhythmical overtones and undertones. That is
to say, there is a metrical rhythm which belongs to the skilful
use of metre — any good poet can manage that; but besides that
there is a music which rises up out of this rhythm or a music that
underlies it, carries it as it were as the movement of the water carries
the movement of a boat. They can both exist together in the same
line, but it is more a matter of the inner than the outer ear and I am
afraid I can't define farther. To go into the subject would mean a
long essay. But to give examples —

> Journeys end in lovers meeting,
> Every wise man's son doth know,[2]

is excellent metrical rhythm, but there are no overtones and undertones.
In

> Golden lads and girls all must,
> As chimney-sweepers, come to dust[3]

there is a beginning of undertone, but no overtone, while the "Take,

---

[1] *Fifty Poems of Nirodbaran*, p. 19.

[2] *Twelfth-Night*, II. iii. 46–7.

[3] *Cymbeline*, IV. ii. 262–3.

O take those lips away"[1] (the whole lyric) is all overtones.
Again

> Friends, Romans, countrymen, lend me your ears;
> I come to bury Caesar, not to praise him[2]

has admirable rhythm, but there are no overtones or undertones.
But

> In maiden meditation, fancy-free[3]

has beautiful running undertones, while

> In the dark backward and abysm of Time[4]

is all overtones, and

> Absent thee from felicity awhile,
> And in this harsh world draw thy breath in pain,[5]

is all overtones and undertones together. I don't suppose this
will make you much wiser, but it is all I can do for you at present.

> *"Break that chain, find in the soul's lonely sign*
> *A fountain of volcanic deluge-fire,*
> *The rock-embedded source of spirit-mine*
> *The immortal wine of sovereign Desire."*

Sir, this is a surrealistic tangle. You find a fountain of volcanic
fire in a sign and that fountain is the source of a mine (rather difficult for the miners to get at through the volcanic fire) and also in that
source is a wine-cellar, — perhaps in the rocks which embed the
source, but all the same a strange place to choose. Perhaps for the
miners to drink.

> *Nothing in A's stools [8.5.37]. Some Vichy water may do*
> *him good.*

Vichy water has to be taken fresh — stale from France in bottles
it is not safe.

> *May I take a "sea bath" twice a week? It will help in fil-*

---

[1] *Measure for Measure*, IV. i. 1.
[2] *Julius Caesar*, III. ii. 79–80.
[3] *A Midsummer-Night's Dream*, II. i. 164.
[4] *The Tempest*, I. ii. 49.
[5] *Hamlet*, V. ii. 361–2.

SRI AUROBINDO   935

> ling up my *clavicular depressions and developing my pec-*
> *toral and intercostal muscles, perhaps. If Mother doesn't*
> *want, I won't.*

Mother is not encouraging the practice but neither is she forbidding it, — except for some. She is neutral. She leaves you free
to choose.

> [*The following questions were put by J:*]
> *Is there a difference between blank verse and poetry which*
> *is* quite epic *and blank verse and poetry which is written*
> *only in the epic style, model or manner?*

I don't quite understand the point of the question. Poetry is epic
or it is not. There may be differences of elevation in the epic style,
but this seems to be distinction without a difference.

> *Surely there must be some difference between an epic, true*
> *and genuine throughout, and a poem which is only in the*
> *epic style or has the epic tone?*

An epic is a long poem usually narrative on a great subject written
in a style and rhythm that is of a high nobility or sublime. But
short poems, a sonnet for instance can be in the epic style or tone,
e.g. some of Milton's or Meredith's sonnet on Lucifer or, as far as
I can remember it, Shelley's on Ozymandias.

> *What are the qualities or characteristics that tell one —*
> *"This is an epic"?*

I think the formula I have given is the only possible definition.
Apart from that each epic poet has his own qualities and characteristics that differ widely from the others. For the rest one can
feel what is the epic nobility or sublimity, one can't very well
analyse it.

> *In Sanskrit epics, e.g.* Kumarsambhav, *what has made up*
> *the rhythm? And how does it sound so grave, lofty, wide and*
> *deep?*

936   CORRESPONDENCE WITH

It is a characteristic that comes natural to Sanskrit written in the classical style.

How can one have all these qualities together?

Why not? they are not incompatible qualities.

English seems to have the necessary tone more easily, but is it possible in Bengali?

I don't know why it shouldn't be. Madhu Sudan's style is a lofty epical style; it is not really grave and deep because his mind was not grave or deep—but that was the defect of the poet, not necessarily an incapacity of the language.

Kumarsambhav was my textbook in I.A., but I have not read all of it. May I ask Kapali Shastri to help me read it?

I don't know if it is necessary for a poetic, not scholarly reading of the poem.
     It is only the 1st seven cantos that need to be read.

May 11, 1937

What does the double line indicate against lines 11, 12?

Double line means double fine.

Good God, Sir, you have made the Spirit a swine!

No, sir, I haven't, though the spirit often becomes a swine. But you have made the spirit-mine into the spirit's mine which is a deterioration.

I take my pen to write, a fear creeps in saying that perhaps what I shall write will be un-English and surrealistic and all labour will be lost. You are taking so much trouble and giving your precious time, is it worth while?

It is because you are finding your way. You have got the inspiration,

SRI AUROBINDO   937

but the mental mixture rises from time to time; that has to be got rid
of, so I am taking trouble. I wouldn't if it were not worth while.

Ishwarbhai is suffering from inability to eat or digest what he has
eaten. Mother proposes to treat him like Amrita with nux vomica
and with syrup of bitter orange. He will probably come to you for
them; give and instruct him.

May 12, 1937

> *A says his trouble has increased: headache, flatulence,
> many motions (due to Soda Sulph.). So we shall give him
> another mixture. . .*

No need of that — he has been having good motions since he is
taking Triphala.

> *[The following question was put by J:]*
> *I would like my present poems to come in a few lines, but
> the epical tone to be more and more perfect every day.*

The epic movement is something that flows; it may not be good to
try to shut it into a few lines. There might be a danger of making
something too compact. If that can be avoided, then of course it
is better to write a few lines with a heightened epic tone than many
with the lesser tone.

May 13, 1937

> *I am having a blessed fever since the morning; aches all
> over the limbs; a damn business it is, Sir! Could not do any
> work. Read a detective story as treatment. Taking one
> Pulv. Glyc. Co.*

Detective story as treatment, and Pulv. Glyc. and Company as
amusement? Right!

May 14, 1937

> *A enquired if too many purgatives were good. I wrote to
> him that they have been stopped. Dr. Becharlal recom-
> mends a dose of castor oil or enema, to clear out the bowels.*

938 CORRESPONDENCE WITH

More purgatives? after the triumph of the soda sulph. and A's own pathetic question?

May 15, 1937

> *Please give a few examples of conceit in English poetry. Not very clear about it. . . .*

Conceit means a too obviously ingenious or far-fetched or extravagant idea or image which is evidently an invention of a clever brain, not a true and convincing flight of the imagination. E.g. Donne's (?) comparison of a child's small-pox eruptions to the stars of the milky way or something similar. I have forgotten the exact thing, but that will serve.

> This hill turns up its nose at heaven's height,
> Heaven looks back with a blue contemptuous eye —

that's a conceit.

> O cloud, thou wild black wig on heaven's bald head,

would be another. These are extravagant specimens. I haven't time to think out any ingenious ones, nor to discuss trochees adequately—have given one or two hints in the margin.

Some more conceits, ingenious all of them:

> Am I his tail and is he then my head?
> But head by tail, I think, is often led.

Also

> Like a long snake came wriggling out his laugh.

Also

> How the big Gunner of the upper sphere
> Is letting off his cannon in the sky!
> Flash, bang bang bang! he has some gunpowder
> With him, I think. Again! Whose big bow-wow
> Goes barking through the hunting fields of Heaven?
> What a magnificent row the gods can make!

And don't forget

> The long slow scolopendra of the train.

Or if you think these are not dainty or poetic enough, here's another:

> God made thy eyes sweet cups to hold blue wine;
> By sipping at them rapture-drunk are mine.

Enough? Amen!

> *. . . About Rajani's blood report, urine and blood are*

SRI AUROBINDO   939

> *connected as* রজনী *[rajani] to* দিবস *[divas]*,[1] *or blood*
> *circulating through the kidney contributes to the formation*
> *or excretion of urine. When blood sugar rises beyond the*
> *normal it is excreted in the urine. But since his sugar is high*
> *with a consequent high sugar percentage in the urine, it has*
> *been marked* + + *in the report.*

Well, you haven't told me if there is any meaning in the ++ 2.5
except that it corresponds to the blood urine like রজনী পালিত
[*Rajani Pālit*] to Diwakar.[2] Does it matter if it is 2.5 or 250 so long
as it is ++? When is it considered a high amount and when is it
considered very serious? You have said nothing about stool.
Nothing abnormal? R is supposed to be suffering from dysentery.

May 16, 1937

> *You said [9.5.37]: ". . . For overhead poetry to come with*
> *a faultless rush one must be very very", and left the sentence*
> *unfinished. Is it "very very Sri Aurobindo-like"?*

But I am not aware that I write overhead poetry with a rush.

> *Everybody is aspiring to write from the overhead plane,*
> *so why not I? Possible?*

Maybe.

> *If one can write all from the highest plane, i.e. overmind*
> *and supermind plane—as you have done in* Savitri, *is it*
> *evidently going to be greater poetry than any other poetry?*

Nobody ever spoke of supermind plane poetry.
Is Savitri all from overhead plane? I don't know.

> *. . . You lay down certain features of overhead poetry, e.g.*
> *greater depth and height of spiritual vision, inner life and*
> *experience and character of rhythm and expression. But*

---

[1] Night to day.

[2] *rajani pālit:* moon (fostered by the night); *diwākar:* sun.

> *it won't necessarily outshine Shakespeare in poetic excellence.*

Obviously if properly done it would have a deeper and rarer substance, but would not be necessarily greater in poetic excellence.

> *You say also that for overhead poetry technique, it must be the right word and no other in the right place, right sounds and no others in a design of sound that cannot be changed even a little. Well, is that not what is called sheer inevitability which is the sole criterion of highest poetry?*

Yes, but mental and vital poetry can be inevitable also. Only in O.P. there must be a rightness throughout which is not the case elsewhere — for without this inevitability it is no longer fully O.P., while without this sustained inevitability there can be fine mental and vital poetry. But practically that means O.P. comes usually by bits only, not in a mass.

> *You may say that in overhead poetry expression of spiritual vision is more important. True, but why can't it be clothed in as fine poetry as in the case of Shakespeare? The highest source of Inspiration will surely bring in all the characteristics of highest poetry, no?*

It can, but it is more difficult to get. It can be as fine poetry as Shakespeare's if there is the equal genius, but it needn't by the fact of being O.P. become finer.

> *Your* Bird of Fire *which I take as overhead poetry, is full of excellent poetry.*

Is it?
Nobody said that O.P. could not be excellent poetry.

> *If one could write like that, is there not going to be a greater creation in all respects?*

Maybe; it has to be seen.

SRI AUROBINDO 941

> *. . . I suppose all spiritual poetry does not come from over-head planes.*

No, it may come from the spiritualised mind or vital.

> *I don't see really why overhead poetry will only excel in expressing spiritual things and not also excel in a superior form than the lower plane poetry.*

It may perhaps if the floodgates are fully opened.

> *Could you enlighten me on your overhead and underhead poetry?*

In what way?

> *In Rajani's report, you seem to make $++$ separate from 2.5%. It is not so.*

Not at all, I simply wanted to know exactly what 2.5 indicated, if anything.

> *We examine chemically first a sample of urine, i.e. by chemical reagents, which is called qualitative test. You ought to know that from your English Public School chemistry, Sir!*

Never learned a word of chemistry or any damned science in my school. My school, sir, was too aristocratic for such plebeian things.

> *Good Lord, the fellow is harbouring all sorts of organisms! Of course, it is in a way expected, for diabetes diminishes resistance to infection. But he is, I gather, coming to supramental treatment soon! Everything clear now? . . . He doesn't seem to be taking Insulin treatment.*

The Civil Surgeon Fisher who fished him into the hospital, talked vaguely of a possibility of Insulin in the future if the examination proved the necessity, but the new civil Surgeon Kapur who is

942   CORRESPONDENCE WITH

making him caper out of hospital, positively forbids the use of
Insulin. So!

May 17, 1937

[*Rajani's case.*] *Oh, it is Kapur! Lt. Colonel N. C. Kapur?*

I suppose. Can't be two C. S. fellows with a name like that.

It is very strange your school had no chemistry.

It may have had in a corner, but I had nothing to do with such stuff.

But for I.C.S. you had no science?

Certainly not. In I.C.S. you can choose your own subjects.

Perhaps these newfangled things hadn't come out then?

They were newfangled and not yet respectable.

*The D.R. cart servant has elephantiasis of the left leg.
Now it has increased — the whole foot is swollen. He was
complaining of pain. . . Are we not likely to be responsible
for any accident (a remote possibility)?*

What accident?

*. . . He ought to be given leave for some days till the pain
subsides, for with pain to carry on the work will only set up
a vicious cycle.*

Evidently he ought to be on leave without pay. If pay is given
they don't care. Cart service seems hardly suitable for that illness.
There is however a hammerman in the smithy who goes on with
a leg like that.

*I am afraid my source of English poetry is exhausted before
it has begun. The Guru is supposed to take up the shishya's
troubles!*

SRI AUROBINDO   943

It seems to me to be rather J's trouble. She writes fine epic verse
and says she is unable to do anything worth while—you write a
fine sonnet and decide that your inspiration is exhausted. Queer.

> *Tell me, please, how I should improve. The details are
> very difficult to manage.*

You have the inspiration, whatever you may say. The management
of details still defective can come only by practice.

> *By a lot of reading and writing or only reading?*

Either.

> *Please bring me back that buoyance, faith and joy, force
> and confidence. Otherwise finished! Your working is ex-
> tremely fine and diplomatic, I must say. Gave me an ex-
> ceedingly fine poem to begin with and cheered me up. Then—
> "Go on, my dear fellow—spading, efforting, labouring and
> perspiring! Oh it will come, it will come!"*

It is not my working, but your moods that are queer. You get
something no reasonable being would expect under the ordinary
laws of Nature and then you fancy you haven't got it and wail
because everything is not absolutely, continuously, faultlessly,
increasingly, illimitably miraculous through and through and
always and for ever. In no sadhana that I know of does absolute
sustained perfection in everything come with a rush and stay ce-
lestially perfect for ever more. If it were so there would be no need
for sadhana—one would only have to gaze at heaven a little and
grow wings and fly into the spheres a triumphant godhead.

> *Your overhead poetry, Sir, not a snatch of it has ever come
> into Bengali poetry—our Bengali poetry?*

I can't say. I can recognise the thing well enough in English, because I know the symptoms of the O.P. abnormality there. In
Bengali it is more difficult for me to detect. I suppose I must try
to train my ear for that.

May 18, 1937

> *"Tapering fingers of an infinite Force*
> *Mould life's grey mire to a bright rhythm of sun:*
> *Through a gold network of vessels lustre-spun*
> *Its luminous blood into earth's darkness pours."*

Sir, what the hell is the meaning of lines 5,6? What are these clumsy vessels doing there, either? Into whose kitchen have you trespassed? Cooking blood? But why not then "earth's cauldron"?

Anyhow kick the vessels out. A gold (something) network lustre-spun would sound fine, but I don't know what something to put as I have not the least idea what you are after. Cryptic, by God!

> *I am greatly surprised to hear that you have to train your ear to judge the source of Bengali poetry. Is it a question of the ear?*

Great Scott, man! Poetry and *no* question of the ear?

> *Just the other day you wrote that by the inner vision, inner feeling, etc. one must understand and judge the source of poetry. How does the ear come in now?*

Have you read only that sentence and not other things I have written about overmind rhythm etc.? Only the other day I said, I think, that Amal's line changed (Flickering no longer) would lose the overtone (rhythmic) and with it the overmind touch.

> *If you put the stress on the ear, O.P. would only be a question of rhythm, or at least principally, no?*

Very largely. The same words, thought, substance with a different rhythm would cease to be overhead at all. I said that clearly and gave the instance "No longer flickering" instead of "Flickering no longer". How is it you miss these things?

> *... Right word in the right place, apart from the substance, of course, is the first criterion.*

Why apart from the substance?

SRI AUROBINDO   945

> *All this you can see at a shot, ear or no ear, as if a line is rocketing down from the O.P. just before your eyes —*

And ears.

> *And you say "Ah, it is illumined, that's Intuition!" That you have to train your ear is a surprise* inattendu!

Strange point! Who does not know that without rhythm poetry is nothing? If poetic rhythm is unessential, pray why not write in prose?

> *Nishikanta's translation of Amal's poem[1] is really splendid, but is it also from the same plane as the original? Perhaps not, for Nishikanta's plane appears to be rather subtle vital.*

Maybe. I don't remember what plane Amal's poem came from.

> *Is the spiritual value of a poem lost in translation by the difference of the planes, though it may be poetically excellent?*

If you mean the spiritual substance, I suppose it would be lost. I was looking at the poetic beauty of Nishikanta's rendering which is on a par with the original. As for the subtle vital, the vital sublimated enters largely into Amal's poem, even if it is a sort of supervital.

> *[D.R. cart man's case.] By "accident", I meant sudden heart failure. But Rajangam says there's hardly any danger of the sort. I saw the man in the smithy—his condition has now become chronic. This D.R. fellow's condition it seems, diminishes as soon as he takes rest, and comes back with work.*

Mother is under the impression he was relieved from cart work. But if it is like that he must take rest.

> *A "cheer brother" again! [28, 29.4.37] N.P. has hydrocele*

---

[1] Agni Jatavedas.

946   CORRESPONDENCE WITH

> *on the left side, Sir. Dr. R is a specialist in that. Shall we pass him on?*

No.

> *But I hear that R himself is unwell. What's the matter? Ear trouble? Self-drugging?*

(Vital up, perhaps.)

> *Given A more M.T.*

A finds your M.T. — which he says is reduced in dose — ineffective. He says he was as well with Sudarshan or with Triphala.

(I see he says that he is worse than eight days ago — says that Sudarshan and the pills were stopped to try the mixture, but the mixture is not helping perhaps because it is reduced in dose without any compensation such as S or T. He asks also whether it is worth while being treated if the cause of his illness is not known or if it cannot be cured. In fact you have not said for what you are treating him or on what base, so I could not answer. I said I would ask you.)

May 19, 1937

> *How is today's poem? Not very successful, perhaps.*

Miraculously successful, sir, except for one ornithological detail.

> *It sounds rather big.*

Not only sounds, but is.

> *Oh yes, you didn't understand my "vessels"? Because you forgot, Sir, that I am a medical poet. Vessels are not for cooking only — there are also blood vessels; and you should have made it out as blood was also there.*

Let me point out to you that vessels of gold can only mean pots and things, not blood vessels. If you say "golden vessels", it might

SRI AUROBINDO   947

be otherwise provided you put a footnote "N.B.: physiological
metaphor". For non-medical poetry veins would be better and not
puzzle the layman.

> *... Why the devil does A write all these things to you?*
> *Are you prescribing or are we? and what the devil is the*
> *use of his knowing the medicines and doses, pray? He could*
> *have asked me.*

Well, what about the free Englishman's right to grumble? This is
not London and there is no "Times" to write to, so he writes a letter
to me, instead of to the "Times".

> *Surely, there is a twist somewhere.*

There is always a twist, sir, always.

> *And, didn't I tell him and report to you that it is his chronic*
> *liver trouble — liver enlarged? He has forgotten it evidently!*

I knew it was liver, but I had myself forgotten about the enlargement.

> *Anyway, I won't fume.*

Don't. Losing one's hair is always a useless operation. Keep your
hair on.

> *Only tell him, please, that he ought to let us know instead*
> *of sending a boy with an empty bottle, if he doesn't want*
> *to present his honourship himself, or shall I tell him myself?*

Dear Sir, tell him yourself, tell him yourself. I will pat you on the
back in silence from a safe distance.

> *A servant boy has hookworm; we suggest Eucalyptus +*
> *castor oil mixture. So?*

Right you are. Go for him, give him castor and pollux.

948   CORRESPONDENCE WITH

Nirod   20.5.37
   We are informed that P has got boils, ringworm and other
privileges all over his body and he is scratching himself and wip-
ing the dishes with his busy fingers. This, I believe, is objectionable according to medical science as well as to common sense?
You had better interview him and insist on his taking some kind
of treatment, also your good advice. What?
                                            SRI AUROBINDO
                                              May 20, 1937

        There are plenty of alternatives and questions in this poem;[1]
        I hope they don't annoy you.

No, it doesn't annoy — but, sir, you have written a magnificent poem
without knowing it and that is absurd. The foam-washed shore on
the edge of time is splendid, twilight's starry heart-beat is splendid;
lines 7, 8, 9, 12 are O.K., while the couplet, sir, the couplet is a miracle. If these are not O.P., they ought to be.
   Quite awfully fine. *Gaudeamus igitur.*[2]

        The bakery servant's ulcer is varicose ulcer. Rather dif-
        ficult to heal, for according to medical science the first
        step in treatment is rest of the parts affected. But since it is
        not bad, we may hope to cure it. About the risk, Mother
        has taken the responsibility.

Mother was told it was a wound and nothing much and the varicose affair was separate.
   What responsibility and what risk? No one is responsible for
the effects of an illness.
                                              May 22, 1937

        Why do you call it "absurd", Sir, writing a magnificent
        poem without knowing? If I knew I would have been glad,
        but there is a greater pleasure in surprises, isn't there?

[1] *Fifty Poems of Nirodbaran*, p. 13.
[2] Let us therefore rejoice.

SRI AUROBINDO   949

Surprise of what? Surprise of not knowing till somebody tells you?

> *Your remarks are rather mysterious. "If these are not
> O.P., they ought to be" means they are not? and "these"
> means also lines 7, 8, 9, 12, I suppose, but you say they are
> O.K.*

I mean just what I say. It is evidently the overhead inspiration
that is trying to come, that it changes into something more mental
in the transmission. Lines 7, 8, 9 are those that can be suspected
of being actually O.P. in rhythm, movement, spirit and turn of the
language. But the poetry of the rest is not the less fine for the mental
intervention.

> *O.K. in English is something like all right, quite fit, etc. no?*

In American English.

> *Can your remark on my poem, with the Latin put right,
> go into circulation?*

No.

> *Amal says it is* Gaudumus igitur.

What's that — that's not Latin! There is no such word as *gaudumus*. I wrote "gaudeamus".[1]

> ... *About the bakery servant — as the Mother knows,
> standing occupation is not good for these conditions; they
> tend to increase it. The risk I spoke of is no doubt remote;
> what happens, at times, is that blood in these veins clots
> and in that case one may be cured; if that does not happen,
> the clot can travel to deeper vessels and then to the heart
> too, or to the brain*. . .

Well, those are things that happen in the course of illness and the
employer is not responsible. As for risk, he has to work for his
living and it won't help him if we refuse him work. In Europe a

---

[1] "Gaudumus", Amal says, is my misconstruction of his correct reading.

950   CORRESPONDENCE WITH

large percentage of the working class have varicose veins, yet their work is standing work all day and they go on with it.

May 23, 1937

> *In the couplet, Amal says, especially your line "Light through her [earth's] dead eclipse of mind is poured," is magnificent. Is it?*

Yes.

> *How I struggled with the line, and you, Sir, by just a touch here and there fixed it up! I wish I could do that.*

It is a question of getting the right words in the right places instead of allowing them to wander haphazard. Naturally it depends on inspiration, not on any clever piecing together. One sits still (mentally), looks at the words and somebody flashes the thing through you.

> *Oh, this blessed mind! But how the hell does it intervene?*

By suggesting an inspiration of its own or a form of its own for the inspiration that is coming and in a hundred other ways. The mind is very active and clever for interference.

> *At times there are good lines, at others utter failures. If I had doubted at every moment, questioned, I can understand.*

The mind can suggest as well as question.

> *I don't seem to have still caught the metrical rhythm.*

It is not the metrical rhythm you have not caught — it is the fact that in English words the stresses cannot be shifted about at pleasure. It can only be done occasionally and within judicious choice.

> *About the poem of yesterday, this remark will do: "Quite awfully fine . . . A magnificent poem".*
> *[Sri Aurobindo put brackets around "Quite awfully fine".]*

SRI AUROBINDO   951

This is too jocular a form for a solemn "remark". The rest by
itself sounds as if you had written the Iliad. Better say more modestly "An extremely fine poem".

> *By the way, I know that Mother's programme is too*
> *crammed; still, I was wondering if I could be occasionally*
> *or rarely put in edgeways as one of the interviewers. Any*
> *decision will be taken with yogic* samatā.

Better not press that now. Wait for better times.

                                                        May 24, 1937

> *You seem to have had no time yesterday to read my poem.*
> *Golden silence of indifference?*

All that was really there last night? How astonishing! I didn't see it.
However I have answered now.

   N.P. is complaining of violent pains "just below the joint of
the thigh" connected with the rapid enlargement of his hydrocele.
Is there any danger of a complication such as hernia — something
of the kind was suggested once by somebody in connection with
another case of hydrocele, I do not know with what authority.
If there is, it ought to be looked to, without alarming a very alarm-
able patient. What are the pains due to anyway?

                                                        May 25, 1937

> *In N.P.'s case there is no "rapid enlargement" of the*
> *hydrocele. It is of the same size as we saw before.*

It was his hallucination then? or fear made him see double?

> *By the way, can you not send one or two sonnets already*
> *written, of yours?*

Impossible at present.

                                                        May 26, 1937

> *Rajlakshmi has eczema, can I try the medicine Mother*
> *gave for that servant?*

952 CORRESPONDENCE WITH

Pavitra has some medicine for eczema, you might ask him for it. Mother was thinking to keep the other medicine for some time in case there should be any recurrence of the ulcer of Krishnaswami.

May 27, 1937

> *In this poem should I put "faint murmur" or "radiant murmur"?*

Faint away, — all right — better than radiation.

> *At night I felt damnably sleepy over the writing. What's the matter, Sir? Had to jump into bed disgusted.*

Result of inspiration I suppose — sends you to sleep.

> *... P has a very rotten physique, Sir!*

Well, you will have to pull him out of this before we send him home.

> *Shall we show N.P. to Philaire, tomorrow? Operation out of the question, perhaps?*

You can exhibit him to Philaire, but operation out of the question.

May 28, 1937

> *Exhibited N.P. to Philaire. Operation is the only remedy, so?*

Mother says NO — So?

> *The rubber sheet Mother gave for the dispensing table is worn out. She had given a shawl which is very good. Shall we use it then?*

You can buy a rubber sheet for it.
Mother does not recollect about the shawl.

SRI AUROBINDO   953

> *There is hardly any substantial result of my writing po-*
> *etry every night. Should one store up and then spend econo-*
> *mically, effectively, splendidly now and then, say twice a*
> *week, like Amal? Which method do you advise?*

Can't say. You have progressed much by the present method.
Could try the other now and then for perfection if you like.

> *Perhaps in all the poems there is a touch of inspiration,*
> *but is that going to be heightened by storing up for some*
> *time and then allowing the gush—that's the question*
> *before you.*

It is a question before you, sir—not before me.

> *Guru, J has been terribly puzzled and worried, myself a*
> *little less, about your "too overmental style"!*

Ornamental, not overmental.

> *. . . She exercised her mental faculty too much? Epic move-*
> *ment has to surpass that?*

No, sir—You must read my epic handwriting properly first—
afterwards exercise your mental faculty.

May 29, 1937

> *By the way, you have absolutely forgotten to send that*
> *"Presse Médicale" with your notes [2.2.37]. Brooding over*
> *it?*

No. Went to limbo.

> *I have progressed much, you say? Very glad and thank you,*
> *Sir. But the latest poems don't seem to come to much, do*
> *they?*

What the big H do you mean? Don't come to much? What did you
expect more than the praise that has been given? Want to be told

954   CORRESPONDENCE WITH

that Homer, Aeschylus and Shakespeare all rolled into one were not a patch on you? What's the idea?

> *The poem which you have marked throughout with single and double marginal lines, is only a fine sonnet?... Not that I mind very much, but I was surprised to see the remark. Can you clarify?*

Again what the damn do you mean? When an English poet achieves a fine sonnet, he feels like a peacock and spreads his tail — and you say "only a fine sonnet". Well, I'm damned! Surprised myself to see your remark on my remark.

> *About the poem of yesterday, I don't feel like changing the last line. The poem hasn't come to much except as an exercise. You have said nothing about it.*

Don't talk blithering nonsense. Change that line and send the poem back to me.

> *D seems to be wounded by our and your silence. Do you think he may be more Pondicherry-minded by a little connection: soothing words, one or two poems, etc.?*

Yes. Better send some soothing remarks from time to time.

> *May I know why Mother says No to N.P.'s operation? I want to know your viewpoint. Hydrocele operations are supposed to be without any risk at all. If we leave it as it is, it will grow bigger.*

What operation? tapping? I have known cases of hydrocele operation being performed times and times but the thing always came back. It is N.P. who is asking for operation?

May 30, 1937

> *Will you wake up from limbo and scratch something on the paper?*

SRI AUROBINDO   955

How can I when the whole thing has gone to limbo?

May 31, 1937

June 1937

> *"Sitting alone under the shade of the tree*
> *Wrapt in a hushed profundity of night. . ."*

A tree gives shade in the day—here it is night when all is shade!
Please change.

> *I was struck by R's sonnet! By Jove, looks like a sheer*
> *genii—I mean genius, what?*

Perhaps both—genii producing genius.

> *[The following question was put by J:]*
> *What is the best way to get to the source of epic poetry*
> *and have it securely established?*

One has to grow into it—there is no other way. Once the epic
inspiration has opened, this growth is possible and, if the inspiration is sustained, fairly certain.

> *Arjava has fever again. He thinks it is due to indigestion.*
> *I hear that he takes some syrup cocoa sanctioned and sent*
> *by Mother. When I asked him about his diet, he didn't*
> *mention it. Too much sugar won't do, I think, as already*
> *he can't even digest D.R. vegetables.*

There is no sugar put in—the sweetness is that of concentrated
cocoa. Mother told him he could take it thrice a day; but it is possible
he takes too much of the syrup at a time. The usual rule is to take a
little syrup with much water. He is exhausting a bottle in 4 days
which is immensely rapid. Certainly too much sweet syrup may not
be good for the damaged liver.

June 1, 1937

956   CORRESPONDENCE WITH

Yesterday I had a dream of a very beautiful plump boy — Amal's golden child[1] — who came with tenderness and affection to my side. But he was a lost child whose mother was searching for him, then she found him. I had a very pleasant feeling. Anything in this?

Your higher being, I suppose. Glad you have found him, if only as yet in a dream.

Why don't you give me some experience, Sir? Afraid of breaking my head?

All in good time, I hope.

June 2, 1937

How is it, Sir, you had no remarks at all for my poor poem? No lines[2] either!

Probably was too much in a hurry for remarks or linings.

What about today's poem?

Quite up to the mark.

I am surprised to hear that the beautiful child in my dream, was my higher being. Why did he go away with his mother if he is my being?

He has no other mother than the Mother, so if the Mother accepts him, what is there to lament over?

. . . Could you be a little more generous in your explanation so that I may put in some more vigour to find him in reality? And why does it make you glad simply because I have found him in my dream?

---

[1] "The Sacred Fire", *Overhead Poetry*, p. 91.
[2] Vertical lines in the margin, denoting the quality of the verses.

SRI AUROBINDO   957

What is once found in the inner being is likely to be found in the
outer consciousness — that is why.

June 3, 1937

> [*Question by J:*] *P says that he is going to write an article
> on "the only vernacular epic",* Tulsi Ramayan *in Hindi. But*
> Meghnadbodh *is an epic too in a vernacular. How can he
> say then that* Tulsi Ramayan *is the only one? Won't it be
> wrong to write like that publicly?*

Of course, it is a wrong idea. There is not only Meghnadbodh but
Kamban's Ramayan in Tamil — But I suppose P knows neither
Bengali nor Tamil.

> *I don't know the cause of Y's sudden diarrhoea. He took
> something at Mrs. S's place, or D.R. mango?*

Perhaps. I don't know. He speaks only of oranges as diet after
attack, but he wrote some days ago about [. . .][1] things. He is
asking for green cocoanuts two a day. Mother says green cocoanuts can have a laxative, even a purgative effect. What do you say?

> *This morning, at 4.30 a.m., while returning after urination,
> K fell down unconscious with froth at the corner of the
> mouth. At 6.30, he was complaining of terrible frontal
> headache. . . He says he concentrated in bed for 20 minutes,
> before going for urination, quite conscious throughout.
> He remembers nothing about the fall nor my visit to him,
> but he answered all my questions quite well.*
>
> *There is nothing wrong in the system. We must eliminate
> the possibility of the Force as a cause, since he was con-
> sciously meditating, he says, before getting up. I have
> heard of A falling down once while meditating in standing
> position.*
>
> *No previous history of epilepsy.*

[*No reply.*]

June 4, 1937

1 Illegible words.

Strange that you didn't write a word on K! I wanted you to clear out the possibility of the Force as a cause...

Bunkum about Force. Obviously if a man goes into trance while standing or walking, he may fall down, — Ramakrishna had often to be held up when he went off suddenly while standing. But it doesn't produce results like that. I don't believe he is such a mighty sadhak as to go off into nirvikalpa samadhi[1] for several hours. Moreover it does not give froth at the lips.

Since I've got no instruction, I suppose he has to get the stools and physical examination done independently?

I think so.

About epilepsy, I am not quite sure, for it usually doesn't occur at his age.

Quite so. If he is sure that nothing happened like this before, it can't be epilepsy.

June 5, 1937

"Bury these quivering clay's repeated cries
In the dumb earth's eternal grave of sighs."
Shall I make it "clay's repeated wave" and bring "grave"
at the end of the last line?

Eh! how can there be a wave of clay? I have put pit instead of grave — I am damned if I know what it means, but it sounds awfully fine.

K is all right today. Another examination tomorrow.

It turns out that his statement is a lie as I thought — he has had these fits before.

J has eczema on fingers and legs. Oil and sunbath not very effective. She finds that ice application gives much

---

[1] Total absorption into the formless, supracosmic Brahman.

SRI AUROBINDO   959

> *relief when there is itching. But I don't know really if ice can cure eczema.*

Sahana cured her skin with ice, but it was perhaps not eczema.

> *I thought for eczema the less the water the better it is.*

I cured mine with force + very hot water, but I don't recommend it to others.

> *Will you kindly ask Mother? Last time J was cured by constant and persistent sunbath + oil. This time?*

Mother says she knows only sunbath.

> *We think A's illness is chronic mucous colitis... What do you say to screen-examination, and X-ray, if necessary?*

If you like.

June 6, 1937

> *"This gentle breeze free from all petty cares*
> *And fragrant peace of the blue-hearted noon..."*
> *It is rather funny, no? Breeze free from all cares!*

Care worried breezes are gentlemen we don't know — on earth at least.

> *And breeze rather than the peace should be fragrant, no?*

Why the devil should any fragrance of the breeze prevent peace from being fragrant too?

> *"With a tranced petal of the pale-white moon*
> *Are a vast breath of God that with us shares."*

What does the breath of God share with us? our meals?

> *Instead of saying "... that with us he shares", I have dropped "he" in order to be more English.*

How does the absence of a personal pronoun make something more English?

The couplet seems flat. What do you say?

Flat! the rhythm is like that of a carriage jolting on a road full of ruts.

I hear Mother kept silent about blood-exam for K?

Why should Mother object? They can do what they think necessary.

June 7, 1937

Can there be fear and anger at the same time?

Fear and anger very often go together. Evidently you have not studied cats fighting . . .

Do you think I have a lyrical hand in English poetry or does my gift seem to be more in grave things?

You have acquired the latter better up to now because you have put more practice into it and found your way.

June 9, 1937

I will try lyrics, whatever may happen, what?

All right.

Why do I find your "Songs to Myrtilla" so difficult?

It is a mystery.

I don't understand a single poem there. The English there seems awfully difficult.

Nonsense. There is nothing difficult about it — it is plain ordinary English.

June 10, 1937

SRI AUROBINDO   961

> *I forward X's letter. He supports in this letter, very strongly,*
> *his belief in human affections. Y came to me just now and*
> *recounted her discussion with X on the subject, and her*
> *having lost all faith in human love and affections, as a result*
> *of her past experiences. Is Y far wrong?*

Obviously not. On X's own argument, if his experience justifies him in believing in human affection, Y's justifies her in not believing in it.

> *... One can't say that there is no truth at all in human*
> *feelings and sentiments.*

There is a "truth" in everything, the question is what kind of truth and how much of it.

> *I don't know what you have written to X about it; he says*
> *that he has your support.*

I don't think I wrote anything about that. It was about his power to persuade others and also about his helping a certain person in her illness by prayer.

> *... The fact is that wherever he has gone, the Goddess of*
> *Love has, as if, enjoined all to pour love upon him; so he is*
> *a confirmed believer in these things.*

What is the fact is that he has vital attractiveness of a magnetic character and naturally[1] it works in people when he wants it to do so.

> *By his charm and personality, atheists seem to have be-*
> *come theists, materialists inclined to Yoga, favourable*
> *towards Pondicherry, etc., etc.*

It is to be seen how far that goes.

> *Well then, there is an element of truth in affection...*

---

[1] Doubtful reading.

962   CORRESPONDENCE WITH

I don't believe it was the affection that did it. It is the dominating
vital force in X. People who were not affectionate by nature, have
attached people to them and dominated their minds and lives —
e.g. Napoleon.

> *He also says that he has been betrayed often by friends
> and suffered much. Is it then his robust optimism that up-
> holds him?*

It is a difference of temperament and vital expansiveness.

> *My questions are: why doesn't he remain content with
> these affections? Why does he intend to come here for
> Yoga?*

That is another X.

> *... If human affections were everything or occupy such
> a big place in life, why did Buddha and Ramakrishna leave
> the world? How does Sri Aurobindo leave everything?
> How do patriots die unknown, unnamed, for their country?*

Because they can look beyond their small self to a bigger self
or to the Self of All. . .

> *Please give a satisfactory reply to all these questions.*

I am not going to perorate on this problem but I shall write something brief if you send the book again.

                                                   June 11, 1937

> *Guru, why won't you perorate? Fear of publicity?*

No, Sir. Subject too old and thin.

> *Do you think X's affection for me is genuine? I hear that
> he has spoken very highly of me to others.*

Perhaps he feels like that when he writes or when he gets a letter
from you; perhaps something in him has got that feeling there

SRI AUROBINDO 963

always, expressed or latent in a corner. At the same time he used to
write to me long lamentations in the desert saying he couldn't stay
here because he had no friends in the Asram.

Human affection is obviously unreliable because it is so much
based upon selfishness and desire; it is a flame of the ego sometimes
turbid and murky, sometimes more clear and brightly coloured —
sometimes tamasic based on instinct and habit, sometimes rajasic
and fed by passion or the cry for vital interchange, sometimes more
sattwic and trying to be or look to itself distinterested. But funda-
mentally it depends on a personal need or a return of some kind
inward or outward and when the need is not satisfied or the return
ceases or is not given, it most often diminishes or dies or exists
only as a tepid or troubled remnant of habit from the past or else
turns for satisfaction elsewhere. The more intense it is, the more it
is apt to be troubled by tumults, clashes, quarrels, egoistic disturbances of all kinds, selfishness, exactions, lapses even to rage and
hatred, ruptures. It is not that these affections cannot last —
tamasic instinctive affections last because of habit in spite of everything dividing the persons, e.g. certain family affections; rajasic
affections can last sometimes in spite of all disturbances and in-
compatibilities and furious ruptures because one has a vital need of
the other and clings because of that or because both have that need
and are constantly separating to return and returning to separate or
proceeding from quarrel to reconciliation and from reconciliation
to quarrel; sattwic affections last very often from duty to the ideal
or with some other support though they may lose their keenness,
spontaneity or brightness. But the true reliability is there only
when the psychic element in human affection becomes strong
enough to colour or dominate the rest. For that reason friendship is usually or rather can oftenest be the most durable of the
human affections because there there is less interference of the vital
and, even though a flame of the ego, it can be a quiet and pure
fire giving always its warmth and light. Nevertheless reliable
friendship is almost always with a very few; to have a horde of
loving, unselfishly faithful friends is a phenomenon so rare that it
can be safely taken as an illusion — the enthusiasm of a triumphant
return and his own habit of exaggeration, for he seems to take
easily social kindness for friendship, is probably responsible for X's;
probably if he remained three years in Calcutta, he might change
his tone in spite of his immense capacity for attracting people. In

any case human affection whatever its value has its place, because through it the psychic being gets the emotional experiences it needs until it is ready to prefer the true to the apparent, the perfect to the imperfect, the divine to the human. As the consciousness has to rise to the higher level, so the activities of the heart also have to rise to that higher level and change their basis and character. Yoga is the founding of all the life and consciousness in the Divine, so also love and affection must be rooted in the Divine and a spiritual and psychic oneness in the Divine must be their foundation — to seek the Divine first leaving other things aside or to seek the Divine alone is the straight road towards that change. That means no attachment — it need not mean turning affection into disaffection or chill indifference. But X seems to want to take his vital emotions just as they are — tels quels — into the Divine — let him try and don't bother him with criticisms and lectures; if it can't be done, he will have to find it out himself. Or perhaps he wants to clap on the Divine to the rest as a crowning ornament — shikhara[1] — to his pyramid of loves and affections. In that case —

Good Lord! I have perorated after all.

> *I wrote these three funny stanzas last night in a somnolent consciousness. I don't find any head or tail anywhere.*

There is not any head distinguishable, about tail I don't know.

> *If the stars are of melody, why the deuce should one weep?*

Stars of melody means opera singers, who can I suppose weep. Melodies can also be sorrowful. But if it is real stars you mean, I don't see why they should weep.

> *Should it be stars of misery?*

Certainly not, the phrase has no meaning.

> *The last stanza seems too surrealistic. What?*

Well, well — there is a rather mystifying and alluring incoherence — Still —

---

[1] Summit, peak.

SRI AUROBINDO   965

> *Why the devil am I having so much difficulty in writing?*
> *And so much sleep too? The English stream is drying up or*
> *the lyrical attempt bringing the pain of labour?*

Probably. It is besides I think the melancholy Jacques in your
imagination who is interfering. Perhaps the higher Inspiration
wants to find a lyrical form and he cuts in with the sorrowful
strains of the past—wrinkles on a smooth face, you know. So
the stars can't manage their melody.

June 12, 1937

> *Guru, do you find anything in this poem?*

Very fine lyric—This time you have hit the bull's eye. I have altered
only a few phrases that were weak.

> *"Wandering on the wild seas of thought" won't do perhaps?*

Voyaging through strange seas of Thought, is a piece of highway
robbery—you might just as well write "To be or not to be that
is the question" and call it yours.

> *Please read Surawardy's poems and give your opinion on*
> *the one about the "old man's" tears. Amal says that he*
> *is under Yeats' influence.*

Am obliged to postpone these tears—mine as well as the old man's.

> *At places his poetry is very fine. If only he had left out the*
> *melancholic old man's tears it would have perhaps sounded*
> *better, what?*

Evidently—the old man's tears and the young woman's tennis.

> *[Regarding J's narrative:] This whole part seems very*
> *poetic, but can poetry come in narrative poems?*

Do you mean to say that the rest of the poem is prose or mere
verse? Poetry does not consist only in images or fine phrases.
When Homer writes simply "Sing, Goddess, the baleful wrath of

Achilles, son of Peleus, which laid a thousand woes on the Achaeans and hurled many strong souls of heroes down to Hades and made their bodies a prey for dogs and all the birds; and the will of Zeus was accomplished", he is writing in the highest style of poetry.

June 13, 1937

Guru, here is the tail of the poem I had begun. I am afraid the typing is as pale as the moon's eye and the tail as mistily mystifying as the head! What?

Agree.

I hope you get the link throughout. Is it poetic?

Very. Don't know what it all means, but meaning is superfluous in such poems. The more mystifying the better.

"Voyaging through strange seas of Thought" — highway robbery? Shakespeare's or Sri Aurobindo's?

Wordsworth — one of his best known lines.

Medical report — nothing — all old cases.

A wants a tonic for his debility, Kaviraji if possible. Duraiswami has suggested to him "Chyavanpras". Well?

June 14, 1937

Are some of the lines in today's poem too long for a lyric?

It does not depend on the length of lines but on whether the rhythm sings or not. If it talks instead of singing, then the rhythm is not lyrical.

Had any time for the old man's tears and the young woman's tennis?

No.

[A's case.] For debility, I know little about Chyavanprash.

SRI AUROBINDO

> *Rajangam, Dr. Becharlal and books say that it is a marvellous remedy for debility etc. So, I suppose, we can get some from Madras when Doraiswamy goes.*

Very well.

> *Is he still consuming the same amount of syrup cocoa?...*

He says he has reduced the quantity.

> June 15, 1937

> *You are surely surprised, staggered at the long ethereal lyric I've sent you!*

Staggered is not the word for it. What on earth have you done?

> *See, Sir, I sat down to write and it came. I feel it is a good fish.*

Fish or fishy?

> *I have caught, though I'm not sure whether it is a sprat, trout or a salmon, which?*

A sprat, sir, a sprat and a weird one at that.

> *"Hush, tread softly like a bride,*
> *See, the night is dreaming."*

Good God!

> *"Between the shadows of her curved lips*
> *A white smile is brimming."*

Christ! Woogh!

> *"Oh, what angels have come to kiss*
> *Her virgin face.*
> *What rapture thrills her soul*
> *With diamond rays!"*

Holy Virgin!

> *"Do not wake her, let her sleep*
> *Through the desert-day."*

Who? Night? Where on earth is she sleeping?

> *A bit of philosophy and metaphysics has spoilt the poem*
> *intended to be a fine piece of poetry, no?*

My dear sir, what possessed you to write in this vein of the most tender and infantile Victorian sentimentalism in this year of the Lord 1937? And who or what on earth are you writing about? Night sleeping? What's the idea? It sounds as if it were the sleep of Little Nell (Dickens).

> *"Between the crescent tender lips. . ."*
> [*Sri Aurobindo underlined "tender".*]

Woogh! Night's lips are tender?

> *Please try to restore it to its deserving beauty.*

I am afraid I can do nothing unless you shed some light on what you can possibly mean. At present I am at sea.

> *A rather funny idea, no?*

Very funny.

> *Can Night sleep through desert-day?*

Never heard of her behaving in this way before.

> *It will take 3 or 4 days to get Chyavanprash from Madras.*
> *Meanwhile A can take Kola, if he wants.*

Very well.

June 16, 1937

SRI AUROBINDO   969

> *Sir, I have shoved the poem back to its own century! But that's what comes of hooking! Where does your theory of hooking go?*

It depends on what you hook on to.

> *I suppose you will put in a corollary now: How the devil am I to shed any light when I don't know myself what I'm writing?*

I always did. I never said that whatever you hook on to, the result will be the same. You have hooked on to two things at a time — one which is Victorian, sentimental, melancholy, tragic-pessimistic and thin in its language, images, emotional tone — the other which is from above, full, coloured, packed with suggestion and significance. The first was in you already, I think — the other has come with the upward opening. In today's poem both are there, but neither at its best or worst. In stanzas 4, 5, 6 the second comes out strongly, in the last two the first comes out. I have had therefore to reconstruct these last two which were out of harmony with what went before in their tone.

> *I took the night as a lady who after long travails and seeking arrives at the peace of the Infinite and enjoys the fruit. Is it impossible to symbolise the night or day like that?*

The figure of the lady was terribly small and sentimental, much too domestically human for a power like Night.

> *[Question put by J.:]*
> *I chose this story for trying out the epic style:*
> *Krishna-Gautami whose only son died, prayed to Buddha to give his life back. Later she became a disciple of Buddha ... I feel almost no impulse to write ... I doubt if the subject is a fit one for trying the epic style.*

... As for the fitness of the subject, it depends on how you treat it. The epic tone can be used very well for it, but it must not be pitched too high, as if one were speaking of Gods and Rishis and great heroes as in Homer and Virgil or in Meghnadbodh or similar poems, so the river swelling in echo[1] of the lamentation of one who is an ordinary woman is out of place. The possibility of epic treatment lies in the subject, the universality of death and grief, the calm high wisdom of Buddha etc.

A called me up in the afternoon. Fever! said no liver trouble...

Mother thinks he would like to have his blood examined at the hospital and on the occasion, a consultation with Valle. She sounded him and he seemed to smile at the suggestion. Anyhow you can speak about it to him.

June 17, 1937

> *I sounded A. He says he could wait and see how the new drug is going to act. But what's this blood-examination for? One examines blood for malaria, anaemia and syphilis. . .*

The blood examination is A's own suggestion. He says his uncle died of pernicious anaemia and how can we know that he is not suffering from pernicious anaemia without a blood examination? It is no use discussing the matter scientifically. If you don't want him to die of pernicious anaemia like his uncle or of the imagination of it, the safest course is to have his blood examined and satisfy him that he has not got it — then he may consent to live. Our own idea is the consultation with Valle, for which we have a yet unspoken reason — we will see. If not anaemia pernicious or otherwise, he has got hyperchollericitis.[2] Nothing to do with cholera, by the way.

> *I was rather surprised to hear that Amal has given Dover's powder capsule to L. It contains, as you know, opium, and to give opium without knowing much about it is rather risky.*

L had told Mother Amal wanted to give her something which was not a medicine! Dover's powder is not a medicine?

---

[1] Doubtful reading.
[2] A mock medical term coined by Sri Aurobindo for irascibility.

SRI AUROBINDO   971

> *I would like to have two short-sleeved shirts for opera-*
> *tion purpose.*

Yes. Ask Romen to do them.

> *The word "bright" has been repeated. I suppose I could*
> *have improved the poem.*

Bright, birds, clouds and now the infinite (by my fault) are repeated. Hang it all, sir, let them repeat to their heart's content.

> *Do you think this recent sentimentality could be due to*
> *Harin's influence?*

No.

> *I am reading his lyrics at present, so an unconscious imi-*
> *tation of his style?*

I don't know. Harin's sentimentality is of a different kind.

June 18, 1937

> *A has again pain in the joints, and fever. Shall we then call*
> *Valle without waiting for the effect of the new drug? There*
> *is no harm in calling him, I suppose.*

A attributes the whole thing to climate and spoke also of his increasing irascibility (which is a fact). You might discreetly find out
from Valle if he thinks it is due to climate.

June 19, 1937

> *No answer to the last portion? ["There is no harm in*
> *calling Valle, I suppose."]*

Forgot.
There is no harm. Of course you will ask A first.

> *No news of A today. What's that word please—"spoke*
> *also of his increasing—"?*

972   CORRESPONDENCE WITH

"irascibility" — due to liver, he says.

June 20, 1937

> *In this poem a pale moonlit night appears mist-laden, and leaves seem to smile...*

Well you have sharp eyes to see the leaves smile through a mist-laden night.

> *I have made the leaves quiver, if you won't quiver at it.*

I read it without a quiver.

> *Don't see the link of the first line with what follows... Instead of "weary traveller" it could as well be "weary sheep", I suppose! "I wait and wait like a weary tramp."*

Sheep!!! why not "cat" at once? "I wait and wait like a weary cat" would be very fine and original.

> *As it is, the poem doesn't seem to say much, does it? God knows what to write next.*

If God knows it is all right. Evidently he knows what he is doing.

> *It's a dream which is nothing extraordinary.*

Evidently you don't know when you are inspired.

> *What kind of poetry am I writing now? Very funny surrealism!*

There is nothing surrealist nor funny.

> *And funnier still that I should write these poems — a logical, medical, practical man, what?*

That is your idea of yourself? Queer.

June 21, 1937

SRI AUROBINDO   973

How did you enjoy the mangoes, Sir?

Can't say, as I don't get them till tomorrow.

Mother didn't take them, I suppose.

No; she only tastes sometimes.

I hear Mother doesn't like mangoes at all.

It is not a question of liking.

*Yesterday I thought K had T.B. or pneumonia. But where
are they now? In one night everything over!*

Shobhanallah! With your diagnosis one would have expected him
to be already in Paradise.

*He had sudden severe pain in the chest, cough, and blood in
sputum, with a rise of temperature. On the previous day
he had cold and exhausted himself in a long sea-bath. So
all this gone overnight. Was it just overexhaustion or Force
did it?*

Of course, I put a Force.

June 22, 1937

*As for K, no, Sir, not in Paradise but in hell of agony,
suffering, fever, brown [red] hepatisation, grey hepatisation etc., etc. (nothing to do with liver, though).*

What on earth is this hepatisation? Where? Lungs? pneumonic?
What etc.? Kindly be less cryptic.

*We have got "Chyavanprash" for A. But, they say, it is
specially meant for lung diseases, but it is also a renowned
tissue builder. . . All cold producing things, e.g. cold water,
curds, lime, fruits, cocoanuts must be avoided.*

I don't understand how a medicine for the lungs can be used in his case. He doesn't need tissues either; but nervous energy.

June 23, 1937

> *Rajangam says that Chyavanprash is indicated for every-thing —a panacea. So can we fire?*

Yes, if it can be done without stopping his eating cold water etc. and confining himself to pickles and cayenne pepper.

> *K— Well, red and grey hepatisation are parts of morbid anatomy. When there is pneumonia, the lungs undergo path-ological changes from red to grey and get the solid appear-ance of liver. So the stages are called red and grey hepat-isation. Nothing alarming, you see!*

But hang it all! Has he pneumonia or not? Is there fever now? Alarming or not, what is his present condition?

> *Black despair has swallowed me up to the neck, except for the hand with which I write! As regards sadhana, I don't find any rosy tint anywhere. All clouded, clouded and shrouded. As regards poetry, same, if not more. Have devoted myself to a task utterly impossible and wholly useless —a foolish attempt.*

Whoosh! Anyhow, as regards your poetry, it doesn't seem to me there is any ground for any indulgence in this black luxury.

June 24, 1937

> *I told you long ago that K is hale and hearty and that was the miracle: no fever, nothing at all. You said that according to our diagnosis you expected him to be in Paradise; I said no, not so early, but in a hell of suffering etc.; that's all. That grey hepatisation troubled you, eh?*

Naturally, if you say that a fellow who is supposed to be hale and hearty, is brown and grey with a mysterious hepatisation and suf-

SRI AUROBINDO   975

fering a hell of agony and not yet in Paradise!

> . . . *Please help me to a higher consciousness. Where is the
> higher Being that I had met with? I seem to have lost every-
> thing.*

Everything once gained is there and can be regained. Yoga is not
a thing that goes by one decisive rush one way or the other — it
is a building up of a new consciousness and is full of ups and downs.
But if one keeps to it the ups have a habit of resulting by accumulation in a decisive change — therefore the one thing to do is to keep
at it. After a fall don't wail and say I'm done for, but get up, dust
yourself and proceed farther on the right path.

June 25, 1937

> *There is hardly any improvement in J's eczema. What's to
> be done? I can't try anything else. Kindly ask Mother.*

The medicine is practically exhausted — so you will have to find
another — we don't know of any that is effective. Eczema is a thing
that comes and goes and comes again.

> *Why is it taking such a long time?*

She writes that she has always had it owing to the peculiarity of
her skin — insufficient secretion — some gland responsible. If so —

> *Can't you give her a big dose?*

If it is constitutional, a big dose will not be sufficient — it is only
by a prolonged action that it could cease altogether.

> *Deviprasad has an enlarged gland below the jaw. He has
> been having it for a long time. Looks like a T.B. gland.*

!! [Sri Aurobindo put 2 exclamation marks.]

> *This poem is absolute hooking, Sir! As great poetry usu-
> ally does, you know, the whole thing simply came down, so it
> must be a genuinely great creation, what?*

976   CORRESPONDENCE WITH

Come down it did! As for the great creation, well—

> *Jatin Bal wants to know the last date for permission; is*
> *there such a date?*

No.

> *Can a tentative permission be given?*

Yes.

> *If no rooms are available, can he share my room?*

I suppose so, if it is large enough for two.

                                                        June 26, 1937

> *Yes, about J's gland secretion it is true. Almost every*
> *doctor in England attributed her skin condition to lack*
> *of gland secretion and almost all said it was thyroid, so they*
> *prescribed thyroid pills. And her eczema also is chronic,*
> *due to the skin.*

But deficiency of thyroid gland does not make people fat? J is
not fat. It was thyroid gland medicine which turned T into a life-
long skeleton.

> *Should thyroids be given internally?*

I have no idea what are the effects of these pills. These gland medicines seem to be rather risky—only if you are sure.

> *Can't interpret your exclamations about Deviprasad! What*
> *do you say to cod-liver oil?*

He is already oily and greasy enough.

> *Here is another masterpiece[1]—hooking on again, and*
> *seems a colossal sample of incoherent utterances. Please try*
> *to bring it to a Grecian perfection. And if you succeed in the*
> *task kindly illumine me.*

---

[1] "Soul's Pilgrimage", *Sun-Blossoms*, p. 20.

SRI AUROBINDO   977

I have succeeded. Hooked on again and you must admit that everything is now coherent, cogent and masterly!!!

> *"A solitary pilgrimage of the Soul*
> *Rising from dark tombs of death*
> *Whence began all conscious throbs of life*
> *And end in one ultimate Breath."*
> Is the construction O.K.?

I don't know what you mean by "Whence". Do you mean that it is
from the tomb of death life comes and ends there in the ultimate
breath? That is what the construction would mean. But trusting
to the capital B I have changed to "To whence".

> *How do you find the masterpiece?*

Superb, after my dealings with it.

> *Amal appreciated yesterday's poem[1] very much. He says*
> *that it has become a very fine poem. Agree?*

Of course, very fine indeed!

June 27, 1937

> *J is not fat, but she seems to think so. People say she is in*
> *Tulsi's group which has naturally alarmed her. And she is*
> *thinking of dieting: cutting down rice, bread, etc. What do*
> *you say to that?*

That seems to me nonsense — in any case cutting down food is not
advisable.

> *S came today with a sad and determined face and said that*
> *he could not sleep at all, too much pain. Twice you kept*
> *silent over his treatment. Silent again?*

How can I prescribe? It is your business.

---

[1] "Cry from the Dark", *ibid.*, p. 29.

I admit, Sir, that yesterday's poem is damned masterly and superbly beautiful. Only if I could be the master! I ask myself, "How much of it is yours? Well, since nothing is yours, why shed tears?"

Can't say that nothing is yours.

Do you think hooking like this will continue or a time will come when everything will be a finished product?

Certainly, you have sometimes had it; but still usually there is the mixture of an old poetic mind and your own romantic sentimentalism helping it. That luxury has got to go, so that the inspiration from a higher source may come out clear.

> *"The moon's pale songs ringing in the dark*
> *Are its own mystery-voice..."*
> *Can songs be pale?*

May, but moon's songs are rather toffee.

Have you brushed aside Surawardy's poems?

No, I have combed them only. I send you the results. A few lines are extremely fine, others are very good, others give a fine poetic turn. But he lapses from all that to a modernist rhythmlessness and triviality to which I cannot get accustomed. Anyway—fashion is fashion and the Time spirit has its tricks, — so I leave it there.

June 28, 1937

Yesterday what did you write, Sir—Moon's songs are rather "toffee"? Toffee! Gracious! Bonbon?

Yes, too sweety-sweety.

June 29, 1937

SRI AUROBINDO   979

July 1937

What do you think now of this piece, Sir? What do you think — fine, very fine, eh? Never mind what you say, I find it damn fine!

Sir, I fully admit it. No need to bully me into assent with a damn. Amen!

The revolution in rhythm is not my fault. Sometimes you allow truncations, sometimes you don't. What to do?

Revolutions of rhythm must produce new rhythms, not no rhythm at all.

In the other line ["A voice threading the dimness, faintly heard!"] is it "threading" or "threatening"?

Threading, sir — why the deuce should there be a Pondicherry squabble, however faintly heard, in this business?

July 1, 1937

[The following question was put by J regarding a poem she had begun on Buddha:]
Do you think I should change the lines? I realised that I know nothing of Buddhistic teaching except the word Nirvana. Kindly say a few words on what Buddha stood for or taught his disciples.

I don't know about the change. Buddhist teaching does not recognise any inner self or soul — there is only a stream of consciousness from moment to moment — the consciousness itself is only a bundle of associations — it is kept moving by the wheel of Karma. If the associations are untied and thrown away (they are called sanskaras), then it dissolves; the idea of self or a persistent person ceases; the stream flows no longer, the wheel stops. There is left according to some Sunya, a mysterious Nothing from which all comes; according to others a mysterious Permanent in which there is no individual existence. This is Nirvana. Buddha himself always refused to say what there was beyond cosmic existence; he spoke

980   CORRESPONDENCE WITH

neither of God nor Self nor Brahman. He said there was no utility
in discussing that — all that was necessary was to know the causes
of this unhappy temporal existence and the way to dissolve it.

July 2, 1937

*I can't quite make out the link between the stanzas, and
some things do not seem logical.*

Well, sir, it is quite obvious that your poem is hopelessly incon-
sequent. For a man of logic (?) such divagations must be a release, I suppose.[1] However there is good stuff in it and I have tried
to put the three meanderings right.

*. . . It is not blank verse, Amal says, as there are rhymes
— seas, centuries, memories, etc. What sort of a poem is it
then? Shall I allow rhymes as they come?*

Let us call it modern verse which is never anything, blank or un-
blank, but rhymes when it feels inclined to and doesn't when it
isn't.

July 3, 1937

*I am sure you won't find much inconsequence here, and you
will be charmed by the subtle beauty of the poem. . .*

Great Jehovah!

*. . . except, perhaps, at places it may be too "toffee" for
you!*

The toffee is there!

*S complains of a lot of weakness, buzzing in the ear, no
appetite, sound in the abdomen. . . I am afraid we have to
take an X-ray in order to see if we can do something. Just
now he was complaining of burning pain.*

[1] See last paragraph of 21.6.37, p. 972.

SRI AUROBINDO   981

You can have the X-ray.

July 4, 1937

> *...Unless our blessed nature changes, there is no help*
> *at all. But change of nature is not a question of a day. Till*
> *then suffer like this?*

One can decide not to suffer. But obviously otherwise, until the
nature changes, there will be trouble.

> *I shall write in detail about my trouble...*

All right.

> *For J, André advised auto-haemo therapy or auto-sero*
> *therapy [blood injection into the muscle] which he says is*
> *very good for eczema and asthma.*

It must be done by André, if at all. It is very fashionable now.
If J consents, you can try it.

> *There is Rajlakshmi also with the same trouble, so if you*
> *allow, we may try André's treatment.*

I don't think.

July 5, 1937

> *As for J's case, you seem to be much behind time, Sir!*
> *You don't favour these new discoveries!*

How is that? About the blood injection juggle? I told you it was
fashionable and you could fash along with it if you liked or rather
if J liked — provided André did it.

> *S — no relief! We gave him some alkali tablets.*

There is a blood curdling letter from S. If it is to be taken as accurate,
the whole affair must be nervous, Mother says — She asks if you
have tried charcoal tablets with him.

July 6, 1937

> *You said that it was fashionable, but hinted that you don't like the fashion: "If you liked or rather if J liked, if at all" — don't they mean that?*

Nonsense, sir. Where on earth did I hint anything? Where did I write that? I said it must be done by André if at all — which had to do with the person who was to do it, not with anything else. For the rest I said if J consents, you can try it. Where the hell in that simple phrase is there anything about either my disliking or your liking or anything else that you have put into it? Really now!

> *For S, this time we hadn't tried charcoal, but yesterday we began it and are continuing it. Yes, the letter is blood curdling and his symptoms too, if they are true... God knows how to cure him.*

If he does, send him a telephone!

> *I am almost sure you will howl this time, seeing my poem. But I can't help it.*

I won't howl, but only sigh.

> *By the way, I am reading Harin's lyrics. But I find that his influence does not suit me. My poems become, according to you, sentimental, romantic; while when I read Amal's poems, there come in unconsciously some lines high and lofty and you smile and say "Aha, ha! This fellow has done something!" How is this? Is there some affinity as far as our Inspiration goes? Amal seems to think so, do you?*

Certainly, your real inspiration is nearer Amal's than Harin's — the inspiration that makes you write strong and original things. Under H's influence you seem to become secondhand and reminiscent of past poetry. There is however a lyric vein of another kind which came out in your dream-poems — it is that that sometimes tries to come out in your lyrics — but it is not like Harin's.

July 7, 1937

SRI AUROBINDO   983

> *Do you think then I should stop reading Harin and read more of Amal?*

No, I don't suggest that.

> *What about Arjava's source? Do we have any affinity?*

Maybe. His poetry is very fine and powerful.

> *Guru, C writes that his anti-Mohammedan spirit leads him to violent political speeches and talks. Is it yogic or safe?*

Neither. Especially as there is now Muslim Raj in Bengal.

July 8, 1937

> *S's pain is now setting into a definite character: acme going down before food and then complete relief by food; then after 2 or 3 hours it resumes. These are, I fear, more ulcer pains, but X-ray revealed no ulcer..*

Before food? that seems queer. I don't see how it can be ulcers, if nothing was shown. More likely nerves.

> *My boil seems to have subsided, but the blessed legs are aching terribly: can't walk after my athletic exercises at this old age, Sir. System won't bear it, it seems. Give some embrocation, please.*

You have been doing Olympic sports? What an idea!

July 9, 1937

> *This boil paining all the time. Please do something, otherwise I can't do anything.*

Why so boiled by a boil?

> *I am simply fomenting it 3 or 4 times a day. Anything else?*

984   CORRESPONDENCE WITH

I suppose there is nothing else to do.

> *I suppose these physical impurities are due to the vital,
> what?*

Eventually, yes.

> *You know how my vital is. You must have scented it from
> up there! Still you want us to write* [5.7.37].

It is you who proposed writing and I thought it better to let the
pen draw something out.

> *Otherwise you won't act and will let us go on suffering.
> Divine Law, I suppose, what?*

My dear Sir, I suffer the Divine Law myself — damned slow affair.

> *. . . I have now no push at all for sadhana; vital is peace-
> less, restless and unhappy. Can't concentrate at all. Life
> is dull and deathlike in consequence!*

Well, what can you expect if you go on yielding either within or
without to temptation like that? It sets you at strife with your
own mind and higher vital, to say nothing of the psychic.

> *. . . Darshan is approaching and I can't remain in this con-
> dition and come to you with a glum face, to see you glum
> too.*

I won't be glum — I shall receive you with a cheerful grunt.

> *I kept myself steady for a couple of months, why the devil
> not one month more? You will say — a usual feature in Yoga.
> That is no comfort to me. I'm getting discouraged.*

Rubbish! Be a spider.

> *. . . It's all an old story, Sir, and it will repeat itself till —?*

SRI AUROBINDO   985

Till your vital physical consents to its being kicked out—which
may be, if not tomorrow, day after tomorrow if it chooses.

July 11, 1937

*Here is Dilipda's letter. Please solve the duel between
the homeopath and the surgeon. He looks up to you for
advice. . .*

What's this rash suggestion in the letter about ear? Surely even
a specialist wouldn't perforate the inside of the ear? Besides Dilip
insists on his nose.

But who am I to decide between the two mighty opposites—
homeopathic stalwarts (bigots is an unpleasant word) and allopathic stalwarts? The only safe course for a prudent layman is
to shake his head wisely and murmur "There is much to be said on
both sides of the matter." But it seems to me that the thing is
already done—he has started with the allopathic treatment and
will have to go through to the end.

*I can't say much about the pumping and washing of the ear.
Do you want him to undergo it?*

Pumping and washing sounds very Hathayogic. Harmless therefore let us hope.

*This B. Babu has some cheek, I must say, uttering nasty
things about you.*

Well, it is nothing new. He has been saying nasty things about us
for some years past.

But is he really gifted with some power?

I suppose he has or had some powers, but his mind seems to be
rather chaotic, accepting all sorts of mental, vital and other perceptions and suggestions as the truth, without discrimination.
Barin told me a lot about his wonderful (prophecy and knowing
everything about everybody) powers, but I was disappointed to

986 CORRESPONDENCE WITH

find it a glowing jumble of truth and error both taken as the very truth. No harm in a mixture of truth and error if one observes and goes on steadily clearing out the mixture. But otherwise —

> *X writes that he can't go to see K, though that was one of the motives of his going to Calcutta.*

It is a pity he could not go to K.

> *... Why this bitterness against "Asramites"? From where has he really got this idea that we are unsympathetic towards him?*

He says some of the Asramites!

> *On the other hand, I think, most of us have a deep and genuine feeling for him which he doesn't see because our expression is so different from worldly people's.*

Yes, but X likes universal patting and patting is rare in the Asram, preaching is more usual.

> *You remember he said that he is a great believer in expression. Is expression the only real thing in life?*

No. Expression is all right provided it is the right expression of the right thing. But it is not necessary to be always expressing and expressing.

> *What do you express when you come and sit like the immovable Himalayas at Darshan? Yet people feel joy, peace, etc., etc.*

Of course. But X's difficulty is that he is accustomed to live outside not inside and feel sensible impacts and react to them — expression you know — The inner silent feeling of things is not much in his line.

> *... At any rate I don't believe that the sadhaks are in any way worse than worldly people whose affections and sym-*

SRI AUROBINDO   987

> *pathy have blinded X. This place being small, one's defects
> stand out and criticisms come to one's ears and get magni-
> fied.*

Yes.

> *Can he say that he has no enemies, no backbiters outside?*

Well, outside being large, he can give them a wide berth.

> *I have heard it said that ordinary sadhaks — the Toms,
> Dicks and Harrys — who would be nowhere beside X in the
> outside world and who would have nothing if they did not
> have a shelter here — even such people criticise him.*

? The quality of the sadhaks is so low? I should say there is a considerable amount of ability and capacity in the Asram. Only
the standard demanded is higher than outside even in spiritual
matters. There are half a dozen people here perhaps who live in
the Brahman consciousness — outside they would make a big noise
and be considered as great Yogis — here their condition is not
known and in the Yoga it is regarded not as siddhi but only as a
beginning.

> *They say — why, the sadhaks had nothing to sacrifice; they
> were beggars, and are kept so comfortably here. This is
> an exterior view of things, isn't it?*

Sacrifice depends on the inner attitude. If one has nothing outward to sacrifice, one has always oneself to give.

> *A visitor once said, "Oh, how happy you all are here, so
> comfortably kept, no thoughts and anxieties. Life is plain
> sailing." When he was asked to come and stay here, he
> replied that he had no time!*

The difficulty is that most of the sadhaks are still full of desires, so
their renunciation is not a thing that becomes very perceptible.
If they had the inner tyaga,[1] it would create an atmosphere that
people coming here would feel.

---

[1] *tyāga:* renunciation.

*. . . Now I have decided to keep aloof as much as possible
from tea-table and music, especially before Darshan. It
may hurt X, but I can't help it.*

Perhaps if he understands that it is a preparation for darshan,
he may not be so hurt.

July 12, 1937

*Shall I pass on your observation about K to X ("It is a
pity he could not go to K.")?*

What's the use — since he has to remain in Calcutta.

*Yes, from the description it seems to be the nose and not
the ear. But in a previous letter he spoke of the ear. Doesn't
know what he is talking about? Ear-trouble, nose-trouble?*

Perhaps he had both.

*[The following two questions were asked by J:] Is your
"Love and Death" a narrative poem?*

Certainly.

*Narratives then can be made or written very poetically,
not like a mere fact-to-fact story-telling?*

But what do you mean by poetically? A fact to fact story telling
can be very poetic. Poetry is poetic whether it is put in simple
language or freely adorned with images and rich phrases. The
latter kind is not the only "poetic" poetry nor is necessarily
the best. Homer is very direct and simple; Virgil less so but still is
restrained in his diction; Keats tends always to richness; but one
cannot say that Keats is poetic and Homer and Virgil are not.
The rich style has this danger that it may drown the narration so
that its outlines are no longer clear. This is what has happened with
Shakespeare's Venus and Adonis and Lucrece; so that Shakespeare
cannot be called a great narrative poet.

*How did you find Monomohan Ghosh's poems on Love and
Death?*

SRI AUROBINDO   989

I don't remember anything about them and am not sure that I
have read.

> *S says that he feels very hungry now, especially in the even-
> ing. Only milk not enough. I fear to give him anything else
> at night.*

But why is it so bad with him? T gets on very well with her ptosis,
keeping only a few rules like not moving about for some time after
meals.
                                                                July 13, 1937

> *I think we should replace S's loss of liver by liver-ex-
> tract. It is a rather costly medicine, that's why I hesitate.*

He has sent me another tragic letter.

> *I hear that A has much pain and can't even move about. But
> it shouldn't be so bad, as it is the sole.*

Becharlal did not seem to think much of it — said it should be
all right in 3 days.

> *Self: Nose boil seems to be boiling down slowly; but at
> noon I had a terrible headache, fever too. Feeling fed up,
> really!*

Cellular bolshevism, probably.
                                                                July 14, 1937

> *What's this "cellular bolshevism", Sir?*

Bolshevism of the cells rising up against the Tsar (yourself). Also
the Bolsheviks carry on their propaganda by creating Communistic
"cells" everywhere, in the army, industries etc., etc. You don't
seem to be very up in contemporary history.

> *Guru, there is a whole mass of letters from dear C.*

His Bengali handwriting is too much for me.

990 CORRESPONDENCE WITH

There is a tangled problem which is absolutely beyond me.

I have read his letter, but can't make head or tail out of his problem. He will have to solve it himself.

There is a clash between ethics or spirituality and worldliness, so he seeks your advice.

Anyhow he seems to me to be the most loose and impractical and disorderly fellow that ever was, leaving his papers and debts and everything fluttering about all over the world. It will be no wonder if he loses all he has.

July 15, 1937

Guru,
At last C has dared to ask for August Darshan permission. Do you dare to permit him?

Mother considers it wiser for him to abstain. She says "Better not."

For S, . . . I can't increase his evening meal yet. My idea is to build up gradually the diet so that the system may be accustomed and strengthened at the same time. No use upsetting the stomach, liver, etc. — what?

I suppose so. Don't understand the ways of a fallen stomach sounds too much like a fallen angel — but S is not that, (no angel, that is to say) whatever his stomach may be.

A has gall bladder trouble and I suspect congestion of right kidney too . . . We have to give bile salts, moderate dose of salts . . .

Mother says to be careful about salts, as they often help formation of stones.

July 16, 1937

Does Mother mean common salt? I meant mag. sulph. and soda-sulph.

SRI AUROBINDO   991

No, she meant medical salts.

> *Mind and vital rather restless. No interest. Tried to write
> poetry, wouldn't come. Can't get it back. What to do?
> Forcibly sit down and scratch and scribble?*

You can try. It might dribble back like that.

July 17, 1937

> Guru,
>   *What the deuce is "Brahman consciousness" [12.7.37]?
> The same as cosmic consciousness? Does one come to it
> after the psychic and spiritual transformations?*
>   *Is it something like seeing Brahman in everybody and
> everywhere or what? It is not spiritual realisation, I suppose,
> I mean realisation of Self? You see I am a nincompoop
> in this business. Please perorate a little.*

Eternal Jehovah! You don't even know what Brahman is! You will
next be asking me what Yoga is or what life is or what body is
or what mind is or what sadhana is! No, sir, I am not proposing
to teach an infant class the A.B.C. of the elementary conceptions
which are the basis of Yoga. There is Amal who doesn't know what
consciousness is, even!

Brahman, sir, is the name given by Indian philosophy since the
beginning of time to the one Reality, eternal and infinite which
is the Self, the Divine, the All, the more than All, which would
remain even if you and everybody and everything else in existence
or imagining itself to be in existence vanished into blazes — even
if this whole universe disappeared, Brahman would be safely
there and nothing whatever lost. In fact, sir, you are Brahman
and you are only pretending to be Nirod; when Nishikanta is translating Amal's poetry into Bengali, it is really Brahman translating Brahman's Brahman into Brahman. When Amal asks me what
consciousness is, it is really Brahman asking Brahman what Brahman is! There, sir, I hope you are satisfied now.

To be less drastic and refrain from making your head reel till
it goes off your shoulders, I may say that realisation of the Self
is the beginning of Brahman realisation; — the Brahman consciousness — the Self in all and all in the Self etc. It is the basis

992   CORRESPONDENCE WITH

of the spiritual realisation and therefore of the spiritual transformation; but one has to see it in all sorts of aspects and applica-
tions first and that I refuse to go into. If you want to know you have
to read the Arya.

> *Is living in that consciousness an ideal condition for receiving
> the Supramental descent?*

It is a necessary condition.

> *I heard that no one here was prepared for this Supra-
> mental descent?*

Of course not, this realisation of the Self as all and the Divine
as all is only the first step.

> *What's the next step?*

The next step is to get into contact with the higher planes above
spiritual mind—for as soon as one gets into the spiritual Mind
or Higher Mind, this realisation is possible.

> *Now the big question is: Is the realisation of the Self a state
> of perpetual peace, joy and bliss?*

If it is thoroughly established, it is one of *internal* peace, freedom,
wideness, in the inner being.

> *Is it a state surpassing all struggles, dualities and depres-
> sions?*

All these things you mention become incidents in the external being,
on the surface, but the inner being remains untouched by them.

> *Are all troubles of the lower nature conquered finally —
> especially sex?*

No, sir. But the inner being is not touched.

> *Or is it that sex-desire rises up in the Yogis, but leaves*

SRI AUROBINDO 993

them untouched, unscathed? No attraction for them? It must be so, otherwise how can they be called siddhas?[1] *No danger of a fall from the spiritual state?*

It may be covered up in a way—so long as it is not established in all parts of the being. The old Yogis did not consider that necessary, because they wanted to walk off, not to change the being.

Why do you call it a beginning only? What more do you want to do except perhaps physical transformation?

I want to effect the transformation of the whole nature (not only of the physical)—that's why.

Could you whisper to me the names of those lucky fellows, those "half a dozen people", so that I can have a practical knowledge of what that blessed thing—"the Brahman, consciousness"—is like?

NO, SIR.

How can you have a practical knowledge of it by knowing who has it? You might just as well expect to have a practical knowledge of high mathematics by knowing that Einstein is a great mathematician. Queer ideas you have!

Are they Anilbaran? Pavitra? Datta? Dyuman? Nolini? Radhanand, but he can't be for he is Brahma himself, so keeps himself secluded like him, no?

???????

July 18, 1937

Self—Pus still coming out. Nose also angry!

What a bad-tempered "pussy" cat of a nose!

I dreamt that the Mother was building a very big hospital in which I would be a functionary. . . Dream of a millennium in advance?

---

[1] *siddha:* one who has realised the Divine.

994   CORRESPONDENCE WITH

It would be more of a millennium if there were no need of a hospital at all and the doctors turned their injective prodding instruments into fountain-pens — provided of course they didn't make misuse of the pens also.

July 19, 1937

> *Why so furious about injective instruments, Sir? They are supposed to be very effective.*

That doesn't make an increase of hospitals, illnesses and injections the ideal of a millennium.

> *But why the deuce are those instruments to be replaced by fountain-pens? Want doctors to be poets or clerks? Or is it a hint to me to write more than prescribe?*

I was simply adopting the saying of Isaiah the prophet, "the swords will be turned into ploughshares", but the doctor's instrument is not big enough for a ploughshare, so I substituted fountain-pens.

> *A swelling — size of a cherry — has appeared inside my nose... The tip is damn painful. Knifing is not advisable. I hope it won't leave me with a nose like that of Cyrano de— quoi?[1]*

Let us hope not. That kind of nose wouldn't suit either your face or your poetry.

July 20, 1937

> *What's this devil of a condition I am passing through? No interest in anything — as if the whole world were dead, blank. There is no uprush of sex or desire and all that. But still a negative blank state! Experience of Nirvana? Tamasic vairagya? I am simply inactive, trying to keep myself steady and hoping that it will pass in time. But will it? No active way out?*

---

[1] Cyrano de Bergerac: A character, famed for his enormous nose, in the play of the same name by Edmond Rostand.

SRI AUROBINDO   995

Well, it may be one of two things. (1) The vital has dropped down
and says "if I can't have what I want in this damned world of yours,
alright I non-cooperate and ask for nothing." Hence the flatness—
Result of course, tamasic vairagya. This kind of thing often happens
at a certain stage of sadhana.

(2) Drop into the physical—first complete acquaintance with
the principle of Inertia proper to the physical when it is moved
neither by vital, mind, nor spirit. Lies flat waiting for the breath of
God or any breath to stir it, but making no move of its own.

Hold on and call upon the Spirit to breathe.

> *I think you are exerting a damn lot of pressure, what?*

Not so much as that—or if so, it is automatic.

July 21, 1937

> *Guru, after all some poetry has come out. The head and*
> *tail seem to be all right, but the body has elongated beyond*
> *proportion, no?*

The body is all right as well as the head, except for that impossible
shining face of a voice. It is the tip of the tail that is defective.

> *I was urgently called by R to see his wife who had received*
> *a wound on the head by falling down. . . Two accounts*
> *were given, one in the morning, another in the evening, for*
> *the fall being the cause of the wound in such a place. Both*
> *were unconvincing. Better to trust than distrust, what?*

Amen!

> *I asked R if he was going to write to the Mother about it;*
> *said no! Very funny!! Relying too much on self or auto-*
> *matic action of the Force?*

He did not write when (he says) he was sick unto death recently.
Calling the Force in silence!

July 23, 1937

> *You know V is having difficulty in breathing through the*

left nostril. Maybe due to polypus. Do you know what he does? He has got some string, besmears it with bee's wax, passes it through one nostril, brings it out through the mouth, and then puts it into the other nostril. Feels much better! Hathayogic treatment, he says. I have no idea, have you? Any danger in it? Can't opine myself; only I think the rope is misplaced!

It is done by the Hathayogis with a cloth, I believe, just as they clean their entrails from throat to anus with a cloth. For them there is no danger, for they are trained but if it is done by a self-sufficient ass or even by an untrained amateur simply there may be danger in these things. Mudgaokar the Bombay judge (known to me) tried the cleaning of the nose with water, a simple Hathayoga process, and had trouble with his proboscis in consequence. It did not approve of his way of dealing with it.

Really, Sir, you have caught a magnificent fellow for Supra-mentalisation, what?

Well, sir, in the supramental world all kinds will be needed, I suppose. Then why not a supramental ass?

July 24, 1937

I hadn't understood "Psh" in Chand's letter. Got it at the last moment, by intuition, Sir: Paresh!

Yes.

I see! It needed intuition to find that out!

S's same trouble continues or worse. Why are you silent on liver extract?

Extract liver — no objection.

A new trouble! Taint of acidity, burning in my throat. The Force is experimenting on me my patients' maladies to take them more seriously?

Who knows?

SRI AUROBINDO   997

> *What is the damned meaning of this poem?*[1] *What's this*
> *path? What's the height? Both being illumed by the moon*
> *etc.? It seems I have simply described Nature, giving free*
> *rein to imagination. Mystifying, no?*

Why do you want any damned meaning? It is a mystic picture —
plenty of mystic significance which is best left unintellectualised,
but no damned meaning.

A height is a height of being, sir, and the seas are seas of the soul,
and the path is a path to infinite peace and light. "That is all we
know or need to know" as Keats has been telling you every day
for the last hundred years. The path naturally goes across the tranced
figure — it couldn't possibly get home otherwise.

> *. . . Please clarify.*

Absolutely refuse to clarify anything. Let us leave it in its own
radiant swoon of mystic misty wistful light.

> *Then at the end, what's the "slumbering seas", suddenly?*
> *Can't make out.*

Why suddenly, man — you have been having seas and waters all
the time.

> *No connections! A horrible mess, Sir! The beauty of the*
> *poem is buried under it, I fear, what?*

Lord! Lord! If you had intellectualised the business with your
connections, there would have been no beauty in the poem or at
least no mystic beauty.

> *Through Surawardy's poems? Seems to be a genuine poet,*
> *no?*

Have not inspected the fellow yet. May perhaps do it tonight.

July 25, 1937

---

[1] "Figure of Trance", *Sun-Blossoms*, p. 10.

Please see Surawardy's poems and say something communicable to the old man!

Don't want to communicate — prefer on this point to be incommunicable — not to you of course, but to Calcutta (old man will hear of it.)

July 26, 1937

Old man is done?

How done? How am I to know if he is done or undone (by the young woman?)? He is in Calcutta.

What's this, really? J had eczema and now asthma! Is there any truth in the popular belief that when eczema disappears, asthma appears? Homeopathic theory, they say.

Never heard of it. The eczema of any number of people disappears without their getting asthma. It is the weather and a certain susceptibility in her physical to these things — no need for all these out of the way theories.

S — pain, burning "normal", i.e. you understand, I hope, this means normal pain.

Yes, of course. It is the patient who is abnormal.

July 28, 1937

Surely you know what I meant by "old man is done"?

Surely I did, but he was not at all done by me, so I had to pass on your question to the young woman.

D wants the poems back, you know.

Well, well — I will try to push my way through him.

People say I am getting absolutely bald, Sir. Two things I feared — one a big tummy and another, a smooth baldness.

SRI AUROBINDO 999

> *Couldn't be saved from one. If you can't grow new hair,
> please help to preserve the little I have, Sir.*

What one fears, is usually what happens. Even if there were no
other disposition, the fear calls it in. Who knows, if you had not
feared, you might have had the waist of a race-runner and the hair
of Samson.

> *I read in Mother's* Conversations[1] *that skin, hair and
> teeth "belong to the most material layers of the being",
> so spiritual Force takes a long time to act on them. Is it true?*

Painfully true.

> *Then I have no chance till the Supermind descends?*

I suppose not. And who knows what fancies the Supramental may
have.
> *July 29, 1937*

> *This is absolutely a third-rate poem.[2] What to do?*

What a queer card you are! It is as good as the others.

> *No use asking the virtue of the poem!*

Very fine and glowing, sir.
> *July 30, 1937*

> *Guru, here are Dilipda's letter and poems. He wants to
> know your opinion. Perhaps in the afternoon you will have
> some leisure.*

What an idea!

> *Please read each one of the poems. I have glanced through
> them and they are really wonderful.*

[1] Mother's Centenary Vol. 3, p. 90.
[2] "In Moonlit Silence", *Sun-Blossoms*, p. 21.

4

Have had time to read only two as yet.

> *Dilipda says that his poems are now appreciated. Personality incarnate?. . . . And the "old man"? How is he?*

Old man suspended by the eruption of Personality — perhaps tomorrow.

July 31, 1937

August 1937

> *The last two lines of the poem are too long, perhaps? Oh, N complains of evening fever 100°, for the last few days.*

Part of your poetry? Can't scan it.

I have read Dilip's poem — there is the force of a new inspiration in the language and the building and turns of thought, something more intense and gathered together. I think there is something less mental, a new and more vibrant note.

I have gone through Surawardy. He has certainly a fine poetic vein, but his success is less than his capacity — The two poems, China Sea and Asoca Tree are very fine — the rest are in a lower pitch; there are fewer deliberate descents into the commonplace than in the old man poems, but also not so frequent, intense felicities of expression and powerful lines.

> *. . . You have perhaps said somewhere that when the Supramental descends, everything will be comparatively easier. Do you mean sex-conquest too?*

This force seems to have been pushing strongly in recent days — for there are others who have been stumbling — luckily the stumble gave them a reaction which has made them more awake to the necessity of "no-indulgence".

August 1, 1937

> *The notion of "equality" seems to be a bugbear to people who have personal ties, though the giving up of them will be more than compensated by getting the Divine within, for, after all, what are these human ties of ego or sex?*

SRI AUROBINDO   1001

The Yoga cannot be done if equality is not established. Personal
relations must be founded on the relation with the Divine in himself and the Divine in all and they must not be "ties" to pull one
down and keep bound to the lower nature but part of the higher
unity.

> *What is your idea of special relationship? Won't predict?*

There is nothing to predict. I have been saying the same thing
all along (what I say above) and if there is to be any fulfilment of
this work, it can be on no other basis. As for founding it on this
[. . .]¹, it can't be done.

> *. . .There are situations when one is faced with either
> telling a lie or the truth, and one can't decide which. Sri
> Krishna says in the Mahabharata that lies are permitted
> at times, and that they are as good as truths, e.g. a truthful
> Muni, by showing the robbers the hiding place of travellers
> and causing their death, went to Hell. What's your opinion?*

Naturally — nobody is called upon to expose others to death by
telling a truth like that. But the lie was not the best way from the
spiritual point of view.

> *You say physical sex action must be avoided by all means.
> Why so strict on it while tolerating vital-physical lapses?*

Because the physical action breaks a law without which the Asram
cannot stand and the work cannot be done. It is not a personal
matter, but a blow aimed at the very soul of the Mother's work.
   Outside sadhaks indulge and get a child, e.g. Y and others.
Mother disapproves and the man who does it has no longer the
same grace as before, but he is not in the Asram and his lapse hurts
only himself and his wife.

> *The last portion of your remark² is rather cryptic. "This
> force" means the Supramental Force?*

¹ One word illegible.
² See last para of 1.8.37.

What the devil! I was speaking of the sex force.

Is it descending, then?

The sex force? By God it is, descending and ascending too.

What did you mean by giving them "a reaction"? Physical reaction?

I meant that they got so alarmed at the closeness to a precipitous fall that they stopped indulging the vital physical.

Have I any chance, Guru, of coming out of this vital struggle?

Of course.

If you are with me, I shall be all right. But don't be with me as with X. You couldn't keep him here; forces took him away! Doubt!

I repeat that he took himself away. No Force can take a man away, who really wants not tó go and really wants the spiritual life. X wanted the "Divine Response" only, not spiritual life — his doubts all rose from that.

Why do you lay so much stress on our writing everything to you? Can't we pray to you and ask for help? Isn't it as good as writing?

Not writing means trying to conceal. That is a suggestion of the vital.

August 2, 1937

Consciousness and intensities can rhyme?

Not that I know of, but all things are possible in a world of infinite possibility.

SRI AUROBINDO   1003

> *K's pus in the eye is not getting less; better inject gom-*
> *enol and then vaccine, if not cured. So?*

You know best — or at least can try.

August 3, 1937

> *A's liver again! He has finished 3 Takadiastase bottles.*
> *He finds good effect from it. We require another bottle*
> *now. Should we buy it?*

Buy the take-a-distaste and keep his liver quiet for God's sake.
He shows signs of starting his lamentations again. The bottle to
keep the baby quiet!

> [*The following report was written by Dr. Becharlal:*]
> *D has pain in the abdomen, liquid motions, vomiting. . . He*
> *has no teeth, so it's very difficult to masticate the food,*
> *hence the tendency to indigestion. . . He eagerly wishes to*
> *be instructed by my Holy Mother, what food he should take*
> *tomorrow: usual food or only milk and whey?*

Is it not the rule so long as the teeth are not replaced to take only
liquid food?

August 4, 1937

> *I don't know about Ekalavya's epidermis. Can he be com-*
> *pared to a* বনদেব[1] *without being one? But Gods and God-*
> *desses are supposed to be fair, no?*

Who says? Krishna was নীল,[2] other gods have different colours,
red, white, black, yellow and green. If he had নীলোৎপল আঁখি[3]
what prevents him from being like a বনদেবতা?[4]

August 5, 1937

> *If you have no light, let these poems remain, Sir.*

---

[1] *vanadev:* god of the woods.   [3] *nīlotpal ānkhi:* blue-lotus eyes.
[2] *nīl:* blue.   [4] *vanadevatā:* god of the woods.

1004   CORRESPONDENCE WITH

I have plenty of light and to spare.

> *Why the devil is this sex force descending and ascending so vehemently now, in place of the Supramental?*

If people want it . . . , what else can you expect than that it should rise?

I don't know what you mean by descending. It is not a high force from above that it should descend — It is a force from below or around.

> *Judging by the degree of vehemency, shall I say that the Supramental Force is vehemently coming down in this form? Or it is at least some Divine Force, giving a last kick at the Sex Force?*

The Divine Force has nothing to do with it. It is the sex and other lower forces that are attacking in order to make it impossible for the Divine Force to do its work, or the Supramental to descend. They hope to prevent it altogether or, if by some miracle, it still descends, to limit its extension and prevent anything more than an individual achievement.

August 6, 1937

> *"New centuries open their eyes. . ." You won't agree, perhaps, that centuries have eyes?*

I agree to everything and anything — let them have ears also. When one can write like that, all objections vanish.

> *"Appear to me" doesn't appear very pretty.*

No it isn't pretty — it is first-class.

> *. . . Well, anything to say?*

I have said it. Why the hell can't you always write like that? The inspiration came clean through this time.

> *Z has no fever. I think he should take Chyavanprash; but*

SRI AUROBINDO   1005

> *it is a costly drug, we can't supply much. I wonder if he has friends to help him with some money.*

I believe he has some thousands of rupees stored up with which he is maintaining his populous family in Bhavnagar, (those who have not been able to push themselves in here owing to our stubborn and inhuman or superhuman resistance). But he doesn't want to acknowledge its existence.

August 8, 1937

> *Why the hell can't I write? Why the hell, indeed! Because I don't want to — that's all!*

My why the hell was an ejaculation, not a question.

> *If I were to ask you that question, I know your prompt answer would be — no poet can always maintain a high level! Isn't that the answer?*

Obviously, if it is put as a question, that is the only answer. But it wasn't.

August 9, 1937

> *Can one break a dream?*

I suppose one can. If you are dreaming and somebody pokes you in the ribs and says, "What are you groaning about? Wake up," wouldn't he be breaking your dream?

August 10, 1937

> *S is again bad; pain started right after lunch and other troubles also.*

Does he remain quiet after the meal for a sufficient length of time or prances about?

August 11, 1937

> *Here is a long letter from D. You can skip portions — at the end there is a reference to T. Their quarrel won't be made up in this life, it seems.*

I have glanced through.
Musician-poets at loggerheads — what can you expect?

I thought, in spite of everything, T has a sort of affection for D, no?

So they both said.

There is an engineer who wants to come here for a month. Can't make out whether he is asking for permission. What's your opinion?

Can't make out, myself, anything about any engineer — so have no opinion. Not anxious for a rush this time.

August 12, 1937

J's eczema is still spreading. . . She can't resist scratching it.

How is it to cure if she scratches?

She asks whether it is any good prolonging the treatment with this ointment — Acecholex. So will it be better now to take sun-treatment with oil?

Very difficult to say. This is a thing in its nature obstinate and needing a long treatment. Constant changing of medicaments more often encourages the obstinacy than curing it.

August 16, 1937

The channel is rather choked, as you will see. This poem is no good. Still, better to send it, I thought, to get a contact.

There is much "good" in it, on the contrary.

Too busy to give us Force? Darshan is over, Sir!

SRI AUROBINDO   1007

Darshan is over but karshan[1] is not.

> *August 17, 1937*

>> *"Slumbering birds awake with a start..."*
> *"With a start" O.K.?*

No — it makes me start.

> *Shivalingam (a servant) has a boil on the face. Not very happy about it.*

He is not? Hard to satisfy these people!

> *August 18, 1937*

> *About Shivalingam, I'm sorry! I meant that I was not happy.*

I supposed so.

> *I'm doubtful about this poem. One mind says very fine, another says damn! So?*

Both are right — the damner because you didn't quite get the proper expression, the other because the substance *is* very fine.

> *By the way, do you find plenty of repetitions in the ideas?*

There are repetitions in the last few poems, variations on the same theme. Vedic, what? Variations fine, though!

> *August 19, 1937*

> *For J's eczema and asthma, Dr. André says that anti-anaphylactic injection is very good. Shall we try?*

I don't know what anti-anaphylactic means (my proficiency in quasi-Greek is not very great) but it sounds swell. No objection.

> *Guru, Anjali and Jatin have written to you regarding their*

---

[1] Ploughing, tilling cultivation, (hard labour).

1008 CORRESPONDENCE WITH

visit here. Perhaps you will give them a reply. It seems they are not very definite about how long they will stay. . . Jatin can stay with me, but could you avoid putting Anjali with Y? I can't judge your work, but it is permissible to state the circumstances. . . Inconveniences, sufferings, etc. do not matter if Mother thinks it is needed for Y's good. . .

I have not yet had time to place Jatin's letter before the Mother and decide on an answer. I shall do so as soon as possible and let him know the result.

Please let me know for future guidance if I should at all interfere in this way.

No objection.

August 21, 1937

25.8.37

Nirod

If Jatin and Anjali are to stay till November, Jatin can stay with you as now; the difficulty is about Anjali. Mother has only 2 rooms that she can offer her and they are both bad. There is the room in Belle-Vue, formerly occupied by Narmada who has shifted now into a better one; it is a very bad room, dark and ill-ventilated and it opens into K's with only a curtain between. I suppose you know also that the . . . sadhikas in the house are fairly noisy and can make themselves very unpleasant when they want to! Alternatively, there is the room next to M's — also bad, though not so bad as the other. Perhaps you know what kind of neighbour M is — if the next door neighbour does anything of which she does not approve, it will be tempests without end and howling enough to take the roof off. I can't write these things publicly, . . . and you will put matters in their fierce naked light before Anjali — for her judgment and decision. She must decide with full knowledge of the circumstances so that she may not blame the Mother afterwards if trouble or discomfort is there. (I may add that even a cricket making a noise near her deprives M of sleep and sends her into flames of wrath or gulfs of depression). So there you are.

SRI AUROBINDO
August 25, 1937

SRI AUROBINDO   1009

> ". . . Breaking all crag-teeth distances
>   Of the dark abysmal dominion."

Sir, this "crag-teeth" is a too obvious theft.[1]

> *Y is not pleased with Jatin staying with me. She says be-*
> *cause I wanted him to stay with me you agreed. . . Is it true*
> *that you have acceded to my desire?*

No. But even if it had been a desire, what objection? To want to
put up a friend in one's room is not a crime. For my part, I am glad
to have him there and think it is good for him and you.

> *. . . Please give Y some Peace and Protection.*

She must be ready to receive it — i.e. she must take and keep the
right attitude.

> *Jatin wants to know if you will write anything more to him.*

Yes.

                                                 August 26, 1937

> *Please give me your constant help and protection.*

I will certainly give that.

> *For A's chronic colitis [6.6.37], we have tried our best,*
> *but without any result. Dr. Manilal says why not try homeo-*
> *pathy? Will R take him up?*

I don't know that we are ready to hand him over to R just now at
least. Besides, R himself does not seem eager to take any cases.

                                                 August 27, 1937

> ". . . Recalling to my memory dim-paced
>   Foot-falls of a paradisal star. . ."

---

[1] "The Bird of Fire", *SABCL*, vol. 5 (*Collected Poems*), p. 571.

1010   CORRESPONDENCE WITH

But, my dear sir, a star has no feet and the picture of a star walking
about on 2 feet in the sky is rather grotesque, so I have had to invent
a godhead of a star who can do it all right.

> *Last night I dreamed that I had gone to a distant rela-*
> *tive's house. There I met a friend of mine looking hideous*
> *because his nose had been eaten up by a disease. I thought*
> *of curing him by calling down the Mother's Force. Then I*
> *actually felt the Force coming down; when I put my hand*
> *on him, lo, he was cured! Miracle and concrete Force in*
> *dream?*

A feat on the vital plane. If you begin to be conscious of the force
there, it ought to travel down before long into the physical also!

> *Can Jatin and his wife attend the stores[1] on the 1st?*

Yes.
   Arjava says his medicine for decoction is exhausted, so he has
to stop. How is that? It is Sudarshan I suppose. But that can be
got at any time from Punamchand's father as well as any of his
other medicines — So they should be ordered in time before depletion.
                                                     August 29, 1937

> *My store seems run down! No words, images or ideas, all*
> *gone![2]*

Well, if a run-down store can produce a poem like that, it is a
miraculous run-down store. . .

> *Please give an all-round poking, will you?*

All right — I shall try to give the all-round poke.

> *It seems, according to Ayurveda and common Indian belief,*

---

[1] "Prosperity", as the stores are now called, from where the requirements of the
sadhaks were given by the Mother, on the first day of every month.
[2] "Your Face", *Sun-Blossoms*, p. 2.

SRI AUROBINDO 1011

> *that onions fried in ghee are almost a specific for piles and an*
> *admirable laxative. They also have a cooling effect. I know*
> *that they make the whole body damn hot, but their heat-*
> *properties have a stimulating effect. Any views, popular*
> *or personal, on this remedy?*

Mother does not know that they are laxative or cooling—it has
an energising effect. Perhaps it is effective for tamasic people—
it is doubtful if it helps piles. It is taken like that largely in Japan,
but it is not supposed there to cure piles.

August 30, 1937

> *As for S, we have exhausted our means. One thing remains*
> *—liver extract which I have withheld till now.*

You can try that—since it is his liver—let's see if it extracts him
out of his agonies.

> *R comes to us now and then for allopathic drugs. Today he*
> *came and asked for apomorphine. This drug is only used in*
> *urgent cases of poisoning where evacuation of stomach is*
> *immediately called for. . . We don't know anything about the*
> *case. We are asked to give certain drugs, we give; for*
> *what case etc. we don't enquire because he may not like it.*
> *What should be done in such cases in the future?*

God knows! Perhaps, if it is anything really dangerous, play the
Artful Dodger[1] and, otherwise, pray fervently to God that nobody
may be poisoned. But for whom does he ask this, I wonder? Alys?
He has no other patients except Lakshmi perhaps at the moment.

> *"Half-veiled figures of unknown splendour*
> *Smile with the happy utterance. . ."*
> *Can they smile?*

May or may not, but smiling here risks being inane; so I dodge the
smiles out.

---

[1] A character in Charles Dickens's *Oliver Twist*.

1012 CORRESPONDENCE WITH

Now that X has returned, J wants to publish her novel. . .
Is there any fear of complications?

It can be taken up, but I refuse to prophesy anything about complications. X seems to be in a beatified mood just now; perhaps he will be saintly and good-tempered about it, but one can't be sure.

August 31, 1937

September 1937

I send you the letter of a diabetic sadhak asking me if he can take rice once a day. I can only pass on the question to you. What shall I reply to his piteous and pathetic request? For enlightenment, please.

September 1, 1937

Guru, I hope you won't call this a Victorian, sentimental,
romantic poem and make me crush my bones by a fall from
the sky of ecstasy!

Nothing of that kind in it.
Your bones are safe this time.

September 4, 1937

. . . By the way, you haven't returned my medical report
book. Mother says it is not there! How? I sent it last night!

Forgot to shove it in. Afterwards it got covered with other books and files — so undiscoverable.

September 5, 1937

What does Mother say about making S a hospital bird for
some days? I think he will benefit by it. This neurotics
do you know.
[*Sri Aurobindo underlined the last sentence.*]

What on earth does this cryptic sentence mean?

SRI AUROBINDO   1013

> *Only the place is a bit nasty with lots of flies and pro-*
> *letariats.*

I fear it might depress him greatly. If nothing has any effect, there
might be a consultation with André.

> *If vetoed, I may try Tonekine injections — (containing ar-*
> *senic, eau de mer, etc.).*

But is this dried liver curable by treatment? Mother says she had an
acquaintance who suffered from it, but nothing could cure him.
There was nothing left of him but bones and some appearance
of skin. Only he kept it up to the age of 80 and died after burying
all his relatives and most of his friends. But this S takes just the
wrong attitude, making the most of his illness. Just read the letter
I send you. What is all this jerks, hammering, beatings, lumpings,
movements? Neurotics? facts? if the latter, what do they "indicate"
— to use a favourite phrase of sadhaks when relating their experiences.

> *He said just now that as soon as he took milk in the evening,*
> *there was fierce burning.*

But what about liver extract?
Meanwhile you can try the sea water etc. tonic.

> *"Green locks of virgin woods*
> *Waived by a gentle breeze. . ."*

What the deuce is this "waived" — You waive your claim, not your
hair.

September 6, 1937

> *I don't think S's ailment is curable. They say that the liver*
> *can regenerate. But what about atony of stomach?*

If it can regenerate, how do you say it is incurable?
Well, what about it?

*He says that you have asked him to continue treatment —
treatment which is of no use? Every day must I hear his
long-drawn, ghastly, tragic tales and sit tight and deaf?
He says it gloriously — Faith etc. is natural with him. Um!
I hope the Force can do something.*

I have told him that if he wants to be cured by Force, he must
give up all quarrelling, cantankerousness, rancour, complaining,
etc., etc., because it is these things that have dried up his liver and
debased his stomach — also that agitation and howling stop the
Force.

. . . Anyway, given him Liver pills today.

That's the Liver Extract?

September 7, 1937

*Yes, that is the liver extract. . . His liver can regenerate,
but will depend on the amount of healthy tissue surviving. . .
And atony? How is the stomach going to get back its tone
and its position, its lost glands, epithelium, etc., etc.?
Homeopathy can do it, I hear.*

Well, if H can, then it is possible.

*I don't know about our branch, unless the fellow gets fatty
suddenly, perhaps there's a chance.*

Fatty? Rather difficult, but it sometimes happens like the opposite
process.

*He says he felt a relief yesterday, from 5 p.m. till this morn-
ing. He had a diamond smile (teeth, I mean) today. I took
the opportunity of showing him that the Force has demon-
strated that it can cure and he must satisfy the Force (so
easy to sermonise, alas!), we can do almost zero.*

Of course it can, if he keeps himself open. But will he?

September 8, 1937

SRI AUROBINDO   1015

> *[The first 2 reports were written by Dr. Becharlal.]*
> *P has been getting slight fever nowadays. You will see here*
> *the prescription. . .*

Mother says that it would be better to give him Indian medicines
out of plants, like Sudarshan or something similar instead of
these drugs. Purani had offered some sort of preparation which
is given in such cases. Mother would like to know if it can be given.

> *He is to continue soup of vegetables, if he cannot digest*
> *milk. He says he gets nausea by taking milk. He needs rest.*

He has been given complete rest for several days; but he is rest-
less and wants to do some work. But he did a little yesterday after
the milk which had upset his digestion and become worse. He had
been rapidly getting better before that with a medicine given by
Pavitra, but which is now exhausted. He was asked again to take
complete rest. He says however that you have told him he can do
some light work.

> *I find that Dr. Becharlal has forgotten to mention P's*
> *diagnosis: his eyes were deep yellow, colour of the face*
> *also faintly so. Rate of heart 58. No liver enlargement*
> *or diminution. So it is diagnosed as jaundice.*

Most of these facts were given by B in a letter this morning. But
there was no mention of the non-enlargement of liver. It was that
Mother especially wanted to know.

September 9, 1937

> *Is the sex Force still strong [6.8.37]? What makes it so*
> *strong?*

It is strong — nothing has made it strong. It has simply come up.

September 10, 1937

> *. . . Please give your Force and protection and blessings.*

I shall put it there.

September 11, 1937

Dara has a hoarse cough. Had no sleep last night. Takes only milk; has no appetite.

Mother says when he came to pranam today his head was very hot. He complains of the painfulness of his throat which prevents taking anything but tea and milk. What about one or two teaspoonfuls of honey in a cup of very hot milk? Mother can give him the honey.

Guru, this poem[1] knocked me on the head when you slammed the door on correspondence. Now my head is all right, so it wants to try its luck again. So?

Very beautiful. You seem to have found yourself in English poetry.

". . . Dim reminiscences
Of flights across thy skies. . ."
Too many S's?
[*Sri Aurobindo cancelled the* s *of "flights".*]

I have beheaded one that was in excess.

September 13, 1937

October 1937

[*Sri Aurobindo stopped all correspondence due to some eye-trouble, and the Mother, instead, took up the medical correspondence.*]
Mère, veuillez-vous me dire comment Sri Aurobindo se porte?
[*The Mother put brackets around "veuillez-vous" and wrote above it "Voudriez-vous".*]

Très bien, mais je tiens à ce qu'il ne reçoive pas de correspondance pendant quelques jours encore. Si vous avez quelque chose d'urgent à me communiquer vous pouvez le faire.[2]

---

[1] "Secret Hands", *Sun-Blossoms*, p. 3.
[2] *Mother,*
  Could you tell me how Sri Aurobindo is?
Very well, but I don't want him to receive any correspondence for a few more days. If you have anything urgent to communicate to me, you may do so.

SRI AUROBINDO   1017

> *I am thinking of giving some milk to Jiban [convalescing from jaundice] at night.*

For the milk it might be better to wait a little more —

> *[A letter from Sitabala:] Ma! for the last few days I have been having a severe attack of headache... My head feels empty and I cannot walk with S's steps... I do not have good sleep nor can I eat well. I pray to you for speedy recovery.*
>
> > *With humble pranam at your feet*
> > *your child Sitabala*

Nirod
I would like you to see her — It might be "artério-sclérose". Will you verify it and let me know? I suspect also that she is constipated, it is to be ascertained.
If it is artério-sclérose Pavitra has some good medicine for it —

October 22, 1937

> *I am afraid these are not the signs of arteriosclerosis — except the headache... But she is badly constipated which may be the simple reason of her troubles. We shall examine her urine. Please advise what to do.*

You might first examine the urine and treat the constipation. We shall see for the rest afterwards.

October 23, 1937

> *N was better last night — the temperature remained 102°... He has eructation, especially after taking milk... There is always a persistent rise of temperature in the evening. There are injections for bringing down the fever, e.g. Diéménal and Omnadin.*

Are not these medicines a bit dangerous?

October 25, 1937

> *I wonder why J's eczema, once improved, comes back*

1018

CORRESPONDENCE WITH

> *again. It has been there for 5 or 6 months and is trying to spread...*

Have you ever tried to wash the place with a cotton pad dipped in *Listerine* (pure) dusting afterwards (when dry) with an antiseptic powder?

October 26, 1937

> *No, I have not tried Listerine etc., but only Acecholex. First of all we don't stock Listerine, secondly if it can be procured from the Pharmacie, what antiseptic powder do you suggest? And should there not be a bandage after the dusting?*

Not at the Pharmacie but perhaps it can be found in Appadorai's.

The powder must be a composed one, but for the composition all depends on the patient's reactions.

The bandage seems to me only good to prevent the scratching.

> *You saw Jiban at Pranam. Should there be any change in diet?*

He seems to be progressing.

> *If it is convenient, you may reply in French. It will help me to learn the language.*

Pas de réponse ce soir[1] —

October 27, 1937

> *For J's eczema, I wonder if Acecholex is proving to be too strong now; otherwise why should the wound become so raw after scratching?*

It may be.

> *I think tomorrow we shall buy Listerine.*

If the skin is too raw it may burn.

---

[1] No reply this evening.

SRI AUROBINDO   1019

> *N is not very well. He is much troubled by hiccoughs etc....*
> *I think his mind will be quiet if somebody stays there at*
> *night. Can his adjacent room be spared?*

It is not possible as Chimanbhai is arriving and the room is kept
for him.
                                                    October 29, 1937

> *Last night N slept well except for a little hiccough now and*
> *then, lasting half an hour. But I wonder why he sleeps so*
> *much. We are not giving him any hypnotic except 15 grains*
> *of bromide in one dose. Due to Force?*

It seems to me more the effect of the bromide and it may be safer
not to give him too much of it.

> *Sitabala got a slight headache after a cold bath.... She*
> *asks if she could have hot water.*

Yes, she can have. Inform Amrita.
                                                    October 30, 1937

> *... N is the same. Do you advise any outside consultation*
> *or Dr. R? Or shall we wait?*

We can wait a few days more.
                                                    October 31, 1937

November 1937

> *J's eczema looks very well... Should we try Listerine*
> *now or see again with the present medicine, for the last*
> *time?*
> [*The Mother marked with a vertical line "or see ... time?"*]

Yes, it is better.

> *Jiban is better now. Dr. Becharlal says he can take a cup*
> *of cocoa in the morning. He can also take up his work from*
> *tomorrow. Jiban wants your sanction.*

Surely he can work now. It will do him good.

November 2, 1937

> *Please look at Jiban well tomorrow; we want to know if his diet can be improved.*

On Sunday he seemed almost all right — Diet can be improved.

November 3, 1937

> *. . . Shall we give N some solid food? What about Bovril — we have a bottle in stock, or some brandy?*

Bovril is better than brandy —

> *Shall we give Jiban some vegetables or only milk in the morning, to begin with?*

Do you think he will be able to digest the milk? He can take vegetables but it would be better if they were simply boiled.

November 4, 1937

> *In J's case, the powder composed of acid salicylic, alum, pulv. calamine Bismuth carb., starch, talc powder has to be cleaned each time we apply Listerine, or shall we clean it with Listerine itself?*

Listerine itself can be used for cleaning.

November 8, 1937

> *N is taking now: 5 cups of milk, 1 litre barley water, soup, 1 loaf bread, 2 or 3 oranges. Is it sufficient?*

It seems to me sufficient.

November 9, 1937

> *J says there is much burning by Listerine. I apply it 4 times a day. The powder clings to the surface and forms a sort of hard crust. . .*

SRI AUROBINDO   1021

It may be that you are putting too much Listerine and too much powder at a time. The powder is only to be dusted. Also the composition of the powder may be changed if it is too heavy and sticky. To remove the crusts *once a day* you may try vaseline or "glycérolé d'amidon".

> *Had an urgent call from M. He says he had high fever (only 101°!), aching body, etc. Looks like a contagion from Nishikanta.*

The best would be to disinfect the house with camphor or sulphur or formol.

November 10, 1937

> *Camphor or Sulphur is to be burnt like incense powder, isn't it?*

Yes —

> *I have asked Sitabala to take enema for some days. Can the hot water sent for bath, be used for enema? It is boiled, I suppose.*

This is not quite sure. But you can inquire about it —

November 11, 1937

> *N's hiccough is much less, but he is getting very weak.*

Is he in bed all the time?

> *For Jiban, shall we begin with one cup of cocoa in the morning?*

You can try —

> *S says every symptom has increased after Sudarshan. He is raising other problems. Wants a stove for hot water, wants his food sent home in the rainy season, etc., etc. To give a stove simply for a small quantity of water is*

1022   CORRESPONDENCE WITH

> *absurd. He can take it from the Dispensary. The servant can bring his evening meal with mine.*

This arrangement is all right. No stove needed.

> *What about the morning meal? He is going on with one thing after another.*

It seems to me that he could go without danger to the D.R. for his morning food.

> *Bula's movements of the right arm are still restricted. I don't think there is any fracture. Shall we see under screen costing Rs. 3, or X-ray costing Rs. 6? Which one?*
> *[The Mother marked "screen" with an arrow.]*

Yes, this.

November 14, 1937

> *... For N, shall we call in André who is a T.B. expert? Or wait a few more days?*

It may be better to call André —

> *J asks if she should come to meditation in the rain — as the eczema will be exposed to water.*

But how does she do for her bath?

November 15, 1937

> *J says for the last 6 months she's been taking half bath, i.e. bath up to the thighs with a lot of acrobatic feats. She just sponges the legs... Should we apply Listerine and powder 3 times now instead of 4?*

Yes.

November 16, 1937

> *About N, André says, it may be either pleurisy or some liver abscess. He sees no signs of T.B... N is quite upset be-*

SRI AUROBINDO   1023

*cause we have called in another doctor. So please advise
if anything is to be done.*

We will see after examination.

November 17, 1937

*N's X-ray tomorrow. How shall we carry him? Rickshaw
may be uncomfortable. Will the car be available?*

Both cars are under repair.

*J is having a lot of itching. I feel that olive oil, almond oil
or cocoagem may do her good. Your opinion, please.*

You might try almond oil but see that it is quite fresh. It gets rancid
very quick.

Now we are applying Listerine thrice a day.

You might reduce it to twice.

Can milk be given to Jiban at night, and curds at noon?

You can try.

November 18, 1937

*N's X-ray is done. There is an encysted patch of pleurisy
on the right side, and commencement of T.B. over the whole
area of both the lungs. André says the condition is bad.
He can be shifted to the hospital, but the treatment can
also be done at home. André warns that precaution against
contagion is to be taken. It seems to Dr. Becharlal and me
that the hospital would be better. Here nursing will be
very difficult. I wonder how many will offer their services, if
they know that it's T.B. I am not sure that N will agree to
go to hospital. . . If you want that he should be kept here,
we shall do our best. But if you want him in hospital, the
sooner the better.*

*P.S.: Though the case is serious, I have not lost all hope.
I believe that if you want to cure him, you can do so, as*

1024   CORRESPONDENCE WITH

you said the other day, "by some accident". Our medical treatment for it is next to nil.

[The Mother wrote above "by some accident", within brackets:]

Not accident — <u>miracle.</u>

I am wondering if we should keep him and try to nurse him ourselves. The question of diet too is a little difficult. . .

It is impossible to make proper arrangements here for diet and nursing nor can we run the risk of contagion in an asram of 150 people. Sending him to the hospital is unavoidable. So the sooner he goes the better. It cannot be left to *his* choice.

November 19, 1937

Now that N has been sent to the hospital, his room has to be thoroughly cleaned and disinfected.

It must first be disinfected by burning sulphur with all openings closed. Afterwards the furniture will be removed and thoroughly cleaned and the room itself will be whitewashed entirely.

November 20, 1937

N says he may hire a servant just to be by his side.

That can be done —

S says he can't digest the Asram curry at all, and soup and vegetables did him much good.

It is better to give him soup and boiled vegetables.

November 21, 1937

Guru, I dare to disturb you as daring has become a necessity. I feel utterly blank and am in need of some support, I can't write poetry by myself, without your help. Have you stopped

SRI AUROBINDO 1025

> *the correspondence because of your eye-trouble or for*
> *concentration? In either case, then, I don't insist on your*
> *seeing my poems. You will understand that I don't write for*
> *the sake of writing, but for a support from you. Please give*
> *me a line in reply, after which I won't bother you any more.*

Apart from the eye-question, I have stopped because there are certain things I have positively to get done before I can take up any regular correspondence work again. If I start again now, I shall probably have to stop again soon for a long long time. Better get things finished now — that's the idea. You must hold on somehow for the present.

November 23, 1937

> *"O Beauty, write in immortal scroll*
> *The passion of my creative fire."*

[*Sri Aurobindo*:] I am afraid writing fire in a scroll is too difficult an operation — even for Beauty unless she has become entirely surrealistic since I first made her acquaintance.

November 24, 1937

> *V wants to go to see N in the hospital. Should he?*

No.

> *This old man L.N. has come back worse from home. Don't*
> *you think he had better go to Madras and get himself*
> *treated there?*

That would be the best if he is willing to go —

November 26, 1937

> *I examined Dayakar today. He has continuous fever. I've*
> *asked them to give him milk and soup. Or can soup be*
> *omitted?*

No, soup is very good.

November 27, 1937

1026 CORRESPONDENCE WITH

[*The following report was written by Dr. Becharlal:*]
*For a long time, I have been asking Lakshmi to do some
work — to start some light work; at least to move about in
the Ashram compound, sit for a few minutes in the Reception
Room etc.... But I have been told by Champaklal that she
has been regularly sitting at the gate at Vithalbhai's duty
time and talking. I have asked her today very gently not to
sit at the gate...*

It is better also that she should not sit in the reception room.

November 28, 1937

December 1937

*Sitabala's headache has a definite relation to food. We
suspect ulceration which was previously cured by olive oil.
Definite diagnosis is possible only by X-ray. Do you advise
it?*

Yes, it is better to do it.

December 6, 1937

*Dr. André says that N's is decidedly a hopeless case. Should
his family be informed?*

No, it is better not, for obvious reasons.

Can Jiban take regular Asram food?

He ought to be able to take it —

December 7, 1937

*What should be done with N's things? Shall we distribute
the clothes among the servants? Flask, easy chair, blankets,
etc. . .*

I was thinking of asking André if we can make a present of all these
things to the hospital.

. . . Should we show A and L to André?

They can both be shown to André. What is to be done in A's case will depend on André's diagnosis.

> *N's death has touched me a little. . . If his case had been diagnosed earlier, he might not have died so soon. Here comes in the question of experience as a doctor. Intuition takes a long time to develop and a very energetic sadhana has to be done side by side. If you want to keep me as a doctor, I am tempted to ask you to send me to a big hospital for a period of training. Two or three deaths have occurred since I have come in, and people are perhaps blaming me for my lack of capacity.*

I do not believe in the usefulness of a stay in a hospital — the "energetic sadhana" is much better. I can console you by assuring you that those who died <u>had</u> to die.

December 8, 1937

> *L has astigmatism of both the eyes. The veins in the eyes are congested. For accurate observation, the oculist says, it is better to dilate the eyes with atropine though it is not absolutely necessary.*

Better *not*.

> *She has to stop sewing, I am afraid, because even the eye-examination gave her giddiness.*

Yes, I have told her already to stop embroidery.

> *I think it would be better to try sun-treatment before taking to glasses.*

It can be tried. But you must give her very *detailed* and *exact* instructions as she is a bit careless about herself.

> *I think B's is a case of phlebitis, due to chill. It would be better if he did less walking and took more rest.*

1028 CORRESPONDENCE WITH

Phlebitis requires *an absolute immobility in bed*, but it seems strange that it should be that. Dr. Bannerji told me that the real phlebitis was extremely rare in India. All the same it would be better if he took complete rest for a day or two —

December 15, 1937

> *Sitabala says that for her constipation she used to take bran boiled by S. She finds it a bother, so can it be taken raw?*
> [*The Mother underlined "taken raw".*]

Certainly *not*.

December 17, 1937

> *From tomorrow we shall give Shivalingam iodide and mercury, internally. But I wonder if you will like mercury being given.*
> [*The Mother underlined "if you will like mercury being given".*]

No, I do not like.

December 18, 1937

> *We examined B today as he was complaining of more pain at night. He has no fever and there is no deep pain, so he will be all right in 2 or 3 days, I think.*

Surely it is nothing serious.

> *May we get bran from Bakery House?*

Yes.

December 21, 1937

> *L.N. has appeared again. . . Rajangam spoke to him and he consents to go home after the 31st, if you will sanction.*

Yes, it is better if he goes home.

SRI AUROBINDO   1029

> *N.P. has again that "terrible pain" on the right side. We*
> *are giving him one aspirin and one dose of salt.*

N.P. is fearing the results of the salt and asks not to take it.

December 23, 1937

> *L has again got a relapse. Shall we call André to see her*
> *now or shall we try some tonic injections?*

You can call André.

December 30, 1937

1938

In B's case, I find a small vein is tender and knotty, the muscles are quite free. So has it affected the vein now or was it so from the beginning?

So, most likely it is varicose.

> *"The wandering waters of my life*
> *Wash thy eternal shore. . .*
> *But thy impregnable silence bears*
> *With calm their passionate moans."*

[*Sri Aurobindo:*] Good Lord! don't moan like that.

January 4, 1938

Laxmi is complaining of obstinate constipation. Is she not taking the castor oil recommended by André?

January 9, 1938

. . . I don't see that S's general health is worse.

He does not look so bad.

Don't you find him better? or shall we show him to André?

Not necessary.

January 14, 1938

You have seen our indents for this year, sent by Rajangam. You must have observed that R has asked for 30 or 40 allopathic drugs, and you have sanctioned them. I was wondering how, being a homeopath, he should require these. For what purpose? Is it legal, etc., etc.?
[*The Mother marked "30 or 40 allopathic drugs".*]

CORRESPONDENCE WITH SRI AUROBINDO   1031

Are they poisons? Because in that case it cannot be given and the best way would be to delay the order — until he writes to me and explains for what purpose he wants them.

January 19, 1938

In that list of indents, there are at least 8 or 10 which come definitely under the act of poisonous drugs. . . Rajangam said that these will be potentised by R, in alcohol. I asked, "Then, why doesn't he get them directly from the Homeopathy pharmacy? That would be very safe in every way. . ." Rajangam replied that as we have got a contributor from Alembic, it's easy to get them; but if he gets from the Homeopathy pharmacy, Mother will have to pay for them. . .

Rajangam's explanation is satisfactory. So they can be bought.

January 20, 1938

February 1938

K's scabies and asthma are almost all right. Shall we give him some sodium cacodylate injections as tonic?

Yes, if there is no "contre-indication".

Perhaps you have noticed that there is still a little swelling in B's leg. Do you want André to be called?

We can wait a few days more.

February 1, 1938

What about L? She says she had no motion for 7 days!

February 2, 1938

What do you think of Rushi's cyst? It is not a wart.

It is nothing much. I suppose it will fall by itself.

February 3, 1938

1032   CORRESPONDENCE WITH

> *. . . L doesn't like enema as it has bad after-effects.*
> [*The Mother underlined "as it has bad after-effects".*]

What bad effects?

> *I don't know if habitual laxatives will be good.*

Habitual laxatives are harmful and purgatives still worse.

> *R has difficulty in swallowing. She is another case of constipation. She hasn't got a healthy colour, has she?*

Neither good nor very bad.

February 8, 1938

> *L — The bad effects of enema are weakness, windiness and loss of appetite. Dr. B asked her if she would like to go to Bombay. She is very willing and says she will come back after some time. So shall we ask her to arrange for it?*

Yes, certainly.

P has come with a doubtful skin disease — It is better to take him to the hospital and ascertain what it is.

February 9, 1938

> *Dr. André says that P has leucoderma, and it is not contagious. But it's better to examine the blood. . . Could it be done?*

Yes —

February 11, 1938

> *K [suffering from asthma] wants to take curds. . .*

He might try.

February 12, 1938

> *We examined Rangachari — his heart seems to be dilated. It is also weak. I understand he has come here with the idea*

SRI AUROBINDO   1033

> *of doing Yoga. If we have to bear his responsibility, André had better be consulted.*

We have no responsibility, he is living outside. But if the case is serious advise him to go to the hospital.

February 14, 1938

> *J says that she has dandruff and consequently losing her hair badly. She has heard that you have suggested a "Lemon cream" for such cases, to some others. Will it be good for her also?*

I'm sending her a bottle.

February 15, 1938

> *You have asked Benjamin to take some vegetables. How to give them? Only boiled? They can't be fried, can they?*

I suppose he can take fried things, but you might ask André about it.

It is *pepper* and *spices* he fears, not oil or ghee.

February 18, 1938

> *For Benjamin, are the vegetables to be fried here? Or we can ask Lakshmi to do it as she too would like to take some.*

You might offer him boiled vegetables. We shall see how he likes them.

February 19, 1938

> *Mother, in the last two Pranams, you seemed to have indicated to me that I have done something wrong somewhere.*

[*Sri Aurobindo:*] Nonsense!

> *Coming on just before Darshan it is weighing on me. May I know what it is, if anything?*

[*Sri Aurobindo:*] Nothing at all — quite imaginary.

> *"Brilliance breaking the night-shell*
> *Like laughter-peels of a ringing bell."*

[*Sri Aurobindo:*] Lord, sir! A bell is not an orange.

February 20, 1938

> *Should we give Romen treatment for his enlarged liver?*

You can start the treatment.

> *Benjamin has been advised to take raw tomatoes. Can he buy them himself from the bazaar?*

The tomatoes can be bought from the Bazaar, but surely Benjamin has no strength to go himself to buy them.

> *Guru, please have a look at this poem...*

[*Sri Aurobindo:*] What the deuce is the meaning of "lineage" here? Lineage means ancestry. And what the greater deuce is "liege"?

February 22, 1938

> *"The deliverance from the grave —*
> *Earth's crucifixion of the Light*
> *That is bound like passion's galley-slave —*
> *..."*
>
> [*After Sri Aurobindo's correction on 20.2.38:*]
> *"For thy deliverance from the grave —*
> *Earth's crucifixion of the Light*
> *In the earth-bound, Nature's galley-slave —*
> *..."*
> *You have repeated "earth".*

I should have thought it clear that the repetition is intentional. Earth does that crucifixion in the earth-bound — once the earth-binding ceases, the soul is free. Cf. St. Paul, "O death, where is thy sting? O grave, where is thy victory?"

SRI AUROBINDO   1035

> *I am much delighted and relieved to find that you have not
> lost your sense of humour by your Supramental transfor-
> mation, Sir!*

Where the deuce do you get these ideas? From Dilip? The Supramental being the absolute of all good things, must equally be the
absolute of humour also. Q.E.D.

February 25, 1938

> *Benjamin doesn't like boiled vegetables. He wants them
> fried. The other day Dr. André took the vegetables home
> and had them fried for him.*

[*Mother :*] Is it not possible to have them fried in the dispensary?

February 26, 1938

> *Shall we give a bottle of Lithiné to Charupada? Cost?
> Free?*

[*Mother :*] It can be given but he will have to pay customs.

> *I have a mind to try some injections of liver extract on S, if
> you permit. . .*

[*Mother :*] Yes, you can do.

February 27, 1938

March 1938

> *Here is N's letter. I don't like his tone at all.*

Neither do I.

> *He asks, "Won't Sri Aurobindo see my poems even after 5
> or 6 days?"*

Can't promise anything.

1036   CORRESPONDENCE WITH

> *Have you any answer to give to his letter?*

No.

> March 4, 1938

> *"Nature is apparelled with a poise*
> *Like the wings of a drowsy bird. . ."*

Sir, if you walk through Pondicherry apparelled only with a poise, the police would arrest you at once. What would happen to Nature if she tried a similar eccentricity, I don't know.

> March 5, 1938

> *O dear, dear, what have you done, Sir? Havoc, indeed!*
> *You couldn't get the trochaic rhythm in yesterday's poem?*[1]

My God, that was intended for trochaic? You are sure it was not anapaestic or dactylic or all three together + iambic? That would be a more accurate description of it. I couldn't make out what metre was intended so I reduced all to a single one, octosyllabics.

> *"Incense-woven words thy heaven-reveried."*
> *Words can be woven with incense?*

They may be but can't be woven by incense, but what the deuce is the construction of this line? and the meaning?
    Woven-incense *words* and *heaven-reveried.*

> March 6, 1938

> *[The poem of 6.3.38.] Why, the construction is quite clear; you can take "words" referring to prayer, if you refer "it" to seed, it can be made "word". What do you say? And words are "heaven-reveried", of course. Not clear? But "woven-incense words" don't get me.*

Incense-woven words (or word) thy heaven-reveried—has absolutely no coherence, meaning or syntax, in English at least. In German, Sanskrit or Japanese it might perhaps do. The reference

---

[1] "My Thoughts", *Sun-Blossoms*, p. 39.

SRI AUROBINDO   1037

of words is quite clear, but that does not save the Bedlamic syntax.
"Woven-incense" words is a Hopkinsian compound—that and
my alteration of "thy" to "and" gives the line a clear and poetic
sense, and it is the best I can do with it. Otherwise the whole will
have to be changed. If you dislike Hopkinsese (though your line
is ultra-H), you can do it in straightforward English "Words like
woven incense heaven-reveried."

> *NK's poem? Please see if you can manage it so that I can
> write at least that you have seen it, what?*

Nishikanta later on. Have done too much for one night.

> *[Chand's wire:] "Why silent great struggle protection."
> Guru, I don't know why he says "silent". I have sent the
> Darshan blessings on 23rd or 24th which he must have
> received.*

But you have not given him protection.

> *Reddy's relative has got urticarial rashes all over the body.
> André asks us to wait and see.*
> *[The Mother underlined "urticarial rashes".]*

[*Mother:*] Is it not that she has been given too strong medicines?

> *Benjamin wants onions also in the vegetables. As you don't
> favour onions, I hesitate.*

[*Mother:*] You can give him.

March 7, 1938

> *"In my soul's still moments you bring
> A rapture from the vast untrod
> Spheres of Light through slumbering
> Arches of misty groves. . ."*

Why "misty"? and why is the rapture brought through groves? A
woodland promenade? I think both the mist and the groves ought
to disappear.

1038

CORRESPONDENCE WITH

> *"The scented air your gold locks leave*
> *Haunts like a heavenly piece of art."*

Doesn't it suggest that she was using a fragrant hair-oil?

> *Plenty of romanticism and incoherence and outburst, per-*
> *haps.*

R and I are there in plenty, but O is not in evidence.

> *Should the word "frost" go?*

No, it might be left to freeze.

> *Is this fellow Hopkins or Hopkensise? Whoever he may be,*
> *I am for the new stuff, so I keep your "woven-incense".*

Hopkinsese is the language of Hopkins — quite a famous poet now in spite of your not having heard of him — a fore-runner of present day poetry. He tried to do new things with the English language. A Catholic poet like Francis Thompson.

> *What's Bedlamic, please? Never heard of him, I'm sure!*

Bedlam is or was the principal lunatic asylum in England. You have never heard the expression "Bedlam let loose" etc.? Bedlamic syntax = rollickingly mad syntax.

> *Guru,*
> *Dilipda requests me, as you will see, to type this letter*
> *[Dilip's letter written to Sri Aurobindo, from Allahabad],*
> *for your facility. I will certainly type it out, if required.*
> *Kindly send it in the afternoon. I have helped you here and*
> *there — in pencil. Surely the Supramental is a greater*
> *decipherer than the inframental, what?*

Read — very interesting.

March 8, 1938

> *You said that I have found myself in English poetry [13.9.37].*

SRI AUROBINDO   1039

> *Now it seems I have lost myself, what?*

You are flopping about a bit, but not lost.

March 9, 1938

> *"The rich sun-mirrored fuming blood*
> *Running through choked earth-laden pores."*

What's this bloody fuming phenomenon? Won't do at all. Pores too! It suggests a bloody sweat like Charles IX's (of France).

> *Is the construction all right?*

No, can't make out head or tail of the beast.

March 10, 1938

> *Guru, you must admit that I have hit this time, what?*

Bull's eye!

> *André has prescribed some medicine for S's suspected en-largement of thyroid gland. I send you the prescription.*

[*Mother:*] Considering S's character I do not think it is quite safe to try this medicine.

March 11, 1938

> *"O symbols of His jewelled reverie*
> *Burn myriad-hued*
> *On my diamond altar a prophecy*
> *Of His solitude."*
> *You shift the accent on "prophecy"?*

I don't see how shifting the accent on prophecy (quite impossible) would make it better. There would be no rhyme as *écy* can't rhyme with *rie*, but only with "greasy" or "fleecy" and the whole thing would sound like an Italian talking English. I take "altar a" as a dactyl—a light dactyl can sometimes replace a trochee.

March 14, 1938

5A

Today I missed meditation as the boy whom we operated upon for tonsil stopped breathing; after half an hour's struggle, we succeeded in restoring the pulse. I wish I could know if you had heard my call so that in the future I may call with greater faith.

[*Mother:*] Forgot to tell you yesterday that I heard your call all right.

March 15, 1938

> *"Shine on their path O star-hearted Dawn*
> *With your gold-crested sun*
> *The quest of dumb centuries burn upon*
> *Their dim flame-pinion."*
> *This stanza is no good, I think.*

The first two lines are all right, the last two not. It is a devil of a job to get a true rhyme for dawn! and a true rhyme is badly needed here. "drawn" "fawn" "pawn" "lawn" "sawn" — none will do, not even Bernard-Shawn. Got a stroke of genius with a hell of a compound adjective. For the rest I have sandwiched some of your words in here and there and got out a something. I think it does well as a close.

> Shine on their path, O high-*hearted Dawn*;
> Let *your gold-crested sun*
> Crown *the* dumb *quest of centuries* dim-withdrawn
> With its *flame*-union.

I understand S is taking mercury ointment for a long time. I hope she is not using it continuously.

[*Mother:*] For what is she taking the ointment? and who is giving it to her? Is it not better to stop it?

Guru, Mother is supposed to have said to X that I am one of those who have done harm to him. I would like to know how so that I may correct myself in the future... My impression was quite the contrary, for I thought he felt lonely, so he should ask Mother for permission to come for tea

SRI AUROBINDO

in the morning and how much he should associate him-
self with me. If he wants to come, I should at least be care-
ful not to harm him.

Mother never said anything of the kind about you. On the contrary
she has always approved of his going to you because you give him
a physical support, encourage him to eat, etc. What she said was
about Y (she has told Y himself to that effect) because of his wrong
ideas, advocacy of all kinds of self-will and self-indulgence, etc.,
and recently to X himself about Z.

March 16, 1938

"Heart-beats of a lustrous life,
In myriad images unfurled."

Good Lord! How do you unfurl a heart-beat?

March 17, 1938

Dyuman has sprained his finger. There is evidently no
dislocation. Still if you want screen-exam, we can do it.

[*Mother:*] I think it is not necessary.

Angamathu's swelling and ulcers on feet are better. He is
not working in the smithy now, but he has to come all the
way from near the station, for dressing. Wouldn't it be
better for him to go to the hospital as it is nearer?

[*Mother:*] Yes, it is better.

March 18, 1938

". . . Floating like a nightingale's moon-crested song
On the enamelled ocean-floor."

Nobody can float on a floor. Try it and see!

March 19, 1938

Bala's[1] stye burst. He didn't turn up in the afternoon.

---

[1] A local boy who used to help Pavitra in Atelier.

[*Mother.*] He was driving the car.

March 20, 1938

> *I'm afraid "God" is coming too much in this poem.*

Where is he?

> *Seen my scansion? Too great, perhaps?*

Never heard of such scansion in a trochaic metre. Is it the new prosody?

Much too great.

Besides, what kind of grammar is "a myriad" with a singular noun?

March 21, 1938

> *"Flowing like the rays of gold impregnable*
> *Sun, on sky-blue dome."*

Ugh, sir! Sky-blue dome is as stale as hell.

> *Could you tell X to make some time for taking soup? To-*
> *day it got spoilt. After seeing you he can come this way.*

[*Mother:*] I shall tell him but I'm not quite sure he will listen.

March 22, 1938

> *Chand writes: "... I shall try to come to Pondicherry*
> *after joining service. . ."*
> [*Sri Aurobindo underlined the word "try".*]

"Try!" What about our permission?

March 23, 1938

> *"Voices of some birds are heard. . ."*

Some birds? Very vague and weak — unless some in American sense! Put anything else, e.g. sky-birds—

SRI AUROBINDO   1043

> ". . . Pouring from their luminous-rhythmed feet
> Songs of a magic-hearted moon."
> Songs from feet?

Never! If people began to sing with their feet, the world would
be startled into a magic-hearted swoon.

> Mulshankar has headache and vomiting. They are recurrent
> nowdays. I am thinking of trying to find a remedy by the
> method you suggested ["energetic sadhana", 8.12.37].
> But has it the possibility of success? I raise the question
> because some diseases seem to have no remedy at all, e.g.
> S's, L's and A's. Can't say definitely about Mulshankar's.
> It is also a chronic thing from his childhood. Of course it
> doesn't mean that for that reason it has no cure. Anyway,
> I shall try; please give your help.

[Mother:] Nothing is incurable but it is the hidden cause of the
illness that must be discovered. I'll put in French what I mean:
   C'est un *fonctionnement* qui est mauvais quelque part, *pas
une lésion* — et l'origine de ce mauvais fonctionnement est pro-
bablement nerveuse (due à quelque chose de faussé dans le vital —
ceci est l'ultime cause psychologique).[1]

                                                      March 26, 1938

> Guru, I hope this poem,[2] will pass.

Exceedingly fine.
   Well, that's *some* inspiration! (American sense of some!) O.K.
to the nth degree. . .

                                                      March 28, 1938

> Mrs. Sankar Ram has a very bad defect of the eyes —
> The ophthalmologist suspects something wrong in the fun-
> dus of rt. eye (she had an accident). To be sure, he wants

---

[1] There is a functional disorder somewhere, *not a lesion* — and the origin of this
functional disorder is probably nervous (due to something wrong in the vital — this
is the ultimate psychological cause).

[2] "Haloed Face", *Sun-Blossoms*, p. 45.

to dilate the eyes with Homatropine—but he doesn't promise a cure. Shall we dilate and see?. . .

[*Mother:*] No, it is better not

March 29, 1938

Mrs. Sankar Ram wants me to ask you whether new glasses should be taken.

[*Mother:*] I suppose so.

We are thinking of giving S: 1) Some iodine, 2) Bromides, 3) Quinine and 4) Thyroid extract. If you approve of any of these, kindly let us know which. Of course, they have their somewhat uncertain and harmful side-effects.

[*Mother:*] All these drugs seem to be more dangerous one than the other. It is safer to abstain from them.

Can the Flute be metaphored as a bird, or can it be taken as a mysterious Bird?

Good Lord! no! A flute can't wander about like a bird and have a flaming heart and all. Better leave it vague as it is, to be taken as any blooming mysterious bird.

‖ *My life is veiled in a sleep of light,*
‖ *A hush that nothing breaks;*
‖ *The world before my inward sight*
‖ *Into pure beauty wakes.*

‖ *Life that is deep and wonder-vast,*
‖ *Lost in a breath of sound;*
‖ *The bubbling shadows have been cast*
‖ *From its heart's timeless round.*

‖ *In its lulled silver stream now shines*
‖ *A lustrous smile of God*
‖ *Whose brilliantly curved outlines,*
‖ *Flashing on the memory-trod*

SRI AUROBINDO   1045

> Caverns of slumbering earth, there bring
> A glow of the Infinite,
> While my soul's diamond voices wing
> Into a heaven of light.[1]

Guru, I fear this is only a sprat — not even a perfect one, perhaps; for "earth" has strayed away from "my" without any link between them.

It is not a sprat, sir; it is a goldfish. You seem to be weak in poetical zoology. It is perfect, except for the one fault you have detected. The only alterations, (except the "pure") I find needful, are meant to obviate that defect, by going back to "my", so connecting the first and last lines (also aided by the repetition of "light") and making the rest appear as closely connected with it. Like that it makes a very well-built and finely inspired poem. If you can produce more sprats like that, there will be much wealth in your fisheries. It is much better than the other recent ones, except the stress poem — nothing decorative, — all there!

March 30, 1938

About yesterday's poem, I am still "weak" in finding the "gold" you found in my fish. I don't see what beauty is there to make you mark certain lines thrice — e.g. "Into a heaven of light", which is a very simple, ordinary sort of line, I should say. I admit it is well-built and devoid of decoration, but to see it as you see it — hum! well, could you explain a bit? But I can increase this sort of "wealth" if you are at my back!

There is probably a defect in your solar plexus which makes it refuse to thrill unless it receives a strong punch from poetry — an ornamental, romantic or pathetic punch. But there is also a poetry which expresses things with an absolute truth but without effort, simply and easily, without a word in excess or any laying on of colour, only just the necessary. That kind of achievement is considered as among the greatest things poetry can do. The three lines are put in yesterday's poem wherever that happened.

---

[1] "Sleep of Light", *Sun-Blossoms*, p. 46.

1046   CORRESPONDENCE WITH

A phrase, word or line may be quite simple and ordinary and yet taken with another phrase, line or word, become the perfect thing. If you look you will see that my 3 lines are put against the *two* last lines taken together and not this one only by itself. So taken they express with perfect felicity something that can be seen or felt in spiritual experience. The same reason for the other three line encomiums. E.g. A line like "Life that is deep and wonder-vast" has what I have called the inevitable quality, with a perfect simplicity and straightforwardness it expresses something in a definitive and perfect way that cannot be bettered; so does "Lost in a breath of sound", with less simplicity but with the same inevitability. The two lines that follow are very fine but they have to labour more to express what they want and express it less absolutely — still they do so much that they get 2 lines, but not three. The same distinction applies to the next two lines "In the lulled silver stream etc." and the four that follow. I don't mean that highly coloured poetry cannot be absolutely inevitable, it can e.g. Shakespeare's "In cradle of the rude imperious surge" and many others. But most often highly coloured poetry attracts too much attention to the colour and its brilliances so that the thing in itself is less felt than the magnificence of its dress. All kinds are legitimate in poetry. I only wanted to point out that poetry can be great or perfect even if it uses simple or ordinary expressions — e.g. Dante simply says "In His will is our peace"[1] and in writing that in Italian produces one of the greatest lines in all poetic literature.

> *"And thy magic vastness wraps my secret hours*
> *With its conquering breath of flame. . ."*

Breath won't do. You have breathed once already.

> *Benoy got a scorpion bite at 8.30 p.m. Luckily he didn't*
> *get violent pain as one would expect from the size of the*
> *scorpion. Should such cases be reported to you at once?*

[*Mother:*] Not necessary unless it is a serious case.

                                              March 31, 1938

---

[1] "E'n la sua volontade è nostra pace",
   La Divina Commedia, "Paradiso", canto 3, 85.

SRI AUROBINDO   1047

April 1938

*Guru, D has suddenly stopped writing to me though it's
two weeks since he went to Calcutta. . . I wrote in one
of my short replies that I have nothing to write about.
He might have taken it in a different light. But is he really
as sensitive as all that? God!*

Quite possible with D. He might think that you mean "what a
nuisance it is to have to write to this fellow" or "what can I find to
write to a fellow like you?" Must be careful with D — and in fact
with most people, if you can judge from the sadhaks here.

April 2, 1938

*Tomorrow I shall write D a mild, sweet letter. Alas, Guru,
what you say is so true, so true! One has to be a perfect and
complete Yogi — no joke, not a word in excess. . . Do you
believe that people here are more sensitive than people
outside? Some persons think that the Asram is a "rotten"
place with jealousy and hatred rampant among the sadhaks.*

Outside there are just the same things — The Asram is an epitome of the human nature that has to be changed — but outside
people put as much as possible a mask of social manners and
other pretences over the rottenness — What Christ called in the
case of the Pharisees the "whited sepulchre". Moreover there one
can pick and choose the people one will associate with while in the
narrow limits of the Asram it is not so possible — contacts are
inevitable. Wherever humans are obliged to associate closely,
what I saw described the other day as "the astonishing meannesses
and caddishnesses inherent in human nature" come quickly out.
I have seen that in Asrams, in political work, in social attempts at
united living, everywhere in fact where it gets a chance. But when
one tries to do Yoga, one cannot fail to see that in oneself and not
only, as most people do, see it in others, and once seen, then? Is it to
be got rid of or to be kept? Most people here seem to want to keep
it. Or they say it is too strong for them, they can't help it!

1048   CORRESPONDENCE WITH

> *Dr. Sircar once told me, after that stove incident, that this Asram lacks "fraternity", while the Ramakrishna Mission is ideal in that way.*

I am afraid not. When I was in Calcutta it was already a battle-field and even in the post-civil-war period one hears distressing things about it. It is the same with other Asrams. . .[1]

> *D was disgusted with the sadhaks here, and N also wrote about it, and many others think that the world outside is not so bad.*

If so, then I suppose they will stay there?

> *D finds the world outside much better, to which I would reply that here we don't believe in appearances.*

D associates only with the people who like and praise him and even so he does not know what they say behind his back. For a man who has knocked about so much he is astonishingly candid and easily deceived by appearances.

> *— And life is precisely* inner *here. . .*

Is it? If people here were leading the inner life, these things would soon disappear.

> *Since we have to lead a life in a concentrated atmosphere, all the ugly things become at once prominent, and add to it the action of the Force on the subconscient for purging of all dross.*

No doubt. Also in this atmosphere pretences and social lies are difficult to maintain. But if things become prominent, it is that people may see and reject them. If instead they cling to them as their most cherished possessions, what is the use? How is the purging to be done with such an attitude?

                                                              April 3, 1938

---

[1] MS mutilated from this point.

SRI AUROBINDO   1049

> *I shall be very careful with D, and even if I have nothing*
> *to write to him, I shall write rubbish!*

Right! Rubbish is usually better appreciated than things worth
saying.

> *Formerly I heard that X didn't much appreciate D's singing,*
> *but now — just see! Is it a change in D or a "pretence" of X?*

Everybody agrees that D's singing has undergone a great change —
so it may be that.

> *Doesn't X, a great intellect, realise that whatever D has*
> *achieved, has been done because of some inner gain through*
> *your Force?*

A man may have a great intellect and yet understand nothing
about spiritual things or spiritual force. X's knowledge in these
matters does not seem to go beyond closing his eyes and feeling
nice and peaceful.

> *I wonder why these people don't understand the work you*
> *are doing.*

How the deuce do you expect them to understand something quite
foreign to their own nature and experience?

> *I suppose they don't recognise your spirituality. Other-*
> *wise how to explain X's and others' love for Buddha and*
> *their miscomprehension regarding you?*

Love for Buddha is an established tradition, so anybody can follow it. Even the Europeans praise Buddha.

> *I read the other day a talk between a Moslem and Sarat*
> *Chatterjee about our Asram. The Moslem says that the*
> *whole Asram has grown up from abnormal circumstances as*
> *it were; by which he means that you fled away from the*
> *political field; "defeated, discouraged, disheartened", a*
> *failure, in one word, and started on Asram.*

1050   CORRESPONDENCE WITH

Have read it. The Moslem was K.N., if I remember right — a
flaring atheist and God-beater. So what do you expect?

> *And he says that the Asram, judging by the ideals it stands
> for, is a great enemy to the society. . . It doesn't recognise
> the "individual entity"; somebody gets "Light" and every-
> thing has to be done according to his dictates.*

Very bad that. To do according to the dictates of the masses i.e.
ignorance multiplied to the millionth is so much better!

April 4, 1938

> *"They are, at thy touch, reborn*
> *Into new shapes and thoughts;*
> *And my soul's prayer adorn*
> *With their bright starry dots."*

This is decoration with a vengeance dottily so. One might just
as well write
                    "And my soul's verandah adorn
                    With starry-red rose-pots."
Then the soul of Donne would rejoice. But Donne should be doffed
here.

> *Do you find any meaning in my stanza?*

Yes, except that the dots have too much meaning.

April 5, 1938

> *You have spoken of the original inspiration becoming
> "mentalised". Could you tell me how it gets mentalised?*

This mentalisation is a subtle process which takes place unobserved.
The inspiration, as soon as it strikes the mental layer (where it
first becomes visible) is met by a less intense receptivity of the mind
which passes the inspired substance through but substitutes its
own expression, an expression stressed by the force of inspiration
into a special felicity but not reproducing or transmitting the inspired beat itself.

SRI AUROBINDO   1051

> *P has a dry cough. Some sedative cough mixture will do*
> *her good. She wants your approval before we give her*
> *medicine.*

[*Mother:*] Yes, I told her already to go to you *for medicine.*

                                                    April 6, 1938

> *Guru, this property business has been redirected to me.*
> *All I understand about it is that the zamindars are now*
> *claiming our property. Chand and his mother are also*
> *partners. Shall I ask Chand to do what he thinks best*
> *or approach my people to do something? My people won't*
> *do anything, I fear, and I don't rely on Chand either; he is*
> *lazy except for his own matters.*

I can't say your exposition of the matter is clear. It is your family
property? If so, your family ought to look after it. However you
can tell Chand as you propose.

> *"Dressed in white robes she came*
> *A figure of purity. . ."*

This is not very impressive, these two lines — sounds too much
like a lady's visit.

> *"O rare figure of Light*
> *I pray for thy measureless boon:*
> *The yearning of the night*
> *For the splendour of thy moon."*
> *It breathes a little of Intuition, perhaps?*

Good Lord, no! This is *not* intuition, — it is mind manufacture.

                                                    April 7, 1938

> *"Murmuringly I roll*
> *Along a grey beech. . ."*

What the deuce? Why a beech and not an oak or pine-tree? Or
do you mean beach?

1052 CORRESPONDENCE WITH

> *Guru, I bade the mind keep quiet and allow intuition to flow in and by golly, it has! what?*

By Jove, yes!

April 8, 1938

> *I cherished a wish to flourish as a story-writer long before the English and Bengali Muse sat on me. Now English poetry has caught me and Bengali poetry has gone to sleep. It seems my English poems are much better and deeper than the Bengali ones... Should I try my hand at story-writing?*

Your Bengali poems seem to me to be very good, though less vividly original than the English, except at times. Don't know anything about your stories. Why not keep to poetry at present, writing English usually and Bengali when you can?

April 9, 1938

> *By the way, you are sitting comfortably over Nishikanta's poem. He will make my life uncomfortable when he comes back, saying I have done nothing for him!*

To be able to be comfortable is so rare in this world of discomfort! However I may see whether I can sit up one day and look into the thing.

> *P's cough is less, but she feels rather weak. Shall we wait a few days more for screen-exam or take it tomorrow?*

[*Mother:*] It is better to wait one or two days more.

April 10, 1938

> *As far as I can see P's is a simple case of bronchitis neglected for 15 days! Still as one should always exclude T.B. and screen-exam helps in that, I proposed it.*

[*Mother:*] Yes, but be very careful not to frighten her.

April 12, 1938

SRI AUROBINDO 1053

> *I hesitate to write in this high tone: "I am the Light of the One, Voice" etc. It sounds high and grand. Some don't like this tone at all. D is one. They call it insincere. A poet-sadhak has no justification for using this tone?*

If such poems are put as a claim, or vaunted as a personal experience of Yoga, they may be objected to on that ground. But a poet is not bound to confine himself to his personal experience. A poet writes from inspiration or from imagination or vision. Milton did not need to go to Heaven or Hell or the Garden of Eden before he wrote Paradise Lost. Are all D's bhakti poems an exact transcription of his inner state? If so, he must be a wonderful Yogi and bhakta.

April 14, 1938

> *N.P. showed me Sri Aurobindo's letter to him regarding his ailment. How interesting to know all these factors! We think the Divine can cure us, even magically, if he wanted, but don't see that it is our own resistance that comes in the way. But suppose we had given one injection of morphia, the pain would have subsided and he would have gone to sleep. The subconscient would have failed to act then. I suppose morphia will act on the body and thus stop the subconscient which acts through the body?*

The morphia stuns locally or otherwise the consciousness and its reaction to the subconscient pressure and so suspends the pain or deadens it. Even that it does not always do — Manilal took five morphine injections in succession without even diminishing his liver inflammation pains. What became of the power of the drug over the subconscient in that case? The resistance was too strong just as the resistance of N.P.'s subconscient to the Force.

> *If the patient had been outside and a doctor had cured him, how would he have conquered this subconscient resistance? If you have no time, could I have a few lines on this subject, from Sri Aurobindo?*

In much the same way as Coué's suggestion system cured most of his patients, only by a physical instead of a mental means. The

1054   CORRESPONDENCE WITH

body consciousness responds to the suggestion or the medicine
and one gets cured for the time being or it doesn't respond and
there is no cure. How is it that the same medicine for the same
illness succeeds with one man and not with another or succeeds
at one time with a man and afterwards doesn't succeed at all?
Absolute cure of an illness so that it cannot return again depends
on clearing the mind, the vital and the body consciousness and the
subconscient of the psychological response to the Force bringing
the illness. Sometimes this is done by a sort of order from above
(when the consciousness is ready, but it cannot always be done
like that). The complete immunity from all illness for which our
Yoga tries can only come by a total and permanent enlightenment
of the below from above resulting in the removal of the psychological roots of ill health — it cannot be done otherwise.

> *P is about the same. Pavitra has sent us a bottle of Pneumo-*
> *gein, and one of Pulmoserum. Shall we try Pulmoserum as*
> *it contains Codein which may be more useful?*
> [*The Mother drew a line indicating "Shall we try" and*
> *underlined "Pulmoserum".*]

Yes.

April 16, 1938

> *Dr. André asked me if I had any communications from Sri*
> *Aurobindo on medical things. May I show him yesterday's*
> *letter?*

[*Mother:*] Yes.

April 17, 1938

[*Mother:*] K is complaining of weakness. I told him to ask you
for a *tonic* (*not medicine*).

> *I hope Dilipda is writing to you!*

Telegraphing — Musical conference and still greater musical conference!

April 18, 1938

SRI AUROBINDO   1055

> *Guru, the Muse is too whimsical. Still, I suppose, there is
> some way, what?*

I don't know that there is, except to catch the inspiration by the
hair when it comes, and keep it till the poem is done.

> *If I could know what time you send in the Force or what's
> your best time, I could get an optimum result.*

I have no best or worst time — it depends on God's mercy.

> *Sitabala's boil looks like a carbuncle... We have a good
> anti-vaccine for it, to be applied locally, which we had
> tried in Parkhi's case. But it gave him a severe general re-
> action — fever 104°. So, should we try?*

[*Mother*:] It may not be prudent to try.

April 19, 1938

> *Purani brought Mrs. Sahmeyer here. She had an accident
> in Moscow: suspected fracture of a rib on the left side,
> but the doctor said none, — without X-ray. The pain sub-
> sided, but it has recurred here. I said X-ray is best. But who
> will pay or shall we pay considering her as an Asram
> member?*
> [*The Mother cancelled "Sahmeyer" and wrote below
> "Sammer".*[1]]

It is better to pay — I will pay — Nothing must be asked from her —

April 20, 1938

> *"Through the night's pendulous haze
> Stars wane and glow..."*

Pendulous! You might just as well write "suspensive".

---

[1] Mrs. Sammer, the wife of Francicheck Sammer, one of the Czech architects of
Golconde.

1056   CORRESPONDENCE WITH

> *In the last stanza, instead of "whorl", shall I put "un-furl"?*

Good heavens, no! *Don't* unfurl.

> *The rest of the poem I leave at your mercy, Sir!*

I have had no mercy upon it, as you can see. I have not put double lines because it would be an encomium on my own ravages, but you can consider the lines to be there.

> *You seem to be in an illusion as regards my inspiration! Do you think it comes in a rush or that I feel its glow?*

Never nursed such a thought.

> *No, Sir, no — or exceedingly rarely! I have to wrestle, Sir!*

So have I.

April 21, 1938

> *"A withering ball*
> *Of fire on the wide canvas of time*
> *Fades to a dot. . ."*

What's this ball of fire on a canvas? Have you reflected that the canvas would be burned away in no time?

> *We have caught a parrot which can't fly. What to do with it?*

[*Mother:*] Feed it with grains and fruit until it can fly away.

April 22, 1938

> *"With myriad titan hosts*
> *That gather and conspire. . ."*

Look here, I say! You seem unable now to write a poem without dragging in the word "myriad"!!

April 24, 1938

SRI AUROBINDO   1057

> *Then you will see no "myriad", Sir, though "many" is*
> *peeping like a coward! But I don't understand why you*
> *are so wry over "myriad". In that case, heaven, spirit,*
> *luminous, shadow, dream, etc. have to go and I shall be*
> *left with what?*

"Myriad" is an epithet, not a key-word like heaven, spirit or dream.
An epithet recurring in every poem (even if it were luminous!) ends
by sounding poor.

April 25, 1938

> *Guru, I feel rather dry and barren! The other poem you*
> *have uplifted twice.*

Excuse me, no! You uplifted once, I repeated the operation.
Changed back the second uplift to a mere lift.

> *[Chand's wire:] Inspectors contact uncongenial Trying*
> *avoid.*

What the hell! He seems to have plenty of money to waste on unnecessary telegrams! Why wire about the Inspector's contact?

> *H had pain in the eyes last night... Looks like a mild*
> *attack of iritis. If you want, we can take him to the ost.*
> *tomorrow.*

[*Mother:*] You can wait one or two days.

April 26, 1938

> *"Mystery's heavenly fane" all right?*

Get rid of this *fane*, please. So long as we keep it, all emendations
will be in *vain*.

> *"The flames of a timeless dawn. . ." Can "flames" be made*
> *singular?*

No, it can't be singularised, as intuition will then walk off in a
huff.

". . . the wan shadows are cast
From its sleepless whirl. . ."[1]
. . . End of 1st stanza all right? and the repetition in the
last stanza?

I can't make out for the life of me what are these wan shadows
and why they poke their pale noses in here!

As you wrote it it is a dream-poem. I have tried by a few alterations to wake it up—now, I think it is truly excellent as a vision-
poem. It must be "thy sky" [instead of "the sky"]—for otherwise it is the ordinary sky and since Science has shown us that
that does not exist—it is only a hallucination of blue colour
created by azotes or some other such chemical entity, anything
written about the ordinary sky can only be either unconvincing
or purely decorative. So!

Repetition all right and very effective.

April 28, 1938

[Chand's wire:] "Progressing again debt case Tomorrow."
Voilà, another, Sir! I wrote to him not to waste money on
unnecessary registered letters and telegrams, but Chand
is Chand! So!

Well, well, let us accept the inevitable প্রকৃতিং যান্তি ভূতানি[2] which
means All animals follow their nature.

K—[18.4.38] Melatone didn't give him much good effect.
As it looks like nervous fatigue, Kola may do him good.
If you have any more Nergine, he could resume it, perhaps.

[*Mother:*] I have no nergine.

April 29, 1938

"Haunted by wild desires. . ." Wild is all right?

No, too wild!

---

[1] "Sky Transcendent", *Sun-Blossoms*, p. 79.
[2] *prakritim yānti bhūtāni.*

SRI AUROBINDO   1059

H has slight pain in the eyes today. [Maybe iritis due to
T.B. Prescribed cod-liver oil.] If you have no objection, we
can try salicylates by mouth.
[The Mother drew a line indicating "salicylates".]

It is *so* bad for stomach!

April 30, 1938

May 1938

"I have seen in thy white eyes
   A spark unknown, . . ."

White eyes = eyes without pupils which would be rather terrifying.

By the way, yesterday while meditating, I saw clearly
that you wrote "excellent" for yesterday's poem[1] — almost
the same as "exceedingly fine". This is the third or fourth
time I had such a prevision. Some faculty growing, Sir?
Or a coincidence?

"Coincidence" is a quack scientific word which like many such
words states the fact that two things coincide (here your prevision and my opinion coincide) but does not explain the fact —
If a man sees a snake in dream in the night and each time crosses
one in the day, that would be a coincidence of dream and snake.
But to say so leaves the real question untouched, viz. why the
coincidence?

. . . Don't know how J will react to your remark that you
are too busy to see her poetry now. That is the Lord's
business.

It is rather her business.

She has given up Bengali poetry thinking that you haven't
much time to take it up. Perhaps English will be easy for
you. Well?

[1] "Seeking Thy Light. . . .", *Sun-Blossoms*, p. 60.

1060

She tells me I can do her poem for her in 3 minutes. I have told her it would take half an hour or 20 minutes at the least — which is a fact as it is in a terrible mess.

> *I asked her to take up some other work so long as poetry can't be done. But her sadhana can only be done through her own line, i.e. literature, not through sweeping etc. Alas, alas! Even R and K [artists] have taken up some other work, she can't!*

Of course not — because she is not sincere about it. The idea of sadhana through her own line is a mere excuse — it is a vital satisfaction she is after.

> *What exactly is vital interchange?*

Difficult to specify. There is always a drawing of vital forces from one to another in all human social mixture that takes place automatically. Love-making is one of the most powerful ways of each drawing up the other's vital force, or of one drawing the other's which also often happens in a one-sided way to the great detriment of the "other". In the passage come. many things good and bad, elation, feeling of strength, and support, infiltration of good or bad qualities, interchange of psychological moods, states and movements, depressions, exhaustion — the whole gamut. People don't know it — which is a mercy of God upon them — but when one gets into a certain Yogic consciousness, one becomes very much aware and sensitive to all this interchange and action and reaction, but also one can build a wall against, reject etc., etc.

> *Dr. Rao thinks that it is better to isolate R.L. from public work. We shall have to see the blood result.*

[*Mother:*] Let her be examined first.

The mischief is that she is very useful in the D.R. just now, but I shall see if I can have her replaced as, evidently, it would be better if she did not do public work.

May 2, 1938

> *Guru, I learned from Ishwarbhai that you want me to send*

SRI AUROBINDO   1061

> *up this letter [on vital interchange]. I wonder if you can
> deal with the subject a little more liberally on the typed
> sheet, as it is rather an important and interesting phenom-
> enon.*

My impression was that I had written much more — but that is
probably an *adhyaropa*[1] from the copiousness of my other reply
on the feminine woman. Anyhow I have added a little to the rather
stumpy note. You can type and give a copy to Ishwarbhai.

[*Sri Aurobindo's revised version of the letter of 2.5.38:*]

There is always a drawing of vital forces from one to another in
all human social mixture; it takes place automatically. Love-
making is one of the most powerful ways of each drawing up the
other's vital force, — or of one drawing the other's, which also
often happens in a one-sided way to the great detriment of the
"other". In the passage come many things good and bad, elation,
feelings of strength, fullness, support or weakness and depletion,
infiltration of good and bad qualities, interchange of psychological moods, states and movements, ideas helpful and harmful,
depression, exhaustion — the whole gamut. In the ordinary consciousness one is not aware of these things; the effects come into
the surface being, but the cause and process remain unknown
and unnoticed because the interchange is subtle and covert, it
takes place through what is called the subconscient, but is rather
a behind-consciousness covered by the surface waking mind.
When one gets into a certain Yogic consciousness, one becomes
very much aware of this covert movement, very sensitive to all
this interchange and action and reaction; but one has this advantage that one can consciously build a wall against them, reject, refuse, accept what helps, throw out or throw back what
injures or hinders. Illnesses can also pass in this way from one to
another, even those which are not medically regarded as contagious
or infectious; one can even by will draw another's illness into
oneself as did Antigonus of Macedon accepting death in this way
in order to save his son Demetrius. This fact of vital interchange,
which seems strange and unfamiliar to you, becomes quite intelli-

---

[1] Mental imposition.

1062   CORRESPONDENCE WITH

gible if one realises that ideas, feelings etc. are not abstract things
but in their way quite concrete, not confining their movements to
the individual's mind or body but moving out very much like the
"waves" of science and communicating themselves to anyone who
can serve as a receiver. Just as people are not conscious of the material waves, so it is and still more with these mental or vital waves;
but if the subtle mind and senses become active on the surface —
and that is what takes place in Yoga — then the consciousness
becomes aware in its reception of them and records accurately and
automatically their vibrations.

> *Mother has said in "Conversations" that one can lose*
> *everything (I don't remember the exact words) by just a look*
> *from another.*[1]

Did she deal with this subject at any length? If so and if you remember where, you can indicate the passage to Ishwarbhai.

> *Or one can lose even by passing by somebody unfavourable.*
> *That is something dreadful, Sir!*

Quite true, it often happens. It is the reason why Mother looked
with some uneasiness on tea parties and things.

> *Is that one of the reasons why Anilbaran down-casts his*
> *glance as soon as he meets our eyes?*

It may be — to minimise interchange.

> *As if he has seen a "sin" — to quote D, and which D deeply*
> *resents and complains of.*

D could never bear that Yoga and spiritual inner life could have
any claims as against social intercourse.

> *Is that the way to "build a wall" against anything unde-*
> *sirable?*

[1] Mother's Centenary vol. 3, p. 6.

SRI AUROBINDO   1063

It is a wall of consciousness that one has to build. Consciousness is not something abstract, it is like existence itself or ananda
or mind or prana, something very concrete. If one becomes aware
of the inner consciousness, one can do all sorts of things with it,
send it out as a stream of force, erect a circle or wall of consciousness around oneself, direct an idea so that it shall enter somebody's
head in America etc., etc.

> *Can it be said also that people who are "powerful" love-*
> *makers have a need in some part of their being or part of*
> *their make-up? D surely has no need, he has enough vital*
> *strength and all that to spend.*

People with vital force are not only always throwing it on others
but also always drawing it from others. D does it in the form of
praise, affection, submission to his influence, sexual surrender,
etc. Otherwise why did he feel so much and become miserable,
if he was criticised, refused affection or submission, etc., etc.?
If he had no need, it would not have affected him.

> *I wonder if transmission of diseases also plays a part in*
> *this interchange.*

Yes.

> *I don't understand why you call it "the mercy of God";*
> *just as there is exhaustion, depression, there is also elation.*

Because ignorance is bliss and they would feel very uncomfortable
if they felt these things or were at all aware of them. As for the
elation they get it without needing to know the cause.

> *[Chand's telegram:] "Great inertia again letter follows."*
> *Guru, another bombardment! What an impulsive fellow!*
> *Almost unparalleled. I think he is another fellow who will*
> *find life extremely difficult here.*

Well, there's no inertia in his wrong activities at any rate. He is
full of energy there.

16

1064   CORRESPONDENCE WITH

> *"Replete with the essences. . ." how do you like it, Sir?*

Great Scott! Replete! essences? petrol? This line is terribly philosophic, scientific and prosaic.

May 3, 1938

> *S has had a terrible cough and high fever since yesterday noon. Any mixture to be given?*
> *[The Mother marked the last portion of my question, with a line.]*

It might be better to know first what it is ————

May 4, 1938

> *Guru, I have absolutely gone for the Muse today in a terrible vengeance against her uncharitableness. The weather is splendidly hot and if the Muse makes me perspire still more, well, I shall be turned into a "perspiring idiot"!*

But is a perspiring idiot worse than a dry idiot? I don't think so.

> *"A purple shadow walks along. . ." It sounds rather like a sentry walking along, no? Seems funny!*

"Walking along" suggests not a sentinel but someone taking a constitutional stroll on the beach in the hope of getting a motion. Too colloquial.

> *"Life is a lonely journey. . ."*

? For most it is a chattering peopled journey — Besides "lonely" comes at the end.

> *I've already told Sahana that I shall give her that letter [on vital interchange].*

In that case you can do so, but it is better if she does not show it to others.

> *In the future, I will take her.*

SRI AUROBINDO   1065

? take her where?

> *N.P. came to me with a letter from Agarwal. I asked him
> to forward it to you, for your advice.*

Don't know anything about this.

> *On grounds of medical ethics I can't give any opinion,
> I said, especially as he has approached Agarwal who is
> more competent than I. One thing struck me in his note,
> when Agarwal says that he cured N.P. in a day because
> Mother's force works actively through him. It may be that
> the force works, but so actively as to cure him in a day?*

Why not? If there is sufficient receptivity, then time does not matter.

> *Alas, the force works through me in months, if at all!*

Agarwal has self-confidence and with that one can always succeed. If there are failures, nobody notices, because they are covered
up by the high notes of the song of self-confidence.

> *Don't understand at all these subtle things. The same
> disease, the same treatment, except hip-bath, purging 20
> times, fruit diet, etc., and he cures in a day!*

But even without the force, in ordinary cases, with the same disease and the same treatment there is sometimes cure and sometimes no-cure.

> *By the way, it is very interesting to note the difference
> of appreciation between D and T regarding the famous
> singer Kesarbai. T says, "I am forced to say it is good,
> though I can't say that I like it," while D is absolutely
> beyond words in praise of her.*

Well, doesn't criticism boil down to that "I like it" or "I don't
like it"? What more do you expect?

> *But then T is also a connoisseur!*

1066   CORRESPONDENCE WITH

My dear sir, what is the use of connoisseurs if they don't have opinions entirely different from every other connoisseur?

May 5, 1938

> *"Eternities come and go*
> *Like clouds of drowsy time..."*

How can Eternities come and go like clouds of Time—they wouldn't be eternities any longer.

> *Guru, this is another specimen of "thoughtless" writing, though I had to doze for about an hour. It is a great bother to concentrate on every line and finish a poem, perspiring like an "idiot". I think I shall try the habit of rushing down whatever comes, and then widen or narrow it as required.*

That is my own method—I put down what comes and deal with it afterwards in the calm light of intuitive reflection.

> *Where is this Intuition gone in my case? No chance of returning? What does it mean by giving a flying visit?*

That kind of hide and seek is a frequent phenomenon of poetic inspiration.

May 6, 1938

> *Guru, when I read that your method of writing poetry is the same as mine, I said: "The shishya's method must be the same as the Guru's," but when I read the rest of your letter, I sat down! "Calm light of intuitive reflection"! O Lord, how to do that? Your Intuition says everything to you? Have you nothing to think whether right or wrong? Alas! how then can the shishya follow the Guru!*

Good Heavens! After a life of sadhana you expect me still to "think" and what is worse think what is right or wrong. I don't think, even; I see or I don't see. The difference between intuition and thought is very much like that between seeing a thing and badgering one's brains to find out what the thing can possibly be

SRI AUROBINDO   1067

like. Intuition is truth-sight — The thing seen may not be the truth?
Well, in that case it will at least be one of its hundred tails or at
least a hair from one of the tails. The very first step in the supramental change is to transform all operations of consciousness from
the ordinary mental to the intuitive, only then is there any hope
of proceeding farther, not to, but towards the supramental. I must
surely have done this long ago otherwise how could I be catching
the tail of the supramental whale?

May 7, 1938

> *"My soul keeps its wide calm*
> *Amidst the surge. . ."*

For heaven's sake don't bring calm in at the end of a line. One
has to rhyme with balm, palm or psalm, and to bring any of these
in without an obvious effort of manufacture is a Herculean feat.
Of course if you slam in an Imam or warm up to an alarm, it becomes easier but at the cost of an uneasy conscience.

May 8, 1938

> *These two poems followed as if one piece. But I find some*
> *difference. Both seem to have a similarity in thought.*

They seem to me separate. Probably the broadcaster above forgot
to announce "Here I begin some new stuff."
    Don't get into a fit over the rhyme — it can be done once in a way.

> *Nolini wants a very good recent poem of mine, to try in*
> *Viswabharati (Tagore's paper). I wonder if they will*
> *publish it. Would an "intuitive" poem be better or a coloured*
> *or stressed one?*

Depends on the poetic taste of the Viswabharati editor about
which I know nothing.

> *Roch (an Atelier worker) came today after 4 or-5 days!*
> *Diarrhoea stopped the very day, but no motion since then.*
> *He has pain in the abdomen, fever, weakness. What to do*
> *with these people? They don't want to go to the hospi-*

1068   CORRESPONDENCE WITH

tal, neither do they come here regularly. How to treat such cases?

[*Mother:*] I suppose you have to threaten them with a refusal of treating them if they do not come regularly — We used to be very strict that way before and it had some effect.

May 9, 1938

Though I didn't get into a "fit", I couldn't escape a slight fine tremor over two "beyonds". How do you explain that?

Well, to silence the tremor, the best is to substitute "above" for the second "beyond" — peace be with you!

And is there a suggestion of 3 vertical lines in the 4th stanza, or cancelled as an after-thought?

No, it was a vain attempt to substitute one line for two.

Guru, this fellow Chand wants a power of attorney. It is a bother to find out Notaire Public, buy a French (?) form and all that. Shall I wait for Doraiswamy's coming?

There is no certainty about the time of Duraiswami's coming and meanwhile Chand may have gone to join himself to his better half, the Calcutta Corporation. Why does not Chand send you the power of attorney ready drawn up; you can go with Purani and sign it before the Consul.

Nateshan (a painter in the carpentry dept.) has syphilis. He has ulcer on the foot — an open wound. Rishabhchand says that his habits are also dirty. I'm afraid we shall have to send him to the hospital for injections. I asked Rishabhchand to give him an outside work till we hear from you.

[*Mother:*] Yes the man must go for treatment to the hospital and we cannot give him work until he is cured.

May 10, 1938

"The moon then rises from the grave Of earth. . ."

SRI AUROBINDO   1069

Lord, sir, and what of the astronomers? A moon rising out of the earth. If it is an irresponsible occult moon, that should appear more evidently.

> *Mr. Raymond[1] says he had an attack of influenza and now feels very weak — no appetite, no taste for food. I think he will profit by some bitter tonic. I didn't suggest it to him, though.*

[*Mother:*] You might suggest.

> *May 11, 1938*

> *. . . André gave Mr. Raymond a tonic — Carnine Lefranco, which, I find, is a concentrated meat extract. I would have preferred something else. . .*
> [*The Mother underlined "meat extract".*]

[*Mother:*] Better not give it — meat is not good for him —

> *May 12, 1938*

> *We want a large vessel for preparing soup. What about an aluminium vessel (if you have one in stock), just the kind we have for the milk in D.R.? Soup can't be prepared in such vessels? Enamel ones have been specially ordered from France, I hear. But I don't think there is any chance of getting a fresh stock now.*

[*Mother:*] Aluminum vessels can be used for soup quite well, but I fear there are none in stock. However we can have one from Madras or Calcutta.

> *May 13, 1938*

> *R. L. had vomiting sensation in the afternoon. Wonder if it is due to small doses of arsenic. . . I have stopped it.*

[*Mother:*] Yes beware of the arsenic. Some people cannot stand it at all.

---

[1] Antonin Raymond — a Czech architect of Golconde, settled in the U.S.A.

1070 CORRESPONDENCE WITH

I am tired of these moons, stars, suns, etc. It seems as if spiritual poems can't do without them.

Excuse me, they can. ন তত্র ভাতি চন্দ্রতারকাং।[1]

May 14, 1938

You say "ন তত্র ভাতি চন্দ্রতারকাং", that may be a spiritual experience, but to express it in poetry is rather difficult. Harin has sun and moon in plenty. Amal has "stars" coming in almost every one of his poems, said his friend Saranagata.

That was Amal's own preference, not the spiritual poems' necessity. I read the other day a comment on Keats' poetry that he always writes about stars and that there is a spiritual reason for it.

We haven't had many of your poems to go by. This is one point against spiritual poetry. Another, it seems to me that spiritual poetry is bound to be limited in scope and less full of "রস বৈচিত্র্য"[2] (to quote Tagore) and a little monotonous, every time soul, spirit, etc. coming in in slightly different garbs.

Ordinary poems (and novels) always write about love and similar things. Is it one point against ordinary (non-spiritual) poetry? If there is sameness of expression in spiritual poems, it is due either to the poet's binding himself by the tradition of a fixed set of symbols (e.g. Vaishnava poets, Vedic poets) or to his having only a limited field of expression or imagination or to his deliberately limiting himself to certain experiences or emotions that are dear to him. To readers who feel these things it does not appear monotonous. Those who listen to Mirabai's songs, don't get tired of them, nor do I get tired of reading the Upanishads. The Greeks did not tire of reading Anacreon's poems though he always wrote of wine and beautiful boys (an example of sameness in unspiritual poetry). The Vedic and Vaishnava poets remain immortal in spite of their sameness which is in another way like that of the poetry of the

---

[1] *na tatra bhāti chandratārakām:* "There the moon and the stars shine not."

[2] *rasa vaichitrya:* a variety of sentiments or feelings.

SRI AUROBINDO   1071

troubadours in mediaeval Europe, deliberately chosen. রস বৈচিত্র্য
is all very well, but it is the power of the poetry that really matters.
After all every poet writes always in the same style, repeats the
same vision of things in "different garbs".

> *In connection with J's poetry, you had said long ago that
> there is a danger of repeating in mystic poetry.*

The danger but not the necessity.

> *You know when Sahana sent some of her poems to Tagore,
> he said that the world creation is full of a variety of rasa.
> The poet's mind should not be confined to one single* প্রেরণা[1],
> *however vast it may be.*[2]
> [*Sri Aurobindo underlined "however vast it may be".*]

But Tagore's poetry is all from one প্রেরণা. He may write of different things, but it is always Tagore and his prerana repeating
themselves interminably. Every poet does that.

> *He hints that only spiritual inspiration dealing with things
> spiritual and mystic should not bind a poet's creation. Well?*

Well and if a poet is a spiritual seeker what does Tagore want him
to write about? Dancing girls? Amal has done that. Wine and
women? Hafez has done that. But he can only use them as symbols
as a rule. Must he write about politics, — communism, for instance,
like modernist poets? Why should he describe the outer aspects of
বিশ্ব প্রকৃতি[3] for their own sake, when his vision is of something
else within বিশ্ব প্রকৃতি or even apart from her? Merely for the
sake of variety? He then becomes a mere littérateur. Of course
if a man simply writes to get poetic fame and a lot of readers, if
he is only a poet, Tagore's advice may be good for him.

> *Nishikanta and Harin have more variety, perhaps. But on
> the whole don't you think we are likely to be lacking in this
> rasa and variety?*

---

[1] *preranā:* inspiration.
[2] Original in Bengali.
[3] *viśwaprakriti:* world nature.

It is not a necessity of spiritual poetry; but if it so happens, I don't see that it matters so terribly.

> *Tagore says that it is unbecoming for a poet to mention that his discovery of a metre is new or difficult.*

That is a matter of etiquette. Tagore popularised the স্বরবৃত্ত[1] and there was a big row about it at first; he left it to his admirers to shout about it. Dilip being a prosodist prefers to do the fighting himself, that is all.

> *I wonder why one should not mention that a chhanda is new, if a poet discovers one. He may not say that it is difficult, but why shouldn't he speak of its newness? For instance the discovery of your stress rhythm had to be mentioned in order to be grasped.*

Obviously.

> *Tagore being a master of chhanda, says this?*

Also an inventor of new metres.

> *Dilip seems to have made chhanda a mathematical business; that's why many complain that his poems can't be read.*

Is it true?

> *Once Tagore wrote to Sahana that he couldn't appreciate Dilipda's language and style (didn't say whether of prose or poetry).*

Why did he praise him (to Dilip himself) now?

> *Can't you send some of your poems? You owe me one, you know.*

What poems? I am not writing any, except occasionally my long epic (Savitri) which cannot see the light of day in an embryonic state.

---

[1] *swarabritta:* one of the principal metres of Bengali poetry.

SRI AUROBINDO

1073

> *"The zephyr from an inscrutable height*
> *Blowing like strains of a lyre..."*

Zephyr from an inscrutable height? The zephyr is a sweet little romantic wind incapable of heights.

> *With difficulty I have avoided moon, stars, etc., but in one place I have put "sun" which I hope you will kick out.*

Kicked!

May 15, 1938

> *"No more the dark world calls*
> *With its alluring voice..."*

Lord, sir — let this dark world and its alluring voice be far from us. It jars here, bringing in the note of the often heard obvious.

> *K feels fatigued again. It may be better for him to take another bottle of the tonic. Shall we buy one?*

[*Mother:*] I have sent to the Dispensary a bottle of Wincarnis; you might try it on K.

May 16, 1938

> *Guru, again with a Herculean effort I have kept out most of my blessed "dear" terms, with what effect, you know.*

Yes, only aureole remains. There is of course immortal — and eternal, but these we have allowed. Also "glow, wine, splendour" perhaps; but if we go too far in exclusiveness, your inspiration may cease to glow also. So we will be moderate in our exactions on the Muse.

T has fever (two days) and pain on the left side which makes it difficult to move or even turn on the bed. Better see her and it may be best to call André to see what is the matter with her, for she has been complaining of bad health for long — weakness, inability to work, lassitude, etc.

May 17, 1938

1074   CORRESPONDENCE WITH

T's X-ray taken, and André says that it may be T.B. He says that injection at present is not desirable. I wonder if she could be spared from the kitchen work, for she has become very weak.

[*Mother:*] The best seems to me that she should stop the kitchen work at least for a few weeks until she becomes stronger—

André has prescribed Tricalcine (calcium), shall we buy it?

[*Mother:*] Certainly.

He has also prescribed some extra alimentation: oranges, milk, butter, soup, etc.

[*Mother:*] For a long time I was giving her orange juice, she herself asked that it should be stopped. I am still giving her biscuits every day. She was getting butter and also asked to stop it, because it was making her fat! In fact she had stopped the orange juice because she was taking much milk and her stomach cannot stand both at the same time.

May 18, 1938

... T's diet is strikingly poor. She has agreed to take 2 or 3 oranges a day. But I hear you are short of oranges. If available, papaya will be good, and mangoes and other fruits.

[*Mother:*] Oranges are difficult but "mandarines" (loose jackets) can be found at the bazaar. I suppose it will do—papaya and mangoes can be given daily for the moment.

Then if you have no objection, she should have some other vegetable. At present she has a little distaste for D.R. curry, so she doesn't take much of it. She can either prepare it herself or L can do it. We could even ask Lakshmi.

[*Mother:*] She has dislike of the D.R. food *because she is cooking it herself.* So I do not think it is quite safe to ask her to cook for herself.

SRI AUROBINDO   1075

> *About work, it will be decidedly better to stop cooking,*
> *but she must have some other light work to occupy herself.*

[*Mother:*] She is doing embroidery. Is there any objection to that?
She seems not to want to stop the cooking work although we
wrote to her to stop it. It might be better to tell her that she *must*
stop it.

> *As for medicine, what do you think of Chyavanprash? It is*
> *widely used in India for lung trouble, and is very effective,*
> *they say. She can take it with Tricalcine.*

[*Mother:*] Yes.

> [*A note from the Mother later in the day:*]

Nirod
It is better not to press T to take Lakshmi's food, but perhaps
L would agree to prepare some food for T — You might ask her —
and if she agrees perhaps she could come to the dispensary for
cooking as she may not have the needed things with her.

May 19, 1938

> *... André said he fears T has T.B. ... At present she has no*
> *taste at all due to fever. So I have asked her to take more*
> *fruits.*

[*Sri Aurobindo:*] When it becomes necessary to have special food
for her, you will have to arrange directly with L about it.

> *"Lonelily like a sheep I go*
> *Along the watermark of time. . ."*
> How is this sheep? "Lonelily" Harinian?

[*Sri Aurobindo:*] I don't know if it is Harinian, but it is certainly
impossible. Sheep is too sheepish, — you might just as well say,
"like a mouse".

1076   CORRESPONDENCE WITH

> *Guru, do you find any blessed progress?*[1] *Getting rather*
> *"hopeless"!*

A very fine poem, sir. Progress blessed, *not* hopeless.

May 20, 1938

> *"Lonelily" is impossible? or it's impossible in this context?*
> *Surely you have seen H using it very often. If you haven't,*
> *then I'll show it to you tomorrow, or only H can do it?*

The word simply doesn't exist, any more than "lovelily" or "sillily"
or "wilily". You can say "lonesomely" if you think it worth while,
not "lonelily". H is no authority for the use of English words. I
did not correct his English when I saw his poems — I left the responsibility of his departures to himself, except when he himself
asked on a particular point.

May 21, 1938

> *"A strange intensity glows*
> *Through its wild frame*
> *Sweeping all barriers flows*
> *Its mystery-flame."*

What is this domestic broomstick work on barriers? If you mean,
sweeping away, you have to say so.

> *Guru, I was rather depressed not to find any double lines*
> *in yesterday's poem.*

I said it was a fine poem — that is the equivalent of lines.

> *I have tried to drag the Muse out; has she come out?*

She has come out but trailing three cliché tails behind her. Most
reprehensible conduct for a self-respecting Muse.

> *I am caught by a fear that the store is over and nothing new*
> *will come.*

[1] "Lonely Tramp", *Sun-Blossoms*, p. 56.

SRI AUROBINDO   1077

No fear!
                                                            May 22, 1938

> *I don't understand why Lele told you that because you are*
> *a poet, sadhana will be easy for you through poetry, or*
> *why you quote it either. Poetry is itself a damn hard job*
> *and sadhana through poetry — well, the less said the*
> *better! Or perhaps he saw within your soul the Sri Auro-*
> *bindo of future Supramental glory?*

Because I told him I wanted to do Yoga in order to get a new inner Yogic consciousness for life and action, not for leaving life.
So he said that. A poet writes from an inner source, not from the
external mind, he is moved by inspiration to write, i.e. he writes
what a greater Power writes through him. So the Yogi karmachari
has to act from an inner source, to derive his thoughts and movements from that, to be inspired & impelled by a greater Power which
acts through him. He never said that sadhana will be easy for me
through poetry. Where is "through poetry" phrase? Poetry can be
done as a part of sadhana and help the sadhana — but sadhana
"through" poetry is a quite different matter.

> *Dr. André said that he saw T walking one day. She should*
> *take complete rest for a week.*

[*Mother:*] Rest is all right *provided* she remains in the open (on a
terrace or in a garden). To remain all day shut up in a room is not
so good.
                                                            May 23, 1938

> *T is much better today. But what about some prunes (tinned)*
> *to help her motion?*

[*Mother:*] Yes, you can ask from Dyuman.

> *K found Wincarnis very good. It is over, should he have an-*
> *other bottle?*

[*Mother:*] One bottle costs more than Rs. 3. It must be taken only
if it is quite indispensable.

1078   CORRESPONDENCE WITH

What about the man (B.S. worker) who fell and got wounded? is he not to come for treatment?

May 24, 1938

> *Guru, why for some time has my poetic inspiration waned? Does the Divine want me to stop for the time being or is it a temporary phase? At times I strongly suspect that you have left me to shift for myself, perhaps relieved very rarely whenever your Supramental leisure allows, by a little whiff. Is that so?*

It is probably because you had hitched on to a certain province of insight and inspiration from which the poetry came. Your abandonment of its "standing terms" (which was quite right, for one can't go on writing the same subject and language for ever) has pitched you off and now you are trying to hook on elsewhere but have not quite grappled your "moorings" into the right spot. Sometimes it catches on, sometimes it doesn't. E.g. in stanzas 1 and 3 hooked, in stanzas 2 and 4 dishooked, stanza 5 half-hooked, half-dishooked.

> *Which or what?*

Neither and nought.

May 25, 1938

> *Guru, your theories are irrefutable, Sir! O wonderful, they are! I have hitched, I have pitched, I have hooked and dishooked!*

But that is not a theory. It is a fact.

> *You take a fancy to hook me on to some "insight" and "inspiration" at very little expense of your Force and "golden sprats" are caught! Then suddenly you cut off the threads from below or above and my net is gone!*

Excuse me — did nothing of the sort. It was you who got dissatisfied with the sprats because of the sameness in the shine of their eyes, fins, tails and other accessories.

SRI AUROBINDO   1079

> *Showing me a future possibility, you shut partially at least,*
> *the opening. Now I knock and knock — nothing!*

Not at all! It is you have started tunnelling in another direction.

> *Can't make things so damn cheap, that's your idea, I*
> *suppose.*

I don't "make" anything cheap or dear. They are so by nature.
These, sir, are the usual vicissitudes of the poetic career and unless
you are a Dilip or a Harin writing away for dear life every day with
an inexhaustible satisfaction and producing tons of poetic matter,
you can't escape the said vicissitudes.

> *How far does this poem go in the hooking business?*

Much better. Only one stanza hookless.

> *Now a little about my prose [property]. Doraiswamy said*
> *that the mere fact of the property being in my name is not*
> *enough; for though the joint family is now disjointed, the*
> *other partners can claim a share in that property unless*
> *they have allotted it to me. . .*

But what was the understanding when it was put in your name?

> *You see a tangled business. I don't think then even a pie*
> *will come to me. I don't know why creditors are not taking*
> *up the property. Has it not been allotted to me then?*

You will have to get reliable information as to what is the real
situation.

> *If it is left, it will simply be swallowed up by zamindars*
> *for nothing. If sold at least the creditors will get some*
> *amount and my "fair name" not fouled!*

Certainly, to sell is the only thing — only your right of property
in it must be put beyond doubt. There is no profit in letting the

zamindars get hold of it — except of course the profit to the zamindars. But why should you be philanthropic to that now much abused class? Get what you can out of it; even if it is only for your creditors.

> *Engineer (Mr. Sammer) has hardly had any motion for some days. No pain or mucus. Free purging by salts would have done good, perhaps, but I held off, giving a simple mild laxative. Enema not effective, he says.*

[*Mother:*] Yet it is only "guimauve" enema that would do him good. Laxative is not advisable as he is working hard and must not be weakened. It must be due to exposure to the midday sun.[1]

May 26, 1938

> *Guru, some consolation that you realise I am "tunnelling". Please realise too that at some time the "tunnelling" may come to a bursting point!*

Hold hard! hold hard!

> *The blessed stars have appeared again in this poem.*

Never mind! Once in a way they can peep in provided they don't overdo it.

[*Mother:*] When is André expected to come back?

May 27, 1938

> *André will be going on the 3rd or 4th and will be back within a week. He is not allowed a longer leave as there are all new hands at the hospital.*
>
> *Chand says that one day he will commit suicide due to lack of faith! My Gracious, are you specialising in a lot of sentimental screw-loose fellows as disciples?*

---

[1] In the construction work of Golconde.

SRI AUROBINDO   1081

It looks like it! What a museum! But this kind of collectioning
has been my luck and not my intention.

May 28, 1938

> *In view of my present obstinate difficulty, sometimes I
> think if it wouldn't be better to go out for a while and come
> back perhaps changed, transformed. If it is so, please allow
> me and many others to go every year. Your Supramental
> work will be made half easier!*

Logically, that would mean everybody in the Asram taking a
month's trip to the Himalayas, Calcutta, Cape Comorin etc. and
returning, if not as supermen, yet as fully-fledged psychic angels.
Easy!

May 29, 1938

> *I've marked that at times Mulshankar doesn't like my in-
> terference or "orders".*

That will not [do]. He must accept your orders, as he is there only
as your assistant.

> *Reading Y's letter, if you have any suggestions to make re-
> garding Mulshankar's work, please let me know. I am not
> satisfied with the way we are going on at present.*

I don't know that there is anything to change. Datta and others
give very good reports of Mulshankar's behaviour and attention
to them when they go to the Dispensary in your absence. I am not
prepared to believe otherwise on the strength of Y's solitary statement.

> *A hospital clerk requested me to speak to Dr. R to treat
> him for his heart-disease. If he is treating cases, shall I ask
> the clerk to approach him directly?*

[*Mother:*] R is not taking cases just now —
[*Sri Aurobindo:*] S is complaining of a mysterious illness (fever)
in which she gets very cold in the full heat of the day and her skin

1082   CORRESPONDENCE WITH

is cold outside but as hot as chillies inside. Perhaps as she is always complaining of catastrophic physical states like this, she might be shown to André like the other specimens.

May 30, 1938

> *S had slow fever for the last few days with plenty of perspiration. André finds nothing in the lungs. He thinks it is neurasthenia. . .*

[*Sri Aurobindo:*] That was the Doctor's (Dr. Banerji's) view also.

> *He has given urotropine and gardinal for her nervousness, shall we give them?*

[*Sri Aurobindo:*] She refuses medicines with contumely. She has by the way always had exceedingly scanty and difficult menstruation.

> *Here is a letter from X. You will see that a portion of it is addressed to Z. But Z told me I must not give her X's letters. So I hesitated to give it before asking you. I find that one has to be careful at every step to see on which sentiment, emotion etc. one is trampling. So, Sir, shall I give it to her?*

I couldn't decipher X altogether. But if there is anything Z has to know (there is something about copies of something that has come out?) you can tell her without giving the letter — It is better to shut up about the rest. Z and X both in talk and otherwise have always upset each other and caused crises and shindies — no use risking a disturbance now that in his absence she is going on very nicely.

> "*Oceans or rocks of solitude*
> *For a winged release aspire. . .*"
> *Weak?*

It is not weak, but rather obscure. What is a winged release of oceans and rocks? However, it sounds well.

May 31, 1938

SRI AUROBINDO   1083

June 1938

Why can't you understand oceans and rocks aspiring to winged release? Haven't you read Tagore's Balākā *where the earth, hills, rocks yearn to fly also, seeing the flight of a flock of cranes? Surely you have!*

I am not an expert in Tagore. In English, rocks *might* just manage to aspire to be birds, but it would be regarded as fanciful — if oceans started that sort of thing, it would be regarded as beginning to be excessive.

June 1, 1938

In yesterday's poem, you seem to have put paeon in 3 or 4 places. Is that so?

Paeon? I don't think I did it consciously, — don't remember. In this metre I generally run to anapaestic-iambic, but I may occasionally plunk in a paeon or two in the exuberance of my soul.

R.B.'s pain is more marked just below the apex. I couldn't touch a single spot without her crying "Pain, pain." I can't make head or tail of the thing. It has been with her for 7 years, she says. I might consult André.

[*Mother:*] Yes, it is better.

June 2, 1938

B's piles still quite the same.

[*Mother:*] What "pommade" are you giving him? is it Anthémor? He was complaining that the pommade was increasing his pain.

Should we stop giving K honey? He has taken it for quite a long time.

[*Mother:*] No harm, he can continue.

J has a small pimple in the left eye. I think saline eye bath and drops of argyrol will do. What does Mother say?

1084   CORRESPONDENCE WITH

Yes, I suppose it is all right.

> *We have no* kājal.

If kajal is wanted, why not have some prepared? People are asking, but Mother can't supply everybody.

> *I am sending you the power of attorney draft sent by Chand. It's in Bengali; you will see how difficult it is to translate the terms into English. What the hell am I to do?*

I have not the hell of an idea!

> *Doraiswamy is coming this Sunday, I hear. Shall I ask him?*

He may be coming, but as yet he has not announced it.

> *Or your I.C.S. knowledge would be help enough? I.C.S. people are supposed to be Gods, you know, knowing everything!*

Good Lord, sir! I was a probationer only and had nothing to do with these elaborate idiocies. If I had been a practising civilian, I might have had to do it, but probably I wouldn't have done it and they would have chucked me out for insubordination and laziness.

> *With whom am I to go to the Consul? nothing to pay?*

Purani will take you and find out everything and arrange everything.

                                                        June 3, 1938

> *Any influence of Wordsworth in my poem?*

Good Lord, any? There are whole chunks of Wordsworth — esp. the childhood's days and growing years etc.

> *This poem has opened a new vista for me and gives me the hope that perhaps long poems and new things are not impossible, what?*

SRI AUROBINDO   1085

> *If I can improve it further, give me the suggestions, and I shall do it.*

It is a very uncertain mixture. Some lines and stanzas are so merely Wordsworth that they can't pass. The whole childhood and fading business is Wordsworth and everybody would ask, what's this old stuff copied here for? Much of the rest is Wordsworth romanticised. On the other hand there are blocks of mysticism. The poetry is good and there are very fine lines and stanzas, but as a whole it must be more inspired and Wordsworth chucked out and replaced by Nirod.

> *R.B. has very little pain [below the navel] even while walking. But no appetite at all.*

[*Mother:*] I find her rather yellow in colour.

June 4, 1938

> *Yes, I also marked R.B.'s coloration. She was better in the morning, but her pain has increased. I can't find out at all what sort of trouble it is. It has been with her for the last 7 years!*

[*Mother:*] Have you seen if it is not a moving kidney?

> *Guru, I have come to the end of my tether. Blessed Wordsworth took all the worth out of my words. So I have kicked out every blessed remnant and sentiment, lakes and rills and years, I hope. How do you find it[1] now?*

It is a true রূপান্তর,[2] the Deformed Transformed — the whole poem is now exceedingly fine throughout. No need of lines; all would have to be double-lined.

June 6, 1938

> *Thank you, Sir, for yesterday's unexpected success. I was raging against you that you have left me alone! Even a dribbling Inspiration can be miraculous, what?*

[1] "Childhood Dream", *Sun-Blossoms.* p. 61.
[2] *rupāntar:* transformation.

Often more miraculous than the flowing ones.

> *Did you receive the letter Dilipda mentions?*

I had a letter from him some days ago.

June 7, 1938

> *"Slowly unfold before my vision*
> *World after world of light. . ."*
> *These 2 lines seem to be a theft from your sonnet.*

No. Anybody can see worlds unfolding before the vision. It is only if the language is reproduced that it can be called a theft.

> *I think it is better to open Bala's abscess. Shall we do it here or in the hospital?*

[*Mother:*] It might be better to take him to the hospital.

P.S. Arjava told me to-day that he had gone to you, almost a week ago, for a tonic and that you had given one which did him a lot of good, and then you told him that there was no more of it in the dispensary and gave him something else which had not a good effect. Can you tell me what was this first tonic and if it is available here?

June 8, 1938

> *R.B. says she has no pain today even while walking. She can take more oranges.*

[*Mother:*] I fear we cannot go on increasing oranges like that. They are not easily found in the market and they are costly.

> *We gave Arjava an Ayurvedic tonic called "Lohasava" containing iron. It is available in Madras.*

[*Mother:*] It is better to order for some.

[*Sri Aurobindo:*] S has started taking douches daily — she writes that she is taking salt lotion (is it permanganate?) in the douche, and has taken from the dispensary but not in liquid form and has to melt in hot water "till she gets the right colour". Now in the old

SRI AUROBINDO   1087

Doctor's time S once as an experiment took a tenfold dose of
permanganate in her douche just to see whether it would not cure
her at once in a trice! So Mother considers she cannot be trusted
in these matters (she believes too much in her own cleverness) and
she says the exact amount needed should be given her every day so
that no "mistakes" may be possible.

> X came to me with the letter you have written to him. He
> said that he showed the letter to D but D had not done
> anything, not even spoken to Mother about it saying that
> he had to make some changes and arrangements. I was
> much surprised that D hadn't put it before the Mother. He
> should have at least done that.

But why on earth should things be done in a slap-dash hurry just
to please X? Mother said nothing to D and did not ask him to make
the new arrangement at once. There are many things beside the
mere displacing of one sadhak by another that have to be considered and he was quite entitled to consider all that was involved
before placing the matter definitely before the Mother for orders.

> I thought that perhaps D did not want X in the kitchen, as
> he would not be able to do with him as he did with N and
> that your praise of X's cooking might not be palatable to him.

It would be quite natural if he felt like that. Since N and S are
working, there has been a halcyon peace in the kitchen (in the D.R.
also for different reasons) which are unprecedented in their annals.
For years and years it has been a cockpit of shouts and quarrels and
disagreements, all the "big" workers quarrelling with each other,
each trying to enforce his own ideas and all (except Charu) trying
to ignore and push aside D, all getting furious against the Mother
because she did not "side" with them (X has also written that if
Mother "sides" with D in a clash between them, he would not stand
it), and the "little" workers quarrelling with each other or with
some big worker. It was like the present state of Europe or worse.
Things got so bad that Mother had to eliminate J, M and others
and quiet down other would-be-bosses in order to still the uproar,
for each time somebody who was till then less boisterous arose to
take up the inheritance of quarrel and revolt. Finally we had

1088   CORRESPONDENCE WITH

arrived, as I say, at a halcyon peace — it might have been the tail
of the supramental, it might have been only a lull; but anyhow it
was precious. When we got X's letter showing by signs with which
we were familiar that he was preparing to take up the inheritance,
our immediate reaction was "No, thank you!" — hence my letter.
We were determined to put our foot down at the first sign and not
wait for farther developments.

> *X told me that he has definitely told D that he won't make any*
> *independent move; whatever D gives, he will cook with that.*

In his letter to us he wrote that he did that because he did not
want to increase his own disquietude. He said that his idea was
after a month or so to improve the cooking after his own ideas. He
spoke of independence in the work and intimated that D's duty
should be only to give whatever the রাঁধুনী[1] asked for and not exercise any farther control as he was quite ignorant of these matters. His whole tone was that of one preparing for militant self-
assertion. Now he seems to deny or forget all that and wonders
why I wrote any letter to him at all.

X seems to be going off the trail altogether. His letters are full
of the kind of stuff we used to get from B, Y at his worst, and many
others. Abhiman, revolt, demands, challenges, ultimatums, com-
mands "You will give me the D.R. upstairs room or I won't remain;
you will answer without delay; you ought to have done this, you
must do that," charges against the Mother of falsehood, bad
treatment meted out to him alone and to no other, etc., etc., also
the wickedness of other sadhaks against him (P.S., S etc.); announcement of his coming departure etc. Announcements also that
he will stop eating. Also a vital mind taking up partial and misrepresented facts stated by others and without any knowledge of the
real situation making false inferences (e.g. that the Mother had
not spoken in truth) etc., etc. All that built up into a dark and
dismal farrago of which we have had a hundred examples in the
past. But it is now long since I have decided not to answer letters of
that kind, leave the revolters to their own devices. They expect
us to flatter them, soothe them, fall at their feet and beg them
not to go, comply with their demands, inundate them with anxious

---

[1] *rāndhunī:* cook.

SRI AUROBINDO 1089

love and affection of the vital kind and generally dandle and pet their vital ego. We have seen that to do anything of that kind is disastrous and makes things a thousandfold worse; the vital ego and its movements increase and reach an Asuric stature. So no more of that. I wanted to answer X and put the truth of his state plainly before him in the most quiet and temperate way because it was his first outbreak; I have already pointed out to him that there is one remedy and only one, for him to reject and fight out his vital mind and ego. But he listens only for a moment and the next day "*cela continue*". I have no time now to go on answering this kind of letter. If he wants to do what I say, there is a chance for him; but if he doesn't, we are not responsible for his failure.

Because I did not at once assure him of the increase of his work, he has now written announcing fasting and departure, refusal of the work — accompanied by some damn fool nonsense about Mother's frowning eyes, and serious face which is his own imagination. *Et voilà.*

June 9, 1938

Didn't you receive my private note-book yesterday? I positively sent it. It must be mysteriously lying somewhere there. I hope it hasn't gone to someone else!

I kept it because I thought of writing something about X and his antics but had no time.

R.L. wants half a cup of extra milk as she feels hungry in the morning. . . Can she have it?

[*Mother:*] Yes, *for a time.*

L has again a vomiting sensation and a headache. Last time we gave her Santonin twice with no apparent effect. Shall we repeat?

[*Mother:*] May not be advisable.

June 10, 1938

Guru, oh Lord! what a lot you have written! I feel called upon to respond to it a little. I had a talk with X and asked

1090   CORRESPONDENCE WITH

> *him all that he had written to you and Mother. First he said it wasn't anything much; then I told him about your letter to me and he said: "I wrote that I had a mind to try to improve the D.R. cooking gradually, but I realised it is impossible, so I have given up the idea. . ."*

? I saw nothing in that letter about giving up the idea of improving the cooking.

> *"And that if D goes against Mother and Mother supports him against me, then it will be natural for me to have abhiman. . ."*

Why should Mother support D against herself?

> *X came to me today with your letter which has pacified him. . . . I am almost sure if you hadn't replied, he would have gone away, and he did express such a desire, I hear.*

He says he went up to the station and came back.

He had decided already not to come back to Pondicherry after he went out — so it is not new. He came back because when at Cape Comorin he meditated on Shiva and Krishna, they none of them showed up and he could only see Mother and myself!

> *From what I learn from you and Kanai, I find that things have not been very well with X, from the beginning. His asking for a room in D.R. etc. was revealed to me only now. This incident only set the flame to his heaped-up grievances; otherwise I don't see how a man could write like that from a single instance of this sort. . .*

He had any number of grievances

    (1) not getting an easy chair,

    (2) not getting an almirah,

    (3) not getting the D.R. room on the terrace (reserved especially for visitors),

    (4) my letter which was quite general about poetry, Yoga etc., he says I told him that his poetry was all humbug (ভণ্ডামি) and that

---

¹ *bhaṇḍāmi.*

SRI AUROBINDO   1091

his sadhana was humbug and all our efforts on him were পণ্ডশ্রম¹ —
Needless to say I never wrote or suggested anything of the kind and
in fact wrote nothing about *his* poetry or *his* past sadhana. There
were other grievances, but I have forgotten them.

> *God allow that I may be left some common sense even in*
> *the vortex of my troubles. You surprise me by saying that*
> *Y also wrote such letters to you!*

At least a dozen in which he was going to take the next train to
commit suicide decently in some distant place. You don't know
what a tug of war it was for some years together. Of course his
letters were not so crude as X's but they were bad enough. All
that was very confidential however. We both "kept up appearances"
outwardly, and saved his face as much as possible.

> *I hope it is a lesson enough for X.*

One can never be sure — when a thing like that has seized a fellow,
it is apt to turn up again and again. But I hope for his sake it won't —
for I have no longer my old unwearied patience which I showed to
B, R or Y and many others. Also I have no longer time for endless
soothing letters. However his present attitude in his last letter is
blameless — he seems to have understood.

> *Z has a slight temperature. Given her an Ayurvedic drug*
> *galoye. Should we give her soup?*
> [*The Mother underlined "soup".*]

Yes, it is better.

> *Our rose water is exhausted. Pavitra asked me to enquire*
> *if you have any.*

[*Mother:*] I have some but it arrived from France in an iron drum.
In spite of filtering there is still in it a slight tinct of rust. For any
toilet preparation it is not harmful, but for eyes?——— If you want
I can send you a bottle —

                                                    June 11, 1938

---

¹ *paṇḍashrama:* useless efforts.

1092   CORRESPONDENCE WITH

T says the oranges are very sour.

[*Mother:*] No good oranges can be found and we are receiving no
more from Bombay.

Please send us one bottle of rose water. We can try it.

[*Mother:*] I am sending one bottle.

June 12, 1938

*Guru, I am not lucky enough to be able to follow your
method [6.5.38]. This little piece has taken me about 2
hours and after an hour's slumbering concentration, mind
you! After every line I had to stop for 10 or 15 minutes to
concentrate for the next line — so it went on...*

Let me remind you that Virgil would sit down and write nine lines,
then spend the whole morning perfecting them. Now just compare
yourself with Virgil; you have written 16 lines in 2 hours. That
beats Virgil hollow.

June 13, 1938

*You flatter me by comparing me with Virgil, Sir. But you
forget that my 16, 20 lines are nowhere beside his 9 lines
and that he didn't require Sri Aurobindo's corrections!*

That is why he spent the greater part of the time, trying to correct them himself.

*Today's poem has turned into "prosaic" philosophy. All
philosophies are, I fear, prosaic. But in poetry it is in-
admissible. What's to be done?*

The only remedy is to extend the philosophy through the whole
poem so as to cure the disparateness. Also it must be a figured philosophy. Philosophy can become poetry, if it ceases to be intellectual and abstract in statement and becomes figured and carries
a stamp of poetic emotion and vision.

R.B. is much better today, but is taking very little food.

SRI AUROBINDO   1093

> *Shall we give her an extra cup of milk?*

[*Mother:*] In that case you will have to stop the oranges because much milk with oranges can give pains again.

> *She wants to join work. We advised her to take rest a few days more.*

[*Mother:*] Yes, it is better.

June 14, 1938

> *I want to take up French again, especially conversation, as I find it will be very useful now. To begin with grammar and verbs will be rather dry, perhaps. Can you give me a few practical hints?*

[*Mother:*] The best is to speak – – – courageously at every opportunity.

June 15, 1938

> *Dr. André has prescribed for Z the same medicine as for T, plus Arsenic. Do you sanction Arsenic?*

[*Mother:*] It is to be seen if she can stand arsenic. Perhaps you might make a *very careful* trial.

> *As an alternative, he has suggested sodium cacodylate injections.*

[*Mother:*] If the arsenic fails, this might be tried—

> *Her diet is very poor, she feels very weak. I don't know what to do. Can you suggest something?*

[*Mother:*] But, evidently, the most important is the food—Unhappily these young ladies are very fanciful with their food; it is the palate and not the hunger that governs their eating.

> *Have you any honey in stock, or shall we buy some from the bazaar?*

1094   CORRESPONDENCE WITH

[*Mother:*] We have just received honey; you can ask from Datta.

> [*A separate note:*]
> *Guru, please read T's medical report tonight. I am abso-*
> *lutely staggered at her sudden voracious appetite. Finished*
> *one cabbage in the evening! Have you pumped some Supra-*
> *mental Force into her stomach or what?*

[*Sri Aurobindo:*] I have of course put pressure for no fever and a
good appetite, but did not expect any supramental effects in the
latter direction.

> *By the way, I find her quite sweet and simple. . .*

[*Sri Aurobindo:*] You seem to be easily impressed by surfaces. You
ought to know by this time that "girls" are almost always complex
and often psychoanalytically so. Someone whom I know might tell
you if he answered sincerely to the question that he had found her
one damned incarnate complex. She is simple of course in the
sense that she has not a sophisticated mind or intentions.

June 16, 1938

> *It would be advisable to give Z now and then some vegetables*
> *like karela, cucumbers, potatoes — which she can eat raw or*
> *boiled, at home; extra milk too.*
> [*The Mother marked the whole question with a vertical line.*]

You can propose to her any of these things. She may choose. If
there is any objection to her eating spices, it is better not to let
her cook because she likes food when it is *terribly hot.*

> *I think it would be better to screen-examine Bala's lungs.*

[*Mother:*] Yes.

> *He is very nervous and his diet is very poor.*

[*Mother:*] Yes, he needs badly a tonic — what about Cacodylate injections?

SRI AUROBINDO   1095

> *Guru, even after writing 200 poems, my poetic sense hasn't developed! On the contrary, barring those intuitive poems, these later poems aren't as good as the sonnets and lyrics of the first glorious days. Decadent genius?*

No decadence, but the throes of an attempt at change of cadence.

June 17, 1938

> *This poem is either exceeding or damned — which?*

Damned! that is to say, romantic.

Let me say again that in condemning things as romantic, it is because they are of the wilted echo kind. "Nectarous flow" "fountain music" "bright ethereal voices" "echoing notes" "far wind-blown lyre" "break upon my listening ear" etc. are perhaps new to you and full of colour, but to experienced readers of English poetry they sound as old as Johnny; one feels as if one had been reading hundreds of books of poetry with these phrases on each page and a hundred and first book seems a little superfluous. If they had not been written before, the poem might be pronounced very fine, but — I have tried my best with three of the stanzas to organise them, but except for stanza 2 out of which a very fine image can be made and the two lines marked, with no entire success. The third and fourth stanzas are hopeless. Where the deuce does your inspiration draw these things from? From remembered or unremembered reading? Or just anyhow? It looks as if some unknown nineteenth century poet from time to time got hold of you to unburden himself of all his unpublished poetry.

> *If you could spare, please send those cherries for T. I tasted one; they're very good.*

[*Mother:*] Sending 2 boxes —

June 18, 1938

> *I was the 19th century poet myself, perhaps, trying to take revenge!. . . The lines are coming just anyhow, even after a head-breaking concentration! To see things happen this way after so much labour is very disappointing and discouraging.*

1096

If it is a rebirth effect, it will obviously take time to get rid of it; no use grudging the labour.

> *I couldn't understand clearly whether Z could take the vegetables or milk or both.*

[*Mother:*] Both can be given if she is ready to take.

> *S (a new-comer) complains of weakness, loss of appetite. . . He requires some "pick-me-up", I suppose. Shall we give him something?*

[*Mother:*] Yes.

June 19, 1938

> *R.B. has again a slight continuous pain. . . I wonder if it is a gynaecological case. But how to find it without examination? Will she agree to be examined in the hospital?*

[*Mother:*] You can ask her.

June 20, 1938

> *Guru, nearly the whole of yesterday's poem came in the evening meditation—hence its intuitive character! Today's came through perspiring trance!*

Not intuitive but a very well-inspired perspiration. You seem to have got back your swing.

> *The mangoes given to T are spoilt usually. Are they bought or sent by somebody?*

[*Mother:*] Mangoes are not bought. They must be coming from one or another garden.

> *She proposes to take more rice and bread instead of fruits.*

[*Mother:*] If she takes bread and butter it will help.

> *R.B. has no pain today. Can she begin work?*

SRI AUROBINDO   1097

[*Mother:*] She may try.

> *Does Benjamin still require special cooking?*

[*Mother:*] Ask André —

> *We have a meat extract lying here, bought for Raymond. Shall we give it to Bala?*

[*Mother:*] Yes, but it is better if he takes it in the dispensary itself as a medicine. Because if he takes it to his home, his mother may very well take it instead of he —

June 21, 1938

> *I fear it is a surrealistic business.*[1] *I don't understand anything of it!*

As Baron says, "Why do you want to understand?" It is very fine poetry — according to Housman "pure poetry", for his view is that the more nonsense, the greater — or at least the purer — poetry. Of course it must be divine nonsense or let us say not "nonsense" but "non-sense". So there you are. The last stanza is a masterpiece in that line — the clustered memories in the tree of night make also an exceedingly fine and quite original image. But the whole thing is perfect in its type. There is however nothing really unintelligible — only the transition (e.g. from day to the abyss and night and again to the heart and the caves) can be followed only on the lines of the logic of mystical experience — it is nonsense only to the intellect, to the inner feeling everything is quite clear. You have to look at it not from the brain but from the solar plexus! Anyhow the rise of light is a spiritual illumination to the silent day of the inner consciousness — the night and the abyss are the outer ignorance, its brief mortal existence, but even there it brings a momentary relief and an after-effect (trace on the clustered memories of the dark outer consciousness); within the heart there is the beginning of a trance, of change opening to the caves of the luminous deep of the psychic (hridaye guhâyâm)[2] with its

[1] "Silver Wonder", *Sun-Blossoms*, p. 63.
[2] In the cave of the heart.

psychic fires. See? But that is only a clue for the mind to follow—this significance can rather be felt than understood.

> *R.B. has no pain, but no appetite at all! Shall I try small doses of arsenic? It may give good effects.*

[*Mother:*] You can try—with prudence.

> *Dr. André says that cooking for Benjamin is no longer necessary. I shall inform him tomorrow.*

[*Mother:*] But it must be ascertained that he eats the asram food. It is by not taking it (he does not like it) that he got so bad—

> *For my piles, local injection or operation is the only remedy!*

[*Mother:*] Beware of operation: it does not cure—

> *Purani showed me your reply. Since we are giving Iron to R.B., there is no objection to Purani's preparation.*

[*Mother:*] Then if she takes that preparation, it is better to postpone the arsenic—

June 22, 1938

> *Dr. André suggests that* ওল কচু[1] *(what you call Indian potato) is very good for piles. Can it be given twice a week in the D.R.? It is not for myself only, but for many others who are also suffering from the same complaint.*

[*Mother:*] You might ask Dyuman if they can be found in the market.

> *Bala is getting on very well, so I have postponed the screen exam. But if you think it's better to do it, I can take him for it.*

---

[1] ol kachu.

SRI AUROBINDO   1099

[*Mother:*] No, it is better *not* to have it done as it might make him anxious for his health.

> *Benjamin says that he can't take Asram food at all. He has taken it before "with difficulty and against his heart"! I suppose, we have to continue?*

[*Mother:*] Yes.

June 23, 1938

> *Lalita came with your message to call Dr. André. Do you suspect something else than just boils?*

[*Mother:*] No, but she is a bit nervous about it and is very anxious that all that should disappear quick. The last one in the armpit was very painful. Also she cannot stand medicine internally.

> *For Benoy's artificial eye, Nagaswami writes to Rajangam that it will be absolutely necessary for Benoy to go to Madras as each specimen varies from person to person, though we mentioned about sending our sample.*
> *Our oculist says that the Madras firms are no good. We should send a sample to Bombay and ask from there. So it's better to enquire there, isn't it?*

[*Mother:*] Yes.

> *The same process [in writing poetry] gives wonderful results sometimes and foolish ones at others!*

It depends on the consciousness-Source you strike; the same method will have different results according to the inspiration fount (or level) you get at.

June 25, 1938

> *I suppose Lalita has told you André's opinion and treatment regarding auto-vaccine. You have no objection, I hope.*

[*Mother:*] No, it is all right.

>D's bag and letter. I have to help you (helping Guru, I chuckle!) wherever you are likely to stumble in reading the letter.

In spite of your help I had a slow struggle with D's hieroglyphics—but half way through Intuition came to my rescue and I swam through the rest.

>You will find from the letter that he is a little or much upset by P.S.'s remark...

It seems to be more much than little. I don't see why he should be upset by it at all.

>I can't say if P.S. has said it, nor can I judge D's capacity to understand your Yoga.

The difficulty with D was that he had caught up ideas about Yoga from various quarters and stuck to his ideas like grim death, his mind refusing to understand my ideas and wilfully misunderstanding them. Thus he took supermind for the Vedantic Nirguna Brahman, something dry and high and cold, and the psychic for a pale udasin nirlipta[1] business with no flame in it and persisted in such absurd ideas in spite of my denials. That obviously was not helpful.

>I fear my capacity also is very poor in that direction. But is it necessary to "understand" your Yoga in order to practise it? As far as I understand, it is only your Supermind business that baffles us and some of us are sceptical about it...

Well, it may not be necessary to understand it, but it is advisable not to misunderstand it.

The scepticism is stupid, because how can one pronounce for or against about something one does not know or understand at all?

>And some think it not worth while at present to bother about it.

---

[1] Indifferent, aloof.

SRI AUROBINDO   1101

Certainly it is better not to bother about it and to do what is immediately necessary. The attempt to understand has led many to take for the Supermind something that was not even spiritual and to suppose themselves supermen when all they were doing was to go headlong into the ultravital.

> *You have said that nobody knows or understands anything about it—but I think it is not even necessary, what?*

Not at present.

> *If that is what was meant by P.S. I can see, but to say that D doesn't understand your Yoga is rather—!*

I don't know what P.S. meant. I have explained in what sense D did not understand it. But how many do?

> *But—I ask you again—does one need to understand your Yoga in order to practise it? Or, how far should one understand, grasp and assimilate it?*

If one has faith and openness that is enough. Besides there are two kinds of understanding—understanding by the intellect and understanding in the consciousness. It is good to have the former if it is accurate, but it is not indispensable. Understanding by the consciousness comes if there is faith and openness, though it may come only gradually and through steps of experience. But I have seen people without education or intellectuality understand in this way perfectly well the course of the Yoga in themselves, while intellectual men make big mistakes—e.g. take a neutral mental quietude for the spiritual peace and refuse to come out of it in order to go farther.

> *I admit that D, at times, was sceptical about some well-accepted things of Yoga, e.g. Force curing diseases etc. But that was scepticism rather than lack of understanding.*

Well, but his scepticism was founded on ignorance and non-understanding.

Could you give some light for him and for me?

This is for you, not for him.

> *N and others are interested to see your answers to D. Will it be advisable to show them?*

They might talk and it would reach P.S. and make matters worse.

> *Anilbaran gave me his novel to criticise. He says it is very impressive and he has seen my criticism of J's poetry.*

He says his own novel is very impressive? Or your criticism?

> *He says that I have a good critical faculty. So, Sir, that's something, what?*

Sometimes.

June 26, 1938

> *"The sudden resurrection comes*
> *Within the slow*
> *Fire of unremembered history*
> *In its clustered snow."*

Now, look here, look here! There is a limit — some coherence there must be! This means nothing either to the brain or the solar plexus.

> *". . . That longs like a winged spirit to fly*
> *Beyond the pale*
> *Zone of terrestrial pathways*
> *Under a veil."*

This flying under a veil is an acrobacy that ought not to be imposed on any bird or spirit. Besides the bird was on the moon — how did the terrestrial pathways come in then?

> *Guru, this is a direct effect of reading Amal's lyrics which you praised so much.*

SRI AUROBINDO   1103

A terrible effect!

I am damned puzzled and baffled!

NO WONDER!!!
   The first two and a half stanzas are very fine, but the rest!!
Well, well, well, this is nonsense with a vengeance; but the poetry
is too pure for any plexus to stand. Something might be done with
the fourth stanza if the feathers disappear out of remembered history and the clustered snow goes the same way. But I fear the last
2 stanzas are hopeless. I tried but my inspiration remained weary
and unstirred by any rhythmic wave.

> *"And melts the snow*
> *From its chilled spirit and reveals*
> *Before its gaze*
> *Columns of fire immensities. . ."*

Why should the bird want to go into fire? Hot bath after cold one?

> *". . . The awakened bird*
> *Now voyages with foam-white sails,*
> *That vision stirred!"*

A bird with sails is unknown to zoology! Or do you mean that the
bird hires a sailing vessel to go into the fires? Lazy beast! And what
is it that is stirred by the vision, the bird or the sails? I don't think
the last line can stand. You can say of the bird "Flies like a ship
with foam-white sails," but then how to end?

> *If this poem doesn't stir your plexus, I am undone! The*
> *expressions may not be apt and felicitous but coherence*
> *there is, what?*

Yes, except at the end where you make the bird a surrealistic animal with sails and stir the sails with a vision.

> *Guru, Chand has sent me the power of attorney. But out of*
> *laziness I didn't move. Is it necessary to show it to you or to*
> *Doraiswamy after typing it?*

1104   CORRESPONDENCE WITH

To me, no. You can show it to Duraiswami. Better get the thing done.

> *The oculist advised N to take cod-liver oil. N wants to have your opinion.*

[*Mother:*] He can take it.

> *Whatever Z wants for her diet, e.g. vegetables, fruits, shall I ask Dyuman to get? He has agreed to buy them if you permit.*

[*Mother:*] All right—

> *The honey we got from Datta is exhausted. I think K can discontinue it now.*
> [*The Mother underlined "discontinue it now".*]

Yes.

1) Arjava says that the Asram food is too rich and too spiced for him. Would it be possible to provide him with some boiled vegetables — beetroots, cabbage, potatoes, etc., once a day, at midday?

2) Madanlal since a very long time has a cold which is refusing to go — he is still coughing; it has become almost chronic, I fear. It would be better to interfere and get him rid of it.

I would like you to see to it, even if he says: it's nothing, etc.—

June 28, 1938

> *Dilipda has asked for a poem. I am sending the one enclosed, but how much of your remarks should pass?*

If it is only for Dilip, it doesn't matter. But there's something wrong. What's "this brief mystical experience" coming in without any syntactical head or tail? Either I have dropped something or you have dropped or else misread. Please look again at my original hieroglyphs.

June 29, 1938

> *I am sending you "the original hieroglyphs". I think you*

SRI AUROBINDO 1105

have dropped one "of" before "this brief . . . experience."

I haven't, but as I thought you have transmogrified what I wrote —
It is not mystical but mortal and not experience but existence,
"this brief mortal existence".

*I am sure you have read the eulogies crowned upon Dorai-
swamy's head, on his retirement, and enjoyed them immensely at the same time feeling proud of him and saying,
"Ha, ha, here is the fruit of my Force!" What? It is indeed
a great pleasure to see the prestige of the Asram elevated
by at least one man, though I suppose you care a damn for
prestige.*

Queer idea all you fellows seem to have of the "prestige" of the
Asram. The prestige of an institution claiming to be a centre of
spirituality lies in its spirituality, not in newspaper columns or
famous people. Is it because of this mundane view of life and of
the Asram held by the sadhaks that this Asram is not yet the centre
of spirituality it set out to be?

*I have been really struck by his many-sided qualities. Is
that all achieved by your Force alone?*

These qualities are all Duraiswami's own by nature. But all that
has nothing to do with *spiritual* achievement which is the one thing
needful here.

*His legal genius, social charm, uprightness, noble charac-
ter, etc., were all there or are they your Force's gifts? How
far can one be changed by your or the spiritual Force?*

Changed in what way? There are plenty of upright people (uprightness, straightforwardness, a certain nobility of character are D's
inborn gifts) and plenty of able and successful people outside this
Asram or any Asram and there is no need of my spiritual Force
for that.

*He told me that he began practice with only Rs. 15-30 a
month. But that is not unusual.*

1106   CORRESPONDENCE WITH

Certainly not. It's done in America every day.

> *It was the same with C.R. Das. Apart from legal acumen, I want more to see how far Doraiswamy's character has been changed and moulded by the Force.*

Lord, man, it's not for changing or moulding character that this Asram exists. It is for moulding spirituality and transforming the *consciousness*. You may say it doesn't seem to be successful enough on that line, but that is its object.

> *I suspect, however, that you are closing in your Supramental net and bringing in all the outside fish!*

Good Lord, no! I should be very much embarrassed if all the outside fish insisted on coming inside. Besides D is not an outside fish.

> *But what about our X? When do you propose to catch him or a still longer rope required? I would call that your biggest success, Sir, and the enrichment of your Fishery.*

I would not. You seem to have an exaggerated idea of X's bigness (an example of Einsteinian relativity, I suppose, or the result of his own big view of himself.) Whatever bigness he has is my creation, apart from the fact that he was a popular singer when he came. He would have been nothing else (even in music) if he had not come here. The only big thing he had by nature was a big and lusty vital.

> *We are all watching with interest and eagerness that big operation of yours. But I don't think you will succeed till your Supramental comes to the field in full-fledged colours, what?*

What big operation? There is no operation; I am not trying to hale in X as a big fish. I am not trying to catch him or bring him in. If he comes into the true spiritual life it will be a big thing for him, no doubt, but to the work it means only a ripple more or less in the atmosphere. Kindly consider how many people big in their own eyes have come and gone (B, Q, H to speak of no others) and has

SRI AUROBINDO 1107

the work stopped by their departure or the Asram ceased to grow? Do you really think that the success or failure of the work we have undertaken depends on the presence or absence of X? or on my hauling him in or letting him go? It is of importance only for the soul of X — nothing else.

Your image of the Fishery is quite out of place. I fish for no one; people are not hauled or called here, they come of themselves by the psychic instinct. Especially I do not fish for big and famous and successful men. Such fellows may be mentally or vitally big, but they are usually quite contented with that kind of bigness and do not want spiritual things, or, if they do, their bigness stands in their way rather than helps them. The fishing for them is X's idea — he wanted to catch hold of S.B., S.C., now L.D. etc., etc., but they would have been exceedingly troublesome sadhaks, if they ever really dreamed of anything of the kind. All these are ordinary ignorant ideas; the Spirit cares not a damn for fame, success or bigness in those who come to it. People have a strange idea that Mother and myself are eager to get people as disciples and if any one goes away, especially a "big" balloon with all its gas in it, it is a great blow, — a terrible defeat, a dreadful catastrophe and cataclysm for us. Many even think that their being here is a great favour done to us for which we are not sufficiently grateful. All that is rubbish.

> *I gather from NK that Nirmala doesn't take vegetable at all at noon. Only rice and curds, and that too not much. She is injuring her health!*

[*Mother:*] You might, perhaps, explain that to her —

June 30, 1938

July 1938

> *I understand that the prestige of the Asram is in its spirituality, but at the same time when a member of the Asram behaves caddishly, doesn't it naturally reflect on us a little, or does it reflect because we are accustomed to take a mundane view of life and its usual code of morals and behaviour? Is it not natural for us to feel proud when praises*

1108   CORRESPONDENCE WITH

> *are bestowed on Doraiswamy or feel embarrassed when things are said against X?*

Natural, but mundane.

If the praise and blame of ignorant people is to be our standard, then we may say good-bye to the spiritual consciousness. If the Mother and I had cared for praise or blame, we would have been crushed long ago. It is only recently that the Asram has got "prestige" — before it was the target for an almost universal criticism, not to speak of the filthiest attacks.

> *For instance we feel a little "embarrassed" when things are said against X (if they are true) especially mentioning that after staying so many years in a spiritual place, he should behave so.*

"Behave so" means behave how? I suppose people complain of him because he mixes on one side in "high society" and on the other with cinema girls and singers. But that is from the point of view of social respectability. It is the spirit that matters. If X did it in the right spirit, it wouldn't matter whom he mixed with. It is true that he puts on a Sanyasin's dress which is absurd if he wants to go into that society — but that is an incongruity only.

> *I admit that it is a mundane view, and it doesn't stop your bringing down the Supermind, but it affects us favourably or adversely. In what way should we then look at it?*

Look at what? What you are looking at is the praise and blame of people, not at any "it". One has to look at "it", not from the point of view of whether it is praised or blamed by the public, but from its inherent relation to the spiritual life.

> *I know uprightness, honesty, etc. have nothing to do directly with spiritual achievement. But when a lax and loose sadhak develops the contrary qualities, won't that be a change of character and a way to the change of nature by your Force?*

Who said so?

SRI AUROBINDO   1109

> *Spirituality, in order not to defeat its own object, must develop these.*

Develop what? A change of consciousness and nature, yes; but it is not a question of moralising the character, but of psychising it.

> *A liar can't realise the Divine, can he?*

A liar does not usually realise the Divine, because one is seeking for Truth and lying comes across Truth; it is not because lying lowers his prestige with the public. Sometimes a liar realises the Divine and stops lying.

> *Isn't it because of his change of consciousness resulting in a change of values of life that Doraiswamy could discard all fame, post of honour, etc.?*

I don't think so. He never wanted to be a judge etc., he was never an office-hunter. His weakness was of a social character, desire to be generous, liked, scrupulous in the discharge of social duties, attachment to family, friends etc.

> *Just as you have developed poetry, music, etc., in X, I thought these gifts which Doraiswamy is endowed with, may have been due to your Spiritual Force, not knowing what his born or unborn gifts were.*

No, Duraiswami was always a sattwic man, a very fine sattwic type. But for spirituality one must get beyond the sattwic.

> *Then by X's bigness or big fishness, I didn't mean "big fish" in that sense, nor your biggest success. I meant that he is such a complicated formula —*

Not so complicated as others I have had to deal with.

> *— There are so many warring and contrary elements in him that it will be a job for you to change him, as it has been.*

1110   CORRESPONDENCE WITH

Mainly two—but quite at war with each other. The others in him lean to one side or the other.

> With sadhaks like us, it is, perhaps, an easy walk-over for you! But him?

It is easy with nobody, not even with Anilbaran or Khirod or Shankararama or Duraiswami who are yet all sattwic people without any adverse vital element in them.

> I read a story by the Mother where she says that the joy lies in taming a turbulent and wild horse.[1] Such is X's case, and catching him and taming him will be your biggest success! I hope it's clear?

It isn't.

> Anyhow you are working on him to change his nature, his mind, vital, etc., etc. Well, if that succeeds, it means he will come and live here.

Certainly; but that is a different thing from fishing or pulling in. It is a quite disinterested spiritual idea without any idea of a "big success" or "prestige".

> You said that if people like S.B. came here, they would be extremely troublesome.

Damnably so!

> On the contrary I thought and argued that if such vitally strong people once turned to Yoga, they could put all their vital will on one point and all the other things would become minor problems for them.

X also is vitally strong.

> For example, for S.B. country is the one thing that matters and nothing else.

---

[1] Mother's Cent. vol. 2, p. 169.

SRI AUROBINDO   1111

Excuse me — country is not the only thing for S.B. — there is also
S.B. and he looms very large. You have illusions about these political heroes — I have seen them close and have none.

> *But you say their bigness will come in the way. Then is our*
> *smallness a great privilege?*

Bigness = vanity, ambition, self-assertion, a self-confident inability to surrender etc., etc.
  Smallness at least gives you a chance.

> *Do the unbracketed parts in your replies mean that they are*
> *public?*

No — only that they are not excessively private.

> *I have shown the document to Doraiswamy and he advises not*
> *to go to this Consul who will charge for every erasure, but*
> *to go to the Sub-Registrar's office — 5 miles from here, in*
> *the British territory. Well? In either case I have no money to*
> *pay.*

Where is it? and are you to go alone or with witnesses or with whom?
Let us know a little more clearly. Find out the charges in either
case and we can decide and arrange.

July 2, 1938

> *Guru, the place I mentioned in the British territory is out of*
> *the question. It's only the Sub-Registrar's office, it won't do.*
> *There are two ways:*
> *1) British Consul. Purani enquired. They charge Rs. 6/8,*
> *and 6 annas for every erasure. It'll come to about Rs. 8.*
> *2) French Notaire Public whose signature is also valid. His*
> *charges are Rs. 6-8. . . He says we'll get the form in 24 hrs.*
> *Purani suggests Cuddalore. Doraiswamy believes that it*
> *will be cheaper by a couple of rupees. . . He has friends who*
> *will introduce me to the Magistrate, a witness he can arrange*
> *for, etc. . .*

The simplest way is to go to the British Consul and have it done

1112   CORRESPONDENCE WITH

there. It is a difference of a couple of Rs. only—not worth the
trouble of going to Cuddalore and all the arrangements. Ask
Purani to arrange.

> *Before Dr. André goes, I think we can have R.B.'s X-ray.*
> *André has agreed, shall we take her to the hospital?*

[*Mother:*] Yes.

> *We have to buy barium meal, if you sanction. I enclose a*
> *chit.*

[*Mother:*] Where is the chit?

> *M has hard stools, and passes blood sometimes. May be the*
> *beginning of piles. Shall we give him* haritaki?

[*Mother:*] Yes.

> *S asks for some more liver injections. We have 3 or 4 am-*
> *poules. If you like, we can give them to him.*

[*Mother:*] Is it not too much?
  Tajdar complains of becoming more and more weak and lifeless
(?). She says her stomach refuses to work, her blood has become
very poor, her heart is weak, her liver is out of order, etc., etc. —
She wishes to have her blood examined, her liver X-rayed, her
urine analysed. I was thinking (yesterday) of asking André to do all
that, but now that he is on the point of going I hesitate to give him
all that trouble. But in case you see that it will not bother him you
can take Tajdar to him—

> [*Sri Aurobindo put 3 marginal lines against two lines of*
> *the disciple's poetry with some of his corrections—*
> ‖ *And the* cry of the *centuries*
> ‖ Pass from your *ears*.]

This triple line is a compliment to my correction, not to your
version.

July 3, 1938

SRI AUROBINDO   1113

I showed Tajdar to André. He says the heart is all right.
All her trouble is due to indigestion and constipation. . .
I don't know if it is worth while doing the blood examina-
tion.

[*Mother :*] She was asking blood examination for *anaemia.*

Today André gave an injection to Lalita. Another due on
Wednesday.

[*Mother :*] Wednesday is a very busy day for her — she is asking it
on *Thursday.*

What is meant by your "too much" in relation to S? We
shall give him only one injection at a time as done before.
We gave him 7, if you remember.

[*Mother :*] Has it not a cumulative effect?

                                                            July 4, 1938

No, it has no cumulative effect as it is not a medicine, but
only liver extract. But I was wondering whether it will
do him any good.

[*Mother :*] If he thinks it will do him good there is a chance.

For Tajdar, is it necessary to examine blood for anaemia?
It can be done any day, if necessary.

[*Mother :*] She believes it very necessary as she is convinced "she
is fast declining" (her own words). Of course all I tell you is confidential.

Mrs. Sankar Ram has a lot of sugar in urine even after
giving up rice. Shall we analyse her blood to see how much
blood-sugar she has?

Perhaps. But is not the illness the result of a rheumatic tendency
and if this is treated will not that get better?

1114   CORRESPONDENCE WITH

Bala found the meat extract very good and wants to buy one more bottle himself.

[*Mother:*] We can buy one more for him. After that he will do as he likes.

July 5, 1938

R.B. was X-rayed today. There seems to be a beginning of ulcer in the duodenum, the radiologist says. If it is that she has to stop all solid food. But you had asked me not to stop it. . . She is also so ridiculous, what to do?

[*Mother:*] Before saying anything one must be sure that it *is* an ulcer.

Shall we buy a bottle of Listerine for J?

[*Mother:*] Yes.

She also wants cocogem. Shall we supply it?

[*Mother:*] Yes.

July 6, 1938

> *"The growing heart of day*
> *Is lily-white. . ."*
> Lily-white cheap?

Not only cheap but gratis.

Guru, this again is a riddle of a poem!

Not very cogent, whether realistically or surrealistically. But see how with a few alterations I have coged it. (Excuse the word; it is surrealistic it). I don't put double lines as I don't want to pay too many compliments to myself. I don't say that the new version has any more meaning than the first. But significance, sir, significance! Fathomless!

As for the inspiration it was a very remarkable source you tapped —super-Blakish, but your transcription is faulty e.g. lily-white

SRI AUROBINDO
1115

rising out of the clay, that horrible "various", and constant mistakes in the last four stanzas. Only the third came out altogether right subject to the change you yourself made of destiny to ecstasy and shot to wrought. But obviously the past tense is needed instead of the present so as to give the sense of something that has been seen.

> *How to be sure about R.B.'s ulcer? X-ray was the one definite way. It may be sound to take it as ulcer. André has given a medicine, Histidine, which won't do any harm even if it is not ulcer. It has to be given either* subcutaneously *or intramuscularly.*

[*Mother:*] Give subcutaneously.

> *Dyuman buys vegetables for the soup, once a week. It would be good if Z could have a "garde-manger" for storing them.*

[*Mother:*] Yes — ask Sahana for one —

> *Mrs. Sankar Ram doesn't want to go to the hospital since her nail pain is gone and sugar less, she feels better. I explained that it's better to ascertain [diabetes], but to no avail. So, shall we wait?*

[*Mother:*] Yes.

> *July 7, 1938*

> *The "garde-manger" given to Z is rather small. Perhaps it will be better to have a special one prepared.*

[*Mother:*] Yes, but it may take some time. Meanwhile ask Sahana if it is not possible to exchange this one for one in the room of an absentee.

> *Guru, I have seen how your little touches have "coged" the poem. Does it then show that if my transcription becomes perfect some day, the whole thing will drop perfectly O.K.?*

Of course. At present the mind still interferes too much, catching at an expression which will somehow approximate to the thing meant instead of waiting for the one true word. This catching is of course involuntary and the mind does it passively without knowing what it is doing—a sort of instinctive haste to get the thing down. In so doing it gets an inferior layer of inspiration to comb for the words even when the substance is from a higher one.

Even if I revised it, do you think I could have made it better?

Not necessarily.

But how can I when I don't understand at all what I am writing? How to correct? By inner feeling?

No; by getting into touch with the real source. The defects come from a non-contact or an interception by some inferior source as explained above.

If I try to understand the thing, every bit of it seems ridiculous.

Because you are trying to find a mental meaning and your mind is not familiar with the images, symbols, experiences that are peculiar to this realm. Each realm of experience has its own figures, its own language, its own vision and the physical mind not catching the link finds it all absurd. At the same time the main idea in yesterday's poem is quite clear. The heart of day evolving from clay and night is obviously the upward luminous movement of the awakened spiritual consciousness covering the intermediate worlds (vital, mental, psychic) in its passage to the supreme Ananda (unknown ecstasy transparence wrought, the transparence being that well known to mystic experience of the pure spiritual consciousness and existence). In the light of the main idea the last four stanzas should surely be clear—the stars and the sun being well known symbols.

"Super-Blakish" you say? And what "remarkable source" please, inner or over? Looks something damnably mystic, but neither inner nor overhead.

SRI AUROBINDO   1117

Can't specify—as these things have no name. Inner—over also
in imagery, but not what I call the overhead planes. These belong to the inner mind or inner vital or to the intuitive mind or
anywhere else that is mystic.

July 8, 1938

> *Z is asking again and again if she can join her work. Do*
> *you advise it?*

[*Mother:*] She may try a small amount of work. Days must seem
dull to her if she is doing nothing.

July 9, 1938

> *Guru, I am puzzled! Your additional stanza of yesterday's*
> *poem is magnificent. But how can a "body" be born, either*
> *God's or an animal's, even if we admit God has a body?*
> > *["From which the cosmic fire*
> > *Sprang rhythmic into Space*
> > *That God's body might be born*
> > *And the Formless wear a face." 9.7.38*]

It is I who am awfully puzzled by your puzzlement. A body is not
born? When the child comes out of the womb, it is not a body
that comes out and the coming out is not birth? It has always
been so called in English. You have never heard the expression
"the birth and death of the body"? What is it then that dies after
having been born? The soul doesn't die, nor is it the soul that
comes out of the womb! You think God cannot have a body?
Brahmo idea? Then what of the incarnation—is it impossible?
And how does the Divine appear in vision to the bhakta except by
putting on a form = a body? But if you object to God having or
getting a body, you must also object to the Formless wearing a
face; so the whole significant stanza becomes nonsense. And
therefore, I suppose, pure poetry. All the same one can understand a metaphysical (not a poetic) objection to God having a body
if one believes that the Infinite cannot manifest the finite or as
finite, but that an animal's body is not born is new to me.

July 10, 1938

> *"A fire leaps from range to range*
> *And touches a height*
> *Unshadowed by time's sudden change*
> *Or the bulk of night."*
>
> Night has a bulk?

It may have, but it is not polite or poetic to talk about it — gives the idea that she is corpulent.

> [*Chand's telegram:*] *"Embarkment enquiry 13th July protection." Guru, is he embarking for Mecca? Looks like embankment which, he said, he demolished, of a tenant.*

It is the telegraph office here that is embarking him — otherwise there would be no enquiry. He must be in trouble over his arbitrary abolition of his neighbours' embankment.

> *Here is Dilipda's royal mail! I have copied out the whole letter for you. Hope it is not worse than his original!*

For this relief much thanks!

> *What about Darshan permission for Kalyan, and his staying in Dilipda's house? Both granted?*

<u>Yes.</u>

> *D is facing a lot of criticism, but he says he has resolved not to mind it.*

I hope he will keep to his resolution of not minding what people say. It is a sage resolve and, if kept, will make a huge difference.

> *Any remarks on his songs?*

Nothing particular. They have the usual qualities.

> *Padmasini seems much reduced. She has no appetite. . . May we give her small doses of arsenic with stomach tonics?*

SRI AUROBINDO   1119

[*Mother:*] <u>Yes.</u>

July 11, 1938

> *I suppose what you wrote yesterday on D's "sage resolve"*
> *is meant for my ears only? Or his also?*

It can reach his, but not in that language which he might take as
ironic. You can say that I was very pleased to read what he had
written on that point; the resolution is a good one and I hope he
will keep strength to carry it out. It would make a great difference.

> *"I dive into the fathomless*
> *Riches of God. . ."*

One doesn't dive into riches — a tankful of bank notes!

> *T is quite all right now and can do some light work for a*
> *couple of hours or so.*

[*Mother:*] She is doing some embroidery work. I think it is sufficient for the moment.

July 12, 1938

> *X calls me now and then in the afternoon to taste something*
> *she has prepared. So I spend about 15-20 minutes on my*
> *way to the hospital.*
> *I like X's smile. It's innocent, childlike — nothing co-*
> *quettish or sophisticated or trying to captivate.*

Very dangerous! especially if you begin to luxuriate in the idea
of her unsophisticated simplicity. Unsophisticated or not, if once
the vital attachment is made, she will hold you as tightly as the
other and with a greater violence of *dabi*,[1] *abhiman* and the rest
of it and, finally when the connection is cut, she will say and think
that it was all your fault and that you are a very wicked person
who took advantage of her foolishness and innocence. Well,
well, you know about as much of women as a house-kitten knows

---

[1] Claim.

1120 CORRESPONDENCE WITH

about the jungle and its denizens and it is you who are in this field amazingly naïve.

> *What exactly is meant by a "sophisticated" mind and "naïveté" in English?*

"Sophisticated" means well up to everything, artificial and without simplicity; naïve means ignorantly artless, amusingly simple, *not* up to things.

> *. . . If you think I had better stop this social relationship and check the unyogic enjoyment — I shall.*

I certainly think that you should stop while there is yet time. It is no use getting out of one net to fall into another.

July 14, 1938

> *Guru, you have castigated me for my inexperience, calling me sheep, lamb, house-kitten and what not. You will exhaust the whole zoology on me, methinks!*

Why not? man has all the animals within him as he is an epitome of the universe.

> *Am I really as naïve as all that?*

Certainly, there is the naïveté, otherwise you would not have relied on X's simplicity.

> *Perhaps if X blames me even now, she may be right, for I can't swear that I didn't try to draw her. . .*

But if she joined in, she would have no right to blame anybody but herself. There is no reason. why she should allow herself to be drawn; it would be a proof that she wants it. Besides she is quite capable of drawing herself even if she does it in an unsophisticated manner.

> *I have resolved that next time X and Y call me, I shall go and*

SRI AUROBINDO   **1121**

> *"cleverly" tell them that it is the last time. Will it do, Sir?*

Yes.

> *I've given them mangoes and things before, as once you said regarding S's offer of curry, that it was quite trifling and absolutely harmless.*

In S's case it was harmless, but similar things in another case might not be. All depends on the inflammability of the human materials in relation to each other. If they are mutually inflammable, a mango or a curry can be the match to light the flame.

> *I was alert regarding Z, because I felt she had definite intentions. So I am not altogether naïve, Sir. But as regards X, I wanted to keep just a friendly relation.*

. . . It is certainly naïve to think that because a girl is simple i.e. instinctive and impulsive and non-mental in her movements she can be relied upon to be an asexual friend. Some women can be, but it is usually those who have a clear mental consciousness and strong will of self-control or else those who are incapable of a passion for more than one person in their life and you are lucky enough not to be that person.

> *[Chand's telegram:] "Partial sex failure must succeed." Guru, after the "embarkment", "partial failure"!*

What the deuce does he mean by "partial sex failure" — beginning of the operation but no conclusion? "Embarkment for Cytherea" (land of Venus), and disembarcation in mid-sea? What a phenomenon of a fellow!

> *July 15, 1938*

[Mother:] What about the workman who had his eye wounded?

> *July 16, 1938*

> *I don't understand how I compare myself to a star, and then the sun.*

Well, the Sun is a star, isn't it? and the stars are suns?

What's the name of that place in the "land of Venus"—
Lytheria?

Cytherea, Venus is called Cytherea = the Cytherean in Latin
poetry.
July 17, 1938

". . . Until an omnipotence
Crowned with a white
Immaculate destiny."
Don't white and immaculate have the same meaning?

No, one can be immaculate without being white; but it reminds of
Gandhi's "spotless white khaddar". Your emendation is quite the
right thing.
July 19, 1938

I am most disappointed with this poem,[1] Sir! What do you
think of it?

Doubly damned fine! Close all right. It is only the two "withs"
that are objectionable, but that is soon mended.

By God, I am absolutely staggered by your dragon image!
Such things have been done before?

Not before, but worse things than that are done nowadays.

If at any time I face public criticism, I will say that my
Guru is to be blamed.

Certainly.

May I know why you object to dilatation by atropine drops
in N's case? Is it due to inconvenience to sight? If so it is
only for a few days and that too can be shortened by dropping

[1] "A Throb of the Vast", *Sun-Blossoms*, p. 87.

SRI AUROBINDO
1123

> *eserine which contracts the pupil. Otherwise I don't know that there is any other risk.*

[*Mother:*] I know of people who never recovered fully the sight they had before. But in his case there is nothing much to lose, I suppose.

> *About his deafness, the specialist finds nothing in the ear. But that there is some defect of hearing is certain. It may be either due to a bad throat — he has a bad pharyngitis and some sign of tonsillitis or otosclerosis.*

[*Sri Aurobindo:*] Psychologically it is due to his extreme self-centredness. So shut up in himself that his ear is retiring from outward action. Of course that does not exclude the physical cause which is instrumental.

> *If it is due to the throat, a tonsil operation. . . If it is due to otosclerosis which can be a remote effect of rheumatism (he had it) then there is no specific cure for it, though Iodine in some form sometimes gives a good effect. . .*

One can't iodine him on the basis of an "if" for a problematically occasional good effect.

> *Blood can be tested for hereditary syphilis.*

Can always see.

> *Adenoids and tonsils, you know, to a great extent dull the intellect.*

Aided by self-imprisonment, I believe.

> *So whatever you sanction, please write against each one, otherwise he will bother me about your sanction and permission first.*

What to sanction, when the doctors can't say what's what?

July 20, 1938

Why did you say, in N's case, that doctors can't say?

Because you say "It *may be* either" and "if" and "if". According to any ordinary logic that means "We" doesn't know but either guesses or infers.

As regards his eyes, it is quite definite—he has trachoma for which the said treatment can be instituted.

No objection to that. I wrote in reference to the doubtful ear.

And as regards his deafness, it is either due to bad throat or otosclerosis, i.e. sclerosis of the bones of the middle ear; in either case iodine can be given.

You didn't say that. You said "if throat, operation"—if osteo-scl. iodine.
It may be does not = is.

Iodine is very often given, especially collosal iodine injection which is very good. But I heard from Dr. Banerjee that you don't favour internal iodine medication; is it true?

What's this word? Cousin of colossal?
Mother does not favour in certain cases; as in those cases it has a bad effect. Can't say for N. But his subconscious is contradictory like S's and inclined to say No to any medicine.

And if it is due to his extreme self-annihilation, why not tell him so?

Where did you get this self-annihilation? I wrote self-centredness. N's self is not annihilated; it is there alive and kicking and governing everything.
What's the use of telling him? It won't go by the mere telling.

He comes and bothers and bothers, saying that medicine has no effect, "You are not looking carefully. . ."
Is his sight really so bad that he can't take up any work

SRI AUROBINDO   1125

> *the whole day? I don't know that eyes have to be much
> used in his electric supervision work.*

So he believes.
You don't allow for the potency of auto-suggestion.

> *Kantilal had sudden pain on the left side of the chest. . .
> I don't find any localising sign, but I suspect he is going in
> for pleurisy.*

!!!

> *Guru, what sayest Thou to this poem? Staggered simply,
> what?*

Exceedingly fine again. Often the intuitive again and throughout
almost that.

July 21, 1938

> *Can't this intuitive faculty grow in my medical sphere and
> make me see both the disease and the cure?*

But in medicine you don't hook on to the intuitive source.

> *Self-annihilation is my own diagnosis. For, I think, N
> will revolt if I call him "self-centred" when he is consid-
> ering himself preparing for self-annihilation.*
> *Anyhow, is there any use of internal medication against
> that subconscient "No"?*

His subconscient is not contradictory to medicines alone. One has
to go on in the firm faith that one day it will change. T and others
were also like that, but by perseverance something has been arrived
at as far as treatment goes.

> *That word is collosal—from colloidal. I suggested that
> N should take up some work in the afternoon to which he
> replied he wrote to you and your answer was—let his eyes
> get better and best. Otherwise if Sri Aurobindo says, he
> will surely take up work. Well?*

1126   CORRESPONDENCE WITH

If I tell him to work in the afternoon, he will after a time say his eyes are very bad, very strained, shall he stop? What's the use then?

> *. . . S is really extremely difficult to deal with.*

He always has been.

> *Is it his disease that has made him so or his nature?*

His nature made the disease.

> *His friends and his mother say that at home he was quite another person: doing sadhana so well, not caring for worldly things, etc. An admirable fellow in all respects. But something has happened, God knows what, by which he is now completely changed. What can really be the matter, may I know? What sort of difficulty in sadhana is likely to set up such a perverse psychology?*

In appearance perhaps he was like that, though it seems to me that there is something of a legend in that. So long as I have known him he has always been sharp and obstinate in pursuing his own idea or interest and the claims of his ego. Maybe, in his first stage of experience, something mental-psychic was there, that gave him the appearance his friends describe, but the vital was not changed, and as always happens, the vital came up for change — and he did not change it, but allowed the old unregenerate vital ego to take hold of him. Hence constant quarrels, resentments, obstinate feuds and hatred, fancies of persecution, neurasthenia, a disorganised nervous system, devastation of the organs by his anger, etc. (liver especially affecting stomach etc.).

> *The other day his mother was saying that he pines for his past spiritual experiences and visions. Is that then the reason or what? and I am afraid till he or you put that right, nothing is any good.*

How can he have them while he indulges and obeys his vital ego to such an excessive extent? The difficulty is that he is self-righteous and priggish in his self-righteousness. Speaks of himself as an angel

SRI AUROBINDO   1127

of meekness and forbearance and all others as wicked devils tormenting this angel martyr. What's to be done with an attitude like that? How can he come out if he does not recognise the necessity of change? It is not that he has not been told, but —

> ... *He has then to shut himself up in his room to escape all disturbances. Even then he will quarrel with the air, light and trees!*

Of course.

> *But if you ask me to do according to what he wants for his health, I will surely and ungrudgingly do it. But you understand how difficult it is!*

Do the best you can, knowing that he is both physically and psychically ill.

> *Romen needs a pair of wooden sandals as the leather ones irritate the patches of eczema he has. Could you please sanction a pair?*

[*Mother:*] Surely he must have. It is to be asked from Benjamin.

Romen was telling me to-day that he always feels tired, very tired, and very often he has head-ache. Is it due to liver? Can nothing be done to relieve him?

Nirod

I send you X's latest epistle, as my capacities are not equal to reproduction — please return the precious document. But mark that it is confidential, you are not supposed to have received it as it contains psychological as well as medical confidences.

I may admit that we are rather inclined to sympathise with her about the guimauve and purgatives and weekly laxatives. Well, what about André's "miksar"?[1] Warranted harmless and directed to the purpose she cherishes?

                                                              SRI AUROBINDO
                                                              July 22, 1938

---

[1] X's pronunciation of the word "mixture".

> *R's tiredness can be easily accounted for; he works like a Canadian lumberman and eats like a Tamil labourer, or even less. . . Today he came at about 2 p.m., saying that his head was reeling, the whole body aching. Looked like a heat-stroke. I advised him rest.*

[*Mother:*] Is it not better to give him aspirin or something of the kind?

> *He says he has no appetite in the evening, which may be true and due, I think, to over-exhaustion. How to remedy that? Something to eat or drink at 4 p.m., or an extra cup of milk at bed-time, perhaps?*

[*Mother:*] For a number of days I gave him something to eat at 4 P.M., a fruit or chocolate or biscuits. After a time he refused saying that his stomach was aching—To-day I once more gave him as he told me what you had said.

> *. . . I am sure this headache will go if he takes enough food. I wish some fruits could be given.*

[*Mother:*] I shall give him fruits. I hope he will take them.

> *Guru, today from 1.30 p.m. to 3.45, I waited and waited, but not a line dropped. So I gave up in disgust. . . Wasting so much time sitting idle! Or is that sort of idleness as valuable as activity?*

No. But you can do something else that may be helpful or useful.

> *Anyway, there is some tendency to think the same words, expressions, rhymes and thoughts. Everything is repeated.*

Can't be avoided in everyday writing—or at least, if you avoid, you will be a phenomenon.

> *So, Guru, another star [Naik] dropped from your firmament? And after 6 years' luminous presence too!*

SRI AUROBINDO 1129

Luminous? Not very, and rather a shooting or at least tendency to shoot star. He was always going, going and twice or thrice gone — but — returned; now he is gone.

In spite of his violent temper, we liked the fellow.

He had a very nice side to him as well as an insupportable side.

Sometimes it puzzles me to think that you couldn't save a fellow who had worked so well, keeping himself busy almost the whole day.

Busy in too many directions, unfortunately.

Was his vital so turbulent that you couldn't manage to change him?

Vital turbulence? If that were all, it would be nothing much. It was the intermittent possession by a dark violent force that was the trouble. It was becoming so frequent that I had when he asked to go this time to advise him to do so. But the real cause was deeper down. As for saving, one can't save if the patient cherishes the illness, justifies it and refuses to part with it. It was only recently that he began to admit that it was regrettable and had bad consequences, but even so he was unable to make an effort when the fit came. The shock of having to go may perhaps have a salutary influence.

There is no doubt that he truly loved the Mother; but in this world nothing saves, except those who are blessed extraordinary souls.

What does save is the true will to be saved accompanied by a reliance on the Divine. Those who have gone, did they have it?

I fear moreover, that fate has decreed that doctors must quit! You see three doctors have gone already, R doesn't seem to be on very sure grounds. Rajangam and my dear self remain! Ah, the bullet is passing very close, Sir!

1130   CORRESPONDENCE WITH

Medical profession can't be based on Naik's case — He dropped it with a joyful grunt as soon as he came here and had nothing to do with it afterwards.

> *I heard an interesting thing that you gave him a big shout! Ah, I wish I had heard it! But I thought you had lost your capacity to shout?*

The supramental (even its tail) does not take away any capacity, but rather sublimates all and gives those that were not there. So I gave a sublimated supramental shout. I freely admit that (apart from the public platform) I have shouted only four or five times in my life.

> *My yesterday's outburst [with S in the dispensary] seems to be part of a general movement; for I hear that our Benjamin had the courage to slap M yesterday. The fellow has some guts, I must say. The Supramental seems to be descending this time, the head, I mean! But it is really striking that M kept calm when he could have easily pulverised the fellow!*

Well, that is a result of the supramental also! But perhaps M felt that Benjamin was too small and weakly a figure to demolish. He apologised to the Mother for having lost his control as far as to speak violently to Benjamin!!

July 23, 1938

> *There is some trouble now about Benoy's glass eye that we ordered from the Company in Bombay. It does not suit him; he says we should return this one and he will ask friends in Calcutta to send one. I don't think the Company will return us the money. We can only place an order for something else equivalent to its price — 1/8.*

If you need things from the Company, there is no objection.

> *Our stock of Sudarshan is nearly over. Punamchand said it is ready, he would send it from Bombay, but no news*

SRI AUROBINDO

1131

from him. Many people are taking it now. So shall we get some from Madras for the present?

Can wait and see.

The other day I gave S a new drug, Incretone, as Haemogen was not giving sufficiently good results. That very night I had a dream that the medicine had a good effect: urinary and other troubles were much less. Today the very thing happened. . .

. . . R.B.'s pain has given place to burning. . . Shall we try Histidine injection subcutaneously, or wait?

Wait.

Guru, the same fate today! No poem! You ask me to do something useful or helpful. You mean some reading — poetry or philosophy?

But it seems to me that I have exhausted my source and nothing new will come till after some time, i.e. by some growth of consciousness. Occasionally I may write when even a sameness won't matter much. But to be a "phenomenon" is impossible.

The sameness does not matter much. The use of your writing is to keep you in touch with the inner source of inspiration and intuition, so as to wear thin the crude external crust in the consciousness and encourage the growth of the inner being. The dream you speak of in your medical report shows that the inner being is beginning to awake somewhat, as a result, even in things not having to do with the literary inspiration. For this purpose the "sameness" does not much matter.

In spite of repetitions and sameness, if I persist, I might strike again a new source.

That is right.

Time seems to press very heavily. But to write poetry because of heaviness of time is an unyogic attitude probably. Well!

1132   CORRESPONDENCE WITH

Neither Yogic nor unyogic.

> *Today Mother appeared to show some displeasure (or*
> *disapproval?) either to me or to the forces acting through me.*
> *Cause there must be: my outburst of temper against S, de-*
> *pression due to Naik's departure and my doubt regarding my*
> *own fate, etc., etc. Don't know which.*

It is the usual false imagination. Perhaps you got it by thinking
too much of Naik—for whenever his vital wanted to go wrong
or was dissatisfied with itself or people, that was always its movement, to imagine the Mother displeased and then to revolt against
her. In that way it succeeded in getting itself into a fit. The fit
passed he realised his mistake—but did it again the next time.

> *It's not important, but the effect is still worse. The blessed*
> *vital gets into a revolting attitude and plays mischief by*
> *wrong suggestions—the result being as you can expect:*
> *all aspiration is clogged up.*

Naturally.

> *I ought to know by now that Mother has no likes or dis-*
> *likes and whatever she does is absolutely for my own good.*
> *But the vital—does it listen? I consider it a dangerous spot*
> *in my sadhana. I must cut it out root and branch.*

Cut what out root and branch? The habit of wrong imagination
and revolted attitude? For that your mind must separate itself from
the vital and be able to tell it when it goes wrong, that it is making
a fool of itself and that the mind refuses to go with it even one step
in that direction. It is always the mind allowing itself to be clouded
by the vital that makes these recurrences possible.

July 24, 1938

> *Guru, ah, you do relieve me! If you had said that the*
> *first day, I would have written a poem! Your first day's*
> *answer gave me the impression that it doesn't matter much*
> *if I can't write every day.*

SRI AUROBINDO   1133

I said nothing about that, except that the repetition couldn't be
avoided in constant writing. My answer was about the idleness —
saying it was not good, but if you find writing poetry impossible
every day, you must do something else and not keep the time
vacant.

> *I think you enjoy playing with us a little, Sir, or perhaps
> that's your divine way?*

I have no such bad intentions.

> *... Freed from the long-standing obstacle, I have been
> feeling extremely happy these two days... The thought that
> I shall be able to send you poems again and get back a
> touch from you is apparently the main cause of joy. I wonder
> if behind this there is the awakening of the inner being as
> well.*

It is certainly the inner being that has the feeling.

> *Today I wrote a poem and it gave me great joy — but
> I couldn't write the last two days, so I feel gloomy. How
> do you explain it?*

The joy is good, but the gloom is not.

> *My days would have been still brighter, perhaps, if I had
> kept my vital free! ...*

The vital needs something to hook itself on to, but for a sadhak
women are obviously the wrong things for it to hook itself on to —
it must get hold of the right peg.

> *Twice X brought something to eat for me and Mulshankar.
> I couldn't ask her to stop it. Is it necessary to tell her?
> Won't it drop by itself if I keep myself right?*

If you keep yourself right, yes — but if the attachment continues,
then it is better to break off the occasion.

> *"Worlds have begun*
> *To unroll like a time-wave,*
> *Each measured beat*
> *Filled with an ecstasy*
> *Of its golden heat."*
> I fear you will shout against this "heat".

Certainly, the heat would make anyone shout.

> *Kantilal is steadily improving. He joined work today. Has been advised not to strain himself.*

[*Mother:*] He came back immediately. Could not stand it. Did you tell him that it is bad to sleep in the vérandah? He is asking for a room on medical grounds.

> *You didn't say anything about S's extra milk. Shall I ask him to resume soup leaving it to his choice?*

[*Mother:*] He has got his milk all right. But it seems to me that the soup was better for his health.

July 25, 1938

> *We are supplying bowls to those who take soup here in the Dispensary. Some others also come from time to time, so shall we keep a few in stock or shall we ask them to bring their own bowls?*

[*Mother:*] You can ask a few bowls from Purushottam.

July 26, 1938

> *"A rapturous throb of stars*
> *I feel in my heart, . . ."*

I think the stars might just as well not be there. It is difficult for a heart-throb to be a star.

July 27, 1938

SRI AUROBINDO 1135

> *"A silver-throated nightingale*
> *Has to my spirit brought*
> *Unimaginable ecstasy. . ."*
> *What's this nightingale doing here?*

Damned if I know, but let her sing.

> *"My rock-white will manifests now*
> *Through grey barrenness of time*
> *Infinities crowned with the sun-glow*
> *Of the withdrawn Sublime."*

"Rock-white" would mean "white as a rock", but a white rock is rarer than a white elephant.

July 28, 1938

> *"My heart yearns now for thy divine*
> *Primeval Word,*
> *Bringing a sense of crystalline*
> *Fire-ecstasy, stirred*
>
> *In every cell and lifted high*
> *Into a gold*
> *Vision of thy Infinity,*
> *Fold after fold."*

I don't think infinity can be rolled about like that, but it can be unrolled, that is revealed progressively and continuously before the sight.

> *Guru, I am afraid this poem has many defects in detail.*
> *It was written after a lot of castor-oil drugging!*

The castor-oil seems to have been effective at any rate. Very fine poem — only three lines (in themselves very poetic) lack original force (5th stanza).

July 29, 1938

> *This "correspondence ban" — how far does it affect me?*

It doesn't affect your poetry; the medical report also can come, but it should be quite concise during this period.

> "My heart is steeped in that reverie
> And drinks a passionless wine. . ."
> Being steeped, can one drink?

Well, you can drink when you are wet.

July 30, 1938

> Rajangam writes that J's chronic complaint of nose and throat has increased. He has suggested douching the nose slowly *with cold water and applying menthol-vaseline at the nostrils. She should practise slow breathing exercises, drawing in breath with one nostril and letting it out with the other. She is ready to follow the treatment, if you approve of it.*

[*Mother:*] She can do.

> Bala (Atelier) has finished the other bottle of meat extract. He feels very well. Wants to be without any drug for some time.

[*Mother:*] All right.

July 31, 1938

August 1938

> T asks whether it is any more necessary to continue her special diet. She fears she will grow very fat.

[*Mother:*] It is better if she goes on with her present diet for the moment.

August 2, 1938

> I seem to have an easier flow of inspiration now, but the product is not of such a superior quality, I don't find striking lines and expressions. Is it because of the ease of flow?

SRI AUROBINDO   1137

Yes, partly. The ease is that of practice in this metrical form and a
certain achieved level of style and flow. But that level is not one of
constant striking lines and expressions—that is not possible without some effort—not effort of construction, but vigilance to keep
the inspiration up to the mark.

Don't you think I should now try some other form?

Yes, perhaps. I was thinking so the last 2 or 3 days.

*[I sent Dilip's letter at the end of which I wrote:] Guru,
so permission for Darshan given to S. Majumdar and
staying with Dilipda too? I also know him, he is really
a very fine man.*
*Dilipda promises me a kingdom for a wire. If I can get
your answer today, well, the kingdom will be one day
earlier, as the wire will go today.*

Can wire and become a king at once.
                                                        August 3, 1938

*Guru, thank you for making me a king! But a king without
a queen wouldn't look nice, would he?*
*I tried the new form today, but found it extremely diffi-
cult.*

That is natural after confining yourself so long to one form. You
have to grow a facility in the new one.

*R says that you think it wise not to remove the crust of
his eczema, but press out the pus and apply medicine over
it. But the crust is not healthy; it is formed by the pus itself. . .
[The Mother marked the first sentence with a vertical line.]*

It is his own interpretation of the sympathy I showed to his pains.
I never intended to interfere with the treatment.
                                                        August 4, 1938

*While Agarwal was examining Sundaranand's eyes, he
found that his digestive function has not been at all right for*

1138   CORRESPONDENCE WITH

> *a long time. There are poisons accumulated in his intestine, therefore piles and loss of appetite. He wants to know what may be the cause of the derangement and if it will get all right.*

[*Mother:*] It is sure to get all right — the derangement must have been the result of the summer's heat, I suppose —

August 5, 1938

> *Guru, I got this letter from Jatin today. I don't know how far he wants to keep connection with me, whether he expects me to receive him at the station. If you think I had better, I shall. Will you put in an advice?*

I suppose since he has written informing you of his arrival, you might go to the station.

> *The other day I dreamed that we had gone to the seaside. We found that the embankment had tumbled down, and a boy of 12 or 13 lay dead upon the rocks; though his limbs were caught in the cracks, they weren't mutilated. Suddenly I found his limbs stirring. Then the scene changed: I called my tired friends who were swimming, to rest on a floating bridge. After a while we swam a race and I came first. Now, what's the link between the two? The boy = the psychic? But the psychic is usually a baby! Any personal significance?*

Looks more like a happening in a vital world than symbolic. The psychic does not always appear as a baby, but this is evidently not the psychic — as the whole thing is in the vital. If it is symbolic it could only mean a formation of some vital framework or breakdown of limitations and some inner formation at first overcome by the change, then recovering — the second dream would mean a dealing with the new structure, a swimming to cross the vital, first in fatigue then after rest a renewed vigour in crossing.

But all that is doubtful; for the symbolism of these is not sufficiently marked to be unmistakable.

SRI AUROBINDO   1139

Annapurna's eyes are watering, and there's a burning sensation. Trachoma. Shall I send her to Agarwal?

[*Mother:*] <u>Yes</u>.

August 6, 1938

I hear from Agarwal that you have sanctioned boiled vegetables from here for Sundaranand.

[*Mother:*] I said to ask you *if it would be possible.*

If so, for the noon, it can be boiled with Arjava's, and for the evening, it can be simply fried (without any spice) with Benjamin's.

[*Mother:*] Yes, it is all right.

August 7, 1938

"The whole universe seems to be a cry
To the apocalypt vision of thy Name."

Damn fine, sir!

August 8, 1938

Padmasini has a dry cough. Perhaps it will be better to see her lungs under the screen.

[*Mother:*] Yes, provided she does not get frightened —

August 10, 1938

"My heart lies now at rest; it has begun
To live within a vast kingdom of soul,..."

Well, "lies" had better change; for one can't live much lying down; but one can be at rest (inwardly) and live.

August 11, 1938

Dining Room servant's legs scalded by hot water... Don't

1140   CORRESPONDENCE WITH

> you think it will be advisable to keep some tannic acid
> solution (which is not a poison) in D.R., so that in emer-
> gencies like small burns it can be applied? It is very effective
> and simple in application.

[*Mother:*] Yes, it is better but contents and use must be *clearly
written* on the bottle with a red label (for external use only) to
prevent all possibility of mistake.
    Is not picric acid more effective?

> *Guru, I became desperate and brought down this poem. God
> knows whether its head is in normal condition or is lac-
> erated.*

No harm has happened to the poetry (whatever be the case with the
head) except that rhythm and metre are rather lacerated in some
lines of the last 3 stanzas.

August 13, 1938

> [*I sent a long report regarding Dr. Manilal's treatment
> for Z's suspected T.B. There was no reply.*]

August 17, 1938

> *You didn't say whether you approved of all that Dr. Mani-
> lal recommended for Z as regards the treatment.*

[*Sri Aurobindo:*] No objection.

> *Guru, I expected something new after the Darshan touch,
> but the same old stuff (in poetry) with the same difficulty
> in writing!*

It is very good stuff.

> *The difficulty is perhaps due to these few days' interval?*

Probably.

> *Did you see "the seas of rapture in my heart"? All right?*

SRI AUROBINDO   1141

Seas have not to be seen so much as swum on.

> *And how did you find the Bangalore scientists? They seem
> to have been much moved, God knows by what!*

The supramental, I suppose!

> *One of them, the hardest nut and a "jewel" of the group,
> Govinda, was on the point of tears at the farewell! Just
> think!*

Again the supramental! The supramental is beyond all thinking.

August 19, 1938

> *Please have some divine compassion and give me something
> new.*

Well, well, well! We'll see.

> *How long can one keep this Yogic attitude?*

Why not? A Yogi must always have Yogic attitude.

> *I asked Rajani for some cheese, butter, jam and coffee, for
> R. But R has suddenly stopped coming here for tea in the
> morning. What then am I to do with these articles? May
> I send them to you? R doesn't want them?*

[*Mother:*] Keep the things; he may come back again after some time.

August 22, 1938

> *"Lost in an ecstasy of germinal sound
> That wanders through the night's shadowy bars. . ."*

The deuce! what's an ecstasy of germinal sound? And a wandering
one at that?

> *Please sprinkle your supramental humour now and then. A*

too matter-of-fact dealing takes our breath away, or at least makes life damned harder, you know. Or are your humours also decided by Supramental Truth-sight?

It depends on the state of my inner humerus.

God, alas! What a queer fellow your Supramental will be!

Can't be queerer than the mental human! But I suppose he will seem queer to the queer mental human just as the queer human seems queer to the queer vital monkey and the queer monkey to the queer material jelly-fish. All queer together! and to each other!

August 26, 1938

"O dream of solitude, visionary flame,
  Make the lone deeps of my heart thy home. . ."
"Visionary" O.K.?

No, it isn't very complimentary, means usually an unpractical fellow who has unreal "visionary" ideas.

"Travelling through hollow spaces of day and night
  Towards its rich fruition in the Sublime. . ."

Fruition! would fructify in prose.

The last two stanzas are logical tails, I hope.

The last three hairs of the tail needed a little combing and brushing.

August 27, 1938

Guru, the last stanza took me an hour and yet I fear I couldn't get an original idea or expression.[1]

On the contrary, it is eminently successful and well worth the hour spent on it.

---

[1] "Seeds of Vision", *Sun-Blossoms*, p. 75.

SRI AUROBINDO   1143

> *You said that you would "see" about giving me something*
> *new in poetry. Well, it does not seem that you have "seen"*
> *yet, does it?*

I simply said that we will see, i.e. how things develop. The idea of
these poems is the same as before, but in expression the poetry is
becoming more and more authentic, more "seen" than before and
that after all is the main thing. The last two stanzas are A1.

August 28, 1938

> *I wonder if you could recast or rewrite the whole poem so*
> *that I may be fortunate enough to preface my 2nd volume of*
> *poems with it. Enclosing a paper, — at your leisure.*

Very difficult. In that case I have to keep the two papers and wait
for illumination.

August 29, 1938

> *Please ask Sri Aurobindo to go through Jyoti's letter. . .*
> *Please advise what to do.*

[*Sri Aurobindo:*] Shoot Becharlal at her as requested.

August 30, 1938

> *By writing that letter, everything has disappeared, and*
> *Jyoti is happy.*

> *Guru, this poem[1] is really disappointing. I am sure you*
> *will find plenty of hurdles. . .*

These are indeed very difficult hurdles but I have leaped them
all — only in the process the poem has got considerably reshaped.
So I don't put lines except for a few that have remained almost
as they were. The last line is magnificent ["A fathomless beauty
in a sphere of pain"] — the others mostly needed a revision which
they don't seem to have got.

---

[1] "Reunion", *Sun-Blossoms*, p. 77.

1144

CORRESPONDENCE WITH

> *Day by day things are getting so difficult — more than your Yoga, Sir! My head will break one day. Be prepared for it, please!*

Well, well, when the head is broken, a passage for a superior light is often created — so either way you gain, a safe head or an illumined one.

August 31, 1938

September 1938

> *Z has broken our thermometer. She wants to pay, shall we accept?*

[*Mother:*] If she goes on taking her temperature she must pay as it will make her more careful in future — But is it wise to attract so much her attention on her temperature? It does not seem to help her to cure – – – –

> *In yesterday's poem, you have hurdled very well indeed! You call this line, "A fathomless beauty in a sphere of pain," a magnificent one, but I did not feel its magnificence when I wrote it and am unable to see where you find it. I think you find behind these things some inner truth which magnifies everything to you, no? Otherwise the rhythm and the word music aren't very striking, what?*

Well, have you become a disciple of Baron and the surrealists? You seem to suggest that significance does not matter and need not enter into the account in judging or feeling poetry! Rhythm and word music are indispensable, but are not the whole of poetry. For instance lines like these

> In the human heart of Heligoland
> A hunger wakes for the silver sea;
> For waving the might of his magical wand
> God sits on his throne in eternity,

have plenty of rhythm and word music — a surrealist might pass them, but I certainly would not. Your suggestion that my seeing the inner truth behind a line magnifies it to me, i.e. gives it a false

SRI AUROBINDO   1145

value to me which it does not really have as poetry, may or may not
be correct. But, certainly, the significance and feeling suggested
and borne home by the words and rhythm are in my view a capital
part of the value of poetry. Shakespeare's lines "Absent thee from
felicity awhile And in this harsh world draw thy breath in pain"
have a skilful and consummate rhythm and word combination,
but this gets its full value as the perfect embodiment of a profound
and moving significance, the expression in a few words of a whole
range of human world-experience. It is for a similar quality that
I have marked this line. Coming after the striking and significant
image of the stars on the skyline and the single Bliss that is the
source of all, it expresses with a great force of poetic vision and
emotion the sense of the original Delight contrasted with the world
of sorrow born from it and yet the deep presence of that Delight
in an unseizable beauty of things. But even isolated and taken by
itself there is a profound and moving beauty in the thought, expression and rhythm of the line and it is surprising to me that anyone
can miss it. It expresses it not intellectually but through vision and
emotion. As for rhythm and word music, it is certainly not striking
in the sense of being out of the way or unheard of, but it is perfect —
technically in the variation of vowels and the weaving of the con-
sonants and the distribution of longs and shorts, more deeply in
the modulated rhythmic movement and the calling in of overtones. I don't know what more you want in that line.

September 1, 1938

Guru, no, I don't suggest that significance doesn't matter.
On the other hand, I said it is more probably because of
the significance of the line than rhythm etc. that you call
it magnificent. "Magnifies" was used jokingly, of course.
As I don't yet understand much of longs, shorts, narrows
and thicks of your prosody, I laid the beauty of the line at the
door of significance or inner vision. So "false value" is not
what I meant. I am rather limited, or my solar plexus is
inhibitory to profound things told in a bare and rugged way.
For instance, your three lines against:
*   "A rhythmic fire that opens a secret door,*
*   And the treasures of eternity are found,"*
don't stir my mortal plexus very much, while perhaps your

> *penetrating eyes see all the treasures of eternity behind the door and exclaim with rapturous delight, "How rich!" But the other three-lined one: "My moments pass with moon-imprinted sail" makes me say: "Ah, here is something real, wonderful, flashing!" You will admit that this line is more poetic than the previous two lines, though perhaps the force of poetic vision and truth is less? That will indicate to you probably that I am a bit of a romantic sentimental type who wants to see colour blend with vision before getting the plexus stirred from its depth, what?*

I am afraid the language of your appreciations or criticisms here is not apposite. There is nothing "bare and rugged" in the two lines you quote; on the contrary they are rather violently figured — the *osé* image of a fire opening a door of a treasure-house would probably be objected to by Cousins or any other purist. The language of poetry is called bare when it is confined rigorously to just the words necessary to express the thought or feeling or to visualise what is described, without superfluous epithets, without imagery, without any least rhetorical turn in it. E.g. Cowper's

> Toll for the brave —
> The brave! that are no more —

is bare. Byron's

> Jehovah's vessels hold
> The godless Heathen's wine;

does not quite succeed because of a rhetorical tinge that he has not been able to keep out of the expression. When Baxter (I think it was Baxter) writes

> I spoke as one who ne'er would speak again[1]
> And as a dying man to dying men!

that might be taken as an example of strong and bare poetic language. I have written of Savitri waking on the day of destiny —

> Immobile in herself, she gathered force:
> This was the day when Sathyavan must die. —

that is designedly bare.

But none of these lines or passages can be called rugged; for ruggedness and austerity are not the same thing; poetry is rugged when it is rough in language and rhythm or rough and unpolished

---

[1] The original line reads: "I preach'd as never sure to preach again".

SRI AUROBINDO 1147

but sincere in feeling. Donne is often rugged, —

> Yet dare I almost be glad, I do not see
> That spectacle of too much weight for me.
> Who sees God's face, that is self-life must die;
> What a death were it then to see God die?

but it is only the first line that is at all bare.

On the other side, you describe the line of your preference

> My moments pass with moon-imprinted sail

by the epithets "real, wonderful, flashing". Real or surreal? It is precisely its unreality that makes the quality of the line; it is surreal, not in any depreciatory sense, but because of its supra-physical imaginativeness, its vivid suggestion of occult vision; one does not quite know what it means, but it suggests something that one can inwardly see. It is not flashing — gleaming or glinting would be nearer the mark — it penetrates the imagination and awakens sight and stirs or thrills with a sense of beauty but it is not something that carries one away by its sudden splendour.

You say that it is more poetic than the other quotation —perhaps, but not for the reason you give; rather because it is more felicitously complete in its image and more suggestive. But you seem to attach the word poetic to the idea of something brilliant, remotely beautiful, deeply coloured or strikingly imaged with a glitter in it or a magic glimmer. On the whole what you seem to mean is that this line is "real" poetry, because it has this quality and because it has a melodious sweetness of rhythm, while the other is of a less attractive character. Your solar plexus refuses to thrill where these qualities are absent — obviously that is a serious limitation in the plasticity of your solar plexus, not that it is wrong in thrilling to these things but that it is sadly wrong in thrilling to them only. It means that your plexus remains deaf and dead to most of the greater poetry of the world — to Homer, Milton, Valmiki, Vyasa, a great part even of Shakespeare. That is surely a serious limitation of the appreciative faculty. What is strange and beautiful has its appeal, but one ought to be able also to stir to what is grand and beautiful, or strong and noble, or simple and beautiful, or pure and exquisite. Not to do so would be like being blind of one eye and seeing with the other only very vividly strange outlines and intensely bright colours.

1148   CORRESPONDENCE WITH

I may add that if really I appreciate any lines for something which I see behind them but they do not actually suggest or express, then I must be a very bad critic. The lines you quote not only say nothing about the treasures except that they are found, but do not suggest anything more. If then I see from some knowledge that has nothing to do with the actual expression and suggestion of the lines all the treasures of eternity and cry "How rich" —meaning the richness, not of the treasures, but of the poetry, then I am doing something quite illegitimate which is the sign of a great unreality and confusion in my mind, very undesirable in a critic. It is not for any reason of that kind that I made a mark indicating appreciation but because I find in the passage a just and striking image with a rhythm and expression which are a sufficient body for the significance.

In today's poem the philosophy is old and poetry poor, what?

A poet is not bound to create a new philosophy—he may adopt an existing philosophy, only his expression of it must be his own, individual and true.

René wants tasteless castor-oil. We have plenty of "tasty" castor-oil, but he doesn't fancy that. So shall we buy it?

[*Mother:*] Yes.
                                                        September 2, 1938

> *". . . As if I had become infinity*
> *And God his mystery to me confides. . ."*
> *Is the link missing?*

No. If God confides his mystery to you, the rest follows as a natural consequence of that portentous act of His.

I have become a Father Confessor to God, what?

That's not a father confessor but only a confidant. A father confessor would be one to whom God confesses His sins, but perhaps you think the creation is a big enough sin in itself?

                                                        September 3, 1938

ŚRI AUROBINDO 1149

You found no answer to my questions, so the delay in sending my notebook?

Well, your arguments are not so overwhelming that I would find it difficult to answer; it was the time to answer that I did not find.

You may note that you quoted some time back [31.3.38] Dante's line: "In His will is our peace" and said that written in Italian it is one of the greatest lines in all poetic literature. Well, judging by the translation (not knowing Italian rhythm), I fear again it doesn't stir me much, but it stirs you much more because you see the profound significance behind it.

How can you judge a line of poetry from a translation? That would be an astonishing feat. I simply gave the meaning of the line in order to point out that poetry can be simple and straightforward in expression and yet rank as the greatest poetry. Its not stirring you would only prove that your plexus is not receptive to great and stirring poetry, it would not prove that the poetry is not great and stirring.

R is going tonight, I hear. I would like to offer the coffee tin and cheese to you, if you won't take the jam and butter. But I will be really glad if you accept everything. R won't take them back.

[*Mother:*] Send me the coffee and cheese and keep the butter and jam.

September 4, 1938

". . . Sharing its rapturous wine with every thing
Till all creation be a soliloquy. . ."
What's this blessed soliloquy doing after a bout of wine?

Well, what else do you expect when a fellow is drunk? But it is more decent to change it into an ecstasy.

Still you have no time, now when the correspondence has gone down?

1150 CORRESPONDENCE WITH

Who told you that? Since the first it has gone up or rather swelled up and my table is covered with 4-volume letters from one third of the Asram.

I suppose you are busy doing something high and mighty!

I would like to do something high and mighty, but God knows how I shall do it at this rate.

September 5, 1938

*"The magic breath of God's omnipotent Grace
Comes blowing from his soul's fathomless deep."*

It sounds as if God had lost his breath and was panting in a vast distress!
Also soul's/fathomless does not make a good rhythm.
The first six lines are very perfect and beautiful, but after that histories begin.[1] I think the histories might be replaced by geography or anything else and God must really stop blowing and panting.

*"Now grows a universe of beauty, crowned
With diamond fruits of everlasting ecstasy."*
O.K.?

No; rhythm awkward. I think I should object to a crown of fruits (apples? oranges? jack-fruit?).

Govinda, the Bangalore scientist [19.8.38] writes that he has written to the Mother, but no reply! Asks me to enquire. What is the mystery, please? Usual timelessness or uselessness?

What mystery? Do you imagine I am conducting a voluminous correspondence with people outside? Put that pathetic mistake out of your head. It would have been a marvel and a mystery and a new history begun in the invisible (upstairs) spheres of the Infinite[1] if I had answered him! I don't even remember what he wrote.

---

[1] Two lines of my poem that day were:
"Each moment new histories are begun
In the invisible spheres of the Infinite."

SRI AUROBINDO   1151

> *In the letter to me, he challenges God to give him peace,*
> *force and faith in this life. Only then will he admit its* মূল্য,[1]
> *otherwise no good.*

But what মূল্য is he prepared to pay for these fine things? Does he
imagine that it is God's business to deliver these goods on order?
Queer kind of business basis for the action of the Divine!

> *He seems to think that we are striving for* মোক্ষ[2] *or some*
> *bliss in the next life! But he does not desire that.*
> [*Sri Aurobindo underlined "next life".*]

Why don't you disabuse him of the idea and assure him that we
don't care a damn for মোক্ষ[2] and less than a damn for the next life?

> *He wants peace, Force and nothing more; but in this life.*
> *Well, can the Divine give them?*

Even if he can, why the deuce should he?

                                                    September 6, 1938

> *That was precisely what I had thought of writing to Govinda*
> *Das. Now I can quote you, toning it down, of course.*

No, sir, you mustn't make it a quotation from me, but you can
unload it as your own original merchandise on your unwary cus-
tomer.

> *Dilipda has presented me with a fine pen as you can judge*
> *from my writing!*

<u>Congrats.</u>

> *I fear what was being more and more "seen" in recent poems,*
> *is now getting more and more "unseen", but, at the same*
> *time, giving the same amount of trouble. I can't, for the*
> *life of me, get new expressions or thoughts. What can be*

---

[1] *mūlya:* value, price.
[2] *moksha:* liberation.

1152

> *done? I break my head over them but they remain as damned hard and unprofitable as the Divine! I am paying the penalty of trying to become an English poet and of facing a hard task-master!*

What the deuce are you complaining about? You are writing very beautiful poetry with apparent ease and one a day of this kind is a feat. If the apparent ease covers a lot of labour, that is the lot of the poet and artist except when he is a damned phenomenon of fluency. "It is the highest art to conceal art." "The long and conscientious labour of the artist giving in the result an appearance of divine and perfect ease" — console yourself with these titbits. As for repetitions, they are almost inevitable when you are writing a poem a day. You are gaining command of your medium and that is the main thing. An inexhaustible original fecundity is a thing you have to wait for — when you are more spiritually experienced and mature.

September 7, 1938

> *"The silent spheres of thought have opened now*
> *Their hidden gates; I enter like a god*
> *In triumphal majesty; upon my brow*
> *Is crowned an eagle-sun, infinity-shod."*

Look here now! neither eagles nor suns are in the habit of wearing shoes. Besides this idea of somebody's shoes on your head is extremely awkward and takes away entirely from the triumphal and godlike majesty of your entrance.

> *Please don't give a start when you see me entering like a god! Too much to bear even in poetry?*

Sorry! couldn't help starting. But the start was worse when I got the vision of somebody's shoes on your godlike head.

> *"The starry light of earth grows suddenly pale..."*
> *Does this starry light grow pale because of the sun?*

Yes. Besides the starry light is below and the sun is on your godlike head above.

SRI AUROBINDO   1153

> *Something queer happened when I was concentrating on*
> *these lines:*
>> *"I have known the fathomless beauty of the soul,*
>> *That moon-like shines upon a universe".*
> *I suddenly saw a very bright full moon, and a feminine fig-*
> *ure walking between me and the moon. The face was indis-*
> *tinct.*

I think the vision had nothing to do with the poetry. It was an
independent phenomenon.

> *Well, it gave me joy, but means what?*

Depends on the significance of the feminine figure; but as the face
was indistinct, how to know?

>> *"The footprints of time slowly fade away*
>> *From the threshold of my life. . ."*
> *These 2 lines, you say, have a "prose rhythm". What's*
> *that? Can't be explained?*

How can rhythm be explained? It is a matter of the ear, not of
the intellect. Of course there are the technical elements, but you
say you do not understand yet about them. But it is not a matter
of technique only; the same outer technique can produce successful or unsuccessful rhythms (live or dead rhythms). One has
to learn to distinguish by the ear, and the difficulty for you is to get
the right sense of the cadences of the English language. That is not
easy, for it has many outer and inner elements.

September 8, 1938

>> *"Mortality fades away with dim footfalls*
>> *From the measureless beauty of my life divine."*

"Life" is not the right word; but if you get upon the mysterious
silence of your height divine, all comes in pat enough. Obviously
mortality has to walk off when you become so uppish as that.

September 9, 1938

1154

> *Guru, so I am installed in X's palace! But my reaction was positively unpleasant. I spent 2 or 3 hours in the afternoon and all the time I was feeling lonely, as if I were far away from you. I was quite happy in my little nook! My medical work may suffer. Mother didn't object because I didn't object!! All these thoughts smashed my Muse. . .*

Mother would much prefer that you should be in your own room and she pointed out the objection about your work, but X said you were quite agreeable and, when both you and he seemed to desire the arrangement, she could not very well go on with her objections. Also what she agreed to was your staying there at night, not all the time.

> *The atmosphere also seemed so foreign to me, I don't know due to what.*

The atmosphere of X's room is *not* likely to be good for you; I should say — it cannot be a quiet one at any rate.

> *I almost feel my old room is preferable to this kingdom. If you could find some trustworthy fellow to stay, I would rather go back to my room.*

You should find somebody to replace you and go back to your own room.

At the same time I don't see what was the necessity of this guardianship. Is it against theft or against Y entering his rooms and arranging?

> *Doesn't Mother think my medical work may suffer?*

She does.

> *Couldn't you write something in my notebook tonight?*

I don't expect I shall be able to do so, but will see.

> *Chand writes there is no letter from you. So, one word, Guru!*

SRI AUROBINDO   1155

Well, well! (That's one word twice repeated).

September 11, 1938

*Mother must have told you all about the room incident, so
I needn't go more into it.*

*You must have seen in today's paper the great news:
Prof. Sanjib Chowdhury of Dacca (belonging to Chittagong, hip-hip hurrah!) has got the Nobel Prize in literature — for his book* Songs from the Heights.

Didn't see it. Who the devil is he? The title of the book doesn't
sound encouraging; but I suppose it can't be merely Noble Rubbish.

*But it is extremely surprising that we have heard very
little about him! Have you?*

Never.

This book has hit!

Hit whom?

*Anyway, a great success for India, Bengal, Chittagong!
I wonder if you have read it.*

Never set eyes on it. No use of success unless it is deserved. Can't
forget that Kipling for whose poetry I have a Noble contempt
(his prose has value, at least the Jungle Book and some short
stories) was illegitimately Nobelised by this confounded prize.
Contemporary "success" or fame is a deceit and a snare.

September 12, 1938

*In yesterday's poem, why do you fear the snow will melt
when there is no snow? Only the spaces are white like snow,
aren't they?*

No doubt, but snow and sun together still suggest the incongruity.
However it can remain — sun on snow but a non-melting sun.

September 14, 1938

*"The fathomless beauty on the soul's blue rim
Wakes with a heaven-stirring cry
And mirrors on the heart's horizon glass. . ."*

Lord Christ! what a yell for beauty to emit! Besides the correlation waking with a cry and mirroring is not very convincing. For heaven's sake do something about this.

What is a horizon glass? cousin of opera-glass?

"All drunken shadows of thought fade and pass. . ."

"Drunken shadows"!! If even shadows become bibulous and stagger, what will become of the Congress and its prohibition laws? Besides Rajagopalachari is sure to pass a law soon forbidding the publication of any book with the words "wine" and "drunken" in it.

You may damn as many lines as you like and find as many rabid utterances as you may, but I can't every day go on looking at the void for a line! I have drunk "the wine of Fire", and you see the result!

I have damned only one line and rearranged others. I have even 3 lined the wine of Fire.

I wait for your crushing strokes and then shall see if I can do the repairs.

One line please.

Otherwise down will it go into the W.P.B.

No need.

By the way, you had better hurry up with your Supermind descent, Sir. Otherwise Hitler, Mussolini & Co. will gunfire it like— !

What has Supermind to do with Hitler or Hitler with Supermind? Do you expect the Supermind to aviate to Berchtesgaden? How the

SRI AUROBINDO   1157

devil can they gunfire S; their aeroplanes can't even reach Pondicherry, much less the Supermind. The descent of S depends on S, not on Hitler or no Hitler.

> *Things look damnably bad, what?*

Bad enough unless Chamberlain finds a way to wriggle out of it.

> *Sahana says you have advised her and Amiya to take calcium. We have calcium lactate which is as good. Shall we give that?*

[*Mother:*] She did not speak of a medicine but of some food which is usually taken in Bengal, but I do not remember its name.[1]

September 16, 1938

> *You are neither writing in my notebook nor sending me the poem. The "illumination" hasn't yet descended [29.8.38].*

These things rest on the knees of the gods.

September 17, 1938

> *"Into a flame of vision my heart has grown*
> *And leaves behind this frail mortality. . ."*
> *What follows is not very favourable, what?*

It is the result of your taking French leave of mortality — quite natural.

September 18, 1938

> *Chand writes: "You have said 'Well, well!' The meaning has appeared quite clear to me." [11.9.38]*

Queer! He seems cleverer than myself.

> *About the property tangle, he writes that if I share the sale money with my cousins, they will at once sell the prop-*

---

[1] Kalzana food: a patent form of calcium.

*etry with Chand's help. They are 4 partners. My share
should be half. So?*

A large sum of money?

September 19, 1938

> *"Thy Presence wraps around my reveried sense
> An air burdened with heavenly frankincense. . ."*

I say, this sounds like making a perfumed package. Reveried?

> *"And in my soul I feel an awakening
> Of thy eternal Beauty ring on ring."
> Guru, I smack my lips today in satisfaction, because I
> find the poem damn fine! Though there are a few anoma-
> lies, e.g. heavenly, ring on ring, etc. What do you say?*

Umph! Smack away but I smack also with my hand of correction.
However the first stanza is O.K. and the last stanza the same
when relieved of reveried and heavenly and unwrapped.

> *Perhaps you find the Presence of my romantic-sentimental
> self?*

Well, there are certainly traces of both romance and sentimentality in the 4th line and the lines 9-11 are as weak as they are
incomprehensible. I have corrected but it keeps the romantic
touch.

> *Ah, what a hard Master you are and what a tough customer!*

Can't help being that, otherwise you would fall back into a lax
and feeble imitative romanticism which would be quite inad-
visable. By "romanticism" I mean really "pseudo-romanticism" or
sometimes "reproductive romanticism".

September 20, 1938.

SRI AUROBINDO   1159

> *Guru, I've prepared myself for further smacks or whips!*

Well, well—it doesn't catch exactly—you haven't put enough
verbal or rhythmic vim into it. Lacks vitamin. Have put some
vit. A and B into it. Some lines not lined because too much mine.

> *Oh dear, dear, what a travail to produce a mouse!*

The mouse was all right in intention, but its tail was not frisky
enough in fact.

September 21, 1938

> *"The rich magnificence of the wandering sun*
> *Reflects my splendour from still height to height. . ."*

I say, there ought to be a limit to your splendour.
   If we transfer the splendour from you to God, it becomes all
right—results of your extraordinary condition.

> *Can you tolerate God twice?*

I can't—once is enough for him, so I have turned him out of one
line, but brought him by pronominal implication into the whole
poem throughout. I think that gives it more consistence.

> *I send you one of Nishikanta's recent Bengali poems, to*
> *share my joy with you. The lines I have marked seem to*
> *have your O.P. touch, don't they? He seems to have struck*
> *a new grandeur and beauty, no?*

It is certainly very powerful and beautiful. By O.P. I presume you
mean Overhead Poetry. That I can't say—the substance seems
to be from there, but a certain kind of rhythm is also needed which
I find more difficult to decide about in Bengali than in English.

> *Didn't you find Vasanti [suffering from anaemia] better*
> *than before?*

[*Mother:*] Much better.

1160   CORRESPONDENCE WITH

> *I saw Sankar Ram limping. I called him and examined him... The symptoms point towards Purpura. But the treatment is simple, which as you know, is more dietetic: fresh fruits and vegetables; iron and arsenic by mouth. We can examine his urine also.*
> [*The Mother marked "fresh fruits... urine also".*]

Yes.

> *I fear a simple local treatment won't be very effective. Of course, if you want us to leave him alone, we can.*

It is better to treat him.

                                                    September 22, 1938

> *"I gather from the fathomless depth of the Mind*
> *Transparent thoughts that float through a crystal (trancèd)*
>   *wind*
> *To a spirit-sky and weave a memory*
> *Around the starry flames (glimpse) of Infinity."*

I read your variation [glimpse] first as "stumps". What a magnificent and original image! the starry stumps (or star-stumps) of infinity! But I fear alas that it would be condemned as surrealistic. I can't make out the variation for "crystal". Wearied? Tired of carrying tons of transparent thoughts? Surely not!

> *"... A sun-plumed Bird made of immortal Breath."*

A bird made of breath! Too surrealistic.

> *I have got some joy out of this poem. God knows whether that joy will be justified in your hands, or crucified! What more do you demand, Sir? Now please, fire away!*

Exceedingly fine all through. The other 3 linings are mainly for the splendour and truth of the image (including of course the perfection in the expression, without which no image would have any

SRI AUROBINDO   1161

value), but the outstanding lines are 8-12* which have an extra-ordinary beauty. I might have put 4 lines, but remembering how you shouted against my first four lining effort, I curled back the impulse into myself and put three only.

> *We are sorry to hear that you can't decide about Bengali overhead poetry. I consider it a defect, Sir, in your poetic and supramental make-up, which you should try to remove or mend. A defect in the Supramental Avatar is — is — well, doesn't fit!*

Why a defect? In any case all qualities have their defects, which are also a quality. For the rest, by your logic I ought to be able to pronounce on the merits of Czechoslovakian or Arabic poetry. To pronounce whether a rhythm is O.P. or not one must have an infallible ear for the overtones and undertones of the sound music of the language — that expertness I have not got with regard to Bengali.

September 23, 1938

> *In yesterday's poem, I am much tempted to take the "stumps", even if it is surrealistic. Who cares what it is when you find it magnificent? It was not "wearied wind" but "trancèd wind". Oh dear, dear!*

Don't do it, sir, or you will get stumped. The "star-stumps" are "magnificent" from the humorous-reckless-epic point of view, but they can't be taken seriously. Besides you would have to change all into the same key, *e.g.*
> > "I slog on the boundless cricket field of Mind
> > Transparent thoughts that cross like crystal wind
> > God's wicket-keeper's dance of mystery
> > Around the starry-stumps of infinity."

---

* "Of a Presence in the heart of a diamond prayer.
  No whirling tide of mortal dreams there brings
  Waves of a silver passion on foam-wings:
  Only in the eternal hush of space
  Abides the beauty of the changeless Face."

I am sorry that you didn't put 4 lines. My shout, you see, was due to a shock — seeing 4 lines — a shock of delight.

It didn't sound like it!

You are surprised at Chand's cleverness! Well, Sir, your non-committal Supramental answers are sometimes damned puzzling, so I wouldn't blame him. Anyhow, shall I pass on the remark to him?

You can if you like. But he ought to have known that "Well, well" in English is not a shout of approbation, but philosophically non-committal.

It seems he has disposed of his mother's ornaments which were trustingly deposited with him, to pull out a friend from difficulty. His mother has detected the "robbery" by his own admission.

Obviously it must be that — unless he robbed her more than once which is always possible.

September 24, 1938

"My life grows day by day into a deep
Reverie broken by no mortal dream,
For the mysterious will of the Supreme
Has made it a mirror of His awakened sleep."
. . . Why the devil do I feel so sleepy when I try to write at night?

Probably your inspiration comes from a part of His awakened sleep and goes back to it.

S again complains of frequent micturition. Once we had given him a gland-product containing pituitary, and it had a goos effect, though temporary. Shall we try again?

[*Mother:*] Is it worth while if it has only a temporary effect?

September 26, 1938

SRI AUROBINDO   1163

> "... For thy immutable silences abide
> Like vast glaciers behind my body's door."

A vast glacier behind a door seems rather impossible. But frozen snow behind a door would convict the housekeeper of negli-
gence.

> The doctor in place of Valle asked me about vaccination.
> I replied that we had done it already last year. He said that
> there might be a few new-comers who might not have been
> vaccinated. I think we can say "no" about the inmates, and
> about workers, they can be done at their own place.
> [The Mother marked the last sentence with a vertical line.]

This is right.
I do not think we have new workmen since last vaccination. If
required, we have the letter written by Valle and signed by Gaffiero thanking for the help we gave for vaccination.

September 27, 1938

> I hear that J is now shedding tears of joy at the sight of
> apples, oranges and prunes. Tears of sorrow, tears of joy,
> oh dear!

"fruity" tears of joy. They move me to poetry
> "O apples, apples, oranges and prunes,
> You are God's bliss incarnate in a fruit!
> Meeting you after many desolate moons
> I sob and sniff and make a joyous bruit."

Admit that you yourself could not have done better as a poetic
and mantric comment on this touching situation.

> Any chance for my book or poem [17.9.38]?

The poem not yet illuminated, can't find anything that would be
on the same level as the two opening and one closing stanza. Book
in same condition — virgin of an answer.

September 28, 1938

October 1938

"From the grapes of sleep", "God's vineyard" sound funnily delightful, Sir! You seem to be trying to be modernistic!

Well, I'm blowed! What is there modern about "vineyard"? Vineyards are as old as Adam or almost, at any rate they existed before the flood.

By what modern alchemy do you make — "In God's vineyard of ecstasies" 3 foot?

Why not? I have anapaestised the line, that is all. No alchemy needed modern or ancient. I don't see what is the difficulty.

With "all" you use the verb in singular — harbours? Possible? We say "All are mad", not "All is mad".

What the deuce! You don't know that all can be used collectively in the singular, e.g. "All he does is mad." "All is beautiful here."?

I have been asked to inform the workers that Thursday (8 a.m.) has been fixed for vaccination. Shall I tell Chandulal to circulate it among the workers so that those who want to be vaccinated may go there?

[*Mother:*] Yes.

October 1, 1938

[*About T convalescing from T.B.:*] *It will be better to continue her usual butter, extra milk and tomatoes and fruits. She also feels very hungry.*
[*The Mother marked this paragraph with a vertical line.*]

[*Mother:*] Yes, better continue.

As for work, she says she is ready to take up anything you give. She will welcome it if given by you.

SRI AUROBINDO   1165

[*Mother:*] I have no intention of giving work other than the one
she is doing now.
                                                          October 2, 1938

> *Guru, so after so much trouble and pain, yesterday's poem*
> *was maimed! What a capricious Goddess is the Muse! But*
> *how partial to you!*

Not at all. I have to labour much more than you, except for sonnets
which come easily and short lyrics which need only a single revision.
But for the rest I have to rewrite 20 or 30 times. Moreover I write
only at long intervals.

> *The glacier image is a theft from Mallarmé, and not a*
> *clever one, perhaps?*

It is quite effective here. Thefts from other languages are habitual in poetry.
                                                          October 3, 1938

> *"A tranced silver flame of thy delight,*
> *Within my rapturous solitude I bear*
> *The occult mysteries of the Infinite*
> *Hidden in a bright seed of tranquil prayer."*

A flame bearing mysteries in a seed is a mixed metaphor.

> *"Life breaks no more with multitudinous waves*
> *Upon my luminous silence; its irised fire*
> *Lights only the forlorn shadowy caves*
> *On the edge of time with foams of moth-desire."*

A fire lighting a cave with foam and a moth foaming! In English one must be careful to avoid mixture of metaphors whether
implied or explicit.

> *Where are the sonnets or lyrics you have written? We have*
> *seen very few of them!*

Unseen they count, but not in numbers.

*And what did you mean by "for the rest" which you re-
write 20 or 30 times? Did you mean your "Savitri"?*

Of course.

Do you think it will greet us one day?

Well, perhaps after ten years if I get time.

October 4, 1938

What's this romantic nightingale doing here?

The nightingale perhaps came in answer to the need of a rhyme.
However it can stay perched there provided it ceases to be white.
It has no connection with the preceding lines, so the semi-colon
must go.

*We have no Camomille you have prescribed for Lalita.
Shall we get it from the Pharmacy?*

[*Mother:*] What they have there is generally old and badly kept.
Perhaps we might try a light decoction of *boldo* instead. (She has
pain 15 to 20 minutes after taking food.)

October 6, 1938

*"The agelong faceted memory of life
Is strewn with silences of the Infinite. . ."*

Lord! sir, what on earth *do* you mean? "agelong faceted" is
"strewn"?

"I live like a rock of diamond trancehood. . ."

A rock doesn't live.

*Seeing this incomplete piece of fire-work, you are sure
to swear at me at every step!*

Haven't sufficient energy or time to swear at every step, — only
where blasphemy is needed.

SRI AUROBINDO 1167

I want now to play a different game with the Muse: just note down whatever comes; not the old tedious game of waiting, straining and praying for every line till it descends after half an hour! What's the result of the new process?

Very much the same as in the old.

Last night N had shivering with bad joint pains. Today (5 p.m.) fever 103° and a "hammering" headache. He wants your sanction *for any internal medication.*

[*Mother:*] Better if he takes medicine.

When I went to foment Lila's leg last night, I just enquired about Nirmala and found her very feverish with a bad head-ache. I washed her head with cold water and asked Lila to sponge the body with warm water today. My little inter-ference, I hope, wasn't bad.

[*Mother:*] No, you did well to help.

October 7, 1938

This time I have kicked out "infinite, eternal, solitude, etc." from my poem. God be thanked!

Congratulations!

Lila's swelling of the leg is still there. Should I leave all treatment now and let it disappear by itself, or continue a few days more the present treatment?

[*Mother:*] You can go on for a few days more.

October 8, 1938

Guru, I fear you will find the poem[1] suffering from the first signs of flu! There is no harmony at all. It is all because of my "hammering headache".

[1] *Fifty Poems of Nirodbaran*, p. 98.

A

1168   CORRESPONDENCE WITH

Well, sir, your flu has made you fluid and fluent, and the hammering headache has hammered out a fine poem. Wa Allah!

It doesn't seem to know what it's talking about.

I don't see what's wrong with it. It seems to know what it is talking about; although you may not know it.

October 9, 1938

What the deuce, Sir! Are you aware of the raging epidemic [flu, dengue] havoc in the Asram? Too busy with the Supermind to bother about these trifles? How is it that the Asram has become so vulnerable to it this time — the first?

There has been a "progressive" increase in that respect during the last ten years and this seems to be its (present) culmination. In that respect more people are being "advanced sadhaks".

Better stop this epidemic now, Sir! I hear that Vedabrata is the latest victim!

Ramkrishna is promising to join the dance.

October 10, 1938

Guru, do you see the overhead reflected in this poem? I've hammered it!

I don't know but the overheadache is also reflected, which accounts for the number of alterations that have to be made.

What's this, Sir? My feverishness persists!

Why on earth is your body so attached to the headache and fever?

I don't suppose an illness has any salutary effect on sadhana, that it should linger, what?

Not in the least — needn't keep it on with that idea!

October 11, 1938

SRI AUROBINDO   1169

> *A cement barrel fell on Mohanlal's foot. It's swollen considerably, and there is a wound too. Purani says that fomentation will cure the swelling.*

[*Mother:*] The wound will never close if it is fomented.

> *Miss Wilson[1] is to come for treatment tomorrow. Should we postpone it as Dr. Becharlal is not well and neither am I?*

[*Mother:*] Yes, it is better to *postpone.*

> *Dr. Becharlal was proposing today that we should try to get another helping hand in the Dispensary, as the work has increased a lot. . .*

[*Mother:*] Quite ready to give you a helping hand — but is it a Sadhak or a servant?

> *Mulshankar says the present oven is too small, as people are increasing for soup. Can a big one be ordered from the smithy?*

[*Mother:*] Yes.

October 12, 1938

> *"A touch of thy hand, a brief glitter of thy eyes*
> *Releases unknown springs from my body's earth. . ."*

Perspiration?
"He held him with his glittering eye"? But this is not the Ancient Mariner. "Glitter of eye" suggests anger, greed, etc.

> *"Thy vigilant caress leads pace by pace*
> *The lonely caravan of my God-desire. . ."*

A caress can't lead a caravan.

> *Guru, how is this poem?*

---

[1] The daughter of President Woodrow Wilson of the U.S.A.

1170 CORRESPONDENCE WITH

Well, the scansion and rhythm seem rather forced at places and some of the ideas are rather headachy e.g. a caress leading a caravan and the suggestion of profuse perspiration and the smile of snow-cool fire. However, being free from headache, I have made a fine thing out of it.

There doesn't seem to be any improvement in the medical atmosphere, Sir!

None. Even all the three Doctors gave the example of getting ferociously ill! The city population follow মহাজনো গতো যেন পন্থা।[1]

By the way, I hope you received my prayer for poetry and your poetic chord was touched.

I did, but my Muse refused to work.

Dr. Becharlal says that a sadhak would be better for work in the Dispensary, as a servant won't be able to do the nursing work.

[*Mother:*] Do you have some name to suggest?
[*Sri Aurobindo:*] Arjava is insisting on having paraffin oil in stock in the Dispensary (it appears there is none) to be available in case of (his stomach's) emergency. Ask Rajangam to procure it.

October 13, 1938

Arjava has finished 1 lb. of paraffin in 15 days! . . . I don't know any emergency requiring paraffin so badly. It is not emergency, but his continuous consumption that we have to see about. . .

[*Mother:*] All the same you can buy the paraffin — — — —

We have no name to suggest for our helper, as it is very difficult to choose. I think whomever you send will be good.

[1] *mahājano gato yena panthā:* the path followed by great men.

SRI AUROBINDO 1171

[*Mother:*] Just now I see nobody whom I can send, but someone may turn up.

> *Guru, I almost wanted to stop writing as my recent poems turned out unsatisfactory either due to my head or due to the study of modern English verses.*

You are too easily discouraged. Such drops in the Inspiration are inevitable when one constantly writes poetry.

> *But why should the study of verses have a wrong influence?*

It depends on what you are studying. There are verses and verses.

> *Today's poem won't fare any better, I fear.*

It is better.

October 14, 1938

> *Can a "closed door" seal anything?*

No — never did.

> *You say I am easily discouraged. Oh Lord! in spite of my heroic pulling on, you say that?*

Heroic in spite of easy and frequent discouragement.

> *However, please give me a few names of poets — especially modern poets, whom I should study.*

In what sense modern?

October 15, 1938

> *By "modern poets" I meant those of the 20th century, i.e. writers who have made a name and are trying to do something new.*

I have very little familiarity with the names of modern poets subsequent to A.E. & Yeats and De La Mare, all of whom you know.

1172   CORRESPONDENCE WITH

There are about a hundred of them moderns, Spender $+ x + y + z + p^2$ etc. Before that they were Hopkins and Fletcher and others and before that Meredith and Hardy and Francis Thompson. You can tackle any of them you can lay your hands on in the library. Watson and Brooke and other Edwardians & Georgians would not be good for you.

October 16, 1938

[*After making the corrections in my poem:*[1]]

Ahem! What do you say to that? It seems to me that between us we have produced something remarkable.

> *After being poised, how can anything travel, and with eagle-wings at that?*

But that is what the eagles do. They beat their wings to give themselves an impulsion and then sail for some time with wide wings poised on the air.

> *I find that I have written about 186 poems from March to August, of which only 15 are "exceedingly fine".*

15 poems exceedingly fine in 6 months! It is a colossal number!

> *But in any case, compared to last year's poems, there has been a very satisfactory progress, I think. What do you say?*

Certainly.

October 17, 1938

> *15 — a colossal number! Joking? I am tempted to say like Monodhar — "I beg to differ with you in this respect."*

Not at all; quite serious. If you take the short lyrics and sonnets (not longer poems) of great poets like Keats, Shelley, Wordsworth, how many are there of the first class written in a whole lifetime?

---

[1] "O Light Inviolable", *Sun-Blossoms*, p. 97.

SRI AUROBINDO   1173

Thirty or forty perhaps at the outside. And you have written 15 in
6 months.
                                              October 18, 1938

> *Ah, here am I again! You had three days' respite, no more,*
> *Sir! Now you will have to scratch your head to find the*
> *right words and expressions!*

I don't need to scratch my head—I have only to look at it from
above and the words bubble up óf themselves—at once or after a
time. When they don't, all the scratching in the world is of no avail.

> *I don't expect anything great here, for the head is dry,*
> *mind is weary and the soul languorous, so?*

Well, it isn't either dry or weary or languorous.
                                              October 22, 1938

> *After a long time my old self is trying to assert itself:*
> *lethargy, depression, ennui, lack of interest in everything,*
> *aftermath of fever!*

Obviously—a stage of it like the rash—a sort of psychological
dengue-fall.
                                              October 24, 1938

> *When one will take up my file of poems and turn over the*
> *pages, he will be sick of these poor repetitions. And yet*
> *I don't know how to avoid them. I admit that in daily writing*
> *this is bound to happen, still it annoys me!*

Well, naturally, if the book had to be published, a selection would
have to be made. But as you are writing in order to open yourself
more to the source of full inspiration, it doesn't matter so much.
                                              October 25, 1938

> *Guru, you say that I have "a much greater mastery of*
> *expression" now; that's something. I am now trying to*
> *read some English poems of poets suggested by you.*

1174   CORRESPONDENCE WITH

Which of them?

> *I have doubts here about the lines 4, 7, 12 and the last.*
> [*"Whence leaps the splendour of the Infinite",*
> *"My human heart begins to understand",*
> *"The secret Truth hidden in thy heart's sphere",*
> *"Upon the sombre shore of memories".*]
> *They seem to be simple!*

My dear sir, these lines are simply exquisite (simply in both senses)
— all four indeed, precisely because they are so simple that the
emotion and experience go straight through without a veil.

> *You asked me to read Hardy, Spender, Meredith, Hopkins,*
> *besides De la Mare, A.E. and Yeats . . . But how will Mere-*
> *dith and others help? Their poetry has nothing in common*
> *with ours, except the turn of expression, if that's what you*
> *mean. Please tell me whom I should take up first and how*
> *I should proceed.*

[*No reply.*]

October 27, 1938

> *Guru, you will find in Satya's letter a doubt that you don't*
> *read their letters!*

The doubt is whether the letters reach me — they reach me all right;
do they imagine that Nolini intercepts letters? What the devil
does this N mean by saying that Mother has asked her to wait
there.

Mother is not in correspondence with her and never asked her to
do anything.

October 28, 1938

> *This rainy weather makes it difficult for me to go to the hos-*
> *pital. Shall I hire a rickshaw when necessary?*
> [*The Mother underlined the last sentence.*]

Yes.

October 29, 1938

SRI AUROBINDO   1175

> *"Stubborn clay"—influence of Meredith?*

Meredith? I don't know. By the way, I forgot to answer your
comments on your reading the other day [27.10.38]. I thought you
wanted to read the modern poets in order to help your style, so
I suggested the names. Naturally their substance has little kin-
ship with the things we try to write. They say Thompson's has, but
I don't know his poetry very well.

> *By the way, do you know why Arjava has stopped writing?*

He wrote a beautiful poem the other day—but his inspiration has
become fitful and far between.

October 30, 1938

> *Today I faithfully surrendered myself to inspiration,*
> *hence I can't make any head or tail. I hope it has a head*
> *and a tail. But I fear, you will chop them off and replace*
> *them by something new. If by fluke you find the poem O.K.,*
> *then please tell me what the 2nd and 3rd stanzas mean.*[1]

Well, the result is very creditable and it has an obvious head even
if there is no tail to make. It is only the irruption of the nightingale to which I object, as that is cheap and obvious. The first
two stanzas are very fine; the second develops an admirable image.
I don't see what there is to explain in it. A sleep full of dreams, a
fantasia of half-forgotten memories as it were, can be very well
called "half-forgetful sleep", and such a sleep filled with the im-
portunities of dream-delight (a beautiful phrase) can very well seem
like the vastness etc. What is there so difficult to catch in that? The
3rd stanza is also very fine with its idea of the dreams coming up
from a mysterious or miraculous depth of nothingness into the
silence of the sleep-trance, revealing all that was hidden darkly
behind a veil—it is an admirably profound description of the happenings of deep sleep-samadhi. It seems to me perfectly plain, true
and simple. But the nightingale won't do; it spoils the depth of
the utterance.

---

[1] *Fifty Poems of Nirodbaran*, p. 102.

I didn't want to read the modern poets only to help my style, but also to get acquainted with their various ways of expression. For instance Meredith says, ". . . to drill the stubborn earth to shape". I would have hesitated a thousand times to use "stubborn" if I hadn't seen its use.

Why? it is an admirably apt epithet in that place.

But while I profit in this way, I get an unconscious influence in other ways. Should I then drop reading these poets?

No, you should be able to read and profit by the beautiful language without losing your own inspiration.

Did I send an English poem of Dilip's along with the Bengali ones yesterday?

October 31, 1938

November 1938

No, you didn't send me Dilipda's English poem.

What the deuce has happened to it then? These dematerialisations are very annoying.

Tripura has a nutlike swelling just on the wrist. Looks like bursitis. I wonder if 7 or 8 hrs. of embroidery daily should not be somewhat curtailed.
[*The Mother underlined "7 or 8 hrs."*]

It seems to me also that it is too much and I have said so already several times.

November 1, 1938

[*I sent Sri Aurobindo the typescript of his comment of 31.10.38, leaving a blank for a word I could not read.*]
You have forgotten a word in the other poem. You will see a blank remains. Or you can't make out your own writing? That's fine, Sir!

SRI AUROBINDO   1177

The word looks like "fantasia" but I am not at all sure—it might
be anything else. It is altogether irrational to expect me to read
my own writing—I write for others to read, not for myself —it is
their business to puzzle out the words. I try to read when I am asked,
but I have to make a strong use of second sight with a mélange
of intuition, reasoned conjectural speculation and random guessing.

> *Lila's ankle is still swollen. Some pain on deep pressure*
> *and on walking. No fracture is likely. Would it be advis-*
> *able to see it under screen?*
> [*The Mother marked the last sentence with a vertical line.*]

Yes.
                                                        November 2, 1938

> *Guru, this poem[1] is so simple (and bare at places?) that*
> *I fear it approaches flatness.*

Well, sir—well, sir—well, sir! I force myself not to break out
into strong and abusive language; but really, really, you *must* mend
your defective sense of poetic values. This is another triumph.
You must have had, besides the foiled romantic, a metaphysical
poet of the 17th century latent in you who is breaking out now from
time to time. Donne himself after having got relieved in the other
world of his ruggedness, mannerisms and ingenious intellectuali-
ties, might have written this poem.

> *In English does "journey to God" mean anything?*

It means everything.
                                                        November 3, 1938

> *I am afraid it will take me some time to mend my defective*
> *sense of poetic values. I am too much imbued with 17th*
> *century influence! Perhaps I would have appreciated this*
> *poem more, if it had been written by another person.*

What influence? Nobody spoke of any influence.

---

[1] "Quest Fulfilled", *Sun-Blossoms*, p. 91.

1178

The merits and defects of poetry remain the same whether written by oneself or another.

> *I had written the first line of this poem before* [*"With outstretched arms of prayer I cling to thee"*], *but it didn't stir you so much perhaps because, though beautiful, the necklace of which it was one jewel, wasn't harmoniously beautiful?*

Naturally — poetry is not a matter of separate lines — a poem is beautiful as a whole — when it is perfect each line has its own beauty but also the beauty of the whole.

> *But why metaphysical? Romantic, I understand. Where do you find metaphysics? I hate metaphysics! and who are these 17th century poets?*

"Metaphysical poets of the 17th century school" is a standing description of the group or line of poets, Donne, Vaughan, Traherne, Herbert, Quarles, Crashaw and a number of others who wrote poetry of a religious and spiritual character — metaphysical here means that (truth beyond the physical) and has nothing to do with the "metaphysics" of Kant or Hegel or Bradley.

November 4, 1938

> *Please throw a glance over the names of the metaphysical poets — I couldn't make out one name which I have underlined.*

You seem to have got the names all right.

> *Have you really put 4 lines against*
>   *"Or a delicate tune out of the heart of a lyre*
>   *Borne by the magic air of eternity"?*
> *I had missed them first, then I saw and stared and gulped — Really four?*

The fourth line is a duplicate — it is really three.

November 5, 1938

SRI AUROBINDO 1179

> *Chandradeep wants an English poem of mine for* Kalpataru
> *magazine. Should I give it?*

If you like, though it does not, I think, usually drop into poetry.

> *Last night I got stuck at every stanza and had to send you
> and Mother frequent S.O.S.'s to rescue me. Do you really
> receive these signals, or do your impersonal Forces intercept
> them and do the necessary?*

As we receive some hundreds of such signals daily, we are obliged
to be impersonal about it, otherwise we would have no time for
anything else.

November 6, 1938

> *Guru, ah, now I see! That's why my poems are not always
> uniformly super-successful or even successful, some being
> crippled, some mentally defective, some consumptive and
> so on. Only when your personal Force intervenes, they
> turn out miracles. I thought so, Sir, I thought so!*

Man! Your explanation is too neat to be quite the thing.

> *S has broken 2 eye-cups in 9 months! She wants another
> now.*

[*Mother:*] You can give her one more.

November 7, 1938

> *"Beyond the flickering lamps of thought our mind
> Soars like an eagle from height to greater height. . ."*

An eagle flying beyond lamps! No, sir!

> *Guru, ah, what a difficulty I had in writing this poem!*[1]
> *And yet it is not satisfactory!*

I am afraid not. As it stands it is a struggling failure. Now just look

---

[1] *Fifty Poems of Nirodbaran*, p. 110.

1180   CORRESPONDENCE WITH

at my alterations and see how finely easy it was all the time! Wa Allah! It seems to me at the moment one of the finest poems we have yet written. Praise be!

> *Guru, you seem to be in a mood of swallowing all the Bengali poems — Dilip's and NK's. Mine too the same fate? Please don't swallow it, je vous prie.*

Actually I had Dilip ready last night, but was too lazy to fish out your thing and put him inside you. Here he is now.

> *Have you any honey or shall we get it from the bazaar?*

[*Mother:*] I have some. Shall send after a day or two.

November 8, 1938

> *This time, Sir, the poem[1] looks to me damn fine. I know you will say, "Well, well!" — but we have very rarely agreed on any point! But does it really leave your plexus cold?*

Very fine, yes, and perfect in expression; but I don't know about damn fine, for that is a tremendous superlative. Such a solemn phrase should only be used when you write something equalling Shakespeare at his best.

> *Yes, Sir, your alterations appear extremely easy, but the fact that they didn't come to me even after struggling breaths, proves them otherwise. Of course if I had been the Lord of all Inspiration, I would have told you the same thing. Anyway I am glad that "we" have achieved something. But do you still stick to your yesterday's remark?*

Well, my enthusiasm has abated a little except for the first 2 stanzas and line 3 of the third. The rest is not quite equal to the first two stanzas not having quite the same stamp of original authenticity. There is more in it of fine writing, which makes it less perfect. All

---

[1] "Thy Presence", *Sun-Blossoms*, p. 108.

SRI AUROBINDO   1181

the same it is very successful. Still some changes suggest themselves
to me as necessary. Like that my first glow of appreciation begins
to return, as the last 2 lines are so lifted up more naturally on the
wave of what comes before. The "distances of air" and the "tune"
brought in a wrong note and the "Are" of the 12th line is weak and
does not convey the full significance.

> *Tripura's finger is getting worse. We can't stop the pus-*
> *formation. Shall we take her to the hospital?*

[*Mother:*] I have no confidence in the people who are now in charge
of the hospital. It would be better to consult Duraiswami's friend
Srinivas Rao who is at Cuddalore.

November 9, 1938

[*Mother:*] By mistake yesterday I wrote Bangalore[1] when I meant
Cuddalore. Srinivas Rao comes often here, that is why I mentioned
his name.

> *Guru, "Shakespeare at his best"? The very name of Shakes-*
> *peare makes my breath shake with fear, and to talk of*
> *equalling him at his best, oh, people will call me mad,*
> *Sir. If someone else had told me that, I would have called*
> *him mad! But I don't know what to say to you! You stagger*
> *me so much!*

Well, but look at logic. G.B.S. declares himself the equal, if not
superior, of Shakespeare. You write better poetry than Shaw ever
did (which is easy because he never wrote any). So you are the
equal (if not the superior) of Shakespeare.

> *But, if I remember aright, some of my lines you have called*
> *"damn fine"! So?*

Did I indeed? Then, logically, it must have been equal to the best
of Shakespeare, otherwise it couldn't have been so damned. This
also is logic.

---

[1] The Mother in fact had written "Cuddalore".

1182   CORRESPONDENCE WITH

Now about this poem, I fear to ask you about the merit, as it is so simple, and written so easily.

Simplicity is not the test. There can be a supreme beauty of simplicity and there can be the opposite.

November 10, 1938

Honey? [8.11.38]

[*Mother:*] Ask from Pavitra — He must have forgotten — I have told him the very same day to send a bottle to you.

Guru, not at all satisfied! nothing flashing!

Well, well, you are difficult to satisfy — It may not flash but it gleams all right.

Besides, you broke my power of judgment on yesterday's poem which I thought was a triumph!

Well, perhaps I shall consider it a triumph if I read it again after six months. I won't insist on Horace's rule that in order to judge poetry rightly that has been newly written, you must keep it in your desk unseen for ten years and then read it again and see what you then think of it!

I give you the lines which you have called "damn fine", Sir!
    "While the whole universe seems to be a cry
    To the apocalypt-vision of thy Name."

Mm, yes, I can't deny the fineness — but perhaps I ought not to have damned it without proper regard to Shakespeare.

I know your enthusiasm will abate now, and perhaps you will only say, "Yes, they are very satisfying!"

Why do you object to a poem being called satisfying? It is high praise.

SRI AUROBINDO   1183

> *Or you will say that yesterday's "damn fine" can't be equal*
> *to today's, what? I find your remarks exceedingly myster-*
> *ious, which justifies your being a "Mystery-Man"!*

Which remarks? On Shakespeare? They were logical, not mystic.

> *What about the poem I requested you to write? No head*
> *or tail?*

Which poem?

> November 11, 1938

> *"Which poem?" indeed! My poem I requested you to*
> *rewrite, Sir!*

Oh that! It is still in cold storage. No flame as yet for cooking it.

> *"I gain the summit of thy loneliness*
> *In whose vast spaces like an eagle I dwell*
> *And drink from thy Spirit-cup a measureless*
> *Delight, O Mystery inscrutable!"*
> —*I hope you won't say, "Drink like an eagle?"*

I am afraid I have to—an eagle drinking in vast spaces from a
cup is too extraordinary a phenomenon.

> *By the way, I am surprised to see that in spite of 3 mar-*
> *ginal lines over the whole poem, you call it only "very*
> *fine". Not a mysterious remark?*

How is it mysterious? What do you expect three lines to come to
then? Damn fine? That would be Shakespeare.

> *You seem to have told Doraiswamy that nobody has told*
> *you anything about Tripura. How is that? In yesterday's*
> *report there was her condition stated!*

[*Mother:*] I never said such a thing to Duraiswami. I simply asked
him how Tripura was *to-day.*

Venkatram and Nagin continue the soup. Is it necessary?

[*Mother:*] They might be asked if they still want it.

November 12, 1938

Guru, three poems in one day! What do you think of it?

Stupendous!

I am thinking of giving a little pāyas *to a few friends on the occasion of my birthday* [*17th November*]. *It will be done on Thursday and not Saturday at Anilkumar's place. But if you don't approve of the idea, I will gladly give it up.*

[*Mother:*] It is all right.

November 14, 1938

Guru, this is the 3rd poem I spoke of. I hope you will find it satisfying.

Quite.

But I fear "Beauty" is coming too much in my poems.

Perhaps it had better be suspended for a time.

Do you find something new in most of my recent poems?

Yes.

Or are they repetitions? The expressions and words are yet the same perhaps.

Well, many words and ideas appear frequently, but it does not give the impression of mere repetition.

If we prepare the Ayurvedic drug Sitopaladi *here, one pound will come to Rs. 2/8; whereas the patent rate is Rs. 1/8. So shall we buy?*

[*Mother:*] Yes.

SRI AUROBINDO   1185

*I had a talk with Ravindra about preparing Ayurvedic drugs
here. He asked me what were the drugs we required. I replied that we didn't require any particular ones, but we
now and then tried preparing some, following the directions
on the labels. Moreover we find that whatever Ayurvedic
drugs we indent, are contributed by somebody from Alembic. It is only when our stock gets exhausted in the middle of
the year, that we have to buy.*

*He says it is not worth while to prepare any drug less
than 10 pounds at a time, which is a huge quantity and runs
a risk of getting spoiled. So, I think, under the circumstances we have to give up the project.*

[*Mother:*] Yes.

November 15, 1938

*Guru, I wrote this poem today. It gave me such a damn
thrill that I thought I must share it with you tonight. Don't
you think the thrill is justified?*

The thrill but not the damn.

*It seems tomorrow's affair is going to be a regular feast.
But this is the last one.*

November 16, 1938

*Guru, Chand writes to me to ask your opinion on the "tamp-
ering with figures". Can there be any opinion? Really,
I don't know what to do with this fellow. But I suppose in
worldly life such things are necessary?*

Not in the worldly life, but perhaps in the Corporation life. All
this promises a bad look out when India gets purna Swaraj.
Mahatma Gandhi is having bad qualms about Congress corruption
already. What will it be when purna Satyagraha reigns all over
India?

November 17, 1938

1186 CORRESPONDENCE WITH

[*A note from the Mother:*]

Nirod   18-11-38.

Have no fear, it is not because of your feast that the pranam was stopped and I shall give you your interview to-morrow.

with love and blessings.

November 18, 1938

Guru, I am afraid nothing great is here; all old stuff and expressions rather poor.

I have changed the order of the last stanza's lines, making the first, part of the passion affair and not of the tranquillities. Also I have made slight changes everywhere. I rather fancy the resulting "stuff" — *not* poor, I think. I am inclined to give it three cheers, I mean three lines.

Dilipda asks me to inform you that K is a little sad to hear that he has to stay out. He is coming here for good.

Is he? Has he got permission for that? I thought it was only for darshan.

Is it not possible to give him a room? If not, would it be advisable to share mine with him till Mother can give him a room?

Mother has no separate room for him, but if Hiren Bandhu wants to share his room with K, that can be done. You have not to share your room with K.

November 19, 1938

"Creation born from his motionless delight . . ."
Motionless delight? Have you experienced it, Sir?

Of course. Why on earth shouldn't delight be motionless? What kind of delight should the immutable Brahman have, for instance, if not an immobile delight?

[*Dilip's telegram:*] *"Nirod Asram Pondicherry Arriving to-morrow evening train Heldil".*

SRI AUROBINDO   1187

> *Guru, this is from Dilipda — Heldil is not he, of course.*
> *But who is it then? Can your Supramental Intuition solve it?*
> *But mine has: it is H of Hashi, e of Esha, l of Lila, — Dil*
> *of course, you know. What do you think, Sir, of my Intuition?*
> *He perhaps thought he would beat us!*

I don't see how he could with the Dil there to illume the Hel.

> *Sanjiban has pain in the throat: tonsillitis and pharyn-*
> *gitis. I don't know if I should give him any gargle, as I*
> *understand you like to leave things more to Nature.*

[*Mother:*] In some cases gargles can be quite useful.

November 20, 1938

> *So Dilipda is coming tomorrow morning. . . I shall be ob-*
> *liged to minimise my contact with him as X will be there*
> *most of the time. Dilipda doesn't know perhaps that we*
> *have no connection at all; but of course he will know from*
> *others.*

Well, if he finds out from others, he ought to understand and if
he doesn't you can explain to him the situation.

November 21, 1938

> *Guru, I couldn't give much time today, as I was all the*
> *time thinking of finishing the poem, to catch your train!*
> *I hope it is not altogether a bad business, what? Most of it*
> *looks like repetition.*[1]

It may be repetition but is an exceedingly fine repetition. I was
going to say "damned" but Shakespeare only withdrew the expletive. Lines 4-6, also to a less degree lines 11-12 have an overhead accent in their substance and turn of expression. If you go on
like that, some day you may find yourself writing overhead poetry
without knowing it.

---

[1] "Primal Source", *Sun-Blossoms*, p. 99.

1188　　　　　　CORRESPONDENCE WITH SRI AUROBINDO

> *About yesterday's poem,[1] I dreamt that it was exceedingly fine — only a dream!*

But who said it wasn't?

> *I am sorry I don't understand where you get "lower and supreme consciousness" in yesterday's poem, nor how you make "magic bars separate" them. . .*

I don't get these things anywhere "in" the poem — naturally, because the poem is not a treatise on metaphysics or spiritual philosophy, but only a series of mystic images, but I get it "from" the poem. You asked what was the meaning and I gave you what I gathered from it or, if you like, what it would have meant if I had written it. But anyone can put another intellectual version to it, if he likes.

Bars usually divide something and as they can't very well be dividing the Spirit or supreme Being itself, it must be dividing the supreme from the lower, especially as you have shadow-spaces of sky immediately afterwards filling with transparent peace which can only come from the removal of the "lid" well-known to shut mind from what is beyond mind. Especially as there is an infinity of "thought", the sky must be the sky of mind and mind is part of the lower (non-supreme) consciousness. If that is not the meaning, I am damned if I know what the meaning can be — at any rate, if there is any other, it surpasses my capacity and range of spiritual or occult knowledge. As for the superconscient, the Supreme is the superconscient, so that there can be no doubt of that — the tranquil spirit's deep and the beatitude of sleep are not part of the ordinary consciousness but can only come in the superconscient or by the meeting of the superconscient and subconscient. You speak of Nature being a song of eternity which it can't be (its roots being in the subconscient) unless there is the meeting of the superconscient and subconscient — the latter being a part of the fathomless deep of the spirit. That meeting is effected through the subtle or inner planes and the inarticulate prayer can only be the aspiration that rises from inconscient and half-conscious Nature calling for the union. That's all.

November 22, 1938

[1] "Flames of Vision", *Sun-Blossoms*, p. 106.

Index

Complete Index to Volumes 1 and 2

Abyssinia, 564, 584, 595, 597, 604, 702
Achilles, 249
Action/Activity, 83-4, 132
and right spirit, 1108
as part of sadhana, 41
danger in every great attempt, 29, 94
fluctuating eternally, 683, 684
three sources of, 252
see also Works; Karma-yoga
Adhar Das, 341-3
Aeschylus, 355, 779, 780
Affection, human, see Love, human affection
Agarwal, R.S., 1065
Ahimsa,
killing mosquitoes etc., 339
truth of, 225-6, 230
Allopathy, see Homeopathy, and allopathy
Amal Kiran (K. D. Sethna), ·ix, 333, 402, 403, 453, 493-4, 507, 516, 895, 909, 911, 929, 930, 931, 944, 945, 970, 982, 991, 1070, 1071, 1102
America, 499, 789
Amrita, 920
Anacreon, 1070
Ananda, 98, 277, 482, 637, 774
Brahmananda, 793, 794, 795
Brahman's immutable delight, 1186
experience of, 36, 52, 53, 54, 71, 461, 560-1
and lower nature, 304
of existence, 279
source of all pleasures, 795
see also Happiness
Ananda [disciple of Buddha], 256

Anecdotes, incidents and illustrations,
Antigonus accepts death to save his son, 1061
ass into elephant, 133, 136, 137
a Tamilian and Nirod at the pier, 684
badger in its hole, 532
British Medical Council refusing validity to Sir Herbert Barker's cure, 427
chess: move in, 150; pawns in, 312
child of 9: Vice Chancellor, 454
chisel's pride in being used by sculptor, 363
cleaning nose with string and with water, 996
Communist in a Nazi concentration camp, 482, 756
dog pulling at his leash, 848
dried liver case, Mother's acquaintance, 1013
egg and hen, 308
"Go to the ant ...", 852
guidance: to Chandulal and Punjalal, 885; to General Miaja, 885-6
Guru Govind Singh and Pathan boy, xi
Japanese agriculturist, barren land, 147
labelling or dissecting a symbol, 763
Mahapurush with a woman for 3 years, 75
mountains in labour, 398
mulish sadhika, 317-8
murder of Muse, 399
Muslim fanatic, 349
Nazi mob in action, 311-2
open-air zoos, 323
opening up a man for

"Appendix", 434, 437
Parsi with debts, 8
Pavitra, Khitish and the bother, 920
reaching the top without Guide, 143
rejuvenation by monkey-glands, 191, 195
sadhika attacked by a ruffian, 45-6
saving life of a mosquito, 340
Simpson's discovery of chloroform, 314
sorting sheep from goats, 363
Sri Aurobindo's grandfather and cousin, 429, 695-6
Sri Aurobindo's uncle's daughter, 129
Sultan of Johore ... shot the wrong man, 565-6
Sun's rays of use to somebody, 172-3
system of lollipops, 543
unreal numbers in mathematics, 142
woman operated on for cancer, 346
Yuvarani's visit, 663
see also Medical matters, (5)
Anger, 216-7, 223, 227, 748
see also Work, loss of temper in
Anilbaran Roy (A. B.), 276-7, 279, 280-2, 353-4, 518, 1062, 1102, 1110
Animal(s), 1058, 1120
and man, 323
Bushy, Ashram cat, 448, 466
cats fighting, 960
monkey-glands, 191, 195
sacrifices of, 339-40, 349, 397
Antigonus of Macedon, 1061

Arjava (J. Chadwick), 684, 775, 983, 1175
Arjuna, xi, 171, 256, 479-80
Art, 208, 352, 666
  beauty and Ananda in, 774
  finest, appreciation of, 448, 778
  greatness of different branches of, 447-50
  highest, to conceal art, 1152
  taking up, with Mother's approval, 245
Artist(s), 23, 261, 284, 394-5, 512, 745-6, 775
Arya Publishing House, 296-7, 301-2, 312-3, 812, 859-60, 899fn
Arya [review], 77, 80, 86, 202, 369, 992
Ashram (Asram), Sri Aurobindo, 17, 481, 667, 887
  accommodation in, 15, 549, 550-1, 632-3, 634, 636, 1007-8, 1009, 1186
  and big people, xii, 285, 912, 1106-7, 1109-10
  and common sense in, 156-7
  and other Asrams, 348, 879, 1048
  artists of, 512
  atmosphere: a Force in, 307, 405, 750; and increase of numbers, 705; concentrated, 1048; disturbed, 210, 707; doubt and depression, 264, 271, 702, 705-6; gossip, 290; hostile forces, 221; hostile suggestions, 24; panic, 702, 704, 707, 708-9; peace, 653; rows, 602; sorrows, 263, 264-5; Sri Aurobindo's presence, 313; suggestion of ghost, 724; vital forces, 45; vital troubles, 212, 271
  cars, 1023
  chances & possibilities, 221
  changing people, 564-5
  complaint about eating at home, 670
  considerable ability and capacity in, 987
  cyclo-mania, 510, 556
  Darshan days, 20, 36, 55, 57, 58, 71, 134, 155, 156, 283, 289-90, 291, 315, 388-9, 499, 501, 502, 516-7, 660, 757-8, 759, 840, 984, 986, 1006-7; significance of 24th November, 293-5, 320
  death in, *see* Death, in Asram
  departures from (leaving, going out of), 14, 19-20, 26-7, 51, 90, 120, 122-3, 133, 222, 243-4, 269, 297-8, 299-301, 302, 463, 468, 517, 518, 521, 551, 591-3, 725-6, 727-8, 852, 911-4, 1106-7, 1128-30, 1132; Mahakali's intervention, 848; X's bigness, 1106; X's going out, 846-51, 856, 869, 1002
  Dining Room (Aroumé), 43, 285-7, 580-1, 669-70, 918, 921, 948, 1060, 1069, 1087-8, 1140
  Divine, not J, brought you here, 267-8
  Divine realisation in, 80, 234, 593, 879; experiences that are summit of old yogas, 750, 879; living in Brahman Consciousness, 987, 993
  doctors and faith, 705
  epitome of human nature, xii-xiii, 93, 1047
  establishing, at Pondicherry, 711
  false notions in, 899
  gate duty, 15, 17; talking, 1026
  growth of capacities (poetry etc.) in, 69, 369-70, 459, 468, 491, 515, 543, 596-7, 600, 661, 678, 850, 1106
  individual affairs, 408-11
  many descents in old days, 209
  object of, 1106
  organisation of, by the Mother, vol. 2, vi-vii
  patting rare, preaching more usual, 986
  people in, and outside, 455, 716-7, 899-900, 1047
  people pushing their way in, 122, 301, 551, 727, 1005
  pocket money, 124
  prestige of, 1105, 1108
  protection, conditional, 45-6
  sadhaks here, 74, 84, 92-3, 95, 139, 156, 157, 163, 189, 220, 221, 222, 233, 237-8, 267, 285, 287-8, 304, 348, 393, 401, 485, 541-2, 544-5, 611, 653, 704, 705, 740, 748, 879, 986-7, 1047, 1048,
  sex-force in, 1000, 1001-2, 1004, 1015
  Sri Aurobindo and the Mother and, target of public criticism, 985, 1049-50, 1108
  survives and grows, 912, 1107
  uprush of mud . . . promise of better things, 220
  view of a well-known atheist, 1049-50
  what a mad Asram!, 238
  why revelation of inner story, xii
  what a museum!, 1081
Aspiration, 31, 36, 48, 67, 73, 216, 217, 315, 346, 347, 479, 606, 628, 754, 823, 870, 902
  for poetry, 25, 47-8, 50, 62, 217, 641, 840, 841; demand on the source of poetry, 835, 836-7, 839, 841
  for Supermind, 215-6, 219-20
  nourishing, 72
  (prayer) for patient's cure, 121, 681
Atman, 81, 82, 276
Attachment, double, 730

1191 INDEX **Concentration**

Augustine, St., 347
Aurobindo Bose, 290
Aurobindo, Sri, *see* Sri Aurobindo
Avatar, 140-1, 151, 197, 739,
1117
can a Muthu, Tom or
Dick be changed into
an Avatar?, 140, 147,
148
death and failure of,
168-9, 170, 175, 229
finding fault with prede-
cessors, 223-4, 225
his example and huma-
nity, 135, 138-9, 148-50,
166-77, 351
sufferings and struggles
of, 165, 169, 174-5, 176,
177, 739
working of, 224, 226-7
see also Humour, (1); Sri
Aurobindo, (5)

Badoglio, Pietro, 607
Bahaullah, 126
Balzac, Honoré de, 50, 366
Bande Mataram [anthem],
487
Bankim Chandra Chatterji,
487
Barin (Barindra Kumar
Ghosh), 102-3, 374
Barker, Sir Herbert, 427
Baron, F., 829, 834, 836,
837, 838, 1097
Bates, Dr. W. H., 577
Baudelaire, Charles, 817,
818, 828, 829, 830
Baxter, Richard, 1146
B. Babu, 329, 985-6
Becharlal, Dr. (Dr. B), 103,
104, 125, 305, 306
Bedlam, 1038
Beecham, Sir Thomas, 448
Being,
better, getting a, 243
division in, 270, 614, 725
double, 97-8, 300
hypocrisy in, 725-6, 727-8
made of many parts, 650;
see also Nirodbaran,
(8): different parts of
true, will prevail, 614
see also Central being;

Psychic being; Surface
being
Bejoykrishna Goswami, 75,
218, 219
Benjamin, 556, 742
Bhakta, 530, 531
Bhakti, 80, 238
vital, emotional, 222-3
Bhishma [Pitamah], 349
Bible, 506
Bilwamangal, 347, 364
Binyon, Lawrence, 404, 505
Blake, William, 448, 631,
635, 636, 640, 763-4,
770, 776, 780, 801, 831
Body, 11-2, 431, 732, 884
and soul, 81, 488, 560,
739
exercise and weight, 578,
580
gross and subtle, and
chakras, 560-1
liberation from body-con-
sciousness, 81, 192-3
response of, to the Force,
181, 193, 200, 381, 385,
445, 613, 620, 881, 1054
Brahmacharya, 391-2
Brahman consciousness, 987,
991-2, 993
living in, necessary con-
dition for supramental
descent, 992
Brunton, Paul, 483, 557, 673
Buddha, 107, 114, 115, 117,
152, 167, 169, 172, 173,
218, 219, 256, 334, 343,
575, 576, 738-9, 859,
1049
action on disciples, 335
Christ and, 235-6
death of, 169, 229, 738-9
denial of God, 224, 229
doctrine of Ahimsa, 225-
6, 229, 230
Ramakrishna and, 224,
235
Buddhist sadhana, 229, 311,
334-5
Buddhist teaching, 226, 979-
80
Byron, Lord George, 280,
1146

Calm, 11, 36, 750, 754-6

like a Daniel, 852
see also Peace; Silence
Catullus, Gaius Valerius, 779
Central being, 303
adventure of, 277
and harmonisation, 97,
650, 651
getting into touch with,
652
Centres (chakras), 560
Chaitanya, 170, 172, 218,
219, 256, 343
Champaklal, 228-9
Chamberlain, Neville, 1157
Chand (C), 53, 75, 289, 291,
307, 308, 524-5, 540,
541, 590, 806, 838, 866-
7, 890, 898, 900-1, 904,
983, 989-90, 996, 1037,
1042, 1051, 1057, 1058,
1063, 1068, 1080-1,
1118, 1121, 1154-5,
1157, 1162, 1185
Chandulal Shah, 87, 121
Change, 644, 726, 1105,
1106, 1108-9
of hostile mind, 16
of humanity, 303, 564-5
outward, 745, 750; *see
also* Nature, human,
change of
see also Supramental
change
Charles IX (of France), 1039
Charu, 1087
Chaucer, Geoffrey, 498
Cheerfulness, 33, 68, 110,
605, 618, 754, 756, 923;
gladness, 523
Children,
infant mortality in India,
884
purgative to, 875, 883-4,
892
with rare gift, and elders,
599-600
Christ, 137, 152, 165, 167,
172, 173, 234, 235, 236,
576, 843, 914, 1047
Coincidence, 147, 313, 1059
Columbus, Christopher, 143
Compassion, 226, 229, 334
Concentration, 11, 40, 459
and work, 78, 79, 80
before sleep and after
rising, 8-9

Concentration   INDEX   1192

on the Divine, 679, 872,
873
packed . . . striped, 607
see also Meditation
Confidence (self-confidence),
33
doctors' success and, 361,
384, 420, 421, 422, 426,
428, 433, 570, 824, 825,
894, 1065
Confucius, 575, 576
Consciousness, 3, 991
a concrete thing, 1063
environmental, 252
fall of, and remedy, 37
gets cut up into two, 227
growth of, and opening
of capacities, 204
intuitivising the opera-
tions of, 1067
social, 301, 302
supramental change of, is
vital, 704
see also Dream-consciousness; Inner conscious-
ness; Physical consci-
ousness; Surface con-
sciousness
Conrad, Joseph, 505, 506,
508
Coué, Emile, 1053-4
Courage, 168, 684, 685, 708
Cousins, James, 746, 749,
1146
Cowardice, 92, 684-5, 687
Cowper, William, 1146
Creation, *see* Manifestation
Criticism, 1065
(dispute) and lecture, 846,
964
literary, 214, 240, 404,
492, 745-6, 809-10,
1147-8
of others (*paranindā*),
cause of, 233-4
of the Mother, 234, 411,
733, 1088, 1090, 1108
public, 216-7, 1108, 1118,
1122
see also Sri Aurobindo,
(5): criticism against
C. V. Raman, 313, 314

Dante Alighiori, 926, 1046
Danton, G., 186
Datta (Dorothy Hodgson),
294, 295, 373, 374
Death, 168-9, 248, 812, 1061
conquest of, 189, 193-4,
702-4, 712-3
immunity from, 194-5
in the Asram, 188-9, 697,
702-3, 1027
recession of, 189
those who died had to
die, 1027
warding off, 694, 712, 713
see also Vital, the, becoming ghost, after death
De la Mare, Walter, 404,
505
Depression,
and despair, remedies for,
17, 47, 71, 156, 185,
231, 232, 243, 338,
376-7, 390, 399, 573,
605, 649, 854, 984-5
and opposite forces, 533
and T. B., 698-9
contagious, 6, 7, 264
opening to nightmares, 23
see also Despair; Dilip,
depression; Man of
Sorrows; Nirodbaran,
(2)
Descartes, René, 307
Descent (of Light, Power,
etc.), 36, 98, 104, 129,
210, 660, 700, 902
all "lacks" will be re-
moved by, 678
and dark Force, 720
and fear, 718, 719, 721,
728, 734; *see also* Ex-
perience(s), and fear
and illness, 718, 720-1
and sex, 555; *see also*
Supramental descent,
and sex-force
and uprush of subcon-
scient mud, 220, 221,
242, 246, 265, 287-8,
389, 502
"blocky" feeling in, 647,
651; feeling it like rain
or fall of snow, 533,
555
determining causes of, 36

giving peace in cells, even
if body ill, 752-3
horizontal, 700
see also Experience(s), of
descent of Power; Su-
pramental descent
Despair, 45, 75, 176
and suicide, 53, 265, 748,
749
doesn't help, 215, 870
remorse useless, 399
shake off the hump, 232,
461
wailing, 94, 943, 975
worrying no good,
215
see also Depression; Nirodbaran, (3)
Destiny, *see* Fate
Detachment, 47, 59, 606,
646, 657-8
Devil, 154-5, 172, 680
Dharma, 226, 570
Diana, 107
Dickens, Charles, 50, 156,
366, 681, 682
Difficulties, *see* Yoga, and
difficulties; Life, mis-
fortunes in
Dilip Kumar Roy (D), 69,
73, 290, 504, 514, 515,
517, 580, 618, 640, 667,
689, 728, 770, 829, 831,
954, 985, 1048, 1049,
1054, 1062, 1100, 1104,
1118, 1119, 1180
depression, 156, 510, 516-
7, 623, 660, 721, 749
Man of Sorrows, 649, 656
hyper-sensitive, 526, 746-
7, 1047
Mother's remarks about,
546
Tagore's description of,
369, 661
see also Nirodbaran, (3):
affiliation and differ-
ences with Dilip; Niro-
dbaran, (7): and Dilip;
Poetry, (1): Dilip's
Disease, *see* Medical matters, (3)
Dissatisfaction,
twisting round one's own,
790

1193   INDEX   **Effort, personal**

see also Nirodbaran,(3): about . . .

Divine, the (God etc.), 49, 267-8, 564, 739, 1117, 1151

and old vital moorings, 278, 622

"As people approach me", 545

bears the world-burden, 175, 176; endures burden of human nature, 169

coming down of, 138-9, 169

concentration on, 679, 872, 873

(divinity) in man, 173-4, 175, 176-7

does not recede, 32

D's treatment of, 517, 602; X's treatment of, 593-4, 964, 1002

establishing possibilities of, 303

fit instrument of, 219; *see also* Force, instrumentation

for the Divine's sake, 344

Impersonal, 229, 477

leads us through sorrow and suffering, 276-7

love for, *see* Love

not many, 477, 479

particular about contagion, 540-1

prayer for, 822

protection of, 532; *see also* Ashram, protection . . . ; Sadhana, and hostile forces . . .

rasa of, 72

response of: to aspiration, 479; to prayers, 73, 542, 545

seeing, everywhere, 872

seeking, 33, 65-6, 92, 231, 344, 528, 529-31, 964

separation of soul from, 333

smiles equally on all, 551

success and failure of, 137; *see also* Divine omnipotence, and conditions . . .

soul's turning towards, 303, 454

turning one's back on (kicking), 28, 465, 468, 532, 728

understanding the working of, 269-70, 277, 312, 675, 680, 886, 897

see also Doubt, in the Divine

Divine action,

and sadhak's surface consciousness, 275

method of, 128-9, 337-8

Divine Force, *see* Force, the

Divine Grace (Grace), 468

action of, 118, 119, 142, 147

defects and, 53; *see also* Yoga, and fitness . . .

effort and, 459, 460, 461, 465-8, 469, 471

necessity of aspiring to get, 48; *see also* Divine Presence, necessity to...

soul and, xiv-xv, 461, 465, 580

state of, 48, 465

see also Doubt, in the Divine or Grace

Divine Love,

bearing the pressure of, 209

universal and a special relation, 256-7, 258-9

Divine omnipotence, 27, 29, 896

and conditions of the game, 109, 128-9, 131, 133, 136-8, 140, 141-2, 146, 602, 768

and latency theory, 145-8, 151-4

"He makes the dumb talk", 147

Muthu into an Avatar, 136, 139, 140, 141, 142, 146-7, 150

Divine Power, *see* Descent (of Light, Power, etc.); Force, the

Divine Presence, 316

experience of, 53, 81, 870-3

necessity to concentrate

and call the, 872; *see also* Divine Grace, necessity of

Divine realisation (Realisation), 86, 217-8, 455

and a liar, 1109

and supramental realisation, 215-6

complete, Gandhi and Sri Aurobindo on, 624

through love or through knowledge, 235-7, 239-41

through work, 77-80, 84-6

yoga realisation, 132

see also Ashram, Divine realisation in; Realisation

Doctor(s), *see* Medical matters, (2)

Donne, John, 938, 1050, 1147, 1177, 1178

Doraiswamy, S., 1105, 1109, 1110

Doubt, 33, 176, 333, 639, 707, 750, 752, 872

in the Divine or Grace, doing everything, 457, 458, 459, 465-6

see also Nirodbaran, (8): doubt

Dreams, 248, 686, 1005

discrimination in, 244

on vital plane, 13-4, 48-9, 54, 63, 163, 163-4, 264, 368, 481, 640, 663, 760, 772, 828, 832, 1138

see also Nirodbaran, (4)

Dream-consciousness, 829, 831-2, 838

D. S. (Esculape), 90, 93-4, 99, 104, 108, 122, 193

see also Medical matters, (5): D. S. (Esculape)

Durga, 66, 229, 299

and Asuras, 226

Duryodhan, 137

Effort, personal, 47, 542

and reliance; 64, 65-6, 67, 215, 269, 458-9, 461

and use of will, 42, 651, 659, 1129

Effort, personal

INDEX

1194

Divine Grace and, 459, 460, 461, 465-8, 469, 471
Force and, 370-1, 512-6, 611-2, 659, 776, 867
Herculean, 459, 460, 466, 467, 513, 604
in Buddhism, 229, 334, 335
liking not enough, get the thing done, 316
place of, in poetry, 774; *see also* Inspiration, waiting for, and effort; Poetry, (1): place of ...
sadhana and, 243, 522, 651, 865
without demand of result, 522

Ego, 341, 514
clash of, 408-11
effacement of, 85, 339, 406, 594
exaggerated, 440-1
Intuition and, 358, 363, 364
of bigness, 123, 330-1, 332, 337, 364, 384-5, 724, 746, 861
of instrument, 363
poetry and, 405, 407, 865, 867
rajasic and tamasic, 332, 461
sadhana and, 28, 85, 258, 304, 344, 411, 465, 468, 519, 520, 605, 858, 860, 1089, 1126

Egypt, 673-4

Eliot, T. S., 507

Einstein, Albert, 205, 287, 993

English language, 161, 405

Englishmen,
and language, 507

Essays on the Gita, 151, 340

Europe, 187, 198, 323, 437, 446, 596, 653, 914, 949-50

Evolution, 348, 392
earthly, 139, 148, 624-5
psychic being and, 140, 308-9, 311, 329, 333

Experience(s), spiritual, 123, 183, 514, 724-5

and fear, 11, 735, 736-7; *see also* Descent
and Herculean labour, 460
and married life, 476
and over-reading, 52-3
and significance, 760
and stillness (*stabdhatā*), 67-8, 603, 655, 735-6
and subtle body, 561, 760
and widening, 69, 97, 503
belittling, 23, 53, 66-7; doubt about, 872
complaints about, 458, 503, 594, 601-2, 879, 956
conditions for gaining, 755
feeling in, *see* Descent, "blocky" feeling ...
gets shut off, 71, 461, 603, 878-9
in intermediate zone, 90, 519-20
in meditation, 67, 81, 91, 104
judging, from description, 719, 721
let it grow, 872-3
like gold crown on pig's head, 677-8
love for the Divine before, 528, 529-31
mystical, 793, 794
of Ananda, 36, 52, 53, 54, 71, 461, 560-1
of ascent to Infinite and descent to Muladhar, 750
of cosmic Force ... feeling of being clutched by the Divine, 455
of descent of Power, 555; *see also* Descent
of divided mind, 72-3
of going inside, 91, 104, 725
of liberation, 73, 81, 192-3
of peace, 23, 52-3, 601
of people outside and of Asramites, 455
of pervading Presence, 53, 81, 870-3
of rays trying to pierce the brow, 261

of samadhi, 104, 735-6
of Self, 367-8, 530, 560
of silence, 72, 81
of warm touch on forehead, 390-1
reason for not coming, 72, 603, 755
relief of pressure by ..., 104, 871
settling of, 74, 205-6, 503-4
speaking of, 324, 878-9, 898
Sri Aurobindo's visit, 82
subjective sense of, 872
testing the, 81
trickle of, 460, 461
versus more important things, 22, 289
willed by the Divine, 49
see also Sri Aurobindo, (1): experiences

Faith (belief), 137, 158, 177, 460, 508, 530, 652, 705, 755, 851, 870
and difficulties, 33, 278
and sadhana, 33, 208, 323-4, 459, 572, 625, 912, 1101
in the Force, 428, 429, 431, 572, 612
living, and death, 703, 713
of doctor, 121, 422, 426, 428, 431
of patient, 345-6, 385, 431, 707, 1125

Falstaff, 500, 671

Fame, 25, 70, 217, 224, 483, 646, 1107

Fate (destiny, luck), 432, 581, 674-5, 733

Fear, 34, 213, 685, 737, 738, 775, 999
and anger at the same time, 960
and illness, 619, 738, 951
call the Mother in, 736
descent and, 718, 719, 721, 728, 734
experiences and, 11, 735, 736-7
in concentration, 11

1195 INDEX **Free will**

in dreams, 13-4, 54
Flowers, *see* Mother, the,
flowers given by
Food (diet), 34, 91, 272-3,
431, 565, 648, 672, 800,
977, 1003, 1093
and sadhana, 18, 37-8,
53-4, 54-5, 58, 76-7,
108-9, 204, 274-5, 538,
859, 729-30
and whim, 627, 628
coconut, green, 957
curry 884; pot-au-feu,
791-2, 796
eggs, 523-4, 613
Indian "moon" supersti-
tion, 360, 361
Indians and Europeans,
796
onions, 1010-1
pān-supāri, 785-6
soup, 124, 617-8, 627,
1024, 1025, 1091, 1134
tea and sadhana, 6-7, 16,
18, 33, 34, 37, 58, 59-
60, 62, 162, 163, 213-4,
227-8, 302, 710, 878
see also Medical matters,
(8): Mother's and Sri
Aurobindo's care . . .
Force, the (Divine or spiritual Force), 129, 315, 316,
579, 580, 884
action of, 36, 128-9, 130,
131, 132, 306, 337-8,
372, 480, 626, 639-40,
673, 750, 755, 894-8,
957-8; and exact know-
ledge of circumstances,
182, 626; behind the
veil, 647, 648, 753; on
the subconscient, 1048;
without physical con-
tact, 478
and departures from the
Ashram, 856, 913
and harmonisation, 199,
201
and intuition, 907
and Knowledge, 645
and knowledge of its
working, 886, 894, 897;
see also Divine, the,
understanding the
working of

and personal effort, 370-1,
512-6, 611-2, 659, 776,
867
and Supramental Force,
713-4
and Supramental Nature,
192
application of, its efficacy
and success, 596, 906-7
applying, in work, 87,
99-100
bringing down, 99-100,
678, 680-1
calling for, and being
heard, 508-9, 595, 617,
678, 679, 681, 1040,
1170, 1179; *see also*
Mother, the, calling;
Work, calling in . . .
canalisation of, 673, 677,
679
communication of, 596,
896-8
contact with, 475-6, 478,
480, 595-6, 662
cure by, (or Sri Auro-
bindo's Force), xiii-xiv,
67, 118, 119, 120, 122,
128, 157, 181, 182, 183,
211-2, 249, 284, 345-6,
380-1, 385-6, 422-3,
443, 445, 481, 520, 524,
613, 615, 617, 618, 619,
714, 724, 731, 737, 760,
853, 874-5, 973, 975,
1094; and body's re-
sponse, 181, 193, 200,
381, 385, 445, 613, 620,
881, 1054; and critical
antagonism, 510, 701;
and illness of skin, hair,
etc., 999; and infants,
880-1; and need of ac-
curate report, 200, 379,
382; and need of diag-
nosis, doctors and
medicines, 120-1, 182,
200-1, 384, 385, 420,
438, 440, 647; and
opening, 345, 1014;
and receptivity, 67, 119,
881; and resistance of
the subconscient, 1053;
and right or wrong
medicine, 187, 384, 385,

422, 645; prevents the
working of, 812, 1014;
three ways of, 200-1;
through symptoms,
200, 420, 425, 436, 737;
see also Medical mat-
ters, (3): cure of . . .
descent of, *see* Descent
Divine, and Yogic-Force,
129, 132
faith in, *see* Faith
general operation of, 130,
133-4, 896-8
in Asram atmosphere,
307, 405, 750
instrumentation (medi-
umship), 121, 128, 129,
260, 261, 337, 419, 421,
436; rajasic man, 568-
9; sattwic man, 571; re-
quisites and defects of
a medium, 429-30, 897
intervention of, 129, 524;
see also Mahakali
joy of being used by, 44
not miraculous, 128, 337;
see also under Divine
omnipotence
pulling down, 208, 701,
718, 720, 724, 726
wrong Force, 906
see also Sri Aurobindo,
(3): application of his
Force...; Supramental
Force; Yoga-Force
Forces,
and germs, 738
and suggestions, 24, 30,
724, 734
opposing, 906
play of, 121, 252, 268,
269, 270, 300, 306, 312,
313-4, 315, 317, 329-30,
334, 532, 698, 733, 906
ready to answer a call, 520
see also Hostile force(s)
Francis of Assisi, St., 173
Frankenstein, 298
Freedom,
individual, xiv, 325, 327,
409, 912
of India, 323, 325, 327,
329-30, 340-1, 1185
Free will (will), 28, 269, 270,
298, 300

French language   INDEX   1196

French language, 777, 778, 780, 781
Freud, Sigmund, 247
Friendship, 267, 615, 963

Gandhi, Mahatma, 177, 624
  Gandhian resistance, 228, 243, 532
  qualms about Congress corruption, 1185
Genius, *see* Literary activity, geniuses
Gita [Srimad Bhagavad Gita], 256, 289, 807
Gods, 162, 299, 447-8, 565, 874, 1003, 1157
Goldsmith, Oliver, 405
Gosse, Edmond, 505, 506
Gossip, 233, 290
Govinda Das, 1141, 1150, 1151
Govind Singh, Guru, xi
Grace, *see* Divine Grace
Gratitude, 267, 374
Gray, Thomas, 779
Greatness (bigness),
  and morality, 817
  and spirituality, 171, 176, 224, 344, 1107, 1111
  extraordinary powers and sincere heart, 301
  question of, 141, 143, 312, 748, 779
  see also Ego, of bigness

Hafez Shirazi, 1071
Happiness, 289, 290, 523, 750, 754
  and sorrow in life, 279-80
  motive power in life, 482-4, 486
  the vast is the, 637
Harin (Harindranath Chatterji), 70, 404, 491, 839, 971, 982, 1076, 1079
Hathayogic processes, 996
Henry IV (of France), 685, 688
Heredity, 169, 203, 251, 253
Higgins, Captain John, 143
Hirendranath Dutt, 793-4

Hitler, Adolf, 210, 222, 508, 518, 553, 1156-7
Holmes, Sherlock, 536
Homeopathy, 586-7, 695, 696, 1014
  and allopathy, 360-1, 383, 420, 423-8, 433-40
Homer, 885, 926, 929, 965-6, 970, 988, 1147
Hopkins, Gerard Manley, 779, 1037, 1038, 1172
Horace, 252, 662, 1182
Hostile force(s), 60, 112, 161, 324, 533, 675, 700, 736, 906, 911
  and departures from Ashram, 913, 1129
  and lower nature, 27-8
  awareness of, 532-3
  calling back, 28, 732
  hostile suggestions, 24, 30, 724, 733-4
  marks of, 28
  opening to, 203, 221
  "out of date", 221
  possession by, 203, 732, 1129
  see also Sadhana, and hostile force(s)
Housman, A. E., 449, 491, 631, 763-4, 775, 781-2, 830, 833, 836, 1097
Hugo, Victor, 50
Hukumchand, 368
Human affection, *see* Love, human affection
Human nature, *see* Nature, human
Human relation, 276
  see also Sadhana, relationship in
Humour, Sri Aurobindo's,
  (1) **Avatar:**
  feeding on germs, 540-1
  getting frightened, 197
  irrational answers, 165, 177-8
  Rolls Royce machine, 149
  typescript, hibernating, 180, 184, 242, 243, 525, 715
  (2) **Medical:**
  abduction of a joint, 579
  Achilles' heel, 249
  Allah is great, 826

Anglo-Indians, peg, 786-7
Artful Dodger, 1011
bare clothing, 354
"beaten" by a rat, 664
bottle to keep baby quiet, 1003
chart of fever temperature, 535-7, 555, 557
cod-liver oil: divine nectar, 676
counter-smoking injection, 258
cow dung handy, 157
dispensary to devil, 122
doctors: address in heaven, 378; angels!, 581; hit or miss, 119; human motorcars, 677; ill, 1170; throwing stones at a dog, 355
Durvasa, 456
eye-cases, optical illusion, 180
fallen stomach, angel, 990
"God moves in a mysterious way", 179
God's Force, Codein Phos!, 524
Golden Age: doctors— pooh!, 598
guinea-pig, luck for, 282, 284, 390
Hail, Reason, holy Light!, 186
hard to satisfy these people, 1007
injections into fountain-pens, 993-4
ladies wanting quick service, 799-800
medicine like Brahman, 185
Meibomian cyst, 182-3, 183-4
modern Mithridates!, 158, 160
Mother occupying the stomach, 710, 714
nothing without a cause, 908
"O apples, apples", 1163
Pancrinol, 714
patients' surrealist poetry, 847
phimosis, 473, 488

1197   INDEX   **Humour, Sri Aurobindo's, (3)**

physician-priest, 112
Prasanna, aprasanna...
   dharna, 393
Rajangam kicking down
   Dispensary, 518
recommending smoke
   and wine?, 302
sending Asram to next
   world, 887, 892-3
servant asserting sovietic
   equality, 368
supramental and swelled
   things, 690
supramental hospital, 711
tablet of aspirin and as-
   piration, 307
thinking with fat, 163
tympanum-piercing howl,
   874-5
weeping machine, 443
"whites", 246

(3) Nirod:
Aeschylean expressions,
   354-5, 386, 539, 550,
   573, 866: aphoristic
   style, 855; Delphic oracles, 297; mysterious
   language, 196, 211, 355,
   366, 538, 561, 562, 572,
   573; Tacitean writer,
   550, 973, 1012
"almost" for accuracy's
   sake, 232
and Nishikanta, 292, 401,
   440, 620-1
Asram doctor going mad,
   209
Avatar!, 168
avoided railway train, 91,
   94
being: solid?, 228
blockhead, 647
boil, 327, 553-4, 556, 562,
   563, 668, 669, 686, 690,
   760, 761, 983, 989, 993,
   994
born supramental, 366
bourgeois mind, 142
break your head, 311;
   broken head, 756, 1144
bullying Sri Aurobindo,
   979
butter and milk-tea, 162,
   163
"By the Guru", 757-8

candid baby, 502
"Cast your bread...", 372
cease to Hamletise, 396
centenary of arrival, 37
chubby cherub, 297, 298
circle M. V. Ph., handle
   sticky, 336
coagulate, 469
conscious ass, 390
correspondence: a Maha-
   bharat, 854-5, 867-8
critic, easiest, 214; logician, not easy, 194
Dance of Harmony!, 374
"De l'audace, ...", 186
deserve only a cane, 359
Dhanwantari overnight,
   205
diagnosis, Paradise, 973,
   974-5
don't blow up Asram, 655
don't tear your hair, 549,
   550, 947
easy the descent to Hell,
   155
English poetry such, what
   of Bengali?, 262
Falstaff-like, 671
Fascist Yogi, 359
father confessor to God,
   1148
forsake never, beat a lot,
   151, 154
Gandhilike logician, 862
gigantic forehead, 328
golden age: 32nd year,
   373
Hail, Rishi: past lives, 466
hair-raising proposal, 214
handwriting, 246, 355,
   725, 751, 801
Homer etc. not a patch on
   you, 953-4
ignorance no defence,
   145, 298
Iliad or Nirodiad, 398
"infinity-shod", 1152
"jack-in-the-boxing",
   503-4
Jivanmukta, no need of
   prayer, 545
kicked along, 269, 285-6
laugh and grow fat, Niro-
   dian jollity, 156
letters in meditation, 161

licking the lips, 802, 803
low current: dynamo, 315
Madam Doubt, 423
Mahomed perhaps will
   help?, 268
mantra: OM Tut tut,
   554, 558, 562, 563, 572,
   766
many ingredients, 228,
   582
medical explanation of
   experience, 91
medical profession, use of
   Rs. 20 000, 99, 121
merciless whipping, 762
mess of explanation, 164
Micawber, 355
mighty hero at the pier,
   684
misfortunes, 881-2
modest poet, 548, 549
mosquitos, Manubhai's
   mercy, 676
mules useful animals, 607
naïve about women,
   1119-20
neighbour of the Divine,
   109, 545
Nirvana, 579
obligatory pursuits, 390
O favoured unapprecia-
   tive, 317
O happy blindness, 212
Old Man of the Sea, 531,
   533
O logical baby, 294
O Nirod of little faith,
   318
other cats to whip, 469
"overnight", 328
Peace, fiery furious spirit,
   141
"peace" like a summer
   dove, 210
persiflage, 143-4
perspiring idiot, 1064,
   1066
petition to Inspiration,
   805, 807, 808
photo, 328, 376, 442, 667
photo's treatment, 561,
   562
pity for "browning", 412
poor Nirod, 92, 96, 442
"Portrait of Nirod", 449

Humour, Sri Aurobindo's, (3)

prescription, 156, 231, 573, 937
private "goāk", 212
profitless debate in your stomach, 399
pulverised, 799
pummelled, 620-1
queer card, 999
read Mark Twain, 701
reading *The Life Divine*, 354-5
say nothing, will sound less foolish, 467
secret sin: *khichuri*, 330, 331
shipwreck in a teacup, 376
sky's my book, 212
smelling salts, 126
smell of lime, 539
spare the poor people's eyes, 337
spelling mistakes, 198, 241, 359, 450, 664, 740, 775, 781-2, 928, 1034, 1051
stupendous financial pressure, 232
supramental species, go forward, 342
surrealist poetry, too much for owls, 827
swan tumbling into dream of medicine, 910
swearing at, 905, 1166
sword at your serivce, 239, 867-8
system of lollipops, 543
Talukdar, 355, 414, 415
timber throne, 98
tummy and baldness, 998-9
Tut, tut, *see above* mantra: Om Tut tut
"walnut" shell, 161
wealth in fisheries, 1045
weight, 578, 580
we weep before and after, 578
whipping boy, 152
why bother about being anything?, 214
word-punctures, 102, 103, 154
W. P. B., 834
you are Brahman, 478, 991

your tail, 321
(4) Poetry:
alchemist taking opium, 346
Baron plexus, 837-8
bird with sails, 1103
bones safe, 1012
broadcaster's announcement, 1067
calm, slam, Imam, 1067; dawn, Bernard Shawn, 1040
carte blanche, 574, 575
champagne bottle, 202
"Clamo, clamavi", 777
clouded soul, 758
condensed milk, 932
Congress prohibition law, 1156
constipation, 262
constitutional stroll, 1064
constructions ... dancing-hall, 819
coupletitis, 904, 906
crown of fruits, 1150
damn fine, tremendous superlative, 1180, 1181, 1182, 1183, 1187
Dara's style, 127, 354
defect in solar plexus, 1045, 1147, 1149
doggerels, 359, 541, 554; *see also* Sri Aurobindo, (2): doggerels
Donne doffed, 1050
don't understand: instand, overstand, 836
dots too much meaning, 1050
dragged out by hair, 255
"Drunken shadows"!!, 1156
every poet a fool, 884
explain the inexplicable ... Christ, 843
fish: gleaming, 835; gold, 1044-5; pentametric, 574; sprat, 967, 1045
fisheries, 1045
flu and headache, 1167-8, 1170
forceps, 245, 254, 255, 263, 286
funniness in, 842-3, 844
Goddesses teasing tails, 356, 357

gulp the whole whale, 305, 306-7
hairs of tail need combing, 1142
illegitimate children, 414
metre: horror for a prosodist, 759; Hitlerian violences to, 552, 761
miraculous run-down store, 1010
misstressing "intestine", 453; "transparent", 497-8
moon's songs toffee, 978, 980
Nature apparelled with a poise, 1036
new soporific, 581
100 million poets writing away, 542
original, aboriginal, co-original, 609
overheadache, 1168
pangs of delivery, 52, 245, 254
parent of irregular menses, 666, 667-8
poem trans-mogrified, 1104-5
poet like a peacock, 954
poets queer cattle, 787
posterity, reaction of, 801-2
refrain, 662
remarks on poems, 809-10, 845, 916-7; "grood", 809
"sea-shells she sells", 924
Shakespeare into shade, 398; spear shake, 490
sing with feet, 1043
sitting behind pardah, 680
sleeve empty, 691
soul's verandah, 1050
"Starry stumps" of Infinity, 1160, 1161
tankful of bank notes!, 1119
weary cat, 972
(5) Sadhana:
advanced sadhaks, 332
ālubhājā and platonic love, 472
ass's bridge, 326, 328
big steamer throwing a yacht, 470

1199 INDEX **Humour, Sri Aurobindo's, (6)**

burst on fell day, 655
calling, not opening, 678, 681
catching head or tail, 681
crying for progress, 26, 644
departures like Japhet, 591-2
devolution, 309
disjointed machines in the lumber-shed, 149
dogs of depression bark, 444; menagerie, 445
Epstein's statues, 315
fall from Purushottama heights, 700, 701
Govt. post, 92
Grand'mère Depression, 609-10
hunting for shaktis, 117
Hurrah for the Himalayas!, 78
kerosene stoves, 852
knocks and shocks, 285
"let us be married", 503-4
Mahomedan with tuft, 755
Maya and fit of the blues, 273
middle Narayan oil, 139, 140, 141
Namo Namo Dilipaya, 515
never to the fruits thereof, 572
not a place to graze in, 266
out of joint, 423
quickening the descent of Supermind, 222
sadhaks: happy-go-lucky, 544; lazy lot the Supramentals, 213; rose-leaf princess, 879; superrational men, 230-1; what delicate people, 740
seeking for safety, 91, 92, 94
seven tails, 321, 322
soul's fun in mud, 305, 311
spiritual culinary joy, 729-30
spree, 919; trip to the Himalayas, 1081
"stand and wait", 319
Supramental ass, 996; in

50 days, 319
supramental police, 197
3 ways of meeting the collision, 607
trials of God-seekers, 231
Yudhishthir's dog, 95
(6) Sri Aurobindo:
"Above" lives opposite, 545
Ahimsuk!, 103
all is well, if it ends well, 604
am I Matter?, 194, 320
and Mother: isolate in the Himalayas, 222; release into beatitude, 594-5; take tickets, 515
"Avataric" sadhana, 151
beast of burden, 905
Beauty's acquaintance, 1025
bewildered by your surrealist prose, 866
biographer's knowledge of, 79; impeccable biography, 101
blessings without garland, 653
calling Sri Aurobindo to bow down, 700
chary of remarks, 590
come down into Erebus?, 156
comfort rare, 1052
cryptic because becoming supramental, 660, 663-4, 665
curvilinear position: fell flat, 597-8
debate with Chellu, 511
Delphic oracles, my monopoly, 297
dharma pāgal, 575
dilate . . . delectations, 452
Expatiate, excavate, 715
father, 123, 126
floating on infinite plasticities, 141
fool being myself, eh?, 167, 173; imbecile, 168, 171
gone off to x loka?, 126
gone out of mind, 247
"Grand First Supramental", 179-80

groan in unAurobindian despair, 156
handwriting, 81, 86-7, 241-2, 246, 247, 538-9, 549, 572, 669, 689, 711, 714-5, 725, 729-30, 783, 788, 803, 855, 860, 868, 953, 1104-5, 1177
hats off, 507
head for Pacific Ocean, 622-3
imitating doctors, 210, 906
insinuate impurity, 211
Joycean neologisms, 463; apo-diaskeptic, 210
mathematics: sleep, 400
menu, pudding and mutton-pie, 541
millions of admirers, 541
modern-minded disciples, kismet!, 859
mukti, 184
my devils: expletive, 155; "why the hell": ejaculation, 1004, 1005
no pumping business for me, 553
off the list of candidates for this Yoga, 231
"overnight": inability to grasp, 328
pineal gland, 559
plague of Prasads, 525
poor in selves?, 808
promise: fulfilment of in 1997, 525; stands, 678
pure and simple, 480
quasi-Greek, 1007
respected person, more than 2 feet, 556
samata, 717, 809
shorthand, 336
stood but not delivered, 295
stylish portfolio, 180
subconscient, my King Charles's head, 254
teaified cells, 228
"Time and I both are shy", 715
verse on correspondence, 126-7
vise and revise, not previse, 722
! ! ! ! ! ! !, 101

Humour, Sri Aurobindo's, (7)   INDEX   **1200**

(7) General:
adhyāropa, 123, 731, 1061
"All animals follow their nature", 1058
all animals in man, 1120
animals and Supermen, 323
baptism of S, 563
"big" balloon with gas, 1107
"Blessed be they . . . ", 234
clout on the head, 824-5
common sense uncommon, 157
dictates of masses, 1050
Divine hungry: goat-chop, 339
ejaculations and swear-words, x, 94, 155, 164, 197, 246, 302, 388, 401, 468, 474, 531, 539, 545, 578, 579, 662, 700, 713, 857, 967, 968, 980, 991, 1004, 1005, 1156, 1180; Donner-wetter! Tausend Teufel, 85; Great Jumble-Mumble, 367; Great Muggins, man, 164; Jehoshaphat, 322; Shobhanallah, 139, 973
élites swarming, 860
embarking for Mecca, 1118
Englishman's right to grumble, 947
erratic genius, 838
everything done, useful, 307-8
feast and *bali*, 206
Gandhi's "spotless white khaddar", 1122
glory be to English language!, 161
Glory to human reason, 139
God knows, 266, 425, 443, 461, 505, 560, 580, 675, 972, 982
God's ways, 675
heat meets heat, 229; shout at heat, 1134
Heldil, 1186-7; Psh, 996
hieroglyphs, 355, 443,

535, 699, 868, 1104
Hitler gunfiring Supermind, 1156-7
human beings making the universe, 277
husband-god, 117
Krishna's Bronchitis, 526
look here, 143, 145
men: exceedingly silly, 108; rational idiots, 109
mosquito curtain, 34
Mother's look at Pranam, 237
paranindā: heavenly Ananda, 233
penal servitude for Avatars, 149
pin-points, 293, 295, 296, 312
Purusha jumps up with an Ooah!, 561
"Queen Mary", 569
rubbish better appreciated, 1049
saving young brains of India, 691
scorpion incident and Socrates, 306
some day, some night, 534
stop being fools, 163
such is life, 145, 853, 874
Supermind may twirl its mustache, 327
super-Tom . . ., 148
Supramental, absolute of humour, 1035
Supramental, a queer fellow, 1142
Thompson's tongue, 504, 507
ticket for Nowhere, 727
time can't stand still, 608
time: one lock of hair, 215
touching proof of unanimity and solidarity, 138
tricks of the Lila, 557
use of connoisseurs, 1066
"Wait and see", 719
What cheer, brothers?, 919, 920
Why one century?, 213
woman will wait, 107-8, 115
women: preservation of

species, 116
Hutchinson, Dr. J., 824, 825

Ignorance, 248, 253, 277, 298, 303, 304, 308, 310, 334, 624, 850, 1063
Illness, *see* Medical matters, (3), (4)
Immortality, 191-2, 196, 197, 713
Impurity(ies), 164, 211, 218, 409, 754, 984
Inconscient, 247, 253, 303
India, 187, 230, 487-8, 691, 884, 914
freedom of, 323, 325, 327, 329-30, 340-1, 1185
people in, keep the books of others, 564
railways, 94
Swadeshi times, 351
Inner being, 38, 146, 153, 178, 183
and the psychic, 82
has to change first, 745
opening of, main thing, 62
Inner consciousness, 171, 829, 833, 1063
Inspiration,
guidance from Sri Aurobindo and the Mother, 885-6, 894-8
Inspiration (poetic), 21, 25, 50, 161, 408, 574, 886
and poetry, 21, 25, 31, 47-8, 260, 292, 513, 516, 542-7, 639, 661-2, 833, 839, 923, 1077, 1099, 1137, 1171, 1173
and widening, 493, 501-2, 503, 513
becoming mentalised, *see* Poetry, (1): mind coming in the way
change in, 818
confinement to one single, 1071
flow of, 371-2, 405, 547, 748, 767-70, 774, 839
getting the, 22, 40-1, 47, 262, 373, 396, 398, 402, 405-6, 413, 546, 547, 1055

1201 INDEX **Life**

going off to another person, 358, 641
hide and seek in, 1066
letting it come through, 43-4, 405-6, 412-3, 634-5, 641, 766, 767
perilous to meddle with, 644
receptivity and, 40-1, 372, 894
transcription of, 22, 396, 405, 490, 516, 545, 635, 641, 769, 831, 1114
vigilance to keep it up to the mark, 1137
waiting for, and effort, 292, 372, 512-6, 547, 678, 743, 747, 768-9
Word comes out of the Silence, 891
see also Mind, silent: and inspiration; Opening...
Integral Yoga, *see* Sri Aurobindo's Yoga
Intellectuals, 236
Intermediate zone, 90, 519
drawing one out of, 519-20
Intuition, 113, 134, 204, 205, 206-7, 246, 282, 678, 885, 886, 907, 909
and thought, 1066-7
bubble and squeak method, 886-7
conditions for getting, 207, 356, 357-8, 364
discrimination in, 338, 358, 363, 365; for poetry, 358
ego in, 358, 363, 364
in medical field, 200, 201, 205, 338, 364-5, 421, 422, 425, 569-70, 887, 893, 1125
poetic and yogic, 487
pseudo-intuitions, 364-5
silent mind and, 356, 357-8, 364
without book-knowledge and experience, 894
Involution, 333
Italy, 564

J [a sadhika], 604, 804, 977
novel of, 284, 296-7, 301-2, 372, 377, 619-20, 1012
see also Poetry, (1): J's
Jadabharat, 219, 579
Jagai and Madhai, 256, 347
Jatakas, 169-70
Jatin Bal (J. B.), 375-6, 442, 475-6, 477-8, 480, 531, 532-3, 534, 548-9, 550-1, 555-6, 611-2, 614, 617, 618, 622, 629, 632-3, 634, 636, 653, 660, 663, 665, 772, 776, 798-9, 976, 1007-8, 1009, 1138; Anjali (J. B.'s wife), 566, 660, 663, 1008
Jeans, Sir James, 540
Jekyl, Dr., and Mr. Hyde, 97-8
Joffre, General Joseph, 161
John, St., 256
Joyce, James, 210, 463

Kabir, 558
Kali, 335, 339, 340, 397
Kalidasa, 395, 399, 498, 926
Karma [past], 308-10, 334, 432, 581, 605-6, 979
Karmayoga, ix, x, 84-8, 411, 557, vol. 2, v, 859, 1077
Kastner, L. E.,
about Mallarmé, 777-81
K. D. Sethna, *see* Amal Kiran
Keats, John, 448, 500, 747, 770, 923, 926, 988, 997, 1070, 1172
Kemal Pasha, Mustafa, 421, 426
Khagananda, 158, 160
Khirod, 100, 915, 1110
Kipling, Rudyard, 448, 1155
Knowledge, 80, 83, 213, 240, 334, 624, 625, 645
Divine realisation through love or through, 235-7, 239-41
higher, and mental, 236
higher, and problems of

ordinary life, 240
outer, and yogic, 88-9
sacrifice of, 350
supramental, and faith, 625
see also Force, the, and knowledge
Krishna (Sri Krishna), xi, 137, 141, 170, 172, 173, 177, 218, 219, 227, 256, 283, 294, 320, 477, 479-80, 522, 529, 602, 859, 1001, 1003
Krishnalal, 23
Krishna Prem, 478
Kundalini, 560

Lawrence, D. H., 682, 743, 746, 747
Lele, Vishnu Bhaskar, 467, 1077
Lenin, Vladimir Ilyich, 129
Liberation, 311, 344
and past karma, 309-10, 334
from body consciousness, 81, 192-3
from Prakriti, 73, 85
Life, 14-5, 139, 145, 239, 240, 278, 435, 625, 653, 853, 874, 1064, 1185
creation of, by man, 148
happiness motive-power in, 482-4, 486
misfortunes in, 881, 882
ordinary and yogic, one's own energy in, 132
petty pleasures of, 303-4, 350, 474, 873
rasa of, 72-3
sorrow and suffering in, 276-7, 279-80, 285-6, 311-2, 981
strife and struggle in, 277, 311, 350, 984; *see also* Avatar, sufferings and struggles of
too complex for simple affirmations, 106, 348; *see also* Mind, mental statements and the truth

Life

worldly, 93, 1185
see also Happiness
Literary activity (pursuits),
and acquaintance with
best literature, 686
and age, 789
and sadhana, 5, 21, 41,
49, 72-3, 89, 451, 683,
744; *see also* Poetry, (1):
sadhana and
best creations, 743
desire for fame, 5, 25;
ambition for success,
683
geniuses, 70, 392, 491,
731, 746; great novel-
ists, 687
growth of capacities, *see*
Ashram, growth of ca-
pacities; Yoga-Force,
growth of capacities
literary man, 61, 284, 744,
745
reading and reliance, 681,
682
reading big writers, 682
reading for style, 52, 61,
365, 366
reading, separate oneself
while, 365, 366
sensibility and hyper-sensitiveness, 745-6
story writing: method and
style, 395-6, 688-9
writers and insincerity,
352
writers and life-experi-
ence, 50-1, 686-7, 1053
writing and *rasa*, 642
writing as a passion, 743-4
see also Criticism, literary
Literature, 217, 666
and transformation of na-
ture, 744
hapax legomenon, 803
impressionist method in,
781
modern novels, 366
publication and public-
appreciation, 631
religious and secular,
351-2
stealing in, 284, 293, 646;
see Poetry, (1): theft in
Lloyd George, David, 171,
274

Lombroso, Cesare, 731
Loneliness,
and isolation, 463
Love, 591-2, 615, 637
and devotion for Mother,
268, 281, 750
and sex, 793-5
Divine realisation through
love or through know-
ledge, 235-7, 239-41
for the Divine, 209, 240,
530, 755; before experi-
ence of the Divine, 528,
529-31
human and real, 452
human affection, 961-4,
986-7; *see also* Sa-
dhana, relationship in
vital, 19, 1060
vital, for the Divine, 793
see also Divine love

Madhusudan, Michael, 404-
5, 936
Mahakali,
intervention of, 517, 848
Maheshwari, 299
Mallarmé, Stéphane, 632,
776-82, 801, 828, 829,
830
Man/Men, 148, 286, 430,
1058, 1120
and women, 95, 100, 104-
7, 112-5, 116-8, 181-3,
581-3, 684
coating of Prakriti over,
166-7, 169, 175, 176
contradictory elements
in, 582
denying the possibility of
change or progress in,
142, 150-1, 154, 166-7,
173-4, 175; *see also* Nature, human, change of
Divine (divinity) in, 173-
4, 175, 176-7
everybody is a problem,
454
he-man, 341; and she-
women, 492-3
nature of, *see* Nature,
human
not a steam-engine, 460
not indifferent to animals,
323

possibilities of, 430, 624-5
reasoning animal but not
reasonable, 717
sattwic, 347, 348, 571,
1109, 1110
unconscious of his hidden
self, 460
uneducated and big
brains, all alike, 717
see also under Being
Manifestation (creation),
and forms, 299
object of, 277, 303
Manilal, Dr., 438, 662, 887,
1053
Man of Sorrows, 263, 264,
265, 278, 280, 317, 338,
445, 457, 461, 521, 531,
601, 649, 650, 656, 673,
680, 775, 799, 802
Old Man of the Sea, 531,
533
Old Nick, 244, 533
strain of, 531, 775, 802
Mantra, 486-7; *see also*
Humour, (3): mantra
Mark Tapley, 156
Marlowe, Christopher, 923
Marriage, 476, 611, 861
of Dharmagurus, 575-6
Marx, Karl, 101
Matter, 121, 194, 205, 294-5,
320-1, 561
Medical matters,
(1) Dispensary:
management, 109-12, 178,
182, 206, 211, 254-5,
266-7, 286-7, 368-9,
386-7, 478-9, 502-3,
518, 521, 524, 535,
561-2, 666, 668, 798,
909, 1030-1, 1067-8,
1069, 1081, 1134, 1140,
1169, 1184-5
medical reports, 159-60,
253, 307, 379, 443
reports confidential, 577
(2) Doctors: 119, 120, 210,
423, 705, 874
death by the mistake of,
429, 695-6
differ, 120, 433, 435, 437,
892
function of, 824, 825
method of, 119, 677, 883,
893

1203 INDEX **Medical matters, (5)**

Mother dealing with, 186, 482, 590, 1137
Mother's epigram on, 456
need of, for Divine Force, 120-1
soft like butter, soothing like . . ., 489, 492, 824, 825
success and intuition, 887, 893
successful qualities of, 121, 186, 384, 422, 426, 428, 429, 431, 489, 568-9, 570, 677, 894, 1065
see also Humour, (2): doctors

(3) Illnesses: 220, 248, 488, 705, 713, 1129
and fear, 619, 738, 951
and flies, 738, 739
and germs, 738
and imagination, 248, 767, 788, 970
and pain-bearing, 180
and peace in the cells, 752-3
and physical consciousness, 508
and physical mind, 517-8
and prayer, 129, 181, 183, 681, 961
and quarrels etc., 1014
and sadhana, 60, 823, 1168
and the subconscient, 248, 518, 738, 1053, 1054, 1124, 1125
cause of infection, 738
clapping a big word on, 488
conquest of, 189, 191
constant change of medicaments, 1006
cooking at home, 34, 283-4, 788, 1094
cure of: 1065; absolute, 1054; caused by spirits, 203; doubts about, 333; many factors—drugs, diagnosis, symptoms, confidence, Force, etc., 361, 422, 426, 428, 430, 431, 432-40; without medicine, 613, 617, 717; *see also* Force, the, cure by

Descent of Force and, 718, 720-1
feeling it coming, 191
help to a patient, 618, 812
human nature as cause of, 1126
interchange of, 1061, 1063
knowing results of examination, 508, 811, 813
most, are connected, 436
Mother's and Sri Aurobindo's ways of dealing with, 434, 435
need of external treatment, 11-2, 183, 270, 438, 617, 707-8, 729, 877, 880, 881
nothing is incurable, 1043
prognostications are confidential, 822
something takes interest in, 230, 508, 620
ultimate psychological cause of, 1043
wrong attitude in, 1013
see also Mother, ailments of; Sri Aurobindo, (5): illness

(4) Illnesses, specific:
cancer, 345-6
cholera, 738
constipation, 595, 613, 620, 866, 892
dandruff, 1033
deafness, 1123
diarrhoea, 40; *see also below* (5): K's baby
dysentery, 739
dyspepsia, 800
eczema, 456, 531, 535, 958-9, 975, 1137; and asthma, 389, 390, 998; *see also below* (5): J
elephantiasis, 942
epilepsy, 187-8, 203
fever, 116, 120
flatulence, 124
hydrocele, 951, 954; *see also below* (5): N.P.
hysteric fits, 196, 198, 203
insanity, 201, 203, 439; *see also below* (5): D.S., madness; M, mental disturbance
"internal discharges",

862-4, 866, 875
jaundice, 614-5, 618, 619, 621, *see also below* (5): S (2)
leprosy, 662-3
lipoma, 509-10, 520-1, 526-7, 716
menstruation: irregular, 198; vicarious, 438-9
phlebitis, 1027-8
plague, 738
pleurisy, 118, 119
skin trouble, 456, 959, 975, 976
stomach ulcer, 67, 241, 630; *see also below* (5): S (3)
T. B., 118, 439, 698-9, 811, 813; *see also below* (5): A (2), K, N (2), T (3)
varicose veins, 949-50

(5) Illnesses, cases:
A(1): enlarged liver, 668, 676, 690, 844-5, 928, 934, 937-8, 946, 947, 955, 966-7, 970, 971-2, 973-4, 1003, 1010
A(2): T.B., 711, 715, 730-1, 800, 801, 811, 812-3, 881, 959, 1009
B.P.: scorpion sting, 305-6, 313; syphilis and eye-trouble, 319-20, 345, 352-3, 359, 361-2, 534, 535, 553, 571, 583, 584, 585-90
D [a child]: colitis, 892, 906, 908, 909, 911, 914-5, 916, 917, 918, 919, 927, 928, 932
D.L.: intestinal affection, 630, 633, 642, 643-4, 647-8, 650, 651, 652-3, 692, 693-4, 695, 696, 697, 701, 722-4, 732-4
D.S. (Esculape): madness, 720-1, 723, 731-2, 856, 858, 861
G: dying patient with high blood-pressure, xiii-xiv, 418-28, 433-6, 441, 443, 444-5, 464
J: eczema, 389, 390, 445-6, 456-7, 494-5, 531, 535, 958-9, 975, 976, 981, 982, 1006, 1007,

Medical matters, (5)　　INDEX　　1204

1017-8, 1019, 1020-2,
1023
K's baby: diarrhoea, 875,
876-7, 878, 879-81, 882-
4, 886, 892
K: T. B., 430-1, 432-4,
438-9, 489, 581, 582,
595, 597, 601, 694-5,
698-9, 729, 735
M: mental disturbance
and D.L.'s ghost, 709,
710-1, 722-4, 731
Mulshankar's accident,
xiii, 473, 474-5, 482,
496-7, 528-9, 578, 579,
583, 654, 761
N(1): eye-trouble and
deafness, 1104, 1122,
1123, 1124, 1125-6
N(2): T. B., 112, 115, 116
118, 120, 123-4, 144,
151, 155, 181, 202, 203,
272-3, 868, 1017, 1019,
1020, 1021, 1022-3,
1024 1026, 1027
N. P.: eye-trouble, 179,
180, 181, 182, 183, 184,
287, 588, 619, 796, 798,
1065; hydrocele, 945,
951, 952, 954, 1029
P: needle stuck in her
palm, 917-8, 919-20,
924
S(1): cerebral haemor-
rhage, 179, 181, 182,
184, 185-9, 193
S(2): jaundice and dried
liver, 613, 614, 617, 618,
619, 621, 622, 626-7,
628, 630, 631, 632, 644,
645, 648, 654, 660, 666,
672, 674, 688, 689, 690,
699, 706, 710, 714, 719,
722, 729, 740, 767, 783,
977, 980, 981, 982, 983,
989, 990, 998, 1005,
1011-4, 1021-2, 1024,
1030, 1035, 1039, 1044,
1112, 1126-7, 1131,
1134, 1162
S(3): stomach ulcer, xiii,
xiv, 228, 230, 253-4,
283-4, 377-83, 384,
385-8, 389, 394, 395,
397, 401, 517

T(1): atony of the
stomach (ptosis), 706-7,
710, 711-2, 714, 715-6,
717-8, 719, 722, 741,
742, 989, 1112, 1113
T(2): kidney infection,
708-9, 716, 718
T(3): T.B., 1073, 1074-5,
1077, 1092, 1096, 1119,
1136, 1164-5
Y: descent and physical
disturbance, 718, 719-
22
(6) Medicines: 187, 384,
385, 422, 613, 617, 717,
877, 878
and Mother's body, 816,
820
effects of strong, 145, 184,
438, 446, 456
Indian, 1015
not a science, 213, 360,
883
(7) Medicines, specific:
arnica, 654
arsenic, 265, 633, 1069,
1093, 1098
atropine, 184, 1027,
1122-3
bismuth, 159, 241, 613
boric solution, 185
bovril, 381, 1020
bromide, 179, 1019, 1044
calomel, 617, 618, 880
camphor lotion, 185
castor-oil, 892, 909, 1030
chicory, 784
coconut (green), 957
cod-liver oil, 671-2, 676,
784
collosal iodine, 1124
eau de cologne, 574
eau sédative, 574
emetine, 444, 876, 877
Fandorine, 874
gland medicines, 976
"guimauve" enema, 159,
927, 1080
kājal, 1084
laxatives, 1032, 1080
Listerine, 1018, 1020
Lithinée, 120, 565
liver extract, 1011
medical salts, 990-1
mercury ointment, 179,

716, 773-4, 1040
morphia, 1053
nux vomica, 632, 633,
937
onions, 1010-1
pān-supāri, 785-6
pastilles charbon, 911
picric acid, 286-7, 1140
pomegranate juice, 463-4,
613, 614
purgatives, 181, 184, 577,
614, 621, 875, 1032
quinine, 184, 446, 752,
788, 1044
salicylates, 185, 249, 1059
Santonin, 1089
soup, 124, 617-8, 627,
1024, 1025, 1091, 1134
spinach soup, 387
Sudarshan, 946, 1010,
1015
sulphersenol, 265
thyroid pills, 248, 976,
1044
yeast, 620, 631
(8) General:
activity of glands, 523,
711
aluminium vessels, 1069
Bates' system, 577
blood-examination, 119,
928, 938-9, 970
book-knowledge useful
with practice, 677
breast-milk, 880
diagnosis not infallible,
420, 697
disinfecting a house,
1021, 1024
epidemics in Asram, 202,
322, 1168
eye-glasses, 248, 796, 798
hieroglyphs, 535, 699
medical etiquette, 178,
335-6, 378-9
medical examination of
candidates, 693, 699,
742
medical knowledge and
Yogic Force, 213
medical theories and
some other power
behind, 696, 698; sur-
gical operations and
Yogic Force, 337-8

Mother's and Sri Aurobindo's care about hygiene, 118, 207, 271, 345, 352-3, 359, 361-2, 496-7, 583, 606, 651, 875-6, 889, 948, 1021, 1022, 1060, 1091
Mother's and Sri Aurobindo's care about sadhak-patients' diet, 124, 159, 228, 230, 253-4, 254-5, 259, 283-4, 345, 382-3, 387, 481, 496-7, 565, 583, 606, 614, 617-8, 619, 626, 627, 628-9, 630, 631, 632, 644, 648, 651, 671, 672, 688, 689, 693, 695, 783, 784-5, 800, 875-6, 889, 892, 915, 917, 918, 926, 948, 955, 957, 977, 1003, 1015, 1020, 1021, 1022, 1024, 1025, 1026, 1028, 1033, 1034, 1035, 1037, 1042, 1060, 1074, 1075, 1077, 1089, 1091, 1093, 1095, 1096, 1098, 1104, 1107, 1128, 1164
Mother's and Sri Aurobindo's views on, 125, 151, 158-9, 181, 185, 259, 266, 375, 401, 408 426-7, 438, 444, 473, 497, 523-4, 548, 587-8, 589, 611, 618, 621, 622, 631, 633, 642, 666, 668, 671-2, 682, 688, 691, 694, 707, 709, 711-2, 715-6, 722, 740, 742, 773, 783, 784-5, 786, 792, 826, 844, 875, 876, 880, 882, 883, 887, 888, 902, 918, 920, 928, 945, 952, 959, 981, 990-1, 1011, 1015, 1016, 1017-37, 1039, 1040, 1041, 1044, 1046, 1052, 1054, 1055, 1059, 1069, 1074, 1075, 1077-8, 1083, 1085, 1086-7, 1094, 1097, 1099, 1112, 1114, 1115, 1117, 1127, 1128, 1134, 1136, 1138, 1144, 1149, 1157, 1164-5, 1167, 1169, 1176, 1187

Mother's views on, far removed, 882
Pondicherry Hospital, 711, 1181
practice here illegal, 250, 336
Presse Médicale, 822, 953, 954-5
sedentary invalids, 670, 691, 730-1
surrealistic method in, 364-5, 886-7, 892-3; *see also* Intuition, in medical field
vaccination in the Asram, viii, 888-92, 896, 900-3, 909, 911, 915-6, 918, 919, 920, 921, 923, 926, 1163, 1164
washing work and nails, 187
see also Humour, (2)
Meditation, 6, 33, 65, 86, 122, 155-6, 161, 240, 526, 602, 607, 735, 820, 821
after rising, 8-9
a *kasrat*, 486
and adverse forces, 736
and work, 77-80, 82-6, 484-6
disturbing thoughts in, 65, 66, 68
experiences in, 67, 81, 91, 104
pressure on the head, 11, 68-9, 97, 104
sitting or walking, 2, 249
sleep in, 1-2, 7, 91
utility of, 40, 64, 83, 484-6
when one cannot do, 7
Mental formation, 872
Mental plane,
forms in, 299
Meredith, George, 935, 1172
Miaja, General José, 885-6, 895, 906
Middle path, 469, 859
Milton, John, 319, 448, 498, 500, 743, 747, 749, 923, 926, 935, 1053, 1147
Mind, 139, 162, 236, 252, 259, 362, 367, 404, 625, 738, 795
and mystic poetry, *see*

Poetry, (1): mystic: intellectual understanding of
and vital world, 772, 828
developing into supermind, 139, 625
divided, 72-3
gathering of, 1
immortality of, 196
mastery of, 59
mental control, removal of, 14
mental statements and the truth, 106, 112-3, 189, 191, 675, 743, 1179; logical not necessarily true, 235, 347
mind-fag and rest, 654
misleading logic, 387; *see also* Nirodbaran, (8): bad logic
nature of, 639
physical, 64, 65, 66, 517-8, 828, 851
plummet and reality, xi-xii, 257, 259
resistance of, 311
silent (passive): 886; and inspiration, 514, 542, 546, 547, 634, 637, 641, 769, 891, 950; and intuition, 356, 357-8, 364; and receptivity, 753; and sadhana, 11-2, 48, 82, 637, 873; and thinkers, 362
sophisticated and naïve, 1120
struggling with vital, 350
stumbling-block in sadhana, 72, 205, 236, 318, 571, 603, 637, 912
supporting the vital, 311, 611, 1132
see also Poetry, (1): mind coming in the way
Mirabai, 1070
Miracle(s), 29, 129, 138, 143, 149, 195, 337, 423, 874, 943, 1024
see also Sri Aurobindo, (5): and miracles
Mithridates, 158, 160
Mohitlal Majumdar, 824fn
Molière, 360, 427

Monomohan Ghosh

Monomohan Ghosh, 286, 331-2, 401, 988-9
Monoranjan Guha Thakurtha, 476
Money, 101, 102, 869
  property, 856
Morality, 432, 817
Mother, the, 49, 74, 84, 165, 168, 177, 220, 222, 228, 282, 349, 350, 400, 434, 723, 737, 885, 956, 1008, 1062
  achievement of indifference, vol. 2, vii
  activity and withdrawal from activity, 83-4
  ailments of, 813, 924; and medicines, 816, 820; and prognostications, 819, 822
  "Always behave as if the Mother was looking at you", 274
  at Pranam and sadhaks' reactions, 2, 10, 12, 13, 15, 19, 31-2, 37-8, 55-6, 76, 162, 237-9, 332, 518, 537-8, 539, 551, 577, 588, 657, 704, 732, 759, 773, 1033, 1089, 1132; misuse of the Pranam, 820-2; no Pranam henceforth, 819, 848; remaining silent after Pranam, 485
  body-transformation, vol. 2, vi
  calling, 7, 9, 54, 87, 651, 736, 1040; see also Force, calling for . . .
  castor-oil in childhood, 892
  concentration on, before writing, 783, 807, 840; see also below her photograph . . .
  conquest of death and illness, 189, 190
  criticism of, 234, 411, 733, 1088, 1090, 1108
  dealing with doctors, 186, 482, 590, 1137
  dealing with sadhaks, 151, 237-8, 264, 920, 922, 924, 1186; see also

INDEX

  Medical matters, (8): Mother's and Sri Aurobindo's care . . .
  effecting transition between human and supramental consciousness, vol. 2, vii
  emanations of, 274, 275-6, 278
  flowers given by, 30-1, 274-5
  Force of, 475, 694, 697, 724, 734, 853; see also under Force, the
  her photograph: bowing down before writing, 402, 405-6; contact through, 475-6, 480; looking at, 2-3
  how many Mothers?, 475-6, 477-8
  knowledge about happenings, 273-5, 313, 721-2
  knowing Sri Aurobindo, vol. 2, vi
  love and devotion for, 268, 281, 750
  misunderstanding statements of, 721, 887, 899
  multitudinous manifestation, 244
  on this correspondence, ix, vol. 2, v-vii
  organiser of the Ashram, vol. 2, vi-vii
  personal relation with, 257, 275, 276
  physical nearness of, 224-5, 951; value of personal touch, 225, 820
  pressure for change, 299, 850
  protection of, xii, 736; see also Sadhana, and hostile force(s) . . .
  pulling at her Force, 208, 726
  remembering, in work, 16-7, 99, 313, 451
  seeing the Divine in, 281, 282
  supramental descent in, 214-5
  taking up medical corres-

1206

  pondence, 1016
  treachery to, 725-6, 727-8
  views of, on medical matters, far removed, 882
  wrong report to, 1040-1
  see also Sadhak(s), wanting to be equal . . . ; Vision, Mother's, about . . ., of Mother
Mother, The, 865, 867
Motilal Roy, 557
Mudgaokar, G. D., 996
Muladhara, 453, 560
Mulshankar, 473, 474-5, 823, 1081; see also Medical matters, (5): Mulshankar
Music, 146, 147, 208, 217, 795
  highest art?, 447-50
Mussolini, Benito, 147, 340, 361, 377
Mysticism, see Poetry, (1): mystic

Naik, Dr. M., 391, 1130, 1132
Napoleon Bonaparte, 231, 421, 426, 962
National mentality, 508
Nature, human, 45, 169, 272, 279-80, 297, 374, 564, 874, 1047, 1126
  change (transformation) of, 86, 132, 138, 150-1, 233, 243, 248, 252, 275, 285, 292, 311, 744, 745, 898, 981, 993, 1127; and freedom, 409; and inner experiences, 677-8; see also Man, denying the possibility of change
  double, 97
  harmonised, rare, 269, 270
  influence of atmosphere on, 264-5
  lower, and hostile forces, 27-8; see also Sadhana, and lower nature; Soul, and Ignorance
  psychisation of, 327, 329

1207   INDEX   **Nirodbaran, (7a)**

same, everywhere, 270,
285
Nature, universal, 311, 434,
739
and subconscient, 247-8,
251-3
and surface being, 252
Universal Energy, and
individual, 514
Nevinson, W. Henry, 144fn
New race, 342, 343
Nietzsche, Friedrich, 101,
102
Nirodbaran,
  (1) **Correspondence**
  with Sri Aurobindo
  and Mother: vii-viii,
  ix, x
  complaint about playing
  pranks with, x, 480
  Mother's remarks on, ix,
  vol. 2, v-vii
  need (purpose) of, xi, xiv,
  2, 10, 20, 76-7, 103,
  208, 281, 1002
  showing it to others, 71,
  75, 207-8, 276, 339, 345,
  509, 600, 714, 900,
  1064, 1102, 1111
  soul-stirring, 595
  special favour, 103, 127,
  281, 641, 1135-6
  subject-matter, x
  (2) **Depression:** 13, 715,
  750, 1173
  and J. B.'s letter, 531-2
  from exaltation to, 47,
  766; Darshan atmo-
  sphere waning, 71, 155-
  6, 291; rosy things and
  poetry died, 266
  inner unquiet, 185
  Jeremiad, 458-62
  moribund, gasping, 376-7
  no faith in effort, 65-6,
  323-4
  no peace, joy, energy, 578,
  605, 622, 624, 655, 790,
  984
  not personal: "regulation
  lathi" attack, 271, 272
  sadness caused: by a
  dream, 48; by a poem,
  787; by better things,
  787

three Ds, 371, 390; and
Dilip's best creation,
372-3
unhappy, 984; don't know
why, 155, 156, 157, 271,
715, 855
upsurge of vital thoughts
and desire, 17, 231, 474
(3) **Despair and dissatisfaction:** 680
about poetry, 31, 64, 263,
266, 317, 346, 407, 457,
498, 504, 578-9, 581,
597, 642, 649, 680, 684,
767-8, 790, 802, 826,
833-4, 854, 885, 891,
942-3, 974, 1151-2
about sadhana, 23-4, 35,
154, 231-2, 315, 316,
317-8, 336, 605, 628,
637, 638-9, 644, 655-9,
715, 730, 744, 748, 752,
790-1, 974, 984, 994-5
affiliation and differen-
ces with Dilip, 372-3,
374, 511, 516, 521, 523,
622-3
apprehension of failure,
see Yoga, failures in,
and apprehension
borrowed your difficulties
from X, 470, 605-6
Dilipian, 54, 156, 622-3
life seems a washout,
277-8
(4) **Dreams:** 3, 6, 13, 23,
48, 54, 69, 244, 727,
1131
about Buddha, 46
about Mother, 44, 163,
164-5, 215, 368, 481,
vol. 2, v, 664, 665, 726-
7, 956
about Sri Aurobindo, 63,
76, 186, 244, 472, 481-2,
664, 665, 916
curing an incurable dis-
ease in, 1010
music in, 264, 640, 760
of a beautiful boy (higher
being), 956-7, 975
of father, 34, 35
of hospital, 993-4
of Shiva's *ansha*, 38
of silver coins, 356

of snakes, 64-5
see also Dreams
(5) **Learning:**
esraj, 20-1
French, 4, 18, 199, 441,
798, 841, 1093
occult science, 199, 728,
730, 913-4
reading *The Life Divine*,
161, 353, 354-5, 356,
730
sitar, 86
study of the English lan-
guage, 161
tabla, 20-1
(6) **Literature:** 687
critical faculty, 214, 1102
desire to be a good writer,
5, 25, 61
literary gift, 25, 42
prose writing, 39-40, 52
resistance in expression,
63-4
story writing, 395, 688-9,
709, 744, 1052'
(7a) **Poetry:**
18, 21, 23, 25, 35-6, 38,
39, 45, 246, 262, 263,
291, 401, 407, 412-3,
452-3, 496, 533, 580,
606-7, 657, 692, 743,
744-5, 761, 788, 809,
833, 845, 868, 884, 904,
914, 918, 924-5, 933,
948, 951, 952, 956, 959,
960, 964, 966, 968, 972,
977, 995, 1003-7, 1011-
2, 1013, 1030, 1034,
1036-8, 1039, 1041,
1042, 1044, 1051, 1055,
1056, 1057, 1058, 1059,
1064, 1066, 1073, 1075,
1076, 1080, 1102, 1114,
1118, 1134, 1135, 1139,
1140-1, 1142, 1156,
1158, 1159, 1163, 1164,
1166, 1173, 1185
"A fathomless beauty in
a sphere of pain", an
estimate, 1143-5
and Amal, 982, 1102-3
and Arjava, 679, 680
and Dilip, 545, 683, 767-8,
769
and Harin, 971, 982

Nirodbaran, (7a)

and J, 744, 745, 767, 768, 943
and NK, 286, 292, 401, 440, 620-1
and Romen, 915, 917
and X, 468
anticipating trouble, and right attitude, 790
attempt at lyrics, 960, 965
Baudelairean fame, 815, 817-8
be a spider, 262, 984; try try again, 262, 372
beaten Virgil hollow, 548, 1092; equalling Shakespeare, 1180, 1181; and Homer, Milton, Keats, etc., 455, 548, 549, 747, 885, 953-4, 1172-3
Bengali, 249, 254, 440, 446, 608-9, 620-1, 637, 907-8, 909, 931; translated into English: by Nolini, 804, 808; by Sri Aurobindo, 835-6
between us we have produced something remarkable, 926-7, 1170, 1172, 1179-80
cease to Hamletise, 396
discouraged easily, 1171
dissatisfaction with his own poems, 787, 790; self-depreciation, 415, 775; see also above (3): about poetry
dozing while writing, 775, 921, 932, 1162
English poems better than Bengali, 490, 1052
expression becoming authentic, 1143; found yourself in English poetry, 1016, 1038-9; gaining command of medium, 1152; getting hold of language, 933; got back your swing, 1096; maturity of poetic power, 647-8, 649; newness, 1184; possibility of finished product, 978
15 poems in 6 months, 1172-3

foiled romantic and metaphysical poet, 1177; nineteenth century poet getting hold of, 1095-6
for the good of others, 598, 843
gift in grave things, 960
grumbler, 338, 802, 942-3, 1152
highway robbery, 965, 1009, 1086
"nower", efforter, 511, 512, 513, 542; plodding vitality, 373
immortalising depression, 537
infant in, 766, 767
joy of creation (enthousiasmos), 43-4, 45, 371, 412-3; no joy of creation, 263, 542, 642, 649, 774; refuse to enthuse, 768, 769
logical, medical man writing poems, 263, 972, 980
magnificent poem without knowing it: Gaudeamus igitur, 948
marginal lines, 936, 956, 1068, 1076, 1112, 1114, 1143, 1156, 1159, 1160-1, 1162, 1171, 1172, 1178, 1183, 1186
Matra-brittas, 919
melancholy Jacques interfering, 965
Muse's response, 288, 317, 597, 650, 1064, 1076; exaction on the Muse, 1073
phenomenon, 1128, 1131, 1152
poet born, now turn of yogi, 254, 255, 286, 647
poetic sense in, 415
poet in the making, 398
poet undeniable, 288
possible verse-maker outside, 596-7, 600
queer moods, 943
remarks on, 249, 606-7, 641, 765-6, 809-10, 845, 902, 916-7, 918, 921,

946, 948, 950-1, 968, 999, 1043-5, 1084-5, 1125, 1139, 1167, 1174, 1180, 1181, 1182, 1183, 1184, 1187
repetition of ideas, 1007
repetition of words, 600, 971, 1056, 1173, 1184
resistance in, 263, 371, 407; see also Poetry, (1): mind coming in the way
romanticised Wordsworth, 1084-5
romanticism, 1095, 1158
Sri Aurobindo hard master, 1158
super-Blakish poem. 1114, 1116-7
surrealist, 804-8, 813, 814, 818-9, 826-7, 828, 830, 834, 837, 864, 934, 1097, 1160; transition from, 862
syntax, Bedlamic, 1036-8
theme not clear, 766
use of writing, 1131, 1132-3, 1173
Victorian and spiritual strains, 969
vs. idleness, 1128, 1133
whole thing dropped, 43-4, 975-6

(7b) Specific poems:

"ālor gandha", 902fn
"ālor pākhi" ("The Bird of Light"), 608, 637
"A Throb of the Vast", 1122fn
bhatiyālī, 608-9
"Childhood Dream", 1085fn
"Cry from the Dark", 977fn
Fifty Poems of Nirodbaran, 933fn, 948fn, 1167fn, 1175fn, 1179fn
"Figure of Trance", 997fn
"First Word", 921fn
"Flames of Vision", 1188fn
"Haloed Face", 1043fn
"In Moonlit Silence", 999fn
"Lonely Tramp", 1076fn
"My Thoughts", 1036fn

"*Nirbhar*", 650fn
"O Light Inviolable",
1172fn
"Primal Source", 1187fn
"Quest Fulfilled", 1177fn
"Reunion", 1143fn
"Secret Hands", 1016fn
"Seeds of Vision", 1142fn
"Seeking Thy Light . . .",
1059fn
"Silver Wonder", 1097fn
"Sky Transcendent",
1058fn
"Sleep of Light", 1045fn
"Soul's Pilgrimage",
976fn; Sri Aurobindo's
success, 977
"Thy Presence", 1180fn
"Your Face", 1010fn

(8) General:
bad logic, 142, 144, 145,
150, 176, 193-4, 196-7,
396-7
birthday, 26, 68, 70, 373,
751, 752, 1184, 1186
breaking the old being,
228
can't understand a joke,
143, 144, 526
chubby chap: ego, 337,
341, 384
complaint from the D.R.,
580-1, 669-70
coward, 92
cycle for melancholiac,
510; cyclo-mania, 556
date of arrival, 494
decision to stay in the
Ashram, 1
"devil of despair" to
"angel of hope", 870
different parts of, 199,
228, 571, 582, 610, 650
difficulties are not yours
alone, xiii, 272, 461,
658, 748
doctor's confidence lack-
ing, 186, 892
doctorship, disappoint-
ment in, 213, 677-8
doubt, 263, 371, 395-6,
431-2, 638; about urge
for the Divine or spiri-
tuality, 23, 209, 232,
454, 466-7, 468-9, 523,

609-10, 623-4; Hamlet,
St. Thomas, etc., 396;
Madam Doubt etc.,
423; *see also under*
Doubt
elixir, 376-7
fatness, seeking from . . .,
163, 671, 934-5
firebrand doctor, 489
fulfilling conditions without knowing, 741
future hope, 46, 57, 71,
287, 315-6, 328, 610,
647, 784, 1002; *see also
above* (7a): poet born ...
Gandhian resistance, 228,
243, 532
growth of yogic con-
sciousness, 73, 74, 82
humorous element in, 351
illness, 36, 40, 59-60, 264,
273, 327, 330, 756,
757-8, 902, 924, 937,
983, 989, 996, 1167,
1168; *see also* Humour,
(3): boil
inertia of physical nature,
thick crust, 609-10, 755
installed in X's palace,
1154
"laugh and grow fat",
156, 163, 520, 523
leechlike tenacity lacking,
457, 461
love for Sri Aurobindo,
209
meditation and poetry,
collision between, 607,
683
mind (mentality, brain)
of, ix-x, 161, 325, 423,
466, 755; active, 48,
542, 767, 769; clear with
deliberate strength,
199, 238; confound-
ed and hesitant, 316,
318, 533, 683, 684; log-
ical brain box, 312,
886; obstructive, 571,
637, 639; wooden head,
xi, 467
not a Sri Aurobindo, 457,
461
opening of heart centre,
68, 240

opening of inner being,
66, 647, 1131
opening up medical chan-
nel, 916; *see also* In-
tuition, in medical field
prestige, and saving the
face, 108, 119
property affairs, 7, 1051,
1068, 1079-80, 1084,
1103-4, 1111-2, 1157-8
putting up a friend in
one's room, 1009, 1186
quite decent, 898
receptive, 752, 753
relation with Sri Auro-
bindo, x, xi-xii, 126,
232, 256, 257, 259, 268-
9, 270, 480, 624; appre-
hension of Sri Auro-
bindo's withdrawal,
623, 799; do not forsake
me, 154, 158, 824
result is gratifying, 628,
629
samatā, exercises in, 29,
717, 809
sea-bath, 934-5
soul-stirring communica-
tions, 595
studying medical books,
927
testing a raw doctor, 119,
198
thirst for Knowledge, x,
208
3 mules, 607
triangle of confusion,
395-6
vairāgya, training in, 605,
606, 608
vital of, 278, 373, 638,
639, 755; lazy, 470, 503,
511, 542, 545, 546, 605,
1132
wanting only peace, 326
weakness, 108
what Sri Aurobindo
wants him to be, 217
work in Ashram: gate
duty, 17, 18; garden,
19, 35; House-painting
Dept., 35; timber-go-
down, 36, 55, 59, 86,
87, 98, 109; talk about
Dispensary charge and

Nirodbaran, (8)

the actual charge, 98-9, 103-4, 108, 109, 486; attending the Hospital, 193, 202, 227-8, 312, 313, 742, 815-6, 1040
yogic strand in, 637
see also Humour, (3)
Nirvana, 80, 115, 117, 206, 309, 317, 579, 902, 979
Nishikanta (NK), 70, 286, 551, 641, 649, 684, 691, 945
and Dilip, 490-1
Bengali poetry, 292, 440, 472, 527, 642, 1159
Brahmaputra of inspiration, 661
English poetry, 402-4, 405-8, 411-2, 413-4, 472, 490-1, 492
fluency in poetry, 401, 405, 543, 547, 748
new channel opened, 642
prodigious and unusual poet, 401, 543, 547
"The Rat and the Cat", 492
vision-poems of, 453-4, 462
Nitai, 256
Nobel Prize, 70, 1155
Nolini Kanta Gupta, 63, 113, 161, 496, 518, 818
Non-violence, 226

Occult faculty, 283
Opening (openness), 16, 36, 62, 72, 203, 205, 211, 258, 270, 338, 601, 647, 649, 678, 680-1, 774, 873, 897, 902, 912, 1101
and cure, 345, 1014
and inspiration, 40, 47, 50, 490, 491, 493, 514, 635, 661-2, 684
meaning of, 12, 21
of mind and other centres, 240-1
passivity and, 514
to hostile forces, 203, 221
vertical, 235
Ouspensky, P.D., 793
Overmind, 141, 156, 477

and supermind, 141, 325, 327
descent of, into Matter, 294-5, 320
in process of supramentalisation, 189, 195, 389
Oxford Dictionary, The, 497, 498, 499, 682

Painting, 72, 88, 146, 148, 202, 208, 369, 447, 448
in Asram, 512
modern, 449
Pallas Athene, 107, 299
Paramhansa,
various forms of, 219, 223
Patriotic sentiments, 348-9, 487-8
Paul, St., 1034
Pavitra (P.B. Saint-Hillaire), 211, 891, 892, 920, 926, 1015
Peace, 47, 72, 85, 98, 209, 210, 223, 289, 316, 326, 409, 637, 653, 655, 659, 750, 752, 753, 754, 773, 959, 986
and mental quietude, 1101
experiences of, 23, 52-3, 601
see also Calm; Silence; Stillness
Peter, St., 147
Physical, the, 76, 201, 321, 841
resistance of, 303, 304, 311
supramental descent into, 179-80, 214-5
Physical consciousness, 252, 303, 453, 483, 508, 544
fall in, 336, 337, 461, 840, 995
obscurity of, and its effects, 821, 822-3
Physical mind, 64, 65, 66, 517-8, 828, 851
Physical world,
and vital world, 163, 164, 314, 664-6, 828
expression of the supraphysical, 739

Pineal gland, 558-60
Plato, 143, 167
Poet(s), 261, 401, 487, 775, 779, 781, 1006
and dreamer, 832-3
born, and made by yoga, 458-9, 491
can't always write well, 885, 1005
epic writers, 926, 935; metaphysicals, 1178; modernists, 448; moderns, 1171-2
greater Power writes through, 1077
greatest, with labour, 922
judgment of one's own poetry, 415, 460, 468, 542, 649, 775, 790, 810, 884; Horace's rule, 662, 1182
limitation of appreciation-faculty of, 1147
manufacture of, 459; *see also* Ashram, growth of capacities in
new *chhanda*, mentioning of, 1072
vicissitudes of poetic career, 1079
works in exalting excitement, 884
Poetry,
(1) **General:** 72, 208, 358, 447, 449, 450-1, 488, 666, 794, 795
A. K.'s, 511
and ego, 405, 407, 865, 867
and novel-writing together, 626
and time factor, 401
appreciation of, 778, 1144-5, 1147-8; *see also* Poet(s), judgment of...
aspiration and passivity, 641
bare and rugged, 1146-7
beautiful, as a whole, 1178
Bengali, 643; *laghu guru chhanda,* 586; of Mohitlal, 824; overhead, 943; possibility of epic style, 936
best, 490, 637-8, 743

1211 INDEX Poetry, (1)

blank verse, 921-3; epic style, 910-1, 925, 935, 937, 955, 957, 969-70 "body" being born?, 1117
coining words, 803
decisive rule for, 50
different minds catching similar things, 358, 641
Dilip's (D's), 50, 69, 369, 512, 513, 515, 543, 547, 631, 644, 661, 684, 767-8, 999-1000, 1072, 1079; and Nishikanta's, 490-1 does not give love and peace but Ananda, 637
dozing while writing; see Nirodbaran, (7a): dozing . . .
dream-poetry, 813, 827, 830, 831-3, 838, 982
ear, question of, 414, 495, 643, 943, 944, 945, 1153
effort in, see below place of Force . . .
epics, 926; see also above blank verse
epithet, recurring, 1056-7
exceptional circumstances, 490, 493, 501-2
expecting success (exceedingly fine), 626, 810, 885
expression main thing, 1143
fear obstacle in, 775
feelings and imaginations in, 599
fine things can come without knowing, 766
fluency and inspiration, 547; see also Inspiration (poetic), flow of
Grand Trunk Road, 542
greatest thing in, 1045-6, 1149
growth of capacities, see Ashram, growth of capacities (poetic etc.); Yoga-Force, growth of capacities
high tone, objection to, 1053
hooking on to the right place, 915, 969, 976-7, 1078, 1079

image: excessive, 1082-3; richness of, 415-6, 491
imitation and reproduction, 552
importance of words, 598
improvement: and egoism, 865, 867; ways of, 516, 835, 839, 840, 841, 842, 845-6, 870, 923, 943, 1116
infancy in, 767
inspiration, poetic, see Inspiration (poetic)
intermittent drops, 490
joy of writing (enthousiasmos), 43-4, 636-7, 769, 774, 923, 927
J's, 585, 634-6, 639, 641, 642, 643, 660-2, 734, 748, 761, 764, 774, 775-7, 791, 801-2, 812, 822, 826, 843-4, 869-70, 902, 921-3, 943, 969-70, 1059-60, 1071
labour not enough, 774
lyrical, 965, 966, 982
mass of works in, 779
matter of factness, 293, 527; see also below, sincerity and verisimilitude
method of writing, 249-50, 262, 372, 396, 398, 547, 839, 840, 953, 1066; each his own technique, 923; same method, different results, 1099
metre (chhanda): 412, 643; variety and Timespirit (yugadharma) in, 864
mind coming in the way, 371, 413, 637, 767, 768, 775, 840, 904, 937, 949, 950, 1050, 1051, 1115-6; see also Mind, silent, and inspiration
modern, 449, 864, 980; and our poetry: difference in substance, 1175
moon, stars, sun in, 504, 964, 1009-10, 1068-9, 1070, 1080, 1121-2, 1134-5

mystic: exact meaning not forte of, 632; intellectual understanding of, 762-5, 770-1, 827, 830, 834-5, 836, 966, 997, 1116; subjective vision, 599; two methods of writing, 782-3; use of sex-imagery, 793
Napoleonic efforts, 468
narrative, 935, 965-6, 988
new technique, 827
not metaphysical treatise, 1188
originality in, 25
overhead, 929-31, 939-40, 943, 944-5, 1117
philosophy in, 35-6, 1092, 1148
place of Force, inspiration and personal effort in, 468, 512-6, 542, 1137, 1152
plodding and easy gallop, 201-2, 204, 206, 207, 215
"poetic power", 652
progress in, and in yoga, 649
pure, 775, 830-1, 1097
reading, help by, 61-2, 768, 925, 943
rhythm: 877, 1153; revolutions of, 979
right words in the right places, 944, 950
rocks aspiring, 1082-3
sadhana and, 22, 62, 70, 72, 217, 283, 410, 594, 784, 1077
sameness in, 1071-2, 1128, 1131, 1133
shunting the train, difficulty of, 869-70; transitional difficulty, 840
significance and feeling in, 1144-5
simple, 415-6
simplicity no test, 1182
sincerity and verisimilitude, 626, 910, 944, 946-7, 955, 958, 959, 968, 1004, 1009-10, 1011, 1013, 1025, 1036, 1038, 1041, 1043, 1059,

Poetry, (1)   INDEX   1212

1066, 1075, 1076, 1082,
1102, 1103, 1134, 1135,
1141, 1152, 1156, 1163,
1166, 1169-70, 1171,
1172, 1179, 1183
"sky", use of, 1058
sources of, 832, 833
spiritual: plane of source,
941; monotony and
variety in, 1070-2
sterile periods, 647
striking different sources,
810-1
style, 415-6
supermind plane of, 806,
939
Surawardy's, 965, 978,
997-8, 1000
surrealist, 813, 827-33,
838; letters to Dilip,
829-33
symbolism and impres-
sionism, 779, 829
technique in, 1153
theft in, 965, 1009, 1086,
1165; see also Litera-
ture, stealing in
thought-power in, 47
value of a poem, 291, 639
vulgarity in, 816, 817
waking up of something
necessary, 42, 52
yoga is skill in works, 808,
915
(2) English poetry:
accent in, 497-9, 1039
and Bengali poetry, 643
by Orientals, 404, 504-8
cadences, right sense in,
1095, 1153
conceit in, 938
metrical rules and rhythm,
402-3, 412, 414, 417-8,
495, 573-4; errors in
rhythm, 552, 960, 1140
mixture of metaphors,
453, 934, 1165
overtones and under-
tones, 933-4
"red tears", 634
rhymes, 403, 500, 546-7,
922, 1067
scansion, 495, 1042
sonnet scheme, 403, 500,
922

spiritual expression in,
405
stresses: fictitious, 453,
497-8, 574; shifting of,
950
see also Amal; Arjava;
Literary activity; Ni-
rodbaran, (7a); Nishi-
kanta
(3) Specific poems:
"Ahana", 746
"Baji Prabhou", 925
"Bird of Fire, The", 763,
782-3, 925fn, 940,
1009fn
"Crimson Rose", 764
"Divine Comedy, The",
926, 1046fn
"Flowers of Evil", 817
"*Gitānjali*", 505, 770fn
"In the Moonlight", 746
"Jackal", 847
"*Kumārsambhav*", 926,
935, 936
"Le Cygne", 779fn, 780-1
"Les Fleurs", 779fn, 786
"Love and Death", 746,
925, 988
"*Meghnādbodh*", 926, 957,
970
"Nirvana", 782, 789fn,
925fn
"Ode to a Nightingale",
770
"Paradise Lost", 749,
925, 926, 1053
"Paradise Regained",
749, 925
"*Rājhaṇsa*", 527
"*Rāmāyan*", 926, 957
"Rape of Lucrece, The",
988
"Rishi, The", 746, 749
"Rose of God", 544,
925fn
"*Shonār Tari*", 770fn
"Skylark", 770-1
"Songs to Myrtilla", 960
"Surrealist", 790fn, 816-7
"*tārā . . . nata āpan hāra*"
("Millions of stars
. . ."), 598-9
"Transformation", 782,
789fn, 925fn
"Urvasie", 925

"Venus and Adonis", 988
see also Nirodbaran, (7b)
Pondicherry, 7-8, 46, 50,
459, 711, 758, 979, 1157
Hospital, 711, 1181
pier, 13, 684
Pope, Alexander, 770, 771
Poverty, 101, 102
Prakriti,
coating of, over man,
166-7, 169, 175, 176
liberation from, 73, 85
separation of Purusha
from, 73, 81, 82, 85
Pranam, see Mother, the, at
Pranam
Prayer, 36, 416, 602
and illness, 129, 181, 183,
681, 961
and rejection, 659
(aspiration) and response,
73, 479, 542, 545
before going to bed, 56-7
call and recession of
death, 189
for a friend, 11, 24
for the Divine, 822
Predestination,
and chance, 268, 269-70,
313-4
Psyche, 329, 832
and desire-soul, 304, 308
Psychic atmosphere, 533
Psychic being (the psychic),
2, 56, 174, 259, 327,
330, 336, 337, 745, 821,
964, 1100, 1138
a flame, not a spark, 140,
329
and Atman, 276
and evolution, 140, 308-9,
311, 329, 333
and inner being, 82
and Jivatman, 308
and personal relation with
the Mother, 276
and psychic fire, 242, 255
and Purusha, 82
awakening of, 174, 363
bringing to the front, 85,
753-4
more developed in some,
329
retracing steps to, 33
taking the lead, 14, 45,

1213 INDEX **Sadhak(s)**

176, 223, 231, 522, 611
weak, 519
see also Soul
Psychic opening, 902
Psychic transformation, 218,
327, 329, 330
Psychology,
criminal, 484
hedonistic, 483
modern, and hidden
forces, 460
Punnuswami, 67
Purification, 555, 611, 1048
Purusha,
and the psychic being, 82
"in the heart", figurative
language, 560, 561
power of, 270, 310-1
separation of, from Pra-
kriti, 73, 81, 82, 85
Pyramids, 674
Pythagoras, 167

Radhaswami sect (of Dayalbagh), 557-61
Rama, 141, 143, 477
and the Golden Deer, 224,
226-7
Ramakrishna, 52, 89, 94,
107, 114, 115, 136, 142,
143, 147, 170, 217-8,
219, 222, 223, 224, 226,
235, 238, 256, 335, 528,
530, 576, 739, 906, 958
Ramakrishna Mission, 1048
Raman, C.V., 313, 314
Raman Maharshi, 298, 477,
483-5, 525
yogi, not Rishi, 486, 487
Raymond, Antonin, 1069fn
Realisation,
of the Self, 82, 215, 367,
530, 992, 993; and
Brahman realisation,
991-2
yogic, 132
see also Divine realisation; Supramental re-
alisation
Reason, 29
or feelings as guide, 134-5
Rebirth, 38-9, 308
change of sex, 117

Receptivity, 100, 363, 753,
897, 1009
and cure, 67, 119, 881
and inspiration, 40-1, 372,
894
wideness and, 69, 502,
503
Rejection (of wrong movements), 3, 24-5, 30, 33,
56, 67, 85, 610, 657,
659, 848, 912, 1047,
1048
procedure, 252-3
Relation, human, 276
see also Sadhana, re-
lationship in
Reliance (*nirbhar*), 650, 651,
657, 658, 914, 1129
and reading literature,
681, 682
effort and, 64, 65-6, 67,
215, 269, 458-9, 461
Religious fanaticism, 349
Religious literature, 351-2
R (homeopathic doctor),
359-61, 378-88, 389,
418-40, 441, 445-6, 464,
493, 508, 510, 563-4,
568-9, 584, 585-90, 679,
691-2, 693-7, 701, 742,
995, 1011, 1030-1
Riddle of this World, The,
277, 280
Rimbaud, Arthur, 829, 830
Rishi,
and yogi, 486-7
Romen, 512, 914, 915, 917,
955
Roosevelt, F.D., 171, 289
Rudrabhava, 227
Rules,
observance of, 685

Sacrifice, 206, 339
depends on inner attitude,
987
of animals, 339-40, 349,
397
self-sacrifice, 349
spiritual, 350-1
(yajna) of works and
knowledge, 350
Sadhak(s), 301, 710
advanced, 330, 332, 1168

amateur Yogis!, 593, 748
and the supramental de-
scent, 142-3, 197-8, 210,
212, 221, 388-9, 440-1,
544-5, 594, 604, 705,
712-3, 852
and women, 1133; *see also*
Sadhana, relationship
in
becoming supramental or
great "overnight", 324,
328, 330-1
bodies abnormally sen-
sitive, 884
civilising the, 669
complete attitude of, 57,
58-9, 289
fashion not to sleep, 206,
700, 772
favourite phrase: "indi-
cate", 1013
following their own ideas
about Yoga, 470-1,
522-3, 593-4, 602, 847,
849, 1100, 1101
homo-intellectualis and
homo-psychicus, 235-7,
239-40
intelligence and interest
rare in, 524
lion-hearts, 531
living in inner self, 253,
750, 751, 753, 819, 820
modern-minded, 859
no Force can take a man
away, 1002
quarrel among, 212,
228-9, 257-8, 408-11,
502, 598, 628-9, 676,
1087, 1130
revolt and upsetting of:
D.S., 93-4; K, 851;
Naik, 1129-30, 1132;
U, 911-2; X (kitchen),
1087-91; Y(1), 297-8,
299-301; Y(2), 725-6,
727-8; Y(3), 1091; re-
medy for revolters,
1089, 1132
sheepishness, 592
shindy in, 653
speeding the, 288
supposing themselves
supermen, 1101
supramentalised, greater

Sadhak(s)   INDEX   1214

than Krishna?, 140-1
surface consciousness of,
and divine action, 275
three possibilities for, 469
wanting to be equal to
Mother and Sri Auro-
bindo, 140, 141, 142-3,
300, 400, 700
yet they arrive, 316, 755,
914
see also Ashram, sadhaks
here; Humour,(5): sa-
dhaks; *see also under*
Mother, the; Sri Auro-
bindo,(3)
Sadhana, 110, 273, 720
alternations in, 11, 45, 47
"Always behave as if the
Mother was looking at
you", 274
and appearances, 750,
1048
and conquest of death,
704, 712-3
and contact with the
world and hostile
forces, 532-3, 555-6
and difficulties, *see* Yoga,
and difficulties; Vital,
the, source of dif-
ficulties
and hostile forces, 23-4,
30, 55, 56, 532-3, 555-6,
700, 720, 757, 821, 914,
1002; and Divine's pro-
tection, 27-9, 109, 275,
299-301, 468, 728, 732,
1129; and safeguards,
29, 96, 222, 253, 555,
914
and illness, 60, 823, 1168
and lower nature, 72,
75, 86, 302, 303, 304,
308, 726, 847-8, 914
and personal effort, *see*
Effort, personal
and sex, 19, 51-2, 476, 532
555, 992-3
and silent mind, 48, 82,
637, 873
and wideness, 69, 97, 312,
503, 639
Buddha's maxim and
Krishna's injunction,
859

building up an inner life,
750-1
comfortable doctrine in,
194-5, 197, 213
conditions for getting
things, 48, 85, 185, 208,
211, 216, 243
conscious at every step,
522
conversion of sinners,
347
dark periods in, 593
descent of, into physical
consciousness, 705
dryness in, 35, 231, 243,
603, 604
dull moments in, 14-5,
605
effective way of, 216
emptiness in, 7, 243, 841
energies directed to, 70
Epicurean austerity in,
197
essential thing: change of
consciousness, 704; in-
ner touch, 820
formula in, 199, 316, 465,
651
fruits by the measure of
the soul, 215, 217
getting back the thread, 8
Grand Trunk Road, 542
harmonisation: of dif-
ferent elements, 97,
199, 201, 269, 650, 651;
of literature (poetry)
and, 607, 683
Heaven in a gallop, 594
increasing pressure for,
710
interruption to, 856
literary activity and, 5,
21, 41, 49, 72-3, 89,
451, 683, 744
living in Asram and out-
side, 899-900
necessary things in, 10,
14, 35, 48, 57, 112, 166,
210, 217, 268, 281, 465,
681, 710, 841, 853, 870,
873, 907, 914, 975, 1101
need of doing, 129, 273,
703, 704, 712-3, 897,
907, 943
need of perfectioning the

instrument, 128, 337,
419, 897
newspapers and, 5
nirbhar, see Reliance
of vital plane, 793
Path (Way), 93, 96, 165,
231, 914; following the,
166, 168, 172-5, 177
peace, balance, sanity,
209, 210, 223, 376
poetry and, 22, 62, 70,
72, 217, 283, 410, 594,
784, 1077
priggishness in 1126-7
progress in, 47, 57, 281,
601, 751
rational attitude, 219
reading and, 3, 52-3, 60-1,
681, 682
relationship in, 8, 19,
114-5, 266-7, 376, 463,
610, 615-6, 629, 729-30,
852-3, 873, 1000-1,
1119-21, 1133
relatives and, 3, 30, 410,
492
resistance in, 58, 63-4,
311; strong resolution
and resistance, 243,
757; *see also* Vital, the,
resistance of
Rome was not built in a
day, 605
satisfaction of desire, 75,
848; lingering look,
311-2
sattwic deeds, 334
secret of, 650, 651, 750
sensible attitude, 24,
376-7, 755
serious mood, 3
singing on the way, 745,
748, 749
slow laborious work, 745
sticking on, xiv-xv, 3, 24,
243, 318, 461, 462, 466,
610, 741, 975, 995
swiftness in, 210
taking, by the right end,
750, 755
talk and, 35
tamasic stage in, 995
through heart, 964
through heart or through
mind, 235-7, 239-41

1215   INDEX   **Sri Aurobindo, (1)**

through literary activity or through work, 451
through one's own line: an excuse, 1060
time taken in, 210, 217, 231, 316-7, 454, 593-4, 673, 755, 912; rule of 12 years, 744, 745, 748, 879
trance, falling down in, 958
ugly things in, 1048
waiting for things to happen, 579-80
wrong way of, 594, 602, 700, 858-9
zeal and patience, 199
see also Ego, sadhana and; Faith, and sadhana; Food, and sadhana; Mind, stumbling block in sadhana; Sri Aurobindo, (3): application of his Force for sadhana; Yoga
Sahana, 1071, 1072
Samata (equanimity), x, xiv, 29, 170, 605, 717, 809, 1001
Sammer, Francicheck, 1055fn, 1080
Sanjiban, 16
Sanjib Chowdhury, 1155
Sannyasi,
bad temper of, 223, 227
Santayana, George, 505
Sarojini Naidu, 505, 506
Schopenhauer, Arthur, 828
Science, 122, 191, 427, 523, 559, 822, 892, 903
and truth, 561
medical, 813
Self, see Experience(s), of Self; Realisation, of the Self
Sex (sexuality), 33, 75, 117, 215, 366, 519, 582, 610, 687, 748, 754
and death, 476
and love, 793-5
and self-control, 21, 796-7
and women, 107, 114, 115, 616
emissions, 56-7, 862-3, 866

for the preservation of species, 116, 582-3, 795
freedom from, 611-2
malpractice, 212-3
sex-energy, 391-5
sex-glands, 391, 392, 393, 394, 395, 396-7
sex-pleasure and Brahmananda, 793-5
see also Ashram, sex-force in; Sadhana, and sex
Shakespeare, William, 224, 398, 490, 500, 631, 639, 794, 803, 922, 923, 929, 940, 954, 988, 1046, 1145, 1147, 1180, 1181, 1182, 1183, 1187
Shankara [Shankaracharya], 78, 343
Shaw, G.B., 240, 1040, 1181
Shelley, Percy Bysshe, 404, 599, 770, 794, 935, 1172
Silence, 72, 73, 74, 81, 891
see also Mind, silent
Sincerity, 19-20, 29, 217, 270, 352, 910, 911-2, 914; earnestness, 281, 755
sincere heart and extraordinary powers, 301
Sircar, Dr. Mahendranath, 591, 722, 730, 1048
Sleep, 59-60, 80, 108-9, 116, 161, 206, 408, 707, 772 859, 871
best time for, 38
conscious, 4-5
in meditation, 1-2, 7, 91
pass into, in concentration, 8-9, 10, 11
Smiles, Samuel, 102
Socrates, 306
S of Dayalbagh, 557
Somnath, 346, 347, 348, 349, 351
Sophocles, 498, 779, 789
Sorrow, 263
see also Life, sorrow and suffering in
Soul, 560
and body, 81, 488, 560, 739
and Grace, xiv-xv, 461, 465, 580

and Ignorance, 303-5, 310-2, 333-4, 606, 850
and Karma, 309-10, 334
turning of, towards the Divine, 303, 454; see also Psychic being, awakening of
see also Psychic being; Sadhana, fruits by the measure of the soul
Southey, Robert, 547
Spirit-entity,
and pineal gland, 558-61
Spiritual consciousness, 54, 173, 639
and praise and blame, 301, 1108
and reading Dickens, 681, 682
Spiritual experience, see Experience(s), spiritual
Spirituality,
and greatness, 171, 176, 224, 344
and marriage, 476, 575-6, 611
and moralising the character, 1106, 1108-9
and sattwic man, 1109
and work in the world, 557-8
high qualities and, 1105
understanding, not by the intellect, 770, 1049
vs. social scale and university education, 142, 144, 145
Spiritual light,
and idealistic or religious notions, 352, 363
Sri Aurobindo,
(1) Yoga/Sadhana: 80, 142, 150, 177, 204, 316
accident to carriage, 368
achieving overmind, 150, 194
and the Divine's help (Grace), 149, 170
anger, upsurge of, 748, 749; shouting, 1130
beginning of Yoga, 367-8; motive behind, 1077
bore every attack, 176; worked on each problem, 204

Sri Aurobindo, (1)

concentration 4-5 hours a day!, 457, 459
doubt and despair, 176
dropped several times, 879; if I fall out, 95
dull moments, 605
experiences: after contact with Lele, 170, 459-60, 467; of Brahman, 467; of Nirvana, 80, 170, 202, 206, 902; of Self, 367-8, 530; of Vasudeva, 367; spiritual, 371
getting out of mind, 170, 247; have never anything in my head, 538; I don't think, 578, 1066, 1141
growth of capacities by Yoga, 62, 70, 88, 133, 148-9, 202, 204, 205, 366, 369-71, 683
Integral Yoga not easy even for me, 149, 282
joyous sacrifice, 350
meditating while walking, 249
mukti, 138, 185, 1151
no spirituality before taking up Yoga, 206
no struggle about Self, 530
physical work, 73-4, 80
Pranayam, 370, 371, 459, 467
retirement, 79, 125-6, 295, 663; question of coming out, 663, 789
samatā (equanimity), x, xiv, 170, 605, 717, 809; not upset, 188
subtle images, 65
suicide, no thought of, 265
vairagya period, 605
see also below (3): his sadhana . . .

(2) Poetry/Prose: 165, 204, 416, 684, 1143
aim in writing poetry, 405, 543-4
alterations in poetry, 544, 846, 929
Cousins' criticism, 746, 749

doggerels, 126-7, 489-90, 493, 494, 497, 520, 668, 756, 1163
fluency in poetry, 748
inspiration, capricious, 260, 516, 1170
labour for, 516, 1056, 1165
method of writing, 62, 1066
must be a bad critic, 1148
mystic poetry, 782-3
no expert: in Bengali *chhanda*, 416, 633, 634, 636, 903, 911, 923; in Bengali overhead poetry, 943, 1159, 1161
not follower of *yuga-dharma*, 864
no time for creative production, 398-9, 544, 686
overhead poetry, 939
poetry and sadhana, 1077
reading, 61, 62, 366; ignorance of other literature, 682
Savitri, 464, 939, 1072, 1146; writing and rewriting of, 543-5, 548, 929, 1165, 1166
scratching my head for words, 1173
self-depreciatory criticism, 775
sonnets, 418, 500, 501, 544, 789, 1165
surrealism, limited province, 815, 838
Surrealist poetry, 489, 790, 807, 814, 816-7
time taken for a poem, 401, 791
"12 recent poems", 925
writing out of silent mind, 356, 362, 370
writing style, 242-3, 366, 370
wrote a lot in England, 748

(3) Help to others: 28-9, 79, 82, 92, 96, 263, 268, 300, 624, 842, 885, 1009
application of his Force: 127-9, 133, 553, 596;

for CURE, *see* Force, the, cure by . . .;
for POETRY, 130, 260, 459, 468, 471, 490, 511-2, 520, 543, 579, 595, 597-8, 602, 604, 621, 625-6, 628, 640, 660, 662, 672, 765, 769, 895, 1010; easier for English, 496; inspirer not the supramental Self, 806, 807-8; metrifying, 826; not responsible for results, 807; running the Poetry Department, 765; strike against many, 843; time and labour on others' poetry, 411-2, 413, 574, 791, 936-7, 961, 1060, 1076, 1114, 1143, 1166; for SADHANA, 131, 133, 317-8, 522, 532, 602, 721, 731-2, 849, 1015; and change of character, 1105, 1108-9; tried the impossible, 325; for STORY-WRITING, 709, 744
correspondence, 78-9, 103, 126-7, 178, 187, 206, 212, 296, 326, 331, 353, 367, 370, 454-5, 469, 473, 501, 509, 525, 541, 553, 584, 597, 604, 609, 618, 623, 641, 655, 678-9, 722-3, 762, 795-6, 799, 800, 804, 811, 812, 921, 1149-50; answers cryptic, 660, 663-4, 665, 679; envelope system, 43; getting letters in vernacular, 589, 658; help through reading letters, 183, 595, 874-5; inner work delayed, 679; misinterpreting (misunderstanding) his writings, 221, 275, 329, 467, 543, 682, 837, 982, 1090-1; no light, 549, 676, 702, 1003-4; no time, 80, 130, 206, 260, 295, 423, 441, 465, 472, 500, 533,

1217 INDEX **Sri Aurobindo, (5)**

618, 678, 701, 806, 858, 887, 903, 1091, 1149; poem, Bengali, 126-7; poem, "Tautology", 103; slip of pen, 305, 460, 527-8; Sundays, 138, 295, 418, 534; suspension of, 127, 134, 281, 501, 641, 658, 664, 1016, 1025; telling the Mother, 418; writing (one day) about: the Avatar, 243; Force, 130, 133-4, 192, 338, 596, 600-1, 714; Intuition, 204, 205, 206-7, 246, 678, 909; physical transformation, 321; supermind, 295, 344, 907; women, 107-8, 115; work, 80; *see also* Nirodbaran, (1)

dealing with sadhaks, xii, 75, 93, 256, 284, 296, 298, 300, 389, 409-11, 502, 600, 851, 861, 924, 1087-9, 1091, 1109; *see also* Ashram, departures . . .; Medical matters, (8): Mother's and Sri Aurobindo's care...; Sadhak(s), quarrelling . . ., revolt . . .

doesn't profess to transform men against their will, 298

his sadhana and terrestrial consciousness, 135, 138-9, 144, 148-9, 151, 166, 216, 288, 704; his difficulties and struggles, 165, 167-8, 174-5, 176, 177; his own example as proof, 80, 135, 138, 140, 148-9, 151, 165, 172-3, 351

meeting, in dreams, 663, 664-5, 772; *see also* Nirodbaran, (4)

receiving S.O.S.'s, 1179; *see also* Force, calling "Trust in Me" . . ., 232

(4) Work [mission]:
advancing (travelling forward), 161, 220, 287,

289, 291, 604

aim of, not Divine Rule, 479

and common clay, xi, xii

and hostile forces, 161, 911

and humanity (world), xii-xiii, 61, 79, 93, 139, 171, 285, 303

and new race, 341-3

and past seers, 343

and the subconscient, 246, 247, 254, 271, 287, 288, 289, 388, 389, 840-1

and the supramental, 79, 121, 131, 137, 142-3, 171, 179-80, 194, 195-6, 197-8, 205, 210, 211, 212, 216, 220, 222, 287-8, 293-5, 301, 320-1, 322, 342, 344, 388, 544, 590, 594, 660, 663-4, 698, 759, 903; Einsteinian formula, 287, 288-9, 291, 388

concentration on work, 78-9, 549, 553

concerned with getting things done, not with words, 192, 344, 852

digging, 852

everything depends on my success, 704

falling flat and recovery, 597-8

not understanding his work, 1049

opened the way, 138, 165, 166, 168, 172, 288

quarrel with Matter, 121, 205; am I Matter?, 194, 320

stillness and march, 604, 608

transformation of overmind, 389

trying to get: a new consciousness in the world, 119, 177; some damned thing done, 584, 1150; supramental Light down, 903, 913; *see also above* and the supramental

what is in the mind of the sadhaks, matters, 301

working easy with nobody, 1110

work of, and big personalities, 1106-7, 1110-1

work of, and Dayalbagh sect, 557-8

(5) General:
and miracles, 119, 128, 135, 148, 204, 283, 300, 317-8, 464, 798, 973, 974

aspiration by post, 479

austere, grave!, 144-5, 156-7, 162

autobiographical hints, 367

Avatar, 138, 139, 165, 169, 174, 177, 748

body-transformation, vol. 2, vi

brilliant career!, 170-1

call (fish for) nobody, 92-3, 171, 1107, 1110

"catch you", 634

choose to be deceived, 557

coming to Pondicherry, 203-4, 549fn, 711

common sense, 157, 340

contact with political heroes, 1111

cowards changed into heroes, xi, 133, 136

criticism against, 149 296, 297, 341-3, 411, 570-1, 602, 691, 789, 851, 1108

daily programme, 295, 296, 464, 553, 595, 628, 672, 765

delightful time, 549

dhotis, 653

did what the Divine wanted, 683

Divine largesse, xiv, xv, vol. 2, v

don't believe in complexes, 732

emanations of, 275

Englishman does not terrify me, 507

facsimiles of, 1, 78, 134

feast, 757

Sri Aurobindo, (5)　　　　INDEX　　　　1218

Goddesses and the Vedas, 356
heredity, 169, 253
horoscope of, 444
humour, 103, 143, 318, 351, vol. 2, vii, 1035, 1141-2; can't joke in public, 489; remarks and criticisms not meant to hurt, xiv, 103, 827; *see also* Humour, Sri Aurobindo's
I. C. S., 942, 1084
illness: eczema, 456, 959; eye-trouble, 178, 180, 186-7, 190, 1016; fragments of, 190; giddiness, 179, 190; pain in heels, 249; smallpox, 901
illness, way of dealing with, 435
immortality, 193-4, 196; conquest of death and illness, 189-94, 712-3; fancy to die, 196, 199-200, vol. 2, vi
inconsistencies in statements, 83, vol. 2, vii
independence and revolutionary movement, 102-3, 170, 488; Swadeshi times, 351
India as the Mother, 487-8
Indian mind and spirit, 506
ink, pad, pen, 496, 500, 521, 525, 541
intellect not dashing, 236
joking all the time, vol. 2, vi
judging, 296, 301
knowledge ineffable, 762
laughing all the time, ix
lifting things from his writings, 646
lived dangerously, 92, 100-3
many-sided Guru, ix, xiv
marriage, 575, 576
Master, 221, 285, 1158
menu, 541, 973
military capacity, 895
misfortunes usual, 881

modern Guru, x
multitudinous manifestations, 244, 808
need nothing, 138, 148
no latent medico, 200, 204-5, 645, 885; not a doctor, 123, 678, 868
no spree, 857
not a moralist, 565
no time to laugh, 667
not jumping at conclusions, 440
occult faculty, 283
opening to Force of Inspiration, 684
outside world for, vol. 2, vii
pān-supāri, 786
pomegranate juice, 464
poverty no terror, 102
publication of his literary work, 631-2
reaction to criticism, 809-10
"reading" photographs, 328, 375-6, 566
safety I would like, 92
science in school, 941, 942
scientific person, 164
seen much of the world, 437
Shiva element, 76
source of Peace, 773, 986
suffering the Divine Law, 984
Supreme!, 478
tea-habit, 228, 878
understanding of, flexible, vol. 2, vii
Upanishads untiring, 1070
vairagya and *samatā*, 605
vishwarup pacifist (amiable), 162, 480
weight, 578
witnessing plague, 738
see also Sadhak(s), wanting to be equal . . . ; Vision, of Sri Aurobindo

Sri Aurobindo Ashram, *see* Ashram, Sri Aurobindo
Sri Aurobindo's Yoga (Integral Yoga), 80, 84, 86, 141, 149, 150-1, 231, 681, 848, 1054

accepts life, xii, xiii, 86, 1077
and former Yogis, 218-9, 993
and Man of Sorrows, 263-5
and old Yogas, 77-80 223, 593, 750
and other Yogas, 879, 898
and paternal or filial love, 591-2
and psychic transformation, 327
cardinal principle of, xii, xiv
denial of, 149, 151
for the Divine, 342, 343-4
Grand Trunk Road, 231, 282
need of balance, 223, 376
no short cuts in everything, 204
not a Vaishnava Yoga, 264
privacy better for work, 860
queer, cold and strange, 858-9
realisation of the Self, a beginning only in, 593, 993
scepticism stupid, 1100, 1101
test in, 593, 993
two kinds of understanding, 1101
why so difficult, 593
Stillness (*stabdhatā*), 67-8, 603, 604, 655, 735-6
Subconscient, the, 254, 592, 594, 829
and illness, 248, 518, 738, 1053, 1054, 1124, 1125
and the general Nature, 247-8, 251-3
revolt of, 221; *see also* Descent, and upsurge of subconscient mud
subconscious belt, 831
see also Sri Aurobindo, (4) Work: and the subconscient
Subliminal, the, 146, 147, 252, 665, 829, 833

1219 INDEX Thought(s)

Success, 137, 224, 355, 683, 1107
and "blue moon", 432, 523, 572
and morality, 432
contemporary, 1155
see also Medical matters, (2)
Suffering, see Life, sorrow and suffering in
Suicide, 53, 265, 608, 616, 674-5, 748, 749
Sukhdev, 107
Sultan of Johore, 565-6
Superman, 93
and man, 323
Supermind (the Supramental), 141, 192, 236, 1100, 1101
and freedom of the individual, 327, 912
and Krishna etc., 219
aspiration for, 215-6, 219-20
does not take away any capacity, 1130
fixing the possibilities of, by the mind, 236-7, 323, 999
highest planes not so accommodating, 544
in physical consciousness, 544
language, 243
mind developing into, 139, 625
nature of, 625
no jurisdiction, 584
only "dead cert" for physical things, 201
peace, poise and sanity first, 209, 210
supramentalisation and divinisation, 342
supramentalisation in parts, 189, 195, 294
tail of, 321, 324, 325, 327, 328, 388, 389, 590-1, 857-8, 1067, 1088, 1130
taking anything other as, 342, 455, 1101
understanding of, 1100-1
will respect Truth only, 327

see also Overmind, and Supermind; Sadhak(s), becoming supramental; Sri Aurobindo, (4): and the supramental
Supramental change, 704
first step in, 1067
Supramental Consciousness, and human consciousness, vol. 2, vii
Supramental descent (bringing down the Supermind), 79, 195-6, 301, 344, 388, 590, 905-6, 999, 1130
and death and illness, 189, 191-4, 703, 704, 712-3
and departures from the Ashram, 913
and human race, 171
and necessity of sadhana, 703, 704, 712-3, 907; 30 years not too slow, 673
and sex-force, 1000, 1004; see also Descent, and sex
and time factor, 213, 214-5, 673, 679
help by, 210, 324, 326-7, 703
in Sri Aurobindo, 194, 293-4, 320
into earth consciousness, 705, 712-3
into the material, 294, 320-1
into the physical!, 179-80, 214-5
necessary condition for, 992
postponement of, 913
why first in Sri Aurobindo and Mother?, 142-3
see also Descent; Sadhak, and the supramental descent
Supramental Force, 907
and Divine Force, 713-4
Supramental Knowledge, and faith, 625
Supramental race, see New race
Supramental realisation, 216, 219-20

Surface being, 147, 252
Surface consciousness, 12, 73, 275
Surrender, 29, 177, 208, 344, 466, 471, 522, 652, 859, 865
Swinburne, A.C., 652
Symbols,
bird, 527
Blue Bird, 822
colours: blue, 686; gold, 686; pale blue, 51; pink, 51; red, 289; violet, 454; white, 686
colours, play of, 31
cross, 76
east, 31
full moon, 76
golden cup, 454
incense sticks, 356
lights: red-crimson, 242; White, 764-5
sea, 33, 208, 1138
silver, 356
silver coins, 356
snakes, 65, 643
Sphinx, 674
sun, 33
swan, 527, 782, 910
wire, 643
Synthesis of Yoga, The, 242-3

Tagore, Rabindranath, xi, 39, 70, 125, 129, 369, 505, 631, 661, 770, 803, 850, 1070, 1071, 1072, 1083
Tennyson, Alfred, 398, 412
Theory, 698
Thomas à Kempis, 173
Thompson [a visitor], 504, 509, 511
Thompson, Francis, 448, 1038, 1172, 1175
Thought(s), 17, 474, 738, 1066
coming of, 357, 358, 362-3, 1062
disturbing, in meditation, 65, 66, 68
hostile, 3, 23-4
"I think, therefore I am", 307

Thought(s)

thought-substance in different persons, 362-3

Tota Puri, 335

Transformation, xi, xiii, 135, 166, 173, 223, 288, 298, 321, 593, vol. 2, vi, 900, 993
complete, 218
of defects, 10
of the nature, *see* Nature, human, change (transformation) of
of the whole nature, required in Sri Aurobindo's Yoga, 593, 993
personal, and of world and hostile forces, 555
physical, 321
psychic, 218, 327, 329, 330
psychic, spiritual and supramental, 218
supramental and spiritual-mental, 219
see also Supramental change

Truth, 83, 226, 304, 327, 483
and error, 986
and shocked reverence for the past, 343
essential and conditional, 142
home-truths, 823
in every proposition, 506, 961
intellectual and real, 764, 771
lies, and observance of, 873, 1001, 1048, 1109
see also Mind, mental statements and the truth

Twelve Years with Sri Aurobindo, ix

Underhill, Evelyn, 793

Universal Nature, *see* Nature, universal

Urvasi, 528

Vairagya, 605-6, 637, 638, 995

Valéry, Paul, 829

Valle, Dr., 379, 383, 386, 418, 435, 697, 877, 888, 890, 891, 892, 926

Valmiki, 201, 202, 498, 1147

Verlaine, Paul, 781, 828, 829

Vidyasagar, Ishwarchandra, 374

Virgil, 401, 548, 743, 747, 926, 970, 988

Virtue, 347, 432

Vision, 31, 33, 208, 643, 686, 689, 832, 1153
Mother's, about Sri Aurobindo and Nirod, xi
of complexion becoming golden, 685-6, 687-8
of J lying dead, 616
of Mother, 617
of Mother and Sri Aurobindo at Cape Comorin, 1090
of Sri Aurobindo, 67
of Sri Krishna, 39
of Sun-Goddess, 415
of violet stream and golden cup, 453-4

Vital, the, 55, 252, 453, 483, 616, 665, 793, 1002
becoming ghost, after death, 723, 733
dealing with, 17, 21, 33, 278, 657, 658, 1089, 1132
magnetic, 961-2
mind struggling with, 350
mind supporting, 311, 611, 1132
nature of, 271, 615, 653, 730, 787
needed qualities of, 164
needs something to hook on to, 1133
non-cooperation, 655-6, 995; Gandhian, 228, 243, 532
old vital moorings, 278 622
resistance of, 14, 64, 278, 303, 304, 311, 655-6, 849, 850, 851, 1129
source of difficulties in sadhana, 56, 72, 113, 463, 470, 519, 605, 606, 1126, 1132

Vital attraction,
double, 730

Vital interchange, 7, 1060-2
building a wall against, 1062-3

Vital love, *see* Love, vital

Vital plane (world), 793
and physical world, 163, 164, 314, 664-6, 828
forms in, 298-9
truth of happenings on, 664-6
understanding, by mind. 772, 828
see also Dreams, on vital plane

Vivekananda, 252, 256, 277, 394, 478, 737, 906

Voronoff, Serge, 191, 195

Vyasa, 498, 1147

War,
and India, 340-1
and justice, 565

Will, 36, 42, 522, 651, 652, 659, 1129
see also Free will

Wodehouse, P.G., 365

Woman/Women, 492-3, 581, 616, 708, 716-7, 735, 1119-20, 1133
and sex, 107, 114, 115, 616
asexual friend, 1121
eternal and Real, 270
"feminine women", 749
"girls" almost always complex, 1094
womanly woman, 823
see also Man, and women

Wordsworth, William, 498, 599, 966, 1084, 1085, 1172

Work, 35, 72
and happiness, 486
and meditation, 77-80, 82-6, 484-6
anticipating trouble, and the right attitude, 790
as an offering, 12, 70, 73-4, 859
calling in the Force for, 87, 99-100
concentration and, 78, 79, 80

1221 INDEX **Yudhishthir**

getting interest in, 55
highest realisation through, 77-80, 84-6
loss of temper in, 87, 257-8, 287, 368-9, 1130
physical, 73-4, 80
physical, and literary, 87, 451
reading when at, 15, 59
remembering the Mother in, 16-7, 99, 313, 451
sacrifice of, 350
spiritual value of, 49
yogic, 73, 85-6, 87
see also Action; Effort; Karmayoga; Sri Aurobindo, (4)
World, 94, 128, 175, 239, 454, 555, 582, 602, 1002, 1052
at present, 279, 280, 292, 826
Divine's way of acting upon, 128-9, 602
Law and Great Wheel, 564
outside, for Sri Aurobindo, vol. 2, vii
riddle of this, 277, 280
things look bad enough, 322-3, 1157, 1185
see also Physical world; Vital plane (world)

Yoga, 24, 29, 231, 239, 361, 649, 764, 808, 872, 915, 1001
aim of, 58, 70, 310, 344, 376, 460, 683, 704, 964
and brilliance, 858
and difficulties, xiii, 14, 17, 32, 33, 92, 93, 96, 113, 168, 263, 264-5, 278, 297, 409, 502, 532-3, 555, 592, 614, 651, 657, 658, 898, 914, 981, 1081; of sattwic and rajasic man, 346-7
and fear, 737
and great personalities

(bigness), 171, 176, 1107, 1111
and headache, 264, 718
and moral obligations, 904
and past karma, 309-10
and physical science, 559, 561
and quarrels, 411
and sociability, 851, 858, 861-2, 1108
and sound body, 11-2; health not enough, 735
and tea-talk etc., 851, 858, 861-2, 907, 988, 1062
becoming conscious: of forces by, 306, 314, 532-3; of one's pretences by, 1047, 1048
building up of a new consciousness, 975
Charvak's way, 858
demanding rational explanation from, 511-2, 514
denial of all possibilities of, 129, 167, 173
effects of, 14, 40, 306, 314, 362, 1060, 1062; see also Yoga-Force, growth of capacities by
failures in, and apprehension, xiv, 26-30, 90-1, 94-5, 298, 302, 303, 308, 592-3, 700-1, 726, 727, 741-2, 748, 750-1, 851-2, 858, 912, 1089
fall in, 95, 96, 593, 700, 748, 797, 914, 975
fitness and unfitness in, 461
food and sleep, 58, 108-9
good "adhar" in, 281, 282
higher being (things) once gained can be regained, 956-7, 975
if absolute surrender, faith, etc. from the beginning were essential . . ., 177
Integral Yoga, see Sri Aurobindo's Yoga

interest in, 72
lila-attitude, 882
not devoid of all reason, 29, 602
not safe or easy, 29, 94-6, 170, 272, 582, 914
one man doing yoga for all, xiii
pressure of, xiii, 14, 30, 592-3, 851
presumptuous demand in, 460
safeguards in, see Sadhana, and hostile force(s) . . .
seeking for safety, 29, 91, 92-6, 1129; see also above failures in, and apprehensions
Sound-Yoga, 558
steps in, 112
ties and, 43, 267, 1000-1
turn for, each has his own time, 11, 24
ups and downs in, 45, 310, 975
see also Sadhana; Sri Aurobindo's Yoga
Yoga-Force (Yogic Force), 133
growth of capacities by, 69-70, 88, 133, 138, 146, 148-9, 202, 204, 206, 207, 208, 369-71, 405, 491, 661, 850, 1106; and inborn qualities, 260, 261, 491, 569; price for, 207, 1151
pressure of, 639-40, 643
producing spiritual results more easily than mental results?, 371
Yogi, xiv, 155-6, 158, 219, 307, 486, 487, 514, 539, 559, 993
Yogic poise, 646, 652
Yogic strand, 637, 638
Yogic vision, about patients, 201, 205
Yogic work, 73, 85-6, 87
Yudhishthir, 95